Papers Relating to the

Foreign Relations

of the

United States

THE LANSING PAPERS
1914–1920

(In Two Volumes)

Volume I

United States
Government Printing Office
Washington : 1939

DEPARTMENT OF STATE
PUBLICATION 1420

For sale by the
Superintendent of Documents, Washington, D. C.
Price $1.50 (cloth)

PREFACE

The documents contained in this and the following volume constitute an extensive selection from the large body of correspondence of Robert Lansing, former Secretary of State, which was secured for the files of the Department of State following Mr. Lansing's death in 1928. These papers were, therefore, not available at the time when the volumes of *Foreign Relations* for the years 1914 through 1919 and the supplementary volumes on the World War and on Russia were compiled. A large number of the papers, however, seemed to have such great public interest that it was deemed desirable to publish these additional supplemental volumes. Although these volumes consist largely of papers received from the collection of Mr. Lansing, a certain number of closely related documents from other official sources, whose publication seemed desirable, have been included.

The papers here published represent, therefore, an additional selection of documents from the period 1914 through 1920 bearing on subjects which have already been presented in the volumes of *Foreign Relations* hitherto published dealing with that period. Accordingly, it must not be expected that the papers published in these two volumes will present a complete or continuous account of the events with which they deal. Such a complete account may be secured by using these volumes in conjunction with the already published *Foreign Relations* volumes. To facilitate such cross-reference numerous footnotes to related documents in earlier volumes of the series have been supplied.

The principles followed with regard to selection of material and inclusion or exclusion of documents or parts of documents are the same as have governed in the preparation of earlier volumes of the *Foreign Relations* series as stated in the Departmental Order approved by Secretary of State Frank B. Kellogg on March 26, 1925, given in full in the preface to *Foreign Relations*, 1914, supplement, pages iii–iv.

The volumes were compiled under the direction of the late Dr. Cyril Wynne, former Chief of the Division of Research and Publication, Department of State; Dr. E. Wilder Spaulding, present Chief of the Division; and Dr. E. R. Perkins, Chief of the Research Section of the Division. The selection and arrangement of the papers and the com-

pilation of the notes were the work of Dr. J. S. Beddie of the Research
Section.

The periods during which Mr. Lansing filled his different posts in the
Department of State were as follows:

Counselor for the Department of State—March 27, 1914–June
9, 1915.
Secretary of State *ad interim*—June 9–23, 1915.
Secretary of State—June 23, 1915–February 13, 1920.

CONTENTS

CONTENTS

LIST OF PAPERS

[Unless otherwise specified, the correspondence is *from* or *to* the Secretary of State or other official of the Department of State.]

THE WORLD WAR:
PERIOD OF AMERICAN NEUTRALITY

EFFORTS AT NEUTRALIZATION OF THE FAR EAST

THE WORLD WAR:
PERIOD OF AMERICAN NEUTRALITY

Peace Proposals—Continued

THE WORLD WAR:
PERIOD OF AMERICAN NEUTRALITY

RECRUITING OF AMERICAN CITIZENS—Continued

ATTITUDE OF THE UNITED STATES TOWARD METHODS OF WARFARE EMPLOYED BY BELLIGERENTS

THE WORLD WAR:
PERIOD OF AMERICAN NEUTRALITY

ATTITUDE OF THE UNITED STATES TOWARD METHODS OF WARFARE EMPLOYED BY
BELLIGERENTS—Continued

THE WORLD WAR:
PERIOD OF AMERICAN NEUTRALITY

ACTION BY THE AMERICAN LEGATION IN BELGIUM ON BEHALF OF MISS EDITH CAVELL—Continued

CONDUCT OF FOREIGN DIPLOMATS IN THE UNITED STATES

THE WORLD WAR:
PERIOD OF AMERICAN NEUTRALITY

CONDUCT OF FOREIGN DIPLOMATS IN THE UNITED STATES—Continued

THE WORLD WAR:
PERIOD OF AMERICAN NEUTRALITY

CONDUCT OF FOREIGN DIPLOMATS IN THE UNITED STATES—Continued

THE WORLD WAR:
PERIOD OF AMERICAN NEUTRALITY

TRANSFER OF FOREIGN VESSELS TO AMERICAN REGISTRY

THE WORLD WAR:
PERIOD OF AMERICAN NEUTRALITY

SALE OF MUNITIONS TO BELLIGERENTS

THE WORLD WAR:
PERIOD OF AMERICAN NEUTRALITY

SALE OF MUNITIONS TO BELLIGERENTS—Continued

THE WORLD WAR:
PERIOD OF AMERICAN NEUTRALITY
LOANS TO BELLIGERENTS

THE WORLD WAR:
PERIOD OF AMERICAN NEUTRALITY

Loans to Belligerents—Continued

THE WORLD WAR:
PERIOD OF AMERICAN NEUTRALITY

ENFORCEMENT OF AMERICAN NEUTRALITY—STATEMENTS CONCERNING AMERICAN
NEUTRALITY POLICY—Continued

THE WORLD WAR:
PERIOD OF AMERICAN NEUTRALITY

ENFORCEMENT OF AMERICAN NEUTRALITY—STATEMENTS CONCERNING AMERICAN
NEUTRALITY POLICY—Continued

THE WORLD WAR:
PERIOD OF AMERICAN NEUTRALITY

ENFORCEMENT OF AMERICAN NEUTRALITY—STATEMENTS CONCERNING AMERICAN NEUTRALITY POLICY—Continued

THE WORLD WAR:
PERIOD OF AMERICAN NEUTRALITY

ENFORCEMENT OF AMERICAN NEUTRALITY—STATEMENTS CONCERNING AMERICAN NEUTRALITY POLICY—Continued

THE WORLD WAR:
PERIOD OF AMERICAN NEUTRALITY

Enforcement of American Neutrality—Statements Concerning American
Neutrality Policy—Continued

THE WORLD WAR:
PERIOD OF AMERICAN NEUTRALITY

INTERFERENCE WITH AMERICAN COMMERCE BY GREAT BRITAIN AND HER
ALLIES—Continued

THE WORLD WAR:
PERIOD OF AMERICAN NEUTRALITY

INTERFERENCE WITH AMERICAN COMMERCE BY GREAT BRITAIN AND HER
ALLIES—Continued

THE WORLD WAR:
PERIOD OF AMERICAN NEUTRALITY

INTERFERENCE WITH AMERICAN COMMERCE BY GREAT BRITAIN AND HER
ALLIES—Continued

THE WORLD WAR:
PERIOD OF AMERICAN NEUTRALITY

INTERFERENCE WITH AMERICAN COMMERCE BY GREAT BRITAIN AND HER
ALLIES—Continued

THE WORLD WAR:
PERIOD OF AMERICAN NEUTRALITY

INTERFERENCE WITH AMERICAN COMMERCE BY GREAT BRITAIN AND HER
ALLIES—Continued

THE WORLD WAR:
PERIOD OF AMERICAN NEUTRALITY

ARMED MERCHANT SHIPS—Continued

THE WORLD WAR:
PERIOD OF AMERICAN NEUTRALITY

ARMED MERCHANT SHIPS—Continued

THE WORLD WAR:
PERIOD OF AMERICAN NEUTRALITY

Armed Merchant Ships—Continued

THE WORLD WAR:
PERIOD OF AMERICAN NEUTRALITY

RELATIONS WITH GERMANY AND AUSTRIA-HUNGARY—GERMAN SUBMARINE
WARFARE—SEVERANCE OF DIPLOMATIC RELATIONS AND OUTBREAK OF WAR
WITH GERMANY—Continued

THE WORLD WAR:
PERIOD OF AMERICAN NEUTRALITY

RELATIONS WITH GERMANY AND AUSTRIA-HUNGARY—GERMAN SUBMARINE WARFARE—SEVERANCE OF DIPLOMATIC RELATIONS AND OUTBREAK OF WAR WITH GERMANY—Continued

THE WORLD WAR:
PERIOD OF AMERICAN NEUTRALITY

RELATIONS WITH GERMANY AND AUSTRIA-HUNGARY—GERMAN SUBMARINE WARFARE—SEVERANCE OF DIPLOMATIC RELATIONS AND OUTBREAK OF WAR WITH GERMANY—Continued

THE WORLD WAR:
PERIOD OF AMERICAN NEUTRALITY

RELATIONS WITH GERMANY AND AUSTRIA-HUNGARY—GERMAN SUBMARINE WARFARE—SEVERANCE OF DIPLOMATIC RELATIONS AND OUTBREAK OF WAR WITH GERMANY—Continued

THE WORLD WAR:
PERIOD OF AMERICAN NEUTRALITY

RELATIONS WITH GERMANY AND AUSTRIA-HUNGARY—GERMAN SUBMARINE WARFARE—SEVERANCE OF DIPLOMATIC RELATIONS AND OUTBREAK OF WAR WITH GERMANY—Continued

THE WORLD WAR:
PERIOD OF AMERICAN NEUTRALITY

RELATIONS WITH GERMANY AND AUSTRIA-HUNGARY—GERMAN SUBMARINE WARFARE—SEVERANCE OF DIPLOMATIC RELATIONS AND OUTBREAK OF WAR WITH GERMANY—Continued

THE WORLD WAR:
PERIOD OF AMERICAN NEUTRALITY

RELATIONS WITH GERMANY AND AUSTRIA-HUNGARY—GERMAN SUBMARINE WARFARE—SEVERANCE OF DIPLOMATIC RELATIONS AND OUTBREAK OF WAR WITH GERMANY—Continued

THE WORLD WAR:
PERIOD OF AMERICAN NEUTRALITY

RELATIONS WITH GERMANY AND AUSTRIA-HUNGARY—GERMAN SUBMARINE WARFARE—SEVERANCE OF DIPLOMATIC RELATIONS AND OUTBREAK OF WAR WITH GERMANY—Continued

THE WORLD WAR:
PERIOD OF AMERICAN NEUTRALITY

RELATIONS WITH GERMANY AND AUSTRIA-HUNGARY—GERMAN SUBMARINE
WARFARE—SEVERANCE OF DIPLOMATIC RELATIONS AND OUTBREAK OF WAR
WITH GERMANY—Continued

THE WORLD WAR:
PERIOD OF AMERICAN NEUTRALITY

RELATIONS WITH GERMANY AND AUSTRIA-HUNGARY—GERMAN SUBMARINE
WARFARE—SEVERANCE OF DIPLOMATIC RELATIONS AND OUTBREAK OF WAR
WITH GERMANY—Continued

THE WORLD WAR:
PERIOD OF AMERICAN NEUTRALITY

RELATIONS WITH GERMANY AND AUSTRIA-HUNGARY—GERMAN SUBMARINE WARFARE—SEVERANCE OF DIPLOMATIC RELATIONS AND OUTBREAK OF WAR WITH GERMANY—Continued

THE WORLD WAR:
PERIOD OF AMERICAN NEUTRALITY

RELATIONS WITH GERMANY AND AUSTRIA-HUNGARY—GERMAN SUBMARINE
WARFARE—SEVERANCE OF DIPLOMATIC RELATIONS AND OUTBREAK OF WAR
WITH GERMANY—Continued

THE WORLD WAR:
PERIOD OF AMERICAN NEUTRALITY

RELATIONS WITH GERMANY AND AUSTRIA-HUNGARY—GERMAN SUBMARINE WARFARE—SEVERANCE OF DIPLOMATIC RELATIONS AND OUTBREAK OF WAR WITH GERMANY—Continued

THE WORLD WAR:
PERIOD OF AMERICAN NEUTRALITY

RELATIONS WITH GERMANY AND AUSTRIA-HUNGARY—GERMAN SUBMARINE
WARFARE—SEVERANCE OF DIPLOMATIC RELATIONS AND OUTBREAK OF WAR
WITH GERMANY—Continued

THE WORLD WAR:
PERIOD OF AMERICAN NEUTRALITY

RELATIONS WITH GERMANY AND AUSTRIA-HUNGARY—GERMAN SUBMARINE
WARFARE—SEVERANCE OF DIPLOMATIC RELATIONS AND OUTBREAK OF WAR
WITH GERMANY—Continued

THE WORLD WAR:
PERIOD OF AMERICAN NEUTRALITY

RELATIONS WITH GERMANY AND AUSTRIA-HUNGARY—GERMAN SUBMARINE WARFARE—SEVERANCE OF DIPLOMATIC RELATIONS AND OUTBREAK OF WAR WITH GERMANY—Continued

THE WORLD WAR:
PERIOD OF AMERICAN NEUTRALITY

RELATIONS WITH GERMANY AND AUSTRIA-HUNGARY—GERMAN SUBMARINE WARFARE—SEVERANCE OF DIPLOMATIC RELATIONS AND OUTBREAK OF WAR WITH GERMANY—Continued

THE WORLD WAR:
PERIOD OF AMERICAN NEUTRALITY

RELATIONS WITH GERMANY AND AUSTRIA-HUNGARY—GERMAN SUBMARINE WARFARE—SEVERANCE OF DIPLOMATIC RELATIONS AND OUTBREAK OF WAR WITH GERMANY—Continued

THE WORLD WAR:

PERIOD OF AMERICAN NEUTRALITY

RELATIONS WITH GERMANY AND AUSTRIA-HUNGARY—GERMAN SUBMARINE
WARFARE—SEVERANCE OF DIPLOMATIC RELATIONS AND OUTBREAK OF WAR
WITH GERMANY—Continued

THE WORLD WAR:
PERIOD OF AMERICAN NEUTRALITY

RELATIONS WITH GERMANY AND AUSTRIA-HUNGARY—GERMAN SUBMARINE WARFARE—SEVERANCE OF DIPLOMATIC RELATIONS AND OUTBREAK OF WAR WITH GERMANY—Continued

THE WORLD WAR:
PERIOD OF AMERICAN NEUTRALITY

RELATIONS WITH GERMANY AND AUSTRIA-HUNGARY—GERMAN SUBMARINE WARFARE—SEVERANCE OF DIPLOMATIC RELATIONS AND OUTBREAK OF WAR WITH GERMANY—Continued

THE WORLD WAR:
PERIOD OF AMERICAN NEUTRALITY

RELATIONS WITH GERMANY AND AUSTRIA-HUNGARY—GERMAN SUBMARINE WARFARE—SEVERANCE OF DIPLOMATIC RELATIONS AND OUTBREAK OF WAR WITH GERMANY—Continued

THE WORLD WAR:
PERIOD OF AMERICAN NEUTRALITY

RELATIONS WITH GERMANY AND AUSTRIA-HUNGARY—GERMAN SUBMARINE
WARFARE—SEVERANCE OF DIPLOMATIC RELATIONS AND OUTBREAK OF WAR
WITH GERMANY—Continued

THE WORLD WAR:
PERIOD OF AMERICAN NEUTRALITY

CORRESPONDENCE BETWEEN THE SECRETARY OF STATE AND AMERICAN
AMBASSADORS IN EUROPE—Continued

THE WORLD WAR:
PERIOD OF AMERICAN NEUTRALITY

CORRESPONDENCE BETWEEN THE SECRETARY OF STATE AND AMERICAN
AMBASSADORS IN EUROPE—Continued

THE WORLD WAR:
PERIOD OF AMERICAN NEUTRALITY

CORRESPONDENCE BETWEEN THE SECRETARY OF STATE AND AMERICAN
AMBASSADORS IN EUROPE—Continued

THE WORLD WAR:
PERIOD OF AMERICAN NEUTRALITY

CORRESPONDENCE BETWEEN THE SECRETARY OF STATE AND AMERICAN
AMBASSADORS IN EUROPE—Continued

THE WORLD WAR:
PERIOD OF AMERICAN NEUTRALITY

CORRESPONDENCE BETWEEN THE SECRETARY OF STATE AND AMERICAN
AMBASSADORS IN EUROPE—Continued

THE WORLD WAR:
PERIOD OF AMERICAN NEUTRALITY

CORRESPONDENCE BETWEEN THE SECRETARY OF STATE AND AMERICAN
AMBASSADORS IN EUROPE—Continued

THE WORLD WAR:
PERIOD OF AMERICAN NEUTRALITY

CORRESPONDENCE BETWEEN THE SECRETARY OF STATE AND AMERICAN AMBASSADORS IN EUROPE—Continued

THE WORLD WAR:
PERIOD OF AMERICAN NEUTRALITY

THE WORLD WAR:
PERIOD OF AMERICAN NEUTRALITY

EFFORTS AT NEUTRALIZATION OF THE FAR EAST

763.72111/34½

The Chinese Legation to the Department of State

MEMORANDUM

In case all means fail to end the present conflict in Europe it is desirable that warlike operations should not be extended to the Far East. For requesting a suspension of hostilities in the East on the part of the belligerent Powers, the United States has a precedent in the war between France and Germany in 1870.

"November 1, 1870, the Ministers of the United States at Paris and Berlin were instructed to propose to France and North Germany a suspension of hostilities between their fleets in the East."

"Soon after the ministers of the United States at Paris and Berlin were instructed to make the proposal information was received that the commanders of the French and Prussian fleets, apparently acting on their own responsibility, had, in view of the situation in China, come to an understanding temporarily to suspend hostilities." Moore's *Digest*, Vol. V, page 440. *Foreign Relations*, 1870.[1]

WASHINGTON, *August 3, 1914.*

763.72111/35½

Memorandum by the Counselor for the Department of State (Lansing) on Course To Be Pursued To Preserve the "Status Quo" in China [2]

The Chinese Government has issued a proclamation of neutrality in the European wars now being waged.

About August 1st the Chinese Minister spoke to the Secretary of State in regard to the feasibility of securing an agreement among the belligerents that the Far East should be neutralized.

On August 3rd the American Chargé at Peking telegraphed the Department:

"The proposal is being mooted to neutralize all foreign settlements concessions in China not including leased areas. I beg to request authorization for the Legation to participate in such an arrangement when laid before diplomatic body." [3]

---

[1] pp. 396–398.
[2] This paper bears the notation: "Handed to Secy of State Aug 8, 1914."
[3] *Foreign Relations*, 1914, supp., p. 161.

To this the Department replied:

"Your cipher telegram of August 3, 5 p. m. The Department authorizes Legation to participate in proposed arrangement to neutralize all foreign settlements in China not including leased areas." [4]

About August 3rd the Netherlands Chargé asked the Counselor of the Department whether this Government would unite with the Netherlands Government in a request to neutralize the western side of the Pacific.

On August 6th the American Chargé at Peking stated [5] that the diplomatic corps were unwilling to take up the matter of neutralization of the treaty ports, but that this Government might take up the question of the observance of the neutrality of China. He further stated that the Chinese Government intended to take up the neutralization of the Far East with this Government and with the Japanese Government.

On August 7th the Belgian Chargé approached the Third Assistant Secretary on the preservation of the *status quo* in China.

It is my judgment that a suggestion to neutralize any portion of the Pacific would be rejected by certain of the belligerents, and that, therefore, it would be unwise to make such a suggestion.

The neutralization of foreign settlements, other than territory leased to foreign governments, such as Wei-hai-Wei, Kiaochow, Kowloon, Kuangchouwan, which are respectively naval bases of Great Britain, Germany, Great Britain, and France should be urged upon the belligerents. It would amount to neutralizing the foreign treaty ports. The Department should take up the matter at once with the belligerent governments.

To further protect the interests of the United States in China and those of the Republic of China, I would suggest that it would be advisable—

(1) to obtain from the belligerent powers specific declarations that they will respect the neutrality of Chinese territory and waters, except areas leased to belligerent powers and except the waters adjacent to such areas.

(2) to obtain from all powers, who have interests in China, whether belligerent or neutral, an agreement that the *status quo* of all foreign rights and interests in China at the beginning of the present wars in Europe shall continue until a state of general peace in Europe.

I believe that it is possible to obtain the foregoing agreements as to neutralization of treaty ports, respect for Chinese neutrality and preservation of *status quo* in China. To ask more would I believe endanger all and would, in any event, so delay an international arrangement as to seriously impair its value when obtained. Further-

---

[4] *Foreign Relations*, 1914, supp., p. 163.
[5] *Ibid.*, p. 162.

more, to ask an agreement of a government, though convinced that it would not be granted, would accomplish no good purpose and give an impression that this Government was impracticable.

I believe that the preservation of the *status quo* to be the most important to American interests.

Appended is a telegram received on August 7th,[6] after the foregoing memorandum was prepared. While it has an important bearing on the situation, it supports the suggestions as to the policy to be pursued by this Government, and emphasizes the desirability of not adopting a course of action which would be unacceptable to the powers interested.

There is also appended a copy of correspondence relating to the action of the French and German naval commanders in Chinese waters during the Franco-Prussian War of 1870.[7] It hardly forms a basis for present action in view of the different conditions which exist today. It was then merely a matter of protection of the lives of foreigners in China against the Chinese. Today it is the protection of national and individual property interests from the attack of belligerents.

ROBERT LANSING

[WASHINGTON,] *August 7, 1914.*

763.72111/55½

The Counselor for the Department of State (Lansing) to the Secretary of State

WASHINGTON, *August 14, 1914.*

DEAR MR. SECRETARY: I have been thinking over the Far Eastern situation which has been, as I understand, submitted to the President to determine a course of action, and the following seems to me as worthy of consideration:

Persistent reports and rumors are that Japan intends to act upon her treaty alliance with Great Britain and declare war upon Germany within a few days, one report stating that this would be done by the 15th of the month. If we should endeavor to secure the neutralization of the treaty ports, the observance of Chinese neutrality and the preservation of the *status quo* before Japan declares war, it would seem to be our duty to approach that government first in accordance with the exchange of notes to which reference is made in the draft of the *Aide Memoire* submitted to you.[8] Presumably if

---

[6] Telegram of Aug. 7, 1914, 2 a. m., from the Chargé in China, *ibid.*, p. 164.
[7] *Ibid.*, 1870, pp. 396–398.
[8] Draft of the *aide-mémoire* to the Japanese Embassy not printed; it referred to the Root-Takahira notes of Nov. 30, 1908, printed in *Foreign Relations*, 1908, pp. 510–512.

Japan determined to begin war against Germany, she would be disposed to ignore or at least delay reply to our communication, and we would therefore gain no benefit by immediate action. On the other hand, if we wait before acting in regard to the questions of neutralization and *status quo* in China, until war between Japan and Germany has been declared, I do not think we would be bound to present the matter in the first instance to the Japanese Government, but with perfect propriety might approach all the belligerents upon the subject simultaneously, including in our note to Japan a statement as to the binding effect of the notes exchanged with her government.

In view of these considerations, I have changed my views as to the necessity of immediate action, and believe that we would gain a diplomatic advantage by waiting until Japan has taken decisive action in regard to her attitude toward Germany.

I am putting this in the form of a letter, in order that it may be more convenient for you to submit these observations to the President, in case you approve.

Very sincerely yours,

ROBERT LANSING

763.72/406

Memorandum by the Counselor for the Department of State (Lansing)

[WASHINGTON,] *August 16, 1914.*

At 10:15 A. M., August 16, 1914, I handed the annexed paper[9] to the Chancellor of the German Embassy at the office of the Embassy. I stated to him that the paper was a copy of a communication received by the Department from the American Ambassador at Berlin, who further telegraphed that the German Foreign Office requested the Department to forward the same to the German Ambassador at Tokio.

I explained to the Chancellor that, as it seemed possible for him to communicate with the German Ambassador in Tokio, it might be considered improper for the Department to be the medium of communication between the German Government and its representative in any other country except the United States. I handed in the paper therefore for him to take such action in regard to it as he might consider advisable.

The Chancellor stated that he understood perfectly the position of the Department and thought its course was the proper one and that

---

[9] Telegram of Aug. 13, 1914, 8 p. m., from the Ambassador in Germany, *Foreign Relations*, 1914, supp., p. 169.

he believed he could communicate by telegraph with the German Ambassador at Tokio.

I further stated that in case he found it impossible to send the communication of his Government to its destination, in such an emergency the Department would consider the propriety of becoming a medium of communication for his Government in forwarding the paper.

The Chancellor asked if the Department had any comments to make upon the declarations set forth in the annexed paper, and I informed him that at the present time, in view of the fact that the German Government had not invited comment, the Department did not think it proper or necessary to make any.

ROBERT LANSING

[There follows this notation in Secretary Bryan's hand:

"On evening of 16th I telephoned German Embassy asking if he had been able to send message. He replied it had been sent and he thought it would reach Tokio. I reiterated statement made by Mr. Lansing that we would send it if he failed to find a way to send it."]

763.72111/88½

President Wilson to the Secretary of State

WASHINGTON, *August 17, 1914.*

MY DEAR MR. SECRETARY: I am returning the enclosed papers [10] because it is evidently too late to pursue the course suggested by them. Things have developed very fast in the East since you were kind enough to submit them to me.

Cordially and faithfully yours,

WOODROW WILSON

---

[10] See Mr. Lansing's memorandum of Aug. 7, 1914, p. 1, and his letter of Aug. 14, 1914, to the Secretary of State, p. 3.

PEACE PROPOSALS

763.72119/36½

President Wilson to the Secretary of State

WASHINGTON, *August 21, 1914.*

MY DEAR MR. SECRETARY: Here is something which looks to me very dangerous. I enclose a copy of the telegram which I sent in reply and hand them both over for your thought pending an answer.

Cordially and faithfully yours,

WOODROW WILSON

[Enclosure 1—Telegram]

The Niagara Section of the New York Peace Society to President Wilson

NIAGARA FALLS, N. Y., *August 20, 1914—3:15 p. m.*

We have an opportunity to raise a peace fund of one million dollars to be used in defraying expenses of a joint commission to be appointed by two neutral governments for the purpose of investigating immediately the cause of the European war and then developing a plan for negotiating satisfactory settlement. Said commission to pave the way for mediation. Will you kindly telegraph whether this project is going to meet with your approval in the interest of peace.

NIAGARA SECTION OF THE NEW YORK PEACE SOCIETY

[Enclosure 2—Telegram]

President Wilson to the Niagara Section of the New York Peace Society

WASHINGTON, *August 21, 1914.*

I fear the plan you speak of might lead to very serious results of a sort that would defeat your purpose. I beg therefore that before proceeding you will let me know more particularly what you have in mind. I would appreciate a letter.

WOODROW WILSON

763.72119/35½a

The Secretary of State to President Wilson

WASHINGTON, *August 28, 1914.*

MY DEAR MR. PRESIDENT: We have at last received an answer from the Czar to your offer of mediation.[1] It is as follows:

"Appreciating the humanitarian sentiments which dictated this step His Majesty has deigned to command me to transmit to the President his sincere thanks. Russia did not desire war and did everything to avoid it, but from the moment this war was imposed upon her she cannot fail to defend her rights by force of arms. Under these circumstances it seems for the moment premature to contemplate the possibility of peace. Nevertheless I beg you to be so good as to be the interpreter to Mr. Woodrow Wilson of the thanks of His Majesty."

If you will examine the five answers received, you will be reminded of that passage in the Scriptures which says "that they all with one accord began to make excuses." Each one declares he is opposed to war and anxious to avoid it and then lays the blame upon someone else. The German Ambassador this morning blamed Russia and congratulates his country that the Emperor did what he could to avoid war. He also commends the efforts of France and Great Britain to avoid war, but the Czar is charged with being the cause, his offense being the mobilization of his army after Austria had assured him that the integrity of Servia would not be disturbed.

The fact that they all declare themselves against war and express regret that it has been gone into would seem to make it easier when a way opens to present the matter again. An appeal could then be reinforced by quotations from their replies.

I hope that you are securing the rest which you so greatly need. With assurances [etc.]   W. J. BRYAN

763.72119/35½b

The Secretary of State to President Wilson

WASHINGTON, *September 5, 1914.*

MY DEAR MR. PRESIDENT: I return the letter of Mr. Rand which you sent me from Cornish.[2] I am afraid of the proposition. A commission of inquiry at this time would not be in position to deal

---

[1] For President Wilson's offer of good offices, see *Foreign Relations*, 1914, supp., p. 42; for the replies, see *ibid.*, pp. 48, 49, 50, 60, 78.
[2] No copy of this letter found in Department files; see correspondence with Niagara Section of the New York Peace Society, p. 6.

with the question as impartially and independently as would be necessary to give the findings weight.   I doubt if there is any other country besides our own which is at present in position to conduct a thorough investigation and announce the result and I do not believe it would be wise for us to do so.   Such a conclusion to have weight would have to locate the blame and it would be impossible to fix the responsibility without arousing protest from the party charged with causing the war.   According to the plan proposed "the commission of inquiry is not to publish these issues (or any other facts unearthed)."   This is admission that publication might jeopardize the cause of mediation and who, after the experience we have had, would imagine that such a commission could investigate the cause of the war in secret or prevent the publication of the facts or findings?

The fifth paragraph in the proposition in Section B promises that all of the work will be in harmony with the policy of the Administration; how could this promise be kept insofar as it affects the foreign members of the commission?   The sixth paragraph proposes the establishment of a Press Bureau "to counteract injurious rumors." It seems to me that the end, however desirable, cannot be reached in this way.   If the time comes for a renewal of the offer you have made, you can determine whether any other nations are at that time in position to join—that question could not be determined many days in advance for we know not how soon other European nations may be drawn into the war.

I venture to suggest, therefore, that the Niagara Section of The New York Peace Society be informed that the offer made is heartily appreciated and the spirit which prompted it warmly commended, but that the plan does not seem practicable at this time.

With assurances [etc.]   W. J. BRYAN

763.72119/35½

President Wilson to the Acting Secretary of State

WASHINGTON, *September 17, 1914.*

MY DEAR MR. LANSING: I had a short interchange of views with the Secretary of State last evening over the telephone about the enclosed dispatch from the German Chancellor.[3]   My own judgment is that it needs for the time, at any rate, no reply from us.   I wonder if your judgment is the same?

Cordially and sincerely yours,

WOODROW WILSON

---

[3] See telegram No. 149, Sept. 14, 1914, from the Ambassador in Germany, *Foreign Relations*, 1914, supp., p. 104.

763.72119/35½

The Acting Secretary of State to President Wilson

WASHINGTON, *September 18, 1914.*

MY DEAR MR. PRESIDENT: I beg to acknowledge your note of the 17th instant enclosing a copy of a despatch from the Imperial Chancellor of Germany regarding proposals of peace. My judgment is the same as yours that the despatch needs for the present no reply.

Respectfully yours,

ROBERT LANSING

763.72119/35½c

The Secretary of State to President Wilson

WASHINGTON, *October 7, 1914.*

MY DEAR MR. PRESIDENT: In conference with some of the Latin-American representatives, I find that suggestions have come from Europe to some of them in regard to the possibility of mediation.

I have put off all discussion of the question of united action, on the ground that until there was an opening for mediation it would not be proper to discuss it. There is a good deal to be said on both sides of the proposition. We will find less embarrassment if we act alone than if we act with a number of others. At the same time, it would be hard to refuse the other nations desiring it the honor of joining with us, and I have no doubt they would be disposed to follow the lead of this nation.

There are three propositions that I think we may be considering in advance, even though we are not prepared to discuss them with others:

First: Whether in case of mediation this government should act alone:

Second: Whether, if we invited others, we should confine the invitation to the three large republics of South America, and let it be an American mediation; or

Third: Whether we should include European nations in the invitation.

The embarrassment about the third proposition would be to determine just whom to include.

The Spanish Minister has expressed an interest in the matter, as has also the Danish Minister and, I think, the Netherlands. I have no doubt all of them would be glad to take part.

I lay the matter before you so that you can be thinking about it at your leisure moments, if you are so happy as to have leisure moments among your many cares.

With assurances [etc.]

W. J. BRYAN

763.72119/35½d

The Secretary of State to President Wilson

WASHINGTON, *December 1, 1914.*

MY DEAR MR. PRESIDENT: I beg to submit for your consideration the following:

(*a*) The war is throwing a heavy burden upon the United States and deranging business. The cotton growers have suffered a loss of not less than $100,000,000 by the restriction of their market; several other lines of industry have suffered severely; the loss to business generally, due to a suspension of credits, has amounted to many hundreds of millions. The Government has been compelled to resort to new forms of taxation to make good the decrease in import duties.

(*b*) Transportation is interrupted both on land and sea and the railroad situation is likely to become embarrassing.

(*c*) Delicate questions are constantly arising in connection with our efforts to maintain neutrality. These may not only affect our relations with the belligerents but they disturb political conditions in this country and threaten to turn attention from our economic problems.

2nd. We owe it to other neutral nations to do everything in our power to bring the war to a close. They are suffering relatively more than we are and are less able than we to endure the hardships which, without their fault, have been thrown upon them. Complaint has already been made against some of the neutral nations that they have not enforced neutrality; other neutral nations are complaining of the acts of belligerents in interfering with neutral commerce—the friction and irritation are increasing. These neutral nations look to us to represent the third party—"the bystanders" who, though innocent, suffer while the combatants fight.

3rd. We owe it to the belligerent nations, as a friend to all of them, to earnestly advise them to consider the peaceful settlement of their differences. Their feelings are so deeply stirred that they take counsel of their anger rather than of their sober judgment; they cannot consider the question with calmness and their pride will not allow them to ask mediation—the offer must come from us.

Four months have elapsed and each of the nations at war has witnessed a failure of its plans and calculations—the uncertainty of the result must now be apparent to all. The chance is decreasing that either side can win such a decisive victory as to enable it to dictate terms, and even if either side should win such a victory the peace that would follow would be built upon fear, and history proves that permanent peace can not be built upon such a foundation.

Mediation does not mean that any of the combatants shall accept terms that are unsatisfactory, but that they shall propose terms, and surely these Christian nations ought to be willing to state to the world the terms upon the acceptance of which they are willing to cease hostilities, leaving responsibility for a continuance of the war to rest upon those who propose unreasonable terms or reject reasonable terms. All disclaim responsibility for the beginning of the war and there is no tribunal to fix the blame, but responsibility can be fixed for a continuation of the war if any nation is unwilling to state its terms or if, in stating its terms, it makes demands which are not just and fair.

When, at the beginning of the war, you proposed mediation, none of the nations expressed a willingness to consider a conference, but now, after appalling losses on both sides; now when all must confess failure to accomplish what they expected; now when the cup of sorrow is overflowing and when new horrors are being added daily, it would seem to be this nation's duty, as the leading exponent of Christianity and as the foremost advocate of worldwide peace, to approach the warring nations again and earnestly urge them to consent to a conference with a view to coming to an understanding which will enable them to lay down their arms and begin the work of reconstructing a permanent peace on the basis of justice and friendship.

With assurances [etc.]   W. J. BRYAN

763.72119/55a

The Secretary of State to President Wilson

WASHINGTON, *April 19, 1915.*

MY DEAR MR. PRESIDENT: As a matter of precaution I return these letters [4] and answer your note concerning them with my pen. The one sent out by O'Laughlin [5] is frank and bears evidence of correctly stating the situation. There is no doubt as to the sentiment in Germany and the view they take is a natural one. 1st, They have warned Americans not to travel on British ships. Why do Americans take the risk? Not an unreasonable question. 2nd, If we allow the use of our flag, how can we complain, if in the confusion one of our boats is sunk by mistake? 3rd, Why be shocked at the drowning of a few people, if there is no objection to starving a nation? Of course Germany insists that by careful use she will have enough food, but if Great Britain cannot succeed in starving the noncombatants, why does she excite retaliation by threatening to do so?

If we are to prove our neutrality—and unless we do, we are likely to be drawn into the conflict by the growing feeling in Germany—it

------

[4] No copies of these letters found in Department files.
[5] J. C. O'Laughlin, of the Chicago *Herald.*

seems to me we must prevent the misuse of our flag and warn Americans not to use British vessels in the war zone unless we can bring pressure on Great Britain to withdraw threat to make bread or food contraband. Our identical note [6] was well intended and Germany indicated a willingness to negotiate—would it not be wise to make another effort to persuade Great Britain to join in some agreement which will, by permitting food to go into Germany, do away with the torpedoing of merchant vessels? Otherwise, the continued export of arms is likely to get us into trouble. So much for the O'Laughlin letter.

The Münsterburg [7] letter indicates that Germany is ready for peace. I doubt if the terms he proposes are possible. I doubt if it is wise to propose terms, but I feel and have felt for some time that we should urge the Allies to consent to a conference at which terms shall be discussed.

It is impossible for either side to annihilate the other, and a continuance of the struggle not only adds to the horrors but endangers neutrals who have already suffered greatly. I doubt if secret proposals will suffice—a public appeal strongly worded might have effect, and would it not be justified considering the nature of the contest and our relation to the nations at war? All the neutral nations would at once indorse it and it might end the war. I do not see that it could do harm.

I agree with Münsterburg that you are the one to act—no self-appointed com. could or should take the lead. "Who knoweth whether thou art come to the kingdom for such a time as this?"

With assurances [etc.]   W. J. Bryan

763.72119/55b

The Secretary of State to President Wilson

WASHINGTON, *April 26, 1915.*

MY DEAR MR. PRESIDENT: I am not sure whether I reported a very confidential communication which I received a few days ago from the Japanese Ambassador. It was to the effect that the Japanese Minister in Stockholm was approached by the Austrian representative on the subject of Japan entering into a treaty of peace with Germany. Their answer was what might have been expected, namely, that they could not consider the matter independently of the Allies.

He wanted to know whether we had seen any indications of a desire on the part of either side for a cessation of hostilities and I told him that while we had heard rumors we were unable to

---

[6] *Foreign Relations*, 1915, supp., p. 119.
[7] Professor Hugo Münsterburg, of Harvard University.

find any authority for such rumors and that so far as we knew no indication of a desire for peace had been given by either side.

With assurances [etc.]   W. J. BRYAN

763.72119/55½

President Wilson to the Secretary of State

WASHINGTON, *27 April, 1915.*

MY DEAR MR. SECRETARY: This is significant news.

I am, as you know, keeping in as close touch as possible with what the men in authority at Berlin, Paris, and London have in mind, and I am sorry to say that there is only one thing we can truthfully say to the Japanese Ambassador in reply to his inquiry,— and perhaps it will be useful to say it,—namely, that there are no terms of peace spoken of (at any rate in Germany) which are not so selfish and impossible that the other side are ready to resist them to their last man and dollar. Reasonableness has not yet been burned into them, and what they are thinking of is, not the peace and prosperity of Europe, but their own aggrandizement, an impossible modern basis (it might be well for Japan to reflect) for peace.

Faithfully Yours,

W. W.

763.72119/88a

The Secretary of State to President Wilson

WASHINGTON, *August 18, 1915.*

MY DEAR MR. PRESIDENT: You ask me for an opinion in regard to the enclosed communication.[8] I hesitate to give one because I do not agree with the premises on which these good people rest their argument for the commencement of a peace movement in this country.

I do not believe that it is true that the civil leaders of the belligerents would at the present time look with favor on action by the neutral nations; and, even if they did, the military branches of the belligerent governments dominate the situation, and, they favor a continuance of the war. It is the latter element which must be won over or we must wait until the civil branch becomes more influential in the conduct of affairs.

It is probable that Germany and Austria, now triumphant in the East and firmly entrenched in the West, would welcome a peace movement by neutrals. I should think that they would, for they are occupying extensive tracts of their enemies territories. While they are losing large numbers of men, the efficiency of their armies remains

---

[8] No copy of enclosure found in Department files.

unimpaired. They are in the best possible situation to make a peace which will give them, in part at least, the fruits of their victories over Russia and their firm hold on the Belgian and French territory which they occupy. They are in a position to demand compensation in territory and treasure. This would unquestionably be their attitude if peace negotiations should be instituted at the present time. It would be the reasonable and logical attitude.

On the other hand the Allies would not, in my opinion, be willing to consider a peace under the present military conditions. Every reason which would induce the Teutons to make peace would make the Allies unwilling. With their enemy successfully occupying their lands they are in no position to make a peace which would be satisfactory to them. They would consider an agreement to negotiate an evidence of weakness, which I do not think they would admit even indirectly. I understand from several reliable sources that their hope is to continue the war in much the same way that it is being carried on now on the theory that Germany and Austria cannot stand the waste of men and resources resulting. The Allies believe that, while this process of wasting is going on, they will on the other hand be gaining in men and munitions and be prepared at the opportune time to force back their exhausted opponents within their own boundaries.

Whether they are drawing right conclusions or not makes no difference if they believe this will be the consequence of continuing hostilities. I am certain that they have this belief.

Manifestly a suggestion to enter into peace negotiations would be inacceptable at the present time to the Allies who are relying on time to equalize the military strength of the belligerents. I think that the attempt now would not only be rejected but resented.

If this estimate of the situation is correct and if we do not wish to destroy our helpfulness when an effort to restore peace offers some prospect of success, it would be folly to approach the belligerents on the subject at the present time.

As to the second premise, the fitness of the United States to initiate a peace appeal at the present time, I think that it is only needful to say that our usefulness for the future as an intermediary would undoubtedly be lost or greatly lessened by such a step, for the Allies would look upon our activity as in the interest of their foes, while the latter would be glad to use us as tools to secure their conquests and not as friends seeking the common good of all.

Holding these views I would strongly favor discouraging any neutral movement toward peace at the present time, because I believe it would fail and because, if it did fail, we would lose our influence for the future.

Faithfully yours,

ROBERT LANSING

763.72119/10428

The Secretary of State to President Wilson

WASHINGTON, *May 3, 1916.*

MY DEAR MR. PRESIDENT: Enclosed is a most confidential message just received from Gerard.[8a] I am a little puzzled as to the real purpose of introducing the subject at the present time. It would look to me like an attempted diversion on Germany's part in order to create here a sympathetic feeling which would prevent radical action on our part. Of course I may be in error as to the motive of the German official who undoubtedly inspired this telegram but I confess to be very skeptical as to the *bona fides* of the suggestion.

Faithfully yours,

ROBERT LANSING

763.72/2691½

President Wilson to the Secretary of State

WASHINGTON, *15 May, 1916.*

MY DEAR MR. SECRETARY: This is the communication from the Pope to which I referred the other day. I would value your suggestion as to the manner and substance of my reply.

Faithfully Yours,

W. W.

It was brought to the Office by the Apostolic Delegate.

[Enclosure—Translation]

Pope Benedict XV to President Wilson [9]

We pray Your Excellency to be kind enough to suspend your decision on the question of Submarine Warfare with Germany since we see the possibility of peaceful settlement and we hope that as far as you are concerned no incident will embarrass our effort. We are sending the same telegram to His Majesty, the Emperor.

BENEDICT

763.72/2691½

The Secretary of State to President Wilson

WASHINGTON, *May 15, 1916.*

MY DEAR MR. PRESIDENT: I received your letter of today enclosing a copy of the communication which you received from the Pope. I enclose a letter which I suggest as a reply.

[8a] *Foreign Relations,* 1916, supp., p. 27.

[9] Filed separately under file No. 763.72/2690½. This undated file translation bears the notation: "Translation dictated to Mr. Tumulty by Monsignor Bonzano." The original was in French.

This morning Monsignor Russell called upon me with a letter [10] addressed to you from Cardinal Gibbons,[11] which he asked me to read and if I thought you intended to answer the Pope's communication to deliver it to you.

I have also drafted a reply to Cardinal Gibbons which provides for the transmission of your answer to the Pope's communication through him.

Monsignor Russell indicated to me that there was some feeling on the part of the Cardinal that no reply had been made to the Pope before this. I believe, although your letter does not indicate it, that you received the Pope's communication on May sixth. Monsignor Russell said that you had agreed to make answer on Monday, the 8th, and for that reason they were disappointed it had not been received before.

Faithfully yours,

[File copy not signed]

[Enclosure]

Draft Reply to Pope Benedict XV [12]

I greatly appreciate the friendly sentiment of broad humanity that prompted your personal communication to me concerning the questions that have arisen between this country and Germany.

I am gratified to say that before the receipt of your message the discussion had already entered upon a stage of satisfactory understanding.

With great respect I have the honor to be, Your Holiness,
Very sincerely,

763.72119/156a

The Secretary of State to President Wilson

WASHINGTON, May 25, 1916.

MY DEAR MR. PRESIDENT: I had hoped to see you tomorrow at Cabinet meeting but today the Doctor refused to allow me to leave the house this week. I intended when I saw you to say something about the purposes of the League to Enforce Peace, which is to meet here,

---

[10] Not found in Department files.
[11] Archbishop of Baltimore.
[12] Filed separately under file No. 763.72/2692½. No final copy of a letter from President Wilson to Pope Benedict XV has been found in the Department files.

and at the banquet of which I understand you are to speak on Saturday night.[13] I would have preferred to talk the matter over with you but as that is impossible I have taken the liberty to write you this letter, although in doing so I am violating the directions of the Doctor.

While I have not had time or opportunity to study carefully the objects of the proposed League to Enforce Peace, I understand the fundamental ideas are these, which are to be embodied in a general treaty of the nations: First, an agreement to submit all differences which fail of diplomatic adjustment to arbitration or a board of conciliation; and, second, in case a government fails to comply with this provision, an agreement that the other parties will unite in compelling it to do so by an exercise of force.

With the first agreement I am in accord to an extent, but I cannot see how it is practicable to apply it in case of a continuing invasion of fundamental national or individual rights unless some authoritative international body has the power to impose and enforce an order in the nature of an injunction, which will prevent the aggressor from further action until arbitration has settled the rights of the parties. How this can be done in a practical way I have not attempted to work out, but the problem is not easy, especially the part which relates to the enforcement of the order.

It is, however, the second agreement in regard to the imposition of international arbitration by force, which seems to me the most difficult, especially when viewed from the standpoint of its effects on our national sovereignty and national interests. It is needless to go into the manifest questions arising when the *modus operandi* of the agreement is considered. Such questions as: Who may demand international intervention? What body will decide whether the demand should be complied with? How will the international forces be constituted? Who will take charge of the military and naval operations? Who will pay the expenses of the war (for war it will be)?

Perplexing as these questions appear to me, I am more concerned with the direct effect on this country. I do not believe that it is wise to limit our independence of action, a sovereign right, to the will of other powers beyond this hemisphere. In any representative international body clothed with authority to require of the nations to employ their armies and navies to coerce one of their number, we would be in the minority. I do not believe that we should

---

[13] For text of the President's remarks on this occasion, see the *Address of the President of the United States Delivered at the First Annual Assemblage of the League to Enforce Peace, May 27, 1916* (Washington, Government Printing Office, 1916).

put ourselves in the position of being compelled to send our armed forces to Europe or Asia or, in the alternative, of repudiating our treaty obligation. Neither our sovereignty nor our interests would accord with such a proposition, and I am convinced that popular opinion as well as the Senate would reject a treaty framed along such lines.

It is possible that the difficulty might be obviated by the establishment of geographical zones, and leaving to the groups of nations thus formed the enforcement of the peaceful settlement of disputes. But if that is done why should all the world participate? We have adopted a much modified form of this idea in the proposed Pan-American Treaty by the "guaranty" article.[14] But I would not like to see its stipulations extended to the European powers so that they, with our full agreement, would have the right to cross the ocean and stop quarrels between two American Republics. Such authority would be a serious menace to the Monroe Doctrine and a greater menace to the Pan-American Doctrine.

It appears to me that, if the first idea of the League can be worked out in a practical way and an international body constituted to determine when steps should be taken to enforce compliance, that the use of force might be avoided by outlawing the offending nation. No nation today can live unto itself. The industrial and commercial activities of the world are too closely interwoven for a nation isolated from the other nations to thrive and prosper. A tremendous economic pressure could be imposed on the outlawed nation by all other nations denying it intercourse of every nature, even communication, in a word make that nation a pariah, and so to remain until it was willing to perform its obligations.

I am not at all sure that this means is entirely feasible. I see many difficulties which would have to be met under certain conditions. But I do think that it is more practical in operation and less objectionable from the standpoint of national rights and interests than the one proposed by the League. It does not appear to me that the use of physical force is in any way practical or advisable.

I presume that you are far more familiar than I am with the details of the plans of the League and that it may be presumptuous on my part to write you as I have. I nevertheless felt it my duty to frankly give you my views on the subject and I have done so.

Faithfully yours,

ROBERT LANSING

---

[14] See vol. II, pp. 471 ff.

763.72/3261½

Memorandum by President Wilson [15]

BASES OF PEACE

I

Mutual guarantee of political independence,—absolute in all domestic matters, limited in external affairs only by the rights of other nations.

II

Mutual guarantee of territorial integrity.

NOTE. The application of this guarantee to the territorial arrangements made by the terms of the peace by which the present war is ended would, of course, necessarily depend upon the character of those arrangements, that is, their reasonableness and natural prospect of permanency; and would depend, so far as the participation of the United States is concerned, upon whether they were in conformity with the general principles of right and comity set forth in the address of the President to the Senate on the twenty-second of January last. [16]

III

Mutual guarantee against such economic warfare as would in effect constitute an effort to throttle the industrial life of a nation or shut it off from equal opportunities of trade with the rest of the world.

NOTE. This would, of course, not apply to any laws of any individual state which were meant merely for the regulation and development of its own industries or for the mere safeguarding of its own resources from misuse or exhaustion, but only to such legislation and such governmental action as could be shown to be intended to operate outside territorial limits and intended to injure particular rivals or groups of rivals.

IV

Limitation of armaments, whether on land or sea, to the necessities of internal order and the probable demands of cooperation in making good the foregoing guarantees.

[NOTE.] *Provided* the nations which take part in this covenant may be safely regarded as representing the major force of mankind.

GENERAL NOTE: It is suggested that it would not be necessary to set up at the outset any permanent tribunal or administrative agency,

---

[15] This paper bears the notation: "Handed me by Prest Feby 7, 1917 RL."
[16] *Foreign Relations*, 1917, supp. 1, p. 24.

but only an Office of correspondence through which all matters of information could be cleared up, correspondence translated by experts (scholars), and mutual explanations and suggestions interchanged. It would in all likelihood be best to await the developments and suggestions of experience before attempting to set up any common instrumentality of international action.

763.72/3261½

Memorandum by the Secretary of State [17]

NOTES ON BASES OF PEACE

[WASHINGTON,] *February 7, 1917.*

Article I

Would it be better to insert "equal" before the word "rights" in the last line?

Article II

Does this provide for the adequate expansion of territory as a result of increased population or an accumulation of capital desiring investment in territory under national control? That is, should not some provision be made for future colonization? So far as the American nations are concerned, and I think the same is true of Russia with its vast undeveloped territories and Great Britain with its great colonial possessions still but partially settled, a provision of this sort could be applied without danger of being disturbed for many decades, but is the same true of such populous countries as Belgium, France, Germany, Italy, Holland, etc.? Is it possible to make a rigid and permanent delimitation of territory which will not in a short time be the source of trouble from the pressure of population? Will not such conditions cause aggression from necessity and in no sense from national ambition or improper motives? Is it possible to provide some elasticity as to territory which will furnish an outlet for surplus populations?

I do not think that the conditions for the application of a "world" treaty are the same as the conditions for the application of a Pan-American treaty. I have no suggestion to offer now as the problem seems to me to require very careful study. I am merely raising here possible objections to the present terms of this Article.

Article III

Does this provision apply to "economic warfare" by a single state against another state? If it does, then the power to retaliate for

---

[17] This memorandum bears no indication of authorship, but contains corrections in Secretary Lansing's hand.

unjust commercial legislation or regulation by one nation, which though general in terms operates in practice against only one other nation, would be lacking and prevent the injured party from protecting itself from injustice. I assume the basic thought in this article is to prevent such international combinations as the Entente Allies had in mind during the Paris Economic Conference, which as I understand proposed to unite their nations in preferential trade facilities after the war so that they would benefit first the Allies, second, friendly neutrals and third, other neutrals, leaving the Central Powers commercially isolated or at least greatly handicapped in trade opportunities.

I am afraid that in its present form the article would be difficult of application. Who would be the judges as to the purpose of an economic war between states? Whose duty would it be to assume to judge of this matter? And whose duty would it be to enforce the guarantee after the authorized party had decided that action was necessary? This article seems to me much more difficult of practical application than either of the two preceding articles.

As a matter of fact I have never felt that the proposed plan of the Paris Conference could be carried out. Such a combination even if attempted would by the natural laws of trade fall to pieces in a short time.

Would it not be as efficacious and less difficult of application to enter into a mutual agreement not to form any international combination or conspiracy to interfere with the commercial enterprises or to limit the equal trade opportunities of any nation? This would not deprive a single nation of the power to act in its own interests, but would prevent the united or identical action of two or more nations.

Article IV

This seems to me the most difficult of all the articles for proper application. So much depends on the geographical location of territorial possessions and their relation to one another, to the state of civilization attained in colonies, to the proximity of territory to semi-civilized nations, to the restlessness of populations due to lack of intellectual development, to political oppression, to industrial injustice, to other causes of domestic unrest. In limited and settled populations with liberal institutions the difficulties could be easily overcome, but in the larger states where domestic peace depends on an adequate force to suppress uprisings, that force might in the hands of an ambitious and unscrupulous government be a very grave menace to small neighboring states.

I am sure that you will understand I am not arguing against this article. I believe in the purpose but I am endeavoring to raise in my own mind the possible difficulties of the practical operation of the provisions if they should be adopted.

Who would determine what armament a nation was entitled to maintain? What would be the basis for limitation? How would an increase or decrease be determined if conditions changed? How would a proper limitation be enforced, and who would determine when enforcement should take place?

These questions are to me very perplexing and very real, and I cannot feel that they should remain unanswered until after the proposal of such an article as this. They will have to be answered some time and better before than after the nations are committed, because they would then be a source of endless controversy and of possible discord.

GENERAL NOTE. As to this note I have no comment to make. It seems to me sound and to offer the best agency possible under present international conditions.

763.72/3261½

President Wilson to the Secretary of State

WASHINGTON, *9 February, 1917.*

MY DEAR MR. SECRETARY: The Swiss Minister is pressing for a reply to the suggestion of his government.[18] He is a very diligent and pressing gentleman!

What would you think of replying to him in the sense of the enclosed memorandum?

I have tried my hand at a restatement of the bases. What do you think of the result? All that we can hope for is to agree upon definite things and rely on experience and subsequent exchanges of treaty agreement to develop and remove the practical difficulties.

Faithfully Yours,

W. W.

[Enclosure]

Memorandum by President Wilson

BASES OF PEACE

I

Mutual guarantee of political independence,—absolute in all domestic matters, limited in external affairs only by the equal rights of other nations.

[18] See *Foreign Relations,* 1916, supp., pp. 112, 117.

II

Mutual guarantee of territorial integrity.

NOTE. The application of this guarantee to the territorial arrangements made by the terms of the peace by which the present war is to be ended would, of course, necessarily depend upon the character of those arrangements, that is, upon their reasonableness and natural prospect of permanency; and, so far as the participation of the United States in the guarantee is concerned, would depend upon whether they were in conformity with the general principles of right and comity which the President set forth in his address to the Senate on the twenty-second of January.

Such a guarantee would not affect natural expansion peaceably accomplished.

III

Mutual agreement not to take part in any joint economic action by two or more nations which would in effect constitute an effort to throttle the industrial life of any nation or shut it off from fair and equal opportunities of trade with the nations thus in concert or with the rest of the world.

NOTE. This would of course not apply, as its terms indicate, to the laws of an individual state intended for the regulation and development of its own industries or for the safeguarding of its own resources from misuse or exhaustion, but only to cooperative action between states intended or which would operate to injure particular rivals or groups of rivals.

IV

Mutual agreement to limit armaments, whether on land or sea, to the necessities of internal order (including, of course, the internal order of an empire) and the probable demands of cooperation in making good the foregoing guarantees and agreements.

NOTE. *Provided* the nations which take part in these covenants may reasonably be regarded as representing the major force of mankind.

GENERAL NOTE. It is suggested that it would not be necessary to set up at the outset any permanent tribunal or administrative agency, but only an office of correspondence through which all matters of information could be cleared up, correspondence translated by competent scholars, and mutual explanations and suggestions exchanged. It would in all likelihood be best, in this matter of executive organization, to await the developments and lessons of experience before attempting to set up any common instrumentality of international action.

Points To Be Made in Reply to the Suggestion of the Swiss Federal Council

The probable physical impossibility of holding an actual conference.

The embarrassments which it is now evident many neutral governments would feel in seeming to come together to influence the present course of events.

The desirability, nevertheless, of a frank interchange of views.

Suggestion, therefore, that the Swiss Federal Council communicate to the Government of the United States its views as to any present feasible course of cooperative action and any common bases upon which neutrals might at this time draw together in a League of Peace. The United States would be very glad in its turn, or at the invitation of the Council, to submit its own views on these vital and important subjects.

763.72119/544a

The Secretary of State to President Wilson

Washington, *March 17, 1917.*

My Dear Mr. President: This telegram from Mr. Penfield, No. 1757, March 13, 3 p. m.[19] (I enclose another copy as you have probably burned yours) seems to me to possess a possibility that something may be accomplished along the line suggested by Count Czernin, namely a secret meeting between a representative of the Allies and a representative of Austria-Hungary. If these two representatives come together to discuss general terms of peace, they may gradually drift into a discussion of a separate peace; and, if Austria-Hungary once permits her representative to talk even on that subject, I believe that something will have been gained.

It is my belief that the rumors reported in the last sentence of the telegram have substantial foundation, and that the Austrian Government is almost as fearful of its powerful ally as it is of its enemies. It seems to be in the unenviable position that its interests will be at the disposal of others however the war ends, in one case Germany will dictate, in the other the Entente Powers. As a matter of expediency, therefore, the Austrian Government may think it wise to come to some arrangement with the enemy before the war is decided, and takes this way of entering upon the subject. That is what I hoped and still hope. The keen interest shown by Count Czernin further encourages this hope.

---

[19] *Foreign Relations*, 1917, supp. 1, p. 65.

I think that the insistence of Count Czernin, that a secret conference such as he suggests could only discuss the terms of a general peace, ought not to be considered as discouraging, because that is precisely what he should be expected to do. He must of necessity maintain an appearance of perfect loyalty to Austria's allies, not only to satisfy the Austrian sense of honor but also to avoid possible dangers from an enraged Germany in case the matter became public. That he is willing to engage in these secret conferences is, I think, very significant and ought to be encouraged. He must know that no single delegate of the Allies would discuss in any way terms of a general peace, especially with an enemy which could not control the other Central Powers. Knowing this these secret meetings must be proposed by Count Czernin for another purpose which, if it relates to peace, must have to do with terms affecting Austria-Hungary alone. A "separate peace" may be repudiated, but may be discussed nevertheless.

It seems to me that we ought to take the opening offered. We may accomplish nothing or we may accomplish more than we expect. If we fail, I do not see that anything has been lost. We will be no worse off than we are now.

We agreed, you will recall, to treat all communications from the Austro-Hungarian Government as strictly secret. The next step would seem to be to telegraph Penfield to ask Count Czernin if he would object to our making the suggestion of a meeting such as he proposed, to one of the Allied Governments, not as originating with Austria-Hungary but as originating here, explaining to him that, since the idea was his, we would not wish to appear to be violating our pledge of secrecy by even adopting the suggestion as our own unless he authorized us to do so. At the same time we should say that we cannot disclose our other correspondent as we are in that case also communicating in the strictest confidence.

Faithfully yours,

ROBERT LANSING

RECRUITING OF AMERICAN CITIZENS

763.72111/81½

Memorandum by the Counselor for the Department of State
(Lansing)

[WASHINGTON,] *August 22, 1914.*

The German Secretary called my attention to the annexed memorandum in regard to the recruiting in Paris of a body of "Rough Riders," among them many Americans, stating that he believed that his Government would regard such enlisted foreigners as not entitled to be treated as properly in the military service of France, and, therefore, if captured, they might be shot as civilians and not held as prisoners of war.

I replied, that I felt sure that he must be mistaken as to his Government's views in regard to the enlistment of Americans in foreign military service; that it had always been the right of individuals to enter the army of a foreign nation; that I recalled no war, unless perhaps the Russian-Japanese, in which there were not numerous foreigners in both armies and often so-called "foreign legions;" and that never to my recollection had these foreigners, when captured, been treated otherwise than as prisoners of war.

The German Secretary said that in spite of these statements, which he could not deny though he had not studied the cases, he feared that his Government would take the view of the character of Americans serving in the French army such as he had stated.

I replied that, if such a course was followed, it would be entirely unwarranted by international usage, and that this Government would not view such treatment of Americans with indifference, for, although its policy was to discourage its citizens from enlisting in foreign military service, it had always recognized their right to do so. I said further that the effect of treating Americans, who chose to fight for France, as military outlaws would undoubtedly cause general indignation in the United States and arouse a spirit of animosity toward Germany, the results of which it would be difficult to foretell.

The Secretary said that he would consider the question further in view of what I had said.

ROBERT LANSING

[Enclosure]

Anglo-American Rough Riders

PARIS—Anglo-American Rough Riders including many famous western horsemen of America and best riders in England and France are expected to figure largely in operations of Allied troops against Germans.

Minister of War declared services of this body recruited during past week would be accepted by France and men would be called on to act as scouts and interpreters.

All of the Rough Riders have seen actual service some of them being veterans of Spanish-American War—They have provided their own mounts and uniforms but French Government has given the squad 5 automobiles—one of which will carry nurses, surgeons and hospital supplies.

_____

763.72111/82½

President Wilson to the Secretary of State

WASHINGTON, *August 27, 1914.*

MY DEAR MR. SECRETARY: Thank you sincerely for having let me see the enclosed memorandum.[1] I think that Mr. Lansing handled the matter in exactly the right way.

Faithfully yours,

WOODROW WILSON

_____

763.72111/284½

The Chairman of the Committee on Foreign Affairs, House of Representatives (Flood), to the Counselor for the Department of State (Lansing)

WASHINGTON, *September 29, 1914.*

DEAR MR. LANSING: In pursuance of our conversation of some time ago, in reference to a resolution introduced by Representative Burgess, of Texas, I am enclosing a copy of the resolution for your inspection. I would be glad if you would let me know whether you think it advisable to report this resolution.

Very truly yours,

H. D. FLOOD

_____

[1] Memorandum by the Counselor for the Department of State, *supra.*

[Enclosure]

House Concurrent Resolution 48, Submitted September 16, 1914,
Sixty-third Congress, Second Session

Whereas feeling is liable to increase on behalf of one or the other
belligerents in the European war; and

Whereas it is reported that American citizens in Europe are drill-
ing for the purpose of joining one or the other belligerents; and

Whereas the results of such action and many other unforeseen
conditions may arise which might tend to endanger the neutrality
which the President has requested every citizen to help maintain:
Therefore be it

Resolved by the House of Representatives (*the Senate concurring*),
That the Congress of the United States call the attention of the
American people to the necessity of the greatest precaution and con-
scientiousness on the part of every citizen, and especially the press,
by conduct, word, and act, to cooperate with and support the Government in maintaining the strictest neutrality as long as the war
continues.

763.72111/285½

Mr. J. P. Tumulty (*Secretary to the President*) *to the Secretary of*
State

WASHINGTON, *September 30, 1914.*

DEAR MR. SECRETARY: I am herewith returning the letter addressed
to Mr. Lansing by Representative Flood, together with the copy of
H. Con. Res. 48.[2] The President does not think it would be wise to
report the resolution.[3]

Sincerely yours,

J. P. TUMULTY

---

[2] *Supra.*
[3] A memorandum attached to this paper reads: "10/3/14. Telephoned Mr.
Flood Prest's view   RL."

ATTITUDE OF THE UNITED STATES TOWARD METHODS OF WARFARE EMPLOYED BY BELLIGERENTS

763.72116/42½

The Counselor for the Department of State (Lansing) to the Secretary of State

WASHINGTON, *August 28, 1914.*

DEAR MR. SECRETARY: In view of the bombardment by a German military balloon of the city of Antwerp during the night of August 24th–25th, it becomes necessary for us to consider:

(1) Whether or not this Government should formally protest against the act, which appears to have been in violation of certain provisions of The Hague Convention of 1907, No. 4;[1] and

(2) Whether, if it is decided to protest, the ground of the protest should be limited to the endangering of the lives of American citizens in Antwerp or should be general in nature as contrary to the laws of civilized warfare.

As to the policy of making a protest I am not convinced that it is expedient though my inclination is to do so, as the act appears to have been wanton and without military purpose, in fact an outrage against humanity.

In case it is decided to protest, I annex for your consideration drafts of protest based upon the two grounds mentioned. The one confined to American interests would not form a precedent for future protests in case the laws of war are violated unless the acts affected our own citizens. In that it has a decided advantage.

The other draft based on the general ground of violation of the usages of civilized warfare would undoubtedly accord with the almost universal indignation expressed by the press of this country, which I believe in this case represents general public opinion. However strong may be the inclination to express abhorrence of such deeds, if we begin to make protests general in nature as to violations of civilized and humane methods of slaughter where are we going to stop? Already the representatives of the belligerents have filed numerous charges of cruel and uncivilized practices by the military and naval forces of their enemies. If we act upon one on the

---

[1] William M. Malloy (ed.), *Treaties, Conventions, etc., Between the United States of America and Other Powers*, 1776–1909 (Washington, Government Printing Office, 1910), vol. II, p. 2269.

ground of humanity, are we not in fairness bound to act upon others?

It seems to me, therefore, for the sake of our future peace of mind a limitation of a protest, if any is considered expedient, should be based upon the solicitude we feel for our own people who are endangered by the illegal acts of a belligerent, narrow as this policy may seem to be.

While, as I said, I am not convinced that any protest is expedient, silence may be misconstrued by the nations at war and cause criticism at home.

For your information I also annex a letter and memorandum[2] which I have received from Dr. James Brown Scott dealing briefly with the provisions of No. 4 of The Hague Treaties.

Very sincerely yours,

ROBERT LANSING

[Enclosure 1]

Draft Protest on Account of American Citizens

The Government of the United States has been officially advised by its diplomatic representative in Antwerp, Belgium, that a German military dirigible balloon on the morning of August twenty-fifth proceeded over that city under cover of darkness, and, without having previously warned the local authorities, delivered several bombs of high power, which exploding in the thickly populated sections of the city killed and wounded a number of non-combatants, men, women and children, and destroyed and damaged many buildings regardless of their use.

This Government is directly concerned in the bombardment referred to in that there were at the time in Antwerp hundreds of American citizens, including diplomatic and consular officers of the United States, and other neutral non-combatants whose lives were endangered, and further because one of the buildings destroyed belonged to an American citizen.

The bombardment in the opinion of this Government was in violation of Article 26 of the Regulations annexed to No. 4 of The Hague Conventions, 1907,[3] concerning the laws and customs of war on land, in that the officer in command of the attacking German force failed to warn the local authorities of Antwerp of the intended bombardment, which warning would have given opportunity for the American and other neutral non-combatants to have removed from the city or sought places of safety before the attack took place.

---

[2] Neither printed.
[3] Malloy, *Treaties*, 1776–1909, vol. II, p. 2286.

This Government is unwilling to believe that this unnotified bombardment under cover of night was authorized by the German Government, one of the signatories to The Hague Convention No. 4, because of the possibility of indiscriminate slaughter which might result to non-combatants without regard to sex or nationality, and because an attack of this character could in no way lessen the defensive strength of the Belgian military forces in and about Antwerp or contribute to the success of the German arms.

This Government, therefore, considering that the bombardment jeopardized the lives of American officials and citizens and was unwarranted by the laws of war or by military necessity, requests the German Government to take the steps necessary to fix the responsibility for this flagrant violation of Article 26 of the Regulations referred to and to punish the offender, and this Government further expects the German Government to declare that the act was unauthorized by it and to give assurances that bombardments of a similar nature will not be permitted by the German forces in the field without full compliance with the Regulations, to which reference has been made.

[Enclosure 2]

Draft Protest on General Grounds

The Government of the United States has been officially advised by its diplomatic representatives in Antwerp, Belgium, that a German military dirigible balloon on the morning of August twenty-fifth proceeded over that city under cover of darkness, and, without having previously warned the local authorities, delivered several bombs of high power, which exploding in the thickly populated sections of the city killed and wounded a number of non-combatants, men, women and children, and destroyed and damaged many buildings regardless of their use.

The Government of the United States, believing that the Imperial German Government, as a signatory of No. 4 of The Hague Conventions of 1907 concerning the laws and customs of war on land, intends to abide strictly by the provisions of that Convention in the conduct of military operations during the present war, directs its attention to Article 26 and Article 27 of the Regulations annexed to the Convention referred to, which, it appears from the report received, were clearly violated by the officer in command of the German attacking force. Since it is manifest that the destruction of the buildings wrecked was unnecessary to the success of the military operations of the German attacking force, there appears no justification on the ground of military necessity for the sudden attack, which caused the useless loss of the lives and property of non-combatants without in any way lessening the military strength of the Belgian force defending the city. It would seem, therefore, that there was no valid excuse for the violation of the regulations referred to.

The Government of the United States, recognizing the fact that Antwerp is a fortified city and, therefore, subject to bombardment, insists that, if its information is correct and the fortifications are a considerable distance from the city proper, such fact does not permit the indiscriminate slaughter of non-combatants and destruction of property without warning by the officer in command of the attacking force, and, in no event, unless directed against the troops or military stores of the enemy.

In view, therefore, of the plain terms of Articles 26 and 27 of the Regulations the Government of the United States is constrained to protest earnestly against the acts of the officer in command of the German attacking force not only on the ground that they were in violation of the Regulations mentioned but, furthermore, on the ground that they were contrary to that solicitude and regard for the lives and property of non-combatants, which every belligerent is bound to have if it is inspired by those humane sentiments which should animate modern nations in the conduct of a war. The nation, which ignores or fails to respond to these sentiments invites the just condemnation of the civilized world.

763.72116/18a

The Secretary of State to President Wilson

WASHINGTON, *September 3, 1914.*

MY DEAR MR. PRESIDENT: Before coming to the White House this morning I jotted down a number of things about which I wished to speak to you but I forgot to add one item, and an important one.

I wrote you in regard to the throwing of bombs on Antwerp. It has been repeated, although the second throwing did no great harm. They are fearful of the same danger in London, it having been rumored that the Germans intended to send their airships across the Channel and drop bombs on London.

Have you had time to think over the matter and if so to what conclusion have you come in regard to our duty in the premises? Should there be any protest—and if so, should it be based upon danger to Americans, or upon the broader ground that it is an improper method of warfare?

I enclose to you a very interesting telegram which has just been received from Page.[4]

With assurances [etc.]   W. J. BRYAN

---

[4] *Foreign Relations*, 1914, supp., p. 87.

763.72116/18½

President Wilson to the Secretary of State

WASHINGTON, *September 4, 1914.*

MY DEAR MR. SECRETARY: I have thought a great deal about the matter of a protest with regard to the dropping of the bombs and my present judgment is that we do not know in sufficient detail the actual facts and that we ought to be very slow to make formal protests, chiefly because we shall no doubt be called upon by every one of the belligerents before the fighting is over to do something of this kind and would be in danger of becoming chronic critics of what was going forward. I think the time for clearing up all these matters will come when the war is over and the nations gather in sober counsel again.

Cordially and faithfully yours,

WOODROW WILSON

763.72116/43½

Memorandum by the Counselor for the Department of State
(Lansing)

[WASHINGTON, *undated.*]

RECEPTION OF BELGIAN DELEGATION

I asked Mr. Adee [5] whether the President should receive the Belgian Delegation now en route to Washington to present to this Government their complaints against certain alleged atrocities of the Germans in the present European wars. Mr. Adee said that being neutrals, there was no objection to the President receiving this Commission in person, but that he should avoid receiving their representations by referring them in that respect to the Secretary of State, who was the channel of communication in matters of foreign affairs. If it seemed impossible to avoid a discussion of the matter between the Commissioners and the President, it would be best in response to their request for an appointment to the President, to say that he could only receive them personally, but as to their representations he must refer them to the Department of State.

I asked Mr. Adee if it was necessary for them to be introduced to the Secretary of State by the Belgian Minister. Mr. Adee said that if the Minister chose to accompany them, of course the Secretary of State would receive them all, but if they were duly commissioned delegates of their Government, he might receive them without

---

[5] Second Assistant Secretary of State.

any introduction by the Minister. If they were not duly accredited delegates, Mr. Adee thought that then they should be received by the Secretary of State only upon introduction by the Belgian Minister and with his approval of their mission.

I asked Mr. Adee if he knew of any precedents which might be followed in this case. Mr. Adee said he did not recollect any of a similar character, except possibly that of Mason and Slidell, who went as representatives of the Confederate States on a special mission to Great Britain. Mr. Adee did not recollect that any delegation from the Boer States had visited the United States.

763.72116/43½

The Counselor for the Department of State (Lansing) to the Secretary of State

[WASHINGTON,] *September 8, 1914.*

DEAR MR. SECRETARY: In regard to the reception by the President of the representatives of Belgium [6] sent here to lay before him a statement in relation to the destruction of Louvain and the conduct of German military authorities in Belgium, concerning which you today asked my views, I can only give an opinion based upon hypotheses.

1. *If the representatives come without credentials from the King of the Belgians or from the Belgian Government*, it would seem courteous for the President to receive them personally upon the introduction of the Belgian Minister, but it would seem improper for the President to receive any statement from them, on the ground that the channel of communication was the Belgian Minister, who should present the subject to the Secretary of State on their behalf.

2. *If the representatives come with credentials from the Belgian Government as Special Commissioners to this Government*, it would seem proper for the President to receive them personally upon the introduction of the Belgian Minister, but any communication, which they desire to make, should be made to the Secretary of State by them and not through the Belgian Minister.

3. *If the representatives come with credentials as Special Ambassadors or bearing a letter from the King of the Belgians addressed to the President*, it would seem proper for the President to receive them officially and listen to any communication which they may be charged to make.

In the hypothetical cases Nos. 1 and 2 the communications should be made by the Belgian Minister or by the representatives as the case may be, to the Secretary of State before the representatives are introduced to the President by their Minister.

---

[6] For President Wilson's remarks to the Belgian Commission at the White House, Sept. 16, 1914, see *Foreign Relations*, 1914, supp., p. 796.

In the hypothetical case No. 3 the Belgian Minister should introduce the representatives to the Secretary of State in order that they may arrange to be presented as Special Ambassadors or as bearers of a letter from their King to the President.

The foregoing procedure in the three cases considered depends upon the official character of the representatives and not upon the nature of their mission. I do not find a precedent which is applicable, but, reasoning from the generally accepted diplomatic practice I think that this procedure would be free from justifiable criticism.

Very sincerely yours,

ROBERT LANSING

763.72116/336a : Telegram

The Acting Secretary of State to the Ambassador in Germany (Gerard)

WASHINGTON, *October 19, 1914—4 p. m.*

445. Message from the President:

"I venture with not a little hesitation to make this suggestion to you in confidence, that you see some member of the government upon whom you are likely to make the deepest impression in such a matter and whose influence you can count upon as great and say that nothing is making so unfavorable, not to say fatal, an impression in this country as the dropping of bombs from airships upon cities elsewhere than upon fortifications, with no result except terror and the destruction of innocent lives. I am deeply interested in maintaining a real neutrality of public opinion here and a scrupulous fairness of judgment but my efforts are being wholly nullified, I fear, by these occurrences and will be so long as the present use of bombs where they can be of no possible military service continues. I have ventured therefore upon the very unusual course of making this suggestion, a suggestion of sincere friendship. This should be done, of course, as upon your own initiative and entirely unofficially, merely as a voluntary act of personal good will and friendship. Woodrow Wilson."

LANSING

763.72111/1072a

The Acting Secretary of State to President Wilson

WASHINGTON, *November 23, 1914.*

DEAR MR. PRESIDENT: From statements made by certain of our public men and from articles appearing in the press and periodicals of this country I apprehend that during the next session of Congress an effort may be made to have the Administration explain the reason for failure to protest as to violations of The Hague Conventions by belligerents. The basis for such criticism will be that the United States being a signatory of the Conventions is bound to enter a protest, or at least to demand an explanation of conduct contrary to the provisions of the Conventions when evidence of violation filed with this Government makes out a *prima facie* case.

While appreciating that it would be most unwise at the present time to address any belligerent government on the subject, I think that we should be prepared to state the reasons for refraining from doing so. I venture, therefore, to offer the following observations:

First. Evidence obtained *ex parte* is always open to the suspicion of prejudice and exaggeration. Before acting upon it this Government should be convinced that it is true. To do this would require an impartial investigation involving the taking of evidence from both sides. This investigation could only be made by a commission appointed by this Government or composed of members from this and other neutral powers. It is manifestly impractical at the present time, while hostilities are in progress, for such an investigation to be made. The Government is, therefore, in no position to act either by protest or demand for an explanation.

Second. Barring cases where the rights of a neutral or its citizens are unaffected [*affected*] by a violation of the provisions of the Conventions there is nothing in The Hague Conventions which imposes upon a neutral government the duty to act on its own initiative in a judicial capacity and pass upon charges of violation of a treaty nor grant the authority so to act at the instance of an injured party. The propriety of such action, therefore, depends upon the character of the undertakings entered into by the signatories to the Conventions. If they are joint in nature, they may be construed as imposing an obligation to investigate charges; if they are several in nature, no such obligation is implied.

Third. It is a matter of doubt, therefore, whether this Government should act in regard to a violation of The Hague Conventions unless the rights of the United States or its citizens are impaired by the violation. While the form of The Hague Conventions is that of a joint undertaking, the adoption of the form may be considered (and I think rightly) to have been for the sake of convenience, and not for the purpose of binding the parties to joint action in case of violation by one of them in a war with another signatory. That is, the same end would have been attained had each of the parties entered into an identical treaty with each one of the other signatories. To avoid this cumbersome method with the attendant repetition of ratifications and exchanges, the form of The Hague Conventions and provisions for deposit of ratifications were adopted. I think that this view is borne out by the provision which occurs in each Hague Convention of 1907 that any one party may denunciate the Convention but such denunciation shall only have effect in regard to that power. If this view of the several character of the undertakings by a signatory is correct the United States is in no position to protest or demand an explanation of an alleged violation unless its rights or those of its citizens are affected.

As this Department may be asked orally by Senators and Representatives in regard to these matters I hope that I may be informed, as soon as it is convenient, of your opinion as to the soundness of these observations in order that there may be no conflict of statements to persons who are entitled to make inquiry on the subject.

Very sincerely yours,

ROBERT LANSING

763.72111/1072½

President Wilson to the Acting Secretary of State

WILLIAMSTOWN, MASS., *November 26, 1914.*
[Received November 28.]

MY DEAR MR. LANSING: I have your letter of November twenty-third about the questions likely to be asked concerning our obligations under the Hague Conventions to protest against conduct on the part of belligerents contrary to the provisions of the Conventions when evidence of violation filed with this Government makes out a *prima facie* case. I believe your comments and proposed replies to be sound and wise.

In haste,

Cordially and faithfully yours,

WOODROW WILSON

763.72111/1691½

The Counselor for the Department of State (Lansing) to the Secretary of State

WASHINGTON, *February 18, 1915.*

DEAR MR. SECRETARY: In the German Ambassador's note to you, dated the 15th and dealing with the intended operations in a war zone,[7] the following statement appears:

"In addition increased danger from mines is to be looked for as it is proposed to make the widest use of mines in every part of the war zone. Neutral vessels therefore must again be most earnestly warned against getting into that zone; they may, if they wish, unhesitatingly take the Northern course, around Scotland, recommended by the German Admiralty."

In view of this statement and the known use of mines by Great Britain (a large number having drifted on to the coasts of the Netherlands), it would seem to me an appropriate time to protest to Great Britain, France and Germany against the use of mines on the high

---

[7] *Foreign Relations*, 1915, supp., p. 104.

seas. The protest could be identical and being sent to both sides could be made vigorous in language.[8]

I think that the opportunity for identical protests should not be lost, as the use of mines on the high seas is the greatest menace to neutral vessels and the lives of neutrals, and, in my opinion, is the most reprehensible and utterly indefensible method employed in naval warfare.

Very sincerely yours,

ROBERT LANSING

763.72/1868½a

The Secretary of State ad interim to President Wilson

WASHINGTON, *June 15, 1915.*

DEAR MR. PRESIDENT: The British Ambassador, during an interview this afternoon, spoke very strongly (I believe under instructions) about the indifference of this Government and the American press to the recent Zeppelin attack on London. He said in brief that London was an undefended city, that many Americans resident there were in imminent danger if the attacks were repeated, and that he considered it our manifest duty to protest against acts which could have no military advantage to excuse them. He grew rather excited and closed with "I must officially inform you that we cannot protect American citizens or your Embassy in London from these outrages."

I replied that I appreciated the point of view of his Government and would consider the subject.

He then asked me to submit the matter to you and I have adopted this method of complying with his request.

I am [etc.]

ROBERT LANSING

763.72/1869½

President Wilson to the Secretary of State ad interim

WASHINGTON, *17 June, 1915.*

MY DEAR MR. SECRETARY: Of course we understand that the British Government cannot defend our people or our Embassy against these air raids; but we also understand, as Sir Cecil does not when he is under great excitement, that it is none of our business to protest against these methods of "warfare", no matter what our opinion of them may be.

---

[8] For protests to Great Britain and Germany, see *Foreign Relations*, 1915, supp., p. 119.

I feel a great deal of sympathy with the Ambassador, and am quite willing to let these incidents pass with a complete understanding of how they occur.

Cordially yours,

W. W.

763.72/2078

The Secretary of State to President Wilson

WASHINGTON, *August 30, 1915.*

MY DEAR MR. PRESIDENT: You have undoubtedly read the flimsy of Mr. Page's 2716, August 29, two p. m.[9] relative to the attack on the *Nicosian* and the events which followed. To me the conduct of the British naval authorities is shocking, and I sincerely hope that this matter may not become public, as it would seriously affect public opinion in Germany and might result in retaliatory measures of a most rigorous character.

Faithfully yours,

ROBERT LANSING

763.72115/2631a

The Secretary of State to President Wilson

WASHINGTON, *November 15, 1916.*

MY DEAR MR. PRESIDENT: The Belgian Minister has just left me. He came to ask what would be your attitude if the King of the Belgians should send you a request to act more formally in behalf of Belgium in the matter of the deportation of Belgian subjects to Germany. As you know, from the information which we have, it appears that these Belgians are being used to take the place of Germans in various industries in order that the Germans may be released for military service.

I told the Minister that I would submit the question to you and I hope you can give me an answer very soon so that I can communicate it to him.

Faithfully yours,

ROBERT LANSING

[9] *Ibid.*, p. 528.

763.72115/2631b

The Secretary of State to President Wilson

WASHINGTON, *November 15, 1916.*

MY DEAR MR. PRESIDENT: The head-line summaries in the Press this morning gave an erroneous impression that this Government had officially protested to Germany against the deportation of the Belgian civilian population. The real situation is as follows:

Various telegrams during September and October from our representatives in Brussels and Berlin reported [10] that the German Government had determined on the policy of enforcing labor on Belgian civilians, many of whom were to be brought to Germany to work in various industries, thus releasing German workmen to go to the front. On October 10th the American Chargé d'Affaires in Berlin cabled [11] that he had received through the American Legation at Brussels two letters from the President of the Comité National de Secours et d'Alimentation of Brussels stating that the German military authorities had demanded from presidents of local committees complete lists of unemployed workmen who were receiving aid from committees in the district and that where lists were refused the presidents were imprisoned, and asking for instructions. The Department replied on October 19th [12] that he might informally and orally draw the attention of the Minister for Foreign Affairs to the reported action of the military authorities in Belgium if he deemed it advisable; and Mr. Grew reports [13] the receipt of the following memorandum from the Under Secretary of State for Foreign Affairs in reply to his inquiry at the German Foreign Office.

"Against the unemployed in Belgium who are a burden to public charity, in order to avoid friction arising therefrom, compulsory measures are to be adopted to make them work so far as they are not voluntarily inclined to work. The order issued by the Governor General on May 15th, 1916."

Mr. Grew then pointed out the unfortunate impression which this decision would make abroad, and said that he thought it ought at least to be brought to the Chancellor's personal attention in the light of the consequences which the order would entail. Mr. Grew then asked whether the Foreign Office would approve of his seeing the Chancellor if he was so authorized by his Government, to which the Under Secretary replied in the affirmative.

Meanwhile the Belgian Minister here had on several occasions expressed to the Department his Government's deep concern in these

---

[10] See *Foreign Relations*, 1916, supp., pp. 858 ff.; also pp. 70–71, 77–78.
[11] *Ibid.*, p. 859.
[12] *Ibid.*, p. 860.
[13] Telegram No. 4535, Oct. 27, 1916, *ibid.*, p. 862.

deportations; and he has officially transmitted to the Department a copy of a telegram from his Government [14] in which the following paragraph occurs:

"The Government of the King applies to the active intervention of the United States Government in order to stop this deportation of its workmen to Germany and to obtain the freedom of those who have already been taken to Germany."

The Minister concludes his note of transmittal by expressing the hope, "that the Government of the United States . . . will kindly bring its powerful influence to bear to put an end to a condition of things that is as barbarous as it is unjust.["]

On November 2d, in reply to Mr. Grew's inquiry as to whether he would be authorized to take the matter up with the Chancellor, the Department informed him by cable [15] that in view of the possible serious consequences which may result from the proposed policy in Belgium, he was authorized to request an interview with the Chancellor; that the Department left to his discretion the extent which his informal representations with the Chancellor should go, which must necessarily be guided by circumstances and upon his general attitude in the matter; but I authorized him to point out to the Chancellor the unfortunate impression that the proposed policy if carried out would create in neutral countries and in the United States which has the welfare of the Belgian civilian population very much at heart. You will see that our action in the circumstances could not possibly be construed as a protest on behalf of the Government of the United States.

Our course has been analogous to the steps which we have taken with the Turkish Government in an endeavor to stop the further deportation of the Armenian civil population. It is interesting to note in connection with the Armenian deportations that on October 8th [, 1915] Count Bernstorff sent me a copy of a memorandum which was presented to the Turkish Government by the German Ambassador in Constantinople,[16] which was a formal remonstrance of the German Government, and in which the German Government declines any responsibility for the consequences they may involve.

Last spring the Department's attention was called to the deportations of the French civil population from Lille, Roubaix and Tourcoing, very similar in effect to the present deportation of the Belgian civil population; and on June 21 we informed Mr. Gerard [17] that, acting under instructions from his Government, the Belgian Minister

---

[14] Not printed.
[15] *Foreign Relations*, 1916, supp., p. 863.
[16] *Ibid.*, 1915, supp., p. 990.
[17] *Ibid.*, 1916, supp., p. 858.

had brought this matter to my attention, and that the Belgian Government, feeling that a similar measure may be taken with the population of occupied Belgium, had requested this Government to bring to the attention of the German Government that such an act would be in violation of international law as well as the law of humanity. Acting on his own initiative Mr. Gerard utilized the occasion of his visit to headquarters in connection with the *Sussex* matter to express to the Chancellor the hope that the deportations could cease and so avoid the consequences which might seriously affect the existence of the Belgian Relief Commission in the occupied portion of France. The result of Mr. Gerard's friendly conversation was that the deportations from Lille, Roubaix and Tourcoing almost immediately ceased.

This morning I have made it clear to the newspaper correspondents that my recent instruction to Grew in regard to the deportations from Belgium must not be construed in the nature of an official protest of this Government; for it was made wholly on behalf of the Belgian Government and People.

Trusting that the Department's course meets with your approval, and with assurances [etc.]

ROBERT LANSING

763.72115/2631c

The Secretary of State to President Wilson

WASHINGTON, *November 21, 1916.*

MY DEAR MR. PRESIDENT: I have been more and more disturbed by the policy of the German Government in the deportation of the civil population of Belgium as the magnitude and purpose of the removals have become more apparent.

The mere fact of the deportation of civilians from a particular region by military authorities is not, in my opinion, reprehensible. There may be ample justification for such action because of military necessity. Prior to the present case we have had two examples of the removal of civilians from their homes, the Armenians by the Turks, and the French in the neighborhood of Lille by the Germans.

In the case of the Armenians I could see that their well-known disloyalty to the Ottoman Government and the fact that the territory which they inhabited was within the zone of military operations constituted grounds more or less justifiable for compelling them to depart from their homes. It was not to my mind the deportation which was objectionable but the horrible brutality which attended its execution. It is one of the blackest pages in the history of this war, and

I think that we were fully justified in intervening as we did in behalf of the wretched people, even though they were Turkish subjects.

In the case of the French at Lille and other towns in the vicinity I can conceive that military expediency may have furnished good reason for the deportation. Located near the battle lines, as they were, the difficulty of furnishing the population with food and shelter may have warranted the removal of a portion to a greater distance from the war zone. But, as in the case of the Armenians, the German military authorities showed towards the inhabitants of the Lille section a ruthlessness and inhumanity which caused needless distress by the separation of families and by deportation without due regard to age or sex and without opportunity to prepare for departure.

In the case of the Belgians the conditions seem to be utterly different. They do not appear to be deported because they are in the field of active operations or because of the difficulty of furnishing them with food, since that is being done through the Belgian Relief Commission. It is not the helpless or weak who are being transported but only males who are physically fit to work. They are being taken to Germany, according to reports, for the purpose of being placed in factories and fields in order that the Germans now engaged in manual labor may be mustered into military service, thus increasing the military strength of Germany without impairing her industrial efficiency.

Of course these Belgians are going unwillingly and are being forcibly compelled to labor for their conquerors. They are to all intents in a state of involuntary servitude. To use a more ugly phrase, they are slaves under a system of slavery which has not been practiced in regard to civilian enemies by civilized nations within modern times. It arouses in me, as I am sure it must arouse in every liberty-loving man, an intense feeling of abhorrence and a desire to find some way to prevent the continuance of a practice which is a reversion to the barbarous methods of the military empires of antiquity.

Now, Mr. President, I have nothing definite to propose. As you know I have firmly supported the policy of avoiding all protests on account of inhuman methods of warfare by belligerents which are in violation of international law. I still believe that that policy is wise and should be continued. But in all such cases the conduct complained of was never admitted to be the definite policy of a Government, nor was the inhumanity of the individual cases conclusively proven. The present case is different. Germany has not yet denied the act or the purpose of the act. Her Government appears rather to excuse it though, in my opinion, no excuse offered can in any way relieve that Government of the enormity of the crime of making slaves, not of prisoners of war (which would be bad enough), but of peaceable non-combatants who have by the fortunes of war come within its jurisdiction. It is a direct and unjustifiable blow at the principle of individual liberty—an essential element of modern political ideas, if not of our civilization.

As I say, I have nothing to propose at the present time but I feel that we ought to consider very carefully whether some way cannot be found to bring moral pressure upon Germany to cause her to abandon a policy which invites the protest of the civilized world, and which will greatly increase her difficulties when the time comes to negotiate a treaty of peace, unless I misjudge the temper of her enemies. If we desire to see peace restored in Europe, no step would be more efficacious than to convince Germany of the imperative need to abandon this policy. I do not believe that any efforts, which we might make, to bring the belligerents together could possibly succeed while Germany persisted in enslaving the civilian subjects of her enemies who have fallen into her hands. To attempt to do so would, I am sure, arouse bitter resentment and place us in a most embarrassing position.

In this connection I may call your attention to a letter which I wrote you on the 15th [18] reporting an interview with the Belgian Minister in which he desired me to ask what would be your attitude toward receiving from the King of the Belgians a request to act more formally in behalf of the deported population of his country. I have been thinking over the matter and I can see no very strong objection to receiving such a request. Indeed it might offer an opportunity to seek to prevent the carrying out of a policy which, it seems to me, if persisted in, will so arouse the Allies that the possibility of peace in the near future will be almost unthinkable.

At your convenience I would like to discuss this subject with you for I feel that we must determine upon the course of action which should be pursued.[19]

Faithfully yours,

ROBERT LANSING

---

[18] *Ante*, p. 39.

[19] President Wilson's reply, dated Nov. 26, 1916, no copy of which has been found in the Department files, is printed in R. S. Baker, *Woodrow Wilson, Life and Letters* (Garden City, 1937), vol. VI, p. 343. For Secretary Lansing's instruction to the Chargé in Germany containing the text of the protest to be presented to the Chancellor, see *Foreign Relations*, 1916, supp., p. 70.

763.72115/2632½

President Wilson to the Secretary of State

WASHINGTON, *November 27, 1916.*

MY DEAR MR. SECRETARY: This paper enclosed emanates from a group of men who are anything but our friends and many of whom would be very glad indeed to embarrass us, and I would value a suggestion from you as to what reply should be made to the inquiry.

Cordially and faithfully yours,

WOODROW WILSON

[Enclosure—Telegram]

Mr. Frederick W. Whitridge and Others to President Wilson

NEW YORK, *November 25, 1916—1:45 p. m.*

There are many of our citizens who wish to do their part toward an expression of public opinion regarding the deportation of Belgians into Germany and France, which as now reported appears to be in violation of law and humanity. We should be glad to have all the information possible so as to be sure of the facts before taking public action. May we have such information as may be proper as to what facts the State Department has, what our Government has done and what so far as known other neutral governments have done about the violation of international law in this respect. If the facts are not now known by our Government cannot they be obtained from our Minister to Belgium?

FREDERICK W. WHITRIDGE	S. R. BERTRON
Rev. Dr. W. T. MANNING	PIERRE MALI
Senator ROOT	Rev. Dr. SLATTERY
A. J. HEMPHILL	R. FULTON CUTTING
THOS. RYAN	JOSEPH H. CHOATE
ROB'T BACON	BENJ. T. CALLE
FRANCIS L. STETSON	ROBERT T. BRIDES
JAMES M. BECK	JOHN M. PARKER, *New Orleans*
H. L. STIMSON	W. H. KING

763.72115/2632½

The Secretary of State to President Wilson

WASHINGTON, *December 1, 1916.*

MY DEAR MR. PRESIDENT: It is evident to my mind that the gentlemen making the request for information regarding the deportation of Belgians desire to obtain some official statement from the Government which they can reproduce in quoted form in printed circulars to be distributed broadcast over the country for the purpose of arousing public opinion and forcing the Government to take some action unfavorable to Germany, which could be construed as favoring the Allies. If I am correct in this surmise, I think that no good purpose would be served by giving out officially the information desired. As a matter of fact, it has always been a rule of this Department not to make official statements to inquirers regarding confidential matters under diplomatic discussion unless the inquirers are parties in interest. This rule is based on the fact that the correspondence is with foreign governments, who may not desire to have the subject matter given out without their consent. This is peculiarly true in the present case, which is passing into a very delicate stage. I think, therefore, that it is not only appropriate, but necessary, for the moment at least, to answer the committee substantially along these lines. Somewhat later, I suppose, it may be possible, with the consent of the German Government, to give out some of the correspondence in the Belgian matter. Of course, if Germany should prefer to give the matter out without asking us, we could then give out so much as may be desirable to make our position clear.

Faithfully yours,

ROBERT LANSING

763.72115/2633½

President Wilson to the Secretary of State

WASHINGTON, *3 December, 1916.*

MY DEAR MR. SECRETARY: I thank you very much for this. Would you be kind enough to answer these gentlemen to the effect you suggest, as by reference from me? I would be very much obliged to you indeed if you would. I think that the wisest way to handle the case.

Faithfully Yours,

W. W.

763.72115/2612

The Secretary of State to President Wilson

WASHINGTON, *December 7, 1916.*

MY DEAR MR. PRESIDENT: I enclose herewith a confidential telegram received from Mr. Grew [20] in answer to our telegram of November 29th [21]—which is the one we took such care to prevent from becoming public.

---

[20] Telegram No. 4689, Dec. 5, 1916, from the Chargé in Germany, *Foreign Relations,* 1916, supp., p. 868.

[21] *Ibid.,* p. 70.

I cannot say that I find Mr. Grew's telegram very encouraging but I suppose no judgment should be formed until the Chancellor has had an opportunity to consult with Mr. Zimmermann and make a formal answer.

Faithfully yours,

ROBERT LANSING

763.72115/2634½

President Wilson to the Secretary of State

WASHINGTON, *8 December, 1916.*

MY DEAR MR. SECRETARY: This is certainly most disappointing, but it is just about what I expected. Protests that there is no likelihood the government making them will follow up with action make very little practical difference, as this war is going.

Faithfully Yours,

W. W.

ACTION BY THE AMERICAN LEGATION IN BELGIUM ON BEHALF OF MISS EDITH CAVELL

362.412 C31/1

The Minister in Belgium (Whitlock) to the Secretary of State

No. 186   BRUSSELS, *October 19, 1915.*
                                         [Received November 5.]

SIR: I have the honor to transmit herewith enclosed for the information and files of the Department copies of correspondence with the Ambassador at London and with the German Government of Occupation in Belgium in regard to the case of Miss Edith Cavell, an English woman, who was executed last week for assisting soldiers to reach the Dutch frontier.

Further than saying that the Legation exhausted every effort to prevent the infliction of the death penalty, I make no comment upon the facts in this case which are fully shown by the correspondence itself.[1]

I have [etc.]   BRAND WHITLOCK

[Enclosure 1—Translation]

The Minister in Belgium (Whitlock) to the Chief of the Political Department of the German General Government in Belgium (Von der Lancken)

No. 6377   BRUSSELS, *August 31, 1915.*

EXCELLENCY: My Legation has just been informed that Miss Edith Cavell, an English subject living in Rue de la Culture in Brussels, has been arrested.

I should be greatly obliged to Your Excellency if you would let me know if this information is correct, and, if so, what are the reasons for this arrest.

I also wish, in this event, that you would be good enough to furnish the Legation with the requisite authorization of the German

---

[1] The enclosures and subenclosures accompanying this despatch have been rearranged so as to appear in more nearly chronological order.

Correspondence between Walter H. Page, American Ambassador in Great Britain, and Sir Edward Grey, British Secretary of State for Foreign Affairs, on the subject of the Cavell case will be found in Great Britain, Cmd. 8013, Miscellaneous No. 17 (1915): *Correspondence with the United States Ambassador respecting the Execution of Miss Cavell at Brussels.*

judicial authorities in order that Mr. de Leval[2] might confer with Miss Cavell and eventually charge someone with her defense.

I embrace this opportunity [etc.]   BRAND WHITLOCK

[Enclosure 2—Translation]

The Minister in Belgium (Whitlock) to the Chief of the Political Department of the German General Government in Belgium (Von der Lancken)

No. 6614

The Minister of the United States presents his compliments to His Excellency Baron von der Lancken and has the honor to remind him of his letter of August 31, relative to the arrest of Miss Cavell to which letter he has not yet received an answer.

As the Minister has been urged by a despatch[3] to occupy himself immediately with the defense of Miss Cavell, he would be greatly obliged to His Excellency Baron von der Lancken if he would enable him to take immediately the measures necessary for this action and to reply by telegram to the despatch which he has received.

BRUSSELS, *September 10, 1915.*

[Enclosure 3—Translation]

The Chief of the Political Department of the German General Government in Belgium (Von der Lancken) to the Minister in Belgium (Whitlock)

I 6940   BRUSSELS, *September 12, 1915.*

MR. MINISTER: Replying to the note Your Excellency addressed to me under date of the 31st last, I have the honor to advise you that Miss Edith Cavell was arrested on August 5th and that she is at present in the military prison of St. Gilles.

She has confessed, to having hidden in her home English and French soldiers as well as Belgians of the age to bear arms, all desirous of going to the front. She has also confessed to having furnished these soldiers with the money necessary to travel to France and to having aided their departure from Belgium by procuring guides to conduct them secretly across the Dutch frontier.

The defense of Miss Cavell is in the hands of the Attorney Mr. Braun who has put himself into communication with the appropriate German authorities.

---

[2] M. Gaston de Leval, legal adviser to the American Legation in Belgium.
[3] No copy enclosed with this despatch.

Inasmuch as the General Government, for reasons of principle does not permit prisoners to have intercourse with anyone, I regret exceedingly not to be able to procure permission for Mr. de Laval to see Miss Cavell while she is in close custody (*au secret*).

I embrace this opportunity [etc.]   LANCKEN

[Enclosure 4]

The Minister in Belgium (*Whitlock*) to the Ambassador in Great Britain (*Page*)

No. 7161   BRUSSELS, *September 21, 1915*.

SIR: Referring to your telegram of August 27th,[4] in regard to the case of Miss Edith Cavell, who was arrested on August 5th and is now in the military prison at St. Gilles, I beg to enclose herewith for your information copy of a communication which I have just received from Baron von der Lancken [5] in regard to the matter.

The legal adviser appointed to defend Miss Cavell has informed the Legation that she has indeed admitted having hidden in her house English and French soldiers and has facilitated the departure of Belgian subjects for the front, furnishing them money and guides to enable them to cross the frontier.

The Legation will of course, keep this case in view and endeavor to see that a fair trial is given Miss Cavell and will not fail to let you know of any developments.

I have [etc.]   BRAND WHITLOCK

[Enclosure 5]

The Minister in Belgium (*Whitlock*) to the Ambassador in Great Britain (*Page*)

No. 7694   BRUSSELS, *October 9, 1915*.

SIR: I beg to acknowledge the receipt of your letter of September 23rd [4] in regard to the arrest by the German Military Authorities of Miss Edith Cavell, head of a training school for nurses.

Upon receipt of your telegram 448, August 27th,[4] I took the matter up with the German authorities and learned that Miss Cavell had indeed been arrested upon a "charge of espionage". The Belgian attorney appointed to defend her before the court martial called several times at the Legation and will continue to keep me well posted in regard to the case. It seems that Miss Cavell has made several very damaging admissions and there appeared to be no ground upon which I could ask for her release before the trial.

[4] No copy enclosed with this despatch.
[5] *Supra.*

The case will come up for trial next week and I will write you as soon as there is any further development.

I am [etc.]   BRAND WHITLOCK

[Enclosure 6]

The Minister in Belgium (Whitlock) to the Ambassador in Great Britain (Page)

No. 7695   BRUSSELS, *October 11, 1915.*

SIR: Referring to my letter of October 9th in regard to the case of Miss Edith Cavell, I hasten to send you word that her trial has been completed and that the German prosecutor has asked for sentence of death against her and eight other persons implicated by her testimony. Sentence has not as yet been pronounced and I have some hope that the court martial may decline to pass the rigorous sentence proposed.

I have thus far done everything that has been possible to secure a fair trial for Miss Cavell and am assured by her attorney that no complaint can be made on that score.

I feel that it would be useless to take any action until sentence is pronounced. I shall then of course neglect no effort to prevent an unduly severe penalty being inflicted upon her. I shall immediately telegraph you upon the pronouncement of sentence.

I have [etc.]   BRAND WHITLOCK

[Enclosure 7]

The Secretary of Legation at Brussels (Gibson) to the Minister in Belgium (Whitlock)

REPORT FOR THE MINISTER

BRUSSELS, *October 12, 1915.*

SIR: Upon learning early yesterday morning through unofficial sources that the trial of Miss Edith Cavell had been finished on Saturday afternoon and that the Prosecuting Attorney (*Kriegsgerichtsrat*) had asked for a sentence of death against her, telephonic inquiry was immediately made at the Politische Abteilung as to the facts. It was stated that no sentence had as yet been pronounced and that there would probably be delay of day or two before a decision was reached. Mr. Conrad gave positive assurances that the Legation would be fully informed as to developments in this case. Despite these assurances, we made repeated inquiries in the course of the day, the last one being at 6.20 p.m. Belgian time. Mr. Conrad then stated that sentence had not yet been pronounced and specifically renewed his previous assurances that he would not fail to inform us as soon as there was any news.

At 8.30 it was learned from an outside source that sentence had been passed in the course of the afternoon (before the last conversation with Mr. Conrad) and that the execution would take place during the night. In conformity with your instructions, I went, (accompanied by Mr. de Leval) to look for the Spanish Minister and found him dining at the home of Baron Lambert. I explained the circumstances to His Excellency and asked that as you were ill and unable to go yourself, he go with us to see Baron von der Lancken and support as strongly as possible the plea which I was to make in your name that execution of the death penalty should be deferred until the Governor could consider your appeal for clemency.

We took with us a note addressed to Baron von der Lancken and a plea for clemency (*requête en grâce*) addressed to the Governor General; (enclosures 1 and 2 attached to this report).[7] The Spanish Minister willingly agreed to accompany us and we went together to the Politische Abteilung.

Baron von der Lancken and all the members of his staff were absent for the evening. We sent a messenger to ask that he return at once to see us in regard to a matter of utmost urgency. A little after ten o'clock he arrived, followed shortly after by Count Harrach and Herr von Falkenhausen, members of his staff. The circumstances of the case were explained to him and your note presented and he read it aloud in our presence. He expressed disbelief in the report that sentence had actually been passed and manifested some surprise that we should give credence to any report not emanating from official sources. He was quite insistent on knowing the exact source of our information but this I did not feel at liberty to communicate to him. Baron von der Lancken stated that it was quite improbable that sentence had been pronounced, that even if so, it would not be executed within so short a time and that in any event it would be quite impossible to take any action before morning. It was of course pointed out to him that if the facts were as we believed them to be, action would be useless unless taken at once. We urged him to ascertain the facts immediately, and this after some hesitancy, he agreed to do. He telephoned to the Presiding Judge of the Court Martial and returned in a short time to say that the facts were as we had represented them and that it was intended to carry out the sentence before morning. We then presented as earnestly as possible your plea for delay. So far as I am able to judge we neglected to present no phase of the matter which might have had any effect, emphasizing the horror of executing a woman no matter what her offense, pointing out that the death sentence had therefore [*heretofore?*] been imposed only for actual cases of espionage and that Miss Cavell was not even accused by the German

---

[7] Subenclosures 1 and 2, *infra*.

Authorities of anything so serious. I further called attention to the failure to comply with Mr. Conrad's promise to inform the Legation of the sentence. I urged that inasmuch as the offenses charged against Miss Cavell were long since accomplished and that as she had been for some weeks in prison, a delay in carrying out the sentence could entail no danger to the German cause. I even went so far as to point out the fearful effect of a summary execution of this sort upon public opinion both here and abroad and although I had no authority for doing so, called attention to the possibility that it might bring about reprisals.

The Spanish Minister forcibly supported all our representations and made an earnest plea for clemency.

Baron von der Lancken stated that the Military Governor was the supreme authority, (*Gerichtsherr*) in matters of this sort; that appeal from his decision could be carried only to the Emperor, the Governor General having no authority to intervene in such cases. He added that under the provisions of German Martial Law the Military Governor had discretionary power to accept or to refuse acceptance of an appeal for clemency. After some discussion he agreed to call the Military Governor on the telephone and learn whether he had already ratified the sentence and whether there was any chance for clemency. He returned in about a half an hour and stated that he had been to confer personally with the Military Governor, who said that he had acted in the case of Miss Cavell only after mature deliberation; that the circumstances in her case were of such a character that he considered the infliction of the death penalty imperative and that in view of the circumstances of this case he must decline to accept your plea for clemency or any representation in regard to the matter.

Baron von der Láncken then asked me to take back the note which I had presented to him. To this, I demurred, pointing out that it was not a "requête en grâce" but merely a note to him transmitting a communication to the Governor, which was itself to be considered as the "requête en grâce." I pointed out that this was expressly stated in your note to him and tried to prevail upon him to keep it; he was very insistent however and I finally reached the conclusion that inasmuch as he had read it aloud to us and we knew that he was aware of its contents there was nothing to be gained by refusing to accept the note and accordingly took it back.

Even after Baron von der Lancken's very positive and definite statement that there was no hope and that under the circumstances "even the Emperor himself could not intervene", we continued to appeal to every sentiment to secure delay and the Spanish Minister even led Baron von der Lancken aside in order to say very forcibly a number of things which he would have felt hesitancy in saying in the presence of the younger officers and of Mr. de Leval, a Belgian subject.

His Excellency talked very earnestly with Baron von der Lancken for about a quarter of an hour. During this time Mr. de Leval and I presented to the younger officers every argument we could think of, I reminded them of our untiring efforts on behalf of German subjects at the outbreak of the war and during the siege of Antwerp. I pointed out that while our services had been rendered gladly and without any thought of future favors, they should certainly entitle you to some consideration for the only request of this sort you had made since the beginning of the war. Unfortunately our efforts were unavailing. We persevered until it was only too clear that there was no hope of securing any consideration for the case.

We left the Politische Abteilung shortly after midnight and I immediately returned to the Legation to report to you.

HUGH GIBSON

[Subenclosure 1—Translation]

The Minister in Belgium (Whitlock) to the Chief of the Political Department of the German General Government in Belgium (Von der Lancken)

No. 7696   BRUSSELS, *October 11, 1915.*

EXCELLENCY: I have just learned that Miss Cavell, an English subject and therefore under the protection of my Legation, was condemned to death this morning by the Council of War.

Without discussing the causes which occasioned so severe a sentence, which, if my information is correct, is more severe in the present case than in any others of the same character which have been tried by the court, I feel that I must appeal to Your Excellency's sentiments of humanity and generosity in behalf of Miss Cavell, in order that the death sentence pronounced against her may be commuted and that this unfortunate woman may not be executed.

Miss Cavell is indeed the head nurse of the Surgical Institute of Brussels. She has spent her life in tending the sufferings of others, and, at her school, many nurses have had their training who throughout the entire world, in Germany as in Belgium, have watched by sickbeds. At the outbreak of the war, Miss Cavell lavished her care upon German soldiers as well as others.

Were other reasons lacking, her humanitarian career has been such as to inspire every sentiment of pity and incite pardon.

If my information is correct, Miss Cavell, far from concealing anything has acknowledged with laudable frankness, all the charges against her, and it may even be that information supplied by herself and which she only could furnish has caused the extreme sentence to be pronounced upon her.

It is therefore with confidence and with the hope of its favorable reception that I beg Your Excellency to present to the Governor General my plea for clemency for Miss Cavell.

I embrace this occasion [etc.]   BRAND WHITLOCK

My dear Baron,

I am too ill to present my request myself but I appeal to your generous heart to support it and to save this unfortunate from death. Have pity on her.

    Yours

                                                BRAND WHITLOCK

(Written by hand by the Minister) [8]

[Subenclosure 2—Translation]

The Minister in Belgium (Whitlock) to the German Governor General in Belgium (Von Bissing)

No. 7697   BRUSSELS, *October 11, 1915.*

EXCELLENCY: I have just learned that Miss Cavell, an English subject and therefore under the protection of my Legation, was condemned to death this morning by the Council of War.

Without discussing the causes which occasioned so severe a sentence, which, if my information is correct, is more severe in the present case than in any others of the same character which have been tried by the court, I feel that I must appeal to Your Excellency's sentiments of humanity and generosity in behalf of Miss Cavell, in order that the death sentence pronounced against her may be commuted and that this unfortunate woman may not be executed.

Miss Cavell is indeed the head nurse of the Surgical Institute of Brussels. She has spent her life in tending the sufferings of others, and, at her school, many nurses have had their training, who throughout the entire world, in Germany as in Belgium, have watched by sickbeds. At the outbreak of the war, Miss Cavell lavished her care upon German soldiers as well as others.

Were other reasons lacking, her humanitarian career has been such as to inspire every sentiment of pity and incite pardon.

If my information is correct, Miss Cavell, far from concealing anything has acknowledged with laudable frankness, all the charges against her, and it may even be that information supplied by her-

---

[8] This parenthetical note appears in the copy accompanying Minister Whitlock's despatch.

self and which she only could furnish has caused the extreme sentence to be pronounced upon her.

It is therefore with confidence and with the hope of its favorable reception, that I have the honor to present to Your Excellency my plea for clemency in favor of Miss Cavell.

I embrace this occasion [etc.]   BRAND WHITLOCK

[Enclosure 8—Telegram]

The Minister in Belgium (Whitlock) to the Ambassador in Great Britain (Page)

BRUSSELS, *October 12, 1915.*

Your letter September twenty third [9] and my replies October 9th and eleventh. Miss Cavell sentenced yesterday and executed at two o'clock this morning despite our best efforts continued until the last moment.[10] Full report follows by mail.

WHITLOCK

[Enclosure 9]

The Legal Adviser of the Legation at Brussels (de Leval) to the Minister in Belgium (Whitlock)

REPORT FOR THE MINISTER

OCTOBER 12, 1915.

SIR: As soon as the Legation received an intimation that Miss Cavell was arrested, your letter of the 31st of August, of which copy is herewith annexed, No. 1,[11] was sent to Baron von der Lancken. The German Authorities were by that letter requested, *inter alia,* to allow me to see Miss Cavell, so as to have all necessary steps taken for her defence. No reply being received, the Legation, on the 10th of September,[12] reminded the German authorities of your letter.

The German reply, sent on the 12th of September,[13] was that I would not be allowed to see Miss Cavell, but that Mr. Braun, lawyer at the Brussels Court, was defending her and was already seeing the German Authorities about the case.

I immediately asked Mr. Braun to come to see me at the Legation, which he did, a few days later. He informed me that personal friends of Miss Cavell had asked him to defend her before the German Court, that he agreed to do so, but that owing to some unforeseen

---

[9] No copy enclosed with this despatch.
[10] Minister Whitlock states in his book *Belgium Under the German Occupation* (London, 1919), vol. II, p. 24, "I was mistaken in supposing that the execution had taken place at two o'clock."
[11] Printed as enclosure 1, p. 48.
[12] See enclosure 2.
[13] Enclosure 3.

circumstances he was prevented from pleading before that Court, adding that he had asked Mr. Kirschen, a member of the Brussels Bar and his friend, to take up the case and plead for Miss Cavell, and that Mr. Kirschen had agreed to do so.

I therefore at once put myself in communication with Mr. Kirschen, who told me that Miss Cavell was prosecuted for having helped soldiers to cross the frontier. I asked him whether he had seen Miss Cavell and whether she had made any statement to him, and to my surprise found out that the lawyers defending prisoners before the German military Court were not allowed to see their clients before the trial, and were not shown any document of the prosecution. This, Mr. Kirschen said, was in accordance with the German military rules. He added that the hearing of the trial of such cases was carried out very carefully, and that in his opinion, although it was not possible to see the client before the trial, in fact the trial itself developed so carefully and so slowly, that it was generally possible to have a fair knowledge of all the facts and to present a good defence for the prisoner. This would specially be the case for Miss Cavell, because the trial would be rather long as she was prosecuted with 34 other prisoners.

I informed Mr. Kirschen of my intention to be present at the trial so as to watch the case. He immediately dissuaded me from taking such attitude, which he said would cause a great prejudice to the prisoner, because the German judges would resent it and feel it almost as an affront if I was appearing to exercise a kind of supervision on the trial. He thought that if the Germans would admit my presence, which was very doubtful, it would in any case cause prejudice to Miss Cavell.

Mr. Kirschen assured me over and over again that the military Court of Brussels was always perfectly fair and that there was not the slightest danger of any miscarriage of justice. He promised that he would keep me posted on all the developments which the case would take and would report to me the exact charges that were brought against Miss Cavell and the facts concerning her that would be disclosed at the trial, so as to allow me to judge by myself about the merits of the case. He insisted that of course he would do all that was humanly possible to defend Miss Cavell to the best of his ability.

Three days before the trial took place, Mr. Kirschen wrote me a few lines saying that the trial would be on the next Thursday, the 7th of October. The Legation at once sent him, on the 5th of October, a letter, No. 2,[14] confirming in writing in the name of the Lega-

---

[14] See subenclosure, *infra*.

tion the arrangement that had been made between him and me. This letter was delivered to Mr. Kirschen by a messenger of the Legation.

The trial took two days, ending Friday the 8th.

On Saturday I was informed by an outsider that the trial had taken place, but that no judgment would be reached till a few days later.

Receiving no report from Mr. Kirschen, I tried to find him but failed. I then sent him a note on Sunday, asking him to send his report to the Legation or call there on Monday morning at 8.30. At the same time, I obtained from some other person present at the trial, some information about what had occurred, and the following facts were disclosed to me:

Miss Cavell was prosecuted for having helped English and French soldiers as well as Belgian young men, to cross the frontier and to go over to England. She had admitted by signing a statement before the day of the trial, and by public acknowledgement in court, in the presence of all the other prisoners and the lawyers, that she was guilty of the charges brought against her, and she had acknowledged not only that she had helped these soldiers to cross the frontier, but also that some of them had thanked her in writing when arriving in England. This last admission made her case so much the more serious, because if it only had been proved against her that she had helped the soldiers to traverse the Dutch frontier, and no proof was produced that these soldiers had reached a country at war with Germany, she could only have been sentenced for an attempt to commit the "crime" and not for the "crime" being duly accomplished. As the case stood, the sentence fixed by the German military law was a sentence of death.

Paragraph 58 of the German military Code says:

"Will be sentenced to death for treason any person who, with the "intention of helping the hostile power or of causing harm to the "German or allied troops, is guilty of one of the crimes of paragr. "90 of the German penal Code."

The case referred to in above said paragr. 90 consists in:

". . . conducting soldiers to the enemy . . . (viz.: dem Feinde "Mannschaften zuführt.")

The penalties above set forth apply, according to paragr. 160 of the German Code, in case of war, to Foreigners as well as to Germans.

In her oral statement before the Court, Miss Cavell disclosed almost all the facts of the whole prosecution. She was questioned in German, an interpreter translating all the questions in French, with which language Miss Cavell was well acquainted. She spoke without trembling and showed a clear mind. Often, she added some greater precision to her previous depositions.

When she was asked why she helped these soldiers to go to England, she replied that she thought that, if she had not done so, they would have been shot by the Germans, and that therefore she thought she only did her duty to her country in saving their lives.

The Military Public Prosecutor said that argument might be good for English soldiers, but did not apply to Belgian young men she induced to cross the frontier and who would have been perfectly free to remain in the country without danger to their lives.

Mr. Kirschen made a very good plea for Miss Cavell, using all arguments that could be brought in her favor before the Court.

The Military Public Prosecutor however asked the Court to pass a death sentence on Miss Cavell and eight other prisoners amongst the thirty-five. The Court did not seem to agree, and the judgment was postponed. The person informing me said he thought that the Court would not go to the extreme limit.

Anyhow, after I had found out these facts (viz. Sunday evening), I called at the Political Division of the German Government in Belgium, and asked whether, now that the trial had taken place, permission would be granted to me to see Miss Cavell in jail, as surely there was no longer any object in refusing this permission. The German official, Mr. Conrad, said he would make the necessary inquiry at the Court and let me know later on.

I also asked him that permission be granted to Mr. Gahan, the English clergyman, to see Miss Cavell.

At the same time, we prepared at the Legation, to be ready for every eventuality, a petition for pardon, addressed to the Governor General in Belgium, and a transmitting note addressed to Baron von der Lancken.

Monday morning at eleven I called up Mr. Conrad on the telephone from the Legation (as I already had done previously on several occasions when making inquiries about the case) asking what the military court had decided about Mr. Gahan and myself seeing Miss Cavell. He replied that Mr. Gahan could not see her, but that she could see any of the three protestant clergymen attached to the prison; and that I could not see her till the judgment was pronounced and signed, but that this would probably only take place in a day or two. I asked the German official to inform the Legation immediately after the passing of said judgment, so that I might see Miss Cavell at once, thinking of course that the Legation might, according to your intentions, take immediate steps for Miss Cavell's pardon if the judgment really was a sentence of death.

Very surprised to still receive no news from Mr. Kirschen I then called at his house at 12.30 and was informed that he would not be there till about the end of the afternoon. I then called, at 12.40, at the house of another lawyer interested in the case of a fellow-prisoner, and found that he also was out. In the afternoon however the latter lawyer called at my house, saying that in the morning he had heard from the German Commandantur that judgment would be passed only the next morning viz. Thursday morning. He said he feared that the Court would be very severe for all the prisoners.

Shortly after this lawyer left me, and while I was preparing a note about the case, at 8 p. m., I was privately and reliably informed that the judgment had been delivered at five o'clock in the afternoon, that Miss Cavell had been sentenced to death, and that she would be shot at 2 o'clock the next morning. I told my informer that I was extremely surprised at this, because the Legation had received no information yet, neither from the German Authorities nor from Mr. Kirschen, but that the matter was too serious to run the smallest chance, and that therefore I would proceed immediately to the Legation to confer with Your Excellency and take all possible steps to save Miss Cavell's life.

According to Your Excellency's decision, Mr. Gibson and myself went, with the Spanish Minister, to see Baron von der Lancken, and the report of our interview and of our efforts to save Miss Cavell is given to you by Mr. Gibson.[15]

This morning, Mr. Gahan, the English clergyman, called to see me and told me that he had seen Miss Cavell in her cell yesterday night at 10 o'clock, that he had given her the Holy Communion and had found her admirably strong and calm. I asked Mr. Gahan whether she had made any remarks about anything concerning the legal side of her case, and whether the confession which she made before the trial and in court was in his opinion perfectly free and sincere. Mr. Gahan says that she told him she perfectly well knew what she had done, that according to the law of course she was guilty and had admitted her guilt, but that she was happy to die for her country.

G. DE LEVAL

[Subenclosure—Translation]

The Minister in Belgium (Whitlock) to M. Sadi Kirschen

No. 7525   BRUSSELS, October 5, 1915.

MY DEAR SIR: Thank you for the letter you have addressed to Mr. de Leval,[16] informing him that the affair of Miss Cavell would come up before the Council of War on Thursday next at 8 a. m.

As agreed, I would be greatly obliged if, after the hearing, you would be good enough to send me a memorandum, setting forth the causes for which Miss Cavell is being prosecuted and indicating the

---

[15] See enclosure 7, p. 51.
[16] No copy enclosed with this despatch.

charges proven against her during the trial, as, also, the sentence when it shall have been rendered.

Accept [etc.]

For the Minister

G. DE LEVAL

Legal Counselor of the Legation

[Enclosure 10]

The Minister in Belgium (Whitlock) to the Ambassador in Great Britain (Page)

No. 7723   BRUSSELS, *October 13, 1915.*

SIR: Referring to previous correspondence in regard to the case of Miss Edith Cavell, I regret to be obliged to inform you, in confirmation of my telegram of yesterday morning that the death sentence recommended by the Prosecuting Attorney was imposed by the Court Martial and that Miss Cavell was executed early yesterday morning.

I enclose herewith for your information copies of all the correspondence which I have had with the German Authorities in regard to this case, together with copies of previous letters addressed to you on the subject.

I know that you will understand without my telling you that we exhausted every possible effort to prevent the infliction of the death penalty and that our failure has been felt by us as a very severe blow. I am convinced however that no step was neglected which could have had any effect. From the date we first learned of Miss Cavell's imprisonment, we made frequent inquiries of the German Authorities and reminded them of their promise that we should be fully informed as to developments.

They were under no misapprehension as to our interest in the matter. Although the German Authorities did not inform me when the sentence had actually been passed I learned through an unofficial source that judgment had been delivered and that Miss Cavell was to be executed during the night. I immediately sent Mr. Gibson, the Secretary of Legation, to present to Baron von der Lancken my appeal that execution of the sentence should be deferred until the Governor could consider my plea for clemency. Mr. Gibson was accompanied by Maître de Leval, Legal Counselor of the Legation, who had worked from the beginning upon the legal aspect of the case. Mr. Gibson was fortunate enough to find the Spanish Minister, and got him to accompany him on his visit to Baron von der Lancken. The details of the visit you will find in Mr. Gibson's report to me. The other papers which are attached speak for themselves and require no further comment from me.

I have [etc.]   [File copy not signed]

124.556/7 : Telegram

The Minister in Belgium (Whitlock) to the Secretary of State

BRUSSELS, *October 30, 1915.*
[Received October 31—10 a.m.]

416. The wide publication in England and America of the full correspondence in the case of the late Edith Cavell so highly incensed the German authorities, and so greatly increased the difficulty of our position here, that it was only after conferences lasting throughout a trying day that I was able to prevent serious complications. I therefore felt that I should report in full for the Department's information and for such instruction as it may care to give.

The Baron von der Lancken, Chief of the Political Department of the General Government, here, made two specific complaints: First, that the publication of the correspondence was a violation of diplomatic etiquette: that it placed, as it were, an arm in the hands of Germany's enemies and therefore affected our neutrality, and: Secondly: That this seemed to be due to the fact that in the person of Maître de Leval we have in our Legation a Belgian subject and therefore an enemy of Germany. Baron von der Lancken thereupon said that he felt that the German Government was entitled to an expression of regret on my part that the correspondence had been published and he asked that Maître de Leval be immediately dismissed from the Legation adding that if this were not done he feared the military authorities regarding Maître de Leval as "undesirable" might take steps that he and the Governor General would be powerless to prevent. My first concern being to prevent any difficulties arising between Germany and our Government, I said to the Baron that the correspondence had been sent to our Ambassador at London for his information and that I did not know whether or not my Government under its reserved right to make public the official correspondence of its officers abroad had given its assent to its publication by British Foreign Office but that whether this was so or not the responsibility for the publication was not mine and that I could not assume to express regret for it. I told the Baron that he and his Government could rest confident in the assurance that the United States Government would do full and complete justice in the matter and that I should at once communicate to my Government the views of the German authorities here.

As for the case of Maître de Leval, I stated that I of course was responsible for his actions and I protested energetically against any interference with his liberty, adding that I should not dismiss him and that in any event he could be dismissed only by my Government. The objections to Maître de Leval were based upon that portion of his report to me in which he said that he had made frequent inquiries at the Political Department and that he had been assured during the day that the Legation would be informed when judgment was pronounced upon Miss Cavell.[17] From this statement Baron von der Lancken said that the inference had been drawn in England and elsewhere that he, the Baron, had broken his word to me, whereas according to his views the conversations of that nature on the day in question were between Maître de Leval and the Chancellor of his Department, neither of whom he insisted had any diplomatic capacity. He raised other objections to statements in the report, but whatever might be the ultimate determination on these points, and feeling that the statements in Maître de Leval's report were substantially accurate, I pointed out that in the various reports we had expressed no conclusions, had made no comments and advanced no opinions, and that I had had no intention of charging Baron von der Lancken with having broken his word or of making any observation on the action of the German authorities.

The feeling against Maître de Leval was indeed an old grievance, for on several occasions the Baron von der Lancken had complained to me of our having a Belgian in our Legation and at the opening of our adjourned conversation in the afternoon he said to me that Maître de Leval was distinctly *persona non grata* and that they must refuse to have relations with him or to recognize him in any diplomatic connection or in any capacity other than that of a Belgian subject. I then said to the Baron that neither my Government nor [apparent omission] would wish to impose upon the German authorities a person who was not to their liking and that upon that basis it would be possible, I had no doubt, in the future to relieve that [*them?*] of any embarrassment that Maître de Leval's relation to the Legation might cause. I told him that I should communicate with my Government in an effort to adjust that question as well as the first one he had raised in a manner satisfactory to the German Government and that in the meantime Maître de Leval would perform no diplomatic functions. I then told Baron von der Lancken that I would rely upon him to see that Maître de Leval be given every protection and he gave me that assurance.

The Department will realize that the publication in full of this correspondence has rendered still more uncomfortable the already difficult and delicate situation of the Legation: that it has not only aroused resentment which I have with the greatest difficulty succeeded in partially allaying, but it has imperilled those mentioned in the report, such as Maître de Leval and the rector who has done such good charitable work in the English colony. I venture there-

[17] See enclosure 9, p. 56.

fore to lay the Baron's views before the Department for appropriate action. In this connection I think it is only due to state that a confusion may have arisen as to the General Government, which is under the command of His Excellency Baron von Bissing as Governor General, and the military authorities. The case of Miss Cavell did not fall within the jurisdiction of the Governor General and it is due Baron von der Lancken to say that he visited the military authorities on that fateful night in an effort to have the execution at least postponed. The embarrassing feature of the publication was perhaps not so much the facts it set forth as the exposure of names, letters and documents and the resulting comments thereon. Baron von der Lancken also requested that I ask the Department to take some action that would moderate criticism of the affair in the American press. I explained to him that my Government had no control over the press but I venture to report his request to the Department.

As far as Maître de Leval is concerned although he has rendered devoted and efficient service and his conduct has been beyond criticism and beyond reproach, I feel that in view of all the circumstances and especially in view of the expressed statement on the part of the German authorities that he is *persona non grata* his usefulness here is unfortunately at an end: this of course as I trust I have made it plain, without involving any reflection upon him. I feel that consideration for his safety would dictate that he be not dismissed and left in this country but that provision for his dignified departure from Belgium be made. Anticipating the possibility of opposition to his going, I respectfully suggest that the Department, in case there should be concurrence in my views, render my task in that respect easier by authorizing me to express to Baron von Bissing, the Governor General, the desire of our Government that Mr. de Leval be granted safe conduct for himself and his family out of Belgium, and that if necessary the Department make a similar request at Berlin. I think this would be the better way to deal with the situation. Although Maître de Leval has been recognized by the German authorities to the extent of the courtesy of passports for use in Belgium, I feel it would be better to avoid if possible raising the question of his diplomatic status. Inasmuch as Maître de Leval's departure from Belgium will entail a considerable financial sacrifice to him I recommend that the Department continue to pay him his salary for a reasonable period of time. He has served us faithfully and I am brought to consider his departure only because I realize that his situation here is insupportable and that his continuance here might create further difficulties which it is of course in the interest of all to avoid. He himself is willing and indeed anxious to go.

I, therefore, request instruction as to what to say to the German authorities as to the publication of the documents and as to the course to be pursued in reference to Maître de Leval, and any further advice and assistance the Department sees fit to give me.

WHITLOCK

124.556/8 : Telegram

The Minister in Belgium (Whitlock) to the Secretary of State

BRUSSELS, October 29, 1915—6 p. m.

[Received October 30—9 : 45 p. m.]

For the information of the Department. In conference reported in my long telegram filed today at The Hague,[18] Baron von der Lancken and I put in writing a short statement in French which I agreed he might give to the press as follows: "The American Minister expressed surprise at the incident; he stated that he had sent his report to London for the information of the Ambassador and was not himself responsible for the publication. He added that he would report the matter to his Government when [*which?*] he was confident would find a satisfactory solution." Baron von der Lancken has left for Germany and this morning an official poster appeared on the walls of Brussels regarding our conversation. It ends as follows: "The Minister of the U. S. has declared that the publication of the documents in question has greatly surprised him and that he would without delay inform his colleague in London and his Government of the differences existing between the real facts and the statement of them in the written report of the Belgian attorney." The foregoing requires no comment from me.

WHITLOCK

124.556/7 : Telegram

The Secretary of State to the Minister in Belgium (Whitlock)

WASHINGTON, November 2, 1915—5 p. m.

185. Your 416, 30th.[19] The Department shares your views as to Maître de Leval, and instructs you to say to Baron von Bissing that this Government would not wish to retain in the Legation any one who was not *persona grata* to the German authorities and that in the circumstances this Government desires that Mr. de Leval be granted safe conduct for himself and his family to depart from Belgium.

---

[18] *Supra.*
[19] *Ante,* p. 62.

Please make it clear to the German authorities that the case of Miss Cavell was not brought to the attention of this Government, nor was the Department the medium of communication in this instance between Brussels and London. This Government, therefore, had no knowledge of the documents in the case, which were made public by the British Foreign Office without consultation with this Department.

The Department appreciates Maître de Leval's loyal and efficient services, and is glad to continue to pay him his present salary for a period of three months after his actual departure from Legation.

LANSING

362.412 C31/6

The Chargé in Belgium (Gibson) to the Secretary of State

No. 205   BRUSSELS, *November 19, 1915.*
[Received December 7.]

SIR: Referring to Mr. Brand Whitlock's telegram of October 27 [*29*] [20] in regard to official notices posted by the German Authorities concerning his alleged disapproval of the reports made in the Cavell case, I have the honor to transmit herewith enclosed, for the information of the Department, copy and translation of the entire text of the poster in question.

I have [etc.]   HUGH GIBSON

[Enclosure—Translation][21]

Extract From News Poster of the German General Government in Belgium

BRUSSELS, *October 27.* The United States Ambassador in London has placed the papers relative to the Cavell case at the disposal of the English Government. These papers relate to the correspondence exchanged on the subject of the trial between the Legation of the United States in Brussels and the German authorities in that city. The English Government at once turned these documents over to the press and had them published by the Reuter Syndicate. They reproduce the most essential facts in an inexact manner. Above all they allow it to be supposed that the German authorities put off the Minister of the U. S. with false promises, in order to leave him in ignorance that the sentence of death had already been pronounced, and, by proceeding rapidly with the execution, prevented intervention in favor of the persons sentenced. In published comments on the subject, Sir Edward Grey considers as particularly reprehensible the fact that the German authority did not respect its engagement to

---

[20] *Ante*, p. 65.
[21] The original poster was in French, Flemish, and German.

keep the Minister of the U. S. informed of the progress of the trial. Such a promise was never made by the German authority which, therefore, could not break its word.   The Minister of the U. S. at Brussels, in the course of an interview with the German authority recognised himself that this was the case.   The United States Ambassador in London has been misinformed: he was led into error by the statements of a Belgian jurisconsult who in his quality of legal counsellor of the American Legation in Brussels has played a certain role in this affair.   The Minister of the U. S. has stated that the publication of the documents in question had greatly surprised him and that he would, without delay, advise his colleague at London and his Government of the difference between the real facts and their exposition in the written report of the Belgian lawyer.

CONDUCT OF FOREIGN DIPLOMATS IN THE UNITED STATES

701.6711/88

The Turkish Ambassador (Rustem) to the Secretary of State

WASHINGTON, *September 12, 1914.*

SIR: Referring to the conversation I had with you yesterday morning I beg to make the following statement:

The remarks attributed to me in the cutting from the *Star* which you handed to me and which I hereby return are a faithful reproduction of language used by me.

I am fully aware that the course I followed in pointing through the press to certain unfortunate happenings in the United States was an unusual one. But so is the situation against which I desired to react in the interest of both Turkey and this Country.

For years past, Turkey has been the object of systematic attacks on the part of the press of the United States. These attacks, conceived very frequently in the most outrageous language, spare her in none of her feelings. Her religion, her nationality, her customs, her past, her present are reviled. She is represented as being a sink of iniquity. Excesses which have occurred in her midst and which I, with all other educated Ottomans, deeply deplore but of which there are parallels without the same excuses in the life of other nations constitute an inextinguishable theme of violent denunciation of her.

This attitude of the press has poisoned public opinion in the United States in regard to the Turkish people to such an extent that a member of that race is seldom thought or spoken of in this country otherwise than as the "unspeakable" and when Turkey, defeated and bleeding as the result of the Balkan War, was in need of a kind word, mockery and insult of the most cruel nature were poured upon her by almost every American paper.

So far, the distance which separates the two countries has protected the Turkish people from a knowledge of the implacable treatment it was receiving at the hands of the American press, but today, when every eye and ear is strained in Turkey as well as in every other part of Europe to detect signs of the attitude of the United States, the only great Power which has remained neutral in the present conflict of nations, echoes are reaching even the most retired in Turkey of the malignant voices raised against her so persistently in the daily and periodical literature of this country.

As, on the other hand, this is a period when racial and nationalist passions are intensely alive, it is greatly to be feared that these provocations of the United States press added to the effect produced by the sale of the *Idaho* and *Mississippi* to Greece at a time when her relations were extremely strained with Turkey and the rumors that the United States were on the point of making a naval demonstration in Turkish waters may cause a strong reaction in the feeling of friendship entertained so far by the Turkish people for the United States. What is particularly unfortunate is that the press of this country should so persistently indulge in false accusations of a projected massacre en masse of Christians in Turkey. To the baser elements of the Turkish population the perpetual agitation of this calumny may finally act as a suggestion to do the thing it was not thinking of doing and this all the more as it is in the name of Christianity that Turkey has been practically condemned to be an outlaw among nations.

The Imperial Government who has only taken notice of the anti-Turkish excesses in the United States to express the pain they have caused it, is fully conscious of its duties at this critical moment. But the press of a country in the van of civilization like the United States and one officially engaged in circumscribing the present storm should not render the task of the Sublime Porte more difficult than it is. It was imperative to make a strong effort to bring it to a more responsible view of its relationship to Turkey. The Administration is notoriously helpless against the press. It was for the Turkish Ambassador to act.

In proceeding as I did it cannot be fairly said that I attacked or even criticised the United States. It is clear that I was defending my country against an American attack and if my mode of defense was to show that the United States has also things to reproach herself with and to specify those things it appeared to me that it was the only way of inducing the press of this country to take a more charitable view of the Turkish people whose defects are compensated by sterling virtues.

I may have transgressed diplomatic rules but the occasion was one in which I firmly believe that it was not only pardonable but legitimate to depart from conventionalities. The interests of humanity cannot be sacrificed to form.

I am conscious of having fulfilled my moral duty to Turkey, to the United States and to humanity at large.

Accept [etc.]   A. RUSTEM

[Enclosure]

Statement by the Turkish Ambassador (Rustem) as Published in the Washington "Evening Star," September 8, 1914

"According to the newspapers, Great Britain, following in the footsteps of France, has agitated before the eyes of the United States the specter of a massacre of Christians in Turkey, and has made this gruesome picture of the immediate future, drawn with absolute disregard to truth, a pretext for requesting the United States to dispatch warships to Turkish ports. That there have been massacres in Turkey I cannot, unfortunately, deny, but the Armenians and Maronites who were the victims, suffered at the hands of the Moslems, not as Christians, but as political agitators engaged in undermining the Ottoman state, the while flaunting in the face of the government and dominant race the support of Russia, France and England.

"Under the same provocation what would Russia have done, who has given the world the spectacle of not one but twenty programs [*pogroms*] against an innocent race; what France, who smoked to death in caverns the Algerians fighting for the independence of their land, who later on rejoiced in that grand production, the Commune; what England, whose punishment of the 'rebels' in the Indian 'mutiny' was to blow them off guns?

"And, since a large number of American papers are siding with Great Britain and France in this affair, I will permit myself to say that the thought of the lynchings which occur daily in the United States and the memory of the 'watercures' in the Philippines should make them chary of attacking Turkey in connection with acts of savagery committed by her under provocation compared with which the economic competition of an Italian or the sniping of a Filipino, or even the outrage of a negro, are as nothing.

"Supposing, for the sake of argument, what in reality could never happen, that the negroes were discovered to be engaged in a conspiracy with the Japanese to facilitate the invasion of the United States by the latter, how many of them would be left alive to tell the tale?

"Great Britain and France have embarked upon a new campaign of provocation against Turkey, secretly hoping that as a result of it something untoward may happen in that country to confirm their sinister predictions, so that the United States will be finally prevailed upon to dispatch warships to the Levant and thus get mixed up in the European fray on the allies' side, but I believe the administration too sagacious to fall into such a vulgar trap.

"Besides, why should the United States, not one of whose citizens has ever suffered in Turkey, send warships in the waters of that country, with the result that it would only cause irritation against her and could under no circumstances act as a check? Bombard Smyrna, Beirut, which are mostly inhabited by Christians? What of that? And what more could she do? Nothing. But that would be enough to mean war. Do the people of the United States want war?

"The new British move against Turkey is clumsy. It will not cause the United States to modify its attitude. But it has called forth the following telegram from New York to the Turkish embassy.

"'If Turkey goes to war against England, the Hindoos and Mussulmans in India and elsewhere will support her in every way. Thousands of volunteers ready.

> " 'Bhayankar,
> " 'Gadar National Volunteers,
> " '57 East 200th Street.' "

701.6711/103½

The Counselor for the Department of State (Lansing) to the Secretary of State

WASHINGTON, *September 14, 1914.*

DEAR MR. SECRETARY: I have read the Turkish Ambassador's note of the 12th instant containing a statement as to his recent published interview.

The statement is, in my opinion, so arrogant in tone as to be extremely offensive; and the Ambassador has by implication criticised the Government in its permitting the sale of cruisers to Greece and in sending a warship to Turkish waters for the purpose, as he is pleased to term it, of a "naval demonstration."

Furthermore, the Ambassador frankly admits that his conduct may be considered undiplomatic, and seeks to justify it by asserting that the occasion was one which made it "not only pardonable but legitimate to depart from conventionalities."

I do not think that it would comport with the dignity of this Government, after the public utterances of the Ambassador and his statement, which aggravates the situation, to permit him to represent longer Turkey at this capital. His usefulness here has ended and he [is] unquestionably *persona non grata.*

Very sincerely yours,

ROBERT LANSING

701.6711/103½

The Secretary of State to the Counselor for the Department of State (Lansing)

WASHINGTON, *September 16, 1914.*

MY DEAR MR. LANSING: The President has not indicated his wishes in the matter of the Turkish Ambassador's interview. I have suggested to him over the phone that in ordinary times it would seem a reason for immediate recall, but at this time it was wise to make some allowances rather than run the risk of making the situation more acute over there.

We cannot well overlook the matter, and it occurs to me that it might be well to write him a letter saying that we regret exceedingly to note from the tone of his letter that he feels justified in violating the well-established rules universally observed among diplomats—and that he has unfortunately allowed himself to be irritated by a very inconsiderable portion of the press of the United States—for it is impossible that he should have been able to read many of the large number of papers published in this country. That this Government is recognizing the tension caused by the acute situation in Europe and is not disposed to deal as strictly with his breach of etiquette as would seem proper in ordinary times and that if he feels that he can render his country service by remaining here he will express in due form his regret at his public utterances, and give assurance of his intention to conform to those requirements which are necessary if diplomatic intercourse is to be conducted in that friendly spirit which the amicable relations of the countries make proper.

I simply suggest the above for the consideration of yourself and the President, in case the latter thinks that something ought to be said at this time.

Yours very truly,

W. J. BRYAN

701.6711/104½

President Wilson to the Acting Secretary of State

WASHINGTON, *September 17, 1914.*

MY DEAR MR. LANSING: I return herewith the extraordinary letter of the Turkish Ambassador.[1] I believe that Mr. Bryan before leaving last evening made some suggestions as to a letter to be sent the

---

[1] *Ante,* p. 68.

Ambassador. I shall be very glad to confer with you about it when you have drafted it.

In haste

Cordially and sincerely yours,

WOODROW WILSON

701.6711/88

The Acting Secretary of State to the Turkish Ambassador (Rustem)

WASHINGTON, *September 19, 1914.*

EXCELLENCY: I have laid before the President your note of September 12th, which you sent in compliance with an oral request of the Secretary of State that you inform him whether you made certain statements attributed to you which appeared as an interview in a newspaper published in this city on September 8th, and which reflected upon the administration of justice in the United States and its dependencies.

In your note you acknowledge that you were the author of those statements and that the report in the newspaper was accurate. In extenuation you state that the hostility of the press of this country toward Turkey was sufficient reason to justify your violation of the rules of conduct universally observed by diplomatic representatives toward the governments to which they are accredited, and you also take the opportunity to criticize by inference the policy of this Government toward Turkey.

The President desires me to inform Your Excellency that your note is not acceptable in tone, nor is it a satisfactory explanation of your conduct, and that it is regrettable that you permitted yourself to become so irritated over the utterances of a very inconsiderable portion of the press of the United States as to commit so serious a breach of official etiquette as that which you admit and attempt to defend.

The President desires me to state further that, recognizing the tension caused by the acute situation in Europe, he is not disposed to deal as strictly with an offense against the hospitality of the United States, which you as the diplomatic representative of your Government enjoy, as he would, under normal conditions, consider necessary and consistent with the dignity of the United States.

I am, therefore, instructed to inform Your Excellency that, if you feel that your services at this capital can still be useful to your Government, and if you are willing to express your regret for your published utterances, which this Government considers to be offensive, the President is disposed to pass over without further comment your public statement and your note and renew the cordial and friendly intercourse between Your Excellency and the Government of the United States, which existed before this unfortunate incident occurred.

Accept [etc.]   ROBERT LANSING

701.6711/94

The Turkish Ambassador (Rustem) to the Acting Secretary of State

WASHINGTON, *September 20, 1914.*

SIR: I have the honor to acknowledge receipt of your Note of the 19th instant replying to my communication of the 8th [*12th*] concerning certain statements made by me in an interview with a press representative.

In answer I beg that you will inform the President that I regret not to be able to accept his point of view in the matter and that, in consequence, it appeared to me necessary to ask my Government to grant me leave of absence. My departure for Constantinople will take place within a fortnight.

Accept [etc.]   A. RUSTEM

701.6711/95a

The Acting Secretary of State to President Wilson

WASHINGTON, *September 22, 1914.*

DEAR MR. PRESIDENT: I enclose a draft telegram to Mr. Morgenthau, which I propose to send if it meets with your approval. I think in case you do approve, it should be sent immediately.[2]

Very sincerely yours,

ROBERT LANSING

[Enclosure]

Draft Telegram From the Acting Secretary of State to the Ambassador in Turkey (Morgenthau)

You are advised in case the matter is brought to your attention by the Ottoman Government of the following facts.

Rustem Bey, the Ottoman Ambassador here, gave an interview which was published in the newspapers of September eighth and in which he attacked the press of this country for its attitude toward Turkey calling attention to the lynchings here and the water cure in the Philippines. When he was asked as to the interview he acknowledged the authorship and the accuracy of the report and stated that the occasion justified his ignoring conventionalities.

---

[2] This paper bears the notation: "Telegram approved by Prest and sent 9 [*10*] pm Sept 22/14   RL."

The President was much displeased with the published interview and with the tone of the Ambassador's note of explanation, which would have merited immediate dismissal under ordinary conditions. In view, however, of the critical situation in Europe the President was disposed to deal leniently with this flagrant violation of diplomatic propriety by the Ambassador, who was advised that the President considered his explanation of his admitted breach of etiquette unsatisfactory, but that on account of the tension in European affairs he would overlook the offense provided the Ambassador considered his usefulness here had not ceased and provided that the Ambassador expressed regret for his utterances.

The note stating the President's views and decisions was delivered to the Ambassador September nineteenth. On the twenty-first the Department received a note from him dated the twentieth in which he said that he disagreed with the President's point of view as to his conduct and stated he would ask for leave of absence and depart for Constantinople within a fortnight.

On account of the critical situation in Turkey and the uncertainty of Turkish action in relation to the European war the President was loath to introduce another element of possible irritation into the situation, but in view of the uncompromising attitude of the Ambassador in regard to his conduct, the President feels that he went to the extreme of leniency in offering the Ambassador an opportunity to express regret. To have gone further would have been inconsistent with the dignity of the United States and would have made further intercourse between this Government and the Ambassador intolerable.

You will use this information discreetly.

701.6211/279½

The Acting Secretary of State to President Wilson

WASHINGTON, *September 25, 1914.*

DEAR MR. PRESIDENT: I enclose a newspaper interview alleged to have been given by Baron von Schoen, formerly Secretary of the German Embassy at Tokio and now attached to the Embassy here, and also his written repudiation of the interview.[3]

The Baron called on me yesterday morning and asked me if I had seen the reported interview. I replied that I had. He then asked if I had seen his letter denying it. I answered that I had and that, when I read the interview imputed to him, I could not believe that he had uttered such silly remarks or been guilty of such extremely

---

[3] Latter not printed.

bad taste and improper conduct, and I was glad that he had disavowed the report.

His manner, when I spoke thus frankly of the interview, which his repudiation made possible, and subsequent statements made to me by the reporter, who said that he obtained the interview, convince me that he was reported with substantial accuracy.

Do you think that the matter ought to be dropped or that the attention of the German Ambassador should be called to it?

Very sincerely yours,

ROBERT LANSING

[Enclosure]

Extract of Interview With the Secretary of the German Embassy (Schoen) as Published in the Washington "Evening Star," September 23, 1914

"I have heard many persons in Japan say they believe war with the United States is unavoidable," said Baron von Schoen, and he repeated this today to a representative of *The Star*, in confirmation when requested to do so. "From repeated statements of this sort I have come to believe that it is the general opinion of the Japanese people. I have seen frequent evidence of very strong anti-American feeling. There seems to be intense hatred for the United States throughout Japan.

"I have just come from Japan, having been transferred to Washington. An astonishing thing about the war is the complete apathy of the Japanese people toward it. The people have no interest in it at all. In England, Russia and France there was really an anti-German feeling, and patriotic demonstrations for their own countries were held, but nothing of the kind took place in Japan. A stranger in that country would not know from appearances that Japan was at war.

WELCOMED MEXICAN TROUBLE

"Before war was declared there were preparations for it, and the people said, 'Yes, it is for Russia or America.' When the Mexican government sent Senor Francisco de la Barra on a special mission to Tokio there were great demonstrations, although there was no feeling of admiration by the people for the Mexicans, despite the alleged race kinship. It was the trouble between Huerta and the United States that gave the people an opportunity, on the occasion of de la Barra's visit, to vent their feelings in great anti-American demonstrations.

"I remember just after going to Japan in 1913, during the negotiations between Washington and Tokio over the California Webb alien land act, an incident impressed me. I lived rather close to the United States embassy, and one morning as I went by it I saw that some Japanese people had written on the walls big sentences in English insulting the United States government.

"There was a strong pro-Mexican feeling in Japan when the United States had difficulties with that republic on account of the Japanese antagonism to the United States. Should both Japan and England be victorious in this war—which, of course, I do not believe is possible—the danger to the United States will be great.

701.6211/280½

President Wilson to the Acting Secretary of State

WASHINGTON, *September 26, 1914.*

MY DEAR MR. LANSING: I return the enclosed reports of the alleged interview with Baron von Schoen.[4]

I hope that if there is any proper way of opening the matter with the German Ambassador, it may be opened. I feel with you that there can be no real doubt about the substantial authenticity of the interview and I think it not only desirable, but imperative, that this gentleman should not remain here.

Cordially and sincerely yours,

WOODROW WILSON

701.6211/280½a

The Acting Secretary of State to the German Ambassador (Bernstorff)

WASHINGTON, *September 28, 1914.*

MY DEAR MR. AMBASSADOR: The President is much annoyed over an interview in the *Evening Star* of September 23rd, which purported to have been given by Baron von Schoen, a Secretary of your Embassy, and which related to the unfriendly public opinion of the Japanese people for the United States.

Although Baron von Schoen on the 24th publicly denied over his own signature that the interview was correct, or that the views expressed therein conformed to the statement which he made, and although the denial was personally called to my attention by its author, Baron von Schoen admits in his letter of denial that he made some statement to the reporter in regard to this subject.

---

[4] *Supra.*

However disposed the President is to recognize the liability of error in a newspaper report of an oral statement, he cannot but feel that a statement at any time by a diplomatic officer of a foreign government, as to the relations of the United States with another Power, is indiscreet and improper. A statement on such a subject at the present time, when the United States is seeking to preserve a strict neutrality, if it tends to influence American public opinion against one of the belligerents in the war which is being waged, is especially mischievous and arouses suspicion as to the motive which inspired it.

I regret, my dear Mr. Ambassador, to be compelled to call this matter to your attention, and I have done so in this informal way in order that you may take the first convenient opportunity to call at the Department and discuss the propriety of Baron von Schoen's conduct.

I am [etc.]   ROBERT LANSING

701.6211/281½

The Acting Secretary of State to President Wilson

WASHINGTON, *September 30, 1914.*

DEAR MR. PRESIDENT: In accordance with the request of the German Ambassador, I send you a copy of a letter which I have just received from him.

Will you please indicate what other steps, if any, you desire to have taken in the matter?

Very sincerely yours,

ROBERT LANSING

[Enclosure]

The German Ambassador (Bernstorff) to the Acting Secretary of State

NEW YORK, *September 29, 1914.*

MY DEAR MR. LANSING: In answer to your favor of 28th inst. I beg to say, that nobody can regret more than I do that an alleged interview with Baron Schoen appeared in the *Evening Star* on September 23d. Quite apart from its contents, this interview, if it had been genuine, would have thrown a very bad light on the discipline of my Embassy, no member of which would ever publish anything in the newspapers, unless specially authorized by me to give out an official statement of my Government. I quite agree with you as to the impropriety of the language of the alleged interview. As, however, Baron Schön assured me that he had not made the statements of the alleged interview, I right away published a denial in all newspapers and have since then regarded the interview as nonexistent and as one of the many mushroom growths which every day rise out of the mire produced in the press by this awful war.

I should be very much obliged to you if you would kindly submit the above to the President. Of course, I am very willing to call at the State Department to repeat these statements to you verbally.

Very sincerely yours,

J. BERNSTORFF

701.6211/282½

President Wilson to the Acting Secretary of State

WASHINGTON, *October 1, 1914.*

MY DEAR MR. LANSING: Thank you for letting me see the enclosed.[5] I do not feel that we can wisely drop the matter about Baron Schoen. I hope that it will be possible to intimate to Count von Bernstorff that the alleged interview has made so widespread an impression and has been in so many ways called to the attention of the Government that it would be an embarrassment for a great many months to come to Baron Schoen himself and it would be certain seriously to impair his usefulness here. I make this as a suggestion.[6]

Cordially and faithfully yours,

WOODROW WILSON

701.6311/141

The Secretary of State to President Wilson

WASHINGTON, *September 2, 1915.*

MY DEAR MR. PRESIDENT: You have undoubtedly read the flimsy of the strictly confidential despatch from London, No. 2732, September 1, 7 P. M.,[7] in which there is a copy of a letter signed by Ambassador Dumba and which was taken from Archibald who was carrying it to Vienna.

It seems to me that the conduct of the Ambassador is of a very serious nature and that we should consider at once what steps should be taken in regard to it.

Faithfully yours,

ROBERT LANSING

---

[5] *Supra.*

[6] The incident was closed by an interview between the Secretary of State and the German Ambassador in which the latter again expressed regret at the appearance of the interview and stated that Baron von Schoen had been instructed to avoid newspaper comment. (File No. 701.6211/300.)

[7] *Foreign Relations,* 1915, supp., p. 932. For correspondence previously printed concerning the incidents leading to the recall of Ambassador Dumba, see *ibid.,* pp. 932–947.

701.6311/145½

President Wilson to the Secretary of State

WASHINGTON, *3 September, 1915.*

MY DEAR MR. SECRETARY: The contents of the strictly confidential despatch from London, No. 2732, September 1, 7 P. M.[8] are certainly serious enough, and I entirely agree with you that we shall have to take some decided action with regard to the activities of Dumba as well as those of Bernstorff. But when, and how?

I take it for granted that we shall first wish to make sure of Germany's concessions and of their exact terms before dealing with either of these allied Ambassadors about the other matter. So much for the When.

As for the How, what do you think would be the best course, a private intimation to each of them which would allow them to ask to be relieved, without public rebuke, or a direct request on our part to their Governments? I do not know the practice in these matters.

Faithfully Yours,

W. W.

701.6311/146½

The Secretary of State to President Wilson

WASHINGTON, *September 7, 1915.*

MY DEAR MR. PRESIDENT: Ambassador Dumba has just left. We went over quite thoroughly the situation created by his letter to the Foreign Office.[9] In substance his defense is set forth in a memorandum which he left with me and which I enclose to you. I do not think that I can add anything of value to it, though he did elaborate to an extent in conversation.

I also called his attention to the employment of Archibald as a messenger, and pointed out to him the impropriety of a diplomatic representative in this country using one of its citizens, who carried an American passport and was entitled to protection by this Government, as a bearer of official dispatches which were to pass through enemy territory. He seemed surprised at this complaint; said that he had never thought of it; that he had never used an American citizen before, and never should again for such a purpose. He also said that it should be realized that conditions of communication with his Government were very difficult and that they took any practical means to send their official dispatches. I told him that I would like

---

[8] *Foreign Relations,* 1915, supp., p. 932.
[9] See telegram No. 2732, Sept. 1, 1915, from the Ambassador in Great Britain, *ibid.*

to have him think the matter over and if he desired to furnish a memorandum on the subject.

I further gave him the decided impression that you were much concerned, I think I might say irritated, over what had occurred and that I would report the substance of our interview to you and that he would hear from me in a few days.

He is evidently very much distressed because of what has occurred, but I do not think he really repents of his action; he only deplores the fact that he was found out.

Faithfully yours,

ROBERT LANSING

[Enclosure]

Memorandum by the Austro-Hungarian Ambassador (Dumba)

In consequence of the production on a gigantic scale of war supplies for the Allies the Austrian and Hungarian citizens, working in the industrial plants which have filled contracts with the Allies, are in an extremely difficult position.—The Hungarian and Austrian penal laws submit all Austrians and Hungarians working in neutral countries in factories producing warmaterial for enemies to heavy penalties. A warning issued by the two Governments in Vienna and Budapest announced that such citizens, after their return to their country, may be punished with imprisonment of ten to twenty years, and even by capital punishment under certain aggravating circumstances which would qualify their acts as high treason.

I had called the attention of my Government to the great difficulty of exacting an immediate and complete compliance with the above cited laws from the many thousands of our citizens occupied in factories now producing warsupplies for the Allies. I especially mentioned months ago, that for instance in Bridgeport a certain number of Hungarians had of their own and free will, prompted by pure patriotic motives left such factories; but that they had been unable to find work elsewhere and therefore reluctantly compelled to return to their former occupation. But as the great majority of these workmen and especially of the Hungarian citizens are anxious to return to their country after the war, it is incumbent upon me to warn them of the danger which they would incur, if they continued to remain in plants working exclusively for the Allies.

I might have done this by official notification through the respective Il. and Rl. Consulates. Legal advisors pronounced themselves against this method, as the Consuls might lay themselves open to actions for damages for incitement to breaking contracts. The only way remaining would therefore be the exhortation of our citizens by their national papers, to leave the plants unless they preferred to stay permanently in the United States and gave up every thought of seeing again their country of origin. At the same time it was clear that the gradual exit of our workmen by small numbers would only deprive them of their bread without in the least interfering with the production of warsupplies, whereas this object would have been more probably attained by their leaving all in great number at the same time.

My attention was also called to the inhuman labour conditions prevailing in different plants and especially in Bethlehem where our unskilled workmen are supposed to work 12 hours a day and seven days a week. I thought therefore that this would be a good opportunity to protect my countrymen, many of whom are analphabets and utterly helpless against this unscrupulous sweating system by organizing these white slaves in unions which would soon obtain for them a shorter working day and altogether better conditions of work. The plants have every motif to grant now concessions, and once such concessions made, they would benefit our unskilled labourers in a permanent way after the war.

To achieve these ends it would be necessary to subsidise different national papers, which suffer already now through bad labour conditions and to the subsequent nonpayment of subscriptions. Besides certain expenses would be caused by the intended organization of unions and the foundation of an employment Bureau to find work for our countrymen who were to leave their present work, would also necessitate considerable expense. It is for this purpose that I asked Baron Burian for a credit of $15,000.

I should be very thankful if my endeavours to procure work for my countrymen in factories producing no warsupplies could be supported by the Federal Government, especially the Secretary of Labour. This cooperation could save no end of misery to my countrymen and prevent trouble and unrest in the labour conditions of this country.

Lenox, Mass., *September 6, 1915.*

701.6311/147½

President Wilson to the Secretary of State

Washington, *8 September, 1915.*

My Dear Mr. Secretary: I have no doubt that the memorandum handed you by Ambassador Dumba has made the same impression on you that it has made on me. I see no alternative but to follow the course we decided on yesterday. And I think it would be well to apprise Dumba and the press of what that course is to-day, unless there seems to you to be an impropriety in mentioning it before our communication has reached the Foreign Office in Vienna.

Faithfully Yours,

W. W.

701.6311/151½

President Wilson to the Secretary of State

WASHINGTON, *15 September, 1915.*

MY DEAR MR. SECRETARY: Thank you for letting me see this letter.[10] I hope, with you, that the withdrawal of Dumba takes away the king pin from this structure of intrigue.

Faithfully Yours,

W. W.

701.6211/323½

The Secretary of State to President Wilson

WASHINGTON, *November 29, 1915.*

MY DEAR MR. PRESIDENT: I feel that we cannot wait much longer to act in the cases of Boy-Ed, von Papen, and von Nuber.[11] I believe we have enough in regard to the activities of these men to warrant us to demand of the German Government the recall of the two first named and to cancel the exequatur of von Nuber, giving notice to the Austro-Hungarian Government that we have done so.

The increasing public indignation in regard to these men and the general criticism of the Government for allowing them to remain are not the chief reasons for suggesting action in these cases, although I do not think that such reasons should be ignored. We have been over-patient with these people on account of the greater controversies under consideration for several months and did not wish to add to the difficulties of the situation by injecting another cause of difference. In my opinion action now cannot seriously affect the pending negotiations, and it would be well to act as expeditiously as possible.

In case you agree with me as to the action which should be taken would you favor informing Bernstorff orally that his attachés are *personae non gratae* or make a formal written statement to that effect without telling him in advance?

In the von Nuber case I would suggest that the Austrian Chargé be told that we intend to cancel the exequatur of von Nuber.

---

[10] From a New York lady complaining of Ambassador Dumba's conduct. Not printed.

[11] For correspondence previously printed concerning these cases, see *Foreign Relations,* 1915, supp., pp. 932–953.

As you know, I believe that we will soon have to go even higher up in removing from this country representatives of belligerents who are directing operations here. It would appear that these higher officials consider our patience to be cowardice. If this is so, the removal of subordinates would indicate our earnest purpose and would, I believe, help rather than hinder the progress of present negotiations.

I hope a decision can be reached speedily in this matter, as it should in my judgment be done, if at all, before Congress meets.

I enclose memoranda on German and Austrian officials here, among which you will find statements regarding the three mentioned.[12]

Faithfully yours,

ROBERT LANSING

701.6211/324½

President Wilson to the Secretary of State

WASHINGTON, *29 November, 1915.*

MY DEAR MR. SECRETARY: There need be no further delay in this matter. I would be obliged if you would act at once in regard to it. May I advise that you act in the following manner?

1. That you inform the Austrian Chargé that von Nuber's exequatur will be cancelled at once, and that the exequatur be then recalled after a courteous interval, perhaps, in which to await the Chargé's reply;

2. That you informally inform the German Ambassador that Boy-Ed and von Papen are *personae non gratae*, but that we wish to afford him an opportunity to have them promptly withdrawn without forcing us to make the formal demand that they be replaced, as we shall be obliged to do if they are not voluntarily recalled. I think that he will appreciate the courtesy and that it may be well to avoid a public course of action just now, though we should not hesitate to take it if there is no voluntary action.

Cordially,

W. W.

701.6211/325½

The Secretary of State to President Wilson

WASHINGTON, *December 1, 1915.*

MY DEAR MR. PRESIDENT: This morning, at ten-thirty, I saw the German Ambassador and I enclose a memorandum of the conversation which I had with him. I told him that I expected to make public announcement on Friday that we had requested the withdrawal of Boy-Ed and von Papen.

---

[12] Not printed.

This afternoon, at two-thirty, I saw the Austrian Chargé and went over the von Nuber case. I told him that this Government felt that von Nuber was unacceptable and that it was our purpose to revoke his exequatur.

Baron Zwiedinek was very much distressed and showed great feeling. We discussed the case and he was most insistent that von Nuber in his publication of warnings to Austro-Hungarian subjects in regard to work in munition factories acted under instructions from the Embassy, which it had received from the Vienna Government. He told me that he considered the action of his Government in this matter unwise and had so informed the Foreign Office; and that they had subsequently advised those who proposed to participate in strikes to avoid doing so. He plead with me to reconsider the question, and while I gave him no hope that our views would be changed I told him that I would do so. The fact is that his presentation of the case has shaken my judgment as to the wisdom of cancelling the exequatur. It is possible that we are doing an injustice and I should very much dislike being unable to furnish substantial grounds for our action, although, in my own mind, I believe von Nuber has been very active in these matters. It is merely a question of evidence.

Of course we do not need to give our reasons, but in this particular case if we give no reasons the inevitable conclusion is that we have accepted the statements of Goricar, the renegade Austrian Consul,[13] and others who have made unproven allegations against von Nuber.

In any event I think it would be well to consider the matter a few days longer. If you approve of this course will you please advise me tomorrow morning, in order that I may notify Baron Zwiedinek that the exequatur will not be revoked tomorrow, as I told him that was the intention.

I enclose several papers which he left with me [14] bearing on the question and which I would be obliged if you would return to me as soon as possible, in order that I may further study the case.

Faithfully yours,

ROBERT LANSING

P. S. I think I should add that von Nuber sent a cipher report to his Government by Archibald so that we have that substantial ground for revoking his exequatur.

R. L.

---

[13] Josef Goricar, a former Austro-Hungarian consul at San Francisco.
[14] Not enclosed with file copy of this letter.

[Enclosure]

Memorandum by the Secretary of State of an Interview With the German Ambassador (Bernstorff)

[WASHINGTON,] *December 1, 1915.*

I told the Ambassador that I had asked him to come to the Department and that I had an unpleasant duty to perform, which was to say that Captain Boy-Ed and Captain von Papen were both unacceptable to this Government, and we desired them to withdraw from the country.

The Ambassador seemed very much perturbed and asked me if I did not think his Government would desire the reasons for their recall. I said that was possibly so but that of course he appreciated it was only necessary for me to say that they were unacceptable to this Government, without giving any reasons.

However, I told him briefly that their activities in military and naval affairs were such here that they involved violations of our laws, and fraudulent practices, and that on that account they ought not be shielded under diplomatic privileges from being subject to our Courts.

He asked as to particulars and I mentioned Boy-Ed's securing of false affidavits in regard to the shipment of supplies to German war vessels from the port of New York; his being involved in a fraudulent passport case for one Stegler; and also that he had communicated with Huerta who was proposing to enter Mexico. The Ambassador seemed much surprised at the latter statement and said he knew nothing about it. I told him we had very good proofs and certainly were convinced that Captain Boy-Ed had seen Huerta several times, both at the Hotel Manhattan and Hotel Astoria.

We did not discuss the case of von Papen.

The Ambassador asked me just where he stood—was he involved in these matters. I said no, that so far as he was concerned these matters were of a military and naval character and that we had gone no further at present.

I then spoke to him about the *Lusitania* case. He said he was hopeless of securing an agreement along the line suggested by me; that he was convinced his Government would not, in view of public opinion in Germany, dare to do as we desired; that the whole question was one of liability to pay damages.

I said to him that he had informed me that he had sent the formula by mail to his Government [15] and that it seemed to me that more prompt action was required; and I therefore offered to send a cipher message for him through the Department.

---

[15] See the German Ambassador's note of Nov. 25, 1915, p. 496.

He expressed his thanks and said he would avail himself of it; and that he would notify his Government of our wishes in regard to Captains Boy-Ed and von Papen by wireless, which was working very well.

I also told him that I should make public announcement this week probably on Friday, of our request for the recall of his Military and Naval Attachés. He asked me how they could be allowed to depart, and I told him that we would do all we could to secure safe conducts for them.

701.6211/326½

President Wilson to the Secretary of State

WASHINGTON, *2 December, 1915.*

MY DEAR MR. SECRETARY: I do not think that we need accede to the representations and request of Baron Zwiedinek. Our knowledge of von Nuber's activities does not by any means rest wholly on what Goricar said, and I think we have abundant ground for the withdrawal of the exequatur. A little prompt action just at this time will be better in its effect than any amount of action later.

Why was Albert not included in the representation to the German Ambassador? [16] He has been in many ways the head and front of the offending, and it is probable that even the Ambassador is obliged to accept his decisions.

I understand that von Papen has left the country, and that he will at an early opportunity be promoted by the admiring government he serves.

Faithfully,

W. W.

701.6211/326½

The Secretary of State to President Wilson

WASHINGTON, *December 2, 1915.*

MY DEAR MR. PRESIDENT: I have your note of today in regard to the von Nuber case, and while I agree with you that we have ground for the revocation of his exequatur I cannot say that I think it is "abundant". I have had the officers of the Department of Justice give me further information on the subject and am asking them to hasten the digest of other material which they have. If they do not furnish me with further evidence tomorrow I will act in accordance with the

---

[16] Heinrich Albert, commercial attaché of the German Embassy at Washington. For correspondence previously printed concerning Albert, see *Foreign Relations*, 1915, supp., pp. 927, 936, 938–940.

plan adopted—that is, send notice of the revocation of von Nuber's exequatur. I hope though, for my own peace of mind, to have a little more convincing evidence on the subject.

In regard to Albert: My only hesitation in his case was that he has been a very valuable assistant to our people in obtaining from Germany certain articles of commerce—such as beet seed, potash, medicines, etc., which are absolutely necessary for this country, and which cannot be produced here. My own opinion is that he is a more dangerous man than either of the two whom we desire removed. At the same time, it is a question of policy whether he is not of sufficient value to our industries to allow him to remain a little longer. If you, however, think it well to act in his case at once I shall be pleased to do so.

I have not heard that von Papen had departed. It is possibly so and I have no doubt that his services will be amply rewarded—in case he reaches Germany.

Faithfully yours,

ROBERT LANSING

701.6211/328½

Colonel E. M. House to the Secretary of State

NEW YORK, *December 2, 1915.*

DEAR MR. LANSING: Bernstorff has just left. He told me of his interview with you yesterday.

I am glad you have taken this action for the country will sustain you. Bernstorff was anxious that you should not make the announcement for a few days and he was also anxious that you should make it clear that he was in no way involved mentioning him by name. He thinks if this is not done there will be a hue and cry in the press to have him also go.

Would it not be well to make the announcement on Monday and let it come out with the President's message?

I think it is due Bernstorff to help him out where possible. For the first time, he seemed nervous and excited, although as usual he was temperate in his speech and blamed no one.

Sincerely yours,

E. M. HOUSE

701.6211/328½

The Secretary of State to Colonel E. M. House

WASHINGTON, *December 3, 1915.*

MY DEAR COLONEL HOUSE: Your letter arrived too late for me to change the making public the request for the recall of Boy-Ed and von Papen. I did so this afternoon, as you will know before this letter reaches you.

I have seen Bernstorff two or three times in regard to this matter and am impressed with the fact that he was more fearful of his own skin than the skins of his Military and Naval Attachés. I attempted, in making the announcement, to put it on grounds which could not apply to the Ambassador himself, and I agree with you that he is entitled to consideration. I observed, as you have, his nervousness and the fact that he was laboring under more or less suppressed excitement. I am not surprised because he evidently realizes that matters are coming pretty near home.

I return to you the letter from Mr. Frazier.[17] From other sources I have received similar information as to the feeling in France in regard to our relations with both sides. I presume we should expect that. It bears out, I think, what I said to you about our having no friends when this war is over unless we gradually favor one side or the other. I thank you for letting me see the letter.

Very sincerely yours,

ROBERT LANSING

701.6211/327½

The Secretary of State to President Wilson

WASHINGTON, *December 3, 1915.*

MY DEAR MR. PRESIDENT: I have again been over the material which we have about Herr Albert and I do not believe that we have sufficient grounds to ask for his recall. I am convinced that his are the directing brains of German activities and propaganda in this country and that he is the one who controls the large sums of money being expended here. He has, however, protected himself well. We are continuing our investigations and may find substantial proof of improper conduct, but we have not got it now.

The enclosed memorandum [18] covers all the evidence which we have on Albert and I believe that when you read it you will agree that at present there is insufficient grounds for requesting his recall.

Faithfully yours,

ROBERT LANSING

---

[17] Not enclosed with file copy of this letter.
[18] Not printed.

701.6211/327½

President Wilson to the Secretary of State

WASHINGTON, *5 December, 1915.*

MY DEAR MR. SECRETARY: I read this letter [19] after writing my annotation on the evidence you sent me with regard to Albert.

There is a great deal of weight in what you say about the assistance Albert has been able, and willing, to render our trade in many particulars; but my feeling is so strong that his is the directing and the most dangerous mind in all these unhappy intrigues which are now so deeply exciting the resentment of this country that I should like to find sufficient ground to ask his recall.

In view of what Gerard says in his despatch of yesterday,[20] it is plainly wise to move with circumspection in this case and not add it too brashly to the others; but Albert is, I am convinced, the king pin.

Faithfully Yours,

W. W.

701.6211/329½

President Wilson to the Secretary of State

WASHINGTON, *5 December, 1915.*

MY DEAR MR. SECRETARY: No doubt you are right that there is not sufficient evidence of acts here to base a demand for Albert's recall upon; but do you not think that there is evidence enough of his exercise of authority and of his control of the evidently large sums of money which are being spent in the country for purposes of nonneutral activity and outrages against our peace? Since he is attached to the Germany Embassy we do not need evidence enough to convict to justify us in saying that he is *persona non grata.*

Faithfully Yours,

W. W.

701.6211/330½

Memorandum From the Office of the Assistant Secretary of War[21]

[WASHINGTON,] *December 6, 1915.*

About 11:15 today, Captain Franz von Papen, military attache of the German Embassy, telephoned my office asking if he might see me. I asked the Secretary as to the propriety of my seeing him

---

[19] Secretary Lansing's letter of Dec. 2, p. 87.

[20] Telegram from the Ambassador in Germany not printed; it stated that the German Foreign Office wished proof of irregularities on the part of von Papen and Boy-Ed. (File No. 701.6211/321.)

[21] The file copy of this memorandum is unsigned. The Assistant Secretary of War at the time was Henry Breckinridge.

and he suggested that I speak to the Secretary of State about it. I then went to Mr. Polk, Counselor of the State Department, who thought it was all right to see him. I had my office telephone Captain von Papen I should be pleased to see him and he came to the Department at 12 o'clock.

He stated to me that he regretted of course leaving this country under such circumstances, but as a soldier was personally glad that he was able to return to his country at such a time.

He stated that the reason he came to me was that he felt I had a feeling of sincere personal friendship for himself as he had for me and that under the circumstances there was no one else to whom he could turn.

He said that the papers of yesterday carried a news story, stating that agents of the United States Government had reported to that Government that he, von Papen and Boy-Ed, had expended $12,000,-000 to foment conditions which would bring about a war between the United States and Mexico. He said this was an utter falsehood, and that he would tell me in confidence the German Ambassador had written a letter to the American Secretary of State [22] setting forth this press report and asking that the Secretary of State make a public statement to the effect that the story was false; that he, von Papen and Boy-Ed had gone to the German Ambassador and given their words of honor as officers that it was utterly false, that neither of them had directly or indirectly approached any Mexican government, faction, individual or set of individuals for any such purpose; that if the American Government were really desirous of maintaining amicable relations with the German government, the American Government would make public denial of these charges, because if they were left without an official denial, they would tend to stir up the public mind to even a more radical bitterness against the German government and the German people, and he requested that I bring these matters to the attention of the proper authorities, urging that this public denial be made so that he, von Papen, would not have to rest under such an outrageous allegation which was not true, particularly in light of the present situation, which in itself is sufficiently unfortunate.

The above was stated to be the main purpose of his visit. The conversation turned to other matters. He was under a great stress of emotion and at times he found it difficult to control himself.

He stated that ever since his detail here he had worked unceasingly for better relations between his government and the American Government; that he had brought to the attention of his superiors the absolute necessity of the improvement of these relations; that he personally

---

[22] Not printed.

and his military superiors had disapproved the submarine policy of the admiralty and that only through the influence of his chief, von Falkenhayn and the Army General Staff had the Imperial German Government finally overruled the submarine policy of the Admiralty with great difficulty; that this submarine policy was considered by him to be the only real cause of difficulty between the two governments and that after the assurance given in the *Arabic* case by the German Government, he and his colleagues thought the matter was settled, especially in view of the fact that actions which speak louder than words had shown that the government had absolutely departed from the obnoxious policy and had committed no further objectionable acts. That he had felt assured, after the *Arabic* incident, that the American Government would accept the actions of his government without the exaction for further humiliating declarations, especially in view of the fact that great personal regret had been expressed more than once for the American lives lost and offer of reparation therefor made. But that this didn't seem to be the case. Rather the impression was being borne in upon the minds of many Germans that the United States actually wished to make a breach with the German government and was pursuing a fundamental policy of this kind and that this was what rendered the situation particularly distressing to him. That it was not so much individual acts of the American Government but the frame of mind that various acts suggested. That the American Government exacted of Germany the last farthing in compliance with law and propriety but permitted great latitude to the allies. That the American Government did not insist upon Great Britain permitting commerce in non-contraband with neutrals; that Germans and others in this country could not send by parcel post 65,000 cans of condensed milk to be given to the babies of Berlin and Germany. That the immense financial, industrial and sentimental assets of America were mobilized in favor of the allies and that for many purposes, particularly after the last loan to the allies, America had departed from a real neutrality. That milk tickets were now given to mothers in Berlin and other German cities, permitting so many ounces of milk to be given to a baby one year old, so many to a baby two years old, and three years old, and that the American Government would not insist upon the right of America to send this milk to these babies and submitted to a suggestion, for instance, that all commerce be with the Dutch over-sea trust, which, in reality, is an English corporation.

That Germany wanted an honorable peace. That of course he could not speak for his Government but that he thought they would be willing to withdraw from Belgium and France—he didn't know about Poland. That if the allies wanted a war of attrition to the end, his country would fight to the end. That if America wished peace in the world she could secure it.

That he had worked sincerely and assiduously for a better understanding between the American and German governments and that he expected the German Emperor, upon his return, would refer to his activities in this line and say to him "My dear Captain, but what is the use and result of all this work?"

That it had been a dream of his Imperial Master throughout the last twenty years that Germany, England and America should unite to hold the balance of influence in the world, with peace and goodwill among themselves but with a united front to the rest of the world. That every day of the war slaughtered thousands of the white race and made more imminent and real the yellow peril, especially as the yellow man now had learned from the white man the modern art of war.

Finally, that even though he was being sent away as he was, he should continue to urge upon his government better relations with the Government of the United States and continue in peace and friendship with it and that he hoped it was true that really the American Government desired peace with Germany.

701.6211/333

Memorandum by the Secretary of State of a Conversation With the German Ambassador (Bernstorff), December 10, 1915, 4:30 p. m.

The German Ambassador called on me this afternoon and handed me the attached note.[23] He stated that he did so in person because he had received my letter of today [24] in which I expressed the idea that I thought there had been undue delay in compliance with our request for the recall of Captains Boy-Ed and von Papen, and he desired to tell me that he was not responsible for such delay.

I replied to him that I did not consider that he was responsible, but I thought there was responsibility at Berlin.

ROBERT LANSING

763.72111/3288½

Memorandum by the Secretary of State of an Interview With the Austro-Hungarian Chargé (Zwiedinek)

[WASHINGTON,] *December 11, 1915.*

Baron Zwiedinek came this morning to see me about certain circulars which are being sent by a person calling himself Count von Ferri, copies of which are attached.[25] He wished to assure me that

---

[23] *Foreign Relations,* 1915, supp., p. 951.
[24] *Ibid.*
[25] Not printed.

the Austrian Embassy and officials had nothing to do with this propaganda and did not countenance it in any way, and said he believed there was a family of Ferri in Austria but he did not know this man.

The Chargé asked me if I had seen the letter which had been published in one of the morning papers which purported to be from the Embassy and dated August 24, 1914. I told him that I had seen it in the *New York Times* (a clipping from the *Times* is annexed) ; [26] he said that he did not wish to deny the letter, but he had no recollection of ever having written it and presumed he signed it in the regular course and that it was written by someone else; that there was no intention to obtain American passports for Austrian reservists and that the obtaining of passports of other neutral countries did not seem to be an invasion of the sovereignty of the United States. I made no comment but thanked him for his frankness. I asked him if Consul-General von Nuber had obtained false passports and he said that he did not know, but he presumed the reservists were given money to defray their expenses in attempting to reach Austria and that the responsibility rested with them if they did obtain passports of other countries.

He asked me as to the situation in the *Ancona* case and I gave him a copy of the instruction to Ambassador Penfield, dated December 6th,[27] telling him that it would be made public next Monday. I said to him that the admission of the Admiralty at Vienna that the sinking of the *Ancona* had been by an Austrian submarine had created very considerable astonishment in this country as the conduct of other submarine commanders of the Austrian Navy had been of a nature to expect humane conduct on the part of its officers; that I could not view the sinking of the *Ancona* as anything but a wanton and murderous attack and that I felt the only way that Austria could regain the good opinion of the American people was by complying fully with the demands of this Government. He told me that he would communicate at once with his Government and see if something could not be done to meet our wishes.

ROBERT LANSING

The Chargé was in a highly nervous state and evidently laboring under great emotion.

R. L.

---

[26] Not printed.
[27] *Foreign Relations*, 1915, supp., p. 623.

701.6211/369½

Memorandum by the Secretary of State of a Conversation With the German Ambassador (Bernstorff), April 19, 1916, 11:30 a. m.

L   Good morning, Mr. Ambassador.

B   Good morning. I came to see you about a very unpleasant affair. By order of the District Attorney of New York the officers went to the office of our Military Attaché and arrested von Igel by force and by force took away and kept papers.[28] I wish to ask if you will request the return of the papers and the release of von Igel.

L   That we have already done. I sent a dispatch yesterday to the Attorney General that official papers should be returned immediately. The official status of von Igel is a question which I am having studied now in the Department—that is, whether immunity under his diplomatic character follows him for a charge committed before he became an attaché of your Embassy.

B   That is different. I realized that and that is why I did not speak of it yesterday; that I perfectly understand and am not questioning that at all. The thing is that these papers should be returned because they were taken by force and that therefore there could be no doubt but they were in the hands of an attaché and should be returned.

L   The only question as to that would be whether they are official papers or private papers.

B   They certainly are official papers.

L   The police broke no seals. As I understand it it is a question, as I have been informed, (from the fact that they evidently looked to see what the papers were,) whether they were official papers or not. Because if they are official, it might be very embarrassing to you on account of the serious character of the communications.

B   Well—I don't know exactly about that.

L   They have evidently, as local police authorities would do, read the papers. The statements are very serious they say. Now the question is whether you claim that they are official papers or not on account of the statements that appeared in them.

B   Well that would of course simply come to the question whether a Military Attaché—how far a Military Attaché could go, because the office of Military Attaché is for certain purposes and not under the Embassy—but I can not see how they could be anything else but official papers.

---

[28] For correspondence previously printed concerning the arrest of von Igel and the seizure of his papers, see *ibid.*, 1916, supp., pp. 807 ff.

L   I see. Of course they may be official, but I have hesitated to hold them as such because they are of a rather peculiar character. I mean by that there are serious statements of criminal intent. Would it not attach to the Embassy?   That is what I am trying to avoid.

B   I see the point entirely.   What would you advise?

L   I think that is a matter you will have to decide for yourself. Possibly, if the authorities submitted the papers to you, you would know whether they are official.

B   That would be embarrassing I am afraid. I think that they should be at once returned—all of them.

L   We ordered that the official papers be returned immediately, and now I understand the authorities are raising the question whether they are official papers, because of the serious nature of the statements made they did not like to assume that they were official.

B   Well—of course if it is absolutely a case of criminal action——

L   And if these are official papers I think it imposes a very considerable burden of responsibility on the Embassy. That is what I am calling to your attention.

B   Yes, but to my mind Military Attachés are not the same as members of the Embassy.

L   I do not think they should have diplomatic immunity unless the Embassy is willing to take the responsibility for their correspondence.

B   Yes—but as long as Military attachés are attached to the Embassy they are members of the Embassy and papers must be regarded as official.

L   If papers are official we must regard the Government as responsible. The papers contain a statement of the most serious nature and I thought it might involve the Embassy if they were considered official documents.

B   It might involve the Government but not the Embassy.

L   Possibly it would.

B   I know perfectly well there is no document from us there, that is out of the question, but of course there are papers which——

L   Would you include as a member of the Embassy a Commercial Attaché?

B   As to that, taking papers from him would be taking official papers.

L   It is a very difficult position and I am trying to point out the difficulties that we are placed in and the possible difficulties that you will be placed in.

B   Yes, well—I would always think that the papers were immune if the Government so stated.

L   We have asked them to return all the papers.

B   They say they will hold the papers.   I think they ought not to do it if they are official.

L   I simply put that up to you so that you could deny they were official papers, if you thought best.

B   I do not deny for one moment they are official but I only say that if they have been acting wrongly, then they are responsible.   I do not think the Embassy is involved because whatever they have done has not been under orders of the Embassy.   If they had acted under instructions of my Government then the Government is responsible.

L   Well I trust that this will be entirely satisfactory.

B   You sent word for the release?

L   Yes.   I have here the telegram that I spoke to you about that I sent to the Attorney General.[29]   He telegraphed me last night late that he had immediately communicated to the United States Attorney in New York so that I assume they will act on that.

B   I think that is all right.

L   There is one other thing.   Here is a note that went forward to Berlin.[30]   I suppose it will be received there sometime today.   I thought you might wish a copy.

B   Anything I can do in the matter——

L   I think after looking it over you will see there is probably only one thing to do.   This is the note and there is an enclosure containing a full statement of the facts in the case of the *Sussex*.

B   This all went in the telegram?

L   Yes, the whole thing.

B   I do not suppose there is anything in which I can help * * *[31]

L   Nothing today.   Goodbye.

701.6211/370½

The Secretary of State to President Wilson

WASHINGTON, *April 22, 1916.*

MY DEAR MR. PRESIDENT: I send you a letter which I have just received from the Attorney General [29] in regard to the seized papers in the Von Igel case and would like to have your views at the earliest possible moment in regard to the disposition which should be made of them.

I do not believe that these papers can be claimed as archives of the Embassy as they were unsealed and were taken from a room which was rented by an individual as an advertising agency.   Von

-----

[29] Not printed.
[30] *Foreign Relations*, 1916, supp., p. 232.
[31] Asterisks appear in the original.

Igel, as I understand it, rented this room before he was notified to us as an Attaché of the Embassy.

I believe that there are two things that a Government should respect in regard to the papers of a foreign government in its territory: First, papers that are on the premises of the Embassy; and, second, papers that are under seal of the Government. I think that the immunity of even official documents attaches solely from the immunity which applies to the premises of the Embassy or the official seal.

If this is a correct interpretation of the rule I do not see that the Von Igel papers are covered by it. My impression is that the Department of Justice can retain them all.

I would also call your attention to that portion of the Attorney General's letter which points out that these papers in no way pertain to the legitimate purposes of an Embassy—that is, to its relations with the Government to which the Ambassador is accredited, with a few exceptions.

Faithfully yours,

ROBERT LANSING

701.6211/372½

President Wilson to the Secretary of State

WASHINGTON, *23 April, 1916.*

MY DEAR MR. AMBASSADOR [*Secretary*]: This is certainly an unfortunate time for these questions to have arisen. It is, of course, merely fortuitous that this arrest and seizure of papers should have come at about the same time as our last communication to the German Foreign Office,[33] but it can be made to appear, by those whose interest and plan it is to disregard the truth, that we have already begun to cooperate with the Allies in breaking up conspiracies against them, as if we intended something more than a mere execution of our own laws and a mere protection of the United States against violations of her neutrality. But, however unfortunate the coincidence, we must insist upon our rights and exercise them.

I think you took the right course in calling upon the German Ambassador to examine the seized papers and declare which of them he claims as official. Probably it would be well to let him retain those which he thus designates. The rest should be retained.

It seems to me clear that no immunity can be claimed for von Igel for acts committed prior to his designation to the Department as an attaché of the Embassy.

---

[33] *Foreign Relations*, 1916, supp., p. 232.

A full statement of the circumstances of this case to the German Foreign Office ought surely to be conclusive of our rights in the premises; and I think that it would probably be wise to send such a statement to Gerard so that they may not get all their information and impressions from Bernstorff.

Faithfully Yours,

W. W.

701.6211/372½a

The Secretary of State to President Wilson

WASHINGTON, *April 25, 1916.*

MY DEAR MR. PRESIDENT: I have information from an absolutely reliable source that the German Ambassador is not particularly worried over the Von Igel case. The submarine question is absorbing all his attention, and the fact that he is not pressing the Von Igel matter is indicated by the fact that he did not return Monday to Washington as he had planned to do and I have heard nothing for two days about the papers in that case.

Faithfully yours,

ROBERT LANSING

702.6211/265c

The Secretary of State to President Wilson

WASHINGTON, *January 22, 1917.*

MY DEAR MR. PRESIDENT: I am sending you herewith for your signature, the formal revocation and annulment of the exequatur issued to Mr. Franz Bopp as Consul General of Germany at San Francisco.[34]

With assurances [etc.]   ROBERT LANSING

702.6211/267½

President Wilson to the Secretary of State

WASHINGTON, *24 January, 1917.*

MY DEAR MR. SECRETARY: I hope I may say without impropriety that I have signed the enclosed with real pleasure.[35]

Faithfully Yours,

W. W.

---

[34] For correspondence previously printed concerning this case, see *ibid.*, 1917, supp. 1, pp. 597 ff.
[35] See *supra.*

TRANSFER OF FOREIGN VESSELS TO AMERICAN REGISTRY

195.1/14½

Mr. J. P. Morgan to President Wilson

NEW YORK, *August 21, 1914.*

MY DEAR MR. PRESIDENT: Referring to the question of the purchase of ships from the German flag by the United States Government or by American citizens, I feel I should inform you that, on August 18th, I received from my London firm, which is at the moment in very close touch with the British Government, a cablegram from which I quote as follows:

"Our Government have privately intimated to us that such a transaction by a neutral in buying ships from a belligerent would contravene international law since the ships would be sold only to avoid capture. Therefore our Government would not hesitate to capture such ships even if sailing under American flag. This you will agree would create bad feeling between Great Britain and the United States during the war and certain to lead to American claims after the war."

I replied to the cablegram, asking if the British Government was taking the stand that it will recognize the transfer only to the British flag of ships belonging to other belligerents, and whether they would not be satisfied with bonafide transfer to a company wholly under neutral control. To this I received late last night a reply saying:

"In my opinion British Government would certainly decline admit that the transfer of German ships to neutral flag in existing circumstances would be consistent with international rules. Article 56 Declaration London makes this clear.[1] You understand British Government quite satisfied if they know steamers were to be New York until end of war and if your authorities arrange this it would be entire-satisfactory."

The balance of the cablegram consists of suggestions in regard to purchases.

I send you this information for what it is worth, appreciating very fully that your information is certainly more complete than mine, but should I be able to be of service to you in this or any other matter I trust you will let me know.

I am [etc.]   J. P. MORGAN

---

[1] For text of the Declaration of London, see *Foreign Relations*, 1909, p. 318.

195.1/15½

President Wilson to the Counselor for the Department of State (Lansing)

WASHINGTON, *August 22, 1914.*

MY DEAR MR. LANSING: Surely if Mr. Morgan's information is correct as stated in the enclosed letter,[1a] the British Government is in danger of taking a very unjustifiable and high-handed action. I would very much like your carefully considered opinion on the subject.

Cordially yours,

WOODROW WILSON

195.1/15½b

The Counselor for the Department of State (Lansing) to President Wilson

WASHINGTON, *August 24, 1914.*

DEAR MR. PRESIDENT: You ask me for an opinion upon the subject of the transfer of title of German merchant ships, now in American waters, to the United States or its citizens, in connection with certain information contained in a letter to you from Mr. J. P. Morgan under date of August 21, 1914, which letter I herewith return.[2]

I annex copies of two telegrams received by the Department from the American Ambassador at London, dated respectively August 18th and 21st,[3] and also the paraphrase of a telegram received by the British Chargé here from Sir Edward Grey, which the former handed to me on the afternoon of August 22nd.[4]

From these communications it is manifest that there has been a very decided change of policy on the part of the British Government between the 18th and 21st. From a general attitude of opposition on legal and technical grounds to our purchase of the German ships, they now do not oppose the purchase but seek only that this Government shall guarantee that the vessels purchased shall not trade to German ports or neutral ports easily accessible to German territory.

The only condition, which Great Britain now seeks to impose on the purchase of the ships, seems to be a general requirement that their habits shall be changed, assuming of course that the transfer of title is absolute and intended to be perpetual.

[1a] *Supra.*
[2] *Ante,* p. 100.
[3] *Foreign Relations,* 1914, supp., pp. 481, 489.
[4] Not printed.

The question of the legality of sale is a question of *bona fides*, and the accepted rule appears to impose the burden of proof on the parties to the sale, particularly the vendee, to establish such *bona fides*. I think that the condition, which the British Government now urge, is a reasonable one. The presumption that a sale is made to avoid the consequences of belligerent ownership is regarded as very strong if the vessel continues to follow the same trade route which it had pursued prior to the outbreak of hostilities, and as almost conclusive if the route lay between the neutral country and the ports of the belligerent, whose subjects are selling the vessel.

In one way the British condition does not go as far as the general rule, in that it does not appear to apply to trade routes other than with Germany or nearby neutral ports. On the other hand it goes beyond the rule in requiring no trade with ports of Germany or those near German territory regardless of the previous trade routes of the vessels sold.

It seems to me that the foregoing modification of the general rule in a way changes its application from the presumption created against the *bona fides* of the sale, and introduces a new element as to the violation of neutrality by the purchaser.

To illustrate, the change after sale of the trade route of a German vessel, which prior to hostilities had been running between American and German ports would remove the presumption that the sale had not been *bona fides*. On the other hand, a similar change of route by a purchased vessel formerly trading to a South American port would not be required to avoid the presumption, but the condition would be that the route could not be changed to Germany. The first case deals with the presumption of *bona fides;* the latter, with neutrality.

Nevertheless, from this point of view, I do not think the requirement unjustified or one to which this Government should seriously object, in view of the British Government's express willingness to waive all other technical grounds of objection to the sale, which I assume includes the production of evidence to establish *bona fides* in addition to the transfer papers.

In my opinion, therefore, there should be no difficulty in removing any objection by Great Britain to the purchase of German merchant vessels now in neutral harbors. As to the attitude of other belligerents we are not yet advised.

I do not think it necessary to say that in no event should we accede formally to such a condition as one which could properly be imposed. To do so might invite protest from the German Government on the ground that we were not preserving a strict neutrality. But having received notice from Great Britain of its view as to vessels so trading the American owners would naturally avoid the risk by using the vessels in other commerce.

In case you desire a more elaborate consideration of the general subject of the purchase of belligerent merchant ships by neutrals I shall be glad to furnish it.

I am [etc.]
ROBERT LANSING

195.1/16½

President Wilson to the Counselor for the Department of State
(Lansing)

WASHINGTON, *August 25, 1914.*

MY DEAR MR. LANSING: Thank you sincerely for your letter of August twenty-fourth about the purchase of German ships. I think that the situation is clearing up in a very satisfactory way.

Cordially and sincerely yours,

WOODROW WILSON

195.1/148½

The Assistant Secretary of the Treasury (Peters) to the Acting Secretary of State

WASHINGTON, *October 14, 1914.*

MY DEAR MR. LANSING: Our recent conversation on the international aspect of granting foreign-built vessels American registry, was most interesting, and I appreciate your giving me your views. You expressed so much interest that I am writing to present to you the situation which confronts the Bureau of War Risk Insurance.

This Bureau, which is under my supervision, is receiving inquiries almost daily in regard to insurance on vessels which formerly flew a foreign flag and have been granted American registry under the recent act of Congress. The vessels which have taken out United States Registry are of two classes:

(1) Vessels which were owned by Americans at the breaking out of hostilities. To the right of these vessels to receive the protection of this Government and its flag I understand there is no objection, and insurance has already been placed on such vessels to a considerable sum.

(2) Vessels which were owned before the war by citizens of belligerent countries, and which have been purchased by citizens of the United States only since the commencement of hostilities. The right of such vessels to American registry, I understand, has been questioned. No insurance on such vessels has been written as yet, or as yet has been refused. Inquiries, however, relative to such insurance have been made to the Bureau of War Risk Insurance. The owners intimate that if they are unable to get such insurance from the

Bureau, they will be unable to use their vessel and their investment will have gone for naught.

The attention of the Bureau is called to the fact that its purpose is to assist American shippers and that its creation indicates a policy of accepting such a risk as the one referred to.

A direct answer in any one of the cases so far presented has not been demanded of us as yet. Such a demand seems imminent, and when the insurance is applied for an immediate answer will undoubtedly be required.

Unless a definite policy has previously been determined on the Bureau will be placed in a position of considerable embarrassment. Should these vessels not be treated by this Government as other vessels flying the American flag are treated, the usefulness of granting American registry to foreign-built ships may be much curtailed. On the other hand the acceptance of such insurance means that this Government must be prepared to insist on its protection of these vessels, and, should these vessels be seized by a belligerent, might be called upon to pay the loss or damages for detention. It does not seem to me that the Bureau, by its decision, ought to determine the policy of the Government on a question with possibilities so far reaching.

I hope I can get you for lunch.

Sincerely yours,

A. J. PETERS

195.1/148½

The Acting Secretary of State to President Wilson

WASHINGTON, *October 19, 1914.*

DEAR MR. PRESIDENT: Assistant Secretary Peters' personal letter to me of the 14th, a copy of which is enclosed,[5] was the result of a conversation which I had with him a few days ago and in which I expressed the opinion that the transfer of ownership of merchant vessels like the transfer of flag, when bona fide, is legal.

When it came to writing a letter to Mr. Peters, which would doubtless be the basis for the issuance of policies by the Bureau of War Risk Insurance to vessels purchased from nationals of belligerent powers, I hesitated to do so until you had given me authority, since the issuance of a policy covering a vessel of this class will amount to a declaration of the position of this Government as to such transfers, and in case of its subsequent seizure by a French or British warship

[5] *Supra.*

it will be necessary to enter a vigorous protest which will precipitate a diplomatic controversy.

It seems to me that we cannot much longer postpone taking a decided stand on this question of transfer of ownership. We must either support American purchasers of vessels of belligerent nationality or else discourage such purchases. Our citizens ought to know whether they may expect the support of this Government.

You know my views upon the subject, in which I am supported by the Solicitor of the Department and by Professor Wambaugh, who for a time assisted my office as an expert, but in order that you may understand that there is difference of opinion by those who have studied the question I enclose two memoranda of the Joint State and Navy Neutrality Board [6] which is at least in a measure adverse to the legality of such transfers.

I also enclose the opinions of the Solicitor and of Professor Wambaugh.[6]

Your attention should also be called to the fact that the French Government has consistently opposed the validity of such transfers and their naval vessels will undoubtedly act accordingly. The British Government at first took the same view, but later changed their attitude as stated in my letter to you of August 24th. From subsequent conversations with the British Ambassador it appears that his Government have since been impressed with the French argument that the purchase of German vessels would release large amounts of capital, which would otherwise be useless to the German owners. Just what position the British Government will take, therefore, is to an extent uncertain.

Since writing the foregoing I have received a memorandum from the British Ambassador which indicates very clearly what attitude his Government intends to take in the matter of the purchase of vessels of belligerent nationality by citizens of the United States. A copy of the memorandum is herewith enclosed.[7]

In view of the importance of a decision of this question to the Bureau of War Risk Insurance it would seem well to reply to Mr. Peters' letter as soon as possible.

Very sincerely yours,

ROBERT LANSING

---

[6] Not printed.
[7] *Foreign Relations*, 1914, supp., p. 499.

341.115 St 2/37a

The Acting Secretary of State to President Wilson

WASHINGTON, *October 20, 1914.*

DEAR MR. PRESIDENT: The capture by a British cruiser of the Standard Oil tank steamer *Brindilla*,[9] which has arrived at Halifax under a prize crew, brings up for immediate decision one phase of the question, concerning which I addressed you yesterday in submitting a letter from Mr. Peters, Assistant Secretary of the Treasury.

The vessel at the outbreak of hostilities was the *George Washington*, a steamer of German register owned by a German corporation, a subsidiary company of the Standard Oil Company. She was transferred to the Standard Oil Company, the purchase money being paid, was renamed the *Brindilla* and obtained an American register. On a full statement of the facts of the transfer the Bureau of War Risk Insurance issued a policy on the hull of the vessel for a voyage to Alexandria, Egypt, with the privilege of coaling at Sicily or the Azores. The cargo of the vessel consists of illuminating oil.

This case is, therefore, a transfer of flag rather than a transfer of ownership, but, if the British Government intend to deny the right of transfer of flag during hostilities, as this seizure would indicate, it is evident that transfer of ownership will be treated as invalid and vessels purchased from enemies of Great Britain will be seized as prize.

It seems to me that the only course is to make an immediate and vigorous protest against the action of the British authorities in seizing an American vessel bound to a neutral port.

Very sincerely yours,

ROBERT LANSING

341.115 St 2/37½

President Wilson to the Acting Secretary of State

WASHINGTON, *October 22, 1914.*

MY DEAR MR. LANSING: I quite agree with you that the only course to take in the matter of the tank steamer *Brindilla* and in other similar cases is to make an immediate and vigorous protest against the action of the British authorities in seizing an American vessel bound to a neutral port.

In haste

Cordially and faithfully yours,

WOODROW WILSON

---

[9] For correspondence previously printed regarding the *Brindilla*, see *Foreign Relations*, 1914, supp., pp. 325–326.

195.1/149½

President Wilson to the Acting Secretary of State

WASHINGTON, *November 23, 1914.*

MY DEAR MR. LANSING: I am preparing my annual message to Congress. One of the bills I want to urge upon the attention of the Houses is the shipping bill, which would involve, as you know, in all likelihood, the purchase of a number of ships that have been owned hitherto by subjects of one or other of the belligerents. You will remember that a little while ago the attitude of the English Government in this matter of the transfer of flag during hostilities seemed to be very different from the attitude of the French Government. I would like very much before writing my message to know just what you think the attitude of those two governments would be towards the purchase by a corporation in which the United States Government was interested of such ships as those now belonging to the North German Lloyd and the Hamburg-American Companies, and which are interned in our waters.

I know that you have had conversations with M. Jusserand and Sir Cecil Spring-Rice that would throw some light upon this question, and I would like to know your full impressions before going further with my message.

Cordially and sincerely yours,

WOODROW WILSON

195.1/149½

The Acting Secretary of State to President Wilson

WASHINGTON, *November 23, 1914.*

MY DEAR MR. PRESIDENT: I fear that I cannot give a very satisfactory answer to your letter of to-day as to the probable attitude of the French and British Governments in the matter of the transfer of ships of belligerent nationality during hostilities, and particularly of transfers to a corporation in which the United States Government is interested.

In the first place I think that a distinction should be made between the transfer of flag and the transfer of ownership. In the case of the transfer of flag there have been numerous cases of ships of foreign register owned by Americans or by companies subsidiary to American companies which have been transferred to American register without opposition by either the British Government or the French Government. A vessel of this sort was the tank steamer *Brindilla.* It was seized and taken to Halifax, but was later released, the British Government stating that it did so without passing upon the legality of the transfer. In spite of this reservation I think that the British Government will recognize such transfers, and in view of the silence of the French Government it is fair to assume that no objection will be made by them.

The transfer of ownership as well as of flag, which is the type of transfer to which your letter refers, is a different matter.

I have not discussed the subject for some time with Mr. Jusserand, but the last time we did so he was most emphatic in his opposition. There is no question but that the French Government in their official utterances have denied the validity of the sale of a merchant vessel by a belligerent to a neutral on the ground that it is always done for the purpose of avoiding the consequences of belligerency. While this has been their consistent attitude for the past one hundred and forty years I am, nevertheless, unable to find a single case in which a French prize court has condemned a vessel so transferred on account of the illegality of the transfer.

While M. Jusserand referred to the French practice in regard to such transfers, he spoke more feelingly upon a consequence of such sales rather than upon the legal right. He asserted that for Americans to purchase German steamships interned in our ports would release a large amount of German capital and relieve the companies of the constant expense of caring for the vessels and of maintaining their crews. The moneys thus made available, he asserted, would be employed to carry on the war against France, so that it would amount to giving aid to the enemy.

Applying this idea to purchases by this Government the Ambassador said that, if the purchases were made, the action would menace the unbroken friendship of France for this country, for whose liberty Frenchmen had shed their blood and contributed their wealth, etc., etc.

Stripped of its sentimentality the argument came to this, that the purchase of interned German ships by this Government would be of material aid to Germany and that to give such aid would be an unneutral and unfriendly act, which the French Government would resent; and that, being contrary to the French theory of legality of transfer, the purchases would be considered invalid and the vessels liable to condemnation as prize.

I should also call your attention to the fact that at the time the shipping bills were being publicly discussed Ambassador Herrick reported that the French Government were bitterly hostile to the idea, raising objections similar to those urged by M. Jusserand.

The British Ambassador in the conversations, which I have had with him on this subject, has been far less definite than his colleague in expression of his views. I think that this is due to the fact that he is unwilling to differ with the French attitude and yet he cannot agree with it as it would be entirely contrary to the position which the British Government has invariably taken in regard to transfers of belligerent-owned vessels.

He has spoken of the release of German capital, which would result, but I was not impressed with the sincerity with which he advanced it as an argument. Recently, in discussing the withdrawal of the suggestion of this Government as to the Declaration of London and the assertion that our rights and duties would be determined by the existing rules of international law, I made the comment that at least the ambiguity of the article of the Declaration relative to the transfer of belligerent merchant ships would no longer vex us, as the right to make such transfers was well established so far as the practice of the United States and Great Britain was concerned. He admitted that this was probably so, but added that it seemed to him to be unneutral to give assistance to a belligerent, thus falling back on the French argument.

To sum up my impressions from the conversations I have had with the two Ambassadors:

I believe that the French Government will vigorously oppose the purchase of German vessels by this Government on the ground that the purchase is invalid, and also on the ground that this Government by making the purchase would violate its neutrality and would act in an unfriendly manner toward France.

I believe that the British Government, while giving a measure of support to their ally on the second ground mentioned, would not, in view of the long established British doctrine as to the right to make such purchases, seriously oppose the validity of the transfers, though I have no doubt their validity would be subjected to prize-court proceedings.

I regret that I cannot give you a more definite impression as to the probable position of the British Government, but the announced position of the French Government, so adverse to the British doctrine, prevents, I think, a free expression of opinion by Sir Cecil.

Very sincerely yours,

ROBERT LANSING

195.2/300a

The Secretary of State to President Wilson

WASHINGTON, *January 22, 1915.*

MY DEAR MR. PRESIDENT: We have received and read the note as you have prepared it.[10] Will have it put into the private cipher. I think the changes which you made are important. You used more of what I suggested than I had expected you to use. It was written hurriedly and only in the form of suggestions for consideration.

Mr. Lansing and I have been conferring in regard to the general situation, and we are inclined to think that it would go a long way toward relieving the fear that is expressed in Great Britain if an announcement was made by the authorities that the Government had no thought of purchasing German ships under the authority which the shipping bill is intended to confer. I believe that a large part of the alarm in Great Britain arises over the fear that if the *Dacia* sale is allowed to stand the Government would expect to use it as a precedent and proceed to buy the German ships. That was Jusserand's fear and you remember how agitated he was at the time. While I think that private individuals have a right to purchase these ships if the purchase is bona fide, I do not think that our Government could afford to raise an international question by purchases made by a corporation in which the Government had a controlling interest—or even a large interest.

If you said—or authorized me to say:—"To avoid misunderstanding and misrepresentation of the Government's purpose, the press is informed that in case the shipping bill is passed the corporation authorized by that bill being partly owned by the Government will not, in the purchase of ships, acquire any vessel whose purchase would raise any international question or issue."—I believe it would do much to calm the fears across the ocean and it would also remove one of the objections which is made against the shipping bill by its opponents in Congress.

As we could not afford and, therefore, have no intention of raising an issue by purchasing German ships, would it not be worth while to remove the fears that are based upon the possibility of such a purchase? A failure to answer these objections and put them to rest stimulates speculation and causes excitement. If such a statement could be made before the new note reaches London it would smooth the way for the strong statement which I am preparing to send and which I presume you want me to say is sent at your direction.

With assurances [etc.]   W. J. BRYAN

---

[10] For text of the note in question, see telegram No. 1019, Jan. 23, 1915, to the Ambassador in Great Britain, *Foreign Relations*, 1915, supp., p. 684; for correspondence previously printed regarding sale of the *Dacia* and similar matters, see *ibid.*, pp. 674 ff.

195.2/300b

The Secretary of State to President Wilson

WASHINGTON, *January 23, 1915.*

MY DEAR MR. PRESIDENT: I am enclosing a personal statement from the British Ambassador which I think you will find interesting.[11] I was talking with him the other day and he asked me if I would like to know what the British papers were saying and I told him I would—and this letter is intended to furnish the information.

You will notice the stress that they lay upon the purchase of German ships. The fact that the bill authorizes the purchase of ships, without excepting the interned German ships, is the basis for their fears.

You will notice from a clipping which I also enclose,[12] that Lodge [12a] is basing his opposition to the shipping bill—or at least making it one of his objections—upon the possibility of the purchase of these ships. Lodge, as you know, is very pro-British, and both he and Gardner [13] have defended an increase in the army and navy on the ground that we may have war with Germany.

I have just talked with Senator Walsh of Montana and he tells me that Lodge has introduced an amendment to the shipping bill prohibiting the purchase of German ships. He says it will either be necessary to vote for that amendment or else defend the right of the Government to buy those ships. His own position is that the Government has a right to buy the ships. He thinks that even an announcement that the ships are not to be bought under the provisions of this shipping bill would hardly be sufficient because they would ask—"Why not put the prohibition in the bill if there is no intention of buying?"

The question is not logical and I think if an announcement was made that the authority would not be used to purchase ships from belligerents it would be sufficient, because the Democrats could say that it was not necessary to support the President's word in such a matter. And they could object to the adoption of the Lodge amendment because after what he has said in regard to the belligerents his amendment would be accepted as an endorsement of his views and not merely upon its legal effect. It being unnecessary to put that provision in the bill, its adoption would naturally be attributed to other motives and the most natural motive would be that expressed by the man who introduced it, who is anything but neutral in his attitude.

---

[11] *Ibid.*, p. 777.
[12] Not enclosed with file copy of this letter.
[12a] Henry Cabot Lodge, Senator from Massachusetts.
[13] Augustus Peabody Gardner, Representative from Massachusetts.

I only send this to reinforce the suggestion made in the letter of yesterday in regard to the advisability of an immediate statement on the subject. Senator Walsh says they may have to vote on this amendment Monday. In view of the controversy that has arisen it might be wise to make the statement even more specifically than the one I suggested—that is, have it specifically state that the authority would not be used by us to purchase ships of belligerents.

With assurances [etc.]   W. J. BRYAN

SALE OF MUNITIONS TO BELLIGERENTS

763.72112/133½a

The Acting Secretary of State to President Wilson

WASHINGTON, *October 10, 1914.*

DEAR MR. PRESIDENT: The Department has received numerous inquiries and complaints in regard to the effect upon the neutrality of the United States of the sale of contraband articles to belligerents. Yesterday I also had a talk with Senator Stone in regard to this matter and he said that the fact it was permitted by this Government was being used as a political argument among the Germans of St. Louis.

In view of these facts it seemed to me that it might be desirable to issue a public statement upon the subject in order that this misapprehension as to the unneutrality of sales of contraband articles might be removed. Before doing this I thought you should be consulted in the matter, and I therefore submit for your consideration a public statement upon the subject. If this meets with your approval I will show it to Senator Stone, who requested the privilege of seeing it before it was issued.[1]

Very sincerely yours,

ROBERT LANSING

763.72112/134½

President Wilson to the Secretary of State

WASHINGTON, *October 13, 1914.*

MY DEAR MR. SECRETARY: Mr. Lansing was kind enough to submit the enclosed to me.[2] I return it with the assurance that I think it is desirable that such a statement should be issued, and this statement seems to me excellent.

Cordially and faithfully yours,

WOODROW WILSON

---

[1] For the statement as issued, see *Foreign Relations*, 1914, supp., p. 573.
[2] *Supra.*

113

763.72111/634a

The Secretary of State to President Wilson

WASHINGTON, *November 12, 1914*.

MY DEAR MR. PRESIDENT: I enclose an opinion in regard to the sale of Submarines.[3] I fear that we would be "skating on thin ice" if we adopted the rule suggested.

It may be within the rules of neutrality but I am afraid we could not convince the average citizen there was any difference in allowing a vessel to be completed here and allowing the parts to be made so that a complete vessel could be shipped and the parts assembled in another port.[4]

If you are in doubt about the matter I would like to talk with you before the matter is finally settled, as I think there is danger in this proposition.

With assurances [etc.]   W. J. BRYAN

763.72111/1072½a

The Acting Secretary of State to President Wilson

WASHINGTON, *November 28, 1914*.

DEAR MR. PRESIDENT: In view of information reaching the Department in regard to the possible construction of submarines by American manufacturers for belligerent governments, I discussed the matter with Secretary Bryan on November 12th and later on the same day put my opinion in the form of a letter to him, which, I think, he called to your attention.

As my opinion did not, as Mr. Bryan informed me, coincide with the views of neutrality held by you or by him, I submitted the question to the Joint State and Navy Neutrality Board in a letter dated November 17th,[5] in order that the legal aspect of the subject might receive critical consideration. The Board has sent me its report, and, as it is in my opinion correct from the standpoint of international and municipal law, I have approved it.

I am sending you a copy of the report [5] together with a copy of my letter of the 12th [6] with no intention of obtaining a modification of your views as to the propriety of sales of this sort, which is essentially a matter of policy; but I think it my duty to lay before you the fact that in the opinion of the Neutrality Board, which I think

---

[3] No copy of this enclosure found in Department files.
[4] For correspondence previously printed concerning the sale of submarines in parts, see *Foreign Relations*, 1914, supp., p. 577; *ibid.*, 1915, supp., pp. 782–783.
[5] Not printed.
[6] Not found in Department files.

is sound, there is no legal obstacle to such sales, and no authority conferred by law upon this Government to prevent sales or to punish American manufacturers who make them.

In order to carry out your wish, made to me over the telephone a few days ago, that submarines in sections should not be sold here, I think that it would be well for the Department to be advised as soon as possible of the action which it should take in this matter, either formally or informally, since it is possible that the manufacturers may proceed without asking the Department's views if they have been advised by counsel that the sales are not illegal.

Very sincerely yours,

ROBERT LANSING

763.72111/1073½

President Wilson to the Acting Secretary of State

WASHINGTON, *November 30, 1914.*

MY DEAR MR. LANSING: As I intimated to you, I gave the matter very serious thought when the question of the submarines was brought up. I feel that it is really our duty (in the spirit, at any rate, of the *Alabama* decision) to prevent submarines being shipped from this country even in parts, and I hope that you will find a way of checking and preventing this if it is contemplated.

Always

Cordially and faithfully yours,

WOODROW WILSON

763.72111 Em 1/1

The Secretary of State to President Wilson

WASHINGTON, *December 24, 1914.*

MY DEAR MR. PRESIDENT: I am sending for your judgment a rather important communication to the German Ambassador.[7]

You will notice in the papers enclosed a translation of the note received from the German Embassy [8] in which they admit the right of belligerents to buy arms, ammunition, etc., in this country, but complain of the inquiries which we make in regard to ships carrying coal to war vessels.

Mr. Lansing and I have gone over this very carefully and you will notice first that we call attention to the recognition of the right

---

[7] *Foreign Relations*, 1914, supp., p. 647.
[8] See note from the German Ambassador, Dec. 15, 1914, *ibid.*, p. 646.

of belligerents to buy our arms. (See the last sentence on the first page.[10])

In the next place we call attention to the distinction between the rules applicable to the purchase of ammunition and the rules applicable to ships carrying coal.

We also take occasion to assert that these principles have been enforced by this nation with impartiality.

We are wondering whether it might not be well, in view of the criticism we have received, to ask the German Embassy to permit us to give to the public their protest and our answer. It will meet the criticism which has been directed against us by some who seem to be ignorant of the rules of international law.

Please let me know whether you have any changes to suggest in the phraseology, and also whether it is worth while to try to secure publication.

With assurances [etc.]   W. J. BRYAN

763.72111 Em 1/11½

President Wilson to the Secretary of State

WASHINGTON, *26 December, 1914.*

MY DEAR MR. SECRETARY: I think the enclosed reply [11] to the memorandum of the German Government both sound and conclusive, and I sincerely hope that you will be able, as you suggest, to obtain the consent of the German Government to the publication of this correspondence.

Cordially and faithfully Yours,

WOODROW WILSON

763.72111/1403

President Wilson to the Secretary of State

WASHINGTON, *January 7, 1915.*

MY DEAR MR. SECRETARY: I hope that when the opportunity offers you will be kind enough to say to the House Committee on Foreign Affairs that I entirely agree with your judgment that "any action looking to interference with the right of belligerents to buy arms here" taken at the present time "would be construed as an unneutral act." My opinion is very clear, as I think the opinion of everyone must be who is fully cognizant of all the implications that would attend such action.

Cordially and faithfully yours,

WOODROW WILSON

---

[10] *Foreign Relations,* 1914, supp., p. 647, last sentence.
[11] *Ibid.,* p. 647.

763.72111/1552a

The Secretary of State to President Wilson

WASHINGTON, *January 29, 1915.*

MY DEAR MR. PRESIDENT: I am sending you an answer which Mr. Lansing has prepared to Bernstorff's protest on hydroaeroplanes.[12]

Since this letter came to me I have been talking with a man acquainted with the aeroplanes and hydroaeroplanes and he confirms the information received from our army and navy officers to the effect that the hydroaeroplane differs from the aeroplane simply and solely in the machinery provided for its starting.

On land the aeroplane starts on wheels—on the water the hydroaeroplane starts on pontoons. The pontoons have nothing more to do with the hydroaeroplane than the wheels do with the aeroplane and cannot, I think, be a determining factor in deciding whether they are contraband or not. I cannot see that the hydroaeroplane differs from a balloon except in the method of operating it. A battleship could carry balloons for the purpose of scouting or carrying bombs. It would not change the rule if aeroplanes were carried and started from the ship's deck. The rule applying to them, it seems to me, would be the same as a balloon and I cannot see that there is any material difference in this respect between the aeroplane and the hydroaeroplane.

But before mailing this I send it to you for your inspection. As I leave tonight for Raleigh to address the legislature tomorrow (returning tomorrow night) I have signed this and it will be mailed by Mr. Davis if you return it with your approval. If there is anything that you desire to speak to me about in connection with it, I will be back Sunday forenoon.

With assurances [etc.] W. J. BRYAN

763.72111/1930

The Counselor for the Department of State (Lansing) to the Secretary of State

[WASHINGTON,] *April 11, 1915.*

DEAR MR. SECRETARY: I enclose a draft reply [13] to the note and memorandum of the German Ambassador of the 4th instant.[14]

The memorandum impresses me as couched in language, which is unpardonable in the insinuations which it contains as to the motives of this Government, and which therefore deserves some rebuke. The

---

[12] For protest and reply, see *ibid.,* 1915, supp., pp. 776, 780.
[13] Not printed; for text of the note as sent, see *ibid.,* p. 160.
[14] *Ibid.,* p. 157.

fact is that Count von Bernstorff, by making this memorandum public without seeking your consent, has acted in a manner almost as improper and offensive as did Rustem Bey.[15]   I believe that it should be seriously considered whether he ought not to be called personally to account for this breach of diplomatic etiquette.

In any event our reply, in my opinion, should show displeasure at his criticisms and should decline to debate the subject with him. Any treatment more moderate than this would, I believe, displease the American people who are jealous of our national dignity and expect our Government to maintain it.

The course which the Ambassador has taken in this matter indicates to my mind that the memorandum was prepared with the intention of publishing it as an arraignment of the Administration in order that German sympathizers in this country may be aroused to stronger political hostility to the Government. It is in entire accord with the Dernberg-Münsterberg-*Fatherland* propaganda.

Neither the dignity of the Government nor political expediency seems to me to warrant a conciliatory reply to the memorandum.

It is with these thoughts in mind that I drafted the reply.

Faithfully yours,

ROBERT LANSING

763.72111/1930

The Counselor for the Department of State (Lansing) to the Secretary of State

WASHINGTON, *April 13, 1915.*

DEAR MR. SECRETARY: Since I handed you the draft note in reply to the German memorandum of April 4th, I have been wondering whether it would not be advisable to ask Count von Bernstorff if he acted under instructions in delivering the memorandum. If he did, he is in a measure relieved of personal responsibility though the affront to this Government would, it seems to me, be more serious and more difficult to deal with.

The more I study the memorandum the more unpardonable its language seems. It is not only an arraignment of the Government for unneutrality, but by comparing the President's attitude towards the exportation of arms to Mexico and his attitude towards exportations in the present war it insinuates that the President is acting inconsistently and with manifest partiality.

Not only is any reference to the President in a communication of this sort a breach of diplomatic propriety, but an insinuation that he has acted in an unfair way, aggravates the breach.

---

[15] See pp. 68–75.

For these reasons, if for no others, I think that we ought to know definitely whether the Ambassador or his Government is responsible for the memorandum, and I, therefore, enclose a draft note to Count von Bernstorff on the subject,[16] which could be delivered before the reply to the memorandum is sent.

Faithfully yours,

ROBERT LANSING

763.72111/2053½

The Third Assistant Secretary of State (Phillips) to the Counselor for the Department of State (Lansing)[17]

[WASHINGTON,] *April 17, 1915.*

DEAR MR. LANSING: At lunch to-day at the British Embassy I met Mr. Oscar Straus, who had been, this morning, calling upon Count Bernstorff. During his conversation Mr. Straus asked Bernstorff why he had presented the last memorandum criticising the neutrality of this Government. Bernstorff replied that he had received instructions from his Government two months ago to present this particular statement; since which time he had allowed it to remain on his desk because in his opinion it was unwise to present it. He said, however, that the state of feeling was such in Germany that to square himself with his Government he was now obliged to carry out his instructions.

Sincerely,

WM. PHILLIPS

763.72111/1930

President Wilson to the Secretary of State

WASHINGTON, *19 April, 1915.*

MY DEAR MR. SECRETARY: Here is my try at a note in reply to Bernstorff.[18] Please let me know what you and Lansing think of it. I shall be at my desk again on Wednesday and we might finish this at that time.

I enclose the other, earlier, papers in the case.

Faithfully Yours,

W. W.

---

[16] Not printed.
[17] This paper bears the notation: "Handed to the Secy and by him sent to President 4/17/15 RL."
[18] Enclosed draft note not printed.

763.72111/1930

*The Counselor for the Department of State (Lansing) to the
Secretary of State*

[WASHINGTON,] *April 20, 1915.*

DEAR MR. SECRETARY: I enclose herewith a copy of the draft reply
to the note of the German Ambassador of April 4, 1915, prepared
by the President.[20]

The principal change is in the re-arrangement of the sentences in
the second, third and fourth paragraphs of the draft. None of
them has been omitted, but it seemed to me that the harmony of
ideas would be more complete by a change of order, such as suggested. The revised draft of the paragraphs is appended to the reply
and is marked X in blue pencil.[20]

On page 4 I wish to call your attention to the change made in
regard to the acknowledged rights of belligerents referred to. We
have thus far carefully avoided any discussion of the articles included
in the lists of contraband, and therefore it would not seem advisable
to me for us to say "within well defined limits." In place of that
portion of the sentence, I have inserted my idea as to what should
be said.[21]

On pages 4 and 5, it seemed to me well to limit our consideration
of belligerent action to neutral rights and interests. Also on page
5, I suggest the omission of the words "for it had no right in the
matter," [22] because I am not sure we did not have a right, since it
affected our trade. It is possible that the inclusion of the phrase
might open the Government to a further charge of weakness in failure to insist on its just rights.

On page 8, I offer the suggestion that the word "conscience" be
changed to "conscious right." [23] It seems to me that we should convey the idea of righteousness, including in the thought justice.

A minor correction which I have made is to give precedence to
the United States over Germany when the two are connected by a

---

[20] Not printed.
[21] The President's draft read, "It [the American Government] has acknowledged, of course, the right of visit and search and the right, within certain well
defined limits, to declare certain goods contraband of war." In place of "within,
etc." Mr. Lansing suggested the words "to apply the rules of contraband of war
to articles of commerce."
[22] In the President's draft these words appeared following the words "not of
right" in the final text. See *Foreign Relations*, 1915, supp., p. 161, last
paragraph.
[23] *Ibid.*, p. 162, last sentence of the note.

conjunction. This is according to the practice of the Department, and is customary with other governments, who give precedence to their own countries.

You will perceive that I have been very free in my suggestions, as I assume that is your wish and also the President's.

Faithfully yours,

ROBERT LANSING

763.72111/1930

The Secretary of State to President Wilson

WASHINGTON, *April 20, 1915.*

MY DEAR MR. PRESIDENT: I am enclosing a note from Mr. Lansing explaining the changes which he suggests.[24] They refer to the form of expression rather than to the merits of the proposition, and I am inclined to agree with him except in one particular.

On page 8 he suggests the substitution of "conscious right" for "conscience". I prefer your phraseology for I think the word "conscience" harmonizes with the good will which follows it better than the phrase "conscious right".

The only change which I have to suggest is in regard to the right of American citizens to export arms. You will remember that Bernstorff, in his note, bases his whole argument in favor of an embargo on the ground that a nation should not increase its plants for the manufacture of arms, etc. Of course this position is entirely unsound but as we reiterate our position would it not be well to conclude the statement of our position with a statement something like this—"We can find no justification in international law for the restrictions upon the export of arms which your Excellency suggests."? And the answer would be still further strengthened by adding—"and even if the position taken by your Excellency were tenable, it would only relate to the amount of arms and ammunition which it would be proper for belligerents to purchase in a neutral country, and would involve the apportionment of such purchases among belligerents, a thing which would seem to be impossible."

Mr. Lansing does not think it necessary to make any answer to the Ambassador's argument on this subject, but it seems to me that in restating our position we cannot well ignore the argument upon which he bases his criticism of our position.

With assurances [etc.]

W. J. BRYAN

---

[24] *Supra.*

763.72111/1930

President Wilson to the Secretary of State

WASHINGTON, *21 April, 1915.*

MY DEAR MR. SECRETARY: I am glad to accept the emendations suggested (except where I have run my pencil through them) and also the rearrangement of paragraphs, and hasten to return the note to be copied and delivered.[25]

I took advantage of your suggestion to add the words (p. 6) "and I respectfully submit that none of the circumstances urged in Your Excellency's memorandum alters the principle involved." [26]

In haste,

Faithfully Yours,

W. W.

763.72111/2313½

The Counselor for the Department of State (*Lansing*) to Dr. Charles Noble Gregory [27]

WASHINGTON, *June 7, 1915.*

MY DEAR GREGORY: I found time at last to read carefully your paper on "Neutrality and Arms Shipments" [28] and I wish now to congratulate you most heartily on the comprehensive treatment of the subject and the conclusive and convincing character of your arguments. I think you have left nothing unsaid and have deprived those who are clamoring for an embargo without a leg to stand on.

My regret is that the paper has not been given greater publicity. It deserves to be read throughout the country.

Very sincerely yours,

ROBERT LANSING

763.72111 Em 1/26

The Secretary of State to President Wilson

WASHINGTON, *July 8, 1915.*

DEAR MR. PRESIDENT: I think that we could dismiss the Austrian statement regarding the sale of arms and ammunition [29] with an

---

[25] For text of the note as sent, see *Foreign Relations*, 1915, supp., p. 160.

[26] *Ibid.*, p. 162.

[27] Chairman of the Standing Committee on International Law of the American Bar Association.

[28] Published in the *New York Herald*, May 16, 1915. The file copy bears the notation in Mr. Lansing's hand: "June 6, 1915. I have read this with much interest and consider the arguments sound and convincing. It should be used in case the question is officially discussed. Robert Lansing."

[29] *Foreign Relations*, 1915, supp., p. 791.

acknowledgment, as you suggest in your note of yesterday,[30] but it seems to me that it offers an excellent opportunity to make a full and clear statement of our attitude. While the communication would be addressed to Vienna, we could by making the correspondence public present the matter in a favorable and, I believe, convincing way to the American people.

Home consumption would be the real purpose; an answer to Austria the nominal purpose.

Convinced of the strength of our position and the desirability of placing the case frankly before the people in order to remove the opposition to sales of war materials, which many persons have on moral grounds and not because of pro-German sympathy, it seems to me advisable to prepare an answer to the Austrian communication, which I will submit to you as soon as it is drafted.

Faithfully yours,

ROBERT LANSING

763.72/2012½ : Telegram

The Ambassador in Germany (Gerard) to the Secretary of State

BERLIN, *August 2, 1915—5 p. m.*
[Received August 4—8:15 a. m.]

2670. A man who is at general headquarters informed a friend of mine of following conversation with the Emperor:

"The Emperor talked to him for an hour and a half on many subjects. He is very angry with America and Americans; thinks that President Wilson is absolutely pro-English; talked for a long time regarding the export of arms and ammunition; said that the war would have been over four months ago but for America's assistance to the Allies; said that we had forbidden the export of arms and ammunition to Mexico; we should do the same for the whole of Europe.

"Man interposed, 'But international law,' whereupon the Emperor angrily retorted, 'There is no international law.'

"Man remarked that Germany had given ammunition to Russia in the Russo-Japanese war. 'Yes,' said the Emperor; 'because the Russians were fighting against a yellow race.'

"He said it was a crime that his brave educated men were being killed by black and yellow men; that he was disappointed in the Anglo-Saxon race; that they were egging on the yellow races; that China was finished.

---

[30] Not found in Department files. A telegram from President Wilson referring to the Austrian note is printed on p. 453.

"England was responsible for the war. England fully intended to retain Calais after the war; the French Government recently went there and were flabbergasted to find it turned into a British colony; the French were afraid of the British fleet.

"Conscription in England was wholly ridiculous; this could only be built up after generations; it was absurd starting it in the middle of a war. Man remarked that we had done this in our Civil war and it enabled us to defeat the South.

" 'Yes,' said the Emperor; 'but that war lasted four years.'

"The Emperor seemed full of confidence; modestly said that after this war Europe would have to be entirely rebuilt and he was sixty years old.

"He seems to be so carefully surrounded by his officers that he is misinformed on many subjects."

Above is reliable but please do not inform anyone except the President as it might be traced to source and cause great trouble.

GERARD

763.72111 Em 1/26

The Secretary of State to President Wilson

WASHINGTON, *August 2, 1915.*

MY DEAR MR. PRESIDENT: In view of the making public of the Austrian statement in regard to the exportation of arms and ammunition, I hasten to send you a draft of reply.[31] I have not had time to review it with the care I should like to give to it.

You will observe in reading it that it is presented in a popular rather than a technical manner because I think it will be more valuable for the public here in the United States than for its effect upon Austria-Hungary.

I hope you can pass upon it speedily because I believe it would, at the present moment, have a very beneficial effect on public opinion. It is our first opportunity to present in a popular way the reasons why we should not restrict the exportation of munitions of war. If you have noticed in the papers meetings are being held under various auspices looking to the imposition of an embargo on arms and ammunition. The propaganda is being conducted in various parts of the country and if continued may become very embarrassing.

Faithfully yours,

ROBERT LANSING

---

[31] Not printed; for text of the reply as sent, see *Foreign Relations*, 1915, supp., p. 794.

763.72111 Em 1/31½

President Wilson to the Secretary of State

WASHINGTON, *5 August, 1915.*

MY DEAR MR. SECRETARY: I have gone over this paper very carefully indeed, and these questions urge themselves upon me:

1. Can this argument not be taken as an argument in sympathy with Allies and against militarism, which is Germany?

2. Are we not ourselves about to urge the control of the manufacture of arms and munitions by every government in our proposed understandings and undertakings with the Latin-American countries; [32] and do we not wish ultimately to strive for the same thing in the final European settlement?

Of course we are arguing only to the special case, and are absolutely unanswerable in our position that these things cannot be done while a war is in progress as against the parties to it; but how far, do you think, the arguments we urge in this paper will estop us in future deliberations on the peace and security of the world?

Faithfully Yours,

W. W.

763.72111 Em 1/31½

The Secretary of State to President Wilson

WASHINGTON, *August 6, 1915.*

MY DEAR MR. PRESIDENT: I am in receipt of your letter returning in revised form the proposed answer to the Austrian statement regarding arms and ammunition, and I think the changes improve the language very much.

The questions which you raise as to the possibility of the reply being taken as an argument in sympathy with the Allies and against German militarism applies, I presume, to that part of the draft which advances the practical and substantial reason—being on page 6. [33]

I think the question is justified. The argument might, and I have no doubt would by pro-German sympathizers, be construed as you suggest by your question. But, if we do not mean it, do we not run the risk of resting our whole case on the principle that to change our laws in time of war would be unneutral and also on the past usage of nations, and especially the practice of Germany and Austria?

While probably that argument is sufficient to meet the contention of Austria, it may be held to be technical and will not, I am afraid,

---

[32] See vol. II, pp. 471 ff.

[33] See *Foreign Relations,* 1915, supp., p. 796, first paragraph.

satisfy the humanitarians. For that reason, it seemed to me politic to insert the practical reason against prohibition and to show that it would compel general armament and so make for war rather than peace. Mr. Bryan and I talked this subject over on several occasions and I am sure that he considers that the prohibition of the sale of arms upon the advancement of peace would have this effect.

Would it be advisable, if this portion of the argument remains, to insert a paragraph disavowing any purpose of insinuating that Austria and Germany were aggressors?

Would that cure the objection or would it aggravate it? I am not at all sure in my own mind what the effect would be.

I enclose such a paragraph for consideration. It could be inserted between lines 2 and 3 on page 9.[35]

I do not think that the argument would seriously affect the program in regard to the American Republics or to a similar program for Europe. The principle is for governmental regulation and control of arms and ammunition, but with it goes the guaranty of political and territorial integrity. In case an American nation was attacked by a transoceanic nation, or another American nation, would it not be the duty of the guarantors to furnish the nation attacked not only with arms, but with men and ships?

Furthermore, I understand that the regulation of the manufacture and sale of arms is limited to trade between the contracting parties and would not apply to other nations unless they entered into a similar guaranty and agreement to regulate. Without the guaranty of integrity of territory and political independence I believe that an agreement restricting in general the sale of arms and ammunition would be inadvisable. With the guaranty the agreement is practical and will make for peace.

Unless, therefore, Europe sees fit to adopt the guaranty and to enter into the agreement about munitions, the argument advanced in the draft would remain and this country would be as free as it is today to trade in arms and ammunition with belligerents, and would be justified, as a neutral, in doing so.

One other thought in this connection suggests itself. If the guaranty should be adopted by the American Republics, an invasion by one of the territory of another would make every guarantor a belligerent, so that the question of the neutral right to sell arms and ammunition could never arise.

Faithfully yours,

ROBERT LANSING

---

[35] See footnote 36, p. 127.

[Enclosure]

Proposed Insert in Reply to Austria-Hungary

The Government of the United States in the foregoing discussion of the practical reason why it has advocated and practiced trade in munitions of war, distinctly disavows any purpose to suggest that Austria-Hungary and Germany are aggressive powers inspired with purposes of conquest. It makes this disavowal in order that no misconstruction may be placed upon its statements and that it may not be credited with imputations which it had no intention of making.

763.72111 Em 1/32½

President Wilson to the Secretary of State

WASHINGTON, *9 August, 1915.*

MY DEAR MR. SECRETARY: I am satisfied to let the note go out as altered, with the addition of the disavowal appended to be inserted on page 9.[36] It is no doubt just as well to have the argument as candid as possible. I hope you think the disavowal, as altered, safe and unobjectionable.

Thank you for your letter in the matter. Your reply with regard to the pending American agreement is entirely convincing. Indeed, I had thought it out to that effect before your reply came.

Faithfully Yours,

W. W.

763.72111 Em 1/32½

The Secretary of State to President Wilson

WASHINGTON, *August 10, 1915.*

MY DEAR MR. PRESIDENT: I am in receipt of your letter of yesterday in regard to the reply to the Austro-Hungarian statement. I approve very heartily of the change which you made as to the paragraph to be inserted on page 9. I will have our reply prepared and sent as soon as possible, and also arrange for its publication here, as I think it will have a salutary effect upon public opinion which is undoubtedly being seriously affected by the propaganda against the exportation of arms and ammunition.

Faithfully yours,

ROBERT LANSING

---

[36] This disavowal, as altered by President Wilson from Secretary Lansing's draft, appears in the note as sent as the last paragraph on p. 796, *Foreign Relations*, 1915, supp.

812.00/15870½

Mr. W. J. Bryan to the Secretary of State

OSSAWOTOMIE, KANS., *August 16, 1915.*

MY DEAR MR. SECRETARY:

Have just read your note to Austria. It is very conclusive and I am telegraphing an editorial endorsement of it to the *Commoner*, but it may be too late for this month's issue. Am glad you are restraining the jingoes on the Mexican border.

We have enjoyed reading the complimentary notices of Mrs. Lansing and yourself.

With kindest regards [etc.]   W. J. BRYAN

763.72111 Em 1/33½

Colonel E. M. House to the Secretary of State

MANCHESTER, MASS., *August 17, 1915.*

DEAR MR. LANSING: I want to congratulate you and felicitate with you over the note to Austria. It was splendidly done and has met with very wide approval.

It is fortunate that Austria gave you an opportunity to bring the argument out so clearly and well.

Medill McCormick was here the other day and he is very eager to serve if possible in the troubles in Hayti. He knows the West Indies well and he believes you might use him there to advantage. I do not understand that he wants any office, but is willing to give his services if you think they are needed.

Sincerely yours,

E. M. HOUSE

763.72111 Em 1/33½

The Secretary of State to Colonel E. M. House

WASHINGTON, *August 19, 1915.*

DEAR COLONEL HOUSE: I received your letter of the 17th congratulating me upon the reply we made to the Austrian Statement in regard to the sale of munitions of war. I am very glad that you so heartily approve of it. It seems to have been received most favorably throughout the country, and I hope will stop, in a measure, the propaganda which is being carried on by peace societies and other well-intentioned persons who have not appreciated the practical side of the question.

Mr. McCormick called to see me this morning. He seems to have a fund of information in regard to Haiti and I have asked him to discuss the subject with Mr. Long, the Chief of the Latin-American Division. Not having your letter at the time he called I did not realize his desire to be of service to the Government in connection with the situation which exists there. As to that situation, I confess that I dislike very much the idea which was involved in our action, but there was really no other practical way in which to handle the question.

Yesterday I received a telegram from Mr. Polk,[38] who was at Plattsburg to see Mr. Mitchel.[39] His telegram said that the matter was satisfactorily arranged between them, but he asked that in case the President saw fit to appoint him it should not be made public immediately. I assume that the Mayor wishes to have time to make up his own mind as to a successor without being bombarded with applications. I hope very much that the President will act promptly in this matter as I am beginning to feel the wear and tear of doing double work in the Department.

Very cordially yours,

ROBERT LANSING

812.00/15870½

The Secretary of State to Mr. W. J. Bryan

WASHINGTON, *August 20, 1915.*

MY DEAR MR. SECRETARY:

. . . .

I am very much gratified that you so fully endorse the note in reply to Austria's statement regarding the trade in munitions of war. Of course I knew that it embodied your views in regard to the subject and I am sure an editorial in the *Commoner* on the subject will have a very wide influence.

You may be sure we are doing all we can to stop the clamor for intervention in Mexico. You know my views in regard to intervention and that I would use every effort to prevent us from being dragged into a conflict which can only bring unhappiness to this country.

With warm regards to yourself and Mrs. Bryan from Mrs. Lansing and me, believe me [etc.]

ROBERT LANSING

---

[38] Frank L. Polk, corporation counsel for the city of New York, appointed Counselor for the Department of State, August 30, 1915.
[39] Mayor of New York City.

812.00/15871½

President Wilson to the Secretary of State

WASHINGTON, *21 August, 1915.*

MY DEAR MR. SECRETARY: Thank you for having let me see the enclosed letters.

Mr. Bryan's praise of the Austrian note takes me, I admit, a little by surprise. I am sincerely glad he thinks as he does about it.

.   .   .   .

Faithfully Yours,

W. W.

763.72111 Em 1/34½

The Ambassador in Germany (Gerard) to the Secretary of State

BERLIN, *September 14, 1915.*

MY DEAR MR. SECRETARY: Congratulations on your Austrian arms note. It is a beautiful piece of work.

Enclosed tribute to your policy in a German paper may interest you.[40] It is written by a friend of mine. (Not a German Viereck or Marcus Braun[41]).

Yours ever,

JAMES W. GERARD

---

[40] Not printed.
[41] Authors of periodical and newspaper articles favorable to Germany.

LOANS TO BELLIGERENTS

763.72111/35½a

The Secretary of State to President Wilson

WASHINGTON, *August 10, 1914.*

MY DEAR MR. PRESIDENT: I beg to communicate to you an important matter which has come before the Department. Morgan Company of New York have asked whether there would be any objection to their making a loan to the French Government and also the Rothschilds—I suppose that is intended for the French Government. I have conferred with Mr. Lansing and he knows of no legal objection to financing this loan, but I have suggested to him the advisability of presenting to you an aspect of the case which is not legal but I believe to be consistent with our attitude in international matters. It is whether it would be advisable for this Government to take the position that it will not approve of any loan to a belligerent nation. The reasons that I would give in support of this proposition are:

First: Money is the worst of all contrabands because it commands everything else. The question of making loans contraband by international agreement has been discussed, but no action has been taken. I know of nothing that would do more to prevent war than an international agreement that neutral nations would not loan to belligerents. While such an agreement would be of great advantage, could we not by our example hasten the reaching of such an agreement? We are the one great nation which is not involved and our refusal to loan to any belligerent would naturally tend to hasten a conclusion of the war. We are responsible for the use of our influence through example and as we cannot tell what we can do until we try, the only way of testing our influence is to set the example and observe its effect. This is the fundamental reason in support of the suggestion submitted.

Second: There is a special and local reason, it seems to me, why this course would be advisable. Mr. Lansing observed in the discussion of the subject that a loan would be taken by those in sympathy with the country in whose behalf the loan was negotiated. If we approved of a loan to France we could not, of course, object to a loan to Great Britain, Germany, Russia, Austria or to any other country, and if loans were made to these countries our citizens would be divided into groups, each group loaning money to the country which it favors and this money could not be furnished without expressions of sympathy. These expressions of sympathy are disturbing enough when they do not rest upon pecuniary interests—they would be still more disturbing if each group was pecuniarily in-

131

terested in the success of the nation to whom its members had loaned money.

Third: The powerful financial interests which would be connected with these loans would be tempted to use their influence through the newspapers to support the interests of the Government to which they had loaned because the value of the security would be directly affected by the result of the war. We would thus find our newspapers violently arrayed on one side or the other, each paper supporting a financial group and pecuniary interest. All of this influence would make it all the more difficult for us to maintain neutrality, as our action on various questions that would arise would affect one side or the other and powerful financial interests would be thrown into the balance.

I am to talk over the telephone with Mr. Davidson of the Morgan Company at one o'clock, but I will have him delay final action until you have time to consider this question.

It grieves me to be compelled to intrude any question upon you at this time, but I am sure you will pardon me for submitting a matter of such great importance.

With assurances [etc.]   W. J. BRYAN

P. S. Mr. Lansing calls attention to the fact that an American citizen who goes abroad and voluntarily enlists in the army of a belligerent nation loses the protection of his citizenship while so engaged, and asks why dollars, going abroad and enlisting in war, should be more protected. As we cannot prevent American citizens going abroad at their own risk, so we cannot prevent dollars going abroad at the risk of the owners, but the influence of the Government is used to prevent American citizens from doing this. Would the Government not be justified in using its influence against the enlistment of the nation's dollars in a foreign war? The Morgans say that the money would be spent here but the floating of these loans would absorb the loanable funds and might affect our ability to borrow.

851.51/6 : Telegram

The Ambassador in Germany (Gerard) to the Secretary of State

BERLIN, *September 5, 1914.*
[Received September 6—3 : 05 p. m.]

40. It may not be my business, but I hope Americans will not subscribe to French loan. Germans are incensed at its flotation in America and in present state of hostilities loan very unsafe and I have heard rumor that Germany may not recognize it.

GERARD

851.51/6 : Telegram

The Secretary of State to the Ambassador in Germany (Gerard)

WASHINGTON, *September 15, 1914.*

159. Your No. 40, September 5th, also number 108, eleventh.[1] Inquiry has failed to disclose any attempt to float French loan in this country. Press today reports rumor that German loan of fifty millions is contemplated by certain New York bankers. No confirmation of rumor.

BRYAN

861.51/78 : Telegram

The Chargé in Russia (Wilson) to the Secretary of State

PETROGRAD, *October 16, 1914—6 p. m.*
[Received 9:18 p. m.]

67. Count Witte called on me and told me in strict confidence that Russian Government had suggested to him to go to America to raise loan as he is well known there besides being president of Russian financial commission. On account of age and health would prefer not to accept but has told Government he will do so in case decision is made, on two conditions only.

First, Russia must make commercial treaty with the United States whereby all American citizens, Jews, Christians, naturalized or native, furnished with American passport shall have equal treatment in Russia.
Second, he must be assured that Russian Government will pass legislation improving social and economic conditions of working classes, as without these two conditions considers chance of securing loan impossible.

I pointed out difficulty of loan from the point of view of American neutrality. Witte replied that Russia's proposal unlike those of France and Germany. No funds would leave the United States but whole loan would be spent there in purchasing from American manufacturers goods needed in Russia. Transaction therefore very advantageous to the United States.

WILSON

---

[1] Latter not printed.

861.51/78

The Acting Secretary of State to President Wilson

WASHINGTON, *October 19, 1914.*

DEAR MR. PRESIDENT: The enclosed telegram from Petrograd (No. 67, October 16, 6 P. M.)[2] is of so much importance that I would like your approval of the draft telegram in reply before sending it.[3]

It would be most gratifying if a treaty such as is proposed could be negotiated, but even to accomplish this, which would certainly bring much credit to your Administration, as it would be accomplishing the seemingly impossible, it seems to me that we should in no way intimate that a Russian credit loan would be favorably received. I have avoided the subject in the proposed reply. Does it seem to you that it could be possibly construed as an admission that Count Witte's mission would be looked upon with favor by this Government?

Very sincerely yours,

ROBERT LANSING

861.51/78 : Telegram

The Acting Secretary of State to the Chargé in Russia (*Wilson*)

WASHINGTON, *October 20, 1914—3 p. m.*

39. Your number 67, October 16th, 6 P. M. This Government would view with much satisfaction the negotiation of a commercial treaty with Russia along the lines indicated in the first of the two conditions upon which Count Witte makes his acceptance of a mission to the United States depend. Do I understand that it is Count Witte's desire to come as a special envoy to negotiate such a treaty or that he desires the treaty to be signed before he visits this country?

Please advise the Department promptly as to any further developments in regard to the subject. It would be manifestly improper for this Government to take any part in facilitating a loan to one of the belligerent governments. It would not be frank to lead Count Witte, whose stipulations as you report them do him so much honour, to expect this.[4]

LANSING

---

[2] *Supra.*
[3] Not printed; for the reply as sent, see *infra.*
[4] The last two sentences were added on the draft telegram in President Wilson's hand (file No. 861.51/78½).

861.51/74½

The Acting Secretary of State to President Wilson[5]

WASHINGTON, *October 20, 1914.*

DEAR MR. PRESIDENT: I enclose you a copy of a memorandum which was left me to-day by the Russian Ambassador.

This is very much like the proposal Mr. Straight[6] made the other day in regard to French Treasury notes, concerning which I spoke to you. Of course I can see that these proposed obligations of the Russian Treasury amount practically to promissory notes, which could be used in paying for supplies purchased in this country.

This proposition seems different to me from a war loan, so far as its form is concerned, but there is no doubt it is a loan or a series of loans to the Russian Government.

I told the Russian Ambassador that I would present this memorandum to you for your consideration.

Very sincerely yours,

ROBERT LANSING

[Enclosure]

Memorandum by the Russian Ambassador (Bakhméteff)

In consequence of the present situation in Europe our manufacturers are compelled to purchase large quantities of goods in the United States. The American manufacturers do not sell goods in any other way than cash American Port (F. O. B.). In endeavour to help our manufacturers in the matter of payments for the purchased goods and not having sufficient funds in the United States our Government would like to issue short term obligations of the Imperial Russian Treasury (to be issued in dollars). The amount of the issue and the interest rate are to be determined as soon as the Federal Government will declare themselves favourably (not to have any objections to the issue).

It is understood that this issue will help both sides, American manufacturers as well as Russian manufacturers.

---

[5] A notation attached to this paper reads: "Oct. 22/14. Covered by our conversation.   W. W."

[6] Willard Straight, associated with J. P. Morgan & Co.

851.51/167

*The Vice President of the National City Bank (Samuel McRoberts)
to the Acting Secretary of State* [7]

NEW YORK, *October 23, 1914.*

MR. COUNSELLOR: Supplementing our conversation of this morning, I desire to call your particular attention to the following conditions now existing in this country and abroad.

The outbreak of the European War came at a time when this country owed a large amount to Europe, particularly to England in the form of short time drafts, maturing between the outbreak of the war and the end of the year. The amount, while large, was not abnormal, considering the volume of our trade relations and was directly due to the anticipated shipment of cotton during the autumn.

War conditions, as you are aware, have made cotton bills unavailable for the settlement of this balance against us and it can only be wiped out by the shipment of the goods, in lieu of the cotton, that are now needed and desired by the various European countries. This is true, regardless of any temporary bridging over of the situation, and it has been the policy of the National City Bank, as far as possible and proper, to stimulate the unprecedented and unusual buying that is now going on in this country by foreign governments and their nationals. Since the beginning of the war this bank alone has received cabled instructions for the payment of in excess of $50,000,000 for American goods and the volume of this business is increasing. Owing to war conditions, this buying is necessarily for cash and it is of such magnitude that the cash credits of the European governments are being fast depleted. Lately we have been urged by manufacturers who are customers of the bank and, in some cases, by representatives of the foreign governments, to provide temporary credits for these purchases. For that purpose we have recently arranged to advance the Norwegian Government some three million dollars, practically all of which is to be expended for cereals in this country. Very recently the Russian Government has placed directly, and through agents, large orders with American manufacturers—such large orders that their cash credit has been absorbed and they have asked us to allow an overdraft, secured by gold deposited in their state bank, of some five million dollars.

Some of our clients have been asked to take short time Treasury warrants of the French Government in payment for goods and have, in turn, asked us if we could discount them or purchase warrants direct from the French Government for the purpose of replenishing

---

[7] Numerous marginal and interlinear notations on this letter in Mr. Lansing's hand indicate that it was used as a basis in the preparation of the memorandum accompanying his letter of Oct. 23, 1914, to President Wilson, *infra.*

their cash balances. We have also been asked by European interests practically the same question as to English Consols and Treasury securities. Some of our German correspondents have approached us with the suggestion that, without naming a particular security, we sell securities to increase their cash account with us, and we have little doubt this is indirectly for the purposes of the German Government.

We strongly feel the necessity of aiding the situation by temporary credits of this sort, otherwise the buying power of these foreign purchasers will dry up and the business will go to Australia, Canada, Argentine and elsewhere. It may in the end come back to us, but the critical time for American finance in our International relations is during the next three or four months and, if we allow these purchases to go elsewhere, we will have neglected our foreign trade at the time of our greatest need and greatest opportunity.

It is the desire of the National City Bank to be absolutely in accord with the policies of our own Government, both in its legal position and in the spirit of its operations and, while very anxious to stimulate our foreign trade, we do not wish to, in any respect, act otherwise than in complete accord with the policy of our government.

For the purpose of enabling them to make cash payments for American goods, the Bank is disposed to grant short time banking credits to European governments, both belligerent and neutral, and where necessary or desirable replenish their cash balances on this side by the purchase of short time Treasury warrants. Such purchases would necessarily be limited to the legal capacity of the bank and, as these warrants are bearer warrants without interest, they could not and would not be made the subject of a public issue. These securities could be sold abroad or be readily available as collateral in our foreign loans and would be paid at maturity in dollars or equivalent in foreign exchange.

This business which I have attempted to describe to you, we deem necessary to the general good and we desire to proceed along the lines indicated unless it is objectionable from the Government's standpoint, in which case we assume that you will advise us.

Very respectfully yours,

SAMUEL McROBERTS

851.51/167a

The Acting Secretary of State to President Wilson

WASHINGTON, *October 23, 1914.*

DEAR MR. PRESIDENT: I spoke to you the other day about a conversation I had with a representative of certain banking interests in New York regarding the use of Treasury notes of the French Republic in this country in payment for purchases by that Government. Since then I have had conversations with representatives of other banking interests in New York, which relate to a similar type of loan to Russia as well as to France. You will also recall that this same subject was dealt with in a memorandum handed me by the Russian Ambassador a few days ago,[8] which you returned with an oral explanation as to the attitude of this Government.

I have gone over the matter pretty carefully with these gentlemen and without comment submit in a memorandum, for your considera- tion, what I consider to be their views in regard to the situation. I have told them that I could make no statement until I had laid the matter before you. They naturally are anxious to know as soon as possible what your views are.

I should hesitate to ask your direction in this matter, were it not for the fact that there is evidence of a desire on the part of these institutions to do nothing which would in any way embarrass the Government or go contrary to your wishes, even if the law permitted them to do so.

Very sincerely yours,

ROBERT LANSING

[Enclosure—Memorandum]

Summary of Information in Regard to Credits of Foreign Govern- ments in This Country and the Relation to Trade

The outbreak of the European war came at a time when this country owed a large amount to Europe, particularly to England in the form of short time drafts, maturing between the outbreak of the war and the end of the year. The amount, while large, was not abnormal, considering the volume of our trade relations and was directly due to the anticipated shipment of cotton during the autumn.

War conditions have made cotton bills unavailable for the settle- ment of this balance against us and it can only be wiped out by the shipment of the goods, in lieu of the cotton, that are now needed and desired by the various European countries. This is true, regard- less of any temporary bridging over of the situation, and it has been the policy of the financial institutions in New York, as far as possible and proper, to stimulate the unprecedented and unusual buying by foreign governments and their nationals that is now going on in this country. Since the beginning of the war I am informed that one bank alone has received cabled instructions for the payment of more than $50,000,000 for American goods and that the volume of this business is increasing. Owing to war conditions, this buying is nec-

[8] *Ante*, p. 135.

essarily for cash and it is of such magnitude that the cash credits of the European governments are being fast depleted. Lately it has been urged by certain manufacturers and by representatives of some of the foreign governments, that the banks should provide temporary credits for these purchases. Recently the Norwegian Government arranged an advance of some three million dollars, practically all of which is to be expended for cereals in this country. Very recently the Russian Government, it is stated, has placed directly, and through agents, large orders with American manufacturers—orders so large that their cash credit has been absorbed and they have sought to obtain overdrafts, secured by gold deposited in their state bank, of some five million dollars.

Some of the manufacturers have been asked to take short time Treasury warrants of the French Government in payment for goods and have, in turn, asked the banks if they could discount them or could purchase warrants direct from the French Government for the purpose of replenishing their cash balances. The same question has been asked as to English Consols and Treasury securities, while some of the banks have been approached by German correspondents with the suggestion that, without naming a particular security, the banks sell securities to increase their cash account in America.

The representatives of the banks state that they feel the necessity of aiding the situation by temporary credits of this sort, otherwise the buying power of these foreign purchasers will dry up and the business will go to Australia, Canada, Argentine and elsewhere. They say that it may in the end come back to the United States but that, in their opinion, the critical time for American finance in our International relations is during the next three or four months and, if we allow these purchases to go elsewhere, we will have neglected our foreign trade at the time of our greatest need and greatest opportunity.

It seems to be the desire of the banks to be absolutely in accord with the policies of this Government, both in its legal position and in the spirit of its operations and, while very anxious to stimulate our foreign trade, they do not wish to, in any respect, act otherwise than in complete accord with the policy of the Government.

For the purpose of enabling European Governments to make cash payments for American goods, it is suggested to grant to them short time banking credits, to both belligerent and neutral governments, and where necessary or desirable replenish their cash balances on this side by the purchase of short time Treasury warrants. Such purchases would necessarily be limited to the legal capacity of the particular bank and, as these warrants are bearer warrants without interest, they could not and would not be made the subject of a public issue. These securities could be sold abroad or be readily available as collateral in foreign loans and would be paid at maturity in dollars or equivalent in foreign exchange.

ROBERT LANSING

[WASHINGTON,] *October 23, 1914.*

763.72111/630½

Memorandum by the Acting Secretary of State of a Conversation With President Wilson, October 23, 1914, 8:30 p. m.

[WASHINGTON,] *October 23, 1914—9:30 p. m.*

From my conversation with the President I gathered the following impressions as to his views concerning bank credits of belligerent governments in contradistinction to a public loan floated in this country.

There is a decided difference between an issue of government bonds, which are sold in open market to investors, and an arrangement for easy exchange in meeting debts incurred in trade between a government and American merchants.

The sale of bonds draws gold from the American people. The purchasers of bonds are loaning their savings to the belligerent government, and are, in fact, financing the war.

The acceptance of Treasury notes or other evidences of debt in payment for articles purchased in this country is merely a means of facilitating trade by a system of credits which will avoid the clumsy and impractical method of cash payments. As trade with belligerents is legitimate and proper it is desirable that obstacles, such an [*as?*] interference with an arrangement of credits or easy method of exchange, should be removed.

The question of an arrangement of this sort ought not to be submitted to this Government for its opinion, since it has given its views on loans in general, although an arrangement as to credits has to do with a commercial debt rather than with a loan of money.

The above are my individual impressions of the conversation with the President, who authorized me to give them to such persons as were entitled to hear them, upon the express understanding that they were my own impressions and that I had no authority to speak for the President or the Government.

ROBERT LANSING

Substance of above conveyed to Willard Straight at Metropolitan Club, 8:30 p. m. October 24, 1914.

R.L.

Substance of above conveyed to R. L. Farnham [9] at the Department, 10:30 a. m., October 26, 1914.

R.L.

---

[9] Representative of the National City Bank.

851.51/30

J. P. Morgan and Company, the National City Bank, and the First National Bank of New York to the Secretary of State

NEW YORK, *March 25, 1915.*

DEAR SIR: The French Government, finding themselves under very great expense for transferring funds from France to America owing to the position of exchange, consider it necessary to obtain temporary credit in this country to meet their obligations for American products and continue their purchases in this country.

We beg to advise you therefore, that we are arranging to place for them some $50,000,000. One-Year Treasury Notes, the proceeds of which are to be expended in this country.

Very truly yours,

J. P. MORGAN AND CO.
THE NATIONAL CITY BANK
by F. A. VANDERLIP
FIRST NATIONAL BANK
F. L. HINE, *Pres.*

841.51/266

The Secretary of the Treasury (McAdoo) to the Secretary of State

NORTH HAVEN, MAINE, *August 23, 1915.*

DEAR MR. SECRETARY: I enclose copy of a letter from James B. Forgan, of Chicago, to Vice-Governor Delano, of the Federal Reserve Board, in reference to the matter of foreign loans in this country. The foreign exchange situation is so serious that it may become imperative for some of the foreign governments to establish credits in this country in order that they may continue to purchase freely our farm products and other supplies. The attitude of the Government, as expressed in the letter of Secretary Bryan to Senator Stone, January 20th, 1915,[10] may seriously embarrass the creation of such credits in favor of foreign governments as are needed to enable them to continue their purchases in this country. Germany, by the way, disregarded this letter and placed more than ten million of short-time notes in this country through Chandler Brothers, of Philadelphia. It is not my purpose, however, to discuss that; I only mean to direct your attention to the importance of giving very serious thought to the points raised in Mr. Forgan's letter. I have always felt that it was a mistake for our Government to discountenance in any way the establishment of credits in this country in favor of foreign governments, such credits to be employed in purchasing

---

[10] *Foreign Relations,* 1914, supp., p. VII (sec. 13).

supplies in this country. It seems to me entirely inconsistent to say that the purchase of our farm products and manufactured articles and other supplies by foreign governments is lawful and to be encouraged, and then to say that we discourage and discountenance as being unneutral the credit operations which are an essential part of such transactions.

I merely desire to call your attention at the moment to the seriousness of the question and to say that I hope no action will be taken that will add to the embarrassments of the situation by reaffirming or emphasizing the position taken in Mr. Bryan's letter of January 20th, last, until I have had an opportunity to discuss this with you and the President.

I shall certainly be in Washington on the first of September—maybe sooner. I look forward with pleasure to seeing you then.

With warmest regards [etc.]   W. G. McAdoo

[Enclosure]

The President of the First National Bank of Chicago (James B. Forgan) to the Vice Governor of the Federal Reserve Board (F. A. Delano)

Chicago, *August 17, 1915.*

My Dear Mr. Delano: I want to get some information for a very confidential purpose and it has occurred to me that you may be in a position to help me secure it.

It is, to put it bluntly; I would like to know what the attitude of the government administration in Washington would be towards the flotation of a large British loan in this country. Sometime ago I remember seeing in the press that the State Department had discouraged New York bankers on a proposition to float a British loan in this country, but at the same time it was stated that it was not within the province of the government to veto such a transaction. It would seem to me that the present condition of international exchange would deter the government from entering any objection to the flotation of such a loan in this country, or to the sale by Great Britain of American securities in this country. One or other of these transactions would seem to be a business necessity at the present time. As I am in a bit of a hurry to get the information I would appreciate a telegram indicating what you believe the government's attitude would be. You might send me one of the following telegrams to indicate which of the positions you think the government would take in regard to the flotation of a large British loan in this country and I will understand your meaning:

1. Parties would be favorable to and would encourage such a transaction.

2. Parties would take no action either for or against such a transaction.

3. Parties would discourage such a transaction but would not offer any active interference with it.

4. Parties attitude would be such as to make such a transaction practically impossible.

With kind regards [etc.] JAMES B. FORGAN

841.51/22

The Governor of the Federal Reserve Board (Hamlin) to the Secretary of State

WASHINGTON, *August 24, 1915.*

MY DEAR MR. SECRETARY: I beg to enclose copy of a letter from Mr. James B. Forgan, President of the First National Bank of Chicago, to Hon. F. A. Delano, Vice Governor of the Federal Reserve Board.[11] As the matter referred to is one of Governmental policy, I beg to ask you to read it, sending me any reply you may care to make, which I will forward to Mr. Forgan.

Very respectfully yours,

C. S. HAMLIN

841.51/266

The Secretary of State to President Wilson

WASHINGTON, *August 25, 1915.*

MY DEAR MR. PRESIDENT: As the letter of Mr. James B. Forgan, which is enclosed to me by Mr. Hamlin, deals directly with the general policy of the Government I feel that before answering it I should be advised as to your wishes. I therefore enclose Mr. Hamlin's letter [11] and a copy of Mr. Forgan's.[12]

I think we must recognize the fact that conditions have materially changed since last autumn when we endeavored to discourage the flotation of any general loan by a belligerent in this country. The question of exchange and the large debts which result from purchases by belligerent governments require some method of funding these debts in this country.

Faithfully yours,

ROBERT LANSING

---

[11] *Supra.*
[12] *Ante,* p. 142.

841.51/266

President Wilson to the Secretary of State

WASHINGTON, *26 August, 1915.*

MY DEAR MR. SECRETARY: My opinion in this matter, compendiously stated, is that we should say that "Parties would take no action either for or against such a transaction", but that this should be orally conveyed, so far as we are concerned, and not put in writing.

I hope that this is also your own judgment in the matter.

Faithfully Yours,

W. W.

841.51/266

The Secretary of State to the Secretary of the Treasury (*McAdoo*)

WASHINGTON, *August 26, 1915.*

MY DEAR MR. SECRETARY: Mr. Hamlin sent me a copy of the letter of Mr. James B. Forgan which you enclosed to me in your letter of the 23d. I sent the letter to the President on the 25th, a copy of my letter to him is enclosed,[14] and I also enclose his reply of today.[15]

I have read your comments upon the matter of loans to belligerent countries and must say that I concur in your opinion—in fact, from the outset, I have held that opinion of such transactions viewed from the legal standpoint rather than from the standpoint of expediency.

While the President did not authorize me to send a copy of his communication to you I feel that he would wish you to know his position.

Faithfully yours,

ROBERT LANSING

811.51/2624a

The Secretary of State to President Wilson

WASHINGTON, *September 6, 1915.*

MY DEAR MR. PRESIDENT: Doubtless Secretary McAdoo has discussed with you the necessity of floating government loans for the belligerent nations, which are purchasing such great quantities of goods in this country, in order to avoid a serious financial situation which will not only affect them but this country as well.

Briefly the situation, as I understand it, is this: Since December 1st, 1914, to June 30, 1915, our exports have exceeded our imports by

---

[14] *Ante*, p. 143.
[15] *Supra.*

nearly a billion dollars, and it is estimated that the excess will be from July 1st to December 31, 1915, a billion and three quarters. Thus for the year 1915 the excess will be approximately two and [a] half billions of dollars.

It is estimated that the European banks have about three and [a] half billions of dollars in gold in their vaults. To withdraw any considerable amount would disastrously affect the credit of the European nations, and the consequence would be a general state of bankruptcy.

If the European countries cannot find means to pay for the excess of goods sold to them over those purchased from them, they will have to stop buying and our present export trade will shrink proportionately. The result would be restriction of outputs, industrial depression, idle capital and idle labor, numerous failures, financial demoralization, and general unrest and suffering among the laboring classes.

Probably a billion and three quarters of the excess of European purchases can be taken care of by the sale of American securities held in Europe and by the transfer of trade balances of oriental countries, but that will leave three quarters of a billion to be met in some other way. Furthermore, even if that is arranged, we will have to face a more serious situation in January, 1916, as the American securities held abroad will have been exhausted.

I believe that Secretary McAdoo is convinced and I agree with him that there is only one means of avoiding this situation which would so seriously affect economic conditions in this country, and that is the flotation of large bond issues by the belligerent governments. Our financial institutions have the money to loan and wish to do so. On account of the great balance of trade in our favor the proceeds of these loans would be expended here. The result would be a maintenance of the credit of the borrowing nations based on their gold reserve, a continuance of our commerce at its present volume and industrial activity with the consequent employment of capital and labor and national prosperity.

The difficulty is—and this is what Secretary McAdoo came to see me about—that the Government early in the war announced that it considered "war loans" to be contrary to "the true spirit of neutrality." A declaration to this effect was given to the press about August 15, 1914, by Secretary Bryan. The language is as follows: "In the judgment of this Government loans by American bankers to any foreign nation at war is inconsistent with the true spirit of neutrality." [16]

---

[16] See telegram of Aug. 15, 1914, to J. P. Morgan & Co., *Foreign Relations*, 1914, supp., p. 580.

In October, 1914, after a conference with you, I gave my "impressions" to certain New York bankers in reference to "credit loans",[17] but the general statement remained unaffected. In drafting the letter of January 20, 1915, to Senator Stone I sought to leave out a broad statement and to explain merely the reasons for distinguishing between "general loans" and "credit loans". However, Mr. Bryan thought it well to repeat the August declaration and it appears in the first sentence of division 13 of the letter, a copy of which I enclose.[18]

On March 31, 1915, another press statement was given out from the Department which reads as follows:[19]

"The State Department has from time to time received information directly or indirectly to the effect that belligerent nations had arranged with Banks in the United States for credits in various sums. While loans to belligerents have been disapproved, this Government has not felt that it was justified in interposing objection to the credit arrangements which have been brought to its attention. It has neither approved these nor disapproved—it has simply taken no action in the premises and expressed no opinion."

Manifestly the Government has committed itself to the policy of discouraging general loans to belligerent governments. The practical reasons for the policy at the time we adopted it were sound, but basing it on the ground that loans are "inconsistent with the true spirit of neutrality" is now a source of embarrassment. This latter ground is as strong today as it was a year ago, while the practical reasons for discouraging loans have largely disappeared. We have more money than we can use. Popular sympathy has become crystallized in favor of one or another of the belligerents to such an extent that the purchase of bonds would in no way increase the bitterness of partisanship or cause a possibly serious situation.

Now, on the other hand, we are face to face with what appears to be a critical economic situation, which can only be relieved apparently by the investment of American capital in foreign loans to be used in liquidating the enormous balance of trade in favor of the United States.

Can we afford to let a declaration as to our conception of "the true spirit of neutrality" made in the first days of the war stand in the way of our national interests which seem to be seriously threatened?

If we cannot afford to do this, how are we to explain away the declaration and maintain a semblance of consistency?

My opinion is that we ought to allow the loans to be made for our own good, and I have been seeking some means of harmonizing our

[17] See memorandum of Oct. 23, 1914, p. 140.
[18] *Foreign Relations*, 1914, supp., p. VII.
[19] *Ibid.*, 1915, supp., p. 820.

policy, so unconditionally announced, with the flotation of general loans. As yet I have found no solution to the problem.

Secretary McAdoo considers that the situation is becoming acute and that something should be done at once to avoid the disastrous results which will follow a continuance of the present policy.

Faithfully yours,

ROBERT LANSING

811.51/2624a

President Wilson to the Secretary of State

WASHINGTON, *8 September, 1915.*

MY DEAR MR. SECRETARY: I have no doubt that our oral discussion of this matter yesterday suffices. If it does not, will you let me know that you would like a written reply?

Faithfully Yours,

W. W.

811.51/2624

The National Chairman, Friends of Peace (John Brisben Walker), to the Secretary of State

NEW YORK, *September 11, 1915.*

SIR: The newspapers today report Pierpont Morgan and other Americans as in treaty with the English Government through Baron Reading, its Lord Chief Justice, and Basil P. Blackett, C. B., Special Treasury Agent of the English Government to use one thousand millions of American money in aiding the cause of the allies.

These millions are badly needed in America for financing the agricultural interests, especially that of cotton, for the railways, for the building of good roads, et cetera. Jas. J. Hill says that twice that sum is needed to put American Railways in proper condition.

The money which Mr. Morgan proposes to lend can only be obtained by making use of the United States Treasury Reserve, putting commercial paper upon the Government, and using the funds thus relieved; or else by deceiving the small investor into accepting a war loan which may yet fall to 48 cents on the dollar, as did our American war securities, under English manipulation, during the war of the rebellion.

May I ask you to telegraph this organization whether we have, or have not, laws on the statute books which, as construed by you, would prevent this flagrant breach of neutrality, in thus giving aid to the financially distressed allies, while committing a positive injustice against the American people?

We beg at the same time to lay before you the platform adopted at Chicago, on September 6th, by the greatest convention ever brought together in behalf of a moral ideal—voted unanimously by more than two thousand delegates representing societies having a membership of more than ten millions of American citizens.

This convention, composed of a high class of American citizens, was addressed by your great predecessor in the office of the Secretary of State, and cheered allusions by him to President Wilson.

Its proceedings have [been] the object of such suppressions, and so much misrepresentation and vilification by that portion of the American press which is behind the great interests manufacturing armaments and munitions, that its platform has not been published anywhere in the East, so far as I have seen. I therefore enclose a copy,[20] asking your special attention to the marked paragraphs.

Yours sincerely,

JOHN BRISBEN WALKER

811.51/2624

President Wilson to the Secretary of State

WASHINGTON, *15 September, 1915.*

MY DEAR MR. SECRETARY: This is a most extraordinary letter.[21] I am sure you know how to handle it. I am much obliged to you for letting me see it.

Faithfully Yours,

W. W.

861.51/116

The Ambassador in Russia (Francis) to the Secretary of State

PETROGRAD, *May 20, 1916.*

[Received June 16.]

SIR: I was called upon May 18 by Mr. J. J. Korostovetz, member of the Council of Ministers of Foreign Affairs, who told me he had been instructed by M. Sazonoff, Minister of Foreign Affairs, and by M. Bark, Minister of Finance, to make inquiries and submit a report concerning the negotiation of the proposed loan to the Russian Government by some American bankers and financial institutions, headed by the National City Bank of New York.

His first inquiry was whether I, as Ambassador, was disposed to look with favor on such a loan. After making clear to him that our Government could in no way be interested in such a loan, conse-

---

[20] Not printed.
[21] *Supra.*

quently it would in no sense incur any moral obligation in connection therewith,—I explained to him the financial responsibility of the National City Bank and those whom it represented, and furthermore expressed the opinion that such a loan would foster the already friendly relations existing between the two countries and would undoubtedly have the effect of promoting their international trade. He said England had been financing Russia and might not like to see such a loan made without her intermediation, but when I explained to him that there was no occasion for any intermediation whatever and that, in fact, our country had recently loaned $500,000,000 to England and France, he thoroughly concurred with the position I assumed.

Mr. Samuel McRoberts, vice president of the National City Bank, accompanied by another vice president, Mr. Rich, arrived in Petrograd May 15 for the purpose of consummating a loan of $50,000,000., negotiations for which have been pending for three or six months past. M. Sazonoff told me, as I have already advised you, that Russia would not accept the proffered loan because the American bankers demanded specific security in addition to the faith of Russia. Mr. McRoberts assures me that the plan which he has formulated and which he has submitted by special communication—sent by Mr. Young, the Petrograd representative of the National City Bank, who left for America May 17—will meet the objections of the government here. I am rendering all the assistance I consistently can toward the consummation of this loan, as I think it will have a very beneficial effect on the diplomatic, as well as the commercial relations between the two countries.

Respectfully yours,

DAVID R. FRANCIS

861.51/110 : Telegram

The Secretary of State to the Ambassador in Russia (Francis)

WASHINGTON, *June 8, 1916—6 p. m.*

860. Your 563, 565, May 24, and 569 May 25, 1 p. m.[22]

Before delivering messages to Vanderlip and Guaranty Trust Company, I must inquire whether they refer to Russian Government loans of any description. If they do, I regret that the Department can not be a party to their transmission, as such action would submit it to justifiable criticism because of participation by this Government in loan transaction by a belligerent for the purpose of carrying on its hostile operations. Such participation is contrary to the ac-

------

[22] None printed.

cepted rule of international law that neutral Governments should not lend their assistance to the raising of war loans by belligerents.

LANSING

861.51/115 : Telegram

The Ambassador in Russia (Francis) to the Secretary of State

PETROGRAD, *June 10, 1916—10 a. m.*
[Received June 11—9 a. m.]

600. Your 860. Messages to Vanderlip and Guaranty refer to Russian Government loan. Regret troubling you therewith especially since your clear exposition of international law. Most of this 50 million however would be used for paying indebtedness already incurred for noncontraband commodities. Not yet consummated.

FRANCIS

861.51/117 : Telegram

The Ambassador in Russia (Francis) to the Secretary of State

PETROGRAD, *June 19, 1916—6 p. m.*
[Received June 20—8 : 15 a. m.]

619. National City consummated Russian loan $50,000,000, 3 years, following terms: Government deposits roubles 150,000,000 in its bank here upon which bank allows 6½ percent interest and ¼ percent commission quarterly, making total interest 7½ percent. Lenders give Russian Government credit $50,000,000 in America to be drawn as Government requires. Lenders privileged to sell deposited roubles any time during 3 years but must divide equally with Government all obtainable over 33⅓ which value is arbitrarily placed on rouble in loan. If roubles sold before expiration 3 years loan is thereby liquidated. Lenders furthermore have option at 94¾ percent on 5-year, 5½ percent Russian Government loan of $100,000,000, payable in America less agreed commission.

Embassy had no participation in negotiation but I am personally glad loan was effected as will promote better diplomatic relations which fear have become strained by Embassy's persistent efforts for German-Austrian prisoners and by constant Jewish agitation in America.

FRANCIS

ENFORCEMENT OF AMERICAN NEUTRALITY—STATEMENTS CONCERNING AMERICAN NEUTRALITY POLICY

763.72111/32½

Memorandum by the Counselor for the Department of State (Lansing) on the Preservation of Neutrality by the People of the United States [1]

In view of the present inflamed state of the public mind of this country over the European conflict, and the danger of utterances by the American people and press which would cause hostile feeling by one or more of the belligerents toward the United States and from [form] a pretext for involving this Government in the present wars, would it not be appropriate and expedient for the President at the present time to publish a public address to the American people urging them to preserve in every way a strict neutrality and to be discreet in public expressions either in the press or otherwise showing bias or sympathy with any one of the countries at war. Such an address should further point out that we have thousands of American citizens, who because of nativity or blood sympathize with particular nations engaged in the conflict; that, however natural such sympathy is, it is their duty as American citizens to preserve a strict neutrality and avoid offense to their fellow citizens of other nationalities.

The same is true of the press. In whatever language a newspaper may be printed, its first duty is to the United States. It is not performing its duty to this country if it opens its columns to unneutral and partisan expressions of opinion, which may encourage antagonism among Americans of foreign birth and lineage and may give the impression to the government or people of a belligerent nation that the American people are hostile to them and desire their defeat.

The creation of such an impression in any country at war would arouse a spirit of hostility to this nation, which might menace our peace and would undoubtedly expose to mob violence the hundreds of Americans who are now in that country and unable to return to their homes, endangering their welfare and even their lives.

While a public utterance of this nature might appear to be an attempt to restrict the freedom of speech and of the press, I believe

---

[1] This paper bears the notation: "Handed to Secy Aug. 9, 1914   RL."

151

that it would appeal to the sober common sense of the people of the United States and prevent opinions and criticisms of an inflammatory nature.

ROBERT LANSING

[WASHINGTON,] *August 9, 1914.*

August 10, 1914, the Secy informed me that he had sent the foregoing to the Pres't with certain verbal changes which he (the Secy) had suggested.

R. L.

763.72111/48½

Memorandum by the Counselor for the Department of State (Lansing) on the Use by Belligerents of Wireless Stations and Submarine Telegraph Cables on Neutral Territory [2]

[WASHINGTON,] *August 12, 1914.*

The Hague Convention of 1907 respecting the Rights and Duties of Neutral Powers and Persons in Case of War on Land contains the following provisions: [3]

"ARTICLE 3

Belligerents are likewise forbidden to:

a. Erect on the territory of a neutral power a wireless telegraphy station or other apparatus for the purpose of communicating with belligerent forces on land or sea;
b. Use any installation of this kind established by them before the war on the territory of a neutral power for purely military purposes, and which has not been opened for the service of public messages."

"ARTICLE 8

A neutral power is not called upon to forbid or restrict the use on behalf of the belligerents of telegraph or telephone cables or of wireless telegraphy apparatus belonging to it or to companies or private individuals."

A neutral power is not bound to forbid or restrict the use of submarine cables landed on its territory whether belonging to a government or to private persons, or the use of wireless telegraphy unless the station on neutral territory is erected by a government, either before or after the beginning of a war for military purposes.

While a neutral is given full discretion in regulating the use of cables and wireless on its territory, with the exception noted as to

[2] For correspondence previously printed regarding control of wireless telegraphy, see *Foreign Relations*, 1914, supp., pp. 667 ff.
[3] Malloy, *Treaties*, 1776–1909, vol. II, p. 2290.

government owned wireless stations, it appears to me the duty of a neutral power in maintaining an impartial neutrality to prevent communications between a belligerent government and its agents on neutral territory when such communications are of an unneutral character unless both belligerents possess equal opportunities of communication.

The unneutral character of communications to and, under certain conditions, from a neutral territory by means of telegraphy would appear to consist in sending secret information by the agent of a belligerent power to his government relative to military or naval operations and to the movements of merchant ships of belligerents arriving at or departing from neutral ports.

This would apply equally to wireless and submarine telegraphs.

There are, however, some distinctions in the means of communication by wireless and by cable. In the latter case the enemy of the belligerent, in whose territory the cable is landed, may, if he is able, cut such cable in the open sea or in the territorial waters of the belligerent. This may be done by a belligerent under the generally accepted principles of international law.

In the case of wireless telegraphy, however, there being no physical connection between the station on neutral territory and the station on the territory of the belligerent the enemy is physically powerless to prevent communication between a belligerent government and its agent or [on] neutral territory.

A further distinction is that messages may be sent directly from neutral territory, without danger of interruption, to the warships of a belligerent on the high seas. Thus by using a cipher the agent of a belligerent on neutral territory might give to the cruisers of his government information as to the movements of an enemy's war-ships or merchant ships, which would amount to a direction of naval operations from neutral territory. On the other hand, by cable, messages may not be sent directly to vessels at sea. They may however be sent to the territory of a belligerent and by him forwarded by wireless to the vessels at sea, the difference in this case being, provided the cable remains intact, a few hours delay in transmission.

A third distinction is that wireless messages radiate in all directions from the sending station, with a radius depending roughly on the power of the station. With cables, however, the points of contact with foreign countries depend on the number of cables laid. For example, it is understood that most of the cables from the United States reach Europe through England or her possessions and that there are no direct cables to Germany or Austria or Russia.

The advantages that flow from these three distinctions depend largely on whether the message is plain or cipher.

Assuming that all messages are sent open and not in cipher, the advantage would appear to be with the cable system, for I am advised that any receiver of one belligerent, if properly adjusted, may pick up wireless messages intended for another belligerent. The cable messages therefore would have the advantage of secrecy, so long as the cable was unmolested.

On the other hand, if all the messages are in cipher, one belligerent could not read the messages of the other belligerent and the wireless system would have the advantage, owing to its freedom from molestation and to its directness of action.

In this discussion no distinction is made between outgoing and incoming messages, for it is believed that both may serve to give a belligerent information of an invaluable character for the guidance of his warlike operations. An incoming cipher message to a belligerent's agent might ask a question as to certain movements of the enemy which could be answered by the word "Yes" or "No;" or the message might instruct the agent to telegraph in reply a certain sentence plain, which would mean one thing or another sentence which would mean another thing. In either case the plain outgoing message would contain secret information, which might be of a most unneutral character, and so defeat the entire purpose of the prohibition or censorship. It is essential, therefore, that, if cipher messages are prohibited, or if cipher messages are censored, the messages affected should be those received as well as those sent.

On these differences in the physical characters and the obvious advantages of the two systems may perhaps depend the duty of a neutral to regulate the use of its wireless or cable stations for the transmission of warlike information to a belligerent. Frequently in the past the isolation of a belligerent nation by the other belligerent has been considered of prime military importance. To permit the use of the wireless telegraph in furnishing a nation, beleaguered by land and sea, with information as to the strength, location, and condition of its enemy's military and naval forces would, therefore, result in depriving the attacking power of an advantage to which it is legitimately entitled.

It seems to me that, because wireless communication between the territory of a neutral and the territory of a belligerent is entirely beyond the reach of the other belligerent, a neutral is bound to control more strictly the use of wireless stations on its territory than it is to control the use of cables between its territory and that of a belligerent, if it decides to control either.

Whether the immunity of wireless, which is open to public use, from interference is a sufficient reason for prohibiting its use for cipher messages by a belligerent government and its agents is a question which I am not prepared to answer finally although I believe that to do so would be justifiable, and especially so if the enemy of the belligerent power was sufficiently dominant on the high seas to prevent all other means of communication.

While a neutral might be justified in taking this course (a course already adopted and acted upon by this Government in the case of the wireless stations at Sayville, Long Island, and Tuckerton, New Jersey,) the belligerent thus deprived of its sole means of communication with its agents in neutral territory, would undoubtedly protest on the ground of discrimination against it by the neutral in permitting cipher messages by cable and not by wireless. Such a protest would seem to be not unreasonable in view of the results, although the advantage to the belligerent possessing cable communication would be due in fact to its naval superiority and its ability to prevent its enemy from severing its cable on the high seas. On the other hand to permit the free use of the wireless for secret communications between a belligerent government and its agents after it had been deprived of all other means of communication by the naval forces of an enemy would constitute a reasonable ground of complaint against a neutral by such enemy.

To avoid, therefore, a more or less justifiable charge of unneutral conduct by either the one or the other of the belligerents, when one possesses cable connection and the other wireless connection with neutral territory, it would seem advisable to find some compromise course, which would permit a measure of communication to both belligerents with their respective agents on neutral territory.

The following propositions regulating the use of submarine and wireless telegraphy in neutral jurisdiction are submitted for consideration:

1. All cables and wireless telegraphs to be open to all belligerents and their respective agents on neutral territory without restriction.

2. The closing of all cables between belligerent and neutral territory and all wireless capable of sending messages between belligerent and neutral territory to all cipher messages both outgoing and incoming.

3. The closing of such cables and wireless to all cipher messages unless they have been read by an official censor of the United States, who shall be furnished with a code by the sender or recipient for that purpose, and the censor shall have decided that they convey no information of military operations or the movements of ships or other information which may be considered unneutral in character. Plain messages conveying such information to be also excluded by the censor.

In connection with these propositions looking to the preservation of an impartial neutrality attention is called to the practice of other governments in relation to the use by belligerents of submarine cables.

In the war between the United States and Spain (1898) the British Government instructed the Governor of the Barbadoes not to permit messages by cable to be sent out from the colony relative to the movements of warships of either belligerent (Moore's *Digest*, Vol. 7, p. 941.) This instruction to be efficient must have of necessity prevented the sending of untranslatable cipher messages.

During the war between Russia and Japan (1904–5) the Netherlands authorities in the East Indies made regulations for the refusal at certain stations of cable messages the contents of which were not intelligible to the Netherlands officials, messages in cipher unless furnished with a code, and messages regarding the movements of ships or troops which would be of interest to Russia or Japan (Int. Law Situations—Naval War College—1907, p. 155.)

While in theory the United States has been an advocate of the neutralization of submarine cables between belligerent and neutral territories, it has in practice as a belligerent followed a contrary course. During the Spanish war it cut several cables landing on Cuba territory and also others connecting the Philippines with neutral territory.

As to wireless telegraphy there appear to be no cases in which the question of its use has arisen, it can only be considered, therefore, by analogy, (unless the station on neutral territory is erected or used by a belligerent government) though its immunity from interruption by an enemy and its wider field of communication must be recognized in reaching a determination as to its use by belligerents on neutral territory.

I would emphasize in conclusion that, while this Government is not bound as a neutral under Article 8 of The Hague Convention to interfere in any way with the use of submarine or wireless telegraphy by belligerents, Article 8 should be read with Article 3, paragraph *b*. It would be impossible for a belligerent to prevent the use of wireless stations on neutral territory from being used for military purposes. To be effective the prohibition of paragraph *b* of Article 3 must be enforced by the neutral government unless the belligerent, using the wireless, voluntarily discontinues the use, an action which cannot be expected. Though not legally obligated the moral duty of the neutral government would appear to be to carry out the spirit of the treaty, but in doing so it should attempt to avoid giving to either belligerent peculiar advantage by reason of its regulation and control of telegraphic communications between its territory and the territories of the belligerents. Impartiality and, as far as possible, equal treatment should determine the policy of this Government in dealing with this question.

ROBERT LANSING

763.72111/49½

The Counselor for the Department of State (Lansing) to the Secretary of State

[WASHINGTON,] *August 13, 1914.*

DEAR MR. SECRETARY: In connection with the question as to the proper course which this government should pursue in the matter of the belligerent use of wireless and cable telegraphy, I desire to call your attention to a fact of which I was ignorant when I prepared my memorandum on the subject yesterday.

Assistant Secretary of the Navy Roosevelt informs me that a vessel at sea cannot receive a wireless message at a greater distance than half-way across the Atlantic Ocean, no matter how powerful the sending installation may be. This fact seems to me to have a direct bearing on one line of argument which I presented in my memorandum in relation to the ability of a belligerent in control of a cable line sending a message to its home government on the other side of the Atlantic and repeating it by wireless to its war ships on this side of the ocean.

I think this fact should be taken into consideration in determining the policy of the United States in its treatment of cipher messages, whether by wireless or by cable.

Very sincerely yours,

ROBERT LANSING

763.72111/158

The Counselor for the Department of State (Lansing) to the Secretary of State [4]

[WASHINGTON,] *September 13, 1914.*

DEAR MR. SECRETARY: I submit for your consideration a memorandum as to the character of armed merchant vessels and their treatment in neutral ports,[5] which I would suggest be adopted as a basis of instructions to port officers of the United States and be followed by the Department in passing upon cases brought to its attention.

The subject with which this memorandum deals is one of the most vexatious which now confronts us, and one, as to which there is the greatest danger of erroneous and conflicting decisions. It seemed to me, therefore, necessary that the attitude of this Government should be clearly and concisely stated in order that our own officials might have definite rules to guide them in dealing with cases of this nature.

I consider also that, in case the memorandum receives your approval, it would avoid misunderstanding and possible irritation if

---

[4] This paper bears the notation: "Okeh W.W."
[5] *Foreign Relations*, 1914, supp., p. 611.

the diplomatic representatives of belligerent powers were furnished
with the substance of the memorandum as a declaration of the attitude of this Government in the matter of armed merchant vessels
in its ports and of its neutral duties in relation to them.

Very sincerely yours,

ROBERT LANSING

763.72111/175½

*The Counselor for the Department of State (Lansing) to the
Secretary of State* [6]

[WASHINGTON,] *September 13, 1914.*

DEAR MR. SECRETARY: I submit herewith for your consideration a
series of propositions which, it seems to me, it would be advisable
to adopt as a declaration of policy, which will be followed by this
Government in dealing with cases of merchant vessels in American
ports, which are suspected of furnishing supplies to belligerent warships.[7]

While each case brought to the attention of the Government will
require independent consideration, a series of propositions, such as
those suggested, will furnish general rules for the guidance of those
who have to pass upon these questions and also of the officials who
are charged with the immediate duty of detaining merchant vessels
suspected of unneutral conduct and of investigating the charges made
against them.

As cases of this sort are already numerous, it is, in my opinion, advisable that a clearly defined declaration of our policy in dealing
with such cases should be made to avoid inconsistent action by American officials and charges of partiality being made by belligerent
governments.

In case the enclosed declaration meets with your approval I would
suggest that it be furnished to the Treasury Department as a basis
for instructions to its officials stationed at our seaports and that the
diplomatic representatives of the belligerent powers be advised that
this Government will follow the policy thus announced in dealing
with merchant vessels suspected of unneutral conduct in supplying
belligerent warships operating on the high seas adjacent to the coasts
of the United States.

In view of the many reports, reaching this Department from
various sources, of cases of this sort which require immediate deci-

---

[6] This paper bears the notation: "Okeh W. W."
[7] Memorandum of Sept. 19, 1914, issued by the Secretary of State, *Foreign
Relations,* 1914, supp., p. 618.

sion, the issuance of a declaration of policy seems necessary and urgent.

Very sincerely yours,

ROBERT LANSING

763.72111/174½

President Wilson to the Acting Secretary of State

WASHINGTON, *September 17, 1914.*

MY DEAR MR. LANSING: I entirely approve of the enclosed suggestions and rules[8] and would be very much obliged indeed if you would send them with my approval and as by my request to the Departments of the Treasury and of Commerce.

Cordially and sincerely yours,

WOODROW WILSON

763.72112/286½a

The Acting Secretary of State to President Wilson

WASHINGTON, *October 26, 1914.*

DEAR MR. PRESIDENT: I enclose for your perusal an article which appears in the pro-German publication, *The Fatherland,* of October 28, 1914.[9] It is called forth by the recent public statement in regard to "Neutrality and Trade in Contraband," which you will recall was approved by you before being issued (copy enclosed).[10]

Very sincerely yours,

ROBERT LANSING

763.72112/287½

President Wilson to the Acting Secretary of State

WASHINGTON, *October 28, 1914.*

MY DEAR MR. LANSING: Thank you for having let me see the enclosed campaign sheet.[11] It is not, however worthy of attention.

Cordially and faithfully yours,

WOODROW WILSON

---

[8] See circular note of Sept. 19, 1914, to the diplomatic representatives of belligerent states, *ibid.*, p. 611, and memorandum issued by the Secretary of State, *ibid.*, p. 618.
[9] Not printed.
[10] *Foreign Relations,* 1914, supp., p. 573.
[11] The article referred to in the preceding document.

763.72111/628a

The Acting Secretary of State to President Wilson

[WASHINGTON,] *November 5, 1914.*

DEAR MR. PRESIDENT: As you know, the preservation of the neutrality of the United States in respect to the use of its ports by the belligerents or their vessels, is under the control of the Department of the Treasury, through the Customs officers in each district, who may call on the naval vessels for assistance in case of necessity. As an exception to this rule, I am advised that on the West Coast and in the Hawaiian Islands, the preservation of neutrality is in the hands of the Navy, assisted by customs officers. The character of the investigations of suspicious cases, whether initiated by the Government or by foreign representatives here, requires that the collectors endeavor to ascertain among other matters whether certain vessels in their ports are destined to supply belligerent cruisers at sea with coal, provisions, arms and other articles, whether these vessels are themselves prepared or preparing for conversion into armed cruisers to prey upon commerce, and whether the territorial jurisdiction of the United States is being invaded by armed vessels seeking supplies or information. In certain cases it may be necessary to use force to prevent the consummation of any such unneutral designs. In taking any action in such cases it is necessary to have in mind, not only the neutrality laws of the United States, but the Hague Conventions relating to neutrality, and also the rules laid down in the Declaration of London.

While the Collectors of Customs are doing excellent work, and their reports are full and complete in regard to commercial matters, it is believed that the Naval officers are, by reason of their training and experience, better prepared to investigate and report upon certain technical naval matters, and on questions involving violations of international law, and that the Navy Department, by means of the force at its disposal, is better able actually to prevent any proposed violations of neutrality.

It is daily becoming more difficult to preserve our neutrality, owing to various means devised for avoiding the restrictions which it imposes upon freedom of commerce, and the belligerent countries are urging greater vigilance on the part of the United States in preventing possible breaches of neutrality by both foreign and American ships.

This situation presents a question as to whether the preservation and enforcement of neutrality in the United States in the East and South as well as in the West should be placed in the hands of the Navy Department, but with the cooperation and assistance of the officers of the Treasury Department. I have not taken up the matter formally with the Navy Department, as I desired first to ascertain your desires in the matter.

Sincerely yours,

[File copy not signed]

763.72111/628½

President Wilson to the Acting Secretary of State

WASHINGTON, *November 6, 1914.*

MY DEAR MR. LANSING: I am so afraid of getting the delicate and difficult questions arising in connection with our neutrality confused or mishandled in any way that I am going to ask if you will not have a conference with Secretary McAdoo and with Secretary Daniels to effect very definite arrangements for cooperation between the three departments in these matters. I think we cannot be too careful in these things and I believe that these three departments ought to keep in systematic touch with one another.

I know that you will be willing to do this.

Faithfully yours,

WOODROW WILSON

763.72111/1074½

President Wilson to the Acting Secretary of State

WASHINGTON, *December 1, 1914.*

MY DEAR MR. LANSING: I would be very much obliged if you would read the enclosed letter from Professor Münsterberg and send me a memorandum, if you would be so kind, of the answers and comments that might be made upon his statements. Here at last is a very definite summing up of the matters upon which German anti-administration feeling in this country is being built up, and perhaps it would be wise to take very serious notice of it. The case they make out is *prima facie* very plausible indeed.

Cordially and sincerely yours,

WOODROW WILSON

[Enclosure]

Professor Hugo Münsterberg to President Wilson

CAMBRIDGE, MASS., *November 19, 1914.*

DEAR MR. PRESIDENT: A few days ago I wrote to you from New York in reply to your very kind letter of November 10th that I begged to postpone my reply until I reached my desk in Cambridge. Now after my return I indeed ask your permission to enter into some detail with regard to the neutrality question. But let me assure you beforehand that I interpret your inquiry as referring exclusively to the views which are expressed to me by American citizens who sympathize with the German cause or who are disturbed by the vehement hostility to Germany on the part of the American press.

My remarks refer in no way to the views of official Germany. Throughout my correspondence with officials in Berlin and in my conversations with men like Bernstorff, Hatzfeld, Dernburg and so on, the neutrality question has seldom been touched, as from the day of your declaration they were fully convinced of your firm intention to resist any official violation. I never heard a word of complaint from an official source. But as I said in my recent letter the views of the American voters are entirely different. I myself abstain from any judgment, but can say that the points which I want to bring before you are selected because they are the ones which are repeated continually in the circles of German sympathizers. They have most deeply influenced the masses of voters and have led them to the belief that the State Department subordinates its decisions to the wishes of England. Hence the political upheaval, and the firm decision of the hyphenated vote to turn away from an administration to which it would otherwise be bound by many ties. Each matter in itself seems not momentous; yet it is the summation of minor complaints which has often a psychologically stronger effect than one great cause of suffering.

Let me emphasize three points to which my correspondents refer most frequently. First, all cables sent by and received by wire pass uncensored, while all wireless news is censored. This reacts against Germany, because England sends all her news by cable, whereas Germany alone uses the wireless. The matter is of grave importance. Second, the policy of the administration with regard to the holding up, detaining and searching of Germans and Austrians from neutral and American vessels is a reversal of the American policy established in 1812. It has excited no end of bitterness. Third, the United States permitted the violation by England of the Hague Convention and international law in connection with conditional and unconditional contraband. The United States, for instance, has not protested against the transference of copper from the conditional to the absolute list, although on former occasions the United States has taken a spirited stand against onesided interpretations of international agreements. In 1812, in the Russian Japanese War, and in the Boer War the United States insisted that a neutral nation has the right to send conditional as well as unconditional contraband to neutral nations without permitting an inquiry into its ultimate destination. She insisted that the consignee must be accepted in good faith. The United States, moreover, insisted that conditional contraband can be sent in neutral or in American bottoms even to belligerent nations, provided it was not consigned to the government, the military or naval authorities or to any contractors known to represent the belligerent government. By permitting this new interpretation the United States practically supports the starving out policy of the Allies. The nation by reversing its own policy thus seriously handicaps Germany and Austria in their fight for existence.

As I said, I emphasize these three points, because they return most frequently, but numberless similar matters contribute to the general impression. I think that the feeling of the Germans and Irish is correctly expressed in the following remarks of the editor of the *Fatherland*. He writes:

"We permit English warships to nose about in our harbors; we permit them to search our ships. In 1812 we went to war for smaller reasons. We raise no protest when England contemptuously disregards our citizenship papers. We even permit her to seize our cargoes of copper in her hope of monopolizing eventually our entire copper trade. She permits us to export dynamite, but she does not permit us to export oil, even to neutral nations. In other words England, while fighting Germany on the field of battle, is waging war on the United States commercially. She makes it impossible for us to profit by the war for she strangles our trade, except for such contraband as she and her allies need. It is time to reassert our declaration of independence. German-American citizens feel, rightly or wrongly, that the administration is hostile to them, because its interpretation of neutrality has been at all points disadvantageous to Germany."

Many of the complaints refer more to the unfriendly spirit than to the actual violation of the law. Here above all belongs the unlimited sale of ammunition to the belligerents. The administration originally advised Mr. Morgan that the making of loans to the nations at war would not be looked upon with favor by the President, and Mr. Morgan cancelled the plans. This attitude has been given up; the State Department has emphasized that money and arms may be sold to the belligerents, while evidently the friends of peace had firmly hoped that the President would denounce the sale of ammunition or any other sale which would be likely to prolong the war. Indeed our friends of peace must regret this encouraging attitude with reference to the sale of agencies of destruction, but the friends of Germany cannot forget that this sympathetic attitude of the State Department under the conditions which objectively exist is not only helpful to the prolongation of the war, but helpful exclusively to the Allies against Central Europe. The favorite interpretation of the Germans is even that the government makes itself a party to the violation of neutrality by giving clearance papers to vessels loaded with war material for England and France. They say, moreover, that the President as Commander-in-Chief of the Army and Navy could and did restrain the shipment of war material into Mexico. Hence he has the same power to restrain the shipment of such material to Europe.

Let me quote this also from a letter:

"As I read President Madison's message to congress of January 1st, 1812, I find that the Wilson administration has practically subscribed to conditions which in that early stage of our history were considered an intolerable insult to our existence as an independent nation. The blood of every man of German descent must boil with indignation and resentment on reading how even American-born citizens are arrested aboard neutral vessels and in British ports, their passports ignored, confined in jails and basely humiliated because they bear German names or have German physical characteristics. Read the private letter of Mr. J. O. Bennett to the Managing Editor of the *Chicago Tribune*, which introduces a symposium of pro-German essays by native American scholars in the new pamphlet 'Germany's Just Cause.' Read the despatch of James T. Archibald to the *New York World* of October 15th, in which he says: 'Americans are imprisoned, although carrying passports and neutral ships captured.' Similar despatches have been sent to the Associated Press, and similar cases are reported in private letters finding their way into print. The mail of American citizens doing business in London has been rifled by Scotland Yard detectives, according to Mr. Bennett and his wife, and American correspondents threatened with arrest and worse for sending news favorable to Germany to American papers.

The State Department has demanded to know of the Turkish government whether it sanctions Turkish threats to Englishmen and Frenchmen, but it is manifesting a supreme indifference to the thousands of noncombatants of German and Austrian connection languishing in English and French concentration camps who are being judicially murdered, despite the fact that the interests of these nations are in the hands of the United States. I refer you to a remarkable article of Herbert Corey in the *New York Globe* for a graphic description of the barbarous hardships imposed on noncombatants confined in one English concentration camp. We protested against these conditions when they obtained in Cuba under Weyler, and we are preparing to protest to Turkey before anyone has been hurt, but we tolerate this barbarism when its victims are Germans and Austrians.

It seems so obvious that the administration is closing its eyes to all manner of expedients evasive of the laws of nations and of strict neutrality as they affect the Allies that the German-American element is rapidly conceiving an ineradicable spite against the administration. This element is usually submissive, but it is thoroughly aroused now and does not intend to be treated as a negligible factor in American political life."

From many sides very naturally much complaint is raised against the treatment of American mail on Dutch and other neutral steamers.

Since the German Government has published the official reply which it received from the Dutch government saying that England has indeed repeatedly destroyed the mail on board of Dutch steamers this case too is removed from mere newspaper gossip. I myself, like hundreds of thousands of others, have not sent a single letter to Germany in the last three months otherwise than by sending it under cover to friends in Holland, Norway or Italy. This situation is acknowledged as contrary to international law; and yet again America is evidently submitting to the whims of England.

Other letters complain much of the in itself small point that Great Britain ships her own war material and soldiers across the territory of the United States, for the Canadian Pacific, upon which troops and ammunition were shipped to Halifax, passes through the state of Maine. Many are indignant about the Honolulu incident. Others protest against America's serving the interests of England by interfering with possible wireless stations in Mexico and South America. In the last few days the new arrangement as to the coaling of warships in the Panama Zone is the centre of attack, as it is evident that England and France are favored by it, as they have colonies in the neighborhood, while Germany is again put at a disadvantage. I could go on with such details without end. They all contribute to the one general impression that the administration favors the Allies, partly by positive acts of interpretation, decision and interference, partly by submitting silently to English acts hostile to the anti-English belligerents.

Finally I beg for permission to send you as material which may not have reached your office as yet an English translation of an article in the semi-official *North German Gazette* in Berlin, which appeared on October 25th, 1914.[12] It stands, of course, only indirectly in relation to the content of my letter, as this is a complaint of official Germany against England. But since probably in a few days this complaint will become known through the German-American newspapers and since it will strongly reenforce the feeling that England's arbitrary actions on the ocean ought to awake a protest from America in the interest of international commerce, the content of this Berlin article will surely soon be added to the list of German-American complaints. It therefore seems perhaps not unfit to enclose here the translation.

Very respectfully yours,

HUGO MÜNSTERBERG

---

[12] The reference is to the Memorial of the German Foreign Office of Oct. 10, 1914, *Foreign Relations*, 1914, supp., p. 263.

763.72111/1074½

The Counselor for the Department of State (Lansing) to President Wilson

WASHINGTON, *December 9, 1914.*

DEAR MR. PRESIDENT: I have, in compliance with the request in your letter of the 1st instant, prepared and enclose herewith a memorandum on a letter of Professor Münsterberg, dated November 19th.[13]

I regret that the memorandum is so long, but to controvert charges such as these requires argument based on a statement of facts. They cannot be met by denials alone. The memorandum is also unsatisfactory to me because I have been compelled to work on it at odd moments and have not had time to give it uninterrupted consideration.

It seems to me that the falsity of these charges, which are being so widely published and are arousing so much criticism of the Administration among the German element in this country, should certainly be exposed, but I am not convinced that the wisest way to do this is by an answer to Professor Münsterberg's letter. As I point out in the first comment in the memorandum, he is a German subject, in fact an agent of the German Government. I cannot feel that our foreign policy or its political effect upon the American people is a proper subject of discussion with a foreigner, who has not even the excuse of being accredited to this government as a diplomatic representative.

I appreciate that my opinion was not asked as to this matter and I have offered it on that account with some hesitation; but, without considering the proprieties, I think that the activities of these foreigners in our political affairs ought to be brought to the attention of the American people, and that would be difficult to do in a private letter to one of them.

It would seem as if some other channel of publicity could be found which would be more effective, less objectionable and give opportunity to discuss alien interference in the party politics of the United States.

I herewith return Professor Münsterberg's letter.

Very sincerely yours,

ROBERT LANSING

---

[13] Professor Münsterberg's letter printed *supra.*

[Enclosure]

Memorandum by the Counselor for the Department of State (Lansing) on Professor Hugo Münsterberg's Letter to President Wilson of November 19, 1914

PRELIMINARY COMMENTS

I. INTERFERENCE OF ALIENS OF BELLIGERENT NATIONALITY IN THE POLITICAL AFFAIRS OF THE UNITED STATES

Regard for the following facts are [*is*] essential in dealing with a communication of this sort:

Professor Hugo Münsterberg is a German subject. Dr. Bernhard Dernburg is not only a German subject, but is probably (though the evidence at hand is not conclusive) a paid agent of the German Government sent to the United States to create sentiment in favor of Germany. These two are the principal leaders in arousing antagonism in this country to the policy of the Administration in its relations to the belligerent nations.

These two foreign writers have severely criticised this Government's conduct of its foreign affairs, have made charges unfounded in fact or in law, have distorted the truth, and have bitterly assailed the President and the Department of State for alleged injustice to Germany and undue friendliness for the cause of the Allies. In pursuing this campaign of misrepresentation and vilification they have done so by means of addresses and publications which have been widely circulated throughout the country relying upon the freedom of speech and of the press guaranteed to the people by the Constitution. If such criticisms and attacks by aliens had been made in Germany upon the German Government even in time of peace, they would undoubtedly have been summarily suppressed. The impropriety of such attempts by foreigners to influence citizens of the United States in their attitude toward the established Government is manifest.

Open participation in the discussion of our domestic politics and of our foreign policies by agents of a European monarchy, whether they are official or self-appointed, cannot but arouse antagonism to a power who will permit its subjects to forget their obligations as alien visitors owing a temporary allegiance to the United States and to seek openly to create political opposition to the Government.

The American people never have and never will brook foreign interference in their public affairs. They resent, and properly resent, foreign support or opposition when a policy of this Government is at issue. The people of this country are capable of managing their own affairs without the advice of aliens, who are seeking the interests of their own government and not the interests of the United States.

The object of Professor Münsterberg and Dr. Dernburg and other German subjects, engaged in the present pro-German propaganda in this country, appears to be two-fold.

Primarily it is to separate American citizens of German nativity or descent from the general body of the American people, to impress upon them that they are a distinct group of society, which on account of their blood are viewed with suspicion, if not with dislike, by their fellow countrymen, and to make them feel that they are first of all Germans.

Secondly their object is by means of this aroused spirit of racial allegiance to use this great body of citizens of German origin as a political machine, with which to threaten the Administration into showing special favors to Germany and Austria in the performance of the neutral duties of this Government. The menace of political opposition, if the present policy of the Government is continued, is openly proclaimed by aliens, who are devoting themselves to this propaganda and who by education and birth are out of all sympathy with American institutions, interests and ideals.

If the American people as a whole realize that these foreigners are attempting to direct our domestic affairs and are seeking to influence political action in this country to obtain special privileges for their own government, the propaganda, which is being carried on under the leadership of Professor Münsterberg and Dr. Dernburg, will awaken a resentment which will more than counteract the activities of these men and their followers.

II. THE POLICY OF THE GOVERNMENT OF THE UNITED STATES IN ITS RELATIONS WITH THE BELLIGERENTS

There are two general reasons controlling the policy of the Government of the United States in relation to the observance of neutrality during the present war:

First, the duty which the United States as a neutral nation owes to all the belligerents, based upon the legal obligation which is imposed by international law and treaty stipulations.

Second, the desirability to avoid exciting bitter feeling between groups of the American people, whose sympathies are divided because of the composite character of our citizenship. This reason is a matter of domestic policy and expediency.

In addition to these two political reasons is the humanitarian one of preserving impartial friendship toward all the belligerent powers in order that this Government at the proper time may exercise its influence for the restoration of peace.

Neutral duty, which is defined by the established rules of international usage, by conventional agreements and by municipal statutes, is enforceable by the Executive operating under enacted law and the treaties in force. Beyond such legal authority the Executive possesses no power to compel obedience. Law is the sole measure of neutrality and of the government's duty to preserve it.

The second reason, based on expediency, has no legal authority to support it. No power is conferred upon the Executive to compel submission to the policy adopted, but the Government may by the exercise of its influence induce popular acceptance of such policy.

This Government may justly be held responsible for failure to enforce the legal rules of neutrality, but it is not bound to impose restrictions greater than those included in such rules. If the Government, as a matter of policy, advocates neutrality beyond the legal requirements, it cannot rightfully be called to account for infractions of these extra-legal restrictions, since it has no power to prevent or to punish their violation.

III. PRESUMPTIVE EQUALITY OF BELLIGERENTS ESSENTIAL TO STRICT NEUTRALITY

In the enforcement of the laws of neutrality and in advocating an extension of neutral obligations, which domestic interests make expedient, this Government cannot take into account the advantage or disadvantage which may result to any of the belligerents through the enforcement of neutral duties. If one belligerent has by good fortune a superiority in the matter of geographical location or of military or naval power, the rules of neutral conduct cannot be varied so as to favor the less fortunate combatant. To change such rules because of the relative strength of the belligerents and in order to equalize their opportunities would be in itself an unneutral act, of which the stronger might justly complain.

This Government, in the enforcement of the laws of neutrality and in exercising its influence over the people as to their conduct toward the belligerents, must consider the hostile nations to be upon equal footing and to possess equal opportunities in the conduct of the war. Any other course would make the rules of neutrality a fluctuating standard which would result in constant confusion and in innumerable charges of partiality. Whether one belligerent or the other is successful, is not a matter of concern to a neutral government, and it cannot vary its rules or change its policy because of a particular triumph or defeat by either during the progress of the war. It must hold strictly to its obligations and to its general policy, however they may benefit one belligerent or injure another.

NOTE 1. THE THREE PRINCIPAL COMPLAINTS (Münsterberg letter, pages 2–3)[14]

"First, all cables sent by and received by wire pass uncensored, while all wireless news is censored. This reacts against Germany, because England sends all her news by cable, whereas Germany alone uses the wireless. The matter is of grave importance."

The reason that wireless messages and cable messages require different treatment by a neutral government is as follows:

Communications by wireless cannot be interrupted by a belligerent. No physical power to interrupt exists except at the wireless stations. If one station is in neutral territory and another beyond danger in an enemy's country, a belligerent, however superior on the sea, cannot benefit by his superiority, but is powerless to prevent messages from passing unmolested, even though they convey information which materially affects his naval operations. Manifestly a neutral has no right to deprive a belligerent of one of the principal benefits of supremacy on the high seas. With a submarine cable it is otherwise. The possibility of cutting the cable exists, and if a belligerent possesses naval superiority, the cable is cut, as was the German cable near the Azores by one of Germany's enemies, and as was the British cable near Fanning Island by a German naval force. Since a cable is subject to hostile attack, the responsibility falls upon the belligerent and not upon the neutral to prevent cable communication.

A more important reason however, at least from the point of view of a neutral government, is that messages sent out from a wireless station in neutral territory may be received by belligerent warships on the high seas. If these messages, whether plain or in cipher, direct the movements of warships or convey to them information as to the location of an enemy's public or private vessels, the neutral territory becomes a base of naval operations, to permit which would be essentially unneutral.

As a wireless message can be received by all stations and vessels within a given radius, every message in cipher, whatever its intended destination, must be censored; otherwise military information may be sent to warships off the coast of a neutral. It is manifest that a submarine cable is incapable of becoming a means of direct communication with a warship on the high seas; hence its use cannot make neutral territory a base for the direction of naval operations.

"Second, the policy of the administration with regard to the holding up, detaining and searching of Germans and Austrians from neutral and American vessels is a reversal of the American policy established in 1812. It has excited no end of bitterness."

---

[14] The original of Professor Münsterberg's letter was returned to the President. The file copy does not retain the pagination of the original.

So far as this Government has been advised, no Germans or Austrians on an American vessel on the high seas, with two exceptions, have been detained or searched by belligerent warships. One of the exceptions to which reference is made is now the subject of a rigid investigation, and if the facts as alleged are established, vigorous representations will be made to the offending government. The other exception where certain German passengers were made to sign a promise not to take part in the war, has been brought to the attention of the offending government with a declaration that such procedure, if true, is an unwarranted exercise of jurisdiction over American vessels in which this Government will not acquiesce.

An American private vessel entering voluntarily the territorial waters of a belligerent becomes subject to its municipal laws, as do the persons on board the vessel.

There has been no reversal of the century-old American policy, which related to the removal of alleged American citizens and their impressment by Great Britain. It is in no way involved in the present case.

"Third, the United States permitted the violation by England of the Hague Convention and international law in connection with conditional and unconditional contraband. The United States, for instance, has not protested against the transference of copper from the conditional to the absolute list, although on former occasions the United States has taken a spirited stand against onesided interpretations of international agreements. In 1812, in the Russian Japanese War, and in the Boer War the United States insisted that a neutral nation has the right to send conditional as well as unconditional contraband to neutral nations without permitting an inquiry into its ultimate destination. She insisted that the consignee must be accepted in good faith. The United States, moreover, insisted that conditional contraband can be sent in neutral or in American bottoms even to belligerent nations, provided it was not consigned to the government, the military or naval authorities or to any contractors known to represent the belligerent government. By permitting this new interpretation the United States practically supports the starving out policy of the Allies. The nation by reversing its own policy thus seriously handicaps Germany and Austria in their fight for existence."

There is no Hague Convention which deals with absolute or conditional contraband, and, as the Declaration of London is not in force, the rules of international law only apply. As to the articles to be regarded as contraband there is no general agreement. It is the practice of a country, either in time of peace or upon the outbreak of war, to declare what articles it will consider as absolute or conditional contraband. It is true that a neutral government is seriously affected by this declaration, as the rights of its subjects or citizens are impaired. The right of the neutral, however, seems to be that of protest.

The record of the United States in the past is not free from criticism. When neutrals, we have stood for the most restricted lists of absolute and conditional contraband. As a belligerent, we have extended the lists of both according to our conception of the necessities of the case.

The United States has now under consideration the question of the right of a belligerent to include "copper unwrought" in its list of absolute contraband instead of in its list of conditional contraband. As the Government of the United States has in the past placed "all articles from which ammunition is manufactured" in its contraband list, and has declared copper to be among such materials, it necessarily finds some embarrassment in dealing with the subject. The doctrine of "ultimate destination" and of "continuous voyage" to which reference is made in the foregoing complaint but which is not specifically stated, is an American doctrine supported by the decisions of the United States Supreme Court. Against the rule of "continuous voyage" this Government has never in the past protested, nor can it consistently do so now, in view of the fact that, when it was a belligerent, it not only asserted but extended the rule and enforced it in its tribunals.

As no American vessel so far as known has attempted to carry conditional contraband to Germany or Austria, no ground of complaint has arisen out of the seizure or condemnation by Great Britain of an American vessel with a belligerent destination. Until a case arises and the Government has taken action upon it, criticism is premature and unwarranted.

The United States has made earnest representations to Great Britain in regard to the seizure and detention by the British authorities of all American ships or cargoes destined to neutral ports, on the ground that such seizures and detentions were contrary to the existing rules of international law, but our American doctrines have been such that we are seriously handicapped in urging our protests.

We have not accepted the principle that delivery to specific consignees in a neutral port settled the question of ultimate destination. We have claimed and exercised the right to determine from the circumstances whether the ostensible was the real destination. We have also held that the shipment of articles of contraband to a neutral port "to order," from which, as a matter of fact, cargoes had been transshipped to the enemy, is corroborative evidence that the cargo is really destined to the enemy, instead of to the neutral port of delivery. We have also held that a cargo of contraband shipped from one neutral port to another will be presumed to be meant for the enemy if destined to a port contiguous to enemy territory. It is thus seen that the doctrines which appear to bear harshly upon neutrals at the present time are analogous to or outgrowths from policies adopted by the United States when it was a belligerent.

NOTE 2. THE "FATHERLAND'S" COMPLAINTS (Pages 3–4 of Münsterberg's letter)

"We permit English warships to nose about in our harbors; we permit them to search our ships. In 1812 we went to war for smaller reasons."

The complaint is unjustified from the fact that representations were made to the British Government that the presence of war vessels in the vicinity of New York Harbor was offensive to this Government and a similar complaint was made to the Japanese Government as to one of its cruisers in the vicinity of the port of Honolulu. In both cases the warships were withdrawn.

It will be recalled that in 1863 the Department took the position that captures made by its vessels after hovering about neutral ports would not be regarded as valid. In the Franco-Prussian war President Grant issued a proclamation warning belligerent warships against hovering in the vicinity of American ports for purposes of observation or hostile acts. The same policy has been maintained in the present war, and in all of the recent proclamations of neutrality the President states that such practice by belligerent warships is "unfriendly and offensive."

"We raise no protest when England contemptuously disregards our citizenship papers."

American citizenship papers have been disregarded in a comparatively few instances by Great Britain, but the same is true of Germany. Bearers of American passports have been arrested in both countries. In all such cases the United States Government has entered vigorous protests with request for release. The Department does not know of any cases, except one or two which are still under investigation, in which naturalized Germans have not been released upon representations by this Government. There have, however, come to the Department's notice authentic cases in which American passports have been fraudulently obtained by certain German subjects. Such fraudulent use of passports by Germans themselves can have no other effect than to cast suspicion upon American passports in general.

"We even permit her to seize our cargoes of copper in her hope of monopolizing eventually our entire copper trade."

There is no question of the United States "permitting" Great Britain to seize copper shipments. In every case in which it has been done vigorous representations have been made to the British Government and our representatives have pressed for the release of the shipments.

"She permits us to export dynamite, but she does not permit us to export oil, even to neutral nations."

Petrol and other petroleum products have been proclaimed by Great Britain as contraband of war. In view of the absolute necessity of such products to the use of submarines, aeroplanes and motors, the United States Government has not yet reached the conclusion that they are improperly included in a list of contraband. Military operations to-day are largely a question of motive power through mechanical devices. It is therefore difficult to argue successfully against the inclusion of petroleum among the articles of contraband. As to the detention of cargoes of petroleum oil to neutral countries, this Government has, thus far successfully, obtained the release in every case of detention or seizure which has been brought to its attention.

"In other words England, while fighting Germany on the field of battle, is waging war on the United States commercially. She makes it impossible for us to profit by the war for she strangles our trade, except for such contraband as she and her allies need. It is time to reassert our declaration of independence."

The fact that the commerce of the United States is interrupted by Great Britain is consequent upon the superiority of her navy on the high seas. If Germany possessed that superiority, it may be confidently assumed that our trade with Great Britain and France would be interrupted and that no articles useful to those countries in the prosecution of the war would reach their ports from this country.

The above quotation should be read with that in Note 3 below. The one complains of the loss of profit in trade which must mean trade in contraband with Germany and the other demands the prohibition of trade in contraband which of course refers to trade with the Allies. The inconsistency is obvious.

"German-American citizens feel, rightly or wrongly, that the administration is hostile to them, because its interpretation of neutrality has been at all points disadvantageous to Germany."

It is not unnatural that American citizens who are partisans of Germany should feel that the Administration is hostile not "to them" but to Germany. This feeling results from the fact that the German naval power is inferior to the British. It is the duty of a belligerent to prevent contraband from reaching an enemy. It is not the duty of a neutral. The partisans of Germany in this country appear to assume that some obligation rests upon this Government in the performance of its neutral duty to prevent all trade in contraband. No such obligation exists, and it would be an unneutral act of partiality on its part to take such action.

NOTE 3. TRADE IN CONTRABAND AND WAR LOANS (Letter page 4)

"Many of the complaints refer more to the unfriendly spirit than to the actual violation of the law. Here above all belongs the unlimited sale of ammunition to the belligerents. The administration originally advised Mr. Morgan that the making of loans to the nations at war would not be looked upon with favor by the President, and Mr. Morgan cancelled the plans. This attitude has been given up; the State Department has emphasized that money and arms may be sold to the belligerents, while evidently the friends of peace had firmly hoped that the President would denounce the sale of ammunition or any other sale which would be likely to prolong the war."

There is no power in the Executive to prevent the sale of ammunition to the belligerents.

Trade in munitions of war has never been restricted by international law or by municipal statute. It has never been the policy of this Government to prevent the shipment of arms or ammunition into belligerent territory, except in the case of neighboring American republics, and then only when civil strife prevailed. Even to this extent the European governments have never so far as I know limited the sale of munitions of war. It is only necessary to point to the enormous quantities of arms and ammunition furnished by German manufacturers to the belligerents in the Russo-Japanese war and in the recent Balkan wars. No country has been able to compete with Germany in the manufacture and sale of arms and ammunition.

Furthermore, one of the compensations for the disorganization of neutral commerce and the restriction of markets has been the sale of contraband to the warring nations. Such trade has been recognized as a proper substitute for the loss sustained by neutrals as a direct result of war. The lack of profit from trade is complained of in Professor Münsterberg's letter.

The reason why the influence of the Government is not exerted to prevent the sale of contraband to belligerents while such influence has been exerted in preventing the flotation of war loans in this country is this: a war loan, if offered for popular subscription in the United States, would be taken up by those who are in sympathy with the belligerent seeking the loan. The result would be that great numbers of our people would become more earnest partisans, having material interest in the success of the belligerent, whose bonds they hold. This would not be confined to a few, but would spread generally throughout our country, so that our people would be divided into groups of partisans, which would be, in the views of the Government, most unfortunate and might cause a serious condition of affairs. On the other hand, contracts for and sales of contraband are mere matters of trade. The manufacturer, unless peculiarly sentimental, would sell to one belligerent as readily as he would to another. No general spirit of partisanship would be aroused—no sympathies excited. The whole transaction would be merely a matter of business.

This Government has not been advised that any general loans have been made by foreign governments in this country since the President expressed his wish that loans of this character should not be made.

NOTE NO. 4. COMPLAINTS IN PRIVATE LETTER QUOTED ON PAGES 5 AND 6 OF MÜNSTERBERG'S LETTER

It is unnecessary to quote the language of the writer of the letter which Professor Münsterberg furnishes. It is manifestly difficult to answer charges of so general a nature as the writer makes. The general charge as to the arrest of American-born citizens on board neutral vessels and in British ports, the ignoring of their passports, and their confinement in jails, requires evidence to support it. That there have been cases of injustice of this sort is unquestionably true, but Americans in Germany have suffered in this way as Americans have in Great Britain. This Government has considered that the majority of these cases resulted from over-zealousness on the part of subordinate officials. Every case which has been brought to the attention of the Department of State has been promptly investigated, and, if the facts warranted, a demand for release has been made.

As to the censorship of mails, Germany as well as Great Britain has pursued this course in regard to private letters falling into their hands. The unquestioned right to adopt a measure of this sort makes objection to it inadvisable. As to the detention of non-combatants confined in concentration camps, all the belligerents, with perhaps the exception of Servia and Russia, have made similar complaints and those for whom this Government is acting have asked investigations, which representatives of this Government have made impartially. Their reports have shown that the treatment of prisoners is generally as good as possible under the conditions in all countries, and that there is no more reason to say they are "languishing" in one country than in another country or that this country has manifested a "supreme indifference" in the matter. As Department's efforts at investigations seemed to develop bitterness between the countries, the Department on November 20 sent a circular instruction to its representatives not to undertake further investigations of concentration camps.[15]

The representations to the Turkish Government relative to its threatening attitude toward the English, Russians and French and their consular officers were made upon the request of the Governments interested and pressed upon their suggestion.

NOTE No. 5. COMPLAINT AS TO DESTRUCTION OF AMERICAN MAIL
(Letter page 6)

No evidence has been filed with this Government, and no representations have been made that American mail on board of Dutch steamers has been "repeatedly destroyed". Until such a case is presented in concrete form, this Government would not be justified in presenting the matter to the offending belligerent. Complaints have come to the Department that mail on board neutral steamers has been opened and detained but there seem to be but few cases where the mail from neutral countries has not been finally delivered. When mail is sent to belligerent countries open and is of neutral and private character it has not been molested.

NOTE 6. TRANSSHIPMENT OF TROOPS AND WAR MATERIAL ACROSS AMERICAN TERRITORY (Letter page 7)

The Department has had no specific case of the shipment of convoys of troops across American territory brought to its notice. There have been reports to this effect but no actual facts have been presented. The transshipment of reservists of all belligerents including Austria, who have requested the privilege, has been permitted on condition that they travel as individuals and not as organized, uniformed or armed bodies. The German Embassy has advised the Department that it would not be likely to avail itself of the privilege.

Only two cases of the transit of war material across United States territory have come to Department's notice. One case was a request for shipment of Government arms and equipment across Alaska which was refused. Another was in regard to shipment of horses and mules on the Canadian Pacific Railway, to which Department replied that a commercial shipment not in the nature of a convoy of the Government such as is prohibited under Article 2 of Hague Convention No. 5, 1907,[16] was allowable.

---

[15] *Foreign Relations,* 1914, supp., p. 754.
[16] Malloy, *Treaties,* 1776–1909, vol. II, p. 2290.

As this Government is not now interested in the adoption of the Declaration of London by the belligerents, the modifications of the belligerents in that code of naval warfare are of no concern to it except in so far as they affect its rights and those of its citizens under international law. Insofar as these rights have been affected the Department has made every effort to obtain redress for violations suffered.

Note No. 7. The Honolulu Incident (Letter page 7)

It is assumed that reference is made to the internment of H. M. S. *Geier* and the German steamer *Locksun*. The *Geier* entered Honolulu on October 15th in an unseaworthy condition. The Captain reported the necessity of extensive repairs which would require an indefinite period for completion. The vessel was allowed the generous period of three weeks to November 7th to make repairs and leave the port or be interned; but a longer period was concluded to be out of the question, as a vessel could not claim time in which to repair a generally run down condition due to long sea service. A Japanese cruiser soon appeared off the port of Honolulu and the *Geier* chose internment rather than departure from the harbor. On October 30th the Department advised the German Ambassador of the proposed internment.[17]

The arrival of the *Geier* was followed soon after by that of the steamer *Locksun* which, it was found had delivered coal to the *Geier* en route and accompanied her toward Honolulu. As she had thus constituted herself a tender to the *Geier* she was accorded the same treatment and interned on November 7th.

Note No. 8. Coaling of warships in Panama Canal Zone (Letter page 7)

By Proclamation of November 13, 1914,[18] certain special instructions [sic] were placed on the coaling of warships or their tenders or colliers in the Canal Zone. These regulations were framed through the collaboration of the State, Navy and War Departments and without the slightest reference to favoritism to the belligerents. Before these regulations were proclaimed war vessels could procure coal of the Panama Railway in the Zone ports but no belligerent vessels are known to have done so. Under the Proclamation fuel may be taken on by belligerent warships only with the consent of the Canal authorities, and in such amounts as will enable them to reach the nearest accessible neutral port; and the amount so taken on shall be deducted

---

[17] *Foreign Relations*, 1914, supp., p. 584.
[18] *Ibid.*, p. 552.

from the amount procurable in United States ports within three months thereafter. Now it is charged the United States has shown partiality, because Great Britain and not Germany happens to have colonies in the near vicinity where British ships may coal while Germany has no such coaling facilities. Again it is intimated the United States should balance the inequalities of geographical position by refusal to allow any warships of belligerents to coal in the Canal until the war is over.

NOTE NO. 9. GERMAN COMPLAINT AGAINST BRITISH CHANGES IN DECLARATION OF LONDON (Letter page 7)

October 10 the German Foreign Office presented to the diplomats in Berlin a memorandum, calling attention to violations of, and changes in, the Declaration of London by the British Government and inquiring as to the attitude of the United States toward such action on the part of the Allies.[19] The substance of the memorandum was telegraphed to the Department October 22,[20] and was replied to shortly thereafter to the effect that the United States had withdrawn its suggestion made early in the war, for the adoption, for the sake of uniformity, of the Declaration of London as a temporary code of naval warfare during the present war, owing to the unwillingness of some of the belligerents to accept the Declaration without changes and modifications, and that thenceforth the United States would insist that the rights of the United States and its citizens in the war should be governed by the existing rules of international law.

ROBERT LANSING

763.72111/1332½

President Wilson to the Counselor for the Department of State (Lansing)

WASHINGTON, *December 10, 1914.*

MY DEAR MR. LANSING: Here is a telegram I have just received upon which I would value your comment. Are these gentlemen right in the position they take, do you think?

I did not mean to have you take Münsterberg's letter quite so seriously as you did. I fear that I put a great burden of unnecessary work on you, but I am heartily obliged to you for the results which reached me last evening.

Cordially and faithfully yours,

WOODROW WILSON

---

[19] For memorandum of the German Foreign Office, see *ibid.,* p. 263; for text of the Declaration of London, see *ibid.,* 1909, p. 318.

[20] See *ibid.,* 1914, supp., p. 259, footnote 3.

[Enclosure—Telegram]

Messrs. Paul Fuller, Benj. F. Tracy, and Frederic R. Coudert to President Wilson

NEW YORK, *December 8, 1914—8:30 p. m.*

Congressional action altering the rules of neutrality during warfare is contrary to accepted international law. Aiding the inefficiency of one belligerent to protect its purchases of arms by forbidding all exportation of arms to the other belligerent is an absolute violation of neutrality. The bills proposed by Representatives Vollmer and Bartholdt and by Senator Hitchcock, would, if enacted, put the United States surely on record as against the Allies.

PAUL FULLER
BENJ. F. TRACY
FREDERIC R. COUDERT

763.72111/1332½

The Counselor for the Department of State (Lansing) to President Wilson

WASHINGTON, *December 10, 1914.*

MY DEAR MR. PRESIDENT: I am in receipt of your letter of to-day asking me to comment upon a telegram, dated the 8th, from Paul Fuller, Benjamin F. Tracy and Frederic R. Coudert, in which they assert that Congressional alteration of the rules of neutrality during warfare is contrary to accepted international law and is an absolute violation of neutrality.

I think these gentlemen are entirely right in the general principle asserted. Any change in our statutes by amendment or repeal would undoubtedly benefit one or the other of the belligerents. Whatever the purpose of a change the belligerent, whose interests were unfavorably affected, would be justified in protesting on the ground that the legislation was for the advantage of its enemy, and, therefore, unneutral. I have in a general way referred to this in Comment III of the Memorandum on the Münsterberg letter (page 6).[21]

Some days ago I spoke to Secretary Bryan about this matter in anticipation of the introduction of bills in Congress for amendment of our neutrality statutes, and expressed an opinion substantially the same as that asserted by Messrs. Fuller, Tracy and Coudert.

At that time I called his attention to another application of the same principle which would come up at the meeting of the Governing Board of the Pan American Union. Briefly the point was this:

---

[21] *Ante*, p. 169.

If this principle was applied to the various schemes of neutralization of certain sea areas and of changing the general rules as to the treatment of belligerent warships, which had been suggested by certain South American republics, such changes would necessarily be unneutral because they would unequally affect the interests of the belligerents; and, unless the belligerents unanimously consented to them, their adoption would be a justifiable ground for complaint. The conclusion was that, as it was manifestly impossible to obtain unanimous consent, no modification of existing rules should be adopted during the present wars, though neutral rights and duties might be profitably considered informally by a Commission looking to future action after the wars were over.

I also discussed the subject in a confidential way with the Argentine Ambassador, who agreed entirely in the opinion that any present change in the rules would be unneutral and impracticable, and who suggested that a Commission be named for an informal exchange of views upon the subject. This was adopted by the Board at its meeting.

There is, however, another type of legislation in relation to the enforcement of neutral duties, which I do not think can be construed into an unneutral act and which it may be advisable, if not necessary, to enact. There are certain obligations as to neutral conduct imposed by treaties, which have never been incorporated in our laws so that the Executive possesses no power to prevent and the courts no power to penalize violations. The result is that, in attempting to enforce these obligations, we are skating on pretty thin ice, and if the authority of the officials should be questioned I am afraid of the result.

Furthermore, some of the penalties imposed by our present statutes are so inadequate that an offender would willingly suffer the penalty for the privilege of violation.

As legislation of this sort, affecting treaty provisions and statutes, would in no way change the rules of neutral conduct but would only confer powers for the proper enforcement of existing rules, there would be no element of unneutrality in its enactment.

I have taken up this matter with Mr. Warren, the Assistant Attorney General having charge of neutrality cases, with the object of curing in some way this embarrassing state of the law which materially affects the proper enforcement of neutrality.

The telegram is herewith returned.[22]

Very sincerely yours,

ROBERT LANSING

---

[22] *Supra.*

763.72111/1333½

President Wilson to the Counselor for the Department of State
(Lansing)

WASHINGTON, *December 14, 1914.*

MY DEAR MR. LANSING: Thank you very warmly for the trouble you have taken in sending a full reply to my inquiry about the telegram from Messrs. Fuller, Tracy, and Coudert. I now feel fully fortified in the matter.

Cordially and faithfully yours,

WOODROW WILSON

763.72119/35½e

The Secretary of State to President Wilson

WASHINGTON, *December 17, 1914.*

MY DEAR MR. PRESIDENT: Mr. House will call your attention to a suggestion which was made to me by one of the South American Representatives and I am inclined to think there is some force in it. You have not failed to notice the increasing urgency with which the neutral nations are presenting the idea of mediation or of some form of protections from the burdens of this war. The sentiment is unanimous among the South American countries that something ought to be done to protect the neutral nations if the war is to continue. The same idea has been presented by some of the neutral nations of Europe. A recent dispatch says that the kings of Norway, Sweden and Denmark are to meet for the purpose of considering what can be done to lessen these burdens. The Venezuelan Minister yesterday handed me a suggestion to the effect that you call a meeting of all of the neutral nations to be held in Washington for the purpose of considering the proposition to be submitted later to a convention in which all the nations, neutral and belligerent, will be represented. I think, however, that the idea of Mr. House, which I have mentioned, is the most feasible one, namely, that you invite all the nations, belligerent and neutral, to send representatives to a conference to be held in Washington for the purpose of considering ways and means by which the burdens borne by the neutral nations may be minimized with the consent and agreement of the belligerent nations. The belligerents could not take exception of [*to*] it, were it understood that the changes were to be made through agreement with the belligerents, and I am sure it would appeal to all the neutral nations. The one who suggested this plan had in mind the possibility of its opening the way to mediation. He thinks that it would give you an opportunity to make an address of welcome which might be helpful in advancing the cause of mediation without directly referring to it. He thinks that the coming together of these representatives, even for the consideration of questions growing out of the war and yet not involving the subject of mediation might lay the foundation for some coming together of the belligerent nations. I am very much impressed with the idea and with the possibilities for good. It seemed to commend itself to Mr. House also, although he only had time to think of it for a moment. It is at his suggestion that I bring the matter up this evening in order that you may talk with him about it more fully and let me know your impressions.

With assurances [etc.]　　　　　　　　　　　　W. J. BRYAN

763.72111 Em 1/1

The Counselor for the Department of State (Lansing) to President Wilson

WASHINGTON, *December 23, 1914.*

DEAR MR. PRESIDENT: Referring to my letter to you of the 9th instant, enclosing a memorandum on a letter of Professor Münsterberg dated November 19th, I have the honor to enclose as of possible interest to you, a copy of a note of the German Ambassador dated the 15th instant [23] in relation to supplies of coal for belligerent warships, and the use of neutral ports as bases of naval operations. You will recall that in my memorandum, Notes 2 and 3, the complaints in regard to the unlimited sale of ammunition to belligerents were replied to on the grounds of the rights of citizens of neutral countries to trade with the belligerents in time of war. The German note is of particular interest in this connection as it supports the views expressed in my memorandum, in that the Imperial Government admit that the adversaries of Germany in the present war are authorized to draw from the United States "Contraband of war, especially arms worth several billions of marks," and that under the general principles of international law no exception can be taken "to neutral States letting war material go to Germany's enemies from or to neutral territory."

Very sincerely yours,

ROBERT LANSING

---

[23] *Foreign Relations*, 1914, supp., p. 646.

763.72111/1334½

The Counselor for the Department of State (Lansing) to the Secretary of State

[WASHINGTON,] *December 26, 1914.*

DEAR MR. SECRETARY: I prepared sometime ago, as you will recall, a memorandum for the President upon a letter written by Professor Münsterberg setting forth in concrete form the complaints of Germany's sympathizers in this country as to the policy and conduct of the Administration in relation to neutral rights and neutral duties. I believe that these complaints are entirely unjustified and can be answered conclusively, and that the memorandum, which I hastily prepared, forms a basis for such answers.

These complaints are still being widely circulated among our people of German birth and descent and are undoubtedly alienating many of them from their political allegiance to the Democratic Party. This hostility is largely the result of false statements as to the course pursued by the Government and of ignorance of the rights and duties of a neutral nation. However unjustified the complaints may be, there can be no doubt of their political effect. Thousands of former friends of the Administration are being converted into bitter adversaries; and this is going on day after day by reason of the propaganda which is being carried on in an apparent effort to force the Government to adopt a policy favorable to Germany regardless of the fact that to do so would be a breach of neutrality.

It seems to me that as a matter of political expediency some steps should be taken to refute the unjust charges which are being made against the Administration and to explain to the public, particularly the pro-German element, the actual situation and what the Government can do and cannot do as a neutral power.

Furthermore, it seems to me that these steps should be taken as soon as possible. The movement has gained much headway, and, like a snow ball rolling down hill, it increases in size and impetus as it advances. The longer it goes on the more difficult it will be to check it.

I have already spoken to you of this matter in a casual way, but, as I am becoming more and more impressed with the strength of the movement and with the serious political consequences which will follow if nothing is done to interrupt it, I venture to call the matter more definitely to your attention.

Very sincerely yours,

ROBERT LANSING

763.72111/1335½

President Wilson to the Secretary of State

WASHINGTON, *December 29, 1914.*

MY DEAR MR. SECRETARY: I have your letter of December twenty-sixth [24] enclosing the letter from Mr. Lansing, which I herewith return.[25]

I hope you will exercise your own judgment entirely as to the method and subject matter of publicity in regard to the German protest and our reply. I agree with you that the essential matter is to get before the public the admission of the German Government with regard to the sale of munitions of war.

Cordially and faithfully yours,

WOODROW WILSON

763.72111/1394½

The Counselor for the Department of State (Lansing) to the Secretary of State [26]

[WASHINGTON,] *January 1, 1915.*

DEAR MR. SECRETARY: Reverting to our conversation the other day relative to the unjustifiable charges of partiality for Great Britain and her allies in the enforcement of neutrality by this Administration, which are publicly made by Germans and their American sympathizers, I have been considering the means which might be employed to meet these charges which are undoubtedly believed to be true by many of our citizens.

I assume

(1st) that the answer should be made for publication in the press in order that it may reach those who have read the charges;
(2nd) that the answer should traverse the charges seriatim;
(3rd) that the answer should have an official character; and
(4th) that the answer should not be addressed to private individuals who have made complaint to the President or the Secretary of State.

The following means suggest themselves:

First. An address in the Senate by the Chairman of the Committee on Foreign Relations setting forth the charges and answers in detail.

Second. A letter to the Secretary of State from the Chairman of the Committee on Foreign Relations or from the Chairman of the

---

[24] Not found in Department files.
[25] *Supra.*
[26] This paper bears the notation: "Handed to Secy Jany 4/15 RL."

Committee on Foreign Affairs setting forth the charges and asking to be advised as to the facts and the action of the Department.

Third. A public statement by the Secretary of State based upon the fact that numerous communications have been received by the Department showing misapprehension of the facts and the law and consequent unjust criticism of the action of the Government in performing its neutral obligations.

Fourth. A request by the Secretary of State upon the Counselor for the Department for a memorandum setting forth the charges made and the facts and law relative to the several charges for transmittal to the President or the Chairman of the Foreign Relations or Foreign Affairs Committees.

Fifth. An oral statement by the President in a public address or otherwise in which the charges are taken up separately and answered in detail.

As to which means would best accomplish the purpose (i. e., a clear public statement of the facts and a refutation of the several complaints which have been made) I express no opinion. That is largely a question of political expediency and of the degree of official character with which the statement should be impressed. In determining it the fact should be borne in mind that any answer to the charges made is in the nature of a defense of the conduct of the Government and that the charges are not official but are made by private persons in letters and publications. On the other hand, thousands have read and believe the charges. I do not think that unofficial denials and refutations will change this belief. The answers to be effective must be explicit and emanate from an official source.

In regard to the first means suggested (a speech in the Senate) I fear that it would not be given the same weight as a statement issued by the President or by the Secretary of State.

In regard to the fifth means (an oral statement by the President) I am not sure that it could be done in an address since it would be difficult to enter into the details of fact which constitute conclusive answers to the charges. There can be no doubt of course but that an utterance by the President would have the greatest influence in dispelling the misapprehensions which exist; on the other hand, I cannot but question whether the charges should be dignified to such an extent. However, that is a matter upon which I do not presume to make suggestions.

Whatever course is adopted I do not think that it would be wise to answer by letter to a private individual or even to a Senator or Representative unless he acted as Chairman of one of the Committees charged with the conduct of our foreign affairs. To do so would hardly comport with the dignity of the Government and would establish a dangerous precedent. If one correspondent was answered, it would be difficult to avoid answering others making different complaints. Furthermore silence as to some charges might be construed into admission of their truth.

Appended are the principal charges which have been published against the Government by those in the United States who advocate the cause of Germany and Austria.

Very sincerely yours,

ROBERT LANSING

[Enclosure]

Charges of Partiality for Great Britain, France, and Russia Made Against the Government of the United States by Sympathizers With Germany and Austria

1. Freedom of communication by submarine cables but censorship of wireless messages.

2. Submission to censorship of mails and in some cases to the repeated destruction of American letters found on neutral vessels.

3. The search of American vessels for German and Austrian subjects—

(*a*) On the high seas.
(*b*) In territorial waters of a belligerent.

4. Submission without protest to English violations of the rules regarding absolute and conditional contraband, as laid down

(*a*) In the Hague Conventions.
(*b*) In International Law.
(*c*) In the Declaration of London.

5. Submission without protest to inclusion of copper in the list of absolute contraband.

6. Submission without protest to interference with American trade to neutral countries

(*a*) In conditional contraband.
(*b*) In absolute contraband.

7. Submission without protest to interruption of trade in conditional contraband consigned to private persons in Germany and Austria, thereby supporting the policy of Great Britain to cut off all supplies from Germany and Austria.

8. Submission to British interruption of trade in petroleum, rubber, leather, wool, etc.

9. No interference with the sale to Great Britain and her allies of arms, ammunition, horses, uniforms and other munitions of war, although such sales prolong the war.

10. No suppression of sale of dumdum bullets to Great Britain.

11. British warships are permitted to lie off American ports and intercept neutral vessels.

12. Submission without protest to disregard by Great Britain and her allies of

    (*a*) American naturalization certificates.
    (*b*) American passports.

13. Change of policy in regard to loans to belligerents

    (*a*) General loans.
    (*b*) Credit loans.

14. Submission to arrest of native born Americans on neutral vessels and in British ports and their imprisonment.

15. Indifference to confinement of non-combatants in detention camps in England and France.

16. Failure to prevent transshipment of British troops and war material across the territory of the United States.

17. Treatment and final internment of German S. S. *Geier* and the collier *Locksun* at Honolulu.

18. Unfairness to Germany in rules relative to coaling of warships in Panama Canal Zone.

19. Failure to protest against the modifications of the Declaration of London by the British Government.

20. General unfriendly attitude of Government toward Germany and Austria.

QUERY. Should not attention be called to the fact that German subjects are interfering in our domestic politics and seeking to arouse political opposition to the Administration?

763.72111/1396½

The Counselor for the Department of State (Lansing) to the Secretary of State

WASHINGTON, *January 9, 1915.*

DEAR MR. SECRETARY: In compliance with your request I herewith enclose a proposed public statement setting forth the attitude of this Government as to a protest by it for alleged violation of the neutrality of Belgium.

The statement follows the lines of my memorandum to you dated January 7, 1915 [27] and embodies your amendments to that memorandum.

    Very sincerely yours,

                        ROBERT LANSING

---

[27] Not printed.

[Enclosure]

Proposed Statement for the Press

Since the outbreak of the European war and the invasion of Belgium by the armies of the German Empire a great number of communications have been received from individuals and organizations in this country asking or demanding the Government to protest against the violation of Belgian neutrality by Germany on the ground that such neutrality was secured by the Hague Conventions to which the United States and Germany were parties.

It seems expedient that the attitude of this Government in regard to its right and duty as a party to the Hague Conventions in relation to Belgian neutrality should be made public in order that the people may not be deceived by the incorrect assumptions as to our duty as a neutral power which constitute the foundation for criticism of the Administration's failure to protest to the German Government.

In the first place it should be pointed out that those who advocate action by this Government fail to discriminate between a neutralized State and a neutral State. The neutrality of the two classes is essentially different and is founded on different principles.

The neutrality of a neutralized State (such as Belgium, Switzerland, Luxembourg, etc.,) is a matter of conventional agreement between powers, which are interested in preventing the State from being absorbed politically by any one of such powers. The treaty, which declares the neutralization of the State, is in fact a guaranty that the parties to the treaty will not deprive the State of independence or invade its neutrality.

The neutrality of a neutral State is a condition, in which all nations other than the belligerents find themselves immediately upon the outbreak of an international war.

The Hague Conventions have nothing to do with the neutrality of a neutralized State or with the guarantees to preserve such neutrality. Only the powers which are parties to the neutralization agreement have a legal right to complain of its violation. To agreements of that sort the United States is not and has not been a party. It would be manifestly improper for this Government to complain of the violation of a treaty to which it was not a party.

So far, therefore, as the invasion of Belgium may be considered a breach of guaranty by Germany to preserve its character as a neutralized State this Government has neither the duty nor the right to protest.

As regards the violation of the neutrality of Belgium as a neutral State the provision in the Hague Conventions relative thereto is found in Article 1 of Convention No. V of 1907,[28] entitled "Convention respecting the Rights and duties of Neutral Powers and Persons in case of War". It reads as follows:

"The territory of neutral powers is inviolable."

Article 20 of the Convention provides:

"The provisions of the present convention do not apply except between contracting powers, and then only if all the belligerents are parties to the convention.["]

The right or duty to enter protest against a violation of a provision of the Hague Conventions is not affirmatively set forth in the documents themselves. If the right or duty exists it must arise from the nature of the undertakings. It will not be questioned but that this Government has the right to protest against any violation of a convention in force when the interests of the United States or of its citizens are involved. But this is not the case in regard to the violation of the neutral territory of Belgium. It does not affect American rights or interests, but those of the Belgians. It is necessary, therefore, to consider the nature of the undertaking to which the ratifying powers subscribed.

While the form of the Hague Conventions is that of a joint undertaking, the adoption of that form was, in the view of this Government, for the sake of convenience and not for the purpose of binding the parties to joint action in case of violation by one of them; and this is evidenced by the fact that there is no provision authorizing joint action by the parties. The same end would have been attained had each of the parties entered into an identical treaty with each one of the other powers. To avoid so cumbersome a method and the repetition of ratification and exchanges the form of the Hague Conventions was adopted and provision was made for the deposit of the ratifications at The Hague. In a word, the undertaking is several and not joint. It lacks entirely the element of a joint obligation imposed by the guaranty of the treaties which neutralize the Kingdom of Belgium.

In view of the several character of the undertakings incorporated in The Hague Conventions the United States would have no right and would even less be charged with the duty to make protest or demand explanation as to an alleged violation unless the rights or interests of the United States or its citizens are affected.

---

[28] Malloy, *Treaties*, 1776–1909, vol. II, p. 2290.

763.72111/1396½

The Secretary of State to President Wilson

WASHINGTON, *January 9, 1915.*

MY DEAR MR. PRESIDENT: I enclose a statement [29] which, with your approval, I will give out to the press, in regard to the demands made upon us to protest against the invasion of Belgium by Germany. Mr. Lansing prepared a memorandum to which I made some amendments and this statement is the result of our conference on the subject. If you will return Mr. Lansing's letter and this statement with such corrections as you wish to make, I will give the statement out early next week.

With assurances [etc.]   W. J. BRYAN

763.72111/1397½

President Wilson to the Secretary of State

[WASHINGTON,] *12 January, 1915.*

MY DEAR MR. SECRETARY: I find myself regretting that it is necessary to say anything on this subject.

This note is entirely sound and conclusive from the lawyer's point of view; [30] but I fear that it will make the impression of a technical defense against the charge that we have not performed a duty suggested by moral considerations and the general sense of thoughtful men throughout the world.

Will you not think of it again in this light, and give me your final impression?

Faithfully,

W. W.

763.72111/1398½

The Counselor for the Department of State (Lansing) to the Secretary of State

[WASHINGTON,] *January 13, 1915.*

DEAR MR. SECRETARY: The President's comment I feel is justified from the standpoint of policy and I had the moral question in mind when preparing the statement.

The difficulty of considering the moral ground of a protest lies in the fact that, if it can be held that this Government is morally bound to protest against the violation of Belgian neutrality, it has been delinquent in not having done so long ago, since over five months have passed since the act occurred.

---

[29] *Supra.*
[30] The reference apparently is to the proposed statement for the press, p. 189.

Furthermore, if a moral obligation exists in this case, is not the obligation equally strong as to the dropping of bombs on Antwerp and Paris, and possibly as to burning of Louvain and the bombardment of the cathedral at Rheims? If there is no conflict of evidence as to the facts, moral obligation may be appealed to in these cases.

Would we not admit that there is possibly a moral obligation by discussing it?

Our defense that we have no legal right, much less a legal duty, is one which explains our long silence.

If we discuss the moral obligations of this Government as to Germany's treatment of Belgium will it do more than invite controversy and criticism as to the extent of such obligations?

In view of the flood of letters, which the Department has received on this subject, it seemed as if a statement of some sort should be made.

While the argument of legal right is perhaps narrow, can we safely go further?

Very sincerely yours,

ROBERT LANSING

763.72111/1674½

The Counselor for the Department of State (Lansing) to the Secretary of State [31]

[WASHINGTON,] *January 23, 1915.*

DEAR MR. SECRETARY: I have read the President's memorandum of the 12th relative to the proposed statement for the press setting forth the Government's position in regard to a protest against German violation of the neutrality of Belgium.

The necessity of making a statement is of course a matter of debate. We cannot ignore the fact that the Department is receiving daily communications from all over the country asking the reasons for our failure to protest. It is an increasing embarrassment not to be able to reply to these inquiries.

Furthermore, I feel that there is public feeling, which is growing stronger, that the Government is shirking a responsibility, which as a party to The Hague Conventions it is bound to assume. Not only is this shown in private letters but also in articles published in newspapers and periodicals. I may over-estimate the importance of this feeling upon the attitude of many of our people toward the Administration, but it seems to me that something ought to be done to check it. Whether the proposed statement is the best way is another matter.

[31] This paper bears the notation: "Approved W. J. B[ryan]."

I appreciate the force of the President's comment as to the apparent technical character of the explanation which is made in the proposed statement. I think, however, that the violation of a treaty such as that neutralizing Belgium is the violation of a legal right and not a natural right. The guaranty of neutralization was in the interest of the guarantors rather than of Belgium. It was a compromise of conflicting national interests entered into by the parties to preserve the balance of power; the integrity of Belgium was incident to the compromise and not its primary object. The agreement was purely political in character.

I think in all frankness it should be said that, while the German breach of the contract of guaranty may possibly be viewed as an immoral act, it may also be viewed as injurious to the rights of the other guarantor powers and a menace to their national safety in destroying the political equilibrium which it was intended to preserve. Great Britain in making the breach a *casus belli* has declared her action to be based on ethical rather than political grounds and has appealed to the conscience of the world for justification. The fact should not be ignored, however, that her political interest coincides with her conception of international morality in this case. If it were otherwise, I am not convinced that righteous indignation alone would have induced the British Government to declare war.

In the case of violations of the rules of humane warfare, such as the dropping of bombs from aircraft on unfortified towns, the indiscriminate sowing of contact mines in the open sea, and the bombardment of unprotected seaports without even giving notice of the proposed attack, natural rights as well as legal rights are invaded. These practices may well be classed as inhumane and, therefore, immoral. It may not be unreasonable to claim that methods of warfare of this sort invite the condemnation and protest of all civilized nations, and that a neutral power is morally bound to exert its influence to prevent their practice. Yet this Government, in spite of the fact that the evidence of the employment of these improper methods is uncontradicted and conclusive, has remained silent and made no effort to check the belligerents.

I do not refer to our failure to protest against these practices by way of criticism because I believe that the moral duty was doubtful and the policy of silence was wise. I only wish to call attention to the fact that the moral duty, if any, is far more evident in such cases than in the case of a right dependent solely upon a treaty stipulation.

Violations of treaties have occurred frequently in the past without calling forth protests from nations not parties to the treaties unless their interests were affected. The recent breach of the Berlin Treaty by Austria–Hungary when she annexed Bosnia and Herzegovina and the invasion by Great Britain of the South African Republics passed without objection by this Government. Both of these violations of agreements affected the territorial integrity and sovereignty of independent states. That is all that the German invasion of Belgium has done.

A treaty violation of this sort is morally wrong when the motive is bad or when an imperative necessity does not compel the violation. It cannot be denied that national safety may justify a nation in violating its solemn pledges. Who is to judge whether the breach of a treaty is justifiable or unjustifiable? Who is to decide whether a government's motives are good or bad?

It seems to me that a nation, which is not a party to a treaty violated, must assume this judicial character, if it enters protest against the violation and condemns the conduct of the violator as immoral. I do not think that international ethics impose such a responsibility upon a nation or furnish an excuse for it to sit in judgment on the motives and necessities of other nations.

Furthermore, the moral duty of this Government to make protest against Germany's conduct has not been emphasized in the complaints, which have been made as to our failure to protest. The legal right and the legal duty to do so have been constantly asserted and argued on the basis that the United States is a party to The Hague Conventions. If the fallacy of that argument can be shown and it can be established that no legal right or duty to act exists, it is my judgment that the present agitation will decrease and that the Government will be relieved of much unjustifiable criticism by those who honestly believe that we are legally bound to protest.

It comes down then to the following questions:

Is the need to state the Government's policy as to Belgian neutrality sufficient to overcome the expediency of continued silence on the subject?

If a statement is made, is it wise or necessary to go beyond a discussion of legal right and duty?

What replies are to be made by the Department to its many correspondents in case no statement is issued?

Very sincerely yours,

ROBERT LANSING

763.72111/1675½

President Wilson to the Counselor for the Department of State
(Lansing)

WASHINGTON, *January 29, 1915.*

MY DEAR MR. LANSING: The enclosed letter is from a genuine friend of peace and Americanism and who is intelligently active in trying to correct the gross misapprehensions and prejudices which have prevailed among some of our fellow-citizens of German extraction. I think that his suggestion in the enclosed letter is a very interesting and important one. I am writing to ask if the complaints of the friends of the Allies have been formulated in a way which would give us an opportunity to treat them as we have treated the complaints of the other side. Perhaps this could be done in connection with the letter about Belgium.

Cordially and sincerely yours,

WOODROW WILSON

[Enclosure]

The Editor of the "Milwaukee Journal" (L. W. Nieman) to President Wilson

[MILWAUKEE, WIS.,] *January 26, 1915.*

MY DEAR MR. PRESIDENT: I forgot to ask you for a companion statement from the State department, dealing with the complaints of friends of the allies. This would greatly strengthen the answer to the partisans of Germany. In no other way could the difficulties of our government be so strikingly brought home to the crowd on both sides. To be useful, this statement should come soon and should not be confined to the case of Belgium, but should also take up minor matters. I went somewhat into details with Mr. McAdoo and Mr. Tumulty.

Very sincerely yours,

L. W. NIEMAN

763.72111/1689½

The Counselor for the Department of State (Lansing) to President Wilson

WASHINGTON, *February 9, 1915.*

DEAR MR. PRESIDENT: I thought you might like to read the enclosed personal letter which I have received from Judge Dickinson, formerly Secretary of War, which it seemed to me contained much worthy of consideration.

Kindly return the letter to me after reading as I have not replied to it.[32]

Very sincerely yours,

ROBERT LANSING

[32] On February 11 the President replied: "It is a pleasure to read letters like the enclosed. They are so exactly in line with the facts and the right way of dealing with them. Thank you for letting me see it." (File No. 763.72111/1690½.)

[Enclosure]

Judge J. M. Dickinson to the Counselor for the Department of State
(Lansing)

CHICAGO, *February 6, 1915.*

MY DEAR MR. LANSING: Recent international developments are giving very great concern to all thoughtful and patriotic people. It seems to me that it will be a prudent and safe course to make a clear, firm and timely declaration in case the newspaper reports as to the attitude of Germany in respect to neutral ships shall be confirmed.

A reproduction in the *Chicago Tribune* today of editorials from German papers shows clearly that their understanding is that Germany will proceed to enforce what it calls a blockade by destruction of ships by means of submarines. This, in the nature of things, means that there can be no reasonable steps taken in advance to ascertain the nationality of the ships attacked. The reason for this course seems to be founded upon the alleged statement that the British Government has secretly authorized its ships to use the flags of neutral nations. The paper this morning indicates that our State Department will inquire into this. It seems to me that this fact, however it may be, can have no bearing on the question. The British Government by such a course cannot take away our right to hold the German Government responsible if it attacks and destroys the property and lives of Americans under our flag. We probably would have ground to protest against such action of the British Government, but such action could not warrant the German Government in such destruction. It is at most a paper blockade, and is to be carried out not by stopping and examining ships, and determining their nationality, or by taking them into a Prize Court where all questions can be adjudicated, but by destroying them without the possibility of ascertaining the true nationality.

If any Government should do this under such circumstances, it would be a wanton and unjustifiable attack, and would call for immediate action on our part.

My reading and my own observation of personal affairs have led me to the conclusion that a clear and firm declaration in advance generally tends to obviate such extreme action as will force a collision, while on the other hand a failure so to do often brings about the very thing that we most desire to avoid. In this nations and individuals are the same, and a timely and explicit warning is wholesome with both. I have seen many personal difficulties avoided by taking a clear, firm and just stand in the beginning, and have seen them brought about because aggressions have advanced slowly, step by step, and to a point which they would not have reached if the consequences had been clearly understood.

Therefore it seems to me that if it shall become clear that Germany may in the course of events, in pursuance of this policy, destroy American ships while legitimately under the protection of the American flag, we should now make a clear and firm declaration as to what our attitude will be. In my judgment it should be that we will protect our flag at all hazards.

Now you know I am a Peace man. I say this in the interest of Peace and as a Peace measure, for I have often seen for the want of such timely action affairs drift gradually into a condition where drastic action becomes unavoidable.

We are in a most delicate situation, and it requires not only justice but firmness to keep us out of complications. We cannot expect, however just we may be, to escape severe criticism, and that from people and newspapers of all the belligerents.

The papers report much severe criticism of Secretary Bryan in Germany and some in England. This cannot be avoided. It is about the best evidence that the recent position taken by him in his letter was correct.[33] I think it was eminently correct. If it had pleased one side it would not have stood the test. The fact that there are those in both England and Germany who severely criticized it, is no evidence of it being unsound, but is evidence of the highly excited condition in which those people are. Any neutral that pursues a just course is bound to excite more or less the antagonism of both contending parties. You will recall how this was in respect of the attitude of England during the Civil War. Both the North and South criticized it. I do not refer to her example then as a proper one to follow, but merely to illustrate how hard it is for a neutral country to avoid the hostility of contending parties. Many of them think that those who are not actively for them are against them. This is the human nature of the thing, and it often manifests itself in governmental action. While there is some disposition to make party capital out of the action of our Government, I believe that the overwhelming judgment in this country is that the Administration has acted in the main wisely in our foreign relations, including those with Mexico. Even those who at one time advocated a more strenuous attitude toward Mexico now realize that it is fortunate for our country that in the midst of this great international turmoil we have not a Mexican war on our hands.

While such a war in and of itself would not be serious, there is no telling in these complicated conditions what reflex action it might have and what it might lead to. Therefore we breathe easier because we have no such war.

---

[33] Letter of Jan. 20, 1915, to Senator Stone, *Foreign Relations*, 1914, supp. p. VII.

I did not intend to inflict so long a letter upon you but I, in common with many with whom I talk, am deeply disturbed over the situation, and am most anxious that we shall not become involved in any way in this European trouble. I know that the Department of State has information that the people at large have not, and for this reason accept and support whatever course it may take as the wise one, for I am convinced that the Secretary of State is filled with the utmost desire to maintain our neutrality in all honorable ways.

With cordial remembrances to Mrs. Lansing and General and Mrs. Foster, I am [etc.]

J. M. DICKINSON

763.72111/1675½

The Counselor for the Department of State (Lansing) to President Wilson

WASHINGTON, February 10, 1915.

DEAR MR. PRESIDENT: I return herewith the letter from Mr. Nieman [34] which you were good enough to let me see in which he urges the issuance of a statement of the Government's reasons for failure to protest against Germany's conduct as a belligerent.

Confirmatory of Mr. Nieman's opinion as to the advisability of a statement of this sort Mr. McKelway, the correspondent of *Harper's Weekly*, called upon me today, and said that he wished that the Government's position could be made public as recent articles in periodicals showed that "since Colonel Roosevelt set the ball rolling it was still in the public mind." (The metaphor of a "ball" being "in the public mind" I disavow.)

Personally I have felt that criticism on this subject was dying out, but as both Mr. Nieman and Mr. McKelway are better judges of public opinion than I am, I presume that I am wrong.

I am handing to Secretary Bryan today a memorandum for a statement on our position together with a letter explaining the reasons for the treatment of the subject adopted.[35]

I also enclose a reported statement of Sir Edward Grey, appearing in today's papers, which will have a tendency to encourage the critics to renewed activity.[36]

Very sincerely yours,

ROBERT LANSING

---

[34] *Ante*, p. 195.
[35] For the memorandum and its covering letter, see *infra*.
[36] Not enclosed with file copy of this letter.

763.72111/1679½

The Counselor for the Department of State (Lansing) to the Secretary of State

WASHINGTON, *February 10, 1915.*

DEAR MR. SECRETARY: I submit herewith for your consideration a memorandum for a public statement by letter or otherwise relative to the criticisms which have been made of the failure of this Government, as a party to the Hague Conventions, to protest against alleged violations of those conventions by Germany.

I confess that I am by no means satisfied with the tone of the memorandum submitted. It is a cold legal statement of our position. It sounds almost brutal in that it evinces no humanitarian motives, no solicitude for the suffering. While I feel that the arguments are sound and will appeal to those who realize that a government must regulate its conduct by law even at the expense of sentiment, I am not at all sure that the average citizen, who feels abhorrence at a belligerent's disregard of the rules of civilized warfare, will be convinced that this Government had not a right or duty to protest against such practices.

While, as you know, I have felt that the pressure of criticism was such as to require some explanation of the Government's continued silence, I now have some doubts as to whether it is expedient. The presentation of our reasons, in spite of the fact that I have endeavored in the last few paragraphs of the statement to consider the subject from the standpoint of international justice, sounds selfish and cold-blooded. I may be supersensitive and misjudge its effect on public opinion, but I consider it my duty to express to you the uncertainty which I feel as to how far this statement will go in quieting the complaints which have been made. It is in fact possible that it may cause controversy and arouse additional criticism of the Government on the ground that it has adopted a low standard of conduct.

As to whether the need of explanation is sufficiently great to overcome the possible results I am not willing to give an opinion.

I should also direct your attention to the fact that it has seemed to me inexpedient to enter into a full discussion of the nature of the undertakings of the contracting powers in the Hague Conventions. It would require technical treatment and could not in my judgment be put in a form suitable for popular consumption. In view of the facts in each case and the treaty provisions applicable it does not seem necessary.

I have, however, raised the question toward the close of the memorandum in order that it may not be charged that the Department considers the Hague Conventions to be joint in nature and thereby be held to have possibly admitted a legal right to protest in every case of treaty violation by a belligerent, whether or not it affects American rights.

While the several character of these Conventions can, I believe, be conclusively shown by argument as a matter of law, the practical reason for holding this position is the one emphasized. If the Conventions are joint undertakings, which must be held if the general right to protest against a violation by a belligerent can be maintained, then the nullifying articles in the Conventions apply equally to belligerents and neutrals and all the provisions become inoperative in the present war in case one or more of the belligerents has failed to ratify. In such a case (hardly a Convention is not defective in this particular) a neutral contracting power not only is deprived of a general right to protest a violation, but also loses the special right to protest if its rights or those of its nationals are impaired. Thus, nothing is to be gained by maintaining the joint nature of the agreements.

On the other hand, if the Conventions are several in nature, the nullifying articles would be construed as effective between belligerents, but as having no force in matters involving the relations between a belligerent and a neutral. Thus, by adopting this view as to the nature of the Conventions, the United States, while it would have no general right to protest, would have the special right to do so in case its rights or those of its citizens, as defined by the Conventions, were affected by a belligerent's violation of a treaty provision.

From the point of view of expediency as well as of legality the position, that the agreements entered into at The Hague are several and not joint in nature, would conserve American neutral rights as well as relieving this Government of a duty to intervene diplomatically when the rights of other powers appear to be impaired by the breach of a Hague Convention.

Very sincerely yours,

ROBERT LANSING

[Enclosure]

Memorandum for a Statement Relative to the Public Criticism of the Government for Its Failure, as a Party to the Hague Conventions, to Protest Against the Action of the German Military Forces in Invading Belgium, in Dropping Bombs From Aircraft, in Destroying the Cathedral of Rheims and Other Monuments of Religion, History and Art, in Using Dum-Dum Bullets and in Planting Contact Mines in the High Seas [37]

[WASHINGTON,] *February 9, 1915.*

First. In considering the invasion of Belgium it should be pointed out that there appears to be a general failure to discriminate between neutralized states and neutral states, or to appreciate that the neutrality of the two classes is essentially different in purpose and founded upon different principles.

The neutrality of neutralized states is a matter of conventional agreement between powers who are more or less interested in preventing the state from being absorbed politically by any power, or from becoming a base of military operations or from otherwise assisting neighboring rival states. The agreement imposes a condition of permanent neutrality. It is in fact a guaranty not only by the neutralized state that it will not engage in aggressive warfare, but also by the other parties to the treaty that it will not be attacked by any of them. These restraining conditions are purely contractual and are imposed and perpetuated from without. They do not exist by virtue of the rules of international law or the customs of nations, but solely by the treaties creating them.

The neutrality of a neutral state on the other hand, is a condition which a nation other than the belligerents may assume voluntarily and regardless of treaty provisions upon the outbreak of an international war. It is optional with such a nation to join in the war or to remain neutral. If it is determined to choose an attitude of neutrality then international law imposes certain rights and duties upon it as a neutral state. But this attitude may be changed at will and the neutral may enter the war on either side. It is this optional nature of the neutrality of a neutral state that distinguishes it from the permanent neutrality of a neutralized state. It is solely with the rights and duties of a neutral state that the Hague Conventions on neutrality deal. They do not deal with the neutralization of a state or with the guaranties of the interested powers to preserve its neutralized status. Only those powers, which are by agreement mutual guarantors of the neutralization of the state have a legal right under

---

[37] This paper bears the notation: "This memo. was laid before Cabinet today and it was decided not to make a statement at the present time. Robert Lansing. 2/16/15."

the agreement to complain of its violation. To an agreement of that sort in reference to Belgium the United States is not and has not been a party. Such an agreement is a matter of European politics, a condition resulting from conflicting interests. It would manifestly be improper for this Government to complain of the violation of a treaty of neutralization, to which it was not a party.

So far, therefore, as the invasion of Belgium may be considered a breach by Germany of a guaranty to preserve the character of Belgium as a neutralized state this Government has neither the legal right nor duty to protest.

In respect to the violation of the neutrality of Belgium as a neutral state during an international war the Hague Conventions contain certain stipulations in Article 1 of Convention of 1907,[38] entitled "Convention respecting the Rights and Duties of Neutral Powers and Persons in case of War," and in Article 1 of Convention XIII, of 1907,[39] entitled "Convention concerning the Rights and Duties of Neutral Powers in Naval Warfare."

These articles read as follows:

"The territory of neutral powers is inviolable." (Convention V, Article 1.)

"Belligerents are bound to respect the sovereign rights of neutral powers and to abstain, in neutral territory or neutral waters, from any act which would, if knowingly permitted by any power, constitute a violation of neutrality". (Convention XIII, Article 1.)

Article 20 of Convention V further provides:

"The provisions of the present convention do not apply except between contracting powers, and then only if all the belligerents are parties to the convention."

It is not necessary to examine into the question as to whether these treaties were in force by virtue of all the belligerents being parties as required by Article 2 [20] of Convention V, and Article 28 of Convention XIII, for the reason that no Hague Conventions, even if they were in force, were violated by the German invasion of Belgium.

If Germany before invading the territory of Belgium, had declared war against that country, the latter would have been impressed with the character of a belligerent, to whom the provisions of Article 1 of Convention V and Article 1 of Convention XIII relative to the inviolability of neutral territory would not be applicable. In case Germany exercised this sovereign right, it could not be charged that there was a violation of neutral territory in contravention of the terms of the Hague Conventions. This was exactly what Germany did.

---

[38] Malloy, *Treaties*, 1776–1909, vol. II, p. 2290 (Convention V).
[39] *Ibid.*, p. 2352.

The published diplomatic correspondence shows that Germany declared war by ultimatum and that a state of war actually existed between Germany and Belgium before German forces penetrated into the territory of the latter country. Following the provisions of Article 1 of Hague Convention III of 1907 [40] that hostilities must not commence "without previous and explicit warning in the form either of a reasoned declaration of war or of an ultimatum with conditional declaration of war" the German Government presented to the Belgian Government a note proposing among other things that German troops be given free passage through Belgian territory and threatening in case of refusal to treat Belgium as an enemy. Belgium declined to accede to the proposal with a full knowledge that the consequence would be war with Germany. Upon her refusal Belgium lost her neutral character and by operation of the ultimatum became a belligerent. After this status in the relations of the two countries had been reached, German forces began the invasion of Belgium and a state of war resulted.

This may have been a violation of an agreement neutralizing Belgium, but that is a question for the parties to that agreement to determine. In any case it was a declaration of war against a state previously neutral. Germany acted in full conformity with the Hague Conventions and therefore cannot be regarded as having violated them.

A belligerent is not restrained by the Hague Conventions from declaring war against a neutral state for any cause which seems to it sufficient. The Conventions do not restrict such action to any stated *casus belli*. A belligerent under the present international system is at liberty to seek his own *casus belli* and to maintain it before the world. For another neutral to protest and denounce it as unjustifiable would be to exceed the bounds of international duty and custom. A procedure for a third party in a case of this sort is, however, laid down in the Hague Conventions. Convention I of 1907 [41] provides in Article 3 that it is expedient and desirable that "strangers to the dispute should on their own initiative and as far as circumstances may allow offer their good offices or mediation to the states at variance," and that "the exercise of this right can never be regarded . . . as an unfriendly act."

Although Great Britain and Servia had never ratified this Convention, yet in conformity with its provisions the Department of State on August 4th sent to Paris, Berlin, Vienna and St. Petersburg and on August 5th to London, the President's offer to act in the interest of European peace either then or at any other suitable

---

[40] *Ibid.*, p. 2259.
[41] *Ibid.*, p. 2220.

time.[42] It is well known that this offer of mediation has not as yet been accepted by any of the belligerents.

It is difficult to see what further action the United States was called upon to take or could have properly taken in the situation presented at the outbreak of the war.

Second. The dropping of bombs from aircraft was prohibited by a Declaration adopted by the Second Hague Conference in 1907,[43] but, as it was neither signed nor ratified by France, Germany, Russia and Servia and was signed but not ratified by Austria-Hungary, it is not in force in the present war since it provides:

"The present Declaration is only binding on the contracting powers in case of war between two or more of them.

"It shall cease to be binding from the time when, in a war between the contracting powers, one of the belligerents is joined by a non-contracting power."

The question may be raised, however, whether the dropping of bombs from aircraft falls under the provisions of Articles 25 and 26 of Hague Convention IV of 1907,[44] which read as follows:

"The attack or bombardment, by whatever means, of towns, villages, dwellings, or buildings which are undefended is prohibited."

"The officer in command of an attacking force must, before commencing a bombardment, except in cases of assault, do all in his power to warn the authorities."

Without discussing whether or not this Convention is in force in view of the fact that Servia never having ratified it all belligerents are not parties to it, as required by Article 2, the question as to whether a town, village, dwelling or building is "not defended" within the meaning of Article 25 is one of fact, which requires conclusive evidence to establish. Some have assumed that the words "not defended" are synonymous with "unfortified," but, in the ordinary use of language, "not defended" is a much broader term than "unfortified."

As to Article 26 it must be determined whether the dropping of bombs from aircraft should be classed as a "bombardment" or as an "assault". If that method of attack can be properly termed a bombardment, it must be shown affirmatively that a commander of an attacking force did not do all in his power to warn the authorities prior to a bombardment, before he can be charged with a violation of the provision. In the case of attacks by aircraft, evidence of the power to warn and of failure to do so has not been furnished.

---

[42] See telegram of Aug. 4, 1914, to the Ambassador in Austria-Hungary, *Foreign Relations*, 1914, supp., p. 42.
[43] Malloy, *Treaties*, 1776–1909, vol. II, p. 2366 (Convention XIV).
[44] Annex to Convention IV, 1907, *ibid.*, p. 2281.

But, even if this evidence were furnished, it may not unreasonably be asserted that in the case of aerial offense the conditions are quite different from those attending a bombardment by land batteries; that in the former case the element of surprise is essential to success; that preliminary notice would give the enemy opportunity to send his aircraft aloft to intercept the attacking force; and that a warning under these conditions would be an unreasonable requirement. If these assertions are correct, then Article 26 was never intended to apply to an aerial attack.

There appears then to be no substantial reason to affirm that the United States, as a party to the Hague Conventions, should enter a protest against the practice of dropping aerial bombs upon places occupied by the enemy.

It may be added that, while this discussion relates to aerial operations by the German forces, the belligerents of both sides have employed this method of attack upon the enemy.

Third. The question of the violation of the rules of land warfare relative to the immunity from attack of certain buildings is raised under the following provisions in Article 27 of Convention II of the Hague Conventions of 1899: [45]

"In sieges and bombardments all necessary steps should be taken to spare as far as possible edifices devoted to religion, art, science, and charity, hospitals, and places where the sick and wounded are collected, provided they are not used at the same time for military purposes."

"The besieged should indicate these buildings or places by some particular and visible signs, which should previously be notified to the assailants.["]

Similar provisions were incorporated in Convention IV of 1907,[46] with the addition between the words "charity" and "hospitals" of the words "historic monuments."

Convention II of 1899 was ratified by all the belligerents in the present war and by the United States, but Convention IV of 1907 was not ratified by Servia.

To establish a violation of the provisions quoted from Convention II of 1899, or the similar ones of Convention IV of 1907, whichever may be considered to be in force it is requisite to show (1) that certain of the class of buildings mentioned have been injured by bombardment, (2) that "all necessary steps" were not taken to spare them "as far as possible," (3) that they were "not being used at the same time for military purposes," and (4) that they were indicated

---

[45] Convention with Respect to the Laws and Customs of War on Land, 1899, Annex *ibid.*, p. 2048.

[46] See art. 27, Annex to Convention IV, 1907, *ibid.*, p. 2281.

"by distinctive and visible signs" which were notified to the assailant beforehand.

These four propositions, each of which is essential to substantiate a claim of violation of the treaty, have not been all established in any case brought to the attention of this Department, or does it appear that they have even been asserted by those who charge violation of the treaty stipulations.

Furthermore the meaning of "all necessary steps" and "as far as possible" is open to a latitude of interpretation by the commander of an attacking force which involves his conception of the operations necessary to military success. Deplorable as may be the destruction of a cathedral or hospital by a bombardment, the fact alone is not sufficient to constitute a breach of the Hague Convention. The other elements establishing a wanton and needless act must be conclusively shown.

It should also be added in this connection that the treaty itself determines the remedy to be applied in case of an unjustifiable destruction of buildings of the immune class, for Article 3 of Convention IV of 1907 provides:

"A belligerent party which violates the provisions of the said regulations shall, if the case demands, be liable to pay compensation. It shall be responsible for all acts committed by persons forming part of its armed forces."

Obviously this article contemplates an investigation of a more or less judicial nature as to the facts determining liability and the amount of damages sustained. A protest by a third party would be to impute guilt and to charge liability without a full investigation of the facts.

Fourth. The bombardment of seacoast towns by the naval forces of a belligerent is dealt with in the following articles of Convention IX of 1907: [47]

"Article 1. The bombardment by naval forces of undefended ports, towns, villages, dwellings, or buildings is forbidden.

A place can not be bombarded solely because automatic submarine contact mines are anchored off the harbor."

"Article 2. Military works, military, or naval establishments, depots of arms or war *matériel*, workshops or plant which could be utilized for the needs of the hostile fleet or army, and the ships of war in the harbor, are not, however, included in this prohibition. The commander of a naval force may destroy them with artillery, after a summons followed by a reasonable time of waiting, if all other means are impossible, and when the local authorities have not themselves destroyed them within the time fixed.

He incurs no responsibility for any unavoidable damage which may be caused by a bombardment under such circumstances.

[47] Malloy, *Treaties*, 1776–1909, vol. II, p. 2314.

If for military reasons immediate action is necessary, and no delay can be allowed the enemy, it is understood that the prohibition to bombard the undefended town holds good, as in the case given in paragraph 1, and that the commander shall take all due measures in order that the town may suffer as little harm as possible."

"Article 6. If the military situation permits, the commander of the attacking naval force, before commencing the bombardment, must do his utmost to warn the authorities."

This Convention was ratified by the United States and by the belligerents except Servia, Turkey and Montenegro.

Without raising the question of the nullifying effect upon the Convention of its non-ratification by these three belligerents, it may be pointed out that the word "undefended" is not an exact term, but may be variously interpreted. If a camp or barracks for troops are maintained or there is a depot for military or naval supplies it is debatable whether or not the town can be classed as "undefended" in the sense in which the word is used in the treaty.

At all events it must be shown that the port or town was undefended when bombarded or that the commander of the attacking force failed to perform his full duty in accordance with the provisions of the Convention. Thus far this Department has not been furnished with evidence establishing either of these facts, which appear necessary to make out a violation of the treaty.

Fifth. The subject of the use of expanding bullets was first treated at the Hague Conference in 1899, and a provision relative thereto was inserted in a Declaration of the Conference in the following language:

"The contracting parties agree to abstain from the use of bullets which expand or flatten easily in the human body, such as bullets with a hard envelope which does not entirely cover the core, or is pierced with incisions."

This Declaration was ratified or adhered to by all of the present belligerents, but it was never signed or ratified by the United States. The United States, therefore, not being a party to the Declaration, would have no duty or right to interfere in case of violation of its provisions by any of the ratifying or adhering powers.

It may be thought that Hague Convention IV of 1907 relative to the Laws and Customs of War on Land, Article 23e, is broad enough to prohibit the use of expanding bullets. This article reads as follows:

"In addition to the prohibitions provided by special conventions, it is especially forbidden—[48]

.   .   .   .

---

[48] The following omission indicated in the original memorandum.

e. To employ arms, projectiles, or material calculated to cause unnecessary suffering."

This article is identical with Article 23*e* of Convention II of 1899 which was concluded at the same time as the Declaration of 1899 just quoted. It appears to be conclusive, therefore, that the two provisions relate to different matters, for otherwise it would have been unnecessary to execute two separate agreements as was done. That the agreements were regarded by the Conference as distinct is shown by the use in Article 23*e* of the words "In addition to the prohibitions provided by special conventions." Corroborative of this is the fact that Great Britain did not adhere to the Declaration of 1899 until August 30, 1907, while the Hague Conference was in session and was considering Convention IV of which Article 23*e* is a part. The conclusion is inevitable that the prohibition of the use of expanding bullets depends upon the provisions of the Declaration of 1899 to which as already pointed out the United States is not a party.

Sixth. There is omitted from the foregoing discussion any reference to the laying of submarine contact mines on the high seas because the belligerents on both sides have apparently employed this method of naval warfare. It should, however, be pointed out that Russia neither signed nor ratified Convention VIII of 1907,[49] (it was signed but not ratified by Turkey or Montenegro) which restricts the use of such mines, so that the provisions of the Convention do not apply in the present war, for by Article 7 all the belligerents must be parties to put it in operation.

Seventh. In the foregoing review of the specific provisions alleged to have been violated by Germany there is no discussion of the abstract question of the right and duty of the United States when one of the parties to The Hague Conventions mentioned to enter a protest against a violation of any of their provisions.

As to this question, which has a general application, attention should be called to the fact that the right or duty to enter a protest against a violation of a Hague Convention relating to a state of war is not affirmatively set forth in any documents signed at The Hague, and that, if that right or duty exists, it must arise from the nature of the undertaking.

As to whether the Hague Conventions are joint or several in their nature is a subject as to which opinions may differ. If they are joint in nature, the nullifying articles, which have come into operation, affect neutral powers as well as belligerents. If they are several in nature, the nullifying articles apply only to the belligerents, and the Conventions remain in full force between neutrals and belligerents.

---

[49] Malloy, *Treaties*, 1776–1909, vol. II, p. 2304.

Furthermore, if they are joint undertakings, the legal right of protest by a neutral party in case of violation by a belligerent may possibly be presumed; but, if they are several undertakings, such right does not exist.

It seems unnecessary in view of what has been said concerning the alleged treaty violations to express an opinion upon this debatable question, which, while it enters into the legal right of protest by a party to the Hague Conventions, is far more important in its effect upon the neutral rights of the United States and its citizens secured by those Conventions.

To summarize briefly the reasons why this Government has not protested against certain alleged breaches by Germany of the provisions of the Hague Conventions:

It would be improper for the United States to protest the violation of a treaty to which it is not a party.

The Hague Conventions are in nearly every case nullified by the non-ratification of one or more of the belligerents so far as they affect the relations between belligerents.

The evidence before the Department of State is incomplete or entirely *ex parte* so that it fails to establish conclusively the violations alleged.

The legal right to protest against the violation of a Hague treaty by a party whose interests are not affected depends upon the nature of the undertaking, a question which is unsettled.

It is important to note, in connection with this general subject of the violation of the rules of war on land and sea, which are laid down in the Hague Conventions, that the belligerents on both sides of the great European conflict have repeatedly called to the attention of the world the disregard of their opponents for the rules of humane warfare recognized by international usage and treaty stipulations.

The frequency of these charges and the denials of the governments charged indicate the influence, which the public opinion of the world exerts upon the conduct of the belligerents, and shows their earnest desire to avoid the condemnation of civilization on the charge of inhumanity and wanton brutality.

While the conflict of evidence and the impossibility of impartial investigation at the present time prevent neutral nations from determining the truth or falsity of the charges and counter-charges, the denials and defenses, which have been made by the belligerents, and, therefore, furnish no basis for protest, the time will undoubtedly come, when these sanguinary wars are ended and when the nations now arrayed against each other are not blinded by passion in viewing the conduct of their adversaries.

When that time comes the truth as to these charges may be conclusively shown, the reasons for acts, normally reprehensible, considered dispassionately in the light of surrounding circumstances, and the responsibility measured by the standard of international law and justice.   The guilty will thus incur the odium of the civilized world and those falsely charged will be vindicated.   It is this future judgment of enlightened nations which today must restrain the warring powers from inhuman practices rather than condemnations by neutral powers for charges made in the heat of conflict and based upon incomplete knowledge of all the circumstances.

ROBERT LANSING

763.72111/1797½

The Counselor for the Department of State (Lansing) to the Secretary of State

[WASHINGTON,] March 11, 1915.

DEAR MR. SECRETARY: We have received so many memoranda from the British Embassy as to rumors of intended departures of German vessels from American ports without any evidence to support them that I am afraid our investigations of these rumors may be construed into an admission that "due diligence" requires an investigation of every suspicion, however vague, reported to the Department.

To avoid any such construction of our practice, which might seriously embarrass the Government in case future claims based on lack of due diligence are presented, I submit for your consideration a proposed note to the British Ambassador setting forth the position of this Government as to its duty in such cases.[50]

It seems to me that we have shown a great deal of patience in running down the numerous rumors reported by the British Embassy which have proven to be without any foundation in fact.   Not only that, but we have taken action, which I do not think we were required to do on the meagre information supplied by the Embassy. It would be unfortunate and I think subject to criticism if we permitted our good nature to be taken advantage of to found a claim on the ground of an admitted duty as a neutral which international law does not impose.

I think that it would be unwise to remain longer silent, and I, therefore, have drafted the proposed note.

Faithfully yours,

ROBERT LANSING

---

[50] Not printed.

763.72111/1797½

The Secretary of State to President Wilson

WASHINGTON, *March 11, 1915.*

MY DEAR MR. PRESIDENT: I am sending you a letter which Mr. Lansing thinks ought to be sent to the British Ambassador as a matter of precaution.[51]

I fully sympathize with Mr. Lansing's feeling in regard to the number of groundless complaints which he received, but I doubt whether we ought to say anything that would indicate impatience. The Ambassadors on both sides are, of course, charged with a grave responsibility and if they fail to bring to our attention anything, that puts them on inquiry, they would be subjected to severe criticism should the reported thing develop into a menace.

I am inclined to think it is one of those annoyances we must endure and make the best of, considering the stress of the times. My opinion is that we had better attempt to investigate each case, asking for additional information where sufficient evidence is not furnished us, but, at the same time, acting on anything that is given us. If the information given is not sufficiently certain or definite to enable us to find anything we cannot be blamed, provided we do the best we can with the material furnished us. Both sides have presented complaints that proved to be groundless and yet I fear we would expect our representatives to act as they have under similar circumstances.

Will you please let me know how the proposed communication impresses you?

With assurances [etc.]

W. J. BRYAN

763.72111/1798½

President Wilson to the Secretary of State

11 MARCH, 1915.

MY DEAR MR. SECRETARY: I think you are quite right about this matter. We must be infinitely patient.

We can very properly, as these reports and complaints are brought to us, ask that we be supplied with definite particulars and tangible proof, and explain that without them it was impossible for us even to set the processes of investigation afoot. But that, I think, is the most we can do. I do not think that such letters as Mr. Lansing suggests, true and justified in reason though they be, would be wise.

Faithfully Yours,

W. W.

---

[51] Not printed.

763.72111/1799½

*The Counselor for the Department of State (Lansing) to the
Secretary of State*

[WASHINGTON,] *March 11, 1915.*

DEAR MR. SECRETARY: In view of the practical cessation of all commerce in German vessels as a result of British naval operations, it seems to me that any attempt of a German vessel to depart from an American port creates a presumption that the vessel does not intend to engage in peaceful commerce, but intends to engage in offensive operations against enemy commerce, or to furnish supplies to German warships.

In view of this strong presumption of hostile purpose would it not be advisable to request the Treasury Department to instruct its collectors at New York and Boston to withhold clearances for all German vessels in their respective ports until the applications for clearance have been reported to Washington and specific instructions have been issued by the Treasury Department authorizing clearance?

This action can be taken under the Joint Resolution approved March 4, 1915.[52]

Faithfully yours,

ROBERT LANSING

763.72111/1795½

*The Counselor for the Department of State (Lansing) to the
Secretary of State*

[WASHINGTON,] *March 15, 1915.*

DEAR MR. SECRETARY: I enclose a memorandum handed to me on Saturday, the 13th, by the British Ambassador.[53]

While the circular [54] transmitted with the memorandum does not in itself constitute a violation of our Neutrality Laws, it may be a preliminary step to the unlawful acts of secret societies in this country which took place during the "Papineau Rebellion" in 1837 and the Fenian invasions of 1866 and 1870, and which called forth proclamations from President Van Buren in 1837 and 1838, from President Tyler in 1841, from President Johnson in 1866, and from President Grant in 1870.

Would it not be well for this information to be turned over to the Department of Justice with the request that the matter be investigated, so that, in case any hostile expedition against Canada is be-

---

[52] 38 Stat. 1226.
[53] Not printed.
[54] A copy of a circular calling on Germans, Irish, and others to attack Canada from the United States (file No. 763.72111/1794).

ing secretly organized, a proclamation of warning may be issued by the President?

Faithfully yours,

ROBERT LANSING

763.72111/2065

The Counselor for the Department of State (Lansing) to the Secretary of State

[WASHINGTON,] *March 27, 1915—6:15 p. m.*

MY DEAR MR. SECRETARY: The annexed undated memorandum was handed to me this afternoon by Prince Hatzfeldt, and, after carefully reading the statements which it contains, I feel that there is very slender legal ground for refusing clearance to the *Pisa*.[55]

The memorandum is very frank in stating that it is intended to supply a German war vessel, if possible, but we have no evidence that any German war vessel has been supplied from United States territory within the last three months. I hardly know what ground we could urge for refusing clearance in the circumstances; and I furthermore think it would be politic to allow the vessel to depart. I am making only this brief comment because there is not time to prepare a full memorandum on the subject.

Faithfully yours,

ROBERT LANSING

763.72111/2065

The Secretary of State to President Wilson

WASHINGTON, *March 27, 1915.*

MY DEAR MR. PRESIDENT: I am sending you a confidential communication which we have received from the German Ambassador, together with a brief note from Mr. Lansing.[56] I have gone over the matter with him, and while it seems quite clear that it is the intention of this vessel to supply a German war-vessel, still I cannot see how it violates the rules which it lays down and I think we must, therefore, leave with the allies the responsibility of preventing the delivery of the cargo. The German war-vessel would have the right to come into port and take coal and provisions and I do not know by what rule we can refuse clearance papers. It might be our duty to examine and see whether she was prepared to convert herself into

---

[55] A copy of this memorandum dated Mar. 26, 1915, is printed in *Foreign Relations*, 1915, supp., p. 858. For correspondence previously printed concerning the *Pisa* and similar vessels, see *ibid.*, pp. 858 ff.

[56] *Supra.*

a cruiser after leaving our port, but if really a merchant vessel she would seem to be entitled to clearance.

With assurances [etc.]   W. J. BRYAN

763.72111/2065

President Wilson to the Secretary of State

WASHINGTON, *31 March, 1915.*

MY DEAR MR. SECRETARY: I have thought a great deal about this case.

I do not think that we can assent to such a use of our territory for the supply of war ships at sea.

There was a not dissimilar case when vessels sought to obtain coal in England during the Russo-Japanese war which they were to carry to the Russian fleet which was on its way to Japan from the Baltic.

Moreover, the application for a clearance is, there is a strong presumption, fictitious, and that alone would seem to me to render the granting of it irregular.

I had a talk with Mr. Lansing to-day about the case, and feel pretty clear in the propriety and wise policy of these conclusions.

Faithfully Yours,

W. W.

763.72111/1938

The Secretary of State to President Wilson

WASHINGTON, *April 2, 1915.*

MY DEAR MR. PRESIDENT: I enclose a memorandum from Mr. Lansing in the case of the S. S. *Pisa.* I think he has made as strong a case as the facts permit.

With assurances [etc.]   W. J. BRYAN

[Enclosure]

Memorandum by the Counselor for the Department of State (Lansing) of an Interview With the Counselor of the German Embassy (Hatzfeldt), April 1, 1915

Prince Hatzfeldt called to ask about the clearance of the S. S. *Pisa* from New York.

I told him that after a thorough investigation of the case and sympathetic consideration from the German standpoint the Government had reached the decision that the vessel should not be cleared.

He asked me the reasons for this decision.

I replied that it was primarily because the *Pisa* was intended to carry fuel and supplies to German warships for the purpose of carrying on hostile operations and not for the purpose of returning to their home port, that this was admitted. I pointed out that the principle, on which the privilege of obtaining fuel and supplies from neutral ports was based, was that the warship intended to return home, and that no such pretense was made in this case. I further said that the furnishing of supplies to warships proceeding on a warlike expedition or intending to continue hostilities on the high seas was contrary to that principle, and made the neutral port furnishing supplies a base of naval operations, which was contrary to Article 5 of Hague Convention XIII (1907).[57] I cited the cases of the refusal of coal by Great Britain to the French fleet in the North Sea in 1870 and of a similar refusal to the Russian fleet proceeding from the Baltic to the Far East during the Russian-Japanese war.

I also said that it was admitted the port of destination was fictitious and tainted the application for clearance with fraud.

Prince Hatzfeldt asked me if this decision was final. I replied that it was.

ROBERT LANSING

763.72111/1960

President Wilson to the Secretary of State

WASHINGTON, 3 April, 1915.

MY DEAR MR. SECRETARY: I think that Mr. Lansing has stated the case truly and conclusively. It is my own judgment that we could not have adopted any other course consistently with our obligations as neutrals.

Faithfully Yours,

W. W.

763.72111/2082

The Acting Secretary of State to President Wilson

WASHINGTON, April 10, 1915.

DEAR MR. PRESIDENT: I enclose a reply to the German Ambassador relative to the refusal to clear the German steamship Pisa.[58] If it meets with your approval kindly return it to me for transmittal.

Very sincerely yours,

ROBERT LANSING

---

[57] Malloy, *Treaties*, 1776–1909, vol. II, p. 2352.
[58] For the reply as sent, see *Foreign Relations*, 1915, supp., p. 861.

763.72111/2101

President Wilson to the Acting Secretary of State

WASHINGTON, 12 April, 1915.

MY DEAR MR. LANSING: This seems to me admirable and absolutely conclusive.

I have altered one word; and a question arises in my mind as to another. Is it possible to say what the note says about the clearance and yet not use the word fraud?

Cordially and sincerely Yrs.,

WOODROW WILSON

862.20211/1634

The Secretary of State to President Wilson

WASHINGTON, August 6, 1915.

MY DEAR MR. PRESIDENT: I return to you Colonel House's letter of the 2d,[59] in which he states the substance of an interview with the British Ambassador.

Sir Cecil has in the past presented to me very similar ideas to those which he gave to Colonel House, particularly referring to the cotton question.

In regard to the German activity in this country, I believe that Sir Cecil is very much affected by any rumor or report which comes to him from whatever source. That has been my experience with him and with our endeavors to find out the truth of his suspicions.

In regard to finding out about suspicious characters in this country I ought to tell you that about a month ago I called the matter to the attention of Mr. Warren, of the Department of Justice, and since then have spoken to him upon the subject and he tells me that they have been preparing a full list of such persons. As soon as I receive it I will forward it to you.

Faithfully yours,

ROBERT LANSING

763.72111/3139

The Secretary of State to President Wilson

WASHINGTON, November 16, 1915.

MY DEAR MR. PRESIDENT: I enclose to you a letter which I received yesterday from the German Ambassador [60] in reply to one which I sent him, stating that I considered it inadvisable to ask for a post-

---

[59] No copy of this letter found in Department files.
[60] Foreign Relations, 1915, supp., p. 869.

ponement of the trial of the officials of the Hamburg-American Line for violation of our laws.

I confess that I felt a measure of irritation at the point of view which the Ambassador took in his letter, but have not allowed it to influence my proposed reply to him, of which I sent you a copy.[61]

As the cases of these officials have gone to trial in New York I hope that you can return the proposed answer at the earliest possible moment in order that the Ambassador may not complain of delay in setting forth the position of the Department in regard to his arguments for further postponement.

I believe nothing will be lost by telling him frankly what we think of his attitude in this matter.

Faithfully yours,

ROBERT LANSING

763.72111/3139

President Wilson to the Secretary of State

WASHINGTON, *17 November, 1915.*

MY DEAR MR. SECRETARY: I think this reply to the German Ambassador altogether the right one, and take pleasure in returning it with my entire approval.

Faithfully Yours,

W. W.

763.72/2271½a

The Secretary of State to President Wilson

WASHINGTON, *November 17, 1915.*

MY DEAR MR. PRESIDENT: I had a talk this morning with Mr. L. W. Nieman, editor of the *Milwaukee Journal*, whose strong support of the administration and desire to be helpful give weight to his views.

The part of his conversation which particularly interested me was the fact that he tells me that there has been a very decided change in public opinion in the middle west toward this country's participation in the war; that the war spirit is growing on account of the increased hostility toward the Germans, who are being ostracised not only socially but industrially.

As you personally know Mr. Nieman, and the value to be placed upon his judgment, I would suggest if it can be arranged that you see him for ten or fifteen minutes tomorrow or Friday as I think you would find it interesting to have his point of view, which I do

---

[61] *Ibid.*

not feel that I can adequately portray in a letter. I am not making this suggestion at Mr. Nieman's request or with his knowledge.

Mr. Nieman is staying at the New Willard, in case you desire to ask him to come and see you.

Faithfully yours,

ROBERT LANSING

763.72111/3214a

The Secretary of State to President Wilson

WASHINGTON, *November 20, 1915.*

MY DEAR MR. PRESIDENT: While municipal law does not lie in my province unless it relates to neutrality or similar subjects pertaining to our international relations, it occurred to me that it might not be inopportune in connection with your message on national defense to include in it some suggestion as to legislation covering foreign intrigues in our internal affairs such as conspiracies to blow up factories, to encourage strikes, to interfere with industrial operations, to gather information of this government's secrets, etc., etc. In view of the wide interest and indignation manifested throughout the country at the recent disclosures of activities of agents of belligerents I think that notice of the subject in your message would be received with general satisfaction.

Faithfully yours,

ROBERT LANSING

111/23b

The Secretary of State to President Wilson

WASHINGTON, *November 20, 1915.*

MY DEAR MR. PRESIDENT: There has been an unfortunate and probably an unavoidable lack of coordination between the different Departments of the Government charged with investigation of violations of law, growing out of the activity of agents of the belligerent Governments, in this country. It seems to me that it would be advisable to have a central office to which results of investigations could be reported day by day and the proper steps taken to continue such investigations in the most efficient way. With this idea in view I submit to you a memorandum on the subject. This Department is not anxious to assume additional duties but, unavoidably, all these investigations—or at least the majority of them—have an international phase which should be not only considered but, I think, should control the action of other Departments.

The memorandum rests primarily on the idea that the Counselor for this Department should be the clearing house for the secret reports of the various Departments, and he could, if it seems advisable, and I think it does—furnish duplicates of his information day by day to the Secretary of the Treasury and the Attorney-General, who are especially interested in these investigations.

I should be pleased to receive your views upon the subject, or any suggestion which you may have as to a better plan of coordination of work.[62]

Faithfully yours,

ROBERT LANSING

[Enclosure]

MEMORANDUM

A great amount of information, some of it important, much of it trivial and a considerable part of it misleading or absolutely untrue, is coming to various departments of the Government regarding the activities of people throughout the United States, who are alleged to be endangering the friendly relations of this Government with other governments by undertaking unneutral enterprises, some of which are criminal and some of which are merely indiscreet. Almost all of the acts reported, if true, require careful consideration from the viewpoint of our relations with other nations before this Government's action in the matter is determined.

The information may be divided roughly into information as to acts violating a law and for which the offenders can be prosecuted in the courts, and acts which are not technical violations of law, but which are calculated to place the United States in the position of permitting violations of neutrality if they are not stopped. Under the latter may properly come certain acts of accredited representatives of foreign governments. Some of these matters can only be handled by confidential representations to the accredited heads of the foreign governments involved that such acts are distasteful to our Government and must be discontinued.

There is another class of acts committed by citizens of the United States, either entirely on their own initiative or through influences which cannot be definitely traced and which can only be stopped by publicity, and in some cases the matters involved would be of such a

---

[62] On December 5 the President replied:

"This is a most important matter, and I am sorry that I have not acted on it sooner.

"If you will be good enough to supply me with six copies of this memorandum, I will at once communicate it to the Secretaries of the Treasury, War, Navy, and Commerce, to the Attorney-General and the Postmaster-General, and ask them to seek an early joint conference with you to work this matter out." (File No. 111/24.)

delicate nature as to make it inadvisable even to call attention to them in an official way.

This information is at present coming to the Department of State, the War Department, the Navy Department, the United States Secret Service and the Department of Justice. Doubtless other Departments, such as Commerce, Post Office, and even Interior, receive or could gather information as well. It is seldom that information received is sufficiently definite even to warrant investigation and it is only by piecing together information from a number of sources that any practical lead can be obtained. At present there is no assurance that the various scattered scraps of information which when put together make a clear case will go to the same place. For instance, one item may be sent in to Justice mentioning certain activities, another item may be received by the Secret Service, the Navy may receive other information—all of which, when put side by side, makes a fairly clear case, but none of which when scattered through the different Departments seems of importance. It is evident that a single office where all this information must be instantly transmitted without red tape is absolutely necessary to an effective organization.

In view of the diplomatic questions involved it seems obvious that the receiving office should be under the Department of State. Otherwise grave errors may be made by well meaning but misdirected efforts. After this information has been received there are at present three ways in which it may be taken care of: The Department of Justice, the Secret Service and the Post Office Inspectors. The Department of Justice is charged with the gathering of evidence by which the Attorney General may proceed to prosecute for a definite crime; the Secret Service is charged with the protection of the President and the protection against counterfeiting and customs frauds; the Post Office Department is charged with watching for violations of the United States mail. None of these Departments is legally or by organization fitted to handle these matters alone and efficient cooperation without a central directing force with authority to supervise their operations and to assign them their respective work can not be accomplished practically. There is the further objection that a case turned over by the State Department to any one of these investigating departments or bureaus is lost sight of and its daily developments are unknown for weeks and sometimes months.

To cure this situation, it is suggested:

That an Executive Order be issued placing all these matters under the authority of the Department of State, directing all Government officials and Departments to transmit immediately to the Department of State any information received along these lines and to collect at the request of that Department any information asked for. The Order should also direct that the Post Office Department, the Secret Service and the Department of Justice place their men when requested at the disposal of the Department of State for the purpose of investigating these matters.

It is suggested that the Department of State should assign the Counselor, as being able to decide the legal questions which sometimes arise without waiting for reference, as the head of the system, acting, of course, always under the Secretary of State and, through him, under the President himself.

It is not thought that any additional force for the Department of State would be required beyond possibly a thoroughly trustworthy stenographer, and if the work is unusually heavy a filing clerk, as it will be absolutely necessary to maintain a card index and to keep each case separate and up to date.

763.72/2337a

The Secretary of State to President Wilson

WASHINGTON, *December 21, 1915.*

MY DEAR MR. PRESIDENT: I had a long conversation this afternoon with Senator Stone [63] in regard to our relations with the belligerent countries, and I am disturbed at his attitude. He clearly indicated after we had talked awhile that he thought that we were bearing too severely upon the Teutonic Allies and were not pressing Great Britain as strongly as we should in insisting upon observance of our trade rights. When I suggested that loss of life seemed to me to require more drastic treatment than loss of property, he replied that they both involved rights. I said to him that the right of life was an inherent right, the loss of which could never be indemnified, but that the right of property was a legal right, which could be fully remedied by an indemnity. I could see, however, that this in no way satisfied him, for he then referred to German babies dying because Great Britain would not allow us to send them condensed milk, and followed it up with dyes, potash, etc., etc.

This seems to me a serious matter, for, while I believe the Senator will not oppose the policies of the Administration, I do not think he will support them whole-heartedly or enthusiastically. This is especially unfortunate with Senator Lodge radically pro-Ally at the head of the minority of the committee, and ready to take advantage of a situation which offers possibilities of political advantage.

Probably Senator Stone is influenced by the fact that he has a considerable German constituency, which he wishes to keep in good

[63] Chairman of the Senate Committee on Foreign Relations.

humor, but whatever the reason, his ideas of our neutral duty will make it difficult for him to deal with our foreign affairs in a way that will strongly support the Administration and carry through its policies.

I hope that you will find it possible as soon as you return to Washington to ask Senator Stone to come and see you and see if something can not be done to change his attitude, as it will otherwise make the situation one which will be hard to handle. I do not think the case one which permits much delay.

Faithfully yours,

ROBERT LANSING

763.72/2337½

President Wilson to the Secretary of State

HOT SPRINGS, VA., *24 December, 1915.*

MY DEAR MR. SECRETARY: This is indeed not a little disturbing, but I think it comes from other quarters than the Senator's own personal thinking. It makes House's errand all the more pressing and opportune. I shall have a talk with the Senator at the earliest possible moment after my return and shall try my best to make the situation as a whole so clear to him that he will take our view of it.

With much regard,

Cordially and faithfully Yours,

WOODROW WILSON

763.72111 Ap 4/48a

The Secretary of State to President Wilson

WASHINGTON, *March 1, 1916.*

MY DEAR MR. PRESIDENT: I am enclosing a draft of a note in the *Appam* case.[64] The note should be sent tomorrow, so I very much hope you will find time to go over it and return it to me early Thursday. I believe I submitted to you sometime ago a draft of a note in this case, much of which is embodied in this one, particularly the discussion of the interpretation of the treaty.

I would be very much obliged for any suggestions which you may have as to change of thought or language.

Faithfully yours,

ROBERT LANSING

---

[64] For text of the note as sent to the German Ambassador, see *Foreign Relations,* 1916, supp., p. 729; for correspondence previously printed concerning the *Appam* case, see *ibid.,* pp. 722 ff.

763.72111 Ap 4/48½

President Wilson to the Secretary of State

WASHINGTON, *1 March, 1916.*

MY DEAR MR. SECRETARY: I have looked this paper through very carefully, and do not see how we could have taken any other position. I return the papers to you at once, as you requested.

Faithfully Yours,

W. W.

763.72111 Ap 4/60

The Secretary of State to President Wilson

WASHINGTON, *April 3, 1916.*

MY DEAR MR. PRESIDENT: I enclose herewith a proposed note in reply to the memorandum of the German Government on the subject of the *Appam* which was received by me on March 16th.[65]

I do not believe that it is advisable to arbitrate the question but I naturally dislike to refuse arbitration on account of our previous attitude on the subject. The note is prepared with the idea of avoiding arbitration in this particular case.

I would be much obliged if you would make any suggestions as to the form of the note.

Faithfully yours,

ROBERT LANSING

763.72111 Ap 4/80½

President Wilson to the Secretary of State

WASHINGTON, *7 April, 1916.*

MY DEAR MR. SECRETARY: This reply seems to me wholly admirable. I do not see how its contentions can be successfully traversed.

Faithfully Yours,

W. W.

763.72111 H 58/5

The British Embassy to the Department of State

MEMORANDUM

The continuance of German intrigues against British Possessions in the East, known to be carried on by correspondence passing between the United States and China, is causing His Majesty's Government grave concern.

---

[65] For the German memorandum, see *ibid.*, p. 733; for the reply as sent, see *ibid.*, p. 735.

A proposal made by the British Naval Authorities to re-establish a Naval Patrol in Eastern Waters with a view to endeavouring to put a stop to these intrigues has been rejected by Viscount Grey on the ground that he would not assent to the interception on the High Seas of mails between the United States and China.

The position however has grown so serious that His Majesty's Government desire to call once more the earnest attention of the United States Government to the continued toleration of Indian and German intrigues in the United States which constitute a grave menace to the British Empire. They regret that they cannot regard the present negligence of the United States Authorities towards such intrigues, which formed the subject of a Note from this Embassy on February 15th last,[67] as compatible with the duties of a neutral power.

In doing so His Majesty's Government beg to refer to the Memorandum of the American Ambassador in London of April 27th last,[68] on the *China* incident, in which it is stated that if individuals "were intriguing in Chinese territory the complaint of His Majesty's Government was clearly one to be laid before the Government of China;"

In view of the above quoted declaration of Mr. Page that the proper recourse against such intrigues is to the Government of the Neutral Power on whose territory they are carried on His Majesty's Government once more request the United States Government to take the necessary action to put a stop to those intrigues against the British Empire now being fostered on United States territory.

His Majesty's Government relying on the United States Government to take proper action in accordance with the declaration of Mr. Page are meanwhile temporarily refraining from taking their own measures in Eastern waters to prevent the spread of these hostile and seditious movements.[69]

COLVILLE BARCLAY

WASHINGTON, *25 September, 1916.*

763.72111/4185a : Telegram

The Secretary of State to Mr. Charles B. Parker, Representing American Interests in Mexico City [70]

WASHINGTON, *October 27, 1916—6 p. m.*

514. Inform General Carranza that rumors of German submarine activity in the Gulf of Mexico have been received by the representa-

---

[67] Not printed.
[68] Not printed; for contents see *Foreign Relations*, 1916, supp., p. 637.
[69] For the reply to this memorandum, dated Feb. 23, 1917, see p. 237.
[70] This paper bears the notation: "Read to Arredondo [representative in the United States of General Carranza] who agreed to send telegram. 4 pm Oct 27/16 RL."

tive here of Great Britain, who states that the Allies would be compelled to take drastic action if it appeared that assistance was being furnished their enemies from Mexican territory.

Impress upon General Carranza the great importance of taking prompt and effective measures to prevent the possible use of Mexican territory as a base of operations for belligerent men of war and the necessity to devise immediately if it has not already been done a rigid censorship of wireless messages especially those from Mexico to or concerning ships on the high seas.

General Carranza must realize that the least violation of Mexican neutrality in this connection can only have the most far reaching and disastrous results.

LANSING

763.72111/4329½

The Secretary of State to President Wilson

WASHINGTON, *November 23, 1916.*

MY DEAR MR. PRESIDENT: The Swedish Minister called upon me today and handed me the enclosed confidential memorandum relating to the plan of a conference of neutrals which was adopted last September by Sweden, Norway and Denmark, and to which they have agreed to invite Holland, Spain and Switzerland, and to afford an opportunity to this Government to take part if it so desire.[71]

The Minister is very anxious to know our attitude to this proposed Conference and whether we would consider taking part in it. At your convenience I should like to talk the matter over.

Faithfully yours,

ROBERT LANSING

[Enclosure]

Memorandum by the Swedish Minister (Ekengren)

WASHINGTON [*undated*].

At the beginning of September last the following communication was, by agreement between Sweden, Norway and Denmark, confidentially made to the Ministers of Foreign Affairs at The Hague, Madrid and Berne through the Legations of the three northern countries:

"At the meeting of the Ministers of Foreign Affairs of Sweden, Norway and Denmark at Copenhagen in March, 1916, the question of cooperation with other neutral powers for the safeguarding of common interest, jeopardized by the World War, was the object of

---

[71] For correspondence previously printed concerning this projected conference of neutral nations, see *Foreign Relations*, 1916, supp., pp. 696–697.

preliminary deliberations. It is the intention to prosecute this scheme on [in] the forthcoming meeting at Christiania by bringing up the question of issuing invitations to a conference to be held by neutral powers in order to consider common interests especially with regard to commerce, neutrality rules and the application of these rules. In choosing the subjects for discussion it is a leading principle to avoid even appearance of taking sides with either of the belligerent parties. The question of mediation is excluded from the program."

This communication was received with sympathy and interest.

Consequently at the meeting at Christiania it was moved by the Swedish delegate that steps should be taken in order to convoke such a conference.

As special subjects to be brought up at the conference were mentioned:

Treatment of submarines and airships;
Destruction of neutral prizes and the question of granting the right of asylum to such prizes;
Questions arising out of the issuing and application of "black-lists" by the belligerents;
Preparatory steps for adjusting the economic situation after the war and of apprising each other of steps taken during the war for economical-political purposes.

Both Norway and Denmark having expressed their approval of this plan, it was agreed that, as a suitable preliminary measure representatives of the three northern countries and Holland, Spain and Switzerland should meet to discuss how such cooperation as above mentioned should best be established and to draw up proposals for the organisation of a conference and for a final program.

It was also decided that the United States Government should be afforded an opportunity to take part in these deliberations, which could take place, either at a meeting of special delegates, or, if it should be deemed more practical, at a meeting of a member of the Government of the country, in which the meeting was held, and the ministers accredited to that country. Finally it was agreed that the deliberations take place at Stockholm, where all of the States invited have diplomatic representatives.

763.72111/4330½

President Wilson to the Secretary of State

WASHINGTON, *26 November, 1916.*

MY DEAR MR. SECRETARY: I would be very much obliged to you if you would discuss this [72] with me orally at the earliest opportunity,— say after the meeting of the Cabinet on Tuesday next, the 28th. I

---

[72] Memorandum by the Swedish Minister, *supra.*

do not feel certain yet of my instinctive judgment in the matter, which is adverse to any participation by our government in the conference proposed.

Faithfully Yours,

W. W.

763.72111/4331½

Memorandum by the Secretary of State of a Conversation With the Swedish Minister (Ekengren), December 1, 1916

I told the Minister that I had requested him to come to the Department in regard to the Memorandum which he left with me on November 23d in which was outlined a plan for a conference of neutrals regarding certain subjects mentioned in the memorandum, and which proposed to invite Holland, Spain and Switzerland to join with Sweden, Norway and Denmark in such conferences, stating that it was decided to afford an opportunity to the United States Government to take part in these deliberations.

I informed the Minister that after very careful consideration of the subject, and after a conference with the President in regard to the proposed meeting, we had reached the conclusion that it would be inadvisable for this Government to participate in a neutral conference at this time; that the reasons for this decision were that on account of our geographical location our problems in regard to the subjects proposed for discussion were so different from those of countries contiguous to the belligerents that there would be no common ground for discussion; that, furthermore, we were peculiarly related to the American Republics and they were not included as possible conferees; and that it had been our policy heretofore, and seemed to be a wise one, to act independently of other countries although, as far as possible, obtaining identic action with them.

The Minister said that he appreciated our attitude in regard to the proposed conference and would communicate our decision to his Government.

ROBERT LANSING

763.72111/4332½

Memorandum by the Secretary of State

DECEMBER 1, 1916.

Neutrality is a state which becomes increasingly difficult to maintain the longer it lasts. The government charged with its maintenance has no easy task, for as a foreign war progresses the citizens of the neutral country become more and more partisan in their sympathies and less just in viewing the impartial attitude of their own government. Neutrality—that is a real neutrality—satisfies no one who supports the one belligerent or the other, so that they constantly criticize the attitude of the government and complain that it is failing to perform its duty.

When so tremendous a struggle is being waged as the present one which is sapping the energies and eating into the very fibre of the great empires of Europe, and when all nations the world over are affected in their industrial and commercial life by the war, it is to be expected that individuals in neutral countries should become increasingly strong in their sympathies and desire earnestly the success of those powers whose cause they advocate.

And this partisanship is naturally more intense and more irreconcilable to impartiality in a nation like ours which has drawn its blood from the various nationalities of Europe, which are now arrayed against each other in the most bitter and most desperate strife in the annals of history. It is natural that ties of blood should affect the sentiments and through the sentiments the individual judgment of the American people, and make of them sympathizers with the nation from which their ancestors came. We are still a young nation in which national characteristics are in the making. We are only gradually absorbing the millions of people who themselves or whose forebears left the lands of their nativity to find here refuge from oppression or opportunity to win the just reward of their industry. Comparatively few of our citizens have lost touch with the lands across the sea or do not feel the call of kinship and the sympathy which springs from pride of origin.

However intense may be the feeling which would inspire every American if this Republic was in conflict with another nation, it is not strange, when the United States is but a spectator of a war so great that it involves nearly all countries from which we have drawn our people, that every American should become a partisan under the impulse of relationship. Nor is it strange that the people of the United States, thus divided into partisan groups, view the policies of their government with prejudiced eyes and are bitterly critical of any course of action which bears hardly upon the belligerents with whom they sympathize, complaining that the strict neutrality of the Government is unworthy of the United States in view of the great principles at stake in the war.

Thus this Government striving to preserve a free and open mind toward both sides and to resist with equal vigor encroachments upon the rights of Americans by either pleases no one, not even its own citizens, while belligerent public opinion is naturally hostile and contemptuous because the official attitude of this country does not coincide with the viewpoint which forms the basis of that opinion in judging of the merits of the conflict, and which denies all justification to the enemy.

For two years and a half this Government has faced this situation and patiently endured the denunciations and invectives of partisanship at home and abroad. It has done this because it believed that its first duty was to the millions who had confided to it their welfare and their interests, and that the welfare and interests of this great people were best served by keeping the United States at peace. But another duty has impressed itself more and more as the war increased in magnitude and the combatants became more desperate in their efforts to vanquish one another, and that was the duty to preserve one great nation in the world free from the terrible results of the world war, so that its energies might be devoted to the restoration of wasted resources, to the rebuilding of new enterprises on the ruins caused by the innumerable lives sacrificed and by the destruction of vast treasures.

Determined as this Government was to remain neutral because of its duty to the American people and its duty to the future of mankind it realized that it had undertaken no light task. Not alone was it compelled to endure the taunts of cowardice, of heartlessness, of lack of moral fibre, of vacillation, of partiality for one or the other of the belligerents, of every possible motive which was dishonorable and pusillanimous, but it had also to deal with conditions of warfare utterly new, to which the rules which common assent had established could not be applied, or, if applied, were found ineffective.

New means of communication, new methods of locomotion, new engines of destruction which had never been listed in actual war, were introduced and put into practical operation. How these various changes increased the efficiency of the military and naval forces of the warring nations and how manifestly inadequate the old codes of warfare were and the accepted rules defining the relative rights of belligerents and neutrals became almost at once apparent. The whole magnificent system of international law applicable to a state of war which had been constructed with such pains and toil, came tumbling to the ground in a few months. Only the foundation stones of principle were left on which to build temporary structures which would at least give partial shelter from the fury of the tempest which seemed to be sweeping every right from its former place in society.

Relying apparently upon the fact that many of the rules of conduct universally accepted were impossible of application because of changed conditions, the belligerents went further and violated other rules which could have been applied and ought to have been applied. These violations of established rules, some of which were possibly justifiable but many of which were not, were seized upon by their adversaries as ample excuses for violations on their part. Thus every new breach begat another, which in turn begat others, until the standards of right sanctioned by treaties and usage, were torn to bits, and the belligerents ignored more and more the former practices of nations at war.

In stating this situation and the positions taken by the warring powers I do not intend to condemn the course pursued by either side, so far as they affect their respective rights. It is not the part of a neutral to sit in judgment or to compare the conduct of belligerents in carrying on hostile operations against one another. It is practically impossible for those having the administration of foreign affairs not to make such a comparison and not to form a judgment as to the justifiable character of violations of recognized rights, but it is nevertheless their duty to refrain from giving official sanction to such opinions or from in any way departing from the position of an impartial spectator, who while he may deplore the conduct of one combatant more than that of the other remains silent and strives to keep the official mind of the government free from prejudice, even though the public opinion of the nation may denounce acts as beyond the pale of right or of humanity.

When, however, the acts of belligerent[s] seriously infringe the rights of neutrals, a neutral government cannot permit such acts to be passed over in silence. It is a duty, which a government owes to its citizens and for which it was established, to protest against such violations and to endeavor to prevent their repetition. Without passing upon the question as to whether new conditions have made certain belligerent acts, previously condemned, justifiable, or upon the question as to whether they are warranted by way of retaliation for alleged lawlessness on the part of the enemy, a neutral is bound to decide as to their legal character if they impair recognized neutral rights, and in reaching a decision it can only apply existing rules, even though they seem obsolete and insufficient.

It is obvious that, with the belligerent nations engaged in what they believe to be—and what indeed may be—a death struggle, a struggle in which they are determined to employ every means to weaken their opponents, a neutral government seeking to preserve the rights of its citizens, I refer particularly to their commercial rights, has well nigh a hopeless task. What can be done to keep inviolate those rights? Appeal to the established rules governing a belligerent's treatment of neutrals? In the intensity of this extraordinary war the ears of belligerents are deaf or at least dull to neutral appeals, if they are convinced that they are working injury to their enemies. Threaten the offending government with retaliation? Would that have any more effect than an appeal to legality unless the threat was carried out? And if the threatened retaliation did not bear with equal force on both belligerents would it not be held with more or less reason that it was unneutral?

On the other hand to threaten without putting the threat into operation would seem to be worse than useless. It would be humiliating and result in a loss of esteem in foreign lands and at home.

In this situation what course lies open to a neutral nation physically unable to give effect to a declaration that it will maintain its rights at all hazard? Is it wise to make such declaration with the possibility that it will accomplish nothing and only bring discredit upon the one that makes it? I do not believe the most optimistic opportunist would counsel such action. But if not that, then what? Do you not perceive the great difficulty of the problem and the perplexities which face those who have to solve it?

Viewed from every angle is not the most sensible course for a neutral government to show patience and treat the warring powers as if the circumstances of the war had made them in a large measure irresponsible for their improper acts? If such a policy is adopted, a belligerent government must be frankly notified that its conduct is in flagrant violation of neutral rights, that its conduct cannot be forgiven or condoned, and that it will be held responsible for any resulting loss or damage. Of course such a notification amounts merely to a reservation of rights to be determined at some later time, and probably will not have the effect of causing a belligerent to change its policy. But what else can a neutral government do if the nation itself is unwilling or unprepared to have its rights enforced by action? As a reservation of rights, on which to found claims to be adjusted when the war is over, a representation of this sort is manifestly desirable, but as a means of improving a difficult or unpleasant state of affairs it will amount to nothing at all. This might just as well be admitted and understood so that hopes may not be built on so weak a foundation.

To guide the course of this Government with intelligence it is necessary to look at the situation not only from the point of view of the neutral but also from that of the participants in the struggle. And first let me say, that the warring nations and their governments are wrought up to the highest pitch of nervous tension. They are desperate. One supreme purpose controls their conduct. It is to win the war. National independence is to them the prize of victory. To preserve that independence is the supreme motive. Put yourself in their place and then decide what regard you would pay to the rights of other nations, if to do so interfered with efforts to injure your antagonist. You might attempt to pacify a neutral, whose friendship you desired, by certain minor concessions, but would you cease in pursuing a practice which you considered essential in the least degree to gaining an advantage over your enemy unless that practice so seriously affected the rights of a neutral nation that its continuance would force that nation to enter the war as an enemy? I do not say that this attitude is right but I do say that we ought not to be surprised that it is under present conditions the one taken by belligerents.

I think too that we should also accept as a logical consequence that a nation, obsessed with the idea that its life hangs in the balance, that it is engaged in a struggle for life, feels a natural irritation that a neutral nation does not see things in the same light that it does and is not as strongly impressed with the righteousness of its cause as are its government and people. A belligerent government, straining every nerve to conquer on land and sea and in the air, putting forth herculean efforts and making tremendous sacrifices of life and treasure, is in no frame of mind to consider calmly and judicially a request or demand by a neutral which, if granted, would seem to surrender some gain, be it ever so slight, over the enemy. It would be folly to expect a just and dispassionate discussion of a question in such circumstances.

Continue to put yourself in the frame of mind of a belligerent and then answer these questions: What does a government, whose people are dying by the tens of thousands for the sake of their country care about a legal right of neutral property? What is the observance of law, however sanctioned by the world, compared to a nation's life? How much do commercial interests weighed against a possibly greater sacrifice of life by prolongation of a war? Answer these questions from the belligerent's standpoint and you will perceive very clearly the attitude of the governments of warring Europe in their dealings with the United States.

Can you in your heart blame them for their indifference to our legal rights or for their attempts to justify their illegal acts? Can you blame them for making bitter complaints that we, as a people, are mercenary, selfish and unsympathetic when we insist that our rights shall be respected, when insistence appears to be favorable to their enemies? They would not be human if they felt otherwise. We must accept it as a natural consequence of present conditions, and deal with it as best we may.

The conditions are abnormal. Public opinion in the countries at war is abnormal. The state of mind and point of view of belligerent governments are abnormal, and the relations of neutral nations with those which are fighting are consequently abnormal. Manifestly the situations which arise cannot be treated in a normal way. This needs no evidence, the facts are too patent to require proof.

In spite of this temper of the belligerents, which is so essentially human, and in spite of these abnormal conditions which have presented a situation of the greatest delicacy in our international relations, there have been numbers of Americans who seem to have failed to comprehend the conditions or to apprehend the mental attitude of the peoples who are at war. Many of these Americans have been engaged in European trade or have industrial enterprises dependent for their materials on imports from belligerent countries. The personal interests of these people seem to have blinded them to the true state of affairs and to the national interests affected, which are so much greater than their own. They appear to have lost their sense of perspective, and to be unable to understand the reasons which have caused this Government to hesitate in peremptorily demanding that every neutral right previously admitted be strictly observed. They not only call upon the Government to protest and threaten, but numbers have insisted that it should go to extremes in defending their rights. The possible consequences of so radical a policy do not seem to worry them, possibly because they expect that the protests and threats will be heeded, which is further evidence of their failure to realize the situation.

I do not wish to judge too harshly those Americans who have maintained this attitude. Very likely we ought to expect persons, who are suffering financial loss while they see many of their fellow citizens prosperous as a result of the war, to resent bitterly the illegal conduct of the belligerents and to feel that the Government was willfully deaf to their appeals and was failing in its duty as their protector. I can understand their frame of mind. They honestly believe that all this Government has to do is stiffen its back and emphatically demand respect for the rights of its citizens, with the result that the belligerent governments, though they may bluster and fume, will submit rather than have the dispute become actually serious.

Of course these complainants, however legally right they may be, have entirely misunderstood the temper of the belligerents. The Government, however, with a much wider horizon and feeling responsibility for the general welfare, takes into consideration all the circumstances. It realizes that the belligerents have but one object and that they will subordinate everything to military exigency. It knows that the course which the complainants demand would aggravate a state of affairs already very difficult. You might as well try to drive with an ox-whip a bull which has been maddened by the *banderilleros* and which stands in the ring with blood dripping from the colored darts, as to force in this way a belligerent to live up to rules which interfere with the necessities of the conflict.

Furthermore, a stern, unbending policy would close the door to all compromise, through which some measure of relief may be found.

Of course this Government cannot compromise a right but the individual, who is suffering may, as has been done in very many cases. And then we must look into the future and as a nation save out of this wreckage with all its passions and hatreds some friendships on which to build anew the normal trade and commerce between this country and the great European markets.

Why not look at this matter squarely and admit the truth? It is almost a certainty that none of the belligerent governments, which are infringing the neutral rights of Americans is going to change its policies because of diplomatic pressure however vigorous it may be, unless it is firmly convinced that this country intends to declare war if its demands are not complied with. Unless the United States is prepared to back up its threats with force, is it wise to make them? Does any American, who comprehends the situation and has the good of his country at heart, advocate such a course? And, if it is adopted, what would be the result? Would it tend to advance the honor and dignity of the United States or would it have a contrary effect? Of course, even without the physical power to enforce its demand, a nation may be compelled because of gross insult or wrong to sever friendly intercourse with another nation and so invite more radical action, but to do so when the issue may be honorably avoided, would be condemned by men who take a commonsense view of international affairs and do not permit selfish interests to influence their judgment.

A policy of moderation is never pleasing to those who mistakenly believe threats will be heeded. It is not pleasing to the unthinking element of the population who applaud vigor of language as evidence of national greatness and who consider it is patriotic to bluster and brag and abuse. But, for the matter of that it is not agreeable to the government which adopts it as the wise and sane course to pursue. It is a difficult policy, a policy of patience, a policy of extreme forbearance, which under normal conditions would be humiliating and incompatible with the dignity of a self-respecting nation.

But at the present time, when half the world sees red, when great empires are staggering under the sledge-hammer blows of their adversaries and exerting every effort to resist the onslaught, and when governments and individuals are laboring under intense excitement, commonsense, as well as generous sentiment, demands that a neutral should not threaten a belligerent with radical action unless he change his conduct when the neutral is convinced that no change will take place. Is it reasonable to expect that nations struggling for their lives will be willing to step aside and let a neutral pass when those nations are firmly convinced that their enemies would be benefited if they should do so? Ought not a neutral government to seek to give just proportion to its commercial interests in comparison with the great enterprise of war? Is not that the sensible, practical and rational way of viewing the present situation and of dealing with the difficult problems which it presents?

A neutral in time of international war must always show forbearance, but never, since neutrality has been recognized as a legal state, have the patience and forbearance of neutrals been put to so severe a test as in the present conflict. The arbitrary and illegal conduct of the belligerents have very naturally aroused intense indignation. To curb the desire to resist this conduct, to suppress the indignant feelings aroused, to remain cool and self-possessed under great provocation—that is the difficult task which a neutral government has been called upon to perform in spite of repeated storms of criticism and abuse.

It seems to me that neutrality is like a slender cable stretched above a seething torrent of war. Along this swaying narrow bridge a neutral nation must walk from shore to shore, from peace to peace. It is no easy matter to keep one's equilibrium. With a long balancing rod weighed at either end with belligerent rights and carrying on his back the rights of the neutral he sets forth on his precarious journey. He bends a little to this side, then a little to that, recovers his poise, and cautiously takes a step forward. He hesitates; the cable trembles and sways; with increased care he again puts his foot out and feels it firmly fixed before he moves; the balancing rod dips dangerously first this way and then that; again he stops; again slowly advances.

This is the task of preserving neutrality as I see it reduced to physical terms.

The neutral must keep his eyes on the swinging cable which stretches away into the mists where lies the firm ground. He must not lean to either side. He must always move with extreme caution and with the certainty that the step taken will not destroy his balance and plunge him into the gulf. The roar of the rushing waters beneath must not affect his calmness; the dashing spray must not dim his vision. He must be prepared to resist the fierce gusts of passion and abuse which beat in his face. He must always look forward, not downward. Above all he must keep his head even though he is wet by the leaping red waves and though the cable grows slippery with bloody foam.

His goal is the distant shore of peace. To reach it without falling into the gorge where the raging flood of relentless war is engulfing millions of men and great nations and sweeping away the standards of life, the very foundations of civilization, is the supreme purpose of the nation which travels the difficult way of neutrality.

I do not think that I have overdrawn the perils and difficulties which beset a government striving to maintain its neutrality; I doubt if the picture can be overdrawn. With a just appreciation of the forces constantly exerted from within as well as from without to compel the abandonment of a policy of impartiality toward the nations at war, no true American will too harshly judge or be too ready to criticize publicly his own government's conduct of foreign affairs, he will not be eager to believe that the government is pusillanimous, and he will not be one of those who cannot curb their tongues but who seek by abuse and ridicule to excite contempt and condemnation of the government which they are bound to support.

Patriotism, real American patriotism, ought to restrain every loyal citizen from giving free rein to his passions and from open and hostile criticism of his own government in any dispute with a foreign power, and especially if the dispute is of so serious a nature that it may result in a resort to arms. To impress a foreign government with the idea that the United States is a divided nation is to encourage that government to pursue a policy which may bring disaster on the Republic and force an issue which the American Government is seeking to avoid. To encourage a foreign government to continued aggression or to anger it so that it will not cease from aggression is an unpatriotic and disloyal act on the part of an individual citizen. The responsibility lies with the government and to place obstacles in its way is neither wise nor praiseworthy. It is not treason to do so unless a state of war exists, but it comes as near treason as any act can in time of peace.

Thus do I view the state of neutrality; a difficult state, in which a government is tried to the uttermost; a state, the preservation of which wins the favor of decreasing numbers the longer it exists; a state, which invites greater and greater resentment from the people of a neutral nation as day by day more individuals are added to those who complain of rights violated and injustices perpetrated by the belligerents.

Even if a government succeeds in passing through the tempest and shielding the nation from the dread consequences of war, it cannot expect the plaudits of a grateful people. In the avoidance of conflict there is nothing to excite hero-worship or to stir the emotions with patriotic fervor. There may be a flicker of thankfulness that the nation has been spared, but no outburst of rejoicing like a paean of victory. What praise is given will be given grudgingly, it will be mingled with complaints at the methods employed and possibly with regrets that the might of the nation was not exerted in behalf of one belligerent or the other.

So the restoration of peace will find the neutral government which has won a greater struggle than that waged on the battlefield, a struggle which has required the exercise of those traits of human nature which appeal least to the average man, the traits of patience, self-control and forbearance.

It is only in the realization of duty performed and in the confident hope that history will some day do tardy justice, that those, upon whom lies the burden, will find a full recompense for having been faithful to the end and attained the goal in spite of every obstacle which has been placed in their way and of every influence which has sought to force them from the path leading to the peace and prosperity, which their countrymen have enjoyed as the result of their efforts.

763.72111 H 58/5

The Secretary of State to President Wilson

WASHINGTON, *February 27, 1917.*

MY DEAR MR. PRESIDENT: I enclose you a copy of a memorandum which I have prepared in reply to memoranda which the British Embassy delivered to us in September [73] and December [74] of last year relative to the Hindu intrigues in this country. If this involved a continuation of a controversy I would be disposed to let it lie for the present, but in view of the fact that it is merely an answer to serious charges against officials of this Government, I feel we should not delay making a reply.

I would be pleased if you would give me any suggestions you may have as to substance or language.

Faithfully yours,

ROBERT LANSING

[Enclosure]

The Department of State to the British Embassy [75]

MEMORANDUM

The Government of the United States begs to acknowledge the receipt of the memoranda of the British Embassy dated September 25th [73] and December 21st [74] last in regard to alleged intrigues in the United States against British Possessions in the East. As the American authorities are still investigating the matters set out in the memorandum of December 21st, the Government of the United States is not in a position to make a complete answer to the British

---

[73] *Ante,* p. 223.
[74] Not printed.
[75] Filed separately under file No. 763.72111 H 58/11a.

contentions, but the Government of the United States has given careful consideration to the memorandum of September 25th last, and will reply to the serious charges therein made against the Government of the United States and its officials prior to the information disclosed in the memorandum of December 21st.

In the memorandum of September 25th His Majesty's Government call attention to "the continued toleration of Indian and German intrigues in the United States, which constitute a grave menace to the British Empire," and state that "they can not regard the present negligence of the United States authorities toward such intrigues . . . as compatible with the duties of a neutral power." The memorandum also refers to the statement of the Government of the United States in the *China* case, that the complaints of His Majesty's Government in regard to intrigues in Chinese territory were clearly ones to be laid before the Government of China, and in view of this declaration "once more requests the United States to take the necessary action to put a stop to these intrigues against the British Empire now being fostered on United States territory," and states that they are "meanwhile temporarily refraining from taking their own measures in the Eastern waters to prevent the spread of these hostile and seditious movements."

In reply, the Government of the United States begs to announce that it adheres to the principle exemplified in the American Ambassador's note of April 27th last in the *China* case,[78] that the proper recourse against intrigues in neutral territory is to complain to the Government of the neutral power within whose territory they are carried on, and trusts that His Majesty's Government will continue, as the release of the men in the *China* case indicates their intention to do, to adhere to the same principle, by referring complaints as to intrigues in this country to the Government of the United States instead of endeavoring to prevent them by seizing mails on the high seas and by removing insurrectionists and intriguers out of American vessels and from under the American flag—practices in which the British Government should know the Government of the United States can not acquiesce.

The Government of the United States does not hesitate to repudiate emphatically the charges made by the British Government in the memorandum of September 25th last, of the "continued toleration" in the United States of Indian and German intrigues which are being "fostered on United States territory," and of the "present negligence" of American authorities toward such intrigues. The characterization of the conduct of the Government of the United States and its officials in language which seems to it to be intemperate in

---

[78] Not printed; for contents see *Foreign Relations*, 1916, supp., p. 637.

tone and unwarranted by the facts, has been a subject of surprise and concern to the Government of the United States; but it appreciates the circumstances of their utterances and is disposed to discuss the complaints of His Majesty's Government without further notice of the expressions, at which it might be justified in taking offense.

There have been, it is true, suspicious circumstances attending the acts of certain Germans, Americans of German descent, and East Indians in relation to British India, but have not enemy aliens and intriguers in neutral countries always been subjects of extreme suspicion? The activities in the present case, however, as will be shown, have not only received the closest attention of the American authorities, but where of a criminal nature under American laws, have been frustrated by the prompt institution of repressive measures.

From the diplomatic correspondence on the subject up to December last, it would appear that the activities complained of related to the enterprises of certain propagandists on the Pacific Coast, and the movements of the American vessels *Henry S.* and *Maverick*. As these appear to be the main factors in the alleged intrigues, each of them will be discussed in turn.

First. An account of the activities of the propagandists occurs in the documents transmitted to the Department of State with the British Ambassador's note of February 15, 1916,[79] relating to the Lahore Conspiracy Case, in which certain of the reputed leaders and participants in the alleged intrigues in America were tried and condemned in India. It appears that long before the present war there existed revolutionary societies among East Indians in France and other countries, aimed to create a revolt in India by violence and murder; that in America the movement began in Canada, whence it spread to the United States; that "the two main centers (of the conspiracy) were Vancouver and San Francisco"; that the movement was begun in 1913 by Hindu and Mohammedan subjects of the British Empire, who undertook the publication of a newspaper in California called the *Ghadr* (*Mutiny*), advocating violent revolutionary measures in India, the first issue of which appeared in November of that year, and was distributed widely among the East Indians in the United States and Canada; that the originator of the propaganda and newspaper, one Hardial, continued his propaganda and sedition until he was forced by the American authorities to leave the United States, in March, 1914; that Ram Chandar succeeded to the leadership of the movement and the management of the *Ghadr;* that from May, 1913, to September, 1914, meetings of East Indians were held on the Pacific Coast of America, at which "sedition was preached, and Indians were ex-

---

[79] Not printed.

horted to be ready to go to India when occasion arose"; that, apparently in anticipation of the opening of the war, subscriptions were collected and lists of volunteers opened of those "ready to return at once (August, 1914) to India," which "many agreed to do"; that many left the United States and Canada to carry out their revolutionary designs, on the steamer *Korea* August 29th, and on other vessels (some vessels leaving Vancouver, Canada, with East Indians on board, and stopping at San Francisco); that a majority of those on the *Korea* transshipped to the Japanese steamship *Toska Maru* at Hongkong, where others joined them, and proceeded to India via Calcutta; that arms and ammunition had been collected and "one of the probable sources of the arms was the United States of America and Canada"; that "a number of these (persons) on arrival in India were interned, but some of them dispersed themselves about the country" and "committed various murders and deeds of violence until they were arrested and tried"; and that some of these seditionists received encouragement, instructions, and money from German subjects and from officials of the German Government.

From the foregoing, which takes no account of the information contained in the British memorandum of December 21st, it appears that, although intriguers may have been present on the Pacific Coast in considerable numbers, they infested Canada as well as the United States, and carried on their activities in both countries; that, although they may have sailed from American ports in order to carry out seditious designs, nevertheless, it does not appear that they formed any military expedition or enterprise within the United States contrary to the laws thereof, or that they left American ports as a military organization, or that they were supplied with arms and ammunition in the United States, or that they received arms and ammunition on the high seas which had been sent from the United States in pursuance of a plan framed within American jurisdiction, or even that arms were permitted to leave the jurisdiction of the United States destined to India for revolutionary purposes. It is clear, therefore, that none of the elements of a military expedition in violation of the neutrality laws of the United States was present in the activities of the alleged intriguers in the United States or in their supposed movement to the Far East.

In an earlier communication, dated March 27, 1916,[80] the British Ambassador called attention to information which had been received from Canada, that there was great activity among the revolutionary Hindus and Mohammedans on the Pacific Coast, and that arms and

---

[80] Not printed.

ammunition were being sent, with machinery, in cotton-bales and general merchandise, and being re-shipped in the Philippines and from there forwarded to India. This information was referred to the Department of Justice for attention, which, on April 5th, replied [81] that "for a considerable time the alleged activities of Hindus on the Pacific Coast have been the subject of investigation by this Department. No facts as alleged have developed as to shipment of arms and ammunition as stated by the British Ambassador. The matter, however, will be further investigated." This was communicated to the Ambassador of Great Britain in a note dated April 17, 1916.[82]

In this relation may be mentioned also the British memorandum of April 10, 1916,[82] enclosing a letter of H. Dayal, dated Switzerland, January 5, 1915, in which he discloses his intention to publish in San Francisco a newspaper in English, entitled, "The United States of India," as the "official organ of the Ghadr Party," with the object of giving "news of all anarchical movements." This matter was promptly laid before the Department of Justice, which stated, on May 1, 1916,[81] "that the matter would be given consideration, although nothing stated would seem to contain any violation or probable violation of the criminal laws of this country. So far as known, the publication of a newspaper to present anarchical views is not a violation of any federal law."

Second. It appears from the British statements prior to December 21, 1916, that in the summer of 1915, certain persons, including one Wehde and one Boehm, left the United States for Manila, where the former chartered the schooner *Henry S.* and loaded her with arms from German vessels lying in the Philippine ports, with a view to transporting them to Shanghai; that the American customs authorities, regarding the transaction as highly suspicious, refused clearance to the vessel unless the arms were removed; that the arms were removed in accordance with this requirement, and the vessel thereafter cleared for Borneo, July 14, 1915, though it appears that the vessel subsequently put in at Paleleh in a disabled condition, where she seems to have been abandoned.

Regarding this case, the British Ambassador, in his note of September 16, 1915,[82] stated "there can be little doubt that a hostile expedition was being planned and fitted out and was probably frustrated by the vigilance of the local United States authorities." And to the same case the Ambassador, in his note of February 15, 1916,[82] refers as follows: "Money, men, and arms were provided by

---

[81] Letter not printed.
[82] Not printed.

242 THE LANSING PAPERS, 1914–1920, VOLUME I

the German consuls at Chicago and San Francisco, and were dispatched to Manila. Here the scheme failed, owing to the United States Customs officials refusing clearance to the *Henry S.*, which had been chartered on behalf of the Party. * * *[86] I take this opportunity of expressing the thanks of my Government for the energetic measures taken by the authorities in the Philippines in order to prevent any breach of the neutrality laws."

From this it will be perceived that the intrigues on American territory resulting in the proposed shipment of arms on the *Henry S.* were promptly frustrated to the satisfaction of the British Government by the vigilance of American authorities, who suspected that the preparations involving the *Henry S.* constituted the beginning or setting on foot in American territory of a military expedition contrary to the neutrality laws of the United States.

Third. From the communications from the British Embassy of February 15, 1916, and January 6, March 13, May 12, June 14, and June 16, 1915, and from the British Foreign Office of March 29, 1916,[87] it appears that the steamship *Maverick* was purchased by certain Germans in California in March, 1915, and sailed from San Pedro, California, April 22d, for Mexico with "five Indians, who posed as Persians"; that she did not transport arms, although it was believed her real mission was to do so; that she cleared for a Mexican port and thence sailed for Socorro Island, a Mexican possession in the Pacific 400 miles west of Manzanillo; that her movements were highly suspicious; and that through press accounts of her supposed expedition, or other causes, her ulterior plans, if she had any, were frustrated and in consequence the "owners changed their plans and used the vessel for purposes other than the conveyance of arms." It appears further from this correspondence that on March 8th, the American steamer *Annie Larsen* sailed from San Diego with several carloads of arms and ammunition for one Bowen, at Topolobampo, Mexico; but that, according to press reports, she sailed with her arms to Socorro Island, and turned up at Acapulco, Mexico, without her cargo of arms and ammunition. From the investigations of the United States authorities it appears, however, that, notwithstanding the reported plan of the *Maverick* to meet the *Annie Larsen* at Socorro Island and there to transship the latter's cargo of arms and ammunition and proceed to Java, the *Annie Larsen*, as a matter of fact, returned to the United States, where she arrived at the port of Aberdeen, Washington, June 29, 1915, with her cargo of arms and ammunition still on board and intact, and that there the American authorities took charge of the vessel and cargo.

---

[86] Asterisks appear in the original memorandum.
[87] None printed.

It will be realized that at the time these vessels were preparing to leave the Pacific ports of the United States, they were investigated thoroughly by American authorities, who, in the absence of actual evidence tending to show a violation of the United States laws, were impelled to grant them clearances. From the circumstances related above regarding the *Maverick* and *Annie Larsen*, it is clear that neither of them violated the neutrality laws of the United States. Even if there were witnesses who might possibly prove facts constituting in this case a military expedition, these witnesses, the Department of State is advised, like most of those connected with intrigues in this country, are now either in the hands of British authorities as prisoners, or else have suffered capital punishment.

From the foregoing account it seems too obvious to require argument, that in none of the three cases of alleged intrigues were the neutrality laws of the United States contravened, nor were the United States authorities negligent in any respect. In these respects the Attorney-General advises the Department of State in a letter of December 20, 1916,[88] as follows:

"The requirements of proof to establish the crime of beginning or setting on foot, or providing or preparing the means for a military enterprise or expedition (Sec. 13, Criminal Code), and the crime of conspiracy to commit the said offense (Sec. 37, Criminal Code), have been clearly established by decisions of the Supreme Court and of the inferior Federal courts.

"Although active efforts have been made by this Department for many months to obtain evidence relative to German and Indian intrigues in this country which would warrant an indictment, no sufficient evidence has as yet been obtained; nor has any evidence which would warrant such an indictment ever been furnished by any officials of the British Embassy, or otherwise.[89] . . .

. . . .

"There has been no negligence on the part of this Department in prosecuting violations of the criminal laws of the United States.

"Prevention of 'intrigues,' which do not constitute a violation of the laws of this country, I do not conceive to be incumbent upon the United States as a neutral power."

On the point of negligence, it may be further noted that some of the activities described originated in part and were carried on in a measure from Canadian territory, where the British authorities, endowed even with the extraordinary powers incident to a state of war had met with no more success in suppressing them than it is charged had the American authorities in suppressing the activities alleged to have taken place in American territory.

---

[88] Not printed.
[89] The following omission indicated in the original memorandum.

In this relation attention may also be directed to the precedent analogous to the present cases established by the British Government in the Orsini case in 1858. In this case a plot was hatched on British soil, bombs were manufactured, and would-be assassins, under the protection of British passports, took passage from Great Britain with these deadly weapons for the purpose of making an attempt on the life of the French Emperor, Napoleon III. So much excitement was aroused in both France and Great Britain at the monstrous act that the British Government introduced a bill amending the law of conspiracy so as to make it a felony to conspire to commit murder either within or without the United Kingdom. It is noteworthy, however, that this bill failed of passage by the British Parliament.

Having disposed of the earlier phases of the so-called intrigues on United States soil, the memorandum of September 25, 1916, may be considered specifically. That memorandum presents no evidence whatever in itself or in its enclosures of "the continuance of German intrigues against British Possessions in the East," other than the assertion of the Counselor of the Embassy, and from the correspondence just reviewed there appears nothing whatever to bear out the assertion. Nor is the Government of the United States, which has used the information presented by the British Embassy and made thorough and painstaking investigations on its own account of the alleged intrigues, aware from sources of information other than the British Embassy, that these intrigues are being "continued," "tolerated," or "fostered" on American territory. The Government of the United States, therefore, must repel the unfounded charge of negligence on the part of American authorities which the British Government advance in the memorandum of September 25th, without the production of proofs. It is unnecessary to add that any facts that may be presented will be thoroughly investigated by the United States authorities, who will take such action under the laws of the United States as the results of the investigation seem to warrant.

This memorandum should not be closed without reference to the statement made in note of Lord Grey of October 10, 1916,[90] on the British blacklist, that:

"In some cases they (German business establishments) have been used as bases of supply for German cruisers and in other cases as organizers and paymasters of miscreants employed to destroy by foul means factories engaged in making, or ships engaged in carrying, supplies required by the Allies. Such operations have been carried out in the territory even of the United States itself, and I am bound to observe, what I do not think will be denied, that no adequate action yet has been taken by the government of the United States to suppress breaches of neutrality of this particular criminal kind, which I know they are the first to discountenance and deplore."

---

[90] Printed in full in *Foreign Relations*, 1916, supp., p. 462.

At the outset, the Government of the United States may state what the preceding part of this memorandum bears out, that this statement contains a direct charge which, so far as it applies to the United States, is unfounded so far as the Government of the United States was cognizant of the facts, or so far as facts have been presented to it by the British Government.

In regard to this statement, the Department of Justice, which is charged with the duty to prosecute violations of the laws of the United States, and to which are referred all reports of intrigues, activities, and movements of the agents of the belligerent powers, advised the Department of State on November 15, 1916,[91] as follows:

"In no instance, to the knowledge of this Department, has there been in this country a base of supplies for German cruisers, as that term is understood in international law; and wherever there has been any violation of the domestic law of this country by the use of false manifests, etc., and sufficient evidence thereof to warrant indictment, it has been prosecuted criminally by this Department.

"The destruction 'by foul means of factories engaged in making or ships engaged in carrying supplies required by the Allies' is not in any manner a breach of neutrality 'of this particular criminal kind,' or of any kind; and there is no obligation resting upon the United States under international law to prevent or punish such destruction. Such destruction, if it has occurred, is a matter purely of domestic concern; . . .[92]

". . .[92] though persistent and prompt investigation has been made of cases of alleged attempts to destroy factories engaged in making supplies, this Department has been unable to discover any evidence of a violation of Federal criminal law with respect thereto, except in the two cases of indictment for violation of the Sherman Anti-trust Law, which have been, and are now, being prosecuted. With regard to attempts to destroy ships carrying supplies, this Department has promptly investigated every instance brought to its attention and has secured indictments for violation of Federal criminal laws wherever the evidence warranted."

In this relation it is proper to add that, as the Department of State is advised, the greatest difficulty which the Department of Justice has experienced in undertaking prosecutions under the criminal laws in certain cases during this war has been the inability to obtain from the British Government consent for the return of supposed culprits and witnesses who have been seized and held as prisoners of war by British authorities.

WASHINGTON, *February 23, 1917.*

---

[91] Letter not printed.
[92] Omission indicated in the original memorandum.

763.72111 H 58/9½

President Wilson to the Secretary of State

WASHINGTON, *28 February, 1917.*

MY DEAR MR. SECRETARY: This, like Penfield's letter,[93] begins to bear the aspect of ancient history, but it is out of the question to let such charges go uncontradicted, and this is unquestionably the right answer. It seems to me complete, and ought to make the persons who formulated the note of complaint ashamed of themselves.

Faithfully Yours,

W. W.

763.72/3358

The Secretary of State to President Wilson

WASHINGTON, *March 7, 1917.*

MY DEAR MR. PRESIDENT: In regard to the communication from the Minister of Ecuador suggesting a meeting of American neutrals,[94] which I sent you on February 19th and which you returned to me the following day, I feel that the time would not be opportune to pursue the suggestion at present. Conditions have materially changed since the Ecuadorean Government, on February 17th, made the proposal. Unless you feel there is something to be gained I will advise the Ecuadorean Minister that in view of present conditions the endorsement of the proposed Congress of Neutrals by this Government might be misinterpreted and cause division of opinion among American republics.

Faithfully yours,

ROBERT LANSING

---

[93] Penfield's letter not printed.
[94] *Foreign Relations*, 1917, supp. 1, p. 233.

INTERFERENCE WITH AMERICAN COMMERCE BY GREAT BRITAIN AND HER ALLIES

763.72112/126

The Acting Secretary of State to President Wilson

WASHINGTON, *September 27, 1914.*

DEAR MR. PRESIDENT: I am sorry to disturb you today, but I think it very desirable that the enclosed instruction to Mr. Page at London,[1] if it meets with your approval, should go forward by tomorrow's pouch, which closes at 2 P. M.

The subject of the instruction, namely the proposal to make the Declaration of London[2] the law of naval warfare for the present conflict as modified by a British Order in Council,[3] required careful consideration and considerable research before we took a definite position. As a result delay in instructing Mr. Page was unavoidable, although every day's delay was to be regretted.

I hope, therefore, that you will find it possible to examine the papers enclosed so that, if you approve, the instruction may be sent in tomorrow's pouch. Otherwise it will postpone the transmittal four or five days.

I cannot but feel that the action of the British Government calls for unqualified refusal of this Government to acquiesce in its legality and that our objections should be clearly and firmly stated.

The British Order in Council will suggest to you, I think, the obnoxious Orders in Council of the Napoleonic Wars, and will, if its provisions are called to public attention in this country, cause severe criticism in the press.

I inclose in addition to the instruction copies of (A) Mr. Page's dispatch enclosing the Order in Council, and the memorandum of the Foreign Office,[4] (B) the Articles in the Declaration of London which are modified by the Order,[5] and (C) a pamphlet containing the Declaration itself, and the Report of the Drafting Committee. In addition to these documents I also inclose (D) a memorandum by Pro-

---

[1] *Foreign Relations*, 1914, supp., p. 225.
[2] *Ibid.*, 1909, p. 318.
[3] The Order in Council of Aug. 20, 1914; for text, see *ibid.*, 1914, supp., p. 219.
[4] *Ibid.*, p. 218.
[5] Enclosures B through E not printed.

fessor Eugene Wambaugh, and (E) a memorandum by the Joint State and Navy Neutrality Board.

If you think time would be saved by oral explanation of these papers, I can be summoned at any time by telephone as I will be either at the Department or at my residence.

Very sincerely yours,

ROBERT LANSING

763.72112/359a

The Acting Secretary of State to President Wilson

WASHINGTON, *September 28, 1914.*

DEAR MR. PRESIDENT: I enclose a draft of telegram to the American Ambassador at London, in accordance with your direction this morning.[6]

I confess I am not satisfied with it, because there seems so much to say which is not said. I hope you will please indicate any suggestions you may have as to changes.

Very sincerely yours,

ROBERT LANSING

[Enclosure]

Draft Telegram From the Acting Secretary of State to the Ambassador in Great Britain (*Page*)

You will immediately see Sir Edward Grey and state to him informally that this Government has given careful consideration to the intention of the British Government to change the provisions of the Declaration of London by the Order in Council of the twentieth August and to adopt the Declaration thus changed as the code of naval warfare for the present war. This Government as the result of its examination, feels grave concern at all of the proposed changes, especially those in Articles three and five of the Order in Council, which so materially affect the rights of neutral commerce. If the proposed rules are put into force and the matter becomes the subject of public discussion in this country, as it undoubtedly will, it is to be feared that it will arouse a spirit of resentment among the American people toward Great Britain, which this Government would extremely regret but which it would be unable to prevent. You will also point out that the enforcement of these rules by the British Government would furnish to those inimicable to Great Britain an opportunity, which they would not be slow to seize.

You will further say that the President desires, if possible, to avoid a formal protest to these proposed rules and their enforcement

---

[6] For telegram as sent, see *Foreign Relations*, 1914, supp., p. 232.

and hopes that the British Government will carefully consider the advisability of modifying the objectionable features of the Order in Council, which possesses such latent possibilities of disturbing the existing relations between the peoples of the two countries.

You will impress upon Sir Edward Grey the extreme gravity of the situation and the earnest wish of the President to avoid causes of irritation and controversy between this Government and the Government of His Majesty.

In presenting the substance of this instruction to Sir Edward Grey you will assure him that it is done in the most friendly spirit. Telegraph result of interview as soon as possible.

763.72112/181

The Acting Secretary of State to the Secretary of State

[WASHINGTON,] *September 29, 1914.*

DEAR MR. SECRETARY: I prepared this instruction [7] with the idea that it be sent at once so that it could be in Ambassador Page's hands in case his informal representations failed. My idea was to avoid any criticism of the Administration for failure to protest promptly against infringement of American rights. The President, however, thought it would be better to await the result of the telegraphic instruction of last night [8] which was based on the annexed. [7]

ROBERT LANSING

763.72112/178½

Statement for the Press by the Counselor for the Department of State (Lansing)

OCTOBER 1, 1914.

A statement appeared in certain morning papers that the British Ambassador had advised officials of the State Department that Great Britain intended to seize goods listed as conditional contraband, which were destined for Germany or Austria, even if they were carried in neutral ships, and consigned to neutral ports.

When the attention of Counselor Lansing of the State Department was called to this statement, he said that it was without foundation; that the British Ambassador had given no such notice; that the question of the inclusion of certain articles in the British list of conditional contraband had been discussed informally with the Brit-

---

[7] No enclosure with file copy of this letter.
[8] *Foreign Relations*, 1914, supp., p. 232.

ish Ambassador, but that he had not informed the British Government or the British Ambassador that this Government did not accept the British position as to seizure of neutral vessels and cargoes, of which our Ambassador at London has not advised the Department.

He further denied that he had handed the British Ambassador a copy of the regulations issued by the Bureau of War Risk Insurance; that neither these regulations nor the lists of articles classified as conditional contraband appearing in the regulations had ever been discussed in any way with the British Ambassador.

He further stated that this matter had not been called to the attention of the Netherlands Government, either here or at The Hague.

Mr. Lansing further said that he considered statements such as these most mischievous as they tended to excite public feeling in a way which might seriously embarrass this Government, and that he hoped hereafter the officials of this Department would not be credited with assertions which they never made and which they have no intention of making.

He added that, so far as the question of shipment of conditional contraband was concerned, he had no doubt that there would be an arrangement reached which would be satisfactory to all parties concerned.

763.72111/505½

The British Ambassador (Spring Rice) to President Wilson

WASHINGTON, *October 15, 1914.*

DEAR MR. PRESIDENT: I enclose decypher of a telegram which I have just received from Sir Edward Grey.

My Government is doing all in its power to avoid interference with neutral trade, especially with the trade of the United States; but in the life and death struggle in which we are now engaged it is essential to prevent war supplies reaching the German armies and factories.

When the United States was involved in a similar struggle a question arose, that of the trade with the Southern States, through British colonies, on which the British Government accepted the doctrine of continuous voyage, even though it entailed serious loss on their own people. It is this same doctrine which we are now ready to abandon if we can receive adequate security from neutral nations that they will not become the bases for supplies of the forces which are devastating Belgium and France.

My Government, in deference to your wishes, has withdrawn the Order in Council, but until the new one is issued it is impossible to make the arrangements with neutral powers which are so essential for our safety.

If a British force were devastating Mexico I do not suppose that the United States would allow it to draw its supplies either directly or by transit through United States territory; and if any nation protested against an embargo I do not suppose that American public opinion would endorse that protest.

The export figures of American trade show the immense increase of exports of all sorts, so that even from the commercial point of view this country has already found its compensation, and it is now abundantly proved that early last summer Germany was laying in supplies with a view to a war and has stated officially that she has enough to last two years. All that we now aim at is that (having no neutral ports ourselves, through which we can import) Germany may not be allowed to avail herself of her usual ports of supply (for instance in Holland) in order to feed her army and supply her factories with war materials.

We do not for a moment ask that this country should depart from the principles of absolute neutrality but merely that she should acquiesce in the enforcement of a doctrine which she herself has always insisted on—namely that a belligerent has the right to take measures to prevent its enemy from using a neutral as a port of entry for belligerent purposes. All that we ask is that you do not now abandon in the interest of our enemy a doctrine which you have in past times successfully asserted against ourselves.

I have [etc.] CECIL SPRING RICE

[Enclosure—Telegram]

The British Secretary of State for Foreign Affairs (Grey) to the British Ambassador (Spring Rice)

It is essential that we should have United States observations as soon as possible in order that we may issue a list of contraband of war that will not meet with objections from the United States Government.

We do not object to the principle of the Declaration of London provided we can prevent German army and war factories such as Essen being supplied through neutral countries.

To effect this it is essential to depart from strict rules of Declaration of London as to list of absolute contraband and to apply stricter measures as to conditional contraband in cases where a neutral country is being used as a base of supplies for German army and materials for munitions of war.

Does State Department realise that under the Rhine Convention between Holland and Germany goods consigned to Rotterdam may on arrival there be declared in transit and pass on to Germany in spite of any embargo on export by Netherlands Government?

Till our new proclamation is issued we cannot make arrangements with neutral governments for insuring that goods consigned to them, however contraband, are not re-exported. We were hoping to make an arrangement with Netherlands Government; but even this is in suspense pending discussion of new proclamation with United States Government.

We are most anxious to come to an agreement with United States Government for otherwise we shall have to choose between a dispute with United States Government or giving up all attempts to prevent Germany from getting free supplies for her army and materials for all munitions of war: either alternative would or might be fatal to our chance of success and insure ultimate German victory and disappearance of Great Britain as a fully independent Power in Europe. I understand importance to the United States of seeing that there is as little interference as possible with trade. In this interest we have for present ceased to detain any food stuffs for Rotterdam or to demand any guarantee from Netherlands Government about them and these are no doubt going up the Rhine which is direct route to German army.

Petroleum, copper, rubber and everything else will follow suit unless we can speedily come to an arrangement about a new proclamation. Enormous quantities of petroleum are now being shipped to Holland and Scandinavian countries and are causing us much anxiety.

[File copy not signed]

763.72111/505½

President Wilson to the Acting Secretary of State

15 OCTOBER, 1914.

DEAR MR. LANSING: For fear this should not reach you promptly otherwise, I am sending it to you within a few minutes of its receipt here.[10]

The tone of it is so candid and sincere, and so earnest that I am sure you will wish to send our reply at once.

Cordially,

WOODROW WILSON

763.72112/157

The Acting Secretary of State to President Wilson

WASHINGTON, *October 15, 1914.*

DEAR MR. PRESIDENT: Referring to our conversation of last evening in regard to the negotiations relative to the Declaration of London

---

[10] Note from the British Ambassador to President Wilson, *supra.*

I send you herewith the objections to the Draft Order in Council of the British Government,[11] which they propose as a substitute to the Order in Council of August 20th.[12]

The sum total of the objection[s] is that the Order in Council of August 20th is repealed in no particular, but on the contrary is re-enacted with changes and additions which make its provisions even more objectionable.

If these objections seem to you to be sound, they should, I think, be telegraphed to Mr. Page in London [13] as Sir Cecil Spring-Rice today showed me a telegram from Sir Edward Grey [14] asking for our comments on the proposed Order in Council as soon as possible.   It would seem best also to give a paraphrase of the telegram to Sir Cecil in order that he may be fully advised of this Government's views.

Even though the telegram is long, it seems to me advisable that Mr. Page should be supplied with the arguments which will be urged on the British Ambassador here.

I regret to have to trouble you with this matter but in view of Sir Edward Grey's urgent request for the views of this Government, which is not unreasonable in the circumstances, I felt this Memorandum should be in your hands tonight.

A copy of the Order in Council of August 20, 1914, and of the substitute Order in Council now proposed by the British Government are also inclosed.

> Very sincerely yours,
>
> ROBERT LANSING

[Enclosure]

Draft Telegram From the Acting Secretary of State to the Ambassador in Great Britain (Page) [13]

OBJECTIONS TO THE PROPOSED ORDER IN COUNCIL, FORWARDED IN AMERICAN AMBASSADOR'S TELEGRAM NO. 806 OF OCTOBER 9, 1914 [11]

First.   It does not accept the Declaration of London without change, hence this Government is convinced that such modified acceptance would not be satisfactory to other belligerents, who have accepted the Declaration conditionally upon its acceptance by all the belligerent powers.

Second.   If all or a part of the belligerents accepted the Declaration of London the proposed modifications and additions to the Declaration, by increasing the restrictions on neutral commerce be-

[11] *Foreign Relations*, 1914, supp., p. 244.
[12] *Ibid.*, p. 219.
[13] For telegram as sent, see *ibid.*, p. 250.
[14] *Ante*, p. 251.

yond those imposed by the Declaration or by international law, would not be acceptable to neutral nations including the United States.

The foregoing objections to the proposed Order in Council are general in nature, depending upon the fact that the proposed modifications and additions make unanimous acceptance of the Declaration of London as a code of naval warfare impossible.

As to the provisions of the proposed Order in Council considered in detail this Government makes the following objections:

A. The proposed Order in Council leaves unrepealed Articles 2, 3, 4 and 6 of the Order in Council of August 20th. Of these Articles Numbers 3 and 6 are especially objectionable to this Government. Articles 2 and 4, while less objectionable, are amendments to the Declaration and so prevent its unqualified acceptance.

B. The proposed Order in Council, while it purports to repeal Article 1 of the Order in Council of August 20th, in fact reenacts that Article and extends the lists of contraband set forth by many additions. These additions could have been made under Articles 23 and 25 of the Declaration if it had been adopted without change, hence it was needless to modify the Declaration itself. This objection was made to Article 1 of the Order in Council of August 20th, and applies equally to its reenactment in an amended form.

C. The substitution of Sub-Article B of Article 2 of Section 3 of the proposed Order in Council for Article 5 of the Order in Council of August 20th is, from the standpoint of neutral interests, more objectionable than the repealed Article 5. That Article was intended to preserve the doctrine of "continuous voyage" in relation to conditional contraband. While purporting to abandon the doctrine Sub-Article B not only reenacts it but goes even further than Article 5 in applying it. If "continuous voyage" is eliminated, no ship carrying articles listed as conditional contraband is liable to capture when its cargo is to be discharged in a neutral port even if the ultimate destination of the cargo is the enemy government. By Article 5 of the Order in Council of August 20th a ship destined to a neutral port is liable to seizure if the consignee of the cargo of conditional contraband is an enemy government, its agent or a person under its control. By Sub-Article B, in the proposed Order in Council a ship and cargo are liable to capture, if the goods carried are listed as conditional contraband, even though to be discharged at a neutral port, provided "no consignee in that country of the goods alleged to be conditional contraband is disclosed in the ship's papers." In fact the terms of the Sub-Article permit capture of a ship bound for the port of one neutral country, if the cargo is consigned to a person resident in another neutral country. The substitute is manifestly far more obnoxious than the original Article 5.

D. Section Four of the proposed Order in Council introduces a new principle into international law, which imposes upon neutral commerce a restriction without precedent in modern times. An analysis of the provisions of this section shows that, in the discretion of one of His Majesty's Principal Secretaries of State, a neutral country may be clothed with enemy character and that the legitimate trade of another neutral with such country may be subjected to the rules which are applied to contraband trade with enemy territory as such rules are laid down in Article 3 of the Order in Council of August 20th. In brief this section means that articles, listed as conditional contraband, shipped in a neutral vessel to a neutral country makes the vessel and its cargo liable to seizure if the British authorities are satisfied that supplies or munitions of war are entering enemy territory from the neutral country to a port of which the vessel is bound even though the consignee is within neutral country.

The purpose of this provision seems to be to gain all the rights of a belligerent over neutral commerce with enemy territory without declaring war against the neutral country which is claimed to be a base of supply for the military forces of an enemy. If the British Government seek belligerent rights they must bear the burden of belligerency. They cannot declare a nation to be neutral and treat it as an enemy, and expect other neutral nations to submit to having their commerce subjected to rules which only apply to commerce with a belligerent. If a neutral nation's trade with a neighboring belligerent constitutes an unneutral act, the remedy is an ultimatum, not a restriction of the trade of an innocent neutral nation with the nation, whose acts are complained of.

ROBERT LANSING

763.72112/12930b

The Acting Secretary of State to President Wilson

WASHINGTON, *October 20, 1914.*

DEAR MR. PRESIDENT: I enclose you a paraphrase of a telegram to-day from Mr. Page [17] and also copies of two telegrams handed to me by the British Ambassador,[18] all relative to the Declaration of London.

It seems to me that in view of the rigid attitude of the British Government further attempts to obtain an agreement on the Declaration of London would be useless. We must, therefore, stand on the rules of international law which have been generally accepted with-

---

[17] *Foreign Relations*, 1914, supp., p. 253.
[18] *Ibid.*, pp. 254, 255.

out regard to the Declaration. In the matter of the transfer of vessels this will be a decided advantage. The great loss is the failure to have a definite code, which will undoubtedly be the source of numerous controversies.

It is to be regretted that in spite of all that has been done, the purpose of the negotiation has failed.

Probably it would be well to await the new proclamation before acting, although a protest might be entered against certain articles which the British Government on September 21st declared contraband.[19]

Very sincerely yours,

ROBERT LANSING

763.72112/189

The Acting Secretary of State to President Wilson

WASHINGTON, *October 21, 1914.*

DEAR MR. PRESIDENT: I enclose herewith a telegram which I have drafted [20] in accordance with our conversation this morning relative to the Declaration of London.

If it meets with your approval, will you kindly return it so that it may be sent at once to Ambassador Page? [21]

Very sincerely yours,

ROBERT LANSING

763.72112/242½a

The Acting Secretary of State to President Wilson

WASHINGTON, *October 23, 1914.*

DEAR MR. PRESIDENT: In view of the fact that we have notified Great Britain that our suggestion as to the adoption of the Declaration of London is withdrawn and that this Government will stand upon its rights as defined by the existing rules of International Law, should we not give a similar notice to the other belligerent governments stating as a reason for the withdrawal of the suggestion the

---

[19] See telegram of Sept. 30, 1914, from the Ambassador in Great Britain, *Foreign Relations*, 1914, supp., p. 236.
[20] For the telegram as sent, see *ibid.*, p. 257.
[21] A memorandum attached to this paper reads as follows:

"OCTOBER 21, 1914.

"Despatch to Page, Oct. 21, 1914 Declaration of London [R. L.]"

"Approved as altered W. W."

"Would it not be well to show this to S[pring]-R[ice] before you send it,—for any comment or suggestion he might have to make? W. W."

"Shown Amb. who made no suggestions. R. L."

unwillingness of some [of] the belligerents to accept the Declaration without modification? [22]

Very sincerely yours,

ROBERT LANSING

763.72112/223½

The British Embassy to the Department of State

WASHINGTON [undated].

TELEGRAM FROM SIR E. GREY TO SIR C. SPRING RICE, DATED OCTOBER 24, 1914

I am very glad that the United States Government no longer insist upon the Declaration of London in its entirety: this decision will smooth the path very much. I am very sensible of the friendly spirit shown by the President and my conversations with Mr. Page have been most pleasant.

It is absolutely necessary for us in the present circumstances to detain ships carrying oil and copper till we make sure that their cargoes are really going to be landed and consumed in a neutral country; it must not however be assumed that when a ship is detained her cargo is going to be captured or confiscated. In the meanwhile I am doing my best to secure arrangements with neutral countries of such a nature as will avoid delay to neutral shipping while it giving us adequate security. [File copy not signed]

763.72112/545a

The Secretary of State to President Wilson

WASHINGTON, *December 17, 1914.*

MY DEAR MR. PRESIDENT: I am sending you a draft of a proposed instruction [to the Ambassador in Great Britain].[23] This was prepared by Mr. Johnson [23a] and revised by Mr. Lansing and afterwards by myself.

I think, in view of the increasing tension there is on the subject it is well for us to put this Government's views in definite form so that in case inquiry is made as to what has been done it will be manifest that we have exerted ourselves to the utmost to bring about a lessening of the hardships imposed upon neutral countries.

---

[22] This paper bears the notation: "Yes; by all means. W. W."
[23] Not found in Department files. See footnote 27, p. 258.
[23a] Cone Johnson, Solicitor for the Department of State.

It is a matter of such importance, however, that we are anxious to have you go over it carefully and suggest any changes in phraseology or any additions or subtractions that you may think wise.

It does seem as if they[24] could do everything required for the protection of their rights without the great and constant injury which has been done to shipping.

We have had a similar experience in regard to communication by cable. We have many complaints of innocent cables being undelivered and the senders have not even been notified of the failure to deliver, so that great loss has been occasioned. This we have recently brought to the attention of the Government in another telegram,[25] but the proposed telegram which I am enclosing goes over the whole subject more fully than we have heretofore done.

The enclosed clippings[26] indicate the public criticism that is being directed toward the policy of the British Government.

With assurances [etc.]   W. J. BRYAN

763.72112/545½

President Wilson to the Secretary of State

WASHINGTON, *26 December, 1914.*

MY DEAR MR. SECRETARY: This paper is much improved and I am glad to give it my sanction.[27]

I think it might be wise to send our Ambassador in London a cipher copy of the despatch from our Ambassador in Rome[28] which speaks of the change of sentiment which is taking place in Italy; and to suggest to him that he might, in his discretion, make unofficial and confidential use of it in his conversations with the British Foreign Office. Very likely the British representative at Rome has apprised his government of these things, but Walter Page ought to have the information in his possession.

Cordially and faithfully Yours,

WOODROW WILSON

---

[24] i. e., the British Government.
[25] *Foreign Relations*, 1914, supp., p. 526.
[26] Not enclosed with file copy of this letter.
[27] Telegram No. 836, Dec. 26, 1914, to the Ambassador in Great Britain, *Foreign Relations*, 1914, supp., p. 372.

A memorandum attached to this note in Mr. Lansing's hand reads as follows:

"*Department's instruction No. 836 to London, Dec. 26, 1914, 4 pm.*

"An original draft was made about the 20th by Johnson. This I revised and changes were then made by the Secy. It was then submitted to the President who thought that it was too abrupt.

"On its return I drafted a new instruction incorporating two changes suggested by Johnson. It was approved by the Secy and sent to the President. With certain changes shown by pen insertions the redraft was approved and sent. Robert Lansing 12/29/14."

[28] *Foreign Relations*, 1914, supp., p. 156.

763.72/1379½

The Ambassador in Great Britain (Page) to the Secretary of State

LONDON, *December 28, 1914.*
[Received January 11, 1915.]

MY DEAR MR. SECRETARY: Two things have pleased me much during the last few days—your kind letter of Dec. 14,[29] and the admirable tone & the dignity of the long telegraphic protest that is just come about the English treatment of neutral ships and cargoes.[30] It is an admirable paper, & it is a pleasure to present it. It takes the English action at its weakest point—its lack of a consistent plan. It will have a good effect and will supplement and strengthen the work that I have been trying to do.

Its admirable quality consists moreover in this—if I may be allowed to say so—it does not accuse the British Government of deliberate small dealing or littleness. We have made the mistake sometimes to accuse them—or to seem to insinuate—that they are giving us trouble in order to increase their own trade or their profit from trade. However keen they may be in this way in peaceful times (and they surely are good tradesmen!) they are not using the war to gain any such advantage. They are playing the game fairly. But they are playing it very hard now (hard-pressed as they are) and they are guilty of having no fixed policy. About trade-restrictions, they are as they are about the censorship—they don't know how to do it. I think that this perfectly fair protest will hasten them to learn.

I have been somewhat afraid of this sort of misunderstanding between the two Governments. On our side, you have seemed at times to think that the British were using their sea-power to gain commercial advantage. I am persuaded that this is not true. They have but one thought now—to starve out the enemy. In this process they are starving out also many of their own business people. This Government has more protests from its own shippers and merchants than it has from all the neutral countries combined. They even come to me to see if I can't find ways to help them—I mean British merchants—via of the United States. You hear of course the complaints of merchants who wish to get wares into Germany. I hear complaints from British merchants who wish to get wares into the U. S. and other neutral countries.

And on the English side, I have at times been very fearful lest this Government should conclude that the Department has (unwittingly of course) fallen under the influence of the German propaganda in

[29] Not found in Department files.
[30] *Foreign Relations*, 1914, supp., p. 372.

the U. S. There has been danger of this suspicion. For example, our wool-importers have been demanding permission to get the wool they have paid for, from England and from Australia. While this has been going on, wool has been bought in the U. S. for the German Government. This Government knows that; & I have had it confirmed on American authority. Of course neither Government can be held responsible for the tricks of its merchants; but so many of our complaints have been so obviously inspired by merchants who wish to reach the German market that this Government has feared that we are unwittingly playing into the Germans' hands. Of course they have never told me this; but I have felt it in the air & I have had it intimated to me in private. This is, of course, as utterly erroneous as the supposition of some of our merchants that the British Government is making profit out of the war. But it is the untrue things that cause the worst misunderstandings.

The worst of it is, no end is in sight. Everybody here expects a long war. And all troubles will increase as time goes on. I am sometimes surprised that ours are no worse. For example, the troubles of Holland, Sweden, Denmark are vastly greater. They have had their business practically killed. They are between the two great belligerents. Their Ministers make the best arrangements they can— sometimes a new arrangement every week. They are in the direst straits. But they agree that this Government is doing nothing indirect nor underhand. It does its mischief openly—going straight for its arch enemy. This doesn't make the mischief any less, but it makes the way a little clearer for dealing with it.

I try to look far ahead: where shall we stand when it ends? We shall have the hatred of the Germans whatever we do because of the preponderance of American opinion against Germany. We shall have the esteem of a lessened number of the English because we keep our strict neutrality. I feel that constantly and am constantly criticised for the care I give the Germans and the German interests. I have a drawer full of letters (all unanswered) full of criticism even of our Government for having anything to do with the Germans & for refraining from protests about the German conduct of the war. To keep a long look ahead seems wise. When it ends we want first the approval of our own consciences and then the approval, as far as we can get it, of all nations—of this nation in particular because it is worth more to us than any other. We shall win their approval by standing up stoutly for our rights, but not by seeming to accuse them of motives that they have not. You may be sure they go and will go the whole length to keep our good will, provided we credit them with wishing to do the fair thing. They do not wish to do us an unfair turn—only to starve out their enemy; and that they are going to do at all costs. Of course the heaviest cost falls on them. They are not now thinking about their trade—or anybody else's—I mean the Government isn't. You'll find the cue to their actions in their determination to win.

A happy New Year to you and Mrs. Bryan. Praise Heaven you are so far from this horrible and continual depression. It is simply unspeakable. I admire the cheerful and buoyant way in which Mrs. Owen holds up under it; she is wonderful and provokes my heartiest admiration.

> Sincerely yours,
>
> WALTER H. PAGE

763.72112/594

The Counselor for the Department of State (Lansing) to President Wilson

WASHINGTON, *January 11, 1915.*

DEAR MR. PRESIDENT: 1 enclose herewith some notes on Sir Edward Grey's reply of January 7th.[31] They are intended merely as preliminary comments on the British defense of the action of which we complain, and as a possible suggestion of the evidence required to meet Sir Edward's positions.

My general impression of the document is that the tone is conciliatory and that the presentation of the British case is adroit, though transparently illogical in many particulars to one familiar with the facts. It appears to be drafted with the purpose of allaying public irritation in this country without giving any assurance that trade conditions with neutral countries will be relieved.

It seems to me that in acknowledging the note Mr. Page, while expressing gratification at its temperate tone, and stating that comment would be withheld until the complete British reply had been received, should be instructed to urge the delivery of such reply as soon as possible in view of the existing doubt as to British action in the future and the consequent demoralizing effect on American commerce.

I have submitted a copy of the enclosed to Secretary Bryan and I am sending you a copy with his approval.

> Very sincerely yours,
>
> ROBERT LANSING

---

[31] *Foreign Relations*, 1915, supp., p. 299.

[Enclosure]

Notes by the Counselor for the Department of State (Lansing) on the Communication of January 7, 1915, From the British Secretary of State for Foreign Affairs (Grey)

[WASHINGTON,] *January 10, 1915.*

Paragraph 2. The question is raised by the statement, that these are "preliminary observations" and that a detailed answer will be made, whether any answer should be made at the present time to these "observations"?

Paragraph 3. Recognition of friendly tone of United States note and desire expressed to reply in same spirit.

Paragraph 4. Concurrence in the principle that necessity for national defense is measure of interference with neutral trade and assertion that G. B. will endeavor to keep within those limits and make redress for unintentional violation.

There seems to be a distinction made between "bona fide" trade and "trade in contraband destined for the enemy's country". The term "bona fide trade" appears to be novel and requires explanation. Certainly trade in contraband is not *mala fides*. No distinction is made in this assertion between absolute and conditional contraband. Trade in conditional contraband to an enemy's country is not necessarily subject to interference.

Paragraph 5. A ground for complaint is that the danger of seizure or detention deters shippers from sending goods, causes steamship lines to refuse to take cargoes, and prevents shippers from obtaining insurance. The uncertainty of freedom of trade is one of the chief, if not the chief, grounds of complaint.

Paragraph 6. These figures prove nothing, at least not what they are intended to prove. No one denies the fact that the export of certain commodities to neutral countries have greatly increased, that is the normal result of closing the sources of supply from belligerent countries. Those who deal in such articles have unquestionably been benefited. On the other hand, the trade in other commodities, which is viewed with suspicion by G. B. and subject to interference, has fallen off to such an extent that the industries are much depressed. Because the general volume of trade to neutral countries has increased does not meet the argument that certain of the great industries of the U. S. are suffering severely by British action. The equilibrium of our industrial life has been destroyed. We have no market for the surplus production of certain industries, while we cannot produce enough of other commodities to keep down their cost to our own people. Labor as well as capital suffers from the deprivation of markets resulting from G. B.'s closing the trade routes.

Paragraph 7. The cotton situation is an excellent example of the effect of the uncertainty and doubt which prevails in this country, due in large measure to the vacillation which has been shown by the British Government in the matter of contraband. The change of policy in regard to resin and turpentine is an example of this vacillation.

Paragraph 8. Invites statistics of trade. Differentiates between results due to British action and the existence of a state of war. This latter point requires consideration as it appears to be well taken.

Paragraph 9. Elaborates the idea that it is the state of war which is responsible for the disorganization of American trade.

Paragraph 10. Calls particular attention to the detention of copper and the trade in it to Italy.

Paragraph 11. Compares 1913 and 1914 statistics of copper exported to Italy. Fails to take into account that Italy in time of peace imported manufactured copper from Germany and therefore imported comparatively little raw copper from the United States. Fails to consider that copper articles are not exported from Germany. Fails to consider that the Italian demand for copper has increased enormously in view of military preparations. Fails to consider that Switzerland must obtain copper from Italy. In spite of these reasons for increased copper import into Italy, exports from the U. S. have only increased 20 million pounds. Of this increase between 8 and 10 millions of pounds are lying at Gibraltar.

Paragraph 12. Comment on paragraph 11 applies to this paragraph dealing with copper shipped to other neutral countries.

Paragraph 13. The presumption in view of the facts which are not considered is not "very strong", nor is the necessity as imperative as alleged.

Paragraph 14. This Government would be better satisfied if the "positive evidence" that copper consigned to Sweden was bound for Germany were produced. It is said to be "in the possession of His Majesty's Government". To withhold it is inexcusable in view of the discussions which have taken place. One of the serious grounds of complaint is not only the failure to disclose evidence which is asserted to be sufficient to warrant seizure, but the neglect to inform this Government of the charges against the vessels seized. In view of the subscription to the doctrine of "frankness" in Paragraph 3 this secretiveness appears to be paradoxical.

Paragraph 15. The term "suspected cargoes" attracts attention. What is the suspicion? What is the foundation of it? On how strong evidence is it based? Is it based on any evidence save the nature of the cargoes? The term requires explanation before it can be accepted.

So too the term "legitimate means" cannot be passed over without comment. The U. S. does not question the employment of legitimate means by G. B., but what is "legitimate"? Apparently the two Governments may differ as to that. The U. S. would limit the word to its use as interpreted by international law, but G. B. does not seem to be satisfied by such limitation.

Paragraph 16. It is the way that the British Government has applied the admitted rule as to food stuffs, of which the United States complains. It is no excuse that the enemy of G. B. may violate the accepted rules of civilization. Specific instances of violation would be more in point. I think that it can be shown that G. B. has not adhered to the rule which she accepts.

Paragraph 17. Cargoes and vessels held for prize court respectively 45 and 8. Hypothetical case of search of a cotton cargo. Information alleged as to contraband hidden in cotton. No evidence adduced that this has ever occurred. The argument seems to be presented for the purpose of excusing future detention of cotton cargoes on reports based on suspicion other than evidence. This paragraph causes distrust rather than confidence in the policy which G. B. intends to follow in the future.

Paragraph 18. The U. S. raised no question as to the justice which would be rendered in the British prize courts. It is the conduct of the British authorities prior to the prize court proceedings of which it complains.

Paragraph 19. This seems to be a sound argument in regard to the trade in crude rubber. There can little be said in reply.

Paragraph 20. This statement is undoubtedly true as to the danger of contiguous neutral nations becoming bases for supplies for the enemies of G. B., but that is a matter between the governments of those nations and G. B., with which the U. S. has not and ought not to have anything to do. That the goods are consigned to a neutral ought to insure them free passage unless it is positively shown that they are destined to an enemy's armed forces or his government. If by arrangement with G. B. these countries forbid exportation of these goods and the consignee fraudulently attempts to evade the prohibition, the matter is one for the British Government to take up with the government of the consignee. Certainly the innocent American owner should not be made to suffer. Yet this is the course which G. B. has adopted during the past five months.

The phrase "bona fide" neutral as applied to goods would appear to mean that other goods are enemy goods falsely held in the name of a neutral. Can G. B. cite a single case of this sort? She has not done so thus far in spite of the scores of vessels and cargoes detained.

Paragraph 21. The United States should accept the statement that G. B. had no ground to complain of the abandonment of entirely unauthorized publication of manifests and the adoption of a rule that they should not be given general publicity by officials for thirty days. Attention might be called to the fact that another custom was also abandoned, which was that a full manifest did not have to be filed for four days after the vessel sailed. In order to prevent the shipment of coal and supplies to belligerent warships clearance was refused by order of the Treasury Department until the full manifest was filed.

So far as knowledge of the contents of a manifest serves to remove a danger of detention in a British port the claim is without foundation. The vessels which are stopped on the high seas by British warships have their manifests. These can be easily examined at the time of visit. If they are without evidence of unneutral trade, the vessels should be allowed to proceed. As to such visit and detention on the high seas the United States has no ground for complaint. But it does not appear that G. B. is satisfied with the facts set forth in a manifest, actual search must verify them, and this, acccording to British practice, takes place in port and not on the high seas. How then does knowledge of the contents of a manifest prevent detentions since the accuracy of the manifest is always apparently doubted?

If a vessel was immune from interruption provided her manifest showed no goods with enemy destination there might be some reason for giving publicity to the manifest at the time of clearing, but, since it does not, it in no way benefits American shippers to publish it, while for trade reasons many seriously object to such publication.

Paragraph 22. The experience of this Government thus far has been that the reasons for many of the detentions have not been promptly attainable. A change in this particular, in accordance with the promise here made, would remove some of the grounds for complaint which exist. The U. S. has sought in vain in many cases for a statement of the reason for detention. Such a situation cannot but cause irritation and arouse suspicion that the vessel or cargo is held until arrangements have been made with the government of the neutral country to the port of which it is destined. If such a suspicion is justified the detention is manifestly illegal and a proper ground for protest.

763.72112/699½

President Wilson to the Secretary of State

WASHINGTON, *January 14, 1915.*

MY DEAR MR. SECRETARY: I return the English preliminary note with Mr. Lansing's memoranda, and wish to make this suggestion, as I did hurriedly over the telephone the other day:

The two governments being apparently in substantial agreement about the principles involved, it would seem to me best that the whole argument should be directed to practicable methods of handling the whole matter with the least possible delay, unfairness, or friction, and with a view to bringing the British practices to some basis of uniformity and consistency upon which our merchants could reckon. My feeling is that it is not worth while debating details with them. But this is only a judgment preliminary like the note itself.

Cordially and faithfully yours,

WOODROW WILSON

763.72112/700½

Memorandum by the Counselor for the Department of State (Lansing)[33]

[WASHINGTON,] *February 1, 1915.*

THE NEGOTIATIONS FOR THE ADOPTION OF THE DECLARATION OF LONDON BY THE BELLIGERENTS AS A CODE OF NAVAL WARFARE DURING THE PENDING EUROPEAN WAR[34]

The Naval Conference at London in 1908–9 was in consequence of the following facts:

Great Britain objected to Article 7 of Hague Convention No. 12 of 1907 relative to the creation of an international prize court,[35] because of the uncertainty of the law to be applied by that court in the decision of controversies submitted to it; Great Britain made its acceptance of the Convention dependent upon an international agreement by the principal maritime powers as to certain fundamental principles of law for the guidance of the court; and the British Gov-

---

[33] This paper bears the notation: "Written for the Secretary who said on Friday (29th Jan.) that the President desired a statement of these negotiations. L[ester] H. W[oolsey]."

[34] For correspondence previously printed concerning the Declaration of London, see *Foreign Relations,* 1909, pp. 294–336, and *ibid.,* 1914, supp., pp. 215 ff; see also *ante,* pp. 247–257.

[35] For text of this convention, see *The Second International Peace Conference Held at The Hague From June 15 to October 18, 1907,* S. Doc. 444, 60th Cong., 1st sess., p. 165.

ernment in order to obtain such an agreement proposed that a conference be held in London for the purpose of agreeing upon these principles of prize law. This proposal was acceptable to the powers approached and a conference met in December, 1908, composed of representatives of the ten principal maritime powers, who on February 26, 1909, concluded the Convention known as the Declaration of London.

As Great Britain originated the conference, the signatory powers generally awaited her action in ratifying it before they took action. The Declaration failed of approval by the Parliament of Great Britain and has not been ratified by any of the signatories, so far as the Department is advised. The United States Senate advised and consented to the ratification of the Declaration, but the United States has never deposited its ratifications at London as required by Article 67 in view of the action of the British Parliament.

The proceedings of the conference will be found collected in two British public documents entitled "Miscellaneous No. 4 (1909) C. D. 4554," and "Miscellaneous No. 5 (1909) C. D. 4555," "Correspondence and Documents respecting the International Naval Conference held in London, December 1908–February 1909."

Printed in the proceedings are the views of the various governments upon the subjects treated in the Declaration, and from these it will be observed how much at variance the different governments were upon certain topics. The Declaration itself in Article 65 states "The provisions of the present Declaration must be treated as a whole and cannot be separated." The conclusion is inevitable that the Declaration of London is a compromise of conflicting ideas which was reached only through mutual concessions on the part of the assembled powers, and that, having reached an agreement in this way, they desired that the rules adopted should be put in force as a whole without elimination or modification.

On August 6th last, the Department instructed the American diplomatic representatives at London, St. Petersburg, Paris, Berlin, Vienna and Brussels [36] to inquire of the governments, to which they were accredited, whether they would be willing to agree that the laws of naval warfare laid down in the Declaration should be applicable to the European conflict, provided that the other countries engaged in the war also agreed to such application. The Department added that this Government believed that the acceptance of these laws by the belligerents would prevent grave misunderstandings which might otherwise arise as to the relations between belligerent and neutral powers, and it therefore expressed the earnest hope that its inquiry might receive favorable consideration. The act of this Government

---

[36] *Foreign Relations.* 1914, supp., p. 216.

in making this inquiry was one of expediency. It did not consider the Declaration of London standing alone as the best and most equitable code of naval warfare, but it seemed available in the emergency and most probable of unanimous acceptance by the maritime powers involved in or affected by the war. The Government felt that by the general adoption of the Declaration, the differences of opinion as to the rights and duties of nations in time of war, which have heretofore been the cause of controversy long after a war ended, would be in a large measure removed in the present conflict.

On August 13th the Austrian Government replied [37] that it would apply the rules of the Declaration during the present conflict "conditional on like observations on the part of the enemy," and on August 23rd [*22d*] the German Government stated [38] that it would apply the Declaration "provided other belligerents do not disregard its provisions." The French and Russian Governments apparently awaited the reply of the British Government. On August 22nd the British Foreign Office informed the American Ambassador at London [39] that the British Government had decided to adopt generally the rules of the Declaration, subject to certain modifications and additions which they judged "indispensable to the efficient conduct of their naval operations." The Foreign Office then gave a detailed explanation of these additions and modifications in a memorandum.

On August 31st the Foreign Office communicated to Ambassador Page [40] the British Order-in-Council of August 20th, by which it was proclaimed that during the present hostilities the Declaration of London would be adopted and put in force by His Majesty's Government as if the same had been ratified, subject to certain additions and modifications which were fully set forth. This Order-in-Council was made binding upon the officers of the British Government, and upon the courts of Great Britain so far as they had occasion to enforce it. The Russian and French Governments adhered to the Declaration of London with the same modifications as made by Great Britain.

After a careful study of the Order-in-Council, the Department sent an instruction to the American Ambassador at London, dated September 26th,[41] which contained in detail a note to be presented to the Foreign Office, setting forth the objections of this Government to the additions and modifications in the Order-in-Council of August

---

[37] *Foreign Relations*, 1914, supp., p. 217.
[38] *Ibid.*, p. 218.
[39] See telegram No. 483, undated, from the Ambassador in Great Britain, *ibid.*, p. 218.
[40] See despatch No. 428, Sept. 2, 1914, from the Ambassador in Great Britain, *ibid.*, pp. 223–224.
[41] *Ibid.*, p. 225.

20th, and the reasons for the acceptance of the Declaration without change. The Ambassador, however, was instructed not to deliver this note until notified to do so by the Department, but to use it meanwhile as a basis for his conversations with Sir Edward Grey on the subject. As a matter of fact the note was never delivered to the Foreign Office.

Discussions were then held, both at Washington and in London, with a view to obtaining the agreement of Great Britain to the adoption of the Declaration without modifications.

Prior to this, on September 7th, the Austro-Hungarian Government informed the American Ambassador at Vienna that they were not able to judge the exact significance of the modifications of the Declaration of London, and asked for enlightenment on the matter.

The discussions between the representatives of this Department and the Foreign Office along the lines of the instruction of September 26th showed that Great Britain was unwilling to recede from her position. As a result this Government, convinced that further discussion would be useless, on October 22nd withdrew its proposal that the Declaration of London be adopted as a temporary code of naval warfare by belligerents and neutrals during the pending conflict.[42] The notice of withdrawal, based on the failure to obtain unanimous assent, was sent to the governments of the warring powers named, with the statement that this Government would insist that the rights and duties of the United States and its citizens in the present war be defined by the existing rules of international law and the treaties of the United States, irrespective of the provisions of the Declaration of London, and that the United States reserved the right to enter protest or demand in each case in which the rights so defined were violated or their free exercise interfered with by the authorities of the belligerent nations.

On October 29th Great Britain issued a new Order-in-Council,[43] replacing the Order-in-Council of August 20th and adopting the provisions of the Declaration of London with certain modifications set forth in the Order.

On December 23rd the British Government further amended the list of contraband articles in the Order of October 29th.[44]

The Department has followed the policy indicated in its telegram of October 22nd withdrawing its proposal regarding the Declaration of London, of protesting in each particular case in which it deemed that its rights or those of its citizens have been interfered with by the

---

[42] *Ibid.*, p. 257.
[43] *Ibid.*, p. 262.
[44] For amended list, see *ibid.*, p. 269.

authorities of a belligerent power in contravention of the rules of international law and the treaties to which it is a party.

ROBERT LANSING

763.72/1551

The Counselor for the Department of State (Lansing) to the Secretary of State

[WASHINGTON,] *March 2, 1915.*

DEAR MR. SECRETARY: The difficulty of determining action upon the British and French declarations of intended retaliation upon commerce with Germany [45] is the nature of the proposed measures in their relation to commerce by neutrals.

While it appears that the intention is to interfere with and take into custody all ships both outgoing and incoming, trading with Germany, which is in effect a blockade of German ports, the rule of blockade that a ship attempting to enter or leave a German port regardless of the character of its cargo, may be condemned, is not asserted.

The language of the declaration is "the British and French Governments will therefore hold themselves free to detain and take into port ships carrying goods of presumed enemy destination, ownership or origin. It is not intended to confiscate such vessel[s] or cargoes unless they would otherwise be liable to condemnation."

The first sentence claims a right pertaining only to a state of blockade. The last sentence proposes a treatment of ships and cargoes as if no blockade existed. The two together present a proposed course of action previously unknown to international law.

As a consequence neutrals have no standard by which to measure their rights or to avoid danger to their ships and cargoes. The paradoxical situation thus created should be changed and the declaring powers ought to assert whether they rely upon the rules governing a blockade or the rules applicable when no blockade exists.

The declaration presents other perplexities.

The last sentence quoted indicates that the rules of contraband are to be applied to cargoes detained. The rule covering non-contraband articles carried to [*in*] neutral bottoms is that the cargoes shall be released and the ships allowed to proceed. This rule cannot under the first sentence quoted be applied as to destination. What then is to be done with a cargo of non-contraband goods detained under the declaration? The same question may be asked as to conditional contraband cargoes.

---

[45] *Foreign Relations*, 1915, supp., p. 127.

The foregoing comments apply to cargoes destined for Germany. Cargoes coming out of German ports present another problem under the terms of the declaration. Under the rules governing contraband only goods owned by enemy subjects in enemy bottoms are subject to seizure and condemnation. Yet by the declaration it is purposed to seize and take into port all goods of enemy "ownership and origin". The word "origin" is particularly significant. The origin of goods destined to neutral territory on neutral ships is not and never has been a ground for forfeiture except in case a blockade is declared and maintained. What then would the seizure amount to in the present case except to delay the delivery of the goods? The declaration does not indicate what disposition would be made of such cargoes if owned by a neutral or if owned by an enemy subject. Would a different rule be applied according to ownership? If so, upon what principles of international law would it rest? But upon what rule if no blockade is declared and maintained could the cargo of a neutral ship sailing out of a German port be condemned? If it is not condemned, what other legal course is there but to release it?

While I am fully alive to the fact that the methods of modern naval warfare, particularly in the use of the submarine for both defensive and offensive operations, have made the former means of maintaining a blockade a physical impossibility, I think that there should be some limit to "the radius of activity," and especially so if this action by the belligerents can be construed to be a blockade. It would certainly create a serious state of affairs if an American vessel laden with a cargo of German origin should escape the British patrol only to be held up by a cruiser off New York and taken into Halifax.

These are some of the questions which suggest themselves from a hasty examination of the British and French declaration. It seems to me that the documents require careful scrutiny before action is taken by the Department as the whole matter of "blockade" under modern methods of naval warfare must be analyzed and some idea reached as to what is proper and right for belligerents to do and to what extent the previous rules should be modified.

Faithfully yours,

ROBERT LANSING

Respectfully submitted to the President. W. J. B[ryan]

763.72/1551

The Secretary of State to President Wilson

WASHINGTON, *March 3, 1915.*

MY DEAR MR. PRESIDENT: Mr. Lansing and I have decided to submit to you the enclosed telegram which we think ought to be sent to Great Britain.

You will notice it asks for information which seems necessary to enable us to understand the purport of the declaration which you have under consideration. If you agree with us that a telegram ought to be sent will you please make such corrections as you think best in this and send it over to the State Department Telegraph Office to be sent out tonight.

With assurances [etc.] W. J. BRYAN

[Enclosure]

Draft Telegram From the Secretary of State to the Ambassador in Great Britain (Page)

British-French declaration regarding commerce to and from Germany delivered by British and French Ambassadors on March first [46] appears to contemplate a blockade of German coasts but fails to announce establishment of such blockade or to use the word in declaration.

You will please inquire at once of British Government whether they consider a state of blockade exists.

If they reply in the affirmative, you will ask by what means they intend to make it effective, and what will be the radius of activity of the blockading squadron, and what particular ports or coastal area they intend to blockade.

You will further ask, in case of a reply in the affirmative, what is meant by the sentence: "It is not intended to confiscate such vessels or cargoes unless they would otherwise be liable to condemnation."

If they reply in the negative, you will ask under what principle of international law or practice the proposed total interruption of commerce will be enforced and to what extent it is proposed to apply the rules of contraband in dealing with vessels and cargoes detained, which are going to or coming from Germany. You will further ask, in case the reply is in the negative, how the right of immunity from seizure of neutral-owned cargoes is affected by its origin and what rule of international law prevents free passage of a cargo of German origin in a neutral vessel bound to a neutral port.

It is necessary for a proper consideration of the British-French declaration that the foregoing questions be answered categorically and clearly in order that this Government may determine to what extent its rights as a neutral are affected by the declaration. Report as promptly as possible.

---

[46] *Foreign Relations*, 1915, supp., p. 127.

763.72/1554½

President Wilson to the Secretary of State

4 MARCH, 1915.

MY DEAR MR. SECRETARY: The green paper despatch attached hereto [47] seems to me abrupt in expression and also a bit difficult to interpret as it stands. I therefore beg that, in its stead, you will send to Ambassador Page at London Mr. Lansing's letter to you (also attached),[47a] as I have taken the liberty of altering it.[48] It is both lucid and conveys the matter in just the right tone of inquiry.

Faithfully Yours,

W. W.

———————

763.72/1588

Newspaper Text of the British Order in Council of March 11, 1915, With Comments by the Counselor for the Department of State (Lansing) [49]

LONDON, *March 15*[*, 1915*].—The text of Great Britain's order in council declaring war on German commerce was made public today. The order reads:

"Whereas the German government has issued certain orders which in violation of the usages of war purport to declare that the waters surrounding the United Kingdom are a military area in which all British and allied merchant vessels will be destroyed, irrespective of the safety and the lives of the passengers and the crews, and in which neutral shipping will be exposed to similar danger in view of the uncertainties of naval warfare;

"And whereas in the memorandum accompanying the said orders neutrals are warned against intrusting crews, passengers or goods to British or allied ships;

[It does not appear that a vessel engaged in the trade sought to be interrupted becomes liable to forfeiture in the Prize Court for any act committed in such trade.

The O. in C. applies only to cargoes.

This preamble purports to furnish an excuse for the promulgation of the O. in C.

It comes to this: Because Germany menaces neutral vessels going to Great Britain, Great Britain menaces all neutral trade with Germany.

———————

[47] *Supra.*
[47a] *Ante,* p. 270.
[48] This was done; for the telegram as sent, see *Foreign Relations,* 1915, supp., p. 132.
[49] Mr. Lansing's comments are here printed in brackets following quotations from the newspaper text of the Order in Council. For official text of the Order, see *ibid.,* p. 144.

Germany deprives neutrals of rights. Great Britain retaliates by depriving neutrals of other rights. The neutrals are the chief sufferers.

This is a matter between Germany and neutrals. Neutrals can complain but not Great Britain on their behalf, and especially is this so if Great Britain proposes to retaliate by imposing still heavier burdens on neutral commerce.]

"And whereas such attempts on the part of the enemy give to his majesty an unquestionable right of retaliation;

[The measures provided for in the O. in C. are declared to be in retaliation for illegal purposes of Germany.]

"And whereas his majesty has therefore decided to adopt further measures in order to prevent commodities of any kind from reaching or leaving Germany, although such measures will be enforced without risk to neutral ships or to neutral or noncombatant life and in strict observance of the dictates of humanity;

[If this procedure was a blockade it would be a legitimate war measure. It would need no excuse such as is set forth in this preamble. It would not need to be based on an "unquestionable right of retaliation".

Clearly the measures are not considered to constitute a blockade. Furthermore the formal notice of a blockade has not been given.]

"And whereas the allies of his majesty are associated with him in the steps now to be announced for restricting further the commerce of Germany, his majesty is therefore pleased, by and with the advice of his privy council, to order, and it is hereby ordered, as follows:

[The only basis for the measures, which can legalize them, must be founded on international law so far as they affect neutral commerce. No nation can legislate for neutrals on the high seas. An O. in C. is municipal law. It can impose no new obligations on neutrals or deprive them of their rights.]

"First—No merchant vessel which sailed from her port of departure after March 1, 1915, shall be allowed to proceed on her voyage to any German port. Unless this vessel receives a pass enabling her to proceed to some neutral or allied port to be named in the pass the goods on board any such vessel must be discharged in a British port and placed in custody of the marshal of the prize court. Goods so discharged, if not contraband of war, shall, if not requisitioned for the use of his majesty, be restored by order of the court and upon such terms as the court may in the circumstances deem to be just to the person entitled thereto.

[Vessels clearing for German port after March 1st. How does this affect cargoes contracted for prior to Mch. 1st?

Who issues the pass?

It would appear that the pass is not issued by the Court since the custody of the Court takes place after a pass has been refused.

The right of requisition appears to be due to the fact that the vessel is taken into a British port.

The wide discretion given the Court prevents any standard of neutral rights being recognized.]

"Second—No merchant vessel which sailed from any German port after March 1, 1915, shall be allowed to proceed on her voyage with any goods on board laden at such port. All goods laden at such port must be discharged in a British or allied port. Goods so discharged in a British port shall be placed in the custody of the marshal of the Prize Court, and if not requisitioned for the use of his majesty shall be detained or sold under the direction of the prize court.

[This affects goods purchased by neutrals prior to March 1st and owned by neutrals. Not German subjects but neutrals bear the loss.

This permits the seizure of a neutral vessel and its detention until its cargo is discharged. It does not appear, however, that the vessel can be condemned.

The right of requisition in these circumstances seems to be a primary right unlimited in application to any sort of cargo.]

"The proceeds of the goods so sold shall be paid into the court and dealt with in such a manner as the court may in the circumstances deem to be just, provided that no proceeds of the sale of such goods shall be paid out of the court until the conclusion of peace, except on the application of a proper officer of the crown, unless it be shown that the goods had become neutral property before the issue of this order, and provided also that nothing herein shall prevent the release of neutral property laden at such enemy port on the application of the proper officer of the crown.

[The retention of the proceeds until peace is concluded furnishes the British Government with the use of the funds during the war. It amounts to an enforced loan by neutrals owning cargoes sold.[50]

If the goods were neutral owned before the 15th of March then what becomes of them? How far does this modifying clause beginning with "unless" apply? Does it mean that the goods will not be requisitioned or sold? Then why should they be discharged in a British port? If the clause applied to the whole proceeding, why then the last proviso?]

"Third—Every merchant vessel which sailed from her port of departure after March 1, 1915, on her way to a port other than a German port, and carrying goods with an enemy destination or which are enemy property may be required to discharge such goods in a British or allied port.

---

[50] Here the following remark is inserted: "It serves as handle [?] to force neutrals to comply with the suggestions of Gt. Br.—L[ester] H. W[oolsey]."

[This section wipes out all distinction between absolute contraband, conditional contraband and non-contraband and makes all articles subject to the rule of absolute contraband and to the rule of "continuous voyage".]

"Any goods so discharged in a British port shall be placed in the custody of the marshal of the prize court, and unless they are contraband of war shall, if not requisitioned for the use of his majesty, be restored by an order of the court upon such terms as the court may in the circumstances deem to be justified to the person entitled thereto, and provided that this article shall not apply in any case falling within articles 2 or 4 of this order.

[This provision proceeds to restore in a measure the rule of contraband so far as the right of condemnation is concerned, but it makes non-contraband articles subject to requisition although taken by force on the high seas.

This discretionary power conferred upon the court to dispose of neutral owned non-contraband goods is a most objectionable delegation of authority. Instead of giving the owner a right to recover his goods, recovery is left to the whim of court, which can translate "circumstances" as it pleases.]

"Fourth—Every merchant vessel which sailed from a port other than a German port after March 1, 1915, and having on board goods which are of enemy origin or enemy property may be required to discharge such goods in a British or allied port. Goods discharged in a British port shall be placed in the custody of the marshal of the prize court, and if not requisitioned for the use of his majesty shall be detained or sold under the direction of the prize court.

[The same comments apply to Article 4 as those applied to Article 3.]

"The proceeds of the goods so sold shall be paid into the court and be dealt with in such a manner as the court may in the circumstances deem to be just; provided, that no proceeds of the sale of such goods shall be paid out of the court until the conclusion of peace except on the application of a proper officer of the crown, unless it be shown that the goods had become neutral property before the issue of this order, and provided also that nothing herein shall prevent the release of neutral property of enemy origin on application of the proper officer of the crown.

[The rule laid down as to property of "enemy origin" does not bear equally on all neutrals. Neutrals, whose territories border on Germany or Austria are not deprived of trade in articles of "enemy origin", while neutrals, separated by sea are prohibited such trade. Furthermore a neutral legally owning such articles is denied the right to sell his legal property to another neutral.]

"Fifth—Any person claiming to be interested in or to have any claim in respect of any goods not being contraband of war placed in the custody of the marshal of the prize court under this order or in the proceeds of such goods may forthwith issue a writ in the prize court against the proper officer of the crown, and apply for an order that the goods should be restored to him or that their proceeds should be paid to him or for such other order as the circumstances of the case may require.

[This merely provides a means to compel the court to exercise its arbitrary power. It confers no right of restitution or compensation on the owner.]

"The practice and procedure of the prize court shall, so far as applicable, be followed *mutatis mutandis* in any proceedings consequential upon this order:

"Sixth—A merchant vessel which has cleared for a neutral port from a British or allied port or which has been allowed to pass as having an ostensible destination to a neutral port and proceeds to an enemy port shall, if captured on any subsequent voyage, be liable to condemnation.

[If this provision was confined to British ports it might be considered a penalty for false clearance. Including allied ports in the Article makes it obnoxious as a violation of International Law. Even the former is objectionable unless the vessel comes voluntarily within British jurisdiction.]

"Seventh—Nothing in this order shall be deemed to affect the liability of any vessel or goods to capture or condemnation independently of this order.

"Eighth—Nothing in this order shall prevent the relaxation of the provisions of this order in respect of the merchant vessels of any country which declares that no commerce intended for or originating in Germany or belonging to German subjects shall enjoy the protection of its flag."

[No neutral nation can afford to enter into any bargain of this sort. It would be unneutral and highly offensive to the countries at war with Great Britain.]

763.72112/976½

President Wilson to the Secretary of State

WASHINGTON, *19 March, 1915.*

MY DEAR MR. SECRETARY: I am sending you herewith an outline sketch of the substance of a reply to the British note [51] which accompanied the recent Order in Council.

It is intended as a suggestion, and as the basis upon which we may be shaping our thoughts in this important matter. You will see that

---

[51] See telegram No. 1798 from the Ambassador in Great Britain, *Foreign Relations*, 1915, supp., p. 143.

what I have done is little more than to reduce to writing what I roughly indicated in Cabinet to-day.

Faithfully yours,

WOODROW WILSON

[Enclosure]

Outline Sketch by President Wilson of a Note to Great Britain

NOTE IN REPLY TO OURS RECEIVED, NOTIFYING US OF THE ESTABLISH- MENT OF A BLOCKADE OF THE COASTS OF GERMANY WHICH IT IS INTENDED TO MAKE IN ALL RESPECTS EFFECTIVE

The cordon of blockading ships which it is intended to maintain is, however, of such an extent, the blockade as indicated in the plan announced covers so great an area of the high seas, that it seems that neutral vessels must pass through it in order to approach many important neutral ports which it is not Great Britain's privilege to blockade, and which she of course does not mean to blockade.

The Government of the United States takes it for granted, in view of the anxiety expressed by His Majesty's Government to interfere as little as possible with neutral commerce, that the approach of American merchantmen to neutral ports situated upon the long line of coast affected will not be interfered with when it is known that they do not carry goods which are contraband of war or goods con- signed to a destination within the belligerent territory affected. The Government of the United States assumes this with the more confi- dence because it is manifest that His Majesty's Government has undertaken a very unusual method of blockade which it will be dif- ficult to confine within the limits required by the law of nations; and it is natural to infer that the commanders of His Majesty's ves- sels of war engaged in the blockade will be instructed to be very careful that the blockade is not made to involve consequences to the trade of neutrals greater and more burdensome than those which have hitherto been regarded as inevitable when the ports of one belligerent are blockaded by the ships of another.

The Government of the United States of course appreciates the existence of the unusual conditions of modern warfare at sea upon which it understands His Majesty's Government to rely to justify methods of blockade and practices of search and detention which His Majesty's Government, like the Government of the United States, has so often and so explicitly held to be inconsistent with the best usages of warfare in the dealings of belligerents with neutrals at sea; but it does not understand His Majesty's Government to claim exemption from the hitherto accepted principles and obligations in these matters because of those unusual conditions; and it should regard itself as failing in its duty, because failing to maintain the principles for which it has always contended, were it not very earnestly to call the attention of His Majesty's Government to the grave responsibilities it is incurring in its efforts to meet a novel situation.

The Government of the United States notes with gratification the assurances conveyed in the note of His Majesty's Secretary of State for Foreign Affairs that special care will be taken to invade neutral rights no further than the necessities of the blockade make unavoidable; but the possibilities of serious interference are so many, the methods and circumstances of the blockade are so unusual and are likely to constitute so great an impediment and embarrassment to neutral commerce, that the Government of the United States feels that it is only candid and in the interest of avoiding future misunderstandings to say that it apprehends many interferences which may involve His Majesty's Government in heavy responsibilities for acts of His Majesty's naval officers which may make the methods of blockade which are now being adopted clearly obnoxious to the well recognized rights of neutral nations on the high seas. It therefore assumes that His Majesty's Government has considered these possibilities, will take every practicable step to avoid them, and stands ready to make reparation wherever it may be shown to have been in the wrong.

The Government of the United States, in brief, does not understand His Majesty's Government as claiming the right to set aside any accepted principle of international law, or to plan to act in contravention of any such principle; and therefore understands His Majesty's Government to assume full responsibility in case its present course of action should unexpectedly draw its representatives into acts for which it would be responsible in law and in comity.

763.72112/979½

The Secretary of State to President Wilson

WASHINGTON, *March 22, 1915.*

MY DEAR MR. PRESIDENT: I am sending you a memorandum on the Order in Council which Mr. Lansing prepared before he received your memorandum covering the details of the reply. Mr. Lansing has carefully examined the memorandum which you sent over and is preparing a suggestion which I will send you this evening, but I thought you might be interested in reading the enclosed.

With assurances [etc.] W. J. BRYAN

[Enclosure]

Memorandum by the Counselor for the Department of State
(Lansing) on the British Order in Council of March 11, 1915

[WASHINGTON,] *March 20, 1915.*

QUERY. Why did not the British Government proclaim a blockade
of German ports and notify neutral governments of that action?

I think the answer to this query is to be found in the fact that the
British Government by their Order in Council of October 29, 1914,[52]
put in operation during the present war the Declaration of London
with certain modifications and directed the British Courts to apply
its provisions thus modified.

The modifications made by the Order in Council in no way affected
the rules laid down in the Declaration covering the subject of
blockade.

Articles 1, 18 and 19 of the Declaration read as follows:

ARTICLE 1

A blockade must not extend beyond the ports and coasts belonging
to or occupied by the enemy.

ARTICLE 18

The blockading forces must not bar access to neutral ports or
coasts.

ARTICLE 19

Whatever may be the ulterior destination of a vessel or of her
cargo, she cannot be captured for breach of blockade, if, at the
moment, she is on her way to a non-blockaded port.

Manifestly these provisions of the Declaration are directly at
variance with the procedure authorized by the Order in Council of
March 15, 1915.[53]

To have announced a blockade as extensive in effect as the operations contemplated in the Order in Council of March 15th would
have compelled the further modification of the Declaration of London by striking out the three articles quoted. So radical a change
in the accepted theory of a blockade would undoubtedly have aroused
general criticism by neutral governments and would have been embarrassing for the British Government to defend.

To avoid placing themselves in so different [*difficult?*] a position
diplomatically the British Government issued the Order in Council

---

[52] *Foreign Relations,* 1914, supp., p. 262.
[53] i. e., the Order in Council dated March 11, 1915 (*ibid.,* 1915, supp., p. 144).
It is frequently referred to as the Order in Council of March 15, 1915, the date
on which it was made public.

of March 15th carefully avoiding the terms "blockade" in the Order, but in the note of transmittal they not only use the word "blockade" but seek apparently to have this Government adopt the idea that it is a blockade and to discuss it from that standpoint.

It seems to me that the course pursued by the British Government is very adroit. This Government, however, should not be led into the trap of admitting that a blockade has been established by the Order in Council, and should insist that, if it is to be considered a blockade with its attendant belligerent rights, the British Government should conform strictly to the rules of blockade promulgated in their Order in Council of October 29, 1914, namely, the rules laid down in the first twenty-one articles of the Declaration of London.

ROBERT LANSING

763.72112/980½

President Wilson to the Secretary of State

WASHINGTON, *22 March, 1915.*

MY DEAR MR. SECRETARY: I have read this memorandum with a great deal of interest; but I think it practically useless to ask such question of Great Britain or to argue with her questions of consistency, as between one Order in Council and another, for example.

The note might be drawn in this way, however, following the general lines of the sketch I sent you the other day:

After the introductory portion, we might speak, as I did in the sketch, of the unusual character of the blockade, and then say that, reading this Order in Council in connection with the former Order (of such and such a date) in which His Majesty's Government announced its adoption of the Declaration of London except with regard to questions of contraband, we would take it for granted that this, though in appearance a blockade of neutral as well as of hostile coasts, was not meant to be so in effect, and that the instructions given the commanders of His Majesty's ships of war engaged in the blockade would be very explicit in this sense, etc., etc.,—as in other memorandum which I sent.

Faithfully Yours,

W. W.

763.72112/981½

The Counselor for the Department of State (Lansing) to the Secretary of State

[WASHINGTON,] *March 22, 1915.*

DEAR MR. SECRETARY: Since sending you the memorandum in regard to the attempt of the British Government in their Order in

Council and note of transmittal to force us into the recognition of a state of blockade, you handed me the President's suggestions as to a reply to the British note.

As I have approached the subject from an entirely different standpoint from that of the President, who accepts the assertions in the British note that a blockade has been instituted, I have taken the liberty of preparing a suggestion for reply based on the ground that the Order in Council is inconsistent with their statement that a blockade has been established.

By adopting this position we more or less avoid the vexatious problem of the effect of modern methods of warfare on the physical maintenance of a blockade, although leaving the question open for future discussion in case it becomes necessary. I think that any admission that Articles 3 and 4 of the Order in Council may be in accord with the practice of blockade would cause considerable criticism from certain quarters, which is of course to be avoided if possible.

I hesitate to submit this suggestion on account of the President's memorandum but believe it to be my duty to do so.

I also enclose for your consideration some preliminary comments which I prepared a few days ago.[54]

Faithfully yours,

ROBERT LANSING

[Enclosure]

Memorandum by the Counselor for the Department of State (Lansing) on Proposed Reply to the British Note of March 15, 1915, and Order in Council

[WASHINGTON,] *March 22, 1915.*

SUGGESTION FOR ANSWER

The Government of the United States has considered the note of His Majesty's Principal Secretary of State for Foreign Affairs and the Order in Council promulgated on March 15, 1915, and is constrained to inform the Government of His Majesty that the provisions of the Order appear to be an extension of belligerent rights over the commerce of neutral powers for which there is no precedent in the record of international relations.

The British note terms the measures instituted by the Order "measures of blockade," and also asserts that "His Majesty's Government have felt most reluctant at the moment of initiating a policy of blockade to exact from neutral ships all the penalties attach-

---

[54] Not enclosed with file copy of this letter; the reference is possibly to Mr. Lansing's comments on the newspaper text of the Order in Council, p. 273.

ing to a breach of blockade." From these statements it would seem that the British Government consider that by the Declaration of March 1st [55] and the Order in Council of March 15th they have instituted a blockade. Nevertheless neither in the Declaration nor in the Order is the term "blockade" used and no notice, such as is required by international usage, has been given this Government that a blockade of specified ports or coasts has been established.

Furthermore an examination of the Order in Council shows that, while Articles 1 and 2 may be applied to the case of a blockade, Articles 3 and 4 are unknown to that practice and contrary to the provisions of the Declaration of London relating to blockade, which by the Order in Council of October 29, 1914, was, with certain modifications, proclaimed by His Majesty as a temporary code of naval warfare during the present war.

The attention of His Majesty's Government is directed to the following articles of the Declaration of London, with which Articles 3 and 4 of the Order in Council are in conflict:

ARTICLE 1

A blockade must not extend beyond the ports and coasts belonging to or occupied by the enemy.

ARTICLE 18

The blockading forces must not bar access to neutral ports or coasts.

ARTICLE 19

Whatever may be the ulterior destination of a vessel or of her cargo, she cannot be captured for breach of blockade, if, at the moment, she is on her way to a non-blockaded port.

The Government of the United States, in view of the assertions of Sir Edward Grey that the measures are those of blockade and in view of the fact that Articles 3 and 4 are manifestly inconsistent with the practice of blockade, is unable to harmonize the two positions which His Majesty's Government have taken respectively in the Order in Council and in their explanatory note.

In addition to the irreconcilable differences of these positions the preamble of the Order in Council bases the measures adopted upon a right of retaliation and not upon a recognized belligerent right, which requires neither explanation nor excuse for its exercise. The right of a nation to retaliate upon an enemy, when the enemy has violated the established rules of war, is not contested so long as the injury is inflicted directly upon the enemy, but when the retaliation seeks to make neutral nations its agents and at the same time to

---

[55] See *Foreign Relations*, 1915, supp., p. 127.

deprive those nations of rights which they are legally entitled to enjoy, the retaliating power invites the condemnation and protest of the nations, which it has so grievously injured.

Retaliation of the sort proposed in the Order in Council imposes upon neutral commerce burdens and losses, which His Majesty's Government can not expect the injured parties to endure with patience or in silence. Hostilities on the high seas conducted with a scrupulous regard for the generally accepted rules of naval warfare bear hardly upon neutrals and deprive them of many of the rights which in times of peace they freely exercise. These invasions of normal rights this Government accepts without complaint as unavoidable consequences of a naval war in which it is not a participant; but, when a belligerent abandons the recognized rules of warfare, and, invoking the right of retaliation, institutes measures, which are without sanction in the law or usage of nations, and which impair the rights of friendly powers, they may justly hold the belligerent responsible for the consequences.

The Government of the United States is not insensible to the spirit of solicitude of His Majesty's Government manifested in their express desire to lessen the rigors of a strict application of the provisions of the Order in Council to neutral commerce. This relaxation, as His Majesty's Government state, is to be accomplished through the medium of extensive discretionary powers, with which His Majesty's executive and judicial officers are clothed by the Order.

This Government cannot, however, accept as a gift that which it is entitled to as a matter of right, nor can it recognize the propriety of substituting official discretion for conformity to legal right. Furthermore the power to exercise discretion is no guaranty that it will be exercised. Thus the discretionary powers granted in no way modify the illegal standard of rights, which the Order in Council seeks to impose on neutral nations, and by which, if they submit to the Order, they must regulate their conduct.

The Government of the United States, in view of the foregoing considerations, to which it earnestly invites the attention of His Majesty's Government, confidently expects that the provisions of the Order in Council which place illegal restraints upon the commerce between neutral ports will be so modified as to remove their objectionable features, and that in the maintenance of a blockade of German ports and coasts, if a blockade is declared, the British officers charged with the maintenance will observe strictly the rules of blockade recognized by civilized nations and refrain from improper interference with neutral vessels plying between neutral ports.

In case the practices, which seem to be contemplated by the Order in Council, are persisted in by His Majesty's Government despite their manifest infraction of neutra' rights, the Government of the United States reserves the right to make further representations to His Majesty's Government upon this subject and to hold them responsible for any loss or damage which citizens of the United States may incur by reason of any interference on the part of the British authorities with their trade with the neutral countries of Europe.

In making this communication to His Majesty's Government, the Government of the United States does so in that spirit of amity and good will, which has happily for a century characterized the relations between the two countries and which it is the sincere desire of this Government to preserve.

763.72112/981½

The Secretary of State to President Wilson

WASHINGTON, *March 22, 1915.*

MY DEAR MR. PRESIDENT: I sent you, earlier in the day, a memorandum [56] which Mr. Lansing prepared before he received your outline.

I am now sending you his views on the subject, embodied in the form of a suggestion for an answer.[57] It is accompanied by some general comments on the order.[57a]

The difference between you and him seems to me rises first from a failure of the British Government to use the word "blockade" in the Orders in Council. I cannot see that it makes a great deal of difference, because it does not really change the situation and I cannot believe that so much importance can be attached to a single word.

The word "blockade" describes a method of procedure. If the method of procedure is described in other words that mean the same, the difference cannot be material.

If by insisting upon the use of the word blockade Mr. Lansing means to insist upon the rules originally governing the blockade, it seems to me that your position is the better sustained. We cannot, I think, ignore the change in methods of warfare. If we recognize the submarine as a legitimate engine of war, we cannot ignore the change in the location of the blockade line made necessary by the use of the submarine. So far as the blockade of enemy's ports are concerned, I believe the use of the submarine justifies the withdrawing of the cordon to a sufficient distance to protect the blockading ships.

The third point is one that gives me most difficulty—namely, their right to interfere with goods going into, or coming out of,

---

[56] *Ante*, p. 280.
[57] *Supra.*
[57a] See footnote 54, p. 282.

Germany through a neutral country. Unless a belligerent nation has a right to extend its contraband list at will so as to include if it desires to do so every article of merchandise, I do not understand how Great Britain can assert the right to stop non-contraband goods shipped to neutral ports. It seems to me that this is quite a different thing from the right to withdraw its ships from the immediate vicinity and yet establish an effective blockade of German ports. I do not understand that any nation has ever asserted the right to blockade a neutral port merely because non-contraband goods may come out of the enemy country through that neutral port, or enter the enemy country through that port. Unless a blockade can be extended to neutral ports I do not see how merchandise can be stopped unless it is contraband and I do not understand that all merchandise may be declared contraband.

The statement which is appended to Mr. Lansing's suggestion very clearly points out the different propositions covered by the Orders in Council.

It occurs to me that in the note as you propose it you assume that interference with non-contraband goods destined for a neutral port is not intended. The language of the Orders in Council is so clear that I am not sure that we are justified in making such an assumption. If the assumption is clearly inconsistent with the language of the Orders in Council, would it not lead to a contradiction that would embarrass us?

The matter is so important that I would like to go over the situation with you after you have read what Mr. Lansing says.

With assurances [etc.] W. J. Bryan

763.72112/982½

The Counselor for the Department of State (Lansing) to the Secretary of State

[Washington,] *March 23, 1915.*

Dear Mr. Secretary: If we proceed on the assumption that the Order in Council and note of Sir Edward Grey constitute a sufficient notice of the establishment of a blockade of German ports, we could agree that Articles 1 and 2 are applicable to the ports and coasts of Germany on the North Sea, but I do not see how we can admit that they apply to the German territory on the Baltic.

The German ports on the Baltic are open to trade with Sweden and Denmark, and possibly with Norway. An essential element of a blockade is its impartial application to all neutral powers. If vessels from a neutral power can proceed without danger to the port of a belligerent, the ineffectiveness of the blockade is manifest, and if a blockade is ineffective as to any vessels, it ought not to be recognized and the rules of contraband only should apply to trade with the port thus outside the blockade.

This position as to the limited coastal area covered by the blockade established by Great Britain and her Allies, confining it to the ports and coasts of Germany on the North Sea, does not involve the question of the radius of activity or the distance of the blockading vessels from the territory blockaded.

As to the physical maintenance of a blockade under present conditions, I think that we ought to take the position that actual experience can be the only measure of the efficiency of modern methods in maintaining a blockade and that we should reserve for the present the consideration of the subject with the express understanding that no rights are waived and no acquiescence given by failure to discuss at this time the mode of enforcing the proposed blockade.

As to articles passing to and from Germany through neutral territory, with which Articles 3 and 4 of the Order in Council deal, the rules of contraband should be applied. While non-contraband may be legally stopped when destined to the port of an enemy which is under blockade, non-contraband consigned to a neutral port, whatever its ultimate destination, should be allowed free passage. Under the rules of contraband, furthermore, the "enemy origin" of non-contraband does not stamp the articles with the character of contraband or confer on a belligerent the right to detain or divert them from a neutral destination.

It seems to me that the line of difference as to the treatment of cargoes destined to Germany, which are proceeding directly to a blockaded coast, and those destined to Germany, which are proceeding through neutral territory, is clear. In the first case the rules of blockade apply; in the second case the rules of contraband apply. In brief I think that a representation might be made along these lines provided it seems advisable to admit that the declaration of March 1st and the Order in Council of March 15th institute a blockade.

Faithfully yours,

ROBERT LANSING

763.72112/710e

The Secretary of State to President Wilson

WASHINGTON, *March 23, 1915.*

MY DEAR MR. PRESIDENT: I am enclosing a flimsy of a despatch from Gerard.[57b] This is the most interesting communication we have received from him lately.

[57b] *Foreign Relations*, 1915, supp., p. 354.

I also enclose an additional suggestion by Mr. Lansing [57c] (by the way, I learned from one of the messengers in the White House that the envelope which I sent over yesterday evening about half past seven, was laid upon your table and I presume it was while you were at dinner. It contained notes on several subjects.) In the enclosed note Mr. Lansing calls attention to the difference between the law governing blockades and the law governing contraband. This is one of the points to which I called attention in my note of yesterday.[57d]

In the matter of the blockade we can make allowance for the use of new implements of warfare but the changing of conditions does not affect the laws in regard to contraband. Unless a belligerent has a right to add everything to the contraband list we cannot concede their right to interfere with shipments through neutral countries of such merchandise as is not contraband. In refusing to recognize the right we do not necessarily resort to force. My own idea is that we cannot afford to make merchandise a cause for the use of force. If we have any disputes about merchandise which cannot be settled during the war, they can be settled afterwards, and if we have any disputes which cannot be settled by agreement between the parties, they can, in due time, be submitted to investigation and arbitration, but it seems to me that we must distinguish between the rules applicable to blockade and the rules applicable to non-contraband goods shipped to neutral ports, reserving for future consideration any questions which may arise, first, concerning the effectiveness of the blockade, and second, concerning the interference with non-contraband goods.

With assurances [etc.]   W. J. Bryan

763.72112/982½

President Wilson to the Secretary of State

WASHINGTON, 24 March, 1915.

MY DEAR MR. SECRETARY: These notes by Mr. Lansing are admirable and convincing; but they lead only to debate, and debate with the British Government (which for the time being consists of the War Office and the Admiralty) is at present of no practical avail.

Inconsistencies in the Order and inconsistencies between the Order and Sir Edward Grey's note accompanying it are neither here nor there, as it seems to me; neither is the lack of the ordinary forms of notice of blockade. We are face to face with something they are going to do, and they are going to do it no matter what representations we make. We cannot convince them or change them, we can only show them

---

[57c] Supra.
[57d] Ante, p. 285.

very clearly what we mean to be our own attitude and course of action and that we mean to hold them to a strict responsibility for every invasion of our rights as neutrals. In short we must make them understand that the discretion which their officials are vested with must be exercised in such a way that the extraordinary "blockade" they are instituting will <u>not</u> in fact violate our rights as neutral traders on the seas.

Take an instance (in the field of argument). It is true that a previous Order in Council adopted all the Declaration of London except the portions defining contraband, as a temporary code of warfare at sea; but that previous Order did not constitute an agreement with any other nation. It was a piece of domestic legislation; and a subsequent Order no doubt repeals it so far as it is inconsistent with it. So <u>that</u> line leads nowhere, I fear.

If, then, we speak only to the facts, is not this our right course? Ought we not to say, in effect: You call this a blockade and mean to maintain it as such; but it is obvious that it is unprecedented in almost every respect, but chiefly in this, that it is a blockade of neutral as well as of belligerent coasts and harbours, which no belligerent can claim as a right. We shall expect therefore that the discretion lodged by the Order in Council in the administrative officers and courts of the crown will be exercised to correct what is irregular in this situation and leave the way open to our legitimate trade. If this is not done we shall have to hold you to a strict accountability for every instance of rights violated and injury done; but we interpret Sir Edward Grey's note to mean that this is exactly what will be done.

Note, by the way, the sentence in Page's despatch [58] in which he says that they will heed none of our arguments, but that they will be careful not to offend us in act.

Note, also, that, as a matter of fact, our export trade shows no sign of slackening and that there is little left, by the action of Germany herself (See Gerard's recent despatch [59] and several preceding) for us to trade with Germany in. Our cotton ships bring nothing away on their return voyage.

I hope that Mr. Lansing will be kind enough to try his hand at a note such as I have indicated, and then we can get together (perhaps all three of us?) and put the thing into a shape that will thoroughly hold water (and exclude it, too, as a maritime paper should).

Faithfully Yours,

W. W.

---

[58] *Foreign Relations*, 1915, supp., p. 146.
[59] *Ibid.*, p. 354.

763.72112/983½

Memorandum by the Counselor for the Department of State (Lansing) on Proposed Reply to British Note of March 15, 1915, and Order in Council [60]

[WASHINGTON,] *March 24, 1915.*

In formulating a reply to the British note of March 15th transmitting the Order in Council of the same date, I think that it is important to consider the following:

1. *The general effect on public opinion in this country.* Unless the reply contains a declaration of the legal rights of the United States based on the principles of international law, with which the press has made the public more or less familiar, the American people will consider the Government either indifferent to or ignorant of its rights. Furthermore, the declaration must be urged with sufficient vigor to remove any impression that the Government is submitting without objection to violations of such rights.

2. *The political effect of a strong declaration of rights in contrast to a general statement based on expediency rather than legality.* A general statement, I am afraid, which amounts to a practical acceptance of the right asserted by Great Britain to interrupt commerce to Germany passing through neutral ports, regardless of its contraband character, would invite strong criticism and furnish the opponents of the Administration with a plausible argument as to the weakness of our foreign policy.

3. *The benefit of asserting legal rights upon any claims arising from the enforcement of the Order in Council.* If the reply of this Government is so worded that it can be construed into an admission that the measures adopted by Great Britain are justified by the conditions and possess, therefore, a degree of legality, it will make the recovery of a claim very difficult. This will also affect public opinion.

4. *The necessity of declaring neutral rights as heretofore recognized in order to be able after the war to assert that such rights exist and their legality has not been impaired by any admission of justification for the Order in Council.* The United States in the present war is the guardian of neutrality. For the sake of the future it ought to assert firmly the rights of neutrals. I have the impression that Great Britain after the war is over will be glad to recede from certain positions now assumed and admit that the position taken by the United States was legally correct. If this Government does not declare its rights as a neutral, Great Britain will have no opportunity to recede, and the future rights of neutrals will be materially curtailed.

5. *The declaration of neutral rights will amount to a reservation rather than cause a relaxation of the enforcement of the Order in Council.* While the assertion of legal rights may have no practical effect on the present commercial situation, it will in the future be of

---

[60] This paper bears the notation: "Handed to Secretary 11 : 30 am Mch 24/15 RL."

extreme value to those who suffer by reason of the Order in Council and to neutrals in general in case of another maritime war.

6. *The avoidance of asserting legal rights in such a way as to force this Government to employ drastic measures to compel their recognition.* The idea is to file a *caveat*, to permit their violation under protest deferring settlement until peace has been restored.

763.72112/990½

The Secretary of State to President Wilson

WASHINGTON, *March 25, 1915.*

MY DEAR MR. PRESIDENT: I am sending you the telegram drafted by Mr. Lansing.[61] I have just had time to read it but not time to go over it with a view to digesting it sentence by sentence. He has worked in nearly, if not all of your language but the impression it makes upon me is that the tone of it is a little more severe than the tone of your memorandum.[62]

If, after you have had an opportunity to consider it, you desire any exchange of views I am at your service, as is Mr. Lansing.

With assurances [etc.]   W. J. BRYAN

763.72/1606½

Memorandum by the Counselor for the Department of State (Lansing) of an Interview With Mr. Samuel K. Ratcliffe, March 25, 1915

Samuel K. Ratcliffe is a prominent journalist of London and came with a letter of introduction from Louis F. Post.

Mr. Ratcliffe stated that, with Lord Bryce, Arthur Ponsonby, M. P., and others who were in frequent conferences, he was deeply interested in the attitude of the American and British peoples toward each other in the present situation, and that he had come to this country the latter part of January to get into personal touch with American sentiment.

He said there had been a very wide-spread change of public opinion in Great Britain toward the United States, that in fact it was almost universal, and included professional men as well as those engaged in trade. The attitude of the British public from the beginning of the war, he said, had been most friendly up to the time of the receipt of our "contraband note" of December 26th,[63] as there was a general belief that the sympathies of the American people were

---

[61] Not printed; for the telegram as sent, see *Foreign Relations*, 1915, supp., p. 152.

[62] Enclosure to President Wilson's letter of Mar. 19, 1915, p. 278.

[63] *Foreign Relations*, 1914, supp., p. 372.

strongly with the Allies in their struggle, but that the note had had the effect of changing that belief and that the average man in Great Britain felt that American sympathy was measured by selfish interests and that the people of this country would take the side which offered them material benefit in the way of trade.

I replied to him that he must know from having come in touch with many people here that such an idea was entirely unwarranted, and that the American people were not allowing their sympathies in the war to be controlled by their pocket books.

He said that of course he realized this, but that it would be most difficult to convince the British public of the truth of it; that the conviction was increasing on account of the diplomatic representations which the United States had made, and which appeared to be protests adverse to the military necessities of Great Britain, and in favor of Americans who sought profit only out of the situation.

I answered him that so far as appearances went I was not disposed to blame the British public, but that I did blame the press of Great Britain for taking such a position, and I also blamed the British journalists, who knew the facts, from [for] not trying to correct this erroneous impression.

He asked me why I said that.

I replied that every thinking man must realize that the only controversies between the United States and Great Britain must be over questions relating to commerce and trade; that naturally it was considered by the unthinking as matters of profit and loss solely, but that they went much further than that involving the whole subject of neutral rights; that the drastic measures which had been adopted by the British Government, whether justified by necessity or not, certainly infringed the rights of neutrals as recognized by international law; and that for the sake of neutrals in the future, of which Great Britain would probably be one, it was most desirable for this country to assert such rights.

Mr. Ratcliffe replied that he appreciated the importance of the United States doing this, but he wondered if it could not be done in such a way as not to give the impression that materialistic interests were the motives which inspired the action.

I asked him if he had any practical suggestion as to how this might be done.

He said that he had not, but he thought that it was possible to do so.

I said that it seemed to me that this course had been followed thus far in the correspondence, and that I had no reason to expect any change by this Government. I was afraid, however, that, if the friendly and considerate way in which the United States had dealt with the subject, was not appreciated by the British public, nothing could change their opinion that we only thought of the dollars and cents at stake.

He replied that he fully appreciated the friendly tone used by this Government, as did his associates in England; the trouble was that the general public could not understand the protests, which seemed to be directed against measures of vital importance to Great Britain in its struggle with Germany; that to the British public they seemed cold-blooded and unsympathetic and contrary to what they expected from their own flesh and blood. He said, that of course he considered them all wrong about it, and entirely unreasonable, but that it was nevertheless a fact.

I said that the remedy to my mind lay with the press and the men who moulded public opinion in Great Britain; that they should show that the United States could not do otherwise than assert its rights as a neutral, that the rights affected were those which pertained to commerce, and, therefore, to financial interests, and that the assertion of rights was no criterion of public sentiment in this country, but a necessary policy for a government which looked to the future, a policy which Great Britain might after the war be very glad that this Government adopted.

Mr. Ratcliffe said that he would do all that he could to remove the ill-feeling which prevailed in Great Britain, and that he knew that American sentiment was largely in favor of the Allies, but that the British public under the intense emotions aroused by the war would be hard to convince. He, however, hoped for the best.

ROBERT LANSING

763.72112/986½

President Wilson to the Counselor for the Department of State
(Lansing)

WASHINGTON, *28 March, 1915.*

MY DEAR MR. LANSING: Will you not be kind enough to look over the enclosed [64] and tell me what you think of it?

You will see what I have done. I have recast the note as a statement and interpretation: so that there is no argument involved, but it is meant to mean: We have the Order and the note accompanying it. We cannot understand these as notice of illegal action. We shall assume the contrary until actual things done compel us to look upon the matter differently. Then we shall hold the British government responsible in accordance with the well known principles of international law, of which we now remind her, so that she may know just what we understand them to be.

[64] Not printed.

Please make any comment you please either on the statements or the language of what I have written.

Sincerely Yours,

WOODROW WILSON

763.72112/985½

The Counselor for the Department of State (Lansing) to President Wilson

WASHINGTON, *March 28, 1915.*

DEAR MR. PRESIDENT: I return the draft which you sent me this afternoon, and which I have, in accordance with your request, examined critically and suggested without reserve certain changes. These are verbal, being chiefly "pluralizing" pronouns relating to the British Government.

I believe that the reply as drafted fully protects our legal rights, so that in the event of claims arising out of the enforcement of the Order in Council no admission by this Government can be urged by Great Britain in denying liability. It was that feature, which it seemed to me, was of special importance.

I do not believe the method of treatment could be improved upon.

Very sincerely yours,

ROBERT LANSING

I have just been handed by a reporter of the N. Y. *Tribune* the enclosed clipping[65] from its issue of today, which may be the line of defense which will be offered by Great Britain. If you have not read Mr. Balfour's statement, I am sure you will find it interesting.

R. L.

763.72112/987½

President Wilson to the Secretary of State

WASHINGTON, *28 March, 1915.*

MY DEAR MR. SECRETARY: Here is the note as I have rewritten it. I would be very much obliged if you would read it and tell me when I get back from Annapolis just what you think of it. I have tried to construct it in the spirit of our recent discussion in the Cabinet.

Since I had built it chiefly on Mr. Lansing's note, I sent it to him this afternoon, and his note is attached (I mean his comment).[66]

I shall be back Tuesday morning early.

Faithfully Yours,

W. W.

---

[65] Not enclosed with file copy of this letter.
[66] *Supra.*

763.72112/988½

The Secretary of State to President Wilson

WASHINGTON, *March 29, 1915.*

MY DEAR MR. PRESIDENT: I am sending you the note to Page, drawn in accordance with your instructions, with a few changes so indicated that you can either approve them or cross them out.

The note from Mr. Lansing, which I enclose,[67] explains those which he has suggested.

The three which I suggest—(I might add with Mr. Lansing's approval)—are as follows:

1. About the middle of page 5 of your notes, I beg to suggest the substitution of the following: "unusual risks and penalties", instead of "similar risks and in large measure to the same penalties".[68] It would not be quite accurate to say that the risks and penalties are similar, or in a large measure the same, because the Orders in Council clearly discriminate between the treatment of merchandise destined to an enemy country through a neutral country, and the treatment of merchandise that attempts to run the blockade. It is correct, however, to say that the risks and penalties are unusual.

2. On page 8 of your notes, about the middle of the page, I suggest the addition of the words—"insofar as they affect neutral rights".[69] We are speaking of acts of retaliation and I take it for granted that your language is intended to refer to retaliation only insofar as retaliation affects neutral rights.

3. Upon reading the concluding paragraph of the note it struck me as ending rather bluntly, and I suggested to Mr. Lansing a little sweetening in the form of a reiteration of the friendly spirit in which the answer is made. Mr. Lansing and I have gone over it together, and the following is the result of our collaboration:

> "In conclusion you will reiterate to His Majesty's Government that this statement of the views of the Government of the United States is made in the most friendly spirit, and in accordance with the uniform candor which has characterized the relations of the Governments in the past, and which has been in large measure the foundation of the peace and amity existing between the two nations without interruption for a century".[70]

I am sure you will pardon me for making these suggestions, in compliance with your request. They are not very material, but are submitted for your consideration.

Allow me to say in conclusion what I possibly should have said in the beginning of this note, namely that I am very much pleased with the note and believe that it will find popular endorsement. The

---

[67] *Ante*, p. 294.
[68] For the context of this passage in the note as sent, see *Foreign Relations*, 1915, supp., p. 153, end of third paragraph.
[69] *Ibid.*, p. 154, end of first paragraph.
[70] *Ibid.*, p. 156, third paragraph.

position which you take is very clearly and strongly stated and yet due consideration is given to the exigencies that call forth the Order in Council and to the promises which they make in regard to its enforcement.

With Assurances [etc.]   W. J. BRYAN

763.72112/989½

President Wilson to the Secretary of State

WASHINGTON, *30 March, 1915.*

MY DEAR MR. SECRETARY: This note [71] is entirely satisfactory to me with the alterations you have suggested, and I entirely approve of adding the paragraph you have drawn as the concluding passage of the note.

I hope that the encyphering and all the handling of this note will be under the safeguards as to privacy which we agreed upon, so that there may be no garbled versions of it current before it reaches London. I assume that it will be agreed between Washington and London that it will be published here upon its receipt and delivery there.

Faithfully Yours,

W. W.

763.72112/1181½

The Counselor for the Department of State (Lansing) to the Secretary of State

[WASHINGTON,] *May 15, 1915.*

DEAR MR. SECRETARY: I thought over our conversation of yesterday in regard to a note of complaint to Great Britain for violation of American rights on the high seas, and I came to the conclusion that the subject might be treated in a general rather than a specific way, which would avoid the necessity of waiting for complete data.[72]

In accordance with that conclusion I have drafted an instruction to Ambassador Page, which is enclosed. It is an uncompromising presentation and "shows its teeth". Probably you will think it too strong, or rather too strongly expressed. In view, however, of the note to Germany a note to Great Britain ought not to be in more friendly or conciliatory language, if it is to give an expression of impartiality to the German Government which will affect in any way their reply.

---

[71] For text of the note as sent, see *Foreign Relations*, 1915, supp., p. 152.
[72] See also Mr. Lansing's letter of May 14, 1915, to the Secretary of State, p. 404.

I am in favor of sending some note similar to the one enclosed as the British treatment of our vessels and cargoes to neutral countries is in flagrant violation of law and contrary to Sir Edward Grey's assurances.

The opportune time to send a communication of this sort seems to me to be the present, as it will evince our impartial purpose to protect American rights on the high seas, whoever is the aggressor. We have just complaints against both. We have already been too complacent with Great Britain in the enforcement of the Order in Council. For two months they have been violating the rights of neutrals.

Faithfully yours,

ROBERT LANSING

[Enclosure]

Draft Note to the Ambassador in Great Britain (Page) Regarding the Order in Council of March 11, 1915

You are instructed to address a note to His Britannic Majesty's Principal Secretary of State for Foreign Affairs in the following sense:

The Government of the United States in its note [73] relative to the British Order in Council of March 11, 1915,[74] expressed the expectation that the orders issued to His Majesty's naval forces charged with the duty of enforcing the Order in Council would be of such a nature as not "to impose restrictions upon neutral trade more burdensome than those which have been regarded as inevitable when the ports of a belligerent are actually blockaded by the ships of its enemy."

Relying upon this expectation, which was amply warranted by the assurances contained in Your Excellency's note of March 15th [75] transmitting the Order in Council, the Government of the United States has observed with increasing surprise and disappointment the method of enforcement of the Order in Council by the British authorities. Realizing that the institution of a policy of commercial non-intercourse with an enemy presented difficulties of exceptional character in view of the conditions prevailing in the present war the Government of the United States patiently awaited the adaptation of the actual practice under the provisions of the Order in Council to the continued exercise of rights of commerce between neutral nations.

---

[73] *Foreign Relations*, 1915, supp., p. 152.
[74] *Ibid.*, p. 144.
[75] *Ibid.*, p. 143.

Two months have now passed since the British authorities entered upon the enforcement of the Order in Council. The time has been ample for the British Government to put into practice the considerate policy toward neutral trade, which was assured in Your Excellency's note. Yet, in spite of these assurances, neutral rights are disregarded and the long-sanctioned rules of international law governing the freedom of the seas to neutrals are repeatedly violated. There has been no apparent abatement of the rigorous methods adopted at the outset by the British naval authorities.

American and other neutral vessels plying between neutral ports and laden with cargoes destined to neutral consignees have been stopped on the high seas and taken into British ports. American vessels and cargoes have been held without the cause of detention being made known to the Government of the United States. In some instances the cargoes have been preempted and, though compensation has been promised, the owners have been brought to the verge of financial ruin through failure of the British Government to recompense them promptly for the goods thus preempted. Furthermore, no reparation has been offered for irregular or undue detentions of vessels and cargoes which were subsequently released.

The unprecedented procedure of arresting neutral vessels and neutral cargoes on the high seas though in trade between neutral ports, of unduly detaining them in British ports without disclosing the *prima facie* cause, of refusing to permit them in many instances to proceed to their destination, and of practically requisitioning cargoes consigned to neutrals, has caused a situation, which the Government of the United States can no longer view with patience or in silence.

Not only is grievous wrong being done to the American citizens interested in the vessels and cargoes, which have been detained without authority of the law or the usage of nations, but the menace of the British practice is forcing American citizens to incur unknown hazards in the special privileges which they are entitled to enjoy, and is threatening to disorganize if not to destroy regular traffic between the United States and the neutral countries of Europe, to which they should have full liberty to resort in trade and navigation.

The Government of His Britannic Majesty should realize that the practices of the British naval authorities in their enforcement of the Order in Council of March 11th has destroyed the expectation and hope of the Government of the United States, which were based on the assurances of Your Excellency in the note of March 15th; that the conditions of trade between the United States and other neutral nations as a consequence of these practices have become intolerable and can no longer be endured without complaint; and that a continuance of these practices so subversive of neutral rights and so destructive of their enjoyment will invite measures by the Government of the United States, which will restore to American citizens the freedom of the high seas and protect them in the exercise of their just rights.

The Government of the United States sincerely hopes that His Majesty's Government, realizing the gravity of the situation and appreciating the duty which this Government owes to itself and to its citizens, will so modify the present practices of its naval authorities that it will not become necessary for the Government of the United States to make further representations or to take any step to protect American citizens in their commerce with neutral nations.

The Government of the United States, while making this appeal to His Majesty's Government in all friendliness and with a full appreciation of the apparent purposes of their policy, desires it to be distinctly understood that the rights of American citizens on the high seas must be respected and that this Government will not fail to adopt measures necessary to insure that respect and to prevent any impairment of those rights which have been universally recognized by the principles of international law and the usages of maritime nations.

_____

763.72112/1241

The Secretary of State ad interim to President Wilson

WASHINGTON, *June 12, 1915.*

DEAR MR. PRESIDENT: I am sending you a proposed telegram to our Embassy at London, which, if it meets with your approval, will you please return to the Telegraph Room of the Department for transmission.

I would not trouble you with this matter, except that it bears directly upon the policy of our sending a note to Great Britain at this time. Briefly, the situation is this: Great Britain has prepared a reply to our note of March 30th.[76] From the confidential information obtained here as to the contents of the note, it would appear to be largely a defense of retaliation against Germany, based upon further alleged violations of the laws of war and humanity by the German Government. If our information is correct, and I have reason to believe that it is so, it seems to me that such an answer at this time would complicate matters and have an undesirable effect upon Germany. I do not think, therefore, that it would be good policy to encourage the sending of such a reply at the present time.

Of course, knowing that Great Britain has a reply prepared and is only withholding it out of consideration to this Government, in view of the controversy with Germany, we could not in fairness, except in

[76] *Foreign Relations,* 1915, supp., p. 152.

extreme cases, send another note of complaint to Great Britain, until that Government had an opportunity to answer our note of March 30th.

It is on account of this situation that the telegram sent to you for approval is drafted.

I am [etc.]   ROBERT LANSING

[Enclosure]

Draft Telegram From the Secretary of State ad interim to the Ambassador in Great Britain (Page)[77]

Your 2258 tenth.[78] If British reply to Department's note March thirtieth acquiesces in United States position therein taken, Department would be glad to receive it promptly, but if it makes no concession to American views and is calculated merely to aggravate situation, perhaps wiser to withhold it in hope that some practical solution of differences may be found through more intelligent exercise by British Government of discretionary powers reserved under order in council, and greater effort on their part to avoid repetition of present difficulties.

Department has been confidentially informed of contents proposed British note as first drafted, and if this information is correct, transmission of note in that form might bring to a climax increasing agitation against British interference with neutral shipping, which in any event will break out soon, if British authorities continue in their present course, and then it will be more difficult to find a solution.

You may use this orally and unofficially.

763.72112/1258½

President Wilson to the Secretary of State ad interim

WASHINGTON, *14 June, 1915.*

MY DEAR MR. SECRETARY: I think that this despatch [79] ought to be sent. Every word of it is true.

But Colonel House, who comes direct from London, landed in New York yesterday from the *Saint Paul;* and, if a delay of a day or two would not be imprudent, I think we had better wait to get his advice. He is well informed, I happen to know on these very matters and has himself been advising the British Foreign Office of our attitude.

Cordially Yours,

W. W.

---

[77] This paper bears the notation: "Not sent."
[78] *Foreign Relations,* 1915, supp., p. 438.
[79] Draft telegram, *supra.*

763.72112/1381

The Secretary of State to President Wilson

WASHINGTON, *July 27, 1915.*

DEAR MR. PRESIDENT: I enclose a copy of the English note [80] we have received in reply to ours of March 30th. It was intended to have this note published simultaneously in England and the United States Wednesday morning, but last night I received a telegram from Mr. Page,[81] saying that Sir Edward Grey would have ready within a week another note dealing with the practical questions relating to shipping, and he therefore requested that publication be delayed until the latter note had been delivered.

Faithfully yours,

ROBERT LANSING

763.72112/1399½ : Telegram

President Wilson to the Secretary of State

WINDSOR, VT., *July 27, 1915—3:45 p. m.*

Instructions of Sir Edward Grey to Ambassador about cotton gives me deep concern.[82] Am I mistaken in my recollection that the British Government formally notified us that cotton would be regarded as not already contraband and would be continued to be so treated?

WOODROW WILSON

763.72112/1399½ : Telegram

The Secretary of State to President Wilson

WASHINGTON, *July 28, 1915—12 noon.*

Your telegram of 27th concerning cotton. Your recollection as to British assurance that cotton was non-contraband and would continue so is correct. The language of Sir Edward Grey's telegram to British Ambassador,[83] a copy of which was handed me on October 26th, contained the following regarding cotton. "It is therefore as far as we are concerned in the free list and will remain there". On the same day Mr. Page telegraphed: "Sir Edward Grey makes the positive declaration to me that cotton is not contraband and so far as the British Government is concerned will not be".[84] Similar assurances were given by the French Government in December.

---

[80] *Foreign Relations*, 1915, supp., p. 168.
[81] Not printed.
[82] See telegram No. 2510, July 22, 1915, from the Ambassador in Great Britain, *Foreign Relations*, 1915, supp., p. 193.
[83] *Ibid.*, 1914, supp., p. 290.
[84] *Ibid.*, p. 289.

These declarations were given wide publicity by the Department through letters and the press.

The change of policy, which is evidently determined upon by the British Government as shown by the telegram received yesterday afternoon from Mr. Page [86] which I will repeat to you, will cause intense dissatisfaction in this country, and the demands for retaliatory measures which will undoubtedly be made will embarrass us seriously. I am afraid that the question will become a political rather than a diplomatic one.

I had a talk with Spring-Rice on the subject Monday, in which I told him that for his Government to put cotton on the contraband list was a confession that their alleged blockade was ineffective, that if it was effective and their theory of blockade was correct it was needless to declare cotton contraband since all articles regardless of their character would be prevented from entering or leaving Germany. I said that if cotton was made contraband at this time we would have to assume that their theory of blockade so far as neutral ports were concerned had been abandoned and we would proceed on that assumption, which would create a very difficult situation. I also pointed out to him the resentment which would be caused in this country by the proposed action and by the feeling that Great Britain had broken her promise, and that his Government could not hold us responsible for the consequences.

I am telegraphing Page the substance of my statements to Spring-Rice.

The following is the telegram received from Page yesterday afternoon.[86]

ROBERT LANSING

195.1/482½

President Wilson to the Secretary of State

WASHINGTON, *29 July, 1915.*

MY DEAR MR. SECRETARY: I asked Mr. Palmer [87] to send me the enclosed,[88] as specimens of what is being sent to our shippers, and I think that you ought to see them.

The copy of the British note of the twenty-fourth [*twenty-third*] of this month,[89] which you sent me, has been received and read with the closest attention. It seems to me, I must say, to make out a

---

[86] Telegram No. 2538, July 27, 1915, 3 p. m., from the Ambassador in Great Britain, *Foreign Relations*, 1915, supp., p. 489.

[87] A. Mitchell Palmer, judge, United States Court of Claims.

[88] Samples of guarantees required of shippers to insure passage of goods through British blockade.

[89] *Foreign Relations*, 1915, supp., p. 168.

strong case. Pending the receipt of the supplementary note, I should very much like an intimation of your first impressions.

Faithfully Yours,

W. W.

763.72112/1851a

The Secretary of State to President Wilson

WASHINGTON, *October 9, 1915.*

MY DEAR MR. PRESIDENT: I am enclosing you the draft of the note to Great Britain upon which we have been working for so long a time.[90] It is unavoidably long, which, to my mind, takes away a certain measure of strength. At the same time I do not see how it can be well abbreviated. Possibly you will think it better to send it by mail, provided it meets with your approval, rather than by telegraph.

Faithfully yours,

ROBERT LANSING

763.72112/1852½ : Telegram

The Ambassador in Great Britain (Page) to the Secretary of State

LONDON, *October 15, 1915—4 p. m.*
[Received 10:12 p. m.]

3025. . . .

The Government and public opinion here are in about the same mood that Northern opinion and Lincoln's administration were in the week after Bull Run or after Lee crossed the Potomac on his way to Gettysburg. The Balkan situation and the Dardanelles tragedy threaten a political upheaval and the public feeling is far more tense than at any [previous time]. Many of our best friends here fear that it is an unfortunate moment for our long note to be presented [91] while the present crisis lasts. Bryce has this feeling strongly. Northcliffe who has always been most friendly and helpful in his newspapers is greatly excited lest a [violent] feeling be provoked not so much by the note itself as by its coming now. I send you these strong convictions by these men and many more like them for whatever they may be worth and without recommendation of my own. But it is certain that the note will receive no serious attention by the Government till the present tension is relaxed, and its presentation at this moment is likely to result in a public reception that may tend to defeat its purpose [*object*].

AM[ERICAN] AMBASSADOR

---

[90] For the note as sent, see *ibid.*, p. 578.
[91] The note contained in the instruction of Oct. 21, *ibid.*

763.72112/1851¼

President Wilson to the Secretary of State

WASHINGTON, *21 October, 1915.*

MY DEAR MR. SECRETARY: I am returning the note to Great Britain. I have made a few verbal changes, but they do not alter the substance at all, as I think you will agree.

I hope that you will send it by post. It is very important that there should be no leakage at all as to its contents. I hope that you will be kind enough to keep your own eye on the whole handling of the note so as to render a leak impossible, confining the copying, sealing, and mailing to the fewest possible persons, and those only the ones that are in your most intimate confidence. When it has reached the Foreign Office we can publish it as a whole.

Any leakage, or any publication of a garbled version, as happened once before, would create a very disagreeable situation. I would suggest that you let no one know that the note had been sent until Page lets you know by cable that it has arrived and been delivered.

Faithfully Yours,

WOODROW WILSON

763.72112/1851½

The Secretary of State to President Wilson

WASHINGTON, *October 21, 1915.*

MY DEAR MR. PRESIDENT: I am in receipt of the note to Great Britain with your changes and also your letter in regard to it. I am very much gratified that the note meets your approval.

For several days I have felt that the note should go forward as promptly as possible to Great Britain. There has been considerable criticism that we have delayed for so many months to reply to the series of notes which Great Britain sent to us on the subject of neutral trade, although the excuse of our controversy with Germany over submarine warfare seemed to be generally accepted as a reasonable ground for delay. After the practical settlement of the *Arabic* question however, unfavorable criticism was renewed and has been increasing in volume from day to day.

I have not felt it was wise to take up the case of the *Lusitania* and the cases of Von Papen, Boy-Ed and Albert until the note to Great Britain was forwarded. For these reasons it seems to me that we ought not to cause further delay by sending the note by mail. The next pouch to London does not leave the Department until the 30th of this month, so that in all probability the note would not be received by the Foreign Office before the 10th or 12th of November.

During the next month the complaints and criticisms would increase very much in volume. The Department has hundreds of letters from American importers and exporters asking what we are doing to relieve the situation in which they find themselves. Furthermore, if you approve of my policy of delaying a consideration of the further questions with Germany until the note to Great Britain has been sent, these could not be taken up until about the middle of November.

In view of all the circumstances I therefore think that the note should be telegraphed immediately to London. Will you please advise me today if possible as to your wishes in the matter.[92]

Everything will be done to preserve the secrecy of the note and only my confidential men will see it.

> Faithfully yours,

[File copy not signed]

763.72112/2190½ : Telegram

The Ambassador in Great Britain (Page) to the Secretary of State

LONDON, *January 15, 1916—2 p. m.*
[Received 7 : 30 p. m.]

3585. I make the following inquiry for my personal information. Members of the British Cabinet privately and unofficially say that the British submarine blockade of Germany in the Baltic is now effective. Suppose the British Government were to declare a strict blockade of Germany, analogous to and in the terms of the United States blockade of the Confederate States, including the doctrine of continuous voyage, would the [Administration] regard this declaration more favorably than it regards the Order in Council of March 11th?

I shall not use your answer in any way except as a general guide to my personal and informal conversations and in no way to indicate that you have expressed an opinion.

AM[ERICAN] AMBASSADOR

763.72112/2190½ : Telegram

The Secretary of State to the Ambassador in Great Britain (Page)

WASHINGTON, *January 20, 1916.*

2753. Your 3585, January 15, 2 P. M.

While Department would regard with favor return of Great Britain to rules of blockade and contraband, I feel it would be

---

[92] By direction of the President the note was sent by a special messenger leaving October 24 (file No. 763.72112/1851½a).

unwise for me to make any statement of probable attitude of Department toward the hypothetical case stated by you because of its vagueness.

LANSING

763.72112/2200⅜ : Telegram

The Ambassador in Great Britain (Page) to the Secretary of State

LONDON, *January 22, 1916—4 p. m.*
[Received January 23—4 : 30 a. m.]

3622. Great Britain's allies, especially France, strongly insist on Great Britain's allies [*sic*] tightening the economic pressure on Germany. Public opinion here also has become earnestly aroused and demands an absolute blockade. The Government cannot long resist this demand for the country is convinced that a [decisive] victory depends on it. If the war end as a draw Europe will remain under a burden of armaments and there can be no hope of a continuing [*continuous*] peace. The Allies believe that [the question] may largely rest with us whether the war shall end as a draw. If we so object to a blockade as to cause an indecisive peace, Ally opinion will hold us responsible for the burdens of armaments and the political complications that will follow.

The following information which comes to me indirectly from an official source illustrates my meaning : Japan has forced [the tentative consent of some of the Allies to her] acquiring and retaining certain large advantages and privileges after the war ends. She wishes to set up a sort of Monroe Doctrine behind which it is feared she would exploit China and dominate the Pacific. England withholds her consent and has provoked an angry attitude by Japan, who wishes to secure her spoils and privileges while England is helplessly engaged in the [war with] Germany. The British Government . . . is for the moment helpless. England's final attitude to Japan must depend largely on the [feeling] at the end of the war between England and the United States. If the United States should oppose the blockade [of Germany] and the war should end as a draw, Japan will be able to extort her full demands because England will need her Navy indefinitely on this side of the world. If the United States acquiesce in the blockade and the war ends with German defeat, both England and the United States will be in the way of Japan's aggressions and [Japan will be checkmated.] The only hope therefore of a permanent peace lies in such a decisive defeat of Germany as will prevent a new era of armament and a new set of dangerous complications both in Europe and in the Pacific; and a decisive [defeat] may depend on the degree of active sympathy we show by our attitude to the forthcoming blockade.

Our attitude to the blockade therefore will have far-reaching re-sults for us and for the whole world. Permanent peace [depends on the] active sympathy of the two great English-speaking nations. There is [no other] practical and enduring basis [for] it. Besides nothing else can long save us from war. We are the larger in white population and potentially the stronger of these nations [and] per-manent peace cannot come without our active sympathy with the smaller empire which is now spending [itself to withstand] the assault [of] military monarchy on free government. If we accept the forthcoming blockade as England acceded to [*accepted*] our weaker blockade against the Confederacy we shall save the world from the aggressive ambitions both of Germany and of Japan. If we insist [on] technical objections in order to build up a code of naval and marine law, one or both the aggressive military mon-archies will smash our legal structure in their assault on democratic civilization.

Events are pushing us to the necessity of a [sharp] decision. It may be a silent [decision] but it must be clear. We should already have been drawn into this conflict but for England's complete naval supremacy over Germany. If the German Navy had the seas we should have been goaded into war. The only course that can insure peace for us in the future in the world-wide conflict between military monarchy and free government is such a direction of events as will bring an active sympathy between the British Empire and the United States. The forthcoming blockade will give probably the last tactical opportunity for such an active sympathy.

For these reasons this seems the critical moment of this war for us, a moment that demands a constructive and [decisive] suggestion. If you have such a suggestion, however tentative, that I may privately use it may secure a permanent peace after this war ends and change the course of history for a century.

I write this [profound] conviction having in mind only our own interests, our own security, and our own duty to our democratic ideals. This is our only practical lead [to insure a lasting peace.]

PAGE

763.72112/2200½

The Secretary of State to President Wilson

WASHINGTON, *January 24, 1916.*

MY DEAR MR. PRESIDENT: I enclose a confidential telegram received from Ambassador Page at London,[93] which was decoded yesterday. The telegram was in the private cipher and is more or less gar-

---

[93] *Supra.*

bled—however, I think that it is sufficiently clear in expressing Mr. Page's view as to the present situation.

I give more weight to the telegram because he had, at the time of sending it, had the advantage of consultation with Colonel House. Possibly you have received from Colonel House telegrams which will throw light on Mr. Page's point of view and also that of the British Government. I hope that you will have had this called to your attention before determining what course we should take with regard to Germany.

Faithfully yours,

ROBERT LANSING

763.72112/2201½

President Wilson to the Secretary of State

WASHINGTON, *24 January, 1916.*

MY DEAR MR. SECRETARY: This is very obscure, but I think I gather the sense of it.

I doubt if we can assume that it has any admixture or colour of House's views in it. I think it is all Page.

It of course has some force in it and deserves to be thought over on its own merits. Indeed, the arguments it urges are evident enough and of considerable weight.

In any case we ought to wait until we get House's letter to which I refer in the mem.[94] attached to your letter about the latest communication from Bernstorff.

Faithfully Yours,

W. W.

841.711/349

The Secretary of State to President Wilson

WASHINGTON, *May 20, 1916.*

MY DEAR MR. PRESIDENT: I enclose a draft of a note to the British Ambassador on the subject of interference with the mails.[95] I have been delayed in preparing this because it required considerable research and in addition I have not been to the Department for the past three days and may not be for two or three days to come.

I consider it very important that this note should be delivered as soon as possible because the mail detentions are becoming more

---

[94] *Post,* p. 522 (file No. 841.857 L 97/129½).
[95] For text of the note as sent, see identic note to the French Ambassador, *Foreign Relations,* 1916, supp., p. 604. For correspondence previously printed on the subject of interference with the mails, see *ibid.,* pp. 591 ff.

and more irritating to our people. I believe a way can be found for Great Britain to modify her present practice, but such a consideration will come after the note is delivered.

I would be obliged for any suggestions or changes you may see fit to make in the draft, which you will oblige me by sending to my house after you have examined it.

Faithfully yours,

ROBERT LANSING

841.711/488½

President Wilson to the Secretary of State

WASHINGTON, 22 May, 1916.

MY DEAR MR. SECRETARY: I have just been able to complete my careful reading of this note, and hasten to return it to you for transmission. I have made a few alterations in the verbiage which seem to me to make it clearer.

I hope that you are feeling a great deal better. We missed you at the Cabinet Friday very much.

Faithfully Yours,

W. W.

341.622A/154½

The Ambassador in Great Britain (Page) to the Secretary of State

LONDON, May 22, 1916.
[Received June 5.]

DEAR MR. LANSING: There's a little inside history of the *China* case that may interest you.[96] When your first telegram [97] about it came to me there was one of the recurring Cabinet "crises", which at intervals almost paralyze the Government. I laid the case before Sir Edward Grey who was ill and was on the eve of going off to rest. He sent it to the Admiralty and some Admiralty lawyer wrote the first answer we got,[98] declining to release these men. Before this answer came, I jogged Lord Crewe, Sir Edward's *locum tenens* during his absence, and at last the answer came. By this time Sir Edward had returned. When I sent this answer to you, I went over the whole case with Sir Edward, now rested and well again; and I told him I was sure that this answer w^d not be acceptable to you, that, in my judgment, it c^d not be acceptable, that the case

---

[96] For correspondence previously printed concerning this case, see *ibid.*, pp. 632 ff.
[97] *Ibid.*, p. 632.
[98] *Ibid.*, p. 633.

was another *Trent* case, the boot now being on the other foot. Then, I think, for the first time he began himself to look into it.

When, therefore, your next telegram came,[99] instructing me to renew the request for the release of these men, I had practically already presented it. Then I went over it again with Sir Edward, your telegram in my hand, w[h] I read to him, and I left with him the *aide memoire* as a brief record of my presentation of the case—now twice done. This was, of course, the most formal and at the same time the most free and elastic method of presentation and a method w[h], I have found, is likely to bring quicker results in this slow Kingdom than any other. An elaborate Note is handed over to a departmental lawyer and we hear from it—when the cows come home. An *Aide Memoire*, given when a thorough verbal discussion has been made, leaves it in the Secretary's own hands: he's obliged to take it up himself. I shall, however, remember your preference for Notes.—I had by this time brought Sir Edward to see the case as we saw it. He told me as much. But he then had to make the Admiralty back water: it was they who really gave the first answer that he signed. And he did overrule them and told me that the men w[d] be released.

Then a new chapter began. All the while the Intelligence Bureau of the Admiralty (the Spy department, or, as we say, the Secret Service) had information that some of these men were actually incorporated in the armed forces of Germany—were, in fact, officers, receiving officers' pay. But the Intelligence Bureau had not told either Sir Edward nor the head of the Admiralty. When, at last, they did tell Sir Edward, he ask[d], you will recall, if you w[d] consent to the English retaining these men, especially if documentary proof, now in the mails from Hongkong, was forthcoming. . . . I think that they already have pretty clear proof that 6 or 7 of these men (not 15, however,) are German officers, receiving officers' pay. It was this knowledge that caused me to suggest that we permit the English to retain these men till they sh[d] receive all the documents about them. I indulged this impulse to be quite generous—no doubt too generous—because we had already won the case and Sir Edward had granted the principle for w[h] we had contended and stood quite ready to live up to his verbal promise to release them all if we insisted. And before you c[d] answer the telegram in w[h] I made that suggestion, he agreed, without further ado to release them all. So ends the incident.

But it is interesting to see how they bungled the case:

(1) In the first place if the commander of the *Laurentic* had kept his hands off the *China*, all these men w[d] have disembarked at a Japanese port, where they c[d] lawfully have been taken in custody.

---

[99] *Foreign Relations*, 1916, supp., p. 637.

(2) Then, but for a Cabinet "crisis" and Sir Edward's necessary absence, he w^d have taken the case up himself in the first place, and it w^d have been settled long ago.

(3) Then the Intelligence Bureau made a mess of it by withholding their information from their superiors—this, probably to our advantage, but surely much to the confusion of the British Government; and I hear that there is now a good deal of a row between the Departments on this account.

All of which confirms an observation that I have had frequent occasion to make to myself—that, whatever other things may be perfect in this world, no great complex government can be. Surely the one near w^h I reside is not. But I must say, as the issue of this incident again proves, its Chief Foreign Secretary is a man of honor and of his word and it is a pleasure to deal with so true a gentleman, especially when I have, as in this case, the cold end of the poker.

Sincerely yours,

WALTER H. PAGE

600.001/18

The Secretary of State to President Wilson

WASHINGTON, *June 23, 1916.*

MY DEAR MR. PRESIDENT: If you have not had time to read carefully the enclosed telegram of the 20th from Paris [1] reciting the resolutions adopted by the Economic Conference of the Allied Powers,[2] I think that it would be well worth reading as the results of these measures may be very far reaching on the commerce and trade of the whole world after the war is over.

The proposed measures must be viewed from two standpoints, that of their effect on the present and future trade of the enemies of the Allies, and that of their effect on the present and future trade of neutral countries.

The drastic measures against the enemies of the Allies are not only intended to strangle their industries and commerce during the war, which is of course a legitimate war measure, but they go much further and purpose to prevent as far as possible the rebuilding of their industries and commerce after the war. It seems to me that the persistence of the Allied Governments in this policy will make the negotiations of a satisfactory peace most difficult, and that the knowledge of this intention to continue the war industrially after actual warfare ceases will cause the central Powers to hesitate in taking steps toward a restoration of peace. I believe that this Conference will have the effect of prolonging the war.

---

[1] Not printed.
[2] For text of these resolutions, see *Foreign Relations*, 1916, supp., p. 975.

In regard to the trade of neutrals, both now and after the war, the intentions of the Allied Powers are disquieting and I think should receive very careful consideration. We neutrals, as well as the Central Powers, will have to face a commercial combination which has as its avowed purpose preferential treatment for its members. It will be a strong combination of nations, which on account of their colonies and great merchant marine will be able, I fear, to carry through their preferential program. The consequent restriction upon profitable trade with these commercial allies will cause a serious, if not critical, situation for the nations outside the union by creating unusual and artificial economic conditions.

In view of these possibilities as to the future and the present restraints upon free commerce between neutrals as a consequence of blacklisting firms, agreements as to non-exportation, influence upon steamship companies and insurance, with the accompanying censorship of mail, would it not be well to consider the advisability of holding a Congress of Neutrals to take up these various questions and determine upon ways and means to relieve the present situation and to provide for the future?

If some step of this sort is not taken, the neutral countries acting independently will be impotent against this commercial combination. United and with some definite plan to meet the proposed measures of the Allies, I believe that the neutrals could better protect their interests by preventing radical action both during and after the war.

I have up to the present consistently opposed any action other than independent, but this economic and commercial conference of the Allied Powers with the purpose of union when peace is restored has materially changed conditions. The policy, which they propose to adopt, requires different treatment as it will materially affect our industrial and commercial life. It must be met in some practical way, and the best way to fight combination is by combination.

At least it seems to me a subject which we should consider, and the consideration of which ought not to be long delayed.

Faithfully yours,

ROBERT LANSING

341.622A/154½

The Secretary of State to the Ambassador in Great Britain (*Page*)

WASHINGTON, *July 8, 1916.*

MY DEAR MR. PAGE: I have read with a great deal of interest your personal note of the 22d [May] giving the inside history of the *China* case. As you have no doubt judged from my telegrams, I have regarded the British action in this case as wholly unwarranted and without the least semblance of right so far as the facts were known to the commander of the *Laurentic*. The United States could not condone the offense without giving up the principle for which it has fought in the past.

I am determined to do my utmost to prevent the infringements of this principle during the present war.

The *Henry S.* case [3] seems to be on all fours with the *China* case, and it seems to me the British Government should, following the *China* case, if the facts are as I believe them to be, promptly release the men removed from the *Henry S.*

The *Ausable* case [3] is receiving my consideration, and I expect to send you a telegram in reply to your 4384, May 30,[4] in a few days.

I congratulate you on your success in the *China* case, as I believe your efforts have resulted in a real contribution to the protection of neutral rights—rights which are as important to the world as belligerent rights, but which have been considerably battered during the present war.

I trust that you may be able to settle as amicably and successfully the *Henry S.* and *Ausable* cases.

Sincerely yours,

[File copy not signed]

763.72112/3044

The Secretary of State to President Wilson

WASHINGTON, *September 18, 1916*.

DEAR MR. PRESIDENT: I send you a copy of a paper which was handed to me by the British Ambassador yesterday,[5] saying that it was confidentially communicated and must not be regarded as in any way official, and that he gave it to me because he wanted to be perfectly frank in setting forth the feelings of his Government in regard to the public sentiment in Great Britain.

I believe that it will impress you, as it has me, that the temper of the British Government at this time does not make for an amicable settlement of our difficulties with them. Of course, this paper calls for no action on our part, but is valuable in indicating what their reply will be in regard to the questions of the censorship of mails and the blacklist.[6]

Faithfully yours,

ROBERT LANSING

---

[3] For correspondence previously printed concerning the cases of the *Henry S.* and the *Ausable*, see *Foreign Relations*, 1916, supp., pp. 635 ff.

[4] *Ibid.*, p. 648.

[5] *Ibid.*, p. 445.

[6] On October 2 President Wilson replied: "This is a very disappointing and discouraging document. They are sinking further and further into the dark." (File No. 763.72112/3046½.)

763.72112/3010a

The Secretary of State to President Wilson

WASHINGTON, *September 22, 1916.*

MY DEAR MR. PRESIDENT: There is a means employed frequently by the British Foreign Office and occasionally by this Department to communicate in a frank way views which it would be embarrassing to do formally. The way it is done is to send a telegram to a diplomatic representative which he is permitted to show the Secretary of Foreign Affairs on his own responsibility and in an entirely unofficial manner. An example of this practice was the telegram from Viscount Grey to Sir Cecil, a copy of which I sent you in my letter of the 18th. It has the advantage that it avoids note-writing and not being given publicity avoids the charge of being done for political effect.

It has seemed to me that it might be advisable to pursue this method at the present time in bringing home to the British Government the growing irritation in this country at the blacklisting, censorship of mails and other measures adopted by Great Britain, and the indifference shown by the British Government in failure to make prompt reply to our notes. I am afraid that London does not appreciate that the tide of resentment is rising very high in this country, and that there is a tendency to demand drastic action by this Government. The British Government ought to be fully advised of this menace to our cordial relations, because the removal of it lies with them. I do not think that their representatives here have correctly pictured the state of the public mind in this country or impressed them with the conditions which are rapidly approaching a critical stage.

In accordance with the method of communicating information, which I have mentioned, I have prepared a telegram to our Chargé at London very frankly and very bluntly telling the truth about the present situation. This telegram he is confidentially authorized to show to Lord Grey on his own responsibility and unofficially.

A draft of the proposed telegram to Mr. Laughlin is enclosed and I would be obliged if you would give me your views as to the advisability of sending any telegram of this nature and as to the language of the telegram, if you approve sending one. I think the decision should be made immediately.

Faithfully yours,

ROBERT LANSING

[Enclosure]

Draft Telegram From the Secretary of State to the Chargé in Great Britain (Laughlin)

We have received, after waiting over six weeks, no reply to our protest of July 26th[7] in regard to the blacklisting of persons in the United States and its possessions. On the contrary, the results of our recent unofficial representations in specific cases of blacklisted firms, and the intimations given to various American firms not to continue business relations of many years standing or not to make new business connections with certain persons, firms and companies resident in the United States or in other neutral countries, together with other information which has come to my attention, but to which it is not necessary at the present time to refer cause me to conclude that the reply to our note of July 26th will be unsatisfactory.

This Government has taken every means in its power, as it has in dealing with other belligerents in this war, to conduct the relations of the United States and Great Britain on a friendly and cordial basis, though maintaining the rights and duties of neutrality as it was bound to do. I regret to say, however, that in no single instance of any importance have the British Government on their part modified their pretensions to extraordinary belligerent privileges so as to conform their conduct to established usage; nor do they appear to have regard for the rights of the United States or for the public opinion of this country. Some of the British practices, which are causing increasing irritation, cannot, so far as I am able to judge, have any material effect on the outcome of the war. The removal of reservists from American vessels on the high seas, the searching of American vessels in territorial waters of the Philippines, the censorship of genuine letter-correspondence, the refusal of cable privileges in legitimate neutral trade, and the blacklisting of American business houses are some of the matters which are carried on now with as much, if not greater, vigor than before this Government protested against them.

I confess that I have been most unfavorably impressed with the absolutely unrelenting attitude of the British Government, courteous though it be, when their measures have been opposed by this Government on grounds of reason, law or practice. Not a single rule that we have contended for and that Great Britain herself has insisted upon in the past, has been admitted by the British Government. A few isolated cases have been decided in our favor but only upon notification that they were acts of grace and must not be regarded as precedents. It should not be a matter of surprise that the American

---

[7] *Foreign Relations*, 1916, supp., p. 421.

people are resenting more and more this practice of granting favors which are claimed as a matter of right.

When a remonstrance is made by the United States, it is frequently met by the argument that, considering the American attitude toward Germany, Great Britain is surprised that the United States should take such a view of the British action complained of. It would seem needless to point out that the United States is not fighting Great Britain's warfare against submarines. Great Britain should understand that the position which the United States has taken toward submarine warfare, is based primarily on its relations to American rights and interests. I cannot but believe that the apparent purpose of treating our controversies by reference to the conduct of Germany is based on a misapprehension of the relations between our intercourse with Germany on the one hand and with Great Britain on the other, a misapprehension, but which it has constantly sought to avoid. The respective subjects of controversy are entirely distinct, and this Government, therefore, perceives no ground for changing its firm intention to keep them separate.

If the British Government is expecting an attitude of "benevolent neutrality" on our part—a position which is not neutral and which is not governed by the principles of neutrality—they should know that nothing is further from our intention. The freedom of our shores to commerce of the allied powers for the exportation of thousands of shiploads of all kinds of supplies—munitions, food, clothing and metals—while their enemies have been able to obtain scarcely a single cargo, and the forbearance, if not the leniency, shown by this Government toward Great Britain in cases involving grave breaches of international law, have apparently caused the British Government to misjudge the policy of this Government and the attitude of the people of this country, and led them to believe that ours is a neutrality from which the Allied Powers might expect no remonstrance, no matter how grievously American rights are infringed or American interests impaired.

Such apparent indifference to the viewpoint and views of the United States on the varied subjects of controversy cannot but have its effect upon the Government and people in this country. The continuance of palpably objectionable practices creates the impression, whether justified or not, that Great Britain is indifferent to the friendship and good will of the American people or else confidently believes that nothing done in violation of American rights will be seriously resisted because of the profitable trade being carried on at the present time with the United Kingdom and its Allies; and this impression is growing stronger in this country and materially affecting public opinion. This unyielding attitude of Great Britain has, to my personal knowledge, awakened against the Allies a resentful sentiment among the American people which is in marked contrast to the popular sympathy, which earlier in the war was strongly on their side in the conflict. This is probably shown best by the feeling aroused in the last session of Congress, whose committees held hearings on the effects of British measures on the rights and interests of the people of the United States, and whose opinion was crystallized in certain legislation enlarging the powers of the President to deal with the situation resulting from the British measures which were considered not only as illegal but as needless from a military point of view, and as imposing upon our citizens losses and burdens, to which Great Britain seemed entirely indifferent.

Perhaps the one measure more responsible than any other for this result is the blacklisting plan of the British Government, although the improper censorship of the mails has affected thousands of our people. I cannot too earnestly impress upon you the strong public feeling in the United States in regard to the blacklist. This feeling is naturally most hostile among those of our citizens whose business has been directly affected, but they are not alone in their complaints or in their demands on the Government for radical action. I have taken pains to sound the opinion of the more conservative portion of our people and I am convinced that a bitterness of feeling is increasing to such a degree as to endanger the good relations of the United States and Great Britain. To resist this rapidly growing sentiment this Government will be powerless, unless the British Government shows a more considerate and friendly regard for American rights. I do not know what reports are sent home by British Agents here, but whatever they are they are ill advised if they have not reported to their Government this change in public opinion. This change is further augmented not only by the fact that the blacklisting plan results in many cases in the transfer of American trade from American houses to British competitors who reside and carry on their business in the United States, but by the belief, whether true or false, that the blacklisting plan, as it has only an infinitesimal effect on the war, is in reality aimed at the destruction of German trade after the war, a purpose which, if true, cannot be justified before the world.

The objectionable features of blacklisting seem to me so apparent that I cannot understand how the British Government can defend it on any but most technical grounds if indeed it can be defended on any grounds. It is clearly an invasion of the independence and sovereignty of the United States by an endeavor to enforce indirectly, if not directly, British laws upon American soil and to impose restraints upon trade in the United States. Not only do the British Government control the actions of British subjects here but seek to control the actions of the American traders. In fact, as I am advised, British agents in their official capacity have gone so far as to intimidate American citizens against pursuing certain lines of business which are entirely legitimate. The criminal nature of such intimidations is receiving the attention of the law officers of the Government with a view to taking such steps to stamp out the practice as may be proper and necessary. There are even some indications that members of the British Embassy and of certain Consulates are involved in such proceedings. If this should prove to be true, I need not tell you that the case would be most serious, and the unavoidable publicity would still further increase the indignation of Americans.

The British Government appears not to comprehend the fact, for it is a fact, that they are really forcing this Government into a position which cannot but result in strained relations between the two countries. The temper of the American people is now so aroused over the attitude and practices of the Allies, that I fear the consequences unless there is some recession on their part. The blacklist and the mail censorship are the matters which are most in the minds of the American people—particularly so because the annoyance to individuals is so intimate and so general. I anticipate, therefore, that in the near future this Government, however reluctantly, will be forced by the strength of public opinion to take steps to put the retaliatory legislation of Congress into effect. If the Government does not do this, it is easy to foresee that Congress may at its next session make this legislation, which now confers discretionary powers upon the President, mandatory upon the executive authorities.

My great desire is to avoid this possible crisis in Anglo-American relations and to conduct them in conformity with the truest international amity, but I can not view the present situation and its logical outcome with anything but the gravest apprehension. I am therefore sending this to you confidentially and requesting you to let no moment be lost in reporting to me confidentially by telegraph your views on the chances of moving the British Government, first, to an appreciation of the effects of their present policy; second, to a realization of the result which is sure to follow from a continuance of it; and lastly, to a recession from their position by radically changing their objectionable measures.

On your own responsibility you may let Lord Grey read this despatch after deleting this paragraph and heading it merely "Telegram from Mr. Lansing, Secretary of State, to Mr. Laughlin, Chargé d'Affaires" as a frank statement of the views of this Government on the present situation. If he asks for a copy do not hand him one at the time, but have one made and sent to him later marked "unofficial and not to be made a part of the records."

763.72112/3010½

President Wilson to the Secretary of State

WEST END, N. J., *29 September, 1916.*

MY DEAR MR. SECRETARY: I think it would be quite unjustifiable to do anything for the sake of public opinion which might change the whole face of our foreign relations. Therefore I think it would be most unwise to send a message like this.[8]

I had a talk with Walter Page of the most explicit kind, and am sure that he will be able to convey to the powers that be in London a very clear impression of the lamentable and dangerous mistakes they are making. I covered the whole subject matter here dealt with in a way which I am sure left nothing to be desired in the way of explicitness or firmness of tone; and I think that our method had better stop with that for the time being. Let us forget the campaign so far as matters of this sort are concerned.

Faithfully Yours,

W. W.

763.72112/3010b

The Secretary of State to President Wilson

WASHINGTON, *September 30, 1916.*

MY DEAR MR. PRESIDENT: On the 22d I sent you the draft of a proposed telegram to our Chargé at London dealing very frankly with our relations with Great Britain. My letter of transmittal explained the purpose and the method of using the statements in the telegram.

I am taking the liberty of calling the matter again to your attention because I feel that the continued delay of the British Government in replying to our notes on the mails and on the blacklist is creating a public sentiment in this country toward this Department which is bringing it into contempt for submitting to such treatment without vigorous protest. I have sought to avoid a protest to the British Government and thought this telegram might obviate it, but the situation is reaching a stage which will compel some action. Will you please advise me of your wishes?

There is another matter—the *Lusitania* case—which is also causing considerable criticism. It is pointed out that delay in our negotiations was unpardonable, and that now several months have passed since the German submission in the *Sussex* case without any settlement of the *Lusitania* affair.

---

[8] *Supra.*

The delay in the negotiations can be readily explained—in fact I have a statement already prepared upon that, the use of which is only a matter of expediency, but the failure to settle the case is less easy of explanation. As you will remember Count Bernstorff and I reached a satisfactory agreement as to the terms last February.[9] Would it or would it not be advisable at the present time to ask him to make our informal agreement formal? If that could be done, while it would open the settlement to discussion, it would stop the criticism as to delay and end the chapter. I confess that I cannot make up my mind as to the best course to pursue.[9a]

Faithfully yours,

ROBERT LANSING

763.72112/3010½

The Secretary of State to President Wilson

WASHINGTON, *October 2, 1916.*

MY DEAR MR. PRESIDENT: I received your letter of the 29th ultimo in reply to mine of the 22d enclosing a draft of telegram to our Chargé at London, and believe that I understand your desire as to the work of the Department at the present time. After my talks with Mr. Page I felt very doubtful whether he would make the situation here as clear to the British Government as he should. It was for this reason that I drafted the telegram.

As you know I have felt that the conduct of our foreign affairs ought to be divorced entirely from the political campaign and for that reason determined at the outset that none of the higher officials of the Department should take any part in the campaign, a course which I felt corresponded with your wishes.

That policy will be rigidly observed, although I confess that it is difficult to "forget the campaign so far as matters of this sort are concerned", when we are subject daily to unjust criticism based on error or deliberate falsehood. It is not easy to remain silent under such charges and imputations as are being publicly made by the opposition, when they can be so fully and convincingly answered.

Faithfully yours,

ROBERT LANSING

---

[9] See *Foreign Relations*, 1916, supp., pp. 171, 172.
[9a] For additional correspondence on the *Lusitania* negotiations, see pp. 569–572.

841.711/1318

The Secretary of State to President Wilson

WASHINGTON, *October 13, 1916.*

MY DEAR MR. PRESIDENT: I hasten to send you a translation of the reply of the Allied Governments [10] to our note on the mails, of May 24th.[11]

I have only had time to read it through and am not prepared to express any definite opinion. I have, however, from this single reading, gained the impression that the note is couched in most friendly terms, indicating a conciliatory attitude; that it has materially cleared the atmosphere as to the exact issues between the two Governments; and that they entirely fail to meet our charge of diverting neutral vessels proceeding to neutral ports from the high seas to British ports for the purpose of examining their mail bags.

As soon as I have digested the reply of the Allies I will communicate further my views.

Faithfully yours,

ROBERT LANSING

841.711/1588½

The Secretary of State to President Wilson

WASHINGTON, *October 17, 1916.*

MY DEAR MR. PRESIDENT: I am enclosing for your consideration a memorandum which I have made on the general subject of the detention and censorship of the mails. In this memorandum I have not sought to traverse the arguments advanced by the Allied Powers in their reply to our note of May 24th, but have sought to view the subject as impartially as possible from the standpoint of principle and applied common sense. An insistence on technicalities will, I feel sure, get us nowhere as each side can bulwark itself behind many legal precedents, which on account of the facts in each case appear to be reasonable and sound. It seems to me, therefore, that we must go back to general principles and determine by logic some solution of the problem.

In considering the subject I think that we should bear in mind that, while we are neutral in the present war, we may be belligerent in the next and may deem it necessary to do certain things which we now regard as extreme restrictions upon neutrals. It would be most unfortunate to tie ourselves too tightly to a proposition which we would regret in the future.

---

[10] *Foreign Relations*, 1916, supp., p. 624.
[11] *Ibid.*, p. 604.

After you have read the memorandum you will perceive that I have reached the following conclusions:

That there are two classes of mails: First, mails going to or toward the Central Powers; and, second, mails coming from those powers or from contiguous neutral countries.

That, as to mails coming from neutral countries included in the second class, there is no basis at law or in reason for the inspection of either sealed or unsealed mails.

That, as to the first class there exists the right to inspect unsealed mail and to detain contraband articles; but as to the inspection of sealed mail there is a conflict of principles due to the law of contraband and the theory of inviolability, principles which are irreconcilable because the superiority of right of exercise has never been determined.

From these conclusions the only solution of the problem which suggests itself to me is this:

That we insist that mail outcoming from neutral countries in continental Europe shall be treated as inviolable and shall not be subject to detention, inspection or seizure.

That the extent and exercise of the belligerent right to detain, inspect or seize mail ingoing to continental Europe shall be submitted immediately to arbitration or to a joint commission of inquiry, which shall seek to apply the conflicting principles equitably and lay down a series of rules which may be adopted as a *modus operandi* by this Government and those of the Allies.

After I hear from you in this matter, and provided you approve of this plan, I might take up the matter informally with the British Ambassador and get the views of his Government.

Of course the difficulty is as to the procedure while the commissioners are considering the question. I think that all we could do is to get the best terms possible.

  Faithfully yours,

           ROBERT LANSING

[Enclosure]

Memorandum by the Secretary of State on Censorship of Mails

[WASHINGTON,] *October 13, 1916.*

The problem of the seizure and detention or censorship by a belligerent of mails carried in a neutral bottom from a neutral port to an enemy destination or to a neutral destination whither they may without interruption be transmitted to the enemy, results from the conflict of two established principles:

First. The belligerent right to remove from neutral vessels on the high seas articles of contraband and contraband communications; and

Second. The neutral right to have mails between neutral countries, and innocent private correspondence between a neutral country and a belligerent country treated as inviolate by belligerents.

It is manifest that neither of these rights can be exercised to their full extent and the other right maintained to any degree. The unimpaired exercise of both rights is impossible. They cannot be brought into harmony.

The question, therefore, arises as to whether the belligerent right of mail-examination or the neutral right of mail-inviolability is the superior right and should govern any attempted adjustment of the conflict between the two rights.

In the first place, all belligerent rights on the high seas are abnormal and contrary to the usual practice of nations in times of peace. As a general proposition, the belligerent right should be strictly construed against the belligerent exercising it, and liberally construed as to the neutral whose normal rights are impaired by such exercise. As a rule, therefore, when a belligerent right conflicts with a recognized neutral right, the latter should be the controlling factor in reaching an adjustment of the differences.

On the other hand, if the full exercise of the neutral right destroys or renders impossible of exercise a recognized belligerent right, it is open to question whether or not the neutral rights should not be so modified as to permit a reasonable exercise of the belligerent right.

The argument in favor of the modification of a neutral right under such conditions rests primarily on the fact that the national safety of the belligerent is at stake, which is in truth the foundation of all exceptional rights over neutrals and their property on the high seas conferred upon belligerents. If the deprivation of a belligerent right materially reduces the possibility of injury to an enemy, or if such deprivation increases the efficiency of an enemy, is a neutral justified in insisting on the observance of neutral right which deprives the belligerent of the right to which he would be entitled if the neutral right did not exist?

If the neutral right is of vital interest there would seem to be strong justification for insisting upon its full observance even though the belligerent right in conflict was nullified by such observance. But, if the neutral right recognized merely the continuance of a practice usual in times of peace, the interruption of which would not impair the vital interests of a neutral state but would cause much inconvenience and possible pecuniary loss to the nationals of that state, it would be of doubtful justice to insist on the exercise of the neutral right without regard to its effect on the belligerent right.

In large measure the limitations upon neutrals which result from the exercise of belligerent rights on the high seas cause inconvenience and loss to neutrals in their commercial enterprises. It is a consequence which is considered unavoidable and is submitted to because of the recognition of the supreme right of a nation to defend itself by preventing aid from reaching its enemy. Like the right of visit and search, the right to seize articles of contraband and contraband communications is one of the oldest and most universally recognized rights of belligerents. It was established before postal treaties were negotiated and before the post had become a world wide institution and mails measured by tons. The long unquestioned acceptance of the law of contraband raises the query whether the expansion of postal facilities to such an extent as to offer a practical means of transporting contraband articles and correspondence can lessen the full force of the more ancient belligerent right.

To determine whether a mail bag contains contraband articles or contraband correspondence requires inspection by a belligerent. Such an inspection can be easily made of unsealed packets, and little argument can be urged against the propriety of such inspection or against the confiscation of articles of contraband which are found. The chief complaints would arise from the seizure of articles of doubtful contraband character and from undue delay in permitting innocent articles to proceed to their destination.

In the case of sealed mail the real difficulty arises. Admitting that the law of contraband can be applied to all articles and communications found on neutral vessels on the high seas, it is manifest that the law can [not?] be applied to sealed packets without their being opened and inspected. But, if the law of contraband cannot be applied to such mail, a channel of communication and transportation would be open to an enemy, through which might flow uninterruptedly contraband of all sorts because of moderate rates of postage and the size of packages now permitted in first class mail.

It cannot be expected that a belligerent will permit, if there is power to prevent, this means of intercourse to remain free to an enemy; and it is very doubtful whether a neutral is justified in objecting to inspection of sealed mail and to the censorship of correspondence provided the belligerent scrupulously confines the inspection and confiscation of mail matter to that which is unquestionably contraband. If the inspection of correspondence is for the purpose of obtaining information either of a military or civil nature it exceeds the limits of right. The sole legitimate reason for interruption of mail is to prevent contraband articles and information reaching the enemy. When it is manifest that the acquisition of knowledge is a principal ground for the seizure or detention of mail, it can find no warrant in law or in usage.

The foregoing applies to sealed mail destined to the enemy. In the case of sealed mail between neutral countries, one of which is contiguous to the enemy with whom are uninterrupted postal facilities, the problem is more complex. Admitting the doctrine of ultimate destination, how can the ultimate destination of sealed mail be determined unless it is opened and inspected? If it is not opened, but is permitted to pass with the seals unbroken, has not a sure and safe channel been found for the conduct of an extensive trade in contraband with the enemy of the belligerent allowing its passage? Is there not justification for the belligerent in insisting on an inspection of sealed mail going to a neutral country contiguous to enemy territory?

However strong may be the argument in favor of the justice of a belligerent's rights to inspect sealed mail going toward an enemy and to apply the law of contraband to such mail, the argument cannot be urged with equal force in regard to sealed mail, or even unsealed mail, leaving a neutral country adjacent to enemy territory. The law of contraband, depending upon enemy destination, cannot be invoked. It may be claimed that the right of inspection and seizure arises from the fact of enemy origin of articles, but that cannot be conceded as giving legal effect to such an act, and it certainly cannot be invoked in the case of sealed correspondence.

The opening of sealed correspondence would appear to be for the purpose of obtaining information for the use of the belligerent. That is the unavoidable presumption. Such a purpose is illegal and improper and constitutes a very legitimate ground of complaint by the neutral on whose vessel the mail is carried and also by the neutral to which it is destined. Such mail at least should be absolutely inviolate.

841.711/1589½

President Wilson to the Secretary of State

WASHINGTON, *14 November, 1916.*

MY DEAR MR. SECRETARY: I have read this memorandum with a great deal of care, and have the following comments and suggestions to offer:

In form the note [12] seems to me too much an argumentative establishment of the belligerent rights now being claimed and exercised by the Allies. Would it not be better (1) to state the problem, as you do, (2) admit this and that point, with the grounds of the admission briefly stated, and (3) insist on the residuum and offer to set afoot an international inquiry as to the right general grounds of right and adjustment.

---

[12] i. e., the memorandum printed *supra*.

You see my point: it is that it would be better to make admissions than to seem to be formally arguing their case.

Faithfully Yours,

W. W.

___

841.711/1589½

The Secretary of State to President Wilson

WASHINGTON, *November 14, 1916.*

MY DEAR MR. PRESIDENT: I perceive by your note of today in reply to my letter of October 17th, in relation to the interception of the mails by the Allied Powers, that you misconceived the purpose of the memorandum which I enclosed in my letter. I am afraid I did not make my purpose clear.

I did not intend the memorandum as a draft of reply but merely as a discussion of the subject for the purpose of settling in our own minds the policy which we should adopt in continuing the controversy and in accordance with which we should prepare a reply. It was intended to analyze the arguments on both sides and to find, if possible, a solution to a dispute over apparently irreconcilable rights.

In sending you the letter and the memorandum I sought to obtain your views as to the analysis of the subject in the memorandum and as to whether the course of action suggested in my letter seemed to you to offer a practical solution of the problem, which we could adopt and incorporate in proper form in a note in reply to the British note of October 12th.[13] For that reason I did not refer to the British note in the memorandum, dealing with the subject abstractly rather than concretely, and, furthermore I did not send you a copy of their note.

I am enclosing a copy of the note now and you will perceive that there are statements and conclusions set forth which we ought not let go unchallenged. So that, if you approve of the analysis in my memorandum and of the policy outlined in my letter, we will use them as general guides in drafting our reply while traversing as far as seems necessary the arguments advanced by Viscount Grey.

I am returning my letter and memorandum to you for consideration in the light of this explanation and I shall await your instructions as to the adoption of the policy proposed and the preparation of a reply, which will of course be submitted to you when drafted.

Faithfully yours,

ROBERT LANSING

___

[13] See note No. 307 from the British Ambassador, *Foreign Relations*, 1916, supp., p. 629.

341.622A/271a

The Secretary of State to President Wilson

WASHINGTON, *November 23, 1916.*

MY DEAR MR. PRESIDENT: You will recall that I spoke to you about two communications to the British Government which were in the course of preparation in regard to the unwarranted and summary seizure and removal at sea of seamen, officers, and others from American vessels by British cruisers, and that you stated that you desired to see these communications before they were forwarded to London. I therefore enclose copies of these notes for your consideration.

The enclosure marked "A" is the proposed communication on the *China* case,[14] which, as you will perceive, has been settled by the release of the persons seized, although settled unsatisfactorily as to the principle involved. This communication is merely a review of the correspondence which has been exchanged in this case, for the purpose of clearing up certain misapprehensions under which Lord Grey appears to have been laboring in regard to the position of the Government of the United States, and to set forth also for the record the inconsistent grounds advanced by the British Government for the seizure of the men on the *China*, in order that this Government might not, if these cases should go to arbitration, be placed in the light of having acquiesced in the British views. I do not think there is anything new in the enclosure marked "A."

The enclosure marked "B" is a proposed communication to the British Government in regard to cases of the removal of seamen and others from American vessels on the high seas which have occurred since the case of the *China*.[15] It is an attempt to set forth without prejudice the past practice of the American and British Governments in this matter, with a view to showing that what Great Britain is now doing in this respect is without warrant in practice or law and has been in the past regarded by her and by us as a most serious offence. Enclosure "B", therefore, is largely historical, with the exception of the last few pages.

I desire to call your particular attention to the last paragraph of the covering instruction of enclosure "B", in which Mr. Page is informed that this Government has in mind a proposal to arbitrate this controversy after the war, on the condition that the men already seized are released and no other seizures are made during the continuance of the war. As these seizures are a great annoyance to American ship-owners, besides being an affront to the American flag,

---

[14] For text of this communication as sent, see *ibid.*, p. 662.
[15] For text of this communication as sent, see *ibid.*, p. 667.

and without any compensating military advantage to the Allies, it seems to me that this proposal is fair and ought to be acceptable to Great Britain.

I hesitate to send you these long communications at the present time, when you are so fully engaged, as I know, upon matters which have accumulated and upon your annual message, but I am impelled to do so by the pressure under which the Department suffers from the continuous inquiries by Congressmen, ship-owners, and seamen in regard to the pending cases, the rights of American seamen, and the attitude of the British Government. I am also moved to send you these now by the further fact that another case similar to those set forth in enclosure "B" has recently arisen, and if I do not mistake the character of the searches of American vessels at sea for German subjects, other cases are likely to arise at any moment. For these reasons, and on account of the particularly annoying and unnecessary nature of these seizures, I deem it very important that these communications should be forwarded to London as soon as possible.

Faithfully yours,

ROBERT LANSING

341.622 a/273½

President Wilson to the Secretary of State

WASHINGTON, *26 November, 1916.*

MY DEAR MR. SECRETARY: I return the enclosed papers (or, rather, the attached papers)[16] with my approval, except that I hope that you will modify the language of page ten (10) of "A" so as not to carry the implication that the British Foreign Office has been dealing insincerely with us. Whatever the appearances may be to that effect, I think it would be wise, as well as kind, not to indicate such an impression on our part, since it is not necessary to our argument. A little change of phraseology will be easy, I hope.

Both papers seem to me to be unusually interesting and quite unanswerable; and I approve the suggestion of arbitration, to which you especially call my attention.

Faithfully Yours,

W. W.

----

[16] See *supra.*

841.711/1590½

President Wilson to the Secretary of State

WASHINGTON, *26 November, 1916.*

MY DEAR MR. SECRETARY: I fear it was a little stupid in me not to perceive the real character of this memorandum.[17] Thank you for correcting me.

The argument and the position seem to me all right, and I hope that you will prepare our note in reply to the British along these lines. I shall be interested to go over it with you when you shall have completed it.

Faithfully Yours,

W. W.

841.711/1699½

President Wilson to the Secretary of State

WASHINGTON, *27 December, 1916.*

MY DEAR MR. SECRETARY: I have just been going over the papers I brought down with me from Shadow Lawn, and come across these.[18] I fear I have kept them too long. I will be glad to discuss this and other kindred matters with you when we have seen just what the several belligerents are willing to do about discussing terms of peace.

Faithfully Yours,

W. W.

---

[17] *Ante,* p. 322.
[18] Papers regarding interference with the mails.

ARMED MERCHANT SHIPS [1]

763.72111/144 : Telegram

The Secretary of State to the British Ambassador (Spring Rice)[1a]

Washington, *September 9, 1914—1:04 p. m.*

Replying to your note of the 4th instant [1b] it seems unnecessary to answer the inquiry regarding the shipment of the *Merion's* guns to England as cargo in another vessel, for the reason that Department is informed that notwithstanding the assurances of your Government the *Merion* sailed with her guns and ammunition.[1c]

W. J. Bryan

763.72/2142½b

The Secretary of State to President Wilson

Washington, *September 12, 1915.*

My Dear Mr. President: We have for several days held at Norfolk a British merchant vessel [2] because she had on board a mounted 4.7 gun, endeavoring meanwhile to have the British Admiralty direct its removal before the vessel left our port.

We are now advised that the British Admiralty declines to remove the gun and asserts, correctly, that the vessel has complied with our declaration of September 19, 1914,[2a] as to armed merchant vessels. Up to the present time the British Admiralty as a result of an informal understanding have kept guns off British merchant vessels entering American ports. For a year, therefore, the question has not been discussed as no case has arisen.

Meanwhile submarine warfare has developed as a practical method of interrupting merchant vessels. At the time we issued the declaration as to the status of armed merchant vessels this use of the submarine as a commerce destroyer was unknown, and the declaration was based on the means employed prior to that time.

---

[1] For additional correspondence on this subject, see pp. 560 ff., *passim.*

[1a] This telegram bears the notation: "In view of objection raised by British Amb. that the last phrase reflected on British Govt. this telegram was withdrawn. 9/9/14 6 pm Robert Lansing."

[1b] *Foreign Relations,* 1914, supp., p. 606.

[1c] For correspondence previously printed concerning the *Merion,* see *ibid.,* pp. 605, 606–607, 612.

[2] i. e., the *Waimana;* for correspondence previously printed concerning this vessel, see *ibid.,* 1915, supp., pp. 848 ff.

[2a] *Ibid.,* 1914, supp., p. 611.

I feel in my own mind that these changed conditions require a new declaration because an armament, which under previous conditions, was clearly defensive, may now be employed for offensive operations against so small and unarmored a craft as a submarine. On the 4th of this month the German Ambassador called my attention to the fact that on two occasions German submarines were attacked and fired upon by British passenger steamers.[3] While these may be isolated cases the fact that such vessels are attacking submarines makes it difficult to demand that a submarine shall give warning and so expose itself to the heavy guns carried by some of the British passenger vessels.

As to the effect of these cases on our declaration, it would seem to me that we ought to amend it by asserting that in view of the successful employment of submarines as commerce destroyers and the possibility of offensive operations against them by a merchant vessel carrying an armament regardless of the number, size or location of the guns composing it, this Government will hereafter treat as a ship of war any merchant vessel of belligerent nationality which enters an American port with any armament.

The assumption of this position has another advantage and that is that the term "armed" ["*unarmed*"] instead of "unresisting" will be justified, and as it was used I feel that we ought to stand by it.

In the particular case of the vessel at Norfolk I think that we should be less rigid on account of our former declaration. A proposed note to the British Ambassador is enclosed [4] treating the case specially and leniently.

I enclose also the entire docket in the case directing your attention in particular to Count von Bernstorff's note of the 4th instant, and our declaration of September 19, 1914, which immediately follows it.

Faithfully yours,

ROBERT LANSING

763.72/2143½

President Wilson to the Secretary of State

WASHINGTON, *13 September, 1915.*

MY DEAR MR. SECRETARY: I have read this carefully.

I think the course we orally outlined this morning is the best one:

To let this particular vessel go upon a promise by the British Admiralty and a bond by the owners of the vessel that the arms will in no case be used for offense;

---

[3] *Ibid.*, 1915, supp., p. 535.
[4] No enclosures with file copy of this letter; reference is probably to the note of Sept. 11, 1915, to the British Ambassador, *ibid.*, p. 849.

And to prepare the general regulation you suggest, but not publish it or put it into effect until we see what we are going to be able to work out of this *Arabic* business.

Faithfully Yours,

W. W.

763.72/2351a

The Secretary of State to President Wilson

WASHINGTON, *January 2, 1916.*

MY DEAR MR. PRESIDENT: The enclosed copies of telegrams [5] telling of the sinking of the British steamship *Persia* on December 30th about three hundred miles northwest of Alexandria do not, in my opinion, seriously affect the *Ancona* case, since the evidence of torpedoing is inconclusive, the nationality of the submarine, if one was the cause, is unknown, and it is stated that the *Persia* carried an armament.

The fact that the vessel was carrying a 4.7 gun raises a question which, it seems to me, we ought to settle.

Three or four days ago I forwarded to the Italian Ambassador at his request the statement in regard to armed merchant vessels, which we issued in September, 1914.[6] I had discussed the question some four or five weeks before with Mr. Barclay of the British Embassy and told him that, in view of the development of submarines as commerce destroyers, which had been unknown when our statement was issued, I felt that the arming of merchant vessels with any gun, of sufficient calibre to attack a submarine, would make it very difficult, if not impossible, to insist that a submarine should expose itself to attack by coming to the surface and hailing a vessel so armed; and that, while the armament might be termed "defensive", it was capable of being used offensively against a submarine and so, I thought, that a merchant ship carrying a gun or guns would have to be considered and treated as a vessel of war if it entered our ports.

In view of this opinion, which I believe I stated to you orally some time ago, I wrote the Italian Ambassador a letter enclosing the statement of September, 1914, explaining the change of view which the new conditions had forced upon us. I enclose a copy of that letter [7] with our printed statement as to the status of armed merchant vessels.

---

[5] Not printed; for correspondence previously printed concerning the *Persia* case, see *Foreign Relations*, 1916, supp., pp. 143–156, *passim*, and p. 214.

[6] *Ibid.*, 1914, supp., p. 611.

[7] *Ibid.*, 1916, supp., p. 749.

Since we issued the statement of September, 1914, formally, it appears to me advisable to issue a new statement setting forth the new conditions resulting from the successful employment of submarines in interrupting and destroying commercial vessels, the impossibility of a submarine's communicating with an armed merchant ship without exposing itself to the gravest danger of being sunk by gunfire because of its weakness defensively, the unreasonableness of requiring a submarine to run the danger of being almost certainly destroyed by giving warning to a vessel carrying an armament, and that, therefore, merchant vessels should refrain from mounting guns large enough to sink a submarine, and that, if they do, they become vessels of war and liable to treatment as such by both belligerents and neutrals.

The chief difficulty with the situation seems to me to lie in this: If some merchant vessels carry arms and others do not, how can a submarine determine this fact without exposing itself to great risk of being sunk? Unless the Entente Allies positively agree not to arm any of their merchant vessels and notify the Central Powers to that effect, is there not strong reason why a submarine should not warn a vessel before launching an attack?

You will recall the case of the *Baralong* where a German submarine was bombarding a vessel from which the crew had escaped in boats, when a tramp steamer approached flying the American flag. The submarine remained on the surface and awaited the steamer, which on nearing the submarine lowered the American flag, hoisted the British colors, and with a gun mounted on the stern (a defensive armament according to our early definition) opened fire and sank the German vessel killing all the crew. The British Government would urge that this was merely a *ruse de guerre* and entirely allowable, and so it would have been under old conditions, but under the new conditions it presents a strong argument in favor of submarine attack without warning.

Not only, therefore, should we, in my judgment, rewrite our statement as to the status of armed merchant vessels but show that if any vessels of that class is armed, all merchant vessels are in danger of sudden attack without warning. As to the use of the American flag on any merchant ship converted into an armed vessel it might be well also to make representations to the British Government.

In view of the sinking of the *Persia* it would seem to be opportune and advisable to act in this matter, if it is decided to act, as expeditiously as possible.

Faithfully yours,

ROBERT LANSING

763.72/2351½

The Secretary of State to President Wilson

WASHINGTON, *January 7, 1916.*

MY DEAR MR. PRESIDENT: I have been thinking over, as I know you have, some means of placing submarine warfare on a basis which will prevent the horrors which have characterized it in the past.

I think that I appreciate the German point of view in regard to the danger to a submarine in attacking an armed merchant vessel, and have prepared a memorandum on the subject, which I enclose.

If the argument has merit the method of reaching a settlement on a basis which would safeguard human life would seem to be an agreement by Germany and Austria not to torpedo enemy vessels without putting the people on board in safety, provided they did not continue to flee, in consideration of an agreement by the Entente Powers not to permit their merchant ships to carry an armament.

I am sure the Teutonic Powers would agree to this, and I cannot see how the Entente Powers could reasonably object to such an arrangement, particularly in view of the fact that there is no case recorded to my knowledge of a submarine being destroyed by gunfire from a merchant vessel.

This plan would be practically a *modus vivendi* and could be made reciprocal on account of the activities of British submarines in the Baltic.

Would you advise my attempting to obtain such agreements?

Faithfully yours,

ROBERT LANSING

[Enclosure]

Memorandum by the Secretary of State on Armed Merchant Vessels and Submarine Warfare

[WASHINGTON,] *January 7, 1916.*

The arming of merchant vessels is allowable when the armament is of a character which can be only used defensively.

When the statement as to the Status of Armed Merchant Vessels was issued in September, 1914, by the Department of State, the assertions contained as to the limitation of armament, which would give it a defensive character, was based on the use of naval ships in intercepting private commercial vessels. It was predicated manifestly on the defensive strength of ships of war, otherwise there would be no necessity to consider any restriction upon the armament carried by a merchant vessel.

Since the statement was issued the submarine has become a practical and successful agent in the capture and destruction of vessels of commerce, and, as a result, the principle on which the arming of merchant ships is declared to be allowable, should be applied to the new conditions created by this instrument of naval warfare.

Comparison of the defensive strength of naval vessels operating on the surface and submarines shows that the latter are almost defenseless in construction, their only means of protection from an enemy being their power to submerge. A merchant ship carrying a small calibre gun could destroy with one shot a submarine provided it came to the surface within range. Thus an armament, though falling within the limitations of defensive armament as previously defined, may be used effectively against a submarine. If it can be so used, it would appear to lose its defensive character.

The rule of visit, which is the only means of protecting private vessels engaged in commerce from being suddenly attacked and is the only means of putting in force the rule that the people on board shall be put in safety before a vessel is sunk, could hardly be required justly of a submarine, if the observation of the rule compels the submarine to expose itself to almost certain destruction by coming to the surface and offering itself as a target to a gun mounted on the merchant ship which it is required to hail and order to "lie to".

If it is admitted that a submarine may be employed in intercepting enemy's commerce and that in doing this it must hail vessels and put the passengers and crews in places of safety, it would appear to be a reasonable requirement that all merchant vessels should be without armament of any sort since a gun of whatever calibre and wherever mounted could be used offensively against a submarine on the surface with good prospect of destroying it.

A merchant vessel, therefore, carrying an armament should be treated by a belligerent or a neutral as an armed ship of the enemy and not possess the immunities attaching to private commercial vessels of belligerent nationality as now set forth in the rules of international law.

763.72/2352½

President Wilson to the Secretary of State

WASHINGTON, *10 January, 1916.*

MY DEAR MR. SECRETARY: This seems to me reasonable, and thoroughly worth trying.

Faithfully Yours,

W. W.

763.72/2352½a

The Secretary of State to President Wilson

WASHINGTON, *January 17, 1916.*

MY DEAR MR. PRESIDENT: I enclose for your consideration the draft of a letter to the British Ambassador dealing with the submarine question, and suggesting a method by which future loss of life on merchant vessels might be avoided.[8]

My first inclination was to send letters to the German Ambassador and Austrian Chargé, but two reasons prevented; first, I was convinced that the German and Austrian Governments would assent to the proposal as it only required them to conform to the rules of international law, while it required their enemies to modify a present practice which might be construed into the relinquishment of a legal right; and, second, if Germany and Austria acceded promptly to the suggestion, any demur by Great Britain, France, Italy or Belgium would, if it became known (as it would undoubtedly through the German or Austrian Embassies), arouse adverse criticism in the press of this country and excite public resentment against the Entente Powers, which appears to be increasing from day to day.

By adopting this method of approach the proposal can be kept secret if it is refused by the Entente Governments and if it is considered inexpedient to make it public.

Faithfully yours,

ROBERT LANSING

763.72/2353½

President Wilson to the Secretary of State

WASHINGTON, *17 January, 1916.*

MY DEAR MR. SECRETARY: This draft has my entire approval. I hope that you will send it to the Governments you have indicated to me; and I most sincerely hope that they will feel that we are right in our argument and suggestion and will be willing to cooperate with us in attaining the object we have in view, an object which they must surely wish to accomplish as earnestly as we do, and which this seems in the circumstances the only feasible way of reaching.

Faithfully Yours,

W. W.

---

[8] For text of the letter as sent, see *Foreign Relations*, 1916, supp., p. 146.

763.72/2371½

The German Embassy to the Department of State

J. Nr. A 627

The Imperial German Embassy presents its compliments to the United States Department of State and has the honor to enclose herewith one wireless cipher message, in duplicate, to the Foreign Office in Berlin for kind transmission to the Tuckerton Station.

Duplicate copies of the message in plain English are likewise enclosed.

WASHINGTON, *January 26, 1916.*

[Enclosure—Telegram]

The Austro-Hungarian Chargé (Zwiedinek) to the Austro-Hungarian Foreign Office

N° 34. With reference to my radiogram N° 21. For Baron Burian: Italian liner *Verona* two 77 mm. guns on stern arrived New York will be allowed clearance on similar assurance as for *Verdi.* Secretary of State informed me however confidentially that justly measuring gravity of issue for Central Powers he has approached Allies in order to induce them to abstain from arming merchantships against promise already given and counted upon to provide for safety of passengers and crew. Secretary would welcome it if Central Powers now came forward with declaration that merchantmen with one or more guns will be treated as auxiliary cruisers. I understand however that he expects—and Count Bernstorff as well as I would strongly recommend this—that we postpone corresponding instructions to submarine commanders for a reasonable time say one month in order to ascertain if *modus vivendi* proposed by Secretary will not be agreed to.

ZWIEDINEK

763.72/2372½

Memorandum by the Secretary of State [9]

[WASHINGTON,] *January 26, 1916.*

Call attention of Austrian Chargé, if opportunity offers, to use of word "welcome" in his telegram of tonight by wireless.[10] Did not use word "welcome", but said if German and Austrian Govts intended to issue such a declaration the sooner it was done the better.

R. L.

---

[9] This paper bears the notation: "Attended to Feby 9/16". See memorandum by the Secretary of State, p. 341.

[10] *Supra.*

763.72/2372½a

The Secretary of State to President Wilson

WASHINGTON, *January 27, 1916.*

MY DEAR MR. PRESIDENT: The British Ambassador called upon me this morning and handed me the enclosed paper [11] which is the substance of a telegram received by him from Sir Edward Grey in regard to our proposition as to a *modus vivendi* in connection with submarine warfare. I also enclose a telegram upon the same subject, deciphered late yesterday, received from Ambassador Page at London.[12]

It seems to me that the British Government expected us to denounce submarine warfare as inhuman and to deny the right to use submarines in attacking commercial vessels; and that these statements by Sir Edward Grey evidence his great disappointment that we have failed to be the instrument to save British commerce from attack by Germany.

I must say that I am very considerably disturbed as to Mr. Page's attitude on all subjects which in any way affect the policies of Great Britain. He certainly is influenced very strongly by the atmosphere in which he is and I frequently doubt whether he urges the cases involving American rights with the force and vigor which he should as American Ambassador.

In regard to the submarine matter I think there is nothing to be done until we have heard from the Allies of Great Britain but I presume in view of these telegrams that they will be opposed to any arrangement. I do not think it is necessary for us to act immediately upon such refusal but we should consider what course we are going to take in regard to Americans traveling on vessels carrying arms, which can be used offensively against submarines. I doubt whether we can insist that vessels so armed can be considered other than as auxiliary cruisers of the respective navies of the Allies.

I would be very much gratified if you could give me your views on this subject.

Faithfully yours,

[File copy not signed]

---

[11] Copy not found in Department files.
[12] *Foreign Relations*, 1916, supp., p. 151.

763.72/2372½b : Telegram

The Secretary of State to Colonel E. M. House

WASHINGTON, *February 2, 1916—5 p. m.*

Call your attention to confidential telegram January 26, 4 p. m. addressed to Embassy, Paris.[13] Page cables [14] that Grey is seriously disturbed over proposal as he claims it is wholly in favor of central powers and against Allies. Page fears that this proposal will be considered German victory and that all our influence with Allies will be lost. I feel strongly that the proposal is fair and only humane solution of submarine warfare for the future. If merchant ships are armed and guns used to sink attacking submarines as has been done and as merchant ships are now instructed to do then it is unreasonable to insist that submarines should take risk of coming to surface to give warning. Feel that allies' refusal to consider proposal calmly will strengthen Germany's position. This proposal has no relation to *Lusitania* settlement and not yet mentioned to Germany but made necessary by conditions in Mediterranean and as merchant ships are arriving here carrying guns.

Gerard cables [15] that you feel we are asking too much of Germany in *Lusitania* case. Please cable fully your views. We feel any settlement without a disavowal or admission of illegality would not be acceptable to our people. Payment of damages incidental and not the material question.

LANSING

763.72/2374½ : Telegram

The German Foreign Office to the German Embassy

[Translation]

FEBRUARY 6, 1916.

29. Reply to wireless No. 34 [16] [omission?] of cipher addressed to Baron Burian. Germany and Austria Hungary will publish within few days declaration welcomed by Mr. Lansing, that hereafter enemy merchant vessels armed with guns will be treated as auxiliary cruisers. All neutrals will be informed accordingly. Corresponding orders to naval commanders not to be put in force before end Feb. Please inform Mr. Lansing immediately.

---

[13] Not printed; it summarized the *modus vivendi* as proposed in the note of Jan. 18, 1916, to the British Ambassador, *ibid.*, p. 146.

[14] *Ibid.*, p. 151.

[15] Telegram No. 3408, Jan. 29, 1916, 10 p. m., from the Ambassador in Germany, *ibid.*, p. 153.

[16] *Ante*, p. 337.

763.72/2374½

The German Embassy to the Department of State

A 936   WASHINGTON, *February 9, 1916.*

The Imperial German Embassy presents its compliments to the United States Department of State and has the honor to enclose herewith two wireless cipher messages in duplicate, to the Foreign Office in Berlin for kind transmission to the Tuckerton Radio Station.

Duplicate copies of the text of the messages are likewise enclosed.

[Enclosure 1—Telegram]

The German Ambassador (Bernstorff) to the German Foreign Office

No. 48. I have informed Mr. Lansing of contents of your wireless No. 29.[17] He has not yet received reply from our enemies concerning his proposal to disarm merchant vessels. Mr. Lansing does not wish to give me copy of his note till he has received an answer which he expects will be refusal. Mr. Lansing reminded me of fact that from the beginning of controversy with us the American Government always spoke of unarmed merchant vessels (American note of May 13th 1915 [18]). As to objections of Mr. Lansing to the word "welcome" I refer to Baron Zwiedineks wireless No. 52.[19]

[File copy not signed]

[Enclosure 2—Telegram]

The Austro-Hungarian Chargé (Zwiedinek) to the Austro-Hungarian Foreign Office

No. 52. Reply to No. 31. For Baron Burian.

I have informed Mr. Lansing of contents of your radiogram concerning armed enemy merchant vessels. On this occasion Mr. Lansing called my attention to a misunderstanding created by the use of the word "welcome". He did not wish to imply any initiative on his part and would not like this idea to prevail. Mr. Lansing, however, repeated that in his opinion there are certain reasons which might justify such a declaration on our part. Please acknowledge receipt of this wireless as Mr. Lansing wishes to know that his point of view is perfectly clear to my Government.

ZWIEDINEK

---

[17] *Ante,* p. 339.
[18] *Foreign Relations,* 1915, supp., p. 393.
[19] *Infra.*

763.72/2375½

Memorandum by the Secretary of State of a Conversation With the Austro-Hungarian Chargé (Zwiedinek), February 9, 1916

Baron Zwiedinek brought and showed me a wireless telegram, dated February 6th,[20] in reply to his wireless of January 26th,[21] although it appeared to be addressed to the German Embassy. After reading the telegram I pointed out to Zwiedinek that, when it used the words "welcomed by Mr. Lansing" in reference to the declaration which Germany and Austria-Hungary proposed to publish, the Governments were unwarranted in doing so as I had not intended to convey any such meaning in our previous conversation.

The Chargé replied that I had had the opportunity to see the telegram which he sent to his Government on the subject and must recall that he reported I would "welcome" a declaration.

I told him that that was so but that I did not propose to pass on the correctness of a report and thus become sponsor for the truth of the statements made, that I had not done so formerly and did not intend to begin such a practice.

He replied that he had understood me to say "welcome."

I told him that he would recall that he had asked me about the reports that we had approached the Allies on the subject of disarming all merchant vessels and that I confidentially went into some detail as to the *modus* proposed; that I had explained to him that we had not communicated with the Central Powers because we were only asking them to abide by the law while we were asking the Allies to modify the law; that, after some discussion of the use of the submarine, in which the reasonableness of the *modus* was emphasized, he had said that the German and Austrian Governments held the view that they could not warn armed merchant vessels and had in mind the issuing of a declaration to that effect; and that he asked me when I thought it would be well to do this, to which I replied that the sooner it was done the better.

(In making this latter statement I had in mind, though I could not tell Zwiedinek, the desirability of having a declaration of this sort before the final settlement of the *Lusitania* case, if such a policy was to be adopted, as it would materially affect the assurances which the German Government had given respecting merchant vessels, and I did not wish that the case after settlement should be reopened.)

The Chargé said that my language seemed to him to warrant his telegram.

I said that I saw how he might have gained that impression and that my language was unfortunate but that, as I had not intended

---

[20] *Ante,* p. 339.
[21] Apparently No. 34, p. 337.

to convey such a meaning, I hoped that he would so advise his Government.

He left with the assurance that he would at once communicate the substance of our conversation to Vienna.[22]

ROBERT LANSING

763.72/2373½ : Telegram

Colonel E. M. House to the Secretary of State

LONDON, *February 14, 1916—6 : 35 p. m.*
[Received 7 : 06 p. m.]

Thanks for your information concerning the latest phase of the L[usitania] settlement.[23] Germany should, and I think will, agree to German Ambassador's latest proposal. There are so many other issues involved in the controversy concerning armed merchantmen that I sincerely hope you will leave it in abeyance until I return. I cannot emphasize too strongly the importance of this.

EDWARD HOUSE

763.72/2415½a

The Secretary of State to President Wilson

WASHINGTON, *February 25, 1916.*

MY DEAR MR. PRESIDENT: Representative David J. Lewis, of Maryland, called me on the telephone this afternoon and after stating that he was with the Administration in the present difficulty and opposed to any of the resolutions which had been suggested, said that several of the Representatives had been discussing the subject with him and had asked him to communicate with me as to the advisability of proposing arbitration as to the rights of the belligerents in respect to arming of merchantmen and the attack upon armed vessels without warning. It is possible, I conclude, that some such suggestion may be made.

I told Mr. Lewis that I could express no opinion on the suggestion at the present time, but would take the matter under consideration.

Personally I do not think that the situation would be helped by any suggestion of this sort. The practical side would be to have Germany relinquish attack until the Court had made a decision which I am convinced the German Government would not consent to. As the proceedings of a tribunal of this sort would undoubtedly take

---

[22] For correspondence previously printed regarding this misunderstanding, see *Foreign Relations*, 1916, supp., pp. 183–185, 202–204.
[23] See *ante*, p. 339.

considerable time the immediate relief which is necessary could not be obtained.

It would oblige me if you would give me your views in order that I may answer Mr. Lewis if he speaks to me again upon the subject.

Faithfully yours,

ROBERT LANSING

763.72/2550½

President Wilson to the Secretary of State

WASHINGTON, *1 March, 1916.*

MY DEAR MR SECRETARY: Thank you for letting me see the enclosed.[24]   I note what the Ambassador says about my letter to Senator Stone.   He leaves no occasion unimproved to put his understanding (his erroneous understanding) of the point at issue forward.   I wonder if you have yet drafted your correction of his impressions, as a memorandum of the same sort as his?

Faithfully Yours,

W. W.

763.72/2550½a

The Secretary of State to the Chairman of the Committee on Foreign Affairs, House of Representatives (Flood)

WASHINGTON, *March 3, 1916.*

DEAR MR. FLOOD: In compliance with your request, I am enclosing a memorandum giving some arguments against the approval of House Resolution 147.[25]   I expect during the day to send you further memoranda on this subject.

I should call to your special attention that these memoranda are sent so that you may use the substance of the information contained in them, but without quoting the memoranda in any way as being the statements of the State Department, or otherwise referring to them as views of the Department.

If the Department can be of further service to you, please do not hesitate to let me know.

Very sincerely yours,

ROBERT LANSING

---

[24] Note of Feb. 29, 1916, from the German Ambassador, *Foreign Relations,* 1916, supp., p. 182.

[25] The text of H. Res. 147 may be found in *Congressional Record,* vol. 53, pp. 495–496, 530, 542, and elsewhere.

Memorandum on House Resolution 147

Par. (*1*) The actual wording of the notice to neutral powers regarding submarine warfare dated February 10, 1916,[26] is:

"In the circumstances set forth above enemy merchantmen armed with guns no longer have any right to be considered as peaceable vessels of commerce. Therefore the German naval forces will receive orders within a short period, paying consideration to the interests of neutrals, to treat such vessels as belligerents. The German Government brings this state of things to the knowledge of the neutral powers in order that they may warn their nationals against continuing to entrust their persons or property to armed merchantmen of the powers at war with the German Empire."

The preceding part of the declaration purports to show why armed merchant vessels should be accorded such treatment.

Par. (*2*) The alleged secret orders of the British Government were attached to the declaration of February 10th as appendixes and though mailed to the Department from Berlin have not as yet been received. Until they have been received the nature of the orders is only known imperfectly through press reports. It cannot be determined, therefore, whether they substantiate the conclusions drawn from them by the German Government as to the offensive armament which, it is stated, has been placed on British merchant ships, and as to the concealment of such armament while in neutral ports.

Par. (*3*). That a "defensive" or "offensive" gun may shoot and destroy an enemy ship is, of course, true; but the two kinds of guns may be distinguished and, in fact, have been distinguished in naval warfare. Perhaps the simplest rule to follow is that if the gun is used to begin attack it is offensive, otherwise it is defensive, it being understood, of course, that mere warning is not attack, and that attack to be offensive must contain the element of an intention to destroy. But it cannot be said that a mere intention to destroy, without an overt act, is, in naval warfare sufficient to constitute an attack.

Par. (*4*) & (*5*) It is conceived that the interest of the United States in the arming of merchant vessels against submarines and the sinking of merchant vessels by submarines is twofold: the protection of American citizens who may have been riding on board the merchant vessels, and the broader question of humanity involved in the wanton slaughter of noncombatants without warning or opportunity to seek safety.

Par. (*6*) & (*7*) The distinction between "offensive" and "defensive" has been pointed out above. True, the United States is concerned

---

[26] See telegram No. 3474, Feb. 10, 1916, 10 p. m., from the Ambassador in Germany, *Foreign Relations*, 1916, supp., p. 163.

in offering American citizens "advice, counsel and assistance" in avoiding the hazards of war, but the question is, what is the best possible advice, counsel and assistance? The inference is that the warning in this resolution is the best advice and assistance. This will be discussed later.

Par. (*8*) The assurances given by the German Government are dated September 1,[27] October 5,[28] November 29,[29] 1915, and January 7, 1916.[30] Copies of these assurances are attached. As to these assurances it should be noted, that they were intended to cover armed as well as unarmed ships (1) because the words "no longer" in the German declaration of February 10th indicate that armed merchantmen had been included in the previous announcement on the submarine warfare; (2) because the assurance of January 7, 1916, was given shortly after the sinking of the steamship *Persia* which was known by Germany to be armed; (3) because the discussion of the *Lusitania* case for a time referred to the arms which she was supposed to have had on board, as shown by the published diplomatic correspondence; (4) because as indicated in the German note of July 8th [31] the alleged instructions of the British Government to sea captains were known to the German Government some months prior to the assurances of September 1, etc.

Par. (*9*) As the United States should preserve its own "freedom of action" in case of war, it is necessary to be particularly circumspect in the issuance of any notice to American citizens in order to avoid the implication by such a notice that the Government is admitting a practice which may embarrass it later or approving a principle for which it can not stand.

Par. (*10*) This paragraph requests the President to warn Americans from traveling on naval or merchant ships whether the latter carry offensive or defensive guns, and to warn American citizens that they travel at their own risk on such ships.

The objections to this course are: (1) that it is a useless procedure to warn Americans not to travel on armed ships because the present discussion of the question must have brought the matter home to their minds more forcibly than could be done by any Congressional resolution; (2) that American citizens can not be warned from traveling on armed ships except upon the ground that it is merely hazardous for them to do so without regard of the question of the rights involved (and sufficient warning for this purpose has already been given) or on the ground that they have no right to travel on such

---

[27] *Ibid.*, 1915, supp., p. 530.
[28] *Ibid.*, p. 560.
[29] *Ibid.*, p. 644.
[30] *Ibid.*, 1916, supp., p. 144.
[31] *Ibid.*, 1915, supp., p. 463.

vessels. If they have a right to travel on such vessels, then to warn them that they travel at their own risk is to take away from them a right which belongs to them instead of defending a right which they are entitled to enjoy; (3) that to give up a right of travel as a matter of expediency is in a sense to approve the circumstances which force such an expedient act, namely, because submarines will sink merchant vessels without placing persons on board in safety. The consequence would be to take up a position in favor of this kind of inhuman warfare which the United States has denounced from the beginning and to assume a position against carrying out the well-known and fully established simple, practicable rules of naval warfare, which are based on the immutable principles of humanity, that human life is to be protected at sea when not engaged in resistance to belligerent right to warn and visit and search; (4) the President, being the spokesman of the United States in its relations with foreign powers is carrying on negotiations with the belligerents and has been carrying on such negotiations with a view to protecting and maintaining the rights of American citizens. This is, up to the point of declaration of war, under the American system of government almost exclusively an executive function. For the Congress now to interpose itself in these negotiations is disconcerting to say the least to the efforts of the executive, is confusing to foreign Governments and is invading the prerogatives of the President. In a word, there is no just ground for Congressional interference in the effort to change the Government's position or to weaken its position in the midst of pending diplomatic negotiations; (5) Congressional action, in any event, cannot serve to change an international rule or an international right. To say that American citizens shall travel on armed ships at their own risk may absolve the Government from responsibility to protect their lives and property from unjust attack upon the high seas, but it would leave the United States in the illogical position of warning Americans off of armed ships as a matter of expediency but of allowing the same armed ships to enter American ports and to be the recipients of American hospitality as peaceful and harmless merchant traders. (6) finally, to begin now in the midst of a war to give up a right as a matter of expediency is to open the door for similar concessions to either one of the other groups of opposing belligerents. A concession to one side might immediately be called to the attention of the Government by the other side with the request for some sort of concession to that side in order to balance matters. The Government would thus be placed in a most embarrassing position, for it would be subject to the charge of having favored one of the belligerents and refusing to favor the other belligerent—a charge which amounts to saying that the United States had broken its obligation as a neutral in the present war.

Par. (*11*) There is, of course, no objection to a resolution asking for the transmittal of documents so far as may not be incompatible with public interest, but, as stated above, the appendixes containing the reported photographic facsimiles of secret British instructions to merchantmen have not as yet been received by the Department.

The Resolution states that this information is desired for its assistance in performing its "constitutional duty of advising the President of the United States with regard to foreign relations". The President as the executive of the nation is admittedly in charge of the conduct of its foreign affairs and is responsible to the country and not to Congress for his conduct of our relations with foreign Governments. The only constitutional share which Congress has in the conduct of foreign relations is the right delegated by the Constitution to the Senate to approve all treaties between the United States and foreign countries. It can not be said that the House of Representatives has any right or duty under the Constitution to impose its views in regard to diplomatic negotiations upon a co-ordinate branch of the Government which is charged with the conduct of such negotiations. This is quite different from the share which the House of Representatives has in the passage of acts of Congress which repudiate treaties or lay down rules governing persons and property within or coming within the jurisdiction of the United States. It is at least doubtful whether Congress has authority to pass resolutions affecting the rights of American citizens on the high seas on foreign vessels flying a foreign flag and subject to foreign jurisdiction.

Par. (*12*) To say that it is the determination to "uphold all American rights" is exactly opposed to waiving the right which is attempted in paragraph (10) by admonishing American citizens that they travel on armed ships at their own risk. In the absence of proof that belligerent armed ships are under Governmental control and direction with a view to attacking submarines at sight it must be presumed that merchant ships carrying a light armament may be legitimately used by American citizens in the exercise of their rights freely to travel on the high seas. What these rights are, as to armed ships, may be gathered from the complete discussion to be found in the attached list of references.[32]

---

[32] Not printed.

763.72/2479½

The Secretary of State to President Wilson

WASHINGTON, *March 6, 1916.*

My DEAR MR. PRESIDENT: I send you a memorandum[33] which I have prepared setting forth clearly, I think, the negotiations and conversations which I have had in regard to the matter of armed merchant vessels, and the recent declaration of February 10th by the Teutonic Powers in regard to submarine warfare.[34]

I suggest, for your consideration, the advisability of reading this memorandum at the Cabinet meeting tomorrow. I feel that the members of the Cabinet ought to know something of the difficulties which we have had to face and particularly the adroit efforts which have been made by the German Ambassador, for I consider Zwiedinek acting more or less under his direction, to cause embarrassment and place this Government in a false light. I assume that when the Ambassador considers the time opportune he will endeavor to show that the recent declaration was instigated by this Government.

Faithfully yours,

ROBERT LANSING

763.72/2416¾

President Wilson to the Secretary of State

WASHINGTON, *8 March, 1916.*

My DEAR MR. SECRETARY: Pray pardon me for not having replied to this letter sooner.[35] I had overlooked it.

I quite agree with you that it would not be at all wise to act upon the suggestion made by Mr. Lewis.

Faithfully Yours,

W. W.

763.72/2429

The Secretary of State to President Wilson

WASHINGTON, *March 8, 1916.*

My DEAR MR. PRESIDENT: I send you a telegram which if it meets with your approval I will send to Berlin and Vienna.[36] I realize that

---

[33] Not printed; the memorandum bears the notation: "Read to Cabinet by President Mch. 7/16 RL," and is substantially the same as the telegram of Mar. 9, 1916, to the Ambassadors in Germany and Austria-Hungary, *Foreign Relations*, 1916, supp., p. 202.

[34] See telegram No. 3474, Feb. 10, 1916, 10 p. m., from the Ambassador in Germany, *ibid.*, p. 163.

[35] *Ante,* p. 342.

[36] For text of the telegram as sent, see *Foreign Relations*, 1916, supp., p. 202.

the message is a long one but I think the matter is of sufficient importance to advise our Ambassadors in detail as to the exact situation. Furthermore, I think we should have in mind that this will go on the files of the Department and it may be necessary some day to give it publicity.

As soon as you have passed upon it will you kindly return it in order that it may be enciphered and sent?

Faithfully yours,

ROBERT LANSING

763.72/2480½

President Wilson to the Secretary of State

WASHINGTON, *8 March, 1916.*

MY DEAR MR. SECRETARY: Thank you for letting me see this.[37]   I have suggested only one change (on page 6 [38]) in order that you might not even seem to admit any excuse for Zwiedinek's misrepresentation of your position.

Faithfully Yours,

W. W.

763.72/2522

The Secretary of State to President Wilson

WASHINGTON, *March 30, 1916.*

MY DEAR MR. PRESIDENT: I send you herewith the translation of an identical memorandum which was received a few days ago by this Government from the Ambassadors of France, Great Britain, Italy and Russia, and the Minister of Belgium.[39]   The memorandum is in reply to the letter of January 18 [40] in reference to the disarmament of merchant vessels.

I also enclose a proposed answer to be sent to each of the Ambassadors and the Minister. I would be obliged if you would let me know if this answer meets with your approval. I assume that it will close the incident.

Faithfully yours,

ROBERT LANSING

---

[37] Telegram referred to *supra.*
[38] Insertion of the words "never said anything of the kind but had"; for context, see *Foreign Relations*, 1916, supp., p. 204, par. 6.
[39] *Ibid.*, pp. 211, 213.
[40] *Ibid.*, p. 146.

[Enclosure]

Draft Note From the Secretary of State to the British Ambassador
(Spring Rice) [41]

WASHINGTON, *March 31, 1916.*

MY DEAR MR. AMBASSADOR: I have received your courteous letter
of the 23d instant and given careful consideration to the Memorandum enclosed relating to the proposal for an agreement to disarm
merchant vessels by the Entente Powers, which I unofficially submitted to you in my letter of January 18, 1916.

The proposal was made with the humane purpose of removing the
principal reason given by the German and Austro-Hungarian Governments for the failure of their submarines to comply strictly with
the rules of naval warfare in intercepting the merchant vessels of
their enemies on the high seas, a practice which has resulted in an
appalling loss of life among the passengers and crews of vessels
which have been attacked without warning.

Believing that an arrangement, such as I had the honor to propose, would have resulted in the discontinuance by Germany and
Austria-Hungary of a method of attack on merchant vessels which
puts in jeopardy the lives of hundreds of men, women and children
of neutral as well as belligerent nationality, I cannot but regret that
the Governments of the Entente Powers have rejected the proposal
and have declared their unwillingness to agree to refrain from the
use of armament in protecting their property on the high seas.

The Entente Governments having, however, reached a decision
to decline the proposed arrangement, it becomes my duty to accept
their decision as final, although I can assure your Excellency that
I do so with the greatest reluctance and with grave apprehension
for the future.

I am [etc.]

763.72/2638½

President Wilson to the Secretary of State

WASHINGTON, *30 March, 1916.*

MY DEAR MR. SECRETARY: There are several reasons why I think
it would not be wise to send a reply of exactly this sort to these governments; but it would be very unsatisfactory to set them forth in
a letter. I would like the pleasure of an early conference with you,

---

[41] This paper (filed separately under file No. 763.72/2525) bears the notation,
"Not sent." For text of the note as sent on April 7 to the British Ambassador
and, *mutatis mutandis*, to the French, Russian, and Italian Ambassadors and
the Belgian Minister, see *Foreign Relations*, 1916, supp., p. 223.

on this and one or two other pending matters. No doubt we can agree upon a time when I see you at the meeting of the Cabinet to-morrow.

Faithfully Yours,

W. W.

763.72/2522

The Secretary of State to President Wilson

WASHINGTON, *April 3, 1916.*

MY DEAR MR. PRESIDENT: I enclose a proposed letter [42] in reply to the rejection of our proposal of January 18th, relative to the disarming of merchant vessels.

I have already sent you a draft of a letter on this subject,[43] and in the enclosed I have sought to meet your views on the previous draft.

Faithfully yours,

ROBERT LANSING

763.72/2640½

President Wilson to the Secretary of State

WASHINGTON, *7 April, 1916.*

MY DEAR MR. SECRETARY: I have taken the liberty of altering the enclosed a little,[44] for the reasons I expressed to you the other day at Cabinet. I think that we should be as non-committal on this subject now as possible, in view of the use the German representatives have tried to make of the proposal referred to, and have sought to make the letter as colourless as possible. I hope that you will not think that I have altered it too much.

Faithfully Yours,

W. W.

763.72/2634½

The Secretary of State to President Wilson

WASHINGTON, *April 24, 1916.*

MY DEAR MR. PRESIDENT: I enclose a memorandum on the *status* of armed merchant vessels, which I prepared a month ago.[45]

---

[42] No copy of this draft found in Department files.
[43] *Ante,* p. 350.
[44] The draft reply to the Allies' refusal of the proposed *modus vivendi* on armed merchantmen; these alterations, in President Wilson's hand, were made on the draft of Mar. 31, *ante,* p. 350. For the text of the reply as sent, see note of Apr. 7 to the British Ambassador, *Foreign Relations,* 1916, supp., p. 223.
[45] For text of this memorandum as made public on April 27, see *ibid.,* p. 244.

It is possible that Germany may abandon submarine war against merchant vessels, and then attack vessels with armaments, claiming that they are not merchant vessels. I think that we should be prepared to meet this move at the very outset, otherwise they will appeal to the letter of January 18th [46] as an expression of the ideas of this Government.

The memorandum was prepared to show the consistency of the statements in the letter of January 18th with the accepted rules as to the arming of merchant vessels.

I would be obliged if you could let me know at Cabinet tomorrow whether you approve of the memorandum as I may have to use the substance orally in interviews with Count Bernstorff.

Faithfully yours,

ROBERT LANSING

---

[46] *Foreign Relations*, 1916, supp., p. 146.

RELATIONS WITH GERMANY AND AUSTRIA-HUNGARY— GERMAN SUBMARINE WARFARE—SEVERANCE OF DIPLOMATIC RELATIONS AND OUTBREAK OF WAR WITH GERMANY

763.72112/710c

The Secretary of State to President Wilson

WASHINGTON, *February 15, 1915.*

MY DEAR MR. PRESIDENT: I am enclosing three communications which we have received from the German Ambassador in regard to the food situation and the war zone.[1]

The situation is growing more and more delicate and under the proposed war zone plan we are liable, at any time, to have a disaster over there which will inflame public opinion—and we are not in a position to meet this outburst of public opinion unless we have done all that we can do to prevent it.

I am led to believe from Conversations with the German and Austrian Ambassadors that there would be a chance of securing the withdrawal of the military zone order in return for favorable action on the food question.

I do not know in what direction your mind is moving on the subject but I feel myself more and more inclined in the opinion that the British position is without justification. The German Government is willing to give assurances that the food imported will not be taken by the Government and is even willing that American organizations shall distribute that food. This, it seems to me, takes away the British excuse for attempting to prevent the importation of food.

You will notice in the last note the bitterness of the tone in which the German Government speaks of the attempts to starve the noncombatants. If I am not mistaken the efforts to bring this "economic pressure"—as they call it—upon women and children of Germany will offend the moral sense of our country and, of course, still further arouse those who are inclined to sympathize with Germany.

I am constrained to believe that it is worth while for us to make an attempt to adjust the difficulty by setting one of these propositions off

---

[1] Communications from the German Ambassador on these subjects appear in *Foreign Relations*, 1915, supp., pp. 94, 95, 102, 104.

against the other. I mean that we should see whether Great Britain will withdraw her objection to food entering Germany—the same to be distributed there through American instrumentalities, in return for the withdrawal of the German order in regard to the war zone.

If we can secure the withdrawal of these two orders it will greatly clear the atmosphere and if we cannot do it I believe that we are approaching the most serious crisis that we have had to meet.

As soon as you have time to consider this will you please let me know your wishes? I shall be at home this evening until nine or half-past and, of course, can remain at home longer if necessary, although I have promised to go out for a little while later in the evening to attend a meeting of the Alumni of the Nebraska University. I will telephone you between nine and half-after and if you have reached a decision we might send a communication to Great Britain tonight. If anything can be done no time should be lost in acting.

With assurances [etc.]   W. J. BRYAN

763.72/1481

Newspaper Text of the German Note of February 16, 1915, With Comments by the Counselor for the Department of State (Lansing) of February 18, 1915 [2]

BERLIN, via LONDON, *Thursday.*—Following is the text of the German government's answer to the American note [3] protesting against a blockade of British waters:—

"The imperial government has examined the communication from the United States government in the same spirit of good will and friendship by which the communication appears to have been dictated. The imperial government is in accord with the United States government that for both parties it is in a high degree desirable to avoid misunderstandings which might arise from measures announced by the German Admiralty and to provide against the occurrence of incidents which might trouble the friendly relations which so far happily exist between the two governments.

"With regard to the assuring of these friendly relations the German government believes that it may all the more reckon on a full understanding with the United States, as the procedure announced by the German Admiralty, which was fully explained in the note of the 4th instant,[4] is in no way directed against legitimate commerce and legitimate shipping of neutrals, but represents solely a measure of self-defence, imposed on Germany by her vital interests, against England's method of warfare, which is contrary to international law and

---

[2] Mr. Lansing's comments are here printed in brackets following quotations from the newspaper text of the note. For official text of the note, see *Foreign Relations*, 1915, supp., p. 112.

[3] *Ibid.*, p. 98.

[4] *Ibid.*, p. 96.

which so far no protest by neutrals has succeeded in bringing back to the generally recognized principles of law as existing before the outbreak of war.

[Because G. B. violates neutral rights is not a valid excuse for Germany's doing so. Neutrals are entitled to insist on their rights or not to insist as they see fit.]

"In order to exclude all doubt regarding these cardinal points the German government once more begs leave to state how things stand. Until now Germany has scrupulously observed valid international rules regarding naval warfare.

[This is correct.]

At the very beginning of the war Germany immediately agreed to the proposal of the American government to ratify the new Declaration of London [4a] and took over its contents unaltered, and without formal obligation, into her prize law.

[Including it in prize law does not make it valid international law.]

"The German government has obeyed these rules, even when they were diametrically opposed to her military interests. For instance, Germany allowed the transportation of provisions to England from Denmark until to-day, though she was well able, by her sea forces, to prevent it.

[Was not this done, so Germany would be in a consistent position in regard to the import of foodstuffs into Germany?]

In contradistinction to this attitude, England has not even hesitated at a second infringement of international law if by such means she could paralyze the peaceful commerce of Germany with neutrals. The German government will be the less obliged to enter into details as these are put down sufficiently, though not exhaustively, in the American note to the British government dated December 29 [26] [5] as a result of five months' experience.

"All these encroachments have been made, as has been admitted, in order to cut off all supplies from Germany and thereby starve her peaceful civil population—a procedure contrary to all humanitarian principles. Neutrals have been unable to prevent the interruption of their commerce with Germany, which is contrary to international law.

[There is something to be said in favor of this argument in regard to the purpose of G. B.]

"The American government, as Germany readily acknowledges, has protested against the British procedure. In spite of these protests and protests from other neutral States, Great Britain could

[4a] For text of the Declaration of London, see *ibid.*, 1909, p. 318.
[5] *Ibid.*, 1914, supp., p. 372.

not be induced to depart from the course of action she had decided upon. Thus, for instance, the American ship *Wilhelmina* recently was stopped by the British, although her cargo was destined solely for the German civil population, and according to the express declaration of the German government was to be employed only for this purpose.

[What proof is there of this assertion?]

"Germany is as good as cut off from her overseas supply by the silent or protesting toleration of neutrals, not only in regard to such goods as are absolute contraband, but also in regard to such as, according to acknowledged law before the war, are only conditional contraband or not contraband at all. Great Britain, on the other hand, is, with the toleration of neutral governments, not only supplied with such goods as are not contraband or only conditional contraband, but with goods which are regarded by Great Britain, if sent to Germany, as absolute contraband; namely, provisions, industrial raw materials, &c., and even with goods which have always indubitably been regarded as absolute contraband.

[What additional steps does Germany expect protesting neutrals to adopt? Does she expect them to use force to compel the passage of foodstuffs to Germany?]

"The German government feels itself obliged to indicate with the greatest emphasis that a traffic in arms, estimated at many hundreds of millions, is being carried on between American firms and Germany's enemies. Germany fully comprehends that the practice of right and the toleration of wrong on the part of neutrals are matters absolutely at the discretions of neutrals and involve no formal violation of neutrality. Germany, therefore, did not complain of any formal violation of neutrality, but the German government, in view of complete evidence before it, cannot help saying that it, together with the entire public opinion of Germany, feels itself to be severely prejudiced by the fact that neutrals, in safeguarding their rights in legitimate commerce with Germany according to international law, have, up to the present, achieved no, or only insignificant, results, while they are making unlimited use of their right by carrying on contraband traffic with Great Britain and our other enemies.

[The whole question of traffic in arms can be answered in the statement: American markets are open to all belligerents; Germany can buy arms as well as the Allies; as to whether they reach Germany is not the affair of this Government. The complaint of Germany is not as to the sale of arms but as to ability to transport them to Germany. Because of inability to transport munitions to Germany is Germany's misfortune, which it is not our business to cure.]

"If it is a formal right of neutrals to take no steps to protect their legitimate trade with Germany, and even to allow themselves to be influenced in the direction of the conscious and wilful restriction of their trade, on the other hand they have the perfect right, which they unfortunately do not exercise, to cease contraband trade, especially in arms, with Germany's enemies.

[Suggestion that neutrals could retaliate on G. B.'s interference with trade by prohibiting trade in contraband. That is, because part of our trade is stopped, we should stop all our trade. Our merchants would thus be the sufferers by such a policy.]

"In view of this situation, Germany, after six months of patient waiting, sees herself obliged to answer Great Britain's murderous method of naval warfare with sharp counter measures. If Great Britain in her fight against Germany summons hunger as an ally for the purpose of imposing upon a civilized people of seventy millions the choice between destitution and starvation and submission to Great Britain's commercial will, then Germany to-day is determined to take up the gauntlet and appeal to similar allies.

[The appeal is to destroy neutrals on the high seas without regard to the destination or character of their cargoes. It seems to be an effort to compel neutrals by threats to force G. B. to change her policy.]

"Germany trusts that the neutrals, who so far have submitted to the disadvantageous consequences of Great Britain's hunger war in silence, or merely in registering a protest, will display toward Germany no smaller measure of toleration, even if German measures, like those of Great Britain, present new terrors of naval warfare.

[The difference is in the two policies that G. B. proposes to make their enemies suffer, while Germany proposes to make neutrals suffer.]

"Moreover, the German government is resolved to suppress with all the means at its disposal the importation of war material to Great Britain and her allies, and she takes it for granted that neutral governments, which so far have taken no steps against the traffic in arms with Germany's enemies, will not oppose forcible suppression by Germany of this trade.

[Germany has the right to suppress this trade, but she must employ legitimate means.]

"Acting from this point of view, the German Admiralty proclaimed a naval war zone whose limits it exactly defined. Germany, so far as possible, will seek to close this war zone with mines, and will also endeavor to destroy hostile merchant vessels in every other way.

[This is the greatest menace to neutrals since it is directed against all commerce regardless of destination or character.]

While the German government, in taking action based upon this overpowering point of view, keeps itself far removed from all intentional destruction of neutral lives and property, on the other hand it does not fail to recognize that from the action to be taken against Great Britain dangers arise which threaten all trade within the war zone, without distinction. This is a natural result of mine warfare which, even under the strictest observance of the limits of international law, endangers every ship approaching the mine area.

[Comment on the use of mines by all belligerents should be made.]

The German government considers itself entitled to hope that all neutrals will acquiesce in these measures as they have done in the case of the grievous damages inflicted upon them by British measures, all the more so as Germany is resolved, for the protection of neutral shipping even in the naval war zone, to do everything which is at all compatible with the attainment of this object.

"In view of the fact that Germany gave the first proof of her good will in fixing a time limit of not less than fourteen days before the execution of said measures, so that neutral shipping might have an opportunity of making arrangements to avoid threatening danger, this can most surely be achieved by remaining away from the naval war zone. Neutral vessels which, despite this ample notice, which greatly affects the achievement of our aims in our war against Great Britain, enter these closed waters will themselves bear the responsibility for any unfortunate accidents that may occur. Germany disclaims all responsibility for such accidents and their consequences.

[What right has a nation to close the high seas to neutral commerce? If it does so illegally, it cannot hold a neutral responsible for failure to ignore [sic] action.]

"Germany has further expressly announced the destruction of all enemy merchant vessels found within the war zone, but not the destruction of all merchant vessels, as the United States seems erroneously to have understood.

[How can there be restriction in operation of mines?]

This restriction which Germany imposes upon itself is prejudicial to the aim of our warfare, especially as in the application of the conception of contraband practised by Great Britain toward Germany—which conception will now also be similarly interpreted by Germany—the presumption will be that neutral ships have contraband aboard.

[The unjustifiable character of this presumption should be emphatically stated.]

Germany naturally is unwilling to renounce its rights to ascertain the presence of contraband in neutral vessels and in certain cases to draw conclusions therefrom.

"Germany is ready, finally, to deliberate with the United States concerning any measures which might secure the safety of legitimate shipping of neutrals in the war zone. Germany cannot, however, forbear to indicate that all its efforts in this direction may be rendered very difficult by two circumstances; first, the misuse of neutral flags by British merchant vessels, which is indubitably known to the United States; second, the contraband trade already mentioned, especially in war materials, on neutral vessels.

[This is the affair of the U. S. This trade is legitimate but subject to seizure.]

"Regarding the latter point, Germany would fain hope that the United States, after further consideration, will come to a conclusion corresponding to the spirit of real neutrality.

["the spirit of real neutrality" is a phrase which is open to more than one interpretation. If it means to equalize advantages by neutral action, then the fact that Germany possesses superior productive power in the matter of munitions of war must be considered as well as the ability of the Allies to obtain munitions from this country.]

"Regarding the first point, the secret order of the British Admiralty, recommending to British merchant ships the use of neutral flags,

[This allegation appears to be denied by G. B.]

has been communicated by Germany to the United States and confirmed by communication with the British Foreign Office, which designates this procedure as entirely unobjectionable and in accordance with British law. British merchant shipping immediately followed this advice, as doubtless is known to the American government from the incidents of the *Lusitania* and the *Laertes*.

"Moreover, the British government has supplied arms to British merchant ships and instructed them forcibly to resist German submarines.

[Of this the U. S. must have proof.]

In these circumstances it would be very difficult for submarines to recognize neutral merchant ships, for search in most cases cannot be undertaken, seeing that in the case of a disguised British ship from which an attack may be expected the searching party and the submarine would be exposed to destruction.

[A submarine remaining at a safe distance could require a boat to be sent from the vessel stopped with the ship's papers. If it refused or attempted to flee it could be torpedoed.]

"Great Britain, then, was in a position to make the German measures illusory if the British merchant fleet persisted in the misuse of neutral flags, and neutral ships could not otherwise be recognized beyond doubt. Germany, however, being in a state of necessity, wherein she was placed by violation of law, must render effective her measures in all circumstances in order thereby to compel her adversary to adopt methods of warfare corresponding with international law and so to restore the freedom of the seas, of which Germany at all times is the defender and for which she to-day is fighting.

[Germany's proposed policy is the greatest menace of any to freedom of the seas for neutrals.]

"Germany, therefore, rejoices that the United States has made representations to Great Britain concerning the illegal use of its flag and expresses the expectation that this procedure will force Great Britain to respect the American flag in the future. In this expectation commanders of German submarines have been instructed, as already mentioned in the note of February 4, to refrain from violent action against American merchant vessels so far as these can be recognized.

[The exercise of the right of visit, which belligerents possess, neutrals may demand. Any action based on anything short of certainty is lawless.]

"In order to prevent in the surest manner the consequences of confusion—though naturally not so far as mines are concerned—Germany recommends that the United States make their ships which are conveying peaceful cargoes through the British war zone discernible by means of convoys.

[In view of the exception made as to danger from mines this suggestion is without merit and cannot be considered. It would mean, if adopted, placing warships of the U. S. in danger of being destroyed without adequate benefit resulting to American commerce.]

"Germany believes it may act on the supposition that only such ships would be convoyed as carried goods not regarded as contraband according to the British interpretation made in the case of Germany.

[As convoy is out of the question this paragraph needs no discussion.]

"How this method of convoy can be carried out is a question concerning which Germany is ready to open negotiations with the United States as soon as possible. Germany would be particularly grateful, however, if the United States would urgently recommend to its merchant vessels to avoid the British naval war zone in any case until the settlement of the flag question. Germany is inclined to the confident hope that the United States will be able to appreciate in its entire significance the heavy battle which Germany is waging for existence, and that from the foregoing explanations and promises it will acquire full understanding of the motives and the aims of the measures announced by Germany.

[I think that there is opportunity here to recognize the greatness of the quarrel, but to point out at the same time the ineffectual character of the proposed action compared with the menace to friendly relations with neutrals.]

"Germany repeats that it has now resolved upon the projected measures only under the strongest necessity of national self defense, such measures having been deferred out of consideration for neutrals.

"If the United States, in view of the weight which it is justified in throwing, and able to throw, into the scales of the fate of peoples, should succeed at the last moment in removing the grounds which make that procedure an obligatory duty for Germany, and if the American government in particular should find a way to make the Declaration of London respected—on behalf also of those Powers which are fighting on Germany's side—and thereby make possible for Germany legitimate importation of the necessaries of life and industrial raw material, then the German government could not too highly appreciate such a service, rendered in the interests of humane methods of warfare, and would gladly draw conclusions from the new situation."

[This last paragraph offers an opportunity for a compromise agreement between the belligerents.]

[GENERAL COMMENTS

G. B. is more dependent on U. S. for food than Germany. If Germany could effectively carry out the Admiralty plan so as to interrupt trade with G. B., she would be far more benefited than G. B. would in stopping supplies to Germany. Germany is, however, willing to relax policy if G. B. will do so. The conclusion is that Germany does not expect that plan will succeed as she would never consent to forego such an advantage.

Germany fails to define outer limits of so called "war zone". The vagueness of the area is another ground for complaint.

Is Germany's position that, because G. B. seizes foodstuffs going to German ports, therefore Germany will destroy neutral ships within certain areas of the high seas; or that, because neutrals have done no more than protest against interference with their trade by G. B., Germany proposes to punish them by endangering their shipping.]

763.72/13422

The Secretary of State to President Wilson

WASHINGTON, *February 18, 1915.*

MY DEAR MR. PRESIDENT: You will find in the afternoon *Star* a copy of the German note.[6] We understand that this is complete except for the omission of a sentence which is supplied by a flimsy herein enclosed. It relates to the matter of "convoys" and the sentence is—

"Germany believes it may act on the supposition that only such ships would be convoyed as carried goods not regarded as contraband according to the British interpretation made in the case of Germany."—

[6] For official text of this note, see *Foreign Relations*, 1915, supp., p. 112.

that is, I suppose, not carry food if Great Britain continues to regard food as contraband.

I have just received from Page, in the confidential cipher, a despatch which I enclose.[7]

Mr. Lansing and I have gone over the copy of the German note which we have and the Page telegram together, and feel that the Page telegram offers a "ray of hope". Page says that the British Government _may_ propose to the German Government, in answer to the Bernstorff note, that it will not put food on the absolute contraband list if Germany will sow no more mines and will attack no more commercial ships by submarines. This, he adds, is not certain and must not be made known.

If Great Britain will make the proposition above suggested, it is possible that some arrangement may be reached. I think it would be worth while for this Government to undertake the distribution of the food, even though it would entail a large amount of labor. But no amount of labor would be too great to avoid the dangers which now menace us. It would be almost a miracle if our ships avoided the dangers necessarily attendant upon the war zone order in view of the increasing bitterness displayed by the belligerent countries. At least it is worth while to attempt negotiations and the German note indicates the willingness of that Government to enter into negotiations.

Whether Germany would be willing to agree that no mines should be sown and that no merchant vessels should be attacked by submarines remains to be seen. I am inclined to think, however, they may agree to that.

Mr. Lansing and I have been going over the proposition together and suggest for your consideration a proposition like this:—

Food sent to Germany for the use of non-combatants, to be consigned to American agents and by American agents delivered to retail dealers licensed for that purpose by the German Government— the license specifying that the food so furnished was to be sold to non-combatants and not to be subject to requisition. Any violation of the terms of the license could work a forfeiture of the right of such dealers to receive food for this purpose.

In return, let it be agreed—I suppose Great Britain would have to agree to this as well as Germany—

First: That there shall be no floating mines;

Second: That any other mines should be placed only at the entrance of harbors and then only for defensive purposes; all mines to bear the stamp of the Government placing them and to be so constructed as to become inoperative if detached;

Third: As to submarines—the belligerents to agree that submarines will not attack commercial vessels.

---

[7] _Foreign Relations_, 1915, supp., p. 111.

If this agreement is made in regard to submarines it might also be stipulated—

Fourth: That neutral flags shall not be used by merchant vessels of belligerent countries.

We think that an agreement covering these four points—food, mines, the use of submarines against merchant vessels and the use of neutral flags—might be worked out and if so, would be a great triumph for neutral trade and would be appreciated by all neutral countries besides restoring the combatants to normal lines of attack.

We have not yet received the copy of the German note officially. With assurances [etc.]　　　　　　　　　　　　　**W. J. Bryan**

763.72/13422

President Wilson to the Secretary of State

19 February, 1915.

My Dear Mr. Secretary: I am cheered to see the "ray of hope" and we must follow it as best we can.

I would be deeply obliged if you and Mr. Lansing would put the suggestions you here make into shape for immediate use in despatches, against the time when we shall see the full official text of the German note.

Page ought to be told at once that the offensive word complained of was not addressed to Great Britain, but appears only in a note sent to us and confidentially communicated to the British Government by us merely for their information and guidance.[8] It ought not to stand in the way of anything that can be done.

Faithfully Yours,

W. W.

763.72112/710d

The Secretary of State to President Wilson

Washington, *February 19, 1915.*

My Dear Mr. President: I am enclosing a telegram drawn along the line suggested in my letter of yesterday and approved in principle by you.[9]

We have tried to make this telegram as mild and inoffensive as we can make it and yet cover the matters which it was necessary to include. It is submitted for your consideration and criticism.

---

[8] See telegram No. 1668, Feb. 17, 1915, from the Ambassador in Great Britain, *ibid.*, p. 111, and note No. 1062, Feb. 15, 1915, from the German Ambassador, *ibid.*, p. 104.

[9] For the telegram as sent, see *ibid.*, p. 119.

The only suggestion I have to make is in regard to the question as to whether we shall propose to distribute food from this country only or from any neutral country. I am inclined to think that we had better put in parenthesis, after the word "United States", the words "or from any neutral country desiring us to act for it."

My reason for inclining to this is that it might seem selfish of us if our effort was confined to food from this country. It is not likely that any other country would ask us because I think we could persuade Great Britain to let each neutral country distribute food exported by it to Germany. If, however, we confine our offer to our country and Great Britain refuses to extend the same arrangement to other countries, it would create great complaint and the unselfishness of our purpose would be questioned.

However, this is merely a suggestion and relates only to a detail. I am deeply impressed with the importance of this communication. I believe the time is ripe for the proposal and it will be hailed with rejoicing by all neutral countries if it succeeds—and I think the sober second thought of the belligerent countries would support it, for surely they cannot find any excuse except the sternest necessity for the resort to such unusual, not to say cruel, remedies as they propose.

With assurances [etc.]   W. J. BRYAN

763.72/1507½ : Telegram

The Ambassador in Great Britain (Page) to the Secretary of State

LONDON, *February 27, 1915—3 p. m.*
[Received 9 : 15 p. m.]

1716. Evidence multiplies that the British Government will not accept your number 1169, February 20th.[10] I hear indirectly that the Cabinet had agreed, prior to receipt of your 1169, to meet the German war-zone order with a similar move against Germany. Germany declared she would destroy by submarines all in-bound and out-bound British commerce. Great Britain will then stop all in-bound and out-bound German commerce. I hear that this proposition has met the approval of the Allies and that the Allied Governments will at once proclaim it and put it into effect. I cannot today verify this report but I have reason to believe it true.

The substance of your 1169 has been telegraphed from Washington to the London press and the universal comment is unfavorable. The *Times* this morning calls it a German blackmailing proposition. There are signs that the opposition party in England in particular and public opinion in general resent a proposition that they interpret

---

[10] *Foreign Relations*, 1915, supp., p. 119.

to mean free food to Germans after they have done their best by mines and torpedoes to cut off England's food.

AMERICAN AMBASSADOR

462.11 T 41/14½

The Counselor for the Department of State (Lansing) to the Secretary of State

[WASHINGTON,] April 2, 1915.

DEAR MR. SECRETARY: The case of the death of an American citizen through the sinking of the British S. S. Falaba [11] presents a question which will have to be decided and the decision will determine our policy in this case and in the event other Americans meet death in the same way.

I assume that, if the sinking of the Falaba had been the result of an attempt of the vessel to resist or to escape when summoned to stop or to surrender by a German submarine, there would be no ground of complaint for the loss of an American life as a result of the submarine's frustrating such attempt.

In that case the submarine would be exercising a belligerent right recognized by international law.

But the sinking of the Falaba, when no attempt is made to resist or escape, without giving the crew and passengers adequate time to leave the vessel is a different matter. It is a practice unwarranted by international usage.

Now the question is this: Ought we not to hold the German Government responsible for the death of an American through the act of their naval forces, when that act is in violation of the established rules of naval warfare?

An American taking passage on a belligerent merchant vessel is entitled to rely upon an enemy's war vessel conforming to the established rules of visit and search and of protection of non-combatants. He should not be exposed to greater dangers than the enforcement of the rules impose. If this is a correct statement, duty would appear to require a complaint and a demand for damages.

On the other hand, to enter complaint on account of the death of an American in these circumstances would compel this Government to denounce the sinking of merchant vessels in the manner referred to as a flagrant violation of international law. In fact it would be a denunciation of the German "war zone" plan, or at least of the method of carrying it out.

While as yet we are not fully advised as to the facts of the case I think that the policy of the Government should be determined in

---

[11] For correspondence previously printed concerning the sinking of the Falaba, see ibid., pp. 358–360, 361–365, 370.

order that we may act promptly if action seems advisable and necessary, as delay in entering complaint and denunciation would be, in my opinion, a matter of just criticism.

I would like to be advised as to the policy of the Government in order that preparations may be made to act in case it is decided to act.

Faithfully yours,

ROBERT LANSING

462.11 T 41/14½

The Secretary of State to President Wilson

WASHINGTON, *April 2, 1915.*

MY DEAR MR. PRESIDENT: I am enclosing a memorandum by Mr. Lansing [15] in regard to the Thrasher case. The matter has been reported to us by Page and Consul-General Skinner but we have not yet the details. It may be worth while to be considering the matter in advance.

It seems to me that the doctrine of contributory negligence has some bearing on this case—that is, the American who takes passage upon a British vessel knowing that this method of warfare will be employed, stands in a different position from that occupied by one who suffers without any fault of his own.

The first question raised is, What kind of a demand shall we make, if we make a demand? We can hardly insist that the presence of an American on a British ship shall operate to prevent attack unless we are prepared to condemn the methods employed as improper in warfare.

If we are to make a demand, shall we recognize the warfare as proper and ask indemnity for the loss of life? Can an American, by embarking upon a ship of the allies at such a time and under such conditions impose upon his Government an obligation to secure indemnity in case he suffers with others on the ship? I confess I have not yet been able to reach a conclusion which is entirely satisfactory to me, but I send this memorandum that you may revolve it in your mind as the question will probably arise.

With assurances [etc.]

W. J. BRYAN

462.11 T 41/12½

The Secretary of State to President Wilson

WASHINGTON, *April 3, 1915.*

MY DEAR MR. PRESIDENT: I am sending you a memorandum made by Mr. Lansing sometime ago. We have been holding it but in view

---

[15] The letter printed *supra.*

of the complication that may arise from the *Pisa* case I bring his suggestions before you.

With assurances [etc.] W. J. BRYAN

The Counselor for the Department of State (Lansing) to the Secretary of State

[WASHINGTON,] *April 2, 1915.*

DEAR MR. SECRETARY: The enclosed memorandum prepared six weeks ago you may think worthy of consideration in connection with the letter I am sending you to-day regarding the death of Leon C. Thrasher through the sinking of the British S. S. *Falaba* by a German submarine.

Since writing the memorandum I have been informed through different channels that German public opinion takes a very similar view of the situation.

Faithfully yours,

ROBERT LANSING

Memorandum by the Counselor for the Department of State (Lansing) on Relations With Germany and Possibilities

[WASHINGTON,] *February 15, 1915.*

PRESENT SITUATION

No commerce with Germany in any articles of contraband, except a negligible amount smuggled through neutral ports.

Free commerce with Allies in all munitions of war and supplies.

There are interned German vessels in ports of the United States, valued at approximately 100 millions of dollars.

POSSIBLE SITUATION IN CASE OF WAR BETWEEN UNITED STATES AND GERMANY

Commercial situation would not be changed so far as Germany is concerned, except that German naval forces would have greater right to interrupt trade with Allies.

The United States could not send an army to Europe, hence no increased military strength to Germany's enemies on land.

The British Navy being already superior to that of Germany, the addition of the naval force of the United States would have no effect on the situation at sea.

There might be created a state of civil discord, and possibly of civil strife, in the United States, which would cause this Government to retain for its own use the munitions and supplies now being sent in great quantities to the Allies.

The interned German vessels would be seized by the United States.

ADVANTAGES AND DISADVANTAGES TO GERMANY OF WAR WITH UNITED STATES

The *Advantages* would seem to be—

A free hand in interruption of United States trade with the Allies.
A possible situation in the United States which would lessen exports to Allies.
No change in military or naval situation.

The *Disadvantages* would seem to be—

Cessation of influence of United States upon Great Britain to allow Germany to receive food from United States.
Cessation of all trade in non-contraband with United States.
Loss of a small amount of contraband smuggled into Germany from United States through neutral ports.
The loss of about 100 millions of dollars of capital tied up in interned ships, which is now inactive and useless.

The Advantages appear to outweigh the Disadvantages.

ROBERT LANSING

462.11 T 41/15½

President Wilson to the Secretary of State

WASHINGTON, *3 April, 1915.*

MY DEAR MR. SECRETARY: I do not like this case. It is full of disturbing possibilities.

But it is clear to me that this American citizen came to his death by reason of acts on the part of German naval officers which were in unquestionable violation of the just rules of international law with regard to unarmed vessels at sea; and it is probably our duty to make it clear to the German Government that we will insist that the lives of our citizens shall not be put in danger by acts which have no sanction whatever in the accepted law of nations.

I think it would be wise for Mr. Lansing to draw a brief and succinct note in the matter for mature consideration, so that we may formulate our position in precise terms.

Faithfully Yours,

W. W.

462.11 T 41/13½

President Wilson to the Secretary of State

WASHINGTON, *5 April, 1915.*

MY DEAR MR. SECRETARY: I had already seen this memorandum of Mr. Lansing's.[16] I appreciate its force to the full. But it ought not to alter our course so long as we think ourselves on the firm ground of right.

It has, as Mr. Lansing points out, its bearings on the Thrasher case. That case, as I said the other day, troubles me. I should very much like to know what Mr. L's view of it is. We must compound policy with legal right in wise proportions, no doubt.

Faithfully Yours,

W. W.

462.11 T 41/17½

The Counselor for the Department of State (*Lansing*) *to the Secretary of State*

[WASHINGTON,] *April 5, 1915.*

DEAR MR. SECRETARY: In compliance with the President's note to you of the 3rd, I have drafted a memorandum for an instruction to Ambassador Gerard in the Thrasher case.

The tone of the instruction is not conciliatory, and the language is plain almost to harshness. Probably it can be softened without weakening it.

I feel this: If it is decided to denounce the sinking of the *Falaba* as an act indefensible legally and morally, we will have to say so, and I do not see how we can say it in a pleasant way. We are dealing with a tragedy. It seems to me that we must assert our rights, condemn the violation and state the remedy which we expect. If we do this without evincing a firm determination to insist on compliance, the German Government will give little heed to the note and may even show contempt for its weakness.

Furthermore, American public opinion will never stand for a colorless or timid presentation of a case, in which an American has been killed by an atrocious act of lawlessness.

If the note is weak or uncertain, it had better not be sent. The situation does not seem to me to be one for compromise. We can not take the position that Thrasher should have kept out of the war zone. To do so would amount to an admission of Germany's right to perform lawless acts in that area. This would unquestionably arouse a storm of criticism, and I think that it would be justified.

[16] *Ante*, p. 367.

On the other hand, the consequences of a strong, vigorous note may be most momentous.

In spite of the critical situation which may result I do not see how we can let the matter pass without protest.

As I said to you, I think that this case is pregnant with more sinister possibilities than any with which the Government has had to deal. After mature consideration from various points of view, I can not advise against a firm demand, and yet I feel the gravest anxiety as to the results of such a course. It by no means means war, but it means intense hostility and the charge of open support of the enemies of Germany.

Faithfully yours,

[File copy not signed]

[Enclosure]

Draft Instruction to the Ambassador in Germany (Gerard) [17]

The Government of the United States has received a report, confirmed by substantial evidence, that Leon C. Thrasher, a native born American citizen, came to his death by reason of the act of the German naval authorities in sinking the British passenger steamer *Falaba* on the high seas on the 28th of March, 1915, outward bound from Liverpool, and the failure of the commander of the German submarine *U-28* to give ample time for the crew and passengers of the *Falaba* to leave the vessel before sinking her by means of torpedoes. It is further reported that, at the time when the *Falaba* was torpedoed and sunk, she was lying to, making no attempt to escape and offering no resistance.

The circumstances of the sinking of the *Falaba*, by which Thrasher with scores of other non-combatants, irrespective of age and sex, met their death, indicate a wantonness and indifference to the rules of civilized warfare by the German naval officer responsible for the deed, which are without palliation or excuse. This is aggravated by the fact that the vessel was departing from and not approaching British territory. So flagrant a violation of international law and international morality requires from a neutral government, whose citizen has been a victim of the outrage, an unequivocal expression of its views as to such conduct and as to the duty of the belligerent government, whose officers are guilty of the violation.

---

[17] Filed separately under file No. 462.11 T 41/16½. The instruction was not sent.

The Government of the United States considers that a United States citizen is entitled to rely upon the practice, heretofore universally observed by belligerent warships, of visiting and searching merchant vessels of enemy as well as of neutral nationality and of protecting the lives of their crews and passengers whatever disposition may be made of the vessels and their cargoes. No notice by a belligerent government that it intends to depart from this practice within a certain area of the high seas can deprive justly a neutral of his rights or relieve the government disregarding those rights from full responsibility for the acts of its naval authorities performed in accordance with such notice.

The Government of the United States is loth to believe that the German Imperial Government authorized, much less directed, the officers of the Imperial Navy to perpetrate acts as ruthless and brutal as the sinking of the *Falaba* before her helpless crew and passengers had been removed, or that that Government will pass over the offense without condemnation and permit the offenders to remain unpunished.

The Government of the United States, in view of the death of a United States citizen through the wanton act of an officer of the German Imperial Navy, which was in direct violation of the principles of humanity as well as of the law of nations, appeals earnestly to the Imperial Government to disavow the act, to punish the perpetrator, and to make just reparation for the death of Leon C. Thrasher.

It is with extreme reluctance and with a full appreciation of the exceptional conditions, in which Germany is placed in the present war, that the Government of the United States makes these representations and presents this appeal to the justice and humanity of the Imperial Government. This Government owes a duty to itself, to its citizens, and to civilization, which is imperative and which it cannot as a sovereign power ignore. No other course, consonant with its dignity, is open to it. Were the rights at stake those which relate to property, it might continue to show that patience and forbearance which it has manifested so often during the progress of this deplorable conflict, but when a United States citizen is killed through an act of lawlessness and cruelty, committed under the orders of a commissioned officer of the German Imperial Navy, and other citizens are threatened with a like fate if they continue to exercise their just rights, this Government can not remain silent. It sincerely hopes that the Imperial Government, recognizing the justice of these representations, will promptly disavow the act complained of and take the steps necessary to prevent its repetition.

462.11 T 41/8½

President Wilson to the Secretary of State

6 APRIL, 1915.

MY DEAR MR. SECRETARY: Thank you for showing me these.

I will keep Lansing's note about the Thrasher case until we get the information we have asked for and until I can see and meditate upon what you are to put in writing of your own views; and will give my thoughts time to settle before allowing myself to form a conclusion. I feel, as you do, the greatest anxiety about the matter.

Faithfully Yours,

W. W.

462.11 T 41/6a

The Secretary of State to President Wilson

WASHINGTON, *April 6, 1915.*

MY DEAR MR. PRESIDENT: I am trying to get my ideas in shape on this Thrasher question but am not able to send them tonight. As we are not yet fully informed in regard to the case the time for action has not arrived, but, as I told you today, I am very much worried about it—the troublesome question being whether an American citizen can, by putting his business above his regard for his country, assume for his own advantage unnecessary risks and thus involve his country in international complications. Are the rights and obligations of citizenship so one-sided that the Government which represents all the people must bring the whole population into difficulty because a citizen, instead of regarding his country's interests, thinks only of himself and of his interests.

I hope by tomorrow night to be able to send you a note on the subject.

With assurances [etc.]   W. J. BRYAN

462.11 T 41/4½

President Wilson to the Secretary of State

WASHINGTON, *6 April, 1915.*

MY DEAR MR. SECRETARY: The Thrasher case is constantly in my mind. I received your letter of yesterday [18] and the accompanying papers from Mr. Lansing [19] and Mr. Anderson,[20] and have of course read them with the closest attention.

---

[18] Not found in Department files.
[19] *Ante*, pp. 369–371.
[20] Not printed.

Unless you think it premature or unwise to do so, I shall bring the matter up for discussion to-morrow morning at the meeting of the Cabinet.

Meantime, one suggestion for your consideration, in the light of the authorities;

If some British merchantmen were known to be armed, and the British Government had in fact authorized or advised all merchantmen to arm themselves against submarines, and, assuming it to have been impracticable for the German commander to ascertain whether the *Falaba* was armed, was he justified in the circumstances in acting upon the theory that the British authorization had in effect transformed all British merchantmen into public armed vessels and made them liable to attack as such?

Faithfully Yours,

W. W.

462.11 T 41/20½

The Counselor for the Department of State (Lansing) to the Secretary of State

[WASHINGTON,] *April 7, 1915.*

DEAR MR. SECRETARY: The great importance of the Thrasher case, to my mind, lies in the fact that a course of action must be adopted, which can be consistently applied to similar cases, if they should arise in the future. For example, suppose another British vessel should be sunk in the same way as the *Falaba* and ten Americans on board the vessel should be drowned. What would be done in that case? Or suppose a neutral vessel with Americans on board should be torpedoed and the Americans drowned. What then would be done? It seems to me that, for the sake of the future, we cannot afford to allow expediency or avoidance of the issue to control our action in the Thrasher case.

Either one of two courses seems to be open:

1. To warn Americans generally to keep out of the German war zone, if on board a merchant vessel, which is not of American nationality.

2. To hold Germany to a strict accountability for every American life lost by submarine attack on the high seas.

The adoption of the first course amounts to an admission of the legality of establishing a war zone, such as Germany has done, or at least to an admission that the illegality is open to question.

The adoption of the second course would be more nearly in accord with our position denying the legality of the war zone and holding Germany responsible for indiscriminate attack within that area of the high seas.

Expediency in the particular case of Thrasher would favor the adoption of a policy resulting in the first course suggested, but the dignity of the Government and its duty toward its citizens appears to demand a policy in harmony with the second course.

The difficulty with the second course is chiefly that our relations with the German Government are becoming increasingly strained, as shown by the questions pending, namely:

1. The Thrasher case.
2. The *Pisa* case.
3. The *Odenwald* case.
4. The Pinchot affair.
5. The *Prinz Eitel Friedrich* case.
6. The arrest of the German Consul at Seattle.
7. The withdrawal of our military observers from Germany.
8. The demand for an embargo on arms and ammunition.

If any other course can be found, which will relieve the present tension in our relations, and at the same time preserve American rights, so that in the future this Government will not be charged with indifference to the death of Americans, or with a failure to do its duty in supporting its rights, I would strongly favor such a course. I have given careful thought to the subject, but am unable to offer any suggestion which will meet these conditions.

Faithfully yours,

ROBERT LANSING

462.11 T 41/9½

The Secretary of State to President Wilson

WASHINGTON, *April 7, 1915.*

MY DEAR MR. PRESIDENT: In leaving with you the tentative draft prepared by Mr. Lansing [21] I stated that I would submit a note on the subject. I have been considering the questions involved and find that the facts are so incomplete as to make it impossible to reach a satisfactory conclusion as to the representations that should be made.

We do not know yet whether the merchant vessel was armed, or whether, if not armed the fact that the vessel was unarmed was known to the commander of the submarine.

We are informed that Great Britain has permitted the arming of some of her merchant vessels and we have received a note from the British Ambassador saying that if her vessels are permitted to arm it is because of the action of the German submarines. The German government seems to assume that British merchantmen are armed,

[21] *Ante,* p. 370.

and gives that as a reason why her submarines cannot insure the rescue of crew and passengers.

The facts, when fully disclosed, may enable us to make a claim without announcing the position on the entire question. While, however, we are waiting for the facts we can be revolving in our minds the various propositions that may be involved:

First: The use of submarines in attacking merchant vessels;

Second: The right of merchant vessels to arm themselves to resist the submarine; and

Third: The effect of such arming on the rules that govern the conduct of the submarine as to the rescue of passengers. Does the arming of a merchant vessel so change the character of the vessel as to increase the risks of passengers and crew?

It seems to me that the third question may become a very important one and I shall confer with Mr. Lansing in regard to the authorities on this subject.

If the arming of a merchant vessel so changes its character as to affect the rights of those who travel on it, the risks assumed by an American passenger would necessarily be greatly increased and he might occupy the position of a foreigner who goes into a fortified city, or exposes himself when a battle is on.

I feel that this is the most delicate question we have had to meet—not only because it involves the loss of a human life, but because we are dealing with a nation whose people have been made sensitive by the course we have pursued in the matter of the export of arms—a course not only entirely consistent with neutrality, but a course compelled by neutrality. We are aware, however, that a large element of our population, influenced by sympathy with the German side, has criticised us violently, and this criticism has been communicated to the other side until there is widespread evidence of unfriendliness. Whatever we do in the Thrasher case will be viewed with suspicion and we must, therefore, be the more careful to take a position which will be not only defensible but, if possible, so obviously defensible as to appeal to the judgment of the entire country.

I am sure that the almost unanimous desire of our country is that we shall not become involved in this war and I cannot help feeling that it would be a sacrifice of the interests of all the people to allow one man, acting purely for himself and his own interests, and without consulting his government, to involve the entire nation in difficulty when he had ample warning of the risks which he assumed. The world has notice of the bitterness of the struggle in which the belligerents are engaged, and each side has issued warning. While we may regard the belief that both sides have overstepped their international rights, the citizens of our country ought to allow the questions to be decided by governmental action and not attempt to decide the questions themselves.

I hope that by the time action is necessary a course may be found which will satisfy the requirements of the case, without increasing the tension already sufficient to cause anxiety.

With assurances [etc.]   W. J. BRYAN

462.11 T 41/13a

The Secretary of State to President Wilson

WASHINGTON, *April 8, 1915.*

MY DEAR MR. PRESIDENT: I am sending you flimsy of a report from our Consul General at London on the *Falaba* case.[22] While it seems almost certain that Thrasher was among the lost it is not known as a fact but as a conclusion drawn from the fact that he is not reported among those saved.

I am sending the following inquiry:

"Answering your April seven, report on *Falaba* please make following additional inquiries:

"First: Number of passengers on *Falaba* and number rescued.

"Second: Whether there was any communication by signals or otherwise between commanders of *Falaba* and submarine before or after firing torpedo.

"Third: Please report any other facts brought out at inquiry as to time when submarine flew British flag.["]

Mr. Lansing and I will see what authorities we can find on the proposition which you submit.

Allow me to submit this proposition for your consideration:

An American citizen, after being warned of the dangers involved, takes passage on a British ship and loses his life with other passengers as a result of an attack by a submarine—the attacking Government not knowing any intention therefore of doing harm to an American citizen, and having notified this Government of its intended action against British ships:—

QUERY: What claim can this Government rightfully make for unintended loss which ordinary diligence would have avoided?

The above question, it seems to me, presents the problem with which we have to deal, unless we take the position that the method of attack is so contrary to international law that a neutral is justified in ignoring the warning and relying upon his government to vindicate his right to travel on the belligerent ship, notwithstanding the risks involved.

---

[22] *Foreign Relations,* 1915, supp., p. 359.

In view of the importance of the subject I am inclined to think it would be well to bring the matter up at the Cabinet meeting so that we can get the opinions from as many angles as possible.

With assurances [etc.]   **W. J. BRYAN**

462.11 T 41/8

The Counselor for the Department of State (Lansing) to President Wilson

WASHINGTON, *April 10, 1915.*

DEAR MR. PRESIDENT: I enclose the telegrams received from Consul General Skinner regarding the sinking of the *Falaba*.[23]

The significant fact to my mind is that the submarine's commander allowed ten minutes for the crew and passengers to leave the vessel, showing that he did not act on the suspicion that the vessel was armed and might attack him. If he had allowed no time for escape, he might enter that plea, but, since he gave some time, he should have given sufficient.

It seems to me that the question of arming British vessels, or Germany's belief that it is being done, disappears from the *Falaba* case.

Very sincerely yours,

ROBERT LANSING

462.11 T 41/21½

President Wilson to the Secretary of State

WASHINGTON, *22 April, 1915.*

MY DEAR MR. SECRETARY: Although I have been silent for a long time about the case, I have had it much in my mind, as I have no doubt you have, to work out some practicable course of action with regard to the death of Thrasher; and I have the following to suggest as the outline of a note to the German Government:

(1) State the circumstances, as we have officially received them.

(2) We take it for granted that Germany has had no idea of changing the rules (or, rather, the essential principles) of international law with regard to the safety of non-combatants and of the citizens of neutral countries at sea, however radical the present change in practical conditions of warfare; and that she will, in accordance with her usual frankness in such matters, acknowledge her responsibility in the present instance.

(3) Raise in a very earnest, though of course entirely friendly, way the whole question of the use of submarines against merchant vessels, calling attention circumstantially to the impossibility of ob-

---

[23] *Ibid.*, pp. 359, 362, 364.

serving the safeguards and precautions so long and so clearly recognized as imperative in such matters: the duty of visit and search; the duty, if the vessel proves to belong to an enemy and cannot be put in charge of a prize crew, to secure the safety of the lives of those on board; etc.

(4) On these grounds enter a very moderately worded but none the less solemn and emphatic protest against the whole thing, as contrary to laws based, not on mere interest or convenience, but on humanity, fair play, and a necessary respect for the rights of neutrals.

My idea, as you will see, is to put the whole note on very high grounds,—not on the loss of this single man's life, but on the interests of mankind which are involved and which Germany has always stood for; on the manifest impropriety of a single nation's essaying to alter the understandings of nations; and as all arising out of her mistake in employing an instrument against her enemy's commerce which it is impossible to employ in that use in accordance with any rules that the world is likely to be willing to accept.

Faithfully Yours,

WOODROW WILSON

462.11 T 41/14a

The Secretary of State to President Wilson

WASHINGTON, *April 23, 1915.*

MY DEAR MR. PRESIDENT: In a note [24] to you this afternoon I stated that Mr. Lansing would take your instructions to Old Point Comfort and prepare a tentative draft of note in the Thrasher case, during his stay there.

As I have not been able to reach the same conclusion to which you have arrived in this case I feel it my duty to set forth the situation as I see it. The note which you propose will, I fear, very much inflame the already hostile feeling against us in Germany, not entirely because of our protest against Germany's action in this case, but in part because of its contrast with our attitude toward the Allies. If we oppose the use of the submarine against merchantmen we will lay down a law for ourselves as well as for Germany. If we admit the right of the submarine to attack Merchantmen but condemn their particular act or class of act as inhuman we will be embarrassed by the fact that we have not protested against Great Britain's defense of the right to prevent foods reaching non-combatant enemies.

We suggested the admission of food and the abandonment of torpedo attacks upon Merchant vessels. Germany seemed willing to negotiate but Great Britain refused to consider the proposition. I fear that denunciation of one and silence as to the other will be

[24] Not found in Department files.

construed by some as partiality. You do not make allowance for the fact that we were notified of the intended use of the submarine, or for the fact that the deceased knowingly took the risk of travelling on an enemy ship. I cannot see that he is differently situated from those who by remaining in a belligerent country assume risk of injury. Our people, will, I believe, be slow to admit the right of a citizen to involve his country in war when by exercising ordinary care he could have avoided danger.

The fact that we have not contested Great Britain's assertion of the right to use our flag has still further aggravated Germany and we cannot overlook the fact that the sale of arms and ammunition, while it could not be forbidden under neutrality, has worked so entirely for the benefit of one side as to give to Germany—not justification but an excuse for charging that we are favoring the Allies. I have mentioned these things to show the atmosphere through which the Thrasher note will be received by Germany.

Believing that such a note as you propose is, under the conditions that now exist, likely to bring on a crisis, I venture to suggest an alternative, namely, an appeal to the nations at war to consider terms of peace. We cannot justify waiting until both sides, or even one side, asks for mediation. As a neutral we cannot have in mind the wishes of one side more than the wishes of the other side. The neutral nations have both rights and we are the neutral nation looked to to give expression to those.

Nearly nine months have passed since the war began, and after the expenditure of over ten billion dollars and the sacrifice of several millions of the flower of Europe the war is a draw. Surely the most sanguinary ought to be satisfied with the slaughter. I submit that it is this nation's duty to make, not a secret but a public appeal for the acceptance of mediation. All the neutral nations would support the appeal—several have suggested it. Our own interests justify it—we may be drawn into the conflict if it continues. Our obligation to the neutral nations demand it. Our friendship to the nations at war requires it. They cannot reason calmly and neither side is in a position to ask for mediation. As the well-wisher of all we should act; as the leader in the peace propaganda we should act; as the greatest christian nation we should act—we cannot avoid the responsibility. The loss of one American, who might have avoided death, is as nothing compared with the tens of thousands who are dying daily in this "causeless war." Is it not better to try to bring peace for the benefit of the whole world than to risk the provoking of war on account of one man? We cannot foresee the result of such an appeal as you can make, but if it is right to do it, there ought not to be lacking the faith to try. You have such an opportunity as has not come to any man before. I most earnestly urge you to make the appeal.

With assurances [etc.]   W. J. BRYAN

462.11 T 41/20½

President Wilson to the Secretary of State

WASHINGTON, *April 28, 1915.*

MY DEAR MR. SECRETARY: I have thought a great deal about the contents of the letter you wrote me (the letter written in your own hand) about the Thrasher case.[25] It of course made a deep impression on me.

As I told you yesterday at Cabinet, I am not at all confident that we are on the right track in considering such a note as I outlined for Mr. Lansing to work on. I am not sure that my outline really expressed what I would myself say in the note, for, after all, the character of a note is chiefly in the way the thing is said and the points developed. Perhaps it is not necessary to make formal representations in the matter at all.

What I have been thinking about most is your alternative proposition, that we publicly call upon the belligerents to end the war.

I wish I could see it as you do. But in view of what House writes me I cannot. It is known to every government concerned that we believe the war should be ended and that we speak for all neutral nations in that wish. It is known to them that we are seeking to help and that anything they want to say to one another which they are too proud or too prudent to say directly and officially they can say privately through us. They are at present most appreciative and cordial,—ready to accept help when they can accept it. We know their minds and we know their difficulties. They are dependent upon their own public opinion (even Germany) and we know what that opinion is. To insist now would be futile and would probably be offensive. We would lose such influence as we have for peace.

I am afraid, Mr. Secretary, that there is much in this that will seem to you disputable; but I can only state my conviction in the matter, and God knows I have searched my mind and conscience both to get the best, the nearest approach to wisdom, there is in them.

With warmest regard and appreciation,

Faithfully yours,

WOODROW WILSON

[25] *Supra.*

462.11 T 41/23½

*The Counselor for the Department of State (Lansing) to the
Secretary of State*

[WASHINGTON,] *May 1, 1915.*

DEAR MR. SECRETARY: Two events have occurred which bear upon
the Thrasher case and which should be called particularly to the attention of yourself and the President in connection with that case and
the policy which should be adopted.

The first of these is the attack April 29th by a German aeroplane on
the American S. S. *Cushing*, which is reported by Dr. Van Dyke in a
telegram dated April 30th, a copy of which is enclosed.[26]

The second is the publication this morning in some fifty newspapers
of a notice to American citizens not to take passage on British vessels
which will traverse the German "war zone." The notice, a copy of
which is enclosed, is signed by the Imperial German Embassy, and,
as I am informed was a paid advertisement prepared about a week ago
by that Embassy.

While no lives were lost by the attack on the *Cushing*, one bomb is
reported to have struck the vessel and caused considerable damage.
It is, therefore, not so serious in one sense as the attack on the *Falaba*
which caused the death of Thrasher. On the other hand, it is a more
flagrant violation of neutral rights on the high seas, and indicates that
the German naval policy is one of wanton and indiscriminate destruction of vessels regardless of nationality. The fortunate outcome of
this attack in no way removes the grave possibilities which may result
from future attacks of the same character.

The question arises, therefore, what course should be pursued by
this Government. Should we make representations in this case before
we do in the Thrasher case? And, if we do, will it not appear that we
care less for an American life than we do an American ship? I fear
that this course would arouse a great deal of criticism, and might be
interpreted as an admission that an American citizen had no right to
take passage on a British vessel. Such an admission would appear to
me to be a serious mistake. An American citizen legally has such a
right and in my opinion the Government ought to uphold it.

The published notice of the German Embassy has an even more
direct bearing on the Thrasher case. It is a formal threat that American citizens, exercising their just rights on the high seas will not be
protected from the intended attack on all British ships without visiting them or giving the persons on board ample opportunity to escape.

If we do not take up the Thrasher case, in what position are we
placed in the event other American passengers lose their lives? Will

[26] *Foreign Relations*, 1915, supp., p. 378.

not the answer be that we acquiesced by our silence in the propriety of the sinking of the *Falaba*, and that Americans were publicly warned of the danger, and that, therefore, Germany is not to be blamed?

Another thing, the using of the American press to warn Americans not to exercise their legal rights, for a violation of which this Government has said that it would hold Germany to "a strict accountability" seems to me to be highly improper. It is an even more insolent proceeding than the making public of diplomatic correspondence. Communications of this sort should be sent to the Department, which can make the contents public if it pleases, but not to address the Department at all is an impertinent act, which would warrant summary action if it was expedient.

In this case, however, it would seem to me unwise to act, as I believe that would be playing into Count von Bernstorff's hands. I cannot but feel that these two events are in line with Germany's attitude toward the United States, to which I directed attention in my memorandum of February 15th.[27] Everything seems to point to a determined effort to affront this Government and force it to open rupture of diplomatic relations. I hope that I am wrong, but I have that feeling.

For the present, however, the question is how do these events affect the Thrasher case. Do they compel action, or is it wise to continue silent?

Faithfully yours,

ROBERT LANSING

[Enclosure]

Clipping From the New York "Sun," May 1, 1915 [28]

GERMANY MOVES TO STOP TOURS ABROAD; EMBASSY SENDS OUT WARNING TO HEAD OFF AMERICAN TRAVEL IN EUROPE

The German Embassy has begun a campaign to head off American travel to Europe during the coming summer.

The first step in this campaign was taken yesterday, when the embassy caused to be inserted in a number of newspapers throughout the country an advertisement, of which the following is a copy:

"Travellers intending to embark on the Atlantic voyage are reminded that a state of war exists between Germany and her Allies and Great Britain and her Allies; that the zone of war includes the waters adjacent to the British Isles; that in accordance with formal notice given by the Imperial Government, vessels flying the flag of

---

[27] *Ante*, p. 367.
[28] Filed separately under file No. 462.11 T 41/22½.

Great Britain or any of her allies, are liable to destruction in those waters and that travellers sailing in the war zone on ships of Great Britain or her allies do so at their own risk.

IMPERIAL GERMAN EMBASSY

WASHINGTON, D. C., *April 22, 1915.*"

462.11 T 41/24½

The Counselor for the Department of State (Lansing) to the Secretary of State

WASHINGTON, *May 3, 1915.*

DEAR MR. SECRETARY: In view of the aerial attack on the American S. S. *Cushing* and of the reported torpedoing of the S. S. *Gulflight,* of which no official confirmation has yet been received, I think it should be considered whether the draft instruction to Ambassador Gerard [29] regarding the death of Leon C. Thrasher through the sinking of the British S. S. *Falaba* should be sent.

The death of Thrasher loses much of its importance in comparison with these two attacks on American vessels if it is true that three of the crew of the *Gulflight* lost their lives by reason of the vessel's being torpedoed.

If these attacks are confirmed officially, I can not see how this Government can avoid making a vigorous protest; a mere appeal or a deferential complaint will, in my opinion, neither satisfy the American people nor be in accord with the duty of the Government or with the rights of the United States.

The course pursued by the Germans seems to be based on a policy intended to provoke radical action by this Government, which will result in the severance of diplomatic relations. I may be wrong and I most sincerely hope so, but recent events appear to tend strongly in support of that view.

It may be deemed advisable to proceed with the Thrasher case separately. If so, the instruction should be sent without delay, provided it is sent at all, so that it could go out before official reports are received on the facts of the other two cases.

Another course would be to treat all three cases in one instruction. While the draft instruction in the Thrasher case might be taken as a basis for a new instruction covering the three cases, it would require very considerable amendment, and would have to be put in stronger and less conciliatory language.

I need not say to you, Mr. Secretary, that I believe the situation is critical and one to cause the gravest anxiety. We are being forced

---

[29] *Ante,* p. 370.

near to the breaking point in our relations with Germany; and I am
thoroughly convinced that it is being done wilfully through a misconception of the result here in the United States.

Faithfully yours,

ROBERT LANSING

763.72/1434

*The Counselor for the Department of State (Lansing) to the Secre-
tary of State*

[WASHINGTON,] *May 5, 1915.*

DEAR MR. SECRETARY: I have been reading over the annexed instruction to Ambassador Gerard of February 10th [30] to determine how far
a course of action was declared by that document in case of submarine
attack.

The important statements are contained in the three paragraphs at
the top of page 2 [31] which I have underscored in red ink and the key
words I have made "black-faced." They are "indefensible violation," "strict accountability" and "steps . . . necessary . . . to
safeguard."

The term "indefensible violation" eliminates in my opinion any
argument as to the justification of the German naval or aerial authorities for their action in attacking American vessels without warning.
It leaves no room for debate, but is an assertion that the act constitutes an international crime.

"Strict accountability" can only mean that the German Government must make full reparation for the act of their naval force and
must also repudiate the act, apologize for it and give ample assurance
that it will not be repeated.

"Steps . . . necessary . . . to safeguard" can have no other meaning than to protect American lives and property by force unless the
German Government guarantee that American lives and property
will not be molested on the high seas.

In view of these declarations, which are substantially unqualified, a
representation covering the attacks on the *Cushing* and the *Gulflight*
would leave little opportunity to discuss the subject of submarine or
aeroplane activities in the "war zone." Those cases would seem to
require brief and positive protests and demands based on the declarations of February 10th.

In the Thrasher case the circumstances are different. There is room
for argument and a discussion of the use of submarines would be ap-

---

[30] *Foreign Relations,* 1915, supp., p. 98.
[31] *Ibid.,* p. 99, pars. 2–4.

propriate since it is open to question whether the declarations apply to that particular case.

I suggest, therefore, the advisability of acting in the Thrasher case before the full reports are received in the other cases, so that a more moderate and less rigid representation may be made before action is taken in the other cases, which, if the reported facts are confirmed, leave little opportunity for a conciliatory note, unless we recede from our former statements, a course which I assume will not be done.

Faithfully yours,

ROBERT LANSING

841.857 L 97/87

The Assistant Secretary of the Treasury (Peters) to the Counselor for the Department of State (Lansing)

WASHINGTON, *May 8, 1915.*

DEAR MR. LANSING: In response to Mr. Woolsey's request on the telephone this morning, that I obtain certain information from the Collector at New York in regard to the Cunard Liner *Lusitania*,[32] I beg to report as follows:—

1. Whether she had any contraband or ammunition on board at the time she sailed from New York:
Practically all of her cargo was contraband of some kind.
2. The character or nature of such contraband and munitions:
Her cargo included:

32 cases cotton goods & 313 cases raw furs.
Sheet brass, 260,000 lbs.
Copper ingots and base, 111,000 lbs.
Insulated copper wire, 58,000 lbs.
Cheese, 217,000. lbs.
Beef, 342,000. lbs.
Butter, 43,000 lbs.
Lard, 40,000 lbs.
Bacon, 85,000 lbs.
31 packages of hardware, aluminum, brass, iron, old rubber
1271 packages ammunition consigned by Bethlehem Steel Co., consisting of
      6 cases of fuses
      12 cases "   "
      1250 cases " shrapnel
8 packages of motor cycles and parts
89 pieces of leather
2400 [*4200?*] cases of metallic packages [*cartridges*] shipped by Remington Arms Company.
185 cases accoutrements

---

[32] For correspondence previously printed concerning the sinking of the *Lusitania*, see *ibid.*, pp. 384 ff.

3. Whether the vessel had any guns mounted on board.

Neutrality men were on board every day. No guns at any time found mounted, nor, so far as they knew, on board.

4. And whether she had any ammunition for the same, and its character:

Answered above.

Yours sincerely,

A. J. PETERS

763.72/1750b

The Secretary of State to President Wilson

WASHINGTON, *May 9, 1915.*

MY DEAR MR. PRESIDENT: As you do not read the *Post* I am taking the liberty of enclosing an editorial that appeared in it this morning.[33] You will notice that it calls attention to Germany's action in endorsing the requirement of notice to passengers. But my special reason for calling your attention to this editorial is that it makes a suggestion for which I ask your consideration, namely, that ships carrying contraband should not be permitted to carry passengers. The idea occurred to me last night (it was not, of course communicated to the *Post*) that some such rule should be adopted. Germany has a right to prevent contraband going to the allies and a ship carrying contraband should not rely upon passengers to protect her from attack— it would be like putting women and children in front of an army.

You will notice from another clipping that the manifest showed 4200 cases of cartridges & ammunition valued at $152,400. I learned from Mr. Lansing last night that the *Lusitania* carried ammunition, and this information suggested to me the rule which seems to have suggested itself to the editor of the *Post* also. You will notice that Germany refers to this war material in the *Lusitania* cargo. One result will be to make the world realize more fully the horrors of war and pray more earnestly for peace. Ridder's comments which I enclose are suggestive.[33] Our people will, I think, be the more thankful that a believer in peace is in the White House at this time.

With assurances [etc.]

W. J. BRYAN

[33] No enclosure with file copy of this letter.

763.72/2541

President Wilson to the Secretary of State

WASHINGTON, *10 May, 1915.*

MY DEAR MR. SECRETARY: After all, this* does not express Page's own opinion, but what he takes to be public opinion at the moment in Great Britain.

It is a very serious thing to have such things thought, because everything that affects the opinion of the world regarding us affects our influence for good.

Faithfully Yours,

W. W.

763.72111/2236½

The Secretary of State to President Wilson

WASHINGTON, *May 10, 1915.*

MY DEAR MR. PRESIDENT: I am sending you a memorandum by Mr. Lansing in regard to the question of "Warning". As you and I have gone over this matter together I need not re-state my views.

Mr. Villard, of the New York *Evening Post*, called this morning. I do not know what value you attach to his opinions but he presented the idea of calling a conference of neutral nations to discuss the interference with trade, of which both sides have been guilty.

I explained to him that the difficulty about calling a neutral conference was that any position taken by such a conference during the war would be considered, not upon its merits, but as it affected one side or the other. He thought that both sides had done enough so that complaint could be made against the action of both sides.

With assurances [etc.]   W. J. BRYAN

[Enclosure]

The Counselor for the Department of State (*Lansing*) to the Secretary of State

[WASHINGTON,] *May 9, 1915.*

DEAR MR. SECRETARY: I have been thinking over your suggestion that it might be considered that Americans, taking passage in a British vessel bound for a British port and passing through the German "war zone", did so, in a measure at least, at their own peril and, therefore, were not entitled to the full protection of this Government.

---

* Page's despatch about the *Lusitania*, which I find I have burned. [Footnote in the original. The despatch is printed in *Foreign Relations*, 1915, supp., p. 385.]

After carefully considering the suggestion I am convinced that this Government is in no position to adopt that view. To accept it would be to admit that the Government of the United States failed in its duty to its own citizens and permitted them to run risks without attempting to prevent them from doing so.

By its note to the German Government on February 10th [35] this Government declared that it would hold Germany to a strict accountability for the loss of American lives and property within the "war zone." It did not discriminate as to the vessels carrying American citizens and property. If it intended to discriminate, it was its manifest duty to its own people to have said so, and to have issued a public warning to them to keep off British ships and to say to them "If you go, you go at your peril."

On the contrary, this Government has permitted in silence hundreds of American citizens to travel by British steamships crossing the "war zone." It has by its silence allowed them to believe that their Government approved and would stand behind them in case their legal rights were invaded.

I do not see how this Government can avoid responsibility now by asserting that an American in traveling by a British vessel took a risk, which he should not have taken. If it held that point of view it should have declared it at the time it protested against the "war zone."

The Government has even gone further than that. When the German Embassy published its "Warning" [36] (a most improper proceeding diplomatically) just prior to the sailing of the *Lusitania*, this Government continued silent. It did not even then advise Americans not to sail on British vessels. It continued to allow them to believe that the assertions in the note of February 10th were unconditional.

It is my opinion in view of the facts that it would cause general public condemnation and indignant criticism in this country, if the Government should attempt now to avoid vigorous action by asserting that the Americans drowned by the torpedoing of the *Lusitania* were blamable in having taken passage on that vessel. They had the right to rely on the note of February 10th, and they had the right to expect a warning from their Government if it considered that it could not support them if they took risks by going abroad on British vessels.

I think that it would be a serious mistake for this Government to take a position so untenable and so vulnerable to attack if it should be taken.

With great respect [etc.]   ROBERT LANSING

---

[35] *Foreign Relations*, 1915, supp., p. 98.
[36] See clipping from the New York *Sun*, p. 382.

763.72/1771½

The Secretary of State to President Wilson

WASHINGTON, *May 10, 1915.*

MY DEAR MR. PRESIDENT: I am sending you a memorandum prepared by Mr. Lansing, together with a letter to me, suggesting courses to be pursued. While I presume you have already prepared an outline of the note, these may be suggestive.[37]

With assurances [etc.]   W. J. BRYAN

P. S.   I am enclosing also an editorial from the *Springfield Republican* which probably has more weight than any other paper of the same circulation in the country.[38]

[Enclosure 1]

Memorandum by the Counselor for the Department of State (*Lansing*) on the Sinking of the "*Lusitania*" [39]

[WASHINGTON,] *May 10, 1915.*

POSSIBLE GERMAN DEFENSES

First. The "Lusitania" carried in its cargo a large quantity of munitions of war for Great Britain and was, therefore, properly destroyed.

This fact, in order to be effective in defense, must be shown to have been communicated to the German naval force making the attack on the vessel.

If so communicated the information came from the representatives of Germany in this country showing the ability to communicate with Berlin.

The presence of munitions of war in the cargo does not in itself relieve the German naval authorities from stopping the vessel and permitting those on board to take to the boats before the torpedo was launched.

The necessity for attack without warning and without delay must rest upon some other defense, which is stated to be—

Second. The "Lusitania" naturally carried guns to resist attack by German war craft.

This defense must be based on actual knowledge or justifiable suspicion.

---

[37] On May 12 President Wilson replied: "I am sincerely obliged to you for these papers, and would appreciate it if you could ask Mr. Lansing to let me have a copy of these suggestions as to alternative courses of action." (File No. 763.72/1772½.)

[38] Editorial not enclosed with file copy of this letter.

[39] Filed separately under file No. 763.72/1770¼.

The fact is that the *Lusitania* had no guns mounted or unmounted and so was entirely unarmed (Collector Malone's statement [40]).

As the German representatives in this country had means of communicating the fact of the presence of munitions of war on board to their Government they had equal facilities to notify them that the vessel was unarmed. They cannot avoid responsibility by claiming that they suspected the vessel was armed, when they had the means of obtaining actual knowledge showing that the suspicion was unwarranted.

The first defense must rest on knowledge; the second defense on ignorance. If the German Government had knowledge in one case, they are chargeable with knowledge in the second case.

Third. The German Embassy gave public warning through the press to American citizens not to travel through the "war zone" on British vessels.

The German Government cannot relieve themselves of responsibility for doing an illegal and inhuman act by announcing that they intend to violate the principles of law and humanity.

The communication was not addressed to the Government of the United States. The German Embassy went over the head of the Administration and addressed the American people. Such procedure was an act of insolence similar to the giving of publicity to his memorandum by the German Ambassador.[41] Advantage was taken of the American doctrine of the right of freedom of the press to ignore the Government and to address the people directly. A foreign diplomatic representative is accredited to the Government of the United States, not to the People of the United States. An Ambassador's means of communication is through the Department of State. The conduct of the German Ambassador in this case is an indefensible breach of propriety, an insult to this Government.

If the warning had been delivered to this Government, it would have been compelled to decide whether it should be made public. It had no opportunity to do this. It did, however, have opportunity to advise the American people to heed the warning. This it did not do. It ignored the warning, and by remaining silent gave the impression that the warning might be ignored.

---

[40] See p. 385.
[41] Memorandum of Apr. 4, 1915, *Foreign Relations*, 1915, supp., p. 157. See also *ante*, pp. 117–122.

The Counselor for the Department of State (Lansing) to the Secretary of State

[WASHINGTON,] *May 10, 1915.*

DEAR MR. SECRETARY: I offer the following course of procedure in the *Lusitania* case as a basis of discussion:

An earnest protest against the torpedoing of an unarmed passenger steamship on the high seas without giving warning of attack or placing non-combatants in a place of safety.

A declaration that the act violated the established rules of international law and the principles of humanity.

A reaffirmation of the assertion made in the note of February 10th that the German Government would be held to a strict accountability for loss of American lives and property.

A demand (1) that the German Government disavow the act and apologize for it; (2) that the officers guilty of the offense be punished; (3) that the German Government acknowledge liability and promise to pay a just indemnity; and (4) that the German Government will guarantee that in the future ample measures will be taken to insure the safety of the lives of American citizens on the high seas unless they are traveling on a vessel of belligerent nationality, which is armed or being convoyed by belligerent war craft.

In case the German Government refuse to comply with these demands, diplomatic relations could be severed.

The severance of diplomatic relations does not necessarily mean war. It may mean that a government is unwilling to continue intercourse with another government, which has grievously offended against law and right and which refuses to rectify the offense by making proper amends. It is an evidence of extreme displeasure but is not a hostile act.

In presenting the foregoing outline of action for consideration I do not express any opinion.

There is another course of action, which I think worthy of consideration.

The neutral powers, Netherlands, Denmark, Sweden, Norway, Italy and the United States, might jointly agree to send identic notes to Germany and also to Great Britain protesting vigorously against the violations of international law with which each is charged. The protest to Germany would have to cover breaches of inhumanity [*sic*] as well as of international law. The protest to Great Britain would cover illegal interruption of trade between neutrals.

If such a course is wise, the present would seem to be an opportune time. I do not think, however, that this would relieve the Government of a separate protest to Germany on the *Lusitania* case, but it might give a chance to make it more moderate in tone.

Faithfully yours,

ROBERT LANSING

763.72111/2237½

President Wilson to the Secretary of State

WASHINGTON, *11 May, 1915.*

MY DEAR MR. SECRETARY: Mr. Lansing's argument seems to me unanswerable. Even if it were just to take the position that a warning that an unlawful and outrageous thing would be done might operate as an exemption from responsibility on the part of those who issued it, so far as our citizens were concerned, it is now too late to take it. We defined our position at the outset and cannot alter it,—at any rate so far as it affects the past.

Faithfully Yours,

W. W.

Mr. Villard's suggestion interests me very much; but the objections you make are certainly very vital ones.[42] We can turn the matter over in our minds.

763.72/1752c

The Secretary of State to President Wilson

WASHINGTON [, *undated*].

MY DEAR MR. PRESIDENT: Your more than generous note received with draft of protest to Germany.[43] I have gone over it very carefully and will give it to Mr. Lansing at once, for I agree with you that it is well to act without delay in order to give direction to public opinion. I do not see that you could have stated your position more clearly or more forcibly. In one sentence I suggest "as the last few weeks have shown" so that it will read: "Submarines, we respectfully submit, cannot be used against Merchantmen, as the last few weeks have shown, without an inevitable violation of many sacred principles of justice and humanity." [44] The only other amendment that occurs to me relates to the *Cushing* and *Gulflight*. Would it not be wise to make some reference to the rules sent us and the offer to apologize and make reparation in case a neutral ship was sunk by mistake? I suggest something like this: "Apology and reparation for destruction of neutral ships, sunk by mistake, while they may

---

[42] See the Secretary's letter of May 10, 1915, to President Wilson, p. 387.
[43] For this draft, embodying Mr. Lansing's suggested changes, see p. 395; for text of the note as sent, see *Foreign Relations*, 1915, supp., p. 393.
[44] See p. 397, l. 7.

satisfy international obligation, if no loss of life results, can not justify or excuse a practice, the natural and almost necessary effect of which is to subject neutral nations to new and innumerable risks, for it must be remembered that peace, not war, is the normal state and that nations that resort to war for a settlement of international disputes are not at liberty to subordinate the rights of neutrals to the supposed or even actual needs of belligerents." [45] I am in doubt of the propriety of referring to the note published by Bernstorff.[46]

But, my dear Mr. President, I join in this document with a heavy heart. I am as sure of your patriotic purpose as I am of my own, but after long consideration both careful and prayerful, I cannot bring myself to the belief that it is wise to relinquish the hope of playing the part of a friend to both sides in the role of peace maker and this note will, I fear, result in such relinquishment—a hope which requires for its realization the retention of the confidence of both sides. It will be popular in this country for a time at least, and possibly permanently, because public sentiment, already favorable to the Allies, has been perceptibly increased by the *Lusitania* tragedy, but there is peril in this very fact. Your position being the position of the government will be approved—that approval varying in emphasis in proportion to the intensity of the feeling against Germany. There being no intimation that the final accounting will be postponed until the war is over, the jingo element will not only predict but demand war (see enclosed editorial from *Washington Post* of this morning), and the line will be more distinctly drawn between those who sympathize with Germany and the rest of the people. Outside of the country the demand will be applauded by the Allies and the more they applaud the more Germany will be embittered, because we unsparingly denounce the retaliatory methods employed by her, without condemning the announced purpose of the Allies to starve the non-combatants of Germany and without complaining of the conduct of Great Britain in relying on passengers including men, women and children of the United States to give immunity to vessels carrying munitions of war—without even suggesting that she should convoy passenger ships as carefully as she does ships carrying horses and gasoline. This enumeration does not include a reference to Great Britain's indifference to the increased dangers thrown upon us by the misuse of our flag or to her unwarranted interference with our trade with neutral nations. Germany cannot but construe the strong statement of the case against her, coupled with silence as to the unjustifiable action of the Allies as evidence of partiality toward the latter—an impression which will be

---

[45] See p. 398, paragraph beginning, "Expressions of regret."
[46] The advertisement warning travelers against sailing on Allied vessels through the German war zone, p. 382.

deepened in proportion to the loudness of the praise which the Allies bestow upon the statement of this government's position. The only way, as I see it, to prevent irreparable injury being done by the statement is to issue simultaneously a protest against the objectionable conduct of the Allies which will keep them from rejoicing and show Germany that we are defending our rights against aggression from both sides.

I am only giving you, my dear Mr. President, the situation as it appears to me—and praying all the while that I may be wholly mistaken and that your judgement may be vindicated by events.

With assurances [etc.]

[File copy not signed]

763.72/1773½

The Secretary of State to the Counselor for the Department of State (Lansing)[47]

MY DEAR MR. LANSING: I enclose a draft of note to Germany drawn by the President.[48] He asks for our suggestions. I wish you would prepare at once a draft embodying yours—I will submit mine in a letter to accompany the draft when sent back to the President. I shall be detained here for a while but will be down before your draft is completed.

Yours

BRYAN

763.72/1774½

The Counselor for the Department of State (Lansing) to the Secretary of State

[WASHINGTON,] May 12, 1915.

DEAR MR. SECRETARY: I enclose herewith the draft prepared by the President in re Lusitania.

The method which I have adopted in making suggestions is to put in brackets the portions of the President's draft which I would omit, and underscoring the words which I would add.

I feel that the communication loses some of its strength by being too long, but I have not been very successful in the short time I have had to consider it in reducing the length.

You spoke to me about omitting any reference to the public warning given by the German Embassy here. My own view is that it

---

[47] This paper is undated; it bears the following notation in Lansing's hand: "May 12/15 RL."

[48] See footnote 43, p. 392.

would be a mistake to do so, as at once the German Government would employ that as an argument. It might as well be met to begin with as later.

Faithfully yours,

ROBERT LANSING

[Enclosure]

Draft Instruction to the Ambassador in Germany (*Gerard*)

Please call on the Imperial German Foreign Minister and after reading to him this communication leave with him a copy if he so desires.

In view of the recent acts of the German authorities violative of American rights on the high seas which culminated in the torpedoing and sinking of the British steamship *Lusitania* on May 7, 1915, by which over one hundred American citizens lost their lives, the Government of the United States and the Imperial German Government must come to a clear and full understanding as to the grave situation which has resulted.

The sinking of the British passenger steamer *Falaba* by a German submarine on March 28th, through which Leon C. Thrasher, an American citizen was drowned; the attack on April 28th on the American vessel *Cushing*, by a German aeroplane; the torpedoing on May 1st of the American vessel *Gulflight* by a German submarine, by which two or more American citizens met their death; and, finally, the torpedoing and sinking of the *Lusitania*, constitute a series of events, which the Government of the United States has observed with growing concern, distress and amazement.

[The Government of the United States has observed this series of events with growing concern, distress and amazement.] Recalling [, as it did,] the humane and enlightened attitude assumed hitherto by [action of] the Imperial German Government in [hitherto in all] matters of international right and particularly with regard to the freedom of the seas; having learned to recognize the German views and the German influence in the field of international obligation as always engaged upon the side of justice and humanity; and having understood the instructions of the Imperial German Government to its naval commanders to be upon the same plane of humane action prescribed by the naval codes of other nations, the Government of the United States [it] was loath to believe, it cannot now bring itself to believe, that these acts, so absolutely contrary to the rules, the practices, and the spirit of modern warfare, could have the countenance or sanction of that great Government. [It feels it to be its duty, therefore, to address the Imperial German Government concerning them with the utmost frankness and in the earnest hope that it is not mistaken in expecting action on the part of the Imperial German Government which will correct the unfortunate impressions which have been created and vindicate once more the position of that Government with regard to the sacred freedom of the seas.]

The Government of the United States has been apprised that [of the feeling of] the Imperial German Government considered themselves to be [that it has been] obliged by the extraordinary circumstances of the present war and the [drastic] measures adopted by their [of its] adversaries in seeking to cut [its coasts] off Germany from all commerce, to adopt methods of retaliation which go much beyond the ordinary methods of warfare at sea, in the proclamation of a war zone [from] which it has warned neutral ships to avoid.   [keep away. But the waters of that zone touch the coasts of many neutral nations, and] This Government has already informed [had the honor of informing] the Imperial German Government that it cannot admit the adoption of such measures or such a warning of danger to operate as in any degree an abbreviation of the rights of American ship masters or of American citizens bound on lawful errands as passengers on merchant ships of belligerent nationality [ownership]; and that it must hold the Imperial German Government to a strict accountability for any infringement of those rights. [, direct or incidental.   It does not understand the Imperial German Government to question those rights.]   It assumes [is confident, on the contrary,] that the Imperial German Government accept[s, as of course,] the rule that the lives of non-combatants, whether they be of neutral citizenship or citizens of one of the nations at war, cannot lawfully or rightfully be put in jeopardy by the capture or destruction of an unresisting [unarmed] merchantman, and recognize[s] also, as all other nations do, the obligation to take the usual precaution of visit and search to ascertain whether a suspected merchantman is in fact of belligerent nationality [ownership] or is in fact carrying contraband of war under a neutral flag.

The Government of the United States, therefore, calls [takes the liberty of calling] the attention of the Imperial German Government with the utmost earnestness to the fact that the objection to their [danger of its] present method of attack against the trade of their [its] enemies lies in the practical impossibility of employing submarines in the destruction of commerce without disregarding those [in conformity with what all modern opinion regards as the imperative] rules of fairness, reason, justice, and humanity, which the civilized world regards as imperative.   It is practically impossible for the officers of a submarine to visit a merchantman at sea and examine her papers and cargo.   It is practically impossible for them to make a prize of her. [; and, if they cannot put a prize crew on board of her,] They cannot sink her without leaving her crew and all on board of her to the mercy of the sea in her small boats. These facts it is understood the Imperial German Government frankly admit. [In the instances of which we have spoken time enough for even that poor measure of safety was not given, and in at least two of the cases cited not so much as a warning was received.] Manifestly submarines [, we respectfully submit,] cannot be used against merchantmen, as the last few weeks have shown, without an inevitable violation of many sacred principles of justice and humanity.

American citizens act within their indisputable rights in taking their ships and in traveling wherever their legitimate business calls them upon the high seas, and exercise those rights in what should be the well justified confidence that their lives will not be endangered by acts done in clear violation of universally acknowledged international obligations and [—] certainly in the confidence that their own Government will sustain them in the [their] exercise [.] of their rights.[49]

There was recently published in the newspapers of the United States, I [we] regret to inform the Imperial German Government, a formal warning, purporting to come from the Imperial German Embassy at Washington, addressed to the people of the United States, and stating, in effect, that any citizen of the United States who exercised his right of free travel upon the seas would do so at his peril if his journey should take him within the zone of waters within which the Imperial German Navy was using submarines against the commerce of Great Britain and France, notwithstanding the respectful but very earnest protest of his government, the Government of the United States. I [We] do not refer to [speak of] this for the purpose of calling the attention of the Imperial German Government at this time to the surprising irregularity of a communication from the Imperial German Embassy at Washington addressed to the people of the United States through the newspapers, but only for the purpose of pointing out that no warning that an unlawful and inhumane act will be committed, can possibly be accepted as an excuse or palliation for that act or as an abatement of the responsibility for the commission.

Long acquainted as this Government has been with the character of the Imperial German Government and with the high principles of equity by [with] which they have [it has] in the past been actuated and guided, the Government of the United States cannot believe that the commanders of the vessels which committed these acts of law-

---

[49] A marginal notation to this paragraph reads, "Transferred from p. 10." See *post*, p. 398, first paragraph.

lessness did so except under a misapprehension of the orders issued by [under orders from] the Imperial German naval authorities [or with their approval. It takes it for granted that, at least within the practical possibilities of every such case, the commanders even of submarines were expected to do nothing that would involve the lives of non-combatants or the safety of neutral ships, even at the cost of failing of their object of capture or destruction.] It confidently expects, therefore, that the Imperial German Government will disavow the acts of [to] which the Government of the United States complains [takes the liberty of calling its attention]; that they [it] will make reparation so far as reparation is possible for injuries which are without measure, and that they [it] will take immediate steps to prevent the recurrence of anything so obviously subversive of the principles of warfare for which the Imperial German Government have in the past [has always itself so wisely and] so firmly contended.

[American citizens act within their indisputable rights in taking their ships and in traveling wherever their legitimate business calls them upon the high seas, and exercise those rights in what should be the well justified confidence that their lives will not be endangered by acts done in clear violation of universally acknowledged international obligations and [—] certainly in the confidence that their own Government will sustain them in the [their] exercise. of their rights]

The Government and people of the United States looks to the Imperial German Government for just, prompt, and enlightened action in this vital matter with the greater confidence because the United States and Germany are bound together not only by special ties of friendship [not only] but also by the [special] stipulations of the Treaty of 1828 between the United States and the Kingdom of Prussia. [explicit treaty]

Expressions of regret and offers of reparation in case of destruction of neutral ships [, sunk by mistake,] while they may satisfy international obligations, if no loss of life results, can not justify or excuse a practice, the natural and necessary effect of which is to subject neutral nations and neutral persons to new and immeasurable risks; [for it must be remembered that peace, not war, is the normal state, and that nations that resort to war to settle disputes are not at liberty to subordinate the rights of neutrals to the supposed or even actual needs of belligerents.]

The Imperial German Government must realize that [will not expect] this [the] Government will not [of the United States to] omit any word [necessary representation] or any [necessary] act necessary to the performance of its sacred duty of maintaining [in sustaining] the rights of the United States and its citizens and of safeguarding their free exercise and enjoyment. [or in safeguarding the sacred duties of international obligation.]

763.72/1752b

The Secretary of State to President Wilson

WASHINGTON, *May 12, 1915.*

MY DEAR MR. PRESIDENT: I am enclosing copy of the draft of the note made according to your instructions.[50] In most of the cases it is simply a choice of words and usually the words used by Mr. Lansing are a little harsher than words used by you, and I incline to the milder statement where it is clear and certain.

In one case, on page 5, I very much prefer your word to his, namely, the use of the word "unarmed" instead of the word "unresisting"— (line 3, page 5).[51] The difference is quite an important one. If the vessel is armed that, as I understand it, establishes her character and it is not necessary to wait to see whether she will resist. It is presumed that an armed vessel will resist—that is what the arms are for.

At the bottom of page 5 he has substituted—"the civilized world" for "modern opinion".[52] I like your phrase—"modern opinion" better. In his phrase—the word "civilized" would be more offensive because it will virtually charge Germany with being uncivilized. There is no use calling names—there is sufficient force in the plain statement.

About the middle of page 6 the phrase which he leaves out strengthens the statement.[53] It might be qualified a little by adding after "was" and before "not giving [*given*]", the phrase—"according to our information".

You will notice that he has inserted on page 6—fifth line from the bottom—the suggestion which I made to you in my letter of this morning[54]—namely: "as the last few weeks have shown".[55] This, of course, is put in subject to your approval.

He has also indicated a place at the beginning of page 11 for the insertion of "A"[56] which I suggested in my letter this morning, only, he leaves out the phrase "sunk by mistake" which broadens the phrase—an improvement.

He also suggests the omission of the last sentence but I am inclined to think that it is worth while to set it forth as a principle. It will be difficult for her to reply that she is "at liberty to subordinate the rights of neutrals to the supposed or even actual needs of the belligerents", and, if she does not deny it, it may be of value to have it taken as admitted.

---

[50] *Supra.*
[51] See p. 396, l. 28.
[52] See p. 396, last paragraph, l. 7.
[53] See p. 397, l. 4 (sentence beginning, "In the instances").
[54] Apparently the undated letter on p. 392.
[55] See p. 397, l. 8.
[56] i. e., the paragraph beginning, "Expressions of regret," p. 398.

On page 11 you will notice that he uses the words—"must realize that" instead of "will not expect, etc." [57]   I like your phrase better; it is more polite to say that the German Government will not expect us to surrender our rights, rather than to say that the German Government "must realize that we will not."

Mr. Lansing prefers to leave in the reference to von Bernstorff about the propriety of which there is, as I wrote you this morning, a question in my mind.

A question arises as to making the matter public. I think it advisable to have the statement issued as soon as possible—do you think it would be improper to give it out here as soon as it is cabled to Berlin? I presume there is no use of putting it in cipher if we give it out here when it is sent. I am inclined to think that, desirable as it would be to give it out at once, it might be better to put it in cipher and send it by cable and then give it out when it has had time to reach Berlin. It occurs to me it would be a little better to have them in possession of it when it was given out here, rather than have them receive the information by news before it reaches them officially. They gave their last statement to us to the Press there when it was filed for transmission, at least it reached the newspapers here in the evening before it reached the Ambassador, and we read it in the newspapers before it was delivered, but the Ambassador explained that he brought it as soon as he could.

With assurances [etc.]   W. J. BRYAN

763.72/1752a

The Secretary of State to President Wilson

WASHINGTON, *May 12, 1915.*

MY DEAR MR. PRESIDENT: I am so fearful of the embarrassment which the Jingoes will cause by assuming that your note means war— an interpretation which might affect the tone of Germany's reply as well as make it more difficult to postpone final settlement that I venture to suggest the propriety of meeting the issue now by a statement given out at the time the protest is published or before.

To explain what I mean I give the following—not as a draft of such notice or interview but as an illustration: The words "strict accountability" having been construed by some of the newspapers to mean an immediate settlement of the matter, I deem it fitting to say that that construction is not a necessary one. In individual matters friends sometimes find it wise to postpone the settlement of disputes until such differences can be considered calmly and on their merits.

[57] See p. 398, first line of last paragraph.

So it may be with nations. The United States and Germany, between whom there exists a long standing friendship, may find it advisable to postpone until peace is restored any disputes which do not yield to diplomatic treatment.

Germany has endorsed the principle of investigation embodied in the thirty treaties signed with as many nations. These treaties give a year's time for the investigation and apply to all disputes of every character. From this nation's standpoint, there is no reason why this policy should not control as between the United States and Germany. I believe such a statement would do great good—

With assurances [etc.] W. J. B[RYAN]

763.72/1775½

President Wilson to the Secretary of State

WASHINGTON, *12 May, 1915.*

MY DEAR MR. SECRETARY: I am sending you herewith the final form of the note to Germany.[58]

I want to express my deep appreciation of the work you and Mr. Lansing have done on it and the splendid spirit in which you have acquiesced in my decision in this grave matter, which gives me as deep concern as it does you.

I am thinking over the suggestion of your manuscript letter very deeply.[59] If the statement is made, I think it should accompany the publication of the note Friday morning, so I will take the day to revolve the matter a little further in my mind.

Faithfully Yours,

W. W.

763.72/1745a : Telegram

The Secretary of State to the Ambassador in Germany (Gerard)

WASHINGTON, *May 12, 1915—6 p. m.*

1658. In view of sensational conjectures in the press here as to what the note we are about to send to the German Government will contain, please see the minister for foreign affairs at once and ask him to discredit absolutely everything that may reach him through the newspapers or the news agencies and kindly await our official communication.

BRYAN

---

[58] For text of the note as sent, see *Foreign Relations*, 1915, supp., p. 393.
[59] *Supra.*

763.72/1757½

President Wilson to the Secretary of State

WASHINGTON, *13 May, 1915.*

MY DEAR MR. SECRETARY: After sleeping over your suggestion, I have this to propose:

It would not be wise, I think, to give out a direct statement; but I think the same purpose would be served by such a "tip" as the enclosed, accompanying the publication of the note. And it would be best that this tip should be given out from the Executive Office, while the note was given out by the Department of State. What do you think?

If you will return the paper in the course of the morning, I will make the necessary arrangements.

Faithfully yours,

W. W.

[Enclosure]

Proposed Notice for Publication

["]There is a good deal of confidence in Administration circles that Germany will respond to this note in a spirit of accommodation. It is pointed out that, while Germany is not one of the many nations which have recently signed treaties of deliberation and inquiry with the United States upon all points of serious difficulty, as a means of supplementing ordinary diplomatic methods and preventing, so far as feasible, the possibility of conflict, she has assented to the principle of such a treaty; and it is believed that she will act in this instance in the spirit of that assent. A frank issue is now made, and it is expected that it will be met in good temper and with a desire to reach an agreement, despite the passions of the hour,— passions in which the United States does not share,—or else submit the whole matter to such processes of discussion as will result in a permanent settlement."

763.72/1757a

The Secretary of State to President Wilson

WASHINGTON, *May 13, 1915.*

MY DEAR MR. PRESIDENT: In going over the draft of the note which you sent over this morning Mr. Lansing discovered that you had left in the sentence saying that this German war zone touched the coasts of many neutral countries. He calls attention to the fact that the war zone does not touch the coast of any neutral nation. The Netherlands is the only neutral nation affected and thirty miles is left along the coast.

We take it for granted that you would desire to have that sentence left out, but I bring it to your attention so that it can be inserted if you think it best.

In talking over the phone with Mr. Tumulty I said I was very much pleased with the statement you are going to have made—meaning the newspaper statement which you have prepared—and I found that he did not know about it. I told him he would find it out from you and did not attempt to give him the contents of it. I was sorry afterwards that I had said anything about it. While I presume he would not mention the matter you might, if you think it necessary, caution him.

With assurances [etc.]   **W. J. Bryan**

763.72/1757¾

President Wilson to the Secretary of State

Washington, *13 May, 1915.*

My Dear Mr. Secretary: Since I expressed my approval of the statement you suggested for the press I have heard something, indirectly, from the German Embassy which convinces me that we would lose all chance of bringing Germany to reason if we in any way or degree indicated to them, or to our own public, that this note was merely the first word in a prolonged debate. I will tell you what I have in mind when I do not have to write it.

In the meantime, I beg that you will pardon me for changing my mind thus. I am sure that it is the safer course, the one more likely to produce the results we are all praying for. Please withdraw the message (the supplementary statement) altogether. If we say anything of the kind it must be a little later, after the note has had its first effect.[60]

Faithfully Yours,

W. W.

763.72/1757c

The Secretary of State to President Wilson

Washington, *May 13, 1915.*

My Dear Mr. President: When I looked at the last sentence of the note to Germany I was struck with the fact that there is no concluding

---

[60] In a message to the President written on the same day, concerning another matter, Secretary Bryan added the following postscript: "I am very sorry that your judgment is against using the statement you prepared this morning. I fear the use the jingo element will make of the German note." (File No. 763.72/1757b.)

reiteration of our friendship as in the other messages that we have sent. I called Mr. Lansing's attention to it and he said he did not think there ought to be, but as it will probably be an hour yet before it is all in type I venture to ask you whether, on reflection, you think it would be wise to conclude the statement with any formal expression referring to friendly relations. If so, will you please send over what you desire added?

With assurances [etc.]   W. J. BRYAN

763.72/1757½

President Wilson to the Secretary of State

13 MAY, 1915.

MY DEAR MR. SECRETARY: I am sorry to say that in this matter my judgment is with Mr. Lansing. I think the body of the note contains a sufficient tone of sincere friendliness.

In haste,

Faithfully Yours,

W. W.

763.72/1758½

President Wilson to the Secretary of State

WASHINGTON, *14 May, 1915.*

MY DEAR MR. SECRETARY: I was as sorry as you can have been to withdraw the "statement" which we had intended for the press.[61] It cost me a struggle to do so. But the intimation was plain from the German Embassy (and I cannot doubt the source of my information) that we were not in earnest, would speak only in a Pickwickian sense if we seemed to speak with firmness, and I did not dare lend colour to that impression. You will notice that hope of a pacific settlement was expressed. That, in the circumstances, was as far as I dared to go.

Faithfully Yours,

W. W.

341.1153/11

The Counselor for the Department of State (Lansing) to the Secretary of State

[WASHINGTON,] *May 14, 1915.*

DEAR MR. SECRETARY: The memorandum [62] of vessels detained in British ports prepared by Mr. Johnson,[63] which you handed to me

---

[61] *Ante,* p. 402.
[62] Not found in Department files.
[63] Cone Johnson, Solicitor for the Department of State.

this afternoon, covers only "cotton ships." There are a number of other vessels detained which carry different cargoes.

I do not think that it would do to confine a representation to Great Britain to vessels only laden with cotton. It would cause undoubtedly much criticism from owners of other vessels and cargoes. The data is being collected as rapidly as possible, but I do not see how a representation could be prepared before Monday, which would be at all complete.

In regard to your suggestion that the President give public notice advising, asking or directing Americans not to take passage on belligerent steamships while the controversy as to submarine warfare is pending, that could of course be prepared at once.

In compliance with your request that I draft a notice such as is suggested I submit the following:

"The President in view of the present diplomatic situation requests that American citizens, intending to proceed abroad and to traverse waters adjacent to the coasts of Great Britain and France, will refrain from taking passage on vessels of belligerent nationality pending the exchange of views between this Government and the Government of Germany regarding the use of submarines in interrupting vessels of commerce in those waters."

I think that this is the sort of notice, which you had in mind. I doubt if more than a request could be made, as I believe there is no law, by which Americans could be restrained from going on belligerent vessels if they saw fit or by which such vessels could be prevented from receiving American passengers. Furthermore a request like this would be, in my opinion, almost, if not quite, as effective as an order, and presents no legal difficulties.

Do you not think that, if this notice is given, it will be said "Why did the Government not give this notice before? Why did it wait after the sinking of the *Falaba*, *Cushing* and *Gulflight* [64] until a hundred Americans lost their lives on the *Lusitania*?["] Even admitting that the effect on the German Government might be beneficial in influencing their reply, I think that the criticism in this country must be considered. It is a matter of policy which must be viewed from every standpoint.

Faithfully yours,

ROBERT LANSING

---

[64] Actually the *Cushing* and *Gulflight* were not sunk.

763.72/1758a

The Secretary of State to President Wilson

WASHINGTON, *May 14, 1915.*

MY DEAR MR. PRESIDENT: I am sending you a letter from Mr. Lansing.[65] You will notice that he cannot possibly prepare the note to Great Britain before Monday. At my request he prepared a notice such as we discussed, warning passengers against taking these ships pending negotiations. He is doubtful about the wisdom of issuing the notice, fearing that it may raise the question as to why we did not issue an earlier notice. While this question may be asked, I think it is better for us to have the question asked and answered, rather than run the risk of any more attacks. I believe that the issuance of such a notice would not only be likely to protect the lives of some Americans and thus lessen the chances of another calamity, but would have its effect upon the tone of the German reply and might point the way to an understanding. At least it would probably prevent anything like a summary dismissal of our protest. I beg to submit the idea for your consideration and the tentative notice for your criticism in case the idea commends itself to you.

With assurances [etc.]   W. J. BRYAN

763.72/1758¼

President Wilson to the Secretary of State

WASHINGTON, *14 May, 1915.*

MY DEAR MR. SECRETARY: It is hard to turn away from any suggestion that might seem to promise safety for our travellers, but what is suggested seems to me both weak and futile. To show this sort of weak yielding to threat and danger would only make matters worse.

Faithfully Yours,

W. W.

763.72/1758½

President Wilson to the Secretary of State

WASHINGTON, *14 May, 1915.*

MY DEAR MR. SECRETARY: I quite understand why a note about the detained ships cannot be made ready before the beginning of next week.

As to the request to Americans not to take passage on belligerent ships (for I agree with Mr. Lansing that it could be nothing more

---

[65] *Supra.*

than a request), my feeling is this: the request is unnecessary, if the object is to save lives, because the danger is already fully known and those who do not refrain because of the danger will not, in all probability, refrain because we request them to do so; and this is not the time to make it, not only for the reason Mr. Lansing suggests, but also because, as I urged this morning, it weakens the effect of our saying to Germany that we mean to support our citizens in the exercise of their right to travel both on our ships and on belligerent. If I thought the notice necessary, or effective, to save lives, the second objection might be waived, but since I do not, I think the second objection ought to prevail.

Faithfully Yours,

W. W.

763.72/1772½

The Counselor for the Department of State (Lansing) to President Wilson

[WASHINGTON,] *May 17, 1915.*

DEAR MR. PRESIDENT: In compliance with the request contained in your note of the 12th instant [66] to the Secretary of State asking for copies of the suggestions as to alternative courses of action made in my letter to the Secretary on the 10th,[67] it seemed to me better to repeat them in a more detailed form.

The suggestions apply to possible action in the event Germany refuses to comply with the demands made upon her.

First. Diplomatic relations could be severed by the withdrawal of our Ambassador. The natural course would be for the German Government to recall Count Bernstorff or at least to direct him to leave Washington and cease to communicate with this Government.

This action would not necessarily mean war. It might mean that this Government is unwilling to continue intercourse with the German Government because it has grievously offended against the principles of international law and humanity affecting American citizens and has refused to rectify the offense by making proper amends and giving proper assurances. It is an evidence of extreme displeasure but is not in itself a hostile act.

For this method of emphasizing a protest or demand there are several precedents, one of the most recent being the withdrawal of Baron Fava because of the failure of our Government to take steps to punish those persons guilty of lynching Italians at New Orleans and to pay a satisfactory indemnity.[68]

[66] See footnote 37, p. 389.
[67] *Ante*, p. 391.
[68] See *Foreign Relations*, 1891, pp. 675, 712.

The severance of diplomatic relations may, however, be interpreted as an evidence of hostile purpose. As the interpretation of the course of action in this case would lie largely with Germany, it is necessary in taking this step to consider the present temper of the German Government. My own belief is that it would be viewed by them as unfriendly, if not hostile, and that they might consider it to be a practical declaration of war.

Second. The alternative course of action would be to approach the other neutral powers particularly affected by the submarine war, namely, Netherlands, Denmark, Sweden and Norway, as to the sending of identic notes to both Germany and Great Britain protesting vigorously against the disregard shown of neutral rights on the high seas and asserting that, unless ample assurances were given that these rights would be respected, the neutral nations would consider what joint action they should take to protect their citizens on the high seas in the enjoyment of their rights.

If this course of action should be decided upon, I think that as a preliminary step an immediate representation should be made to Great Britain pointing out the failure of the British Government to act in accord with Sir Edward Grey's assurances of consideration for neutral rights given in his note of March 15th.[69] By doing this the disregard of Germany for law and humanity and of Great Britain for law would form substantial grounds for joint protest and, if necessary, for joint action. It would furthermore indicate entire impartiality toward the belligerents and show that the neutrals sought to secure the freedom of the seas for their people, whichever belligerent invaded their rights.

A copy of this letter has been given to the Secretary of State.

I am [etc.] ROBERT LANSING

763.72/1793a

The Secretary of State to President Wilson

WASHINGTON, *May 17, 1915.*

MY DEAR MR. PRESIDENT: As you will not return until Wednesday morning [70] I think I ought to let you know at once of a conversation which I had this morning with Ambassador Dumba, of Austria. I am therefore sending this by special messenger.

The Ambassador first expressed appreciation of your letter to the Czar [71] and then asked me to say to you that he would be pleased to give you any assistance he could in the negotiations with Germany. He said he knew that Germany had no desire for war but, on the

---

[69] *Foreign Relations*, 1915, supp., p. 143.
[70] President Wilson was in New York City.
[71] *Foreign Relations*, 1915, supp., p. 1013.

contrary, was anxious to maintain friendly relations with the United States and asked whether if assurances were given for the future it would not be possible to arbitrate the question so far as past transactions are concerned. I told him I would not feel authorized to discuss the subject without first getting your views, but suggested that he might say to the German Government that he felt sure there was no desire for war in this country and that we expected Germany to answer the note in the same spirit of friendship that prompted ours. He then suggested it might make it easier for Germany if she could, in her reply, say that she expected us to insist in the same spirit upon freedom of trade with neutrals. I pointed out to him that such an expression in the answer might embarrass us and also make it more difficult to deal with the Allies along that line and that I thought Germany ought to assume that we would live up to the position taken in our answer to the Orders in Council. He asked whether we could give any confidential assurances of that kind and I told him it ought not to be necessary and suggested to him that if Germany desired to justify, before her own people, her acceptance of the doctrine set forth in our note she could publish her views in a statement—not to us but to the German people, and say that she took it for granted that we would maintain the position taken in that statement and would insist upon our right to trade with neutrals. I told him if this statement was made to the German people instead of to us it would not require any answer from us and would not embarrass us, but if her answer contained any expression of opinion as to how we would deal with Great Britain it would seemingly link the two cases together and put us in the attitude of acting at Germany's suggestion instead of acting upon our own initiative and for the protection of our own interests, and it might also be construed as a sort of trade, whereby we would settle an account with Germany by opening an account with the Allies.

He saw the force of the objection. I emphasized the two points—first that it was important that Germany should answer in the same spirit in which we had addressed her; and second, that there should be no attempted connection between our dealings with Germany and our dealings with Great Britain.

He asked whether we could not refuse clearance to ships that carried explosives and ammunition. He said that in Germany passenger trains were not allowed to carry explosives and that the regulation was made for the protection of the lives of passengers; he suggested we might, on the same ground, refuse to allow shipowners to carry explosives on passenger boats. I told him that Germany was, of course, at liberty to make any suggestions that she thought proper in her reply, but that we could not consider these suggestions in advance.

I think the call of the Ambassador was rather significant especially as I learned from Villard that he had received some of the same suggestions from von Bernstorff. I believe it would have a splendid effect if our note to Great Britain can go at once. It will give Germany an excuse and I think she is looking for something that will serve as an excuse. There is much discussion of the idea suggested by Dumba—in fact mentioned in the first explanation received from Germany, namely—that passengers and ammunition should not travel together. I have no doubt Germany would be willing to so change the rule in regard to submarines as to exempt from danger all passenger ships that did not carry munitions of war.

I am also enclosing a statement from Page.[72] The closing sentence is interesting. Am glad to note that it will not take a generation to regain the respect with the loss of which we were threatened.[73]

With assurances [etc.]   W. J. BRYAN

P. S. The bearer of this letter—Mr. Yardley—will bring it to the Mayflower tonight and await instructions from you. If you have any answer to send back tonight he will return on the twelve-thirty train—if not, he will return early tomorrow afternoon. If you do not send an answer tonight but desire to send one tomorrow you can instruct him whether he is to call at the Mayflower for it or whether you can send it to the Holland House, Fifth Avenue near 28th street where he will stop.

763.72/1764½

President Wilson to the Secretary of State

WASHINGTON, *20 May, 1915.*

MY DEAR MR. SECRETARY: As I intimated in the little scribbled note I sent back by the special messenger whom you sent with this to New York, I think your position in the conversation with the Austrian Ambassador was admirable. We clearly cannot afford to consult with Germany as to our course toward Great Britain. The two must be kept carefully separate and distinct.

I am glad to be back and at my desk.

Faithfully Yours,

W. W.

---

[72] Telegram No. 2104, May 16, 1915, from the Ambassador in Great Britain, *Foreign Relations*, 1915, supp., p. 397.
[73] The reference is to Ambassador Page's statement in his telegram of May 11, 1915, *ibid.*, p. 391.

763.72/1777½

President Wilson to the Counselor for the Department of State
(Lansing)

WASHINGTON, *May 20, 1915.*

MY DEAR MR. LANSING: May I not thank you very warmly for your
kindness in sending me an amplified copy of your suggestions [74]
as to alternative courses of action should the Imperial German
Government not respond as we hope it will to our note? I shall
keep this by me.

Cordially and sincerely yours,

WOODROW WILSON

———

763.72/1764¼

President Wilson to the Secretary of State

WASHINGTON, *20 May, 1915.*

MY DEAR MR. SECRETARY: The proposed note to Great Britain,[75]
drawn by Mr. Lansing, reached me in New York, and I shall at the
earliest possible moment go over it and work it into what seems to
me its best expression.

But the more I think about this matter the clearer it becomes to
me that we ought not to send this note, or any other on this subject,
to Great Britain, until we have the reply of the Imperial German
Government to our note to it, because we cannot afford even to seem
to be trying to make it easier for Germany to accede to our demands
by turning in similar fashion to England concerning matters which
we have already told Germany are none of her business. It would
be so evident a case of uneasiness and hedging that I think it would
weaken our whole position fatally.

There is no reason to feel that our note to Germany is being looked
upon by them as unfriendly; and it is right that we should oblige
them to consider our rights upon the seas so far as they are concerned
without regard to anything we mean to say or do in the case of
England.

In every such decision I feel very keenly the force of your counter
judgment and cannot claim that I feel cock sure of the rightness of
my own conclusions; but I can only follow what grows more and
more clear to me the more I think the matter out.

Faithfully Yours,

W. W.

———

[74] Letter of May 17, 1915, p. 407.
[75] *Ante*, p. 297.

763.72/1764½

President Wilson to the Secretary of State

WASHINGTON, *20 May, 1915.*

MY DEAR MR. SECRETARY: It is very interesting indeed that this course of action [76] should have occurred to Mr. Johnson quite independently of any knowledge that it should have been in our minds as among the possibilities.

I think, however as I did the other day, that this is at any rate not just the right moment to take such action, even if we have the legal right to take it.

Faithfully Yours,

W. W.

763.72/1795½

President Wilson to the Secretary of State

WASHINGTON, *23 May, 1915.*

MY DEAR MR. SECRETARY: Here is at last a message from House (which I finished deciphering last evening) which seems to afford a gleam of hope.

In compliance with its suggestion, I have prepared a despatch to Gerard. If you approve of it, I hope that you will have it sent at once to-day, since time would seem to be of the essence.[77]

At the same time will you not take extraordinary precautions to keep all of this within the narrowest possible confidential circle and prevent a leak at any cost! I shall myself speak of it to absolutely nobody.

Faithfully yours,

W. W.

From House, London May 21st.

"Sir Edward Grey has talked with the present cabinet ministers and with the opposition members that are to come in and he says in his opinion this government will now consider the suggestion you made to both Germany and England in your note of February 22d [*20th*],[78] provided some additions to cover poisonous gas. There is no question as to bargaining, I think, as far as we are concerned. That is a matter between England and Germany in which we are using our good offices. If successful it will close our contentions with both nations. It looks as if it might be successful if Germany consents to make the proposal. I would suggest it be now unofficially and confidentially taken up with Gerard from Washington. Gerard

---

[76] The reference is probably to the proposal to warn American citizens against traveling on armed merchant ships. See pp. 404-406.

[77] For the telegram as sent, see *Foreign Relations,* 1915, supp., p. 406.

[78] *Ibid.,* p. 119.

could then make it clear to the German government, as I have to the British Government, that you in no way concede any of our rights in the premises."

The above needs this explanation: House had intimated to me in an earlier despatch what he found Sir Edward Grey's views and disposition in this matter to be, and I had asked him to find out how far Sir Edward would be supported in those views. Then came his request that you send the message to Gerard about which you wrote me, asking for delay in the German reply to our recent note. I had heard from House to the same effect when I was in New York. I hastened to cable him that he must take pains to make it very clear indeed, not only in London but also in all that he said to Gerard, that we were proposing no bargaining, so far as our rights were concerned; that what England did to Germany or Germany to England did not release either of them from any part of their obligation to respect our rights.

This will make clear, I hope, the reference in the above.

W. W.

763.72/1794

The Secretary of State to the Austro-Hungarian Ambassador
(Dumba)

WASHINGTON, *May 24, 1915.*

MY DEAR MR. AMBASSADOR: We have just received a telegram from Berlin [79] which informs us that Minister Zimmermann has reported to Ambassador Gerard that you sent a telegram saying in substance that the *Lusitania* note was "not meant in earnest and was only sent as sop to public opinion."

I have cabled Ambassador Gerard [79] to notify the Foreign Office that nothing was said that would justify any such report and that the German Government must not, for a moment, misunderstand either the language or the intent. I also told him that I would secure from you and send him a denial of that report, or a correction of the interpretation placed upon it, and it is for this reason that I have asked you to call this afternoon.

I made a memorandum of our conversation,[80] for the President, immediately after your departure and, refreshing my memory by an examination of the memorandum I give you herewith the substance of our conversation. I feel sure that you could not have misunderstood the points which I endeavored to impress upon you—first,

---

[79] *Ibid.*, p. 407.
[80] See Secretary Bryan's letter of May 17, 1915, to President Wilson, p. 408.

that I would not feel authorized to discuss the subject of arbitration without first getting the President's views.

In answer to your statement that Germany did not desire war and was anxious to maintain friendly relations with the United States, I stated that you might say to the German Government that you felt sure there was no desire for war in this country, and that we expected Germany to answer the note in the same spirit of friendship that prompted ours.

You then suggested that it would make it easier for Germany if she could, in her reply, say that she expected us to insist in the same spirit upon the freedom of trade with neutrals. I pointed out to you that such an expression in the answer might embarrass us and make it more difficult to deal with the Allies and I thought that Germany ought to assume that we would live up to our answer to the Orders in Council.

You asked whether we would give confidential assurances of that kind, and I told you it ought not to be necessary and that if the German Government desired to justify before the people its acceptance of the doctrine set forth in our note it could publish its views in a statement, not to us but to the German people and say that she took it for granted that we would maintain the position taken in that statement and would insist upon our right to trade with neutrals. I pointed out that if her answer contained any expression of opinion as to how we should deal with Great Britain it would seemingly link the two cases together and put us in the attitude of acting at Germany's suggestion, instead of acting upon our own initiative and for the protection of our own interests, and that it might be construed as a sort of trade whereby we would settle an account with Germany by opening an account with the Allies.

When you referred to Germany's prohibition of the carrying of explosives on railways and asked if we could not refuse clearance to ships carrying explosives and munitions I replied that Germany was at liberty to make any suggestions she thought proper in her reply but that we could not consider these suggestions in advance.

I give you this review of the conversation in order that you may either endorse its correctness or submit any changes which your memory suggests. I am sure that you would not intentionally misrepresent what I said and, in order to avoid any misunderstanding I have asked you to call at four o'clock.

Accept [etc.]   [File copy not signed]

763.72/1794½

The Austro-Hungarian Ambassador (Dumba) to the Secretary of State

WASHINGTON, *May 24, 1915.*

MY DEAR SECRETARY OF STATE: I just received your letter and am very thankful to you for giving me an opportunity of clearing up any misunderstanding or misrepresentation which evidently originated at the foreign office in Berlin.

I find the memorandum you had the kindness to send me quite correct and rendering faithfully the substance of our conversation.

As I could only send a short telegram, I had no possibility to touch all the points; so I did not mention at all my suggestion of an arbitration nor your cautious answer that you could not commit yourself, but were ready to reserve any suggestion. In order to vindicate myself I now shall communicate to you quite verbally the text of my telegram as far as it refers to our conversation: It was addressed to Baron Burian Vienna, but went via Berlin:

"Mr. Bryan, with whom I had a long talk about the situation, asked me today to draw, through your kind intervention, the attention of the Berlin Cabinet to two points:

I. The American protest, which with regard to the high waves of indignation roused in American public opinion by destruction of so many lives, was bound to be much more energetic than that of the 30th of March addressed to England,[81] is yet kept in a friendly tone, and he (Mr. Bryan) hopes for an answer in the same friendly tone and spirit.

II. He would not see any advantage if the German Government should yield in the question of the submarine war on condition that the United States Government induces the London Cabinet to respect the law of nations, especially as far as free passage of foodstuffs is concerned. President Wilson would then appear to act in London under German pressure, and this action would not promise success. Mr. Bryan suggested rather an unconditional modification of the submarine warfare by Germany in the sense of the American note; at the same time, in an official statement of the German Government to the German people, the certain expectation could be expressed, that the United States would live up to their statement and press earnestly in London their view of the rights of neutral commerce."—

I hear confidentially from a good source, that President Wilson will spontaneously act in this way in London in two to three days. Perhaps it is therefore advisable to wait so long in Berlin before answering the American note."

---

[81] *Foreign Relations,* 1915, supp., p. 152.

The last sentence does not refer to our conversation. I leave it to your judgment whether I cabled anything which could be construed in the sense indicated by Ambassador Gerard, and deeply regret that my loyal effort to help in a difficult and delicate situation has met with so little success.

Believe me [etc.]   C. DUMBA

_____

763.72/2478

President Wilson to the Secretary of State

WASHINGTON, *27 May, 1915.*

MY DEAR MR. SECRETARY: This is disappointing.[82] House had cabled me a copy of what Gerard had sent him, and I was just about to send it to you.

I cannot help feeling that Gerard might have managed this better, so at least to give us a chance to act as intermediary in some way in an interchange between England and Germany that might have been the beginning of something.

The terms Zimmermann suggests are manifestly impossible of acceptance by England so far as they concern things which, like copper, enter into the manufacture of munitions of war. It looks as if we were again in a blind alley.

What would you think of sending the following to Gerard:

Please point out kindly and unofficially but very earnestly to the Foreign Office that the conditions now prevailing in the marine war zone are rapidly becoming intolerable to the whole world, that their rectification is in the interest of both parties to the present conflict, and that this Government, while it has nothing to propose as between the belligerents, but will confine itself to the protection of its own clear rights, will act with pleasure in conveying any proposals that either the one government or the other has to make for the correction of the present conditions fraught as they are with universal danger.

We can do no more than this; we should, perhaps, do no less.

Gerard has got part of his instructions wrong. We did not say that the new Ministry in England would be willing. We said only that we had reason to hope that they would be. I suppose it would be well to make this clear to him . . .

Faithfully Yours,

W. W.

_____

[82] See telegram No. 2289, May 25, 1915, from the Ambassador in Germany, *Foreign Relations,* 1915, supp., p. 415.

763.72/1859½

The Counselor for the Department of State (Lansing) to the Secretary of State

[WASHINGTON,] *June 1, 1915.*

DEAR MR. SECRETARY: The American note of May 13th[83] was founded on the following principles of law and humanity:

1. Citizens of neutral nationality are entitled to traverse the high seas in merchant vessels of any nationality.
2. They are entitled to be protected from danger to life by the exercise of the belligerent right of visit and by the performance of the belligerent duty of placing passengers and crew of an enemy or neutral merchant vessel in safety in the event that the vessel is destroyed.
3. To destroy a merchant vessel without safeguarding the lives of the persons on board is inhuman and morally wrong.

The German note of May 28th[84] does not admit, deny or even discuss these principles which affect the future as well as the past conduct of the German naval authorities. The note reviews the facts and seeks to raise doubts as to the correctness of those on which this Government relies.

The essential issue between the Governments is one of principle and not of fact. I can see no benefit to be derived from disputing as to the invasion of a right unless both parties agree that the right exists.

The German note appears to have been drafted with the design of drawing this Government into a controversy as to the facts and avoiding the questions of the principles involved.

In my opinion the reply to the German note should state that a discussion of the facts of specific cases would be premature before the rights asserted in the American note had been admitted and assurance given that in future those rights would not be violated; that upon receiving such admission and assurance this Government would consider the conflicting evidence as to the facts; and that the question of liability depends primarily on the principles applicable to the cases which have arisen.

The German note is not expressed in language which evinces a friendly sentiment for the United States. It shows an inflexible purpose to continue a course of action which this Government has frankly asserted to be illegal and inhuman. In view of the tone of the German note I do not think that the reply should be less firm or should repeat the friendly expressions of the note of May 13th, which have been with apparent intention, ignored by the German Government.

Faithfully yours,

ROBERT LANSING

---

[83] *Ibid.,* p. 393.
[84] *Ibid.,* p. 419.

763.72/1860½

The Counselor for the Department of State (*Lansing*) to the Secretary of State

[WASHINGTON,] *June 2, 1915.*

DEAR MR. SECRETARY: In drafting the note of May 13th you will recall that I suggested that the word "unarmed" be changed to "unresisting." There were two reasons for the suggestion.

First. It is entirely legal for a merchant vessel to carry a defensive armament without losing her character of a vessel of commerce. The Department issued a statement to this effect last September,[85] as the law was well settled on that point. The use of the adjective "unarmed," therefore, implied that if <u>armed</u> a vessel changed her status and was subject to different treatment, which practically contradicted the Department's statement.

Second. The adjective "unresisting" appeared broader in application in that it covered not only an armament of the vessel but any use of small arms against a boarding party and any attempt to ram a submarine which had signalled a vessel to stop.

As you will recall you thought the word "unarmed" should be retained, and I think that I was at fault in not explaining my reasons more fully.

The German Government has seized the opportunity in its last note to build up an argument on the allegation that the *Lusitania* was armed and the German Ambassador has sent to the Department several affidavits to support the allegation. While I do not think that these affidavits, if true (which is doubtful) constitute a substantial argument for Germany since they do not show that the German Government knew of the armament on the *Lusitania* before the vessel was sunk, I believe, if opportunity offers, the idea of "unresisting" should be emphasized as the only legitimate reason for attack without visit.

Faithfully yours,

ROBERT LANSING

763.72/1847½

President Wilson to the Secretary of State

WASHINGTON, *2 June, 1915.*

MY DEAR MR. SECRETARY: Would you be kind enough to let me have, for the guidance of my thought on this anxious matter, an outline of the answer you think we should make to the German reply to our note? I feel that I very much need all the counsel I can get,

---

[85] *Foreign Relations,* 1914, supp., p. 611.

and I shall, of course, chiefly value yours. I meant to ask you this yesterday.

I would like very much to have also a similar memorandum from Mr. Lansing, if he will be kind enough to prepare one for me.

With warmest regard,

Faithfully Yours,

WOODROW WILSON

763.72/1847a

The Secretary of State to President Wilson

WASHINGTON, *June 2, 1915.*

MY DEAR MR. PRESIDENT: Responding to your generous request for suggestions as to the reply to be made to the German note, I beg to enclose some suggestions submitted by Mr. Lansing.[86] I have asked him to amplify his statement by giving his opinion as to the points raised in the German note and will send that with comments when it is ready.

You will notice that in proposition one of his note, he leaves out the word "unarmed." You will remember that he suggested the word "unresisting" in place of "unarmed." I have asked him to give such authority as he can find on the distinction between "unarmed" and "unresisting". He has given me a memorandum, dated June 2nd,[87] which I enclose, but he will not be able to prepare today an opinion on the different propositions. I am asking, therefore, that you will allow me to submit a few suggestions and then tonight I will take time to go over the answer and send you a memorandum tomorrow covering all the points raised. I think that Mr. Lansing will by that time be able to complete the memorandum which he has in mind.

There are two thoughts which I beg to submit at this time: First, that we should not feel it necessary to make an immediate answer: (*a*) because it is more important that the answer should be wisely drawn than that it should be speedily sent, (*b*) that time itself is a factor of no mean importance. In our peace plan we have emphasized the advantage of time for investigation and deliberation. The matter with which we are dealing is one of the first magnitude. It involves questions, which have in time passed, furnished an excuse if not a cause for armed conflict. Our note to Germany, while unequivocally stating this Government's position, was couched in friendly language and the German reply is in the same tone. There is apparently no desire on either part for war; and there is always

[86] *Ante,* p. 417.
[87] *Ante,* p. 418.

hope of an amicable adjustment where neither side desires war. So much for the subject of time.

Second: It seems that the note can be properly subjected to legal treatment—that is, we can take up the different points raised by the German Government and, assuming that they are presented in good faith, treat them as we would if it were a case in court, drawing a distinction between material and immaterial propositions. In court, facts which are not material are met by a demurrer, which means that even if the proposition stated is true, it does not affect the issue. If the proposition presents [as] a fact something which if a fact would materially affect the issue, we can then answer the proposition if we believe the statement of fact to be erroneous, or investigate if we are not in the position to deny it. The above is merely a brief suggestion to accompany Mr. Lansing's suggestion.

I do not agree with Mr. Lansing as to the propriety of using the word "unresisting" instead of "unarmed." It seems to me that the character of the vessel is determined, not by whether she resists or not, but by whether she is armed or not. Take, for instance, the cruiser; the fact that she is armed raises the presumption that she will use her arms, therefore, she is not entitled to the same treatment as the unarmed vessel. If we use the word "unresisting" the attacking party would not be entitled to employ force until after the vessel had actually used her arms, which would give the vessel attacked a great advantage over the vessel attacking.

Neither do I agree with him as to the advisability of requiring the German Government [apparent omission] to the principles involved before we discuss the facts of this particular case. It is the custom of the State Department to investigate the facts before taking a position. In the case of the *Lusitania* we stated our position upon a state of facts as we understood them. If a question is raised as to the correctness of the assumed facts, I can see no reason why we should refuse to consider the question of facts. For instance, suppose the German Government had replied that our note was based upon the assumption that certain Americans were drowned by the sinking of the vessel, but that it was Germany's understanding that no Americans were on the vessel and, therefore, none could have been drowned. If that was the fact questioned is there any reason why we should answer "you must first tell us what you would do in case American citizens were drowned and then we will discuss whether they were drowned or not"? If the facts which they set up are not material, that is if we could demur to them, we can so state, but I do not see how we can reasonably refuse to consider a question of fact when it is properly raised.

This I am writing in a hurry and I am simply thinking out loud. I want to go over the note carefully and take it up point by point, and then I shall be pleased to lay before you a more matured suggestion as to its treatment.

With assurances [etc.]   W. J. BRYAN

P. S. I suppose the German Ambassador brought before you the suggestion which he made to me, namely, that this question of fact is raised in order to give the German Government a plausible excuse for accepting our position if the grounds upon which its action was based proved to be erroneous. If Germany is really looking for a way out we cannot do otherwise than assist her. This might not be to the advantage of sensational newspapers, but I am sure that it would meet with unanimous approval throughout the country.

763.72/1847¼

President Wilson to the Secretary of State

WASHINGTON, *2 June, 1915.*

MY DEAR MR. SECRETARY: I am very much obliged to you for the suggestions you have sent me about the note we are to send to Germany, and will welcome anything further you will be good enough to send.

I think that time (though of course not haste) is of the essence in this matter in order that the German Government should be made to feel that we regard it as pressing; for they show not the least inclination or purpose to change their methods even pending this interchange of views.

Faithfully yours,

W. W.

763.72/1847½

President Wilson to the Secretary of State

WASHINGTON, *2 June, 1915.*

MY DEAR MR. SECRETARY: It is interesting and significant how often the German Foreign Office goes over the same ground in different words, and always misses the essential point involved, that England's violation of neutral rights is different from Germany's violation of the rights of humanity.

Faithfully yours,

W. W.

763.72/1849b

The Secretary of State to President Wilson

WASHINGTON, *June 3, 1915, morning.*

MY DEAR MR. PRESIDENT: I have gone over the note carefully [88]
and beg to submit the following suggestions. The first paragraph of
the note, after the one expressing a desire to contribute to the clearing up of the misunderstanding, takes up the cases of the *Cushing* and
Gulflight and explains that there is no intention to injure neutral
vessels and that an apology will be offered and reparation made for
any injury done by mistake. The suggestion is then made that the
investigations made by the parties may be supplemented by the investigation provided for in The Hague Convention. Where they disavow any intention to attack a neutral vessel and offer apology and
reparation, it seems to me that we are justified in accepting such an
answer, except where life is lost. In our note we specifically assert
this principle. In the case of the *Cushing* no lives were lost. In the
case of the *Gulflight* two of the crew jumped overboard and were
drowned. I presume that the manner of death would not change the
rule, since the men jumped with a view to saving their lives and may
be supposed to have acted upon what to them seemed the best means
of escape after the ship was struck.

In the case of the *Gulflight* it may be necessary to consider the fact
that the ship contained contraband of war and was being convoyed by
two British vessels. The German Government reports that the commander of the submarine did not see the flag until after the order
was given to fire the torpedo. Under all the circumstances, it seems
to me, that in this case we can afford to continue investigation with a
view to securing suitable reparation.

The sinking of the *Falaba* presents a different issue. The sinking of the steamer was intentional and the German Government
affirms that the commander had the intention of allowing the passengers and crew "ample opportunity to save themselves." This
indicates a recognition of the rule in regard to dealing with prize
ships. It is asserted that ten minutes were given and that the time
was extended to twenty-three, and then as an excuse for not giving
more time, it is stated that "suspicious steamers were hurrying to the
aid of the *Falaba*." The question raised here is whether the coming
of steamers to the rescue relieved the submarine commander of the
obligation to give sufficient time for the crew to escape. In other
words, is the sinking of the ship a greater importance than the
rescue of the passengers? I shall ask Mr. Lansing to look up the

---

[88] i. e., the German note of May 28, 1915, *Foreign Relations*, 1915, supp., p. 419.

authorities for this question must often have been raised. As the taking of prizes is an old custom, it must frequently have occurred that ships have come to the rescue of a merchantman that has been overtaken. In such case has the attacking ship the right to <u>sink</u> the vessel, passengers and all rather than allow the prize to escape? As we have no information as to the "suspicious steamers", might it not be well to ask further information on this subject, and in so doing ask whether we are to understand that the German Government asserts as a rule of international law, that the right to sink the prize of [*is*] paramount to the obligation to allow the passengers time to escape—that being the real issue presented in the *Falaba* case. If on investigation of authorities, we find that the approach of rescuing vessels does not justify sinking the prize we can so state, an investigation of these facts being in that case unnecessary.

We cannot well object to arbitration where arbitration is possible. Neither can we object to investigation in any case. Our thirty treaties commit us to the doctrine of investigation <u>in all cases</u> and since this form of treaty was offered to Germany and the principle accepted by her (Germany was the twelfth nation to accept the principle) we could not consistently refuse to apply this document [*doctrine?*] to all questions that may arise between us. It seems to me that these treaties not only furnish us the most plausible excuse that we can find for investigation, but leave us no valid excuse for not resorting to the plan. Nothing could more forcibly emphasize the value of this peace plan than the employment of it in this case, and now that we have stated our position and received Germany's reply, the objection urged against making the statement at the time the note was sent would not seem to apply. The use of this idea at this time might even exert a profound influence upon the making of the treaty between belligerent nations at the end of the war. The plan for investigation of all difficulties is the simplest plan that can be found for dealing with disputed questions and, though simple, gives the greatest promise of effectiveness.

When Mr. Lansing finishes his suggestions in regard to the excuses given for the sinking of the *Lusitania*, I will prepare a comment on each one of the excuses. In dealing with the *Lusitania*, it is, in my judgment, necessary to bear in mind that our only concern is with the protection of our people. We have not felt called upon to express an opinion on submarine warfare when other vessels not bearing Americans have been sunk. Whatever views we may have as to the moral character of the means employed by the belligerents, we do not feel it our duty to express opinions merely for the purpose of announcing our views. We could, of course, contribute something towards the formation of public opinion against the belligerent which employs methods which we might denounce and in favor of the belligerent which was the victim of the methods so denounced, but even the most biased among our citizens would hardly feel justified in asking us to make [take?] any position merely for the purpose of helping one side or the other.

It seems to me that, having stated our position without equivocation, we are not only justified but compelled by duty to do what we can to prevent our citizens incurring unnecessary risks. The precedents for this are abundant. Take the case of a riot for instance, the authorities are not absolved from the duty of enforcing order and of punishing those guilty of violence, but as a matter of precaution, they restrain citizens from the exercise of their rights in order to prevent injuries that might otherwise be inflicted unintentionally. The bystander is always in danger when there is shooting upon the street and no government would feel justified in refusing to warn noncombatants away from the dangerous place, merely because the citizens ordinarily have the right to go upon the streets.

For the same reason we advised all American citizens to leave Mexico, not because they did not have a right to stay there, but because we thought it unwise for them to incur the risks involved in staying. We went to the expense of bringing out those who were not able to pay their own way. We did not refuse to give such protection as was possible to those who remained, but we warned them of the extraordinary danger involved in remaining. It seems to me that we cannot well justify a failure to warn American citizens against going into the danger zone on foreign ships—especially on ships which, by carrying ammunition, invite extraordinary risks. It is not sufficient to say that, according to international law, American citizens have a right to go anywhere and that the Government's protection will follow them no matter what risks they take. If the authorities of a city are justified in warning people off the streets of the city in which they reside, surely a nation is justified in warning its citizens off of the water highways which belong to no nation alone, but to all the nations in common.

The German Government pleads as one reason for the attack upon the *Lusitania* that it was carrying 5,400 cases of ammunition "destined for the destruction of brave German soldiers, etc." This ammunition was valued at about $150,000. We have clearly stated the Government's position in regard to the rights of Americans and if it is thought desirable, this right can be restated in language specifically asserting that according to this Government's view of international law, citizens have a right to travel with contraband and that their rights cannot be violated merely because the vessel carries contraband. Still it is not only consistent, but, in my judgment, a matter of imperative duty to not [only] warn our citizens against the exercise of this time [*right?*], but to do whatever lies in our power to prevent the incurring of such risks. Would it not be advisable to reverse the rule by which passenger ships are permitted to carry ammunition? The law says that no ship shall carry gun powder without a license. This has been interpreted by a department order not to apply to gun powder contained in small ammunition. If that order was involved [*invoked?*] and it was interpreted to exclude all ammunition, it would add to the security of passengers.

I believe that Germany is looking for a way out and that, having stated our position unequivocally on the subject of the use of submarines against merchantmen, we would be justified in taking all the precaution possible to prevent our citizens taking risks. If—not for the benefit of Germany but for the benefit of our own people— we announce that passenger ships will not hereafter be allowed to carry ammunition, I think Germany would be very likely to say that no passenger ship would be attacked if assurances were given that it did not carry ammunition. This we could do without invoking any new legislation. In my judgment, you would be justified in going even further and saying that Congress would be asked for legislation authorizing the refusal of clearance to passenger ships carrying contraband. If such a rule was adopted, contraband would be carried on ships without passengers and thus the safety of passenger ships would be assured. But even if you do not feel justified in going so far as to advise the legislation suggested, forbidding the carrying of contraband on passenger ships, I believe the order in regard to ammunition would have a powerful influence upon Germany just at this time, and I feel sure that it would be approved in this country. A person would have to be very much biased in favor of the Allies to insist that ammunition intended for one of the belligerents should be safe-guarded in transit by the lives of American citizens or, for that matter, by the lives of citizens of any country.

I hope you will pardon the length of this note but I am sincerely anxious to render you any service I can in the solution of the difficult problem presented by the *Lusitania* disaster. I recognize, of course, that the responsibility rests upon you and that in the final decision your judgment and your conscience are the only guides upon which you are justified in relying. Those of us who have been honored by being selected as advisors are in duty bound to give you, when desired, the benefit of our judgment and conscience, but none of your associates realize more fully than I that we can only assist insofar as the reason[s] which support our conclusions appeal to you. I know of no other way of discharging the duty of an advisor than to outline the course that I would pursue if the responsibility for action were upon me. The earnestness with which I have spoken in the discussion of these questions measures the depth of my solicitude and the sincerity of my desire that your decisions may, by safeguarding our country's welfare, redound to your own personal credit and to the advantage of our party.

With assurances [etc.]   W. J. BRYAN

763.72/1861½

The Counselor for the Department of State (Lansing) to the
Secretary of State

[WASHINGTON,] *June 3, 1915.*

DEAR MR. SECRETARY: I am submitting a memorandum [89] on the allegations of facts contained in the German note of May 28th. If I had more time, it could be very much abbreviated.

It seems to me that only two of the allegations are relevant to the German defense, namely:

(1) That the *Lusitania* was armed, and
(2) That the commander of the submarine feared the *Lusitania* would ram him.

There is no evidence that the German Government had information that the vessel was armed or information sufficient to found a belief to that effect.

As to the second allegation, the danger of the *Lusitania*, a vessel of over 31000 tons burden, being able to maneuver so as to ram a small swift moving craft like a submarine is too remote to warrant serious consideration. That the commander actually feared being rammed I believe to be false.

The remaining allegations are irrelevant to the defense that the submarine was justified in torpedoing the *Lusitania* without visiting her and without putting her crew and passengers in a place of safety. If the vessel was laden with war supplies, if she flew a neutral flag, if she had Canadian soldiers on board, and if she violated several laws of the United States as to her cargo, these facts in no way affect the question.

While the memorandum reviews these facts, I think that it would be unwise to controvert or discuss them.

Faithfully yours,

ROBERT LANSING

---

[89] Not enclosed with file copy of this letter.

763.72/1849a

The Secretary of State to President Wilson

WASHINGTON, *June 3, 1915, evening.*

MY DEAR MR. PRESIDENT: I am sending you the memorandum prepared by Mr. Lansing.[90] I have not, of course, had an opportunity to examine the authorities upon which he bases his opinion, but the arguments which he presents here are, for the most part, reasonable.

The objection bases [*based*] upon the fact that the *Lusitania* was built by the aid of the Government and is subject to being called into the Government use is, it seems to me, quite effectively answered. I am not sure, however, that I would go as far as he does when he says that if vessel were entirely owned by the British Government and yet put in trade as a merchant vessel, it would occupy exactly the same character as a privately owned merchant vessel.

As to the second argument, namely, that the *Lusitania* had guns on board: It seems to me that that fact would be material if she had any guns other than those made known to us. We have regulations in regard to the size of the guns that can be taken on board a merchant vessel. If it could be shown that the *Lusitania* had concealed guns which were not made known to our authorities, and that the fact was made [known?] to the German Government, it seems to me that it might properly have some bearing, unless we take the position that it is the unresisting ship and not the unarmed ship that is entitled to protection. I think that it might be well for us to state the facts as we understand them and express a willingness to hear any arguments that contradicts this position.

While, as you know, I have felt that we ought to do something to protect our flag from use by belligerents, I do not see that the question of using neutral flags can be raised in this case, because there is no doubt that the *Lusitania* was flying a belligerent flag. What Mr. Lansing says about the impossibility of ramming a submarine with a ship the size of the *Lusitania* would seem to be quite conclusive, although if it is true that secret instructions have been issued instructing merchant vessels to adopt, in regard to submarines, a course different from that occupied by merchant vessels in resisting the attack of armed cruisers, that fact ought to be taken into consideration. In other words, if a submarine is to be bound by the rules applicable to merchantmen, then the merchantman ought also be bound by the rules applicable when the merchantmen are attacked by a cruiser.

It seems to me that the question of ammunition is the most serious one raised and I do not share Mr. Lansing's view that we can ignore

---

[90] See *supra*, footnote 89.

entirely the question raised as to whether our law was violated. Even if we say that the enforcement of our laws must be entrusted to our own officials and not to commanders of submarine[s] of belligerents, still we must consider the moral effect of a position which would make us seem to acquiesce in the carrying of American citizens with ammunition in violation of law. I feel that our position would be very much strengthened by affirmative action on the side which would for the future prevent the carrying of ammunition by passenger ships, and, as I said in my note of this morning, which accompanies this, I believe it would have a very beneficial influence, both on public opinion in this country and on the German Government.

With assurances [etc.]   W. J. Bryan

841.857 L 97/166½

The Collector of Customs of the Port of New York (Malone) to the Secretary of the Treasury (McAdoo)[91]

[NEW YORK,] *June 4, 1915.*

SIR: I beg to make the following reply to your letter of June 1st, 1915, as to the conditions, circumstances, character of equipment, passengers and cargo of the steamship *Lusitania* when she sailed from the Port of New York on May 1, 1915. You submitted eight questions, which I shall answer in the order of your submission:

1. When the *Lusitania* sailed from New York on her last trip to England did she or not have guns on board, mounted on the underdecks and masked?

When the steamship *Lusitania* sailed from the Port of New York on May 1, 1915, on her last trip to England, she did not have any guns of any calibre or description on any deck or decks, on her stern or bow, mounted or unmounted, masked or unmasked. This statement is made of my own official knowledge and is based upon the statements and affidavits of James G. Ross and Israel Finkelstein, United States Inspectors of Customs at the Port of New York, who had charge of discharging the cargo of the steamship *Lusitania* during her last stay in this port; John F. Hoey, United States Inspector of Customs at the Port of New York; William J. Smith, United States Inspector of Customs at the Port of New York, and a member of the Neutrality Squad; Frederick A. Dowsey, a supervising officer of the members of the Neutrality Squad; and Captain David J. Roberts, the Marine and Pier Superintendent of the Cunard Steamship Company.

---

[91] The text of this letter is from an authenticated copy on file with the Mixed Claims Commission, United States and Germany. The summary of the manifest of the *Lusitania* is attached to the letter, but appears not to have been included in the authentication.

These affidavits are affixed under the heading marked "Group A." [92] All of these men examined the steamship *Lusitania* and testify that she was without guns, arms or armament. In addition I, myself, boarded the steamship *Lusitania* on the morning of May 1, 1915, within one hour of the time of her actual departure and, after an inspection of her open bow deck and open stern deck, I can testify of my own personal knowledge that there were no guns of any character, mounted or unmounted, masked or unmasked, nor any blocks or blocking, or marked spaces on which guns might be mounted, on the said bow or stern decks, or the open promenade deck, around which I walked on the ship.

2. Did the *Lusitania* on said trip, to your knowledge, have Canadian troops on board?

The *Lusitania* did not have Canadian troops or troops of any nationality on board when she left the Port of New York on May 1, 1915. Moreover, the *Lusitania* carried no group or groups, no body or organization of passengers as such, with or without uniforms; and if any individual reservists of any nationality sailed on the *Lusitania* on this trip they did so as individuals, paying their own passage and receiving their own individual tickets. The Canadian troops, under my observation, are noteworthy for their military appearance. There were no individuals, and no group or groups of men of any particular military bearing or appearance among the passengers on the *Lusitania* sailing on this trip, which would indicate the presence of any individuals or groups of military. This statement is made of my own official and personal knowledge, and my official knowledge is based upon the statements and affidavits of James G. Ross, United States Inspector of Customs at the Port of New York; Israel Finkelstein, United States Inspector of Customs at the Port of New York; William J. Smith, United States Inspector of Customs at the Port of New York and member of the Neutrality Squad; Captain David J. Roberts, the Marine and Pier Superintendent of the Cunard Steamship Company; and Charles P. Sumner, General Agent of the Cunard Steamship Company, who had charge of the inspection of all passengers before they were permitted to board the *Lusitania* on the day she last sailed from the Port of New York. These affidavits are affixed under the heading marked "Group B." [92]

3. Did the *Lusitania*, to your knowledge, have, on earlier occasions or on any previous trip, Canadian troops on board?

The *Lusitania* has not carried on any trip since the European war began, Canadian troops or troops of any other nationality on board

---

[92] Not printed.

when leaving the Port of New York. This statement is made of my own official knowledge, and is based upon the statements and affidavits of William J. Smith, United States Inspector of Customs at the Port of New York and member of the Neutrality Squad; John F. Hoey, United States Inspector of Customs at the Port of New York and who, from August 7, 1914 to February 15, 1915, was a member of the Neutrality Squad and detailed to the Cunard Piers; Captain David J. Roberts, the Marine and Pier Superintendent of the Cunard Steamship Company; and Charles P. Sumner, General Agent of the Cunard Steamship Company. These affidavits are affixed under the heading marked "Group B." [94]

4. Did the *Lusitania* on her last trip have munitions of war on board? If so, state exactly what said munitions consisted of.

Yes; the *Lusitania* on her last trip from the Port of New York had on board 4200 cases of metallic cartridges, three cases shell castings, 18 cases fuses, 1250 cases shrapnel, and one package containing an empty high explosive shell, cut in half. This statement is made of my own official knowledge, based upon the sworn manifests filed by the individual shippers of these consignments at the Custom House, and vised by the proper clerks of the Marine Division at the Custom House; and is based also upon the supervision and report of William J. Smith, United States Inspector of Customs at the Port of New York and member of the Neutrality Squad.

5. Did the *Lusitania* have on board on said trip 5,400 cases of ammunition? If so, to whom were they consigned?

The *Lusitania* had on board on the said trip, 5468 cases of ammunition. The Remington Arms-Union Metallic Cartridge Co. shipped 4200 cases of metallic cartridges, consigned to the Remington Arms Co., London, of which the ultimate consignee was the British Government. G. W. Sheldon & Co. shipped three lots of fuses of 6 cases each, and 1250 cases of shrapnel, consigned to the Deputy Director of Ammunition Stores, Woolwich, England. W. R. Grace & Co., for the Ingersoll-Rand Company, shipped three cases of shell castings, consigned to Superintendent of Experiments, Shoeburyness, England. Adams Express Company shipped one package of empty high explosive shell, cut in half, consigned to R. Gordon Blackie, Queen Ann's Chambers, Westminster, London, England, who is the British representative of the Adams Express Company in London. The said 4200 cases of metallic cartridges, shipped by the Remington Arms-Union Metallic Cartridge Company, were of the calibre of .303, Mark 7, loaded with either Hivel #2 powder manufactured by the Hercules Powder Company, or Du Pont #19, manufactured by the Du Pont

---

[94] Not printed.

De Nemours Powder Company, packed 20 in a box without clips, 1,000 to a case, and containing 5 pounds of powder to a thousand cartridges. The three lots of fuses of 6 cases each, and the 1250 cases of shrapnel, shipped by G. W. Sheldon & Company, were shipped for the Bethlehem Steel Company of South Bethlehem, Pa. These fuses contained no explosives, and the 1250 cases of shrapnel were packed at South Bethlehem, Pa. and contained no fuses and no explosives of any description whatsoever. The three cases of shell castings, shipped by W. R. Grace & Company for the Ingersoll-Rand Company, consisted of 12 sample shells of a calibre of 5 inch, weighing 408 pounds net and 489 pounds gross, unprimed and unloaded. These shells were packed at Phillipsburg, New Jersey, on April 30th, 1915, and had no ammunition or explosive substance contained in them or in the packages which contained them. The one package of empty high explosive shell, shipped by the Adams Express Company to its British representative, was a single shell cut into sections and containing no explosive.

6. If you answer "Yes" to question 5, state the rules or regulations of the Department under and by virtue of which the *Lusitania* was permitted to carry said cases of ammunition.

The steamship *Lusitania* was permitted to carry the above said cases of ammunition by virtue of a ruling of the Department of Commerce and Labor, dated May 2, 1911, in interpretation and limitation of Section 4472 of the Revised Statutes of the United States. This ruling reads as follows:

(B) (41923)

"DEPARTMENT OF COMMERCE AND LABOR
STEAMBOAT-INSPECTION SERVICE
WASHINGTON

Circular Letter 8516 MAY 2, 1911.

U. S. Supervising and Local Inspectors,
Chief Officers of Customs, and others concerned.

GENTLEMEN:
Tests of the handling of small arms ammunition, and the rough usage to which it may be subjected without risk of danger from fire or explosion, having been witnessed by representatives of this Department, you are advised that the results of these tests justify beyond doubt the conclusion that small arms ammunition may be transported without restriction on steamers carrying passengers, and that it need not be confined to the magazine of the vessel as heretofore required, with the exception that large calibre blank black powder ammunition should be stowed as previously required in the magazine.
All rulings previously made upon the transportation of small arms ammunition, inconsistent with the ruling now made, are hereby revoked.
Respectfully,

GEO. UHLER
Supervising Inspector General, D. N. H.

Approved:
CHARLES NAGEL
Secretary."

7. State whether or not the *Lusitania* on her last voyage carried any explosives of any kind or character. If so, state in detail the character of such explosives, the quantity thereof, when and where loaded upon the ship, and to whom consigned.

The *Lusitania* on her last voyage carried no explosives of any kind or character. The ammunition above set forth as part of the *Lusitania's* cargo on said voyage did not contain explosives within the interpretation of our statutes and regulations as interpreted and promulgated by the Department of Commerce and Labor in the ruling cited above in the answer to question 6.

8. State what examination was made of the ship's manifest before she proceeded on her last voyage, and what steps were taken to verify the same.

When Captain W. T. Turner of the *Lusitania* came to the Custom House on Friday, April 30, 1915, to get clearance for the steamship *Lusitania*, he went to the Marine Division and took the usual master's oath that the manifest which he presented contained a full, just and true account of all goods, wares and merchandise which were actually laden or to be laden on board the steamship *Lusitania*. At this time the acting deputy collector, John Farrell, examined the manifest presented by Captain Turner to ascertain if the fixed preliminary steps had been taken, namely, if the clerks had examined the manifest page by page, and item by item, for the purpose of ascertaining whether or not there were any arms or ammunition included in the cargo and, if so, whether or not the clerks had made such notation in red ink at the side of each such item, so that it might be apparent immediately to the head or acting head of the Marine Division. To see also if the check of the payment of fees in the Cashier's office was attached, and to be certain that all the oaths were properly signed by the master of the vessel. Acting deputy collector Farrell found that the manifest had gone through the usual routine and bore all the checks of all the clerks who were charged with the duty of examining this manifest. This statement is made of my own official knowledge, based upon the statements and affidavits of John Farrell, clerk and acting deputy collector of the First, or Marine Division of the Collector's Office, Customs Service, Port of New York; Fayette T. Brimmer, clerk of the Marine Division of the Collector's Office, Port of New York; and John F. Morrissey, clerk of the Marine Division of the Collector's Office, Port of New York. These affidavits are affixed under the heading marked "Group C." [95]

It is practically a physical impossibility to examine the contents of each case and package that is put aboard or attempted to be put

---

[95] Not printed.

on board each outgoing ship from this port. During the early stages of this European war, I personally gave great thought and attention to the question of verifying the contents of packages and cases to be shipped on outgoing steamers. The particular purpose of such examination would be to ascertain if the contents of the package corresponded with the description of the contents in the sworn manifest. I called a conference here at the Custom House of the larger shippers at this port, together with the more experienced men of the Customs Service here and, after a long discussion and exchange of views, it was decided that it would be entirely impracticable to make a physical examination of each package or case going into the cargo of an outgoing ship. The reasons upon which the judgment of impracticability were based were that the shipments of closed cases at that time, and all the greater now because of the increased export trade, were so tremendous that it would literally take an army of men to open and verify the contents of goods in closed cases, replace the goods and reseal the cases. The expense to the Government would make it almost prohibitive. The delay to shippers and steamship companies would make it an untold hardship and inconvenience. The damage to goods would be immeasurable. Any one of these reasons, in the judgment of the conference, would be sufficient to make impossible and impracticable a plan for the physical examination of closed cases of outgoing cargoes. I was therefore obliged to abandon the project, except to the extent that orders were issued to the Customs officials, and particularly to the members of the Neutrality Squad, to report at once to me any circumstance of a suspicious nature with respect to any cargo, or any part of a cargo; in which case a complete and extensive examination and verification of the contents of the particular consignment of goods and cargo would immediately be made by the Customs officials. This has been the utmost that could be done under the circumstances at this port.

In reply to your inquiry for any information additional to that brought forth by your specific questions, I beg to state that the steamship *Lusitania*, in her construction, was so built that certain sections were reinforced, and in her structure at certain points, bases were laid for mounting guns of a 6 inch calibre. The said bases were riveted to the steel structure of the ship but were entirely covered over at all times by the wooden planking of the decks. The reason why the deck of the *Lusitania* was built with provision for guns was that if the Admiralty should call the *Lusitania* from the merchant service to the service of the British navy, she would be more readily adaptable to naval purposes. Consequently, if any guns had been mounted, or there was any intention to mount guns on the *Lusitania* on her open bow or open stern deck, these guns would have been mounted on the stable gun bases provided for the purpose, and not upon any blocks or blocking or other alleged paraphernalia for this purpose. This statement is merely made to indicate the improbable character of any testimony which states that any guns were mounted on the bow or stern of the *Lusitania* on wooden blocks or blocking.

In order effectively to carry out in the Port of New York the mandate of the President's Proclamation of Neutrality, and the general orders issued from time to time by the Treasury Department, I formed what has been called the "Neutrality Squad," a squad composed of men picked out of the ranks of the Inspectors of Customs for character, alertness, faithfulness to duty and intelligence. To this squad I have assigned the particular duty of specific and special examination of all ships and cargoes to ascertain any possible violation of neutrality. After the Neutrality Squad was formed, each man assigned to neutrality duty was given a copy of the following specific and written instructions, viz.:

1. To report any repairs or alterations showing any intent to convert a merchant vessel into a vessel of war.
2. To report the loading on board, the unpacking or the mounting of guns.
3. To report the storing on board of unusual quantities of coal, except on vessels usually employed as colliers.
4. To report the painting of a vessel in the shade of dull gray, usually known as "war color."
5. To report the transportation of recruits, troops or reservists in bulk or organization.
6. To report any attempt to ship arms or other munitions of war; and
7. To report any single act or circumstance which would arouse any suspicion as to the legitimate purpose for which the vessel or her cargo was intended.

It has been under these instructions and through the medium of this Neutrality Squad that the information about the steamer *Lusitania* had been gathered, which is herewith respectfully submitted.

Respectfully yours,

DUDLEY FIELD MALONE

[Annex]

Summary of the Manifest of the S. S. "Lusitania," April 30, 1915

LIVERPOOL

Sheet Brass	lbs	260000	$49565
Copper	"	111762	20955
Copper Wire	"	58465	11000
Cheese	"	217157	33334

Summary of the Manifest of the S. S. "Lusitania," April 30, 1915—
Continued

LIVERPOOL—Continued

Beef	lbs.	342165	30995
Butter	"	43614	8730
Lard	"	40003	4000
Bacon	"	185040	18502
Casings	pkgs	10	150
Cd. Meat	cs	485	1373
" Veget.	"	2488	744
Cutlery	pkgs	63	10492
Shoes	"	10	726
Tongues	"	10	224
Oysters	bbls	205	1025
Lub. Oil	"	25	1129
Hardware	Pkgs	31	742
Leather	"	30	16870
Furs	"	349	119220
Notions	"	2	974
Confy	"	655	2823
Silverware	"	8	700
Precious Stones	Pkgs	32	13350
Jewelry	"	2	251
Belting	"	2	1243
Auto. Veh. & Pts.	"	5	616
Elect. Mtl.	"	8	2464
Machy	"	2	1386
Steel & Mfs.	"	8	354
Copper "	"	138	21000
Aluminum "	"	144	6000
Brass "	"	95	6306
Iron "	"	33	3381
Old Rubber	"	7	341
Military Goods	"	189	66221
Dry "	"	238	19086
I. R. "	"	1	131
Wire "	"	16	771
Reclaimed Rubber	"	10	347
Staves	pcs	2351	200
Brushes	pkgs	4	342
Ammunition	cs	1271	47624
Salt	pkgs	100	125
Bronze Powder	cs	50	1000

BRISTOL

Dental Goods	pkgs	7	2319
Steel & Mfg	"	4	331

DUBLIN

Engines & Mtl.	pkgs	2	140

GLASGOW

Notions	pkgs	1	479

KOBE

Liquid Glue	pkgs	2	124

Summary of the Manifest of the S. S. "Lusitania," April 30, 1915—
Continued

LONDON

Books	pkgs	9	845
Drugs	"	8	458
Wool yarn	"	1	105
Shoes	cs	1	274
Bronze Powder	"	16	887(?)
Motor Cycles & Pts.	pkgs	8	1650
Paintings	"	1	2312
Furs	"	1	750
Printed Matter	"	14	147
Leather	cs	89	31517
Cartridges & Ammunition	"	4200	152400
Films	"	1	100
Machine Patterns	pkgs	3	1500
Machy	"	6	1149
Electrical "	"	1	1616
Watch Mtl.	"	2	2489
Elect. "	"	4	3200
Auto. Veh. & Pts.	"	4	340
Optical Goods	"	1	1313
Dental "	"	10	3962

MANCHESTER

Sewing Mchs, & Pts.	Pkgs	20	360

763.72/1849c

The Secretary of State to President Wilson

WASHINGTON, *June 4, 1915.*

MY DEAR MR. PRESIDENT: Senator Martin of Virginia and Congressman Flood called this afternoon and asked me to communicate to you the reason of their call. Senator Martin was the spokesman but Mr. Flood concurred in what he said. The Senator spoke with great earnestness to the effect that this country does not want war with Germany and that it expects you to find a way out that will not involve hostilities. He spoke of the question of passports and expressed the opinion that while the demand for or giving of passports is not necessarily an act of war, that it is so near it that it involved risks that ought not to be taken. He said that he had talked with three senators whom he had found in town and that they were all of the same opinion as he is and would vote against a declaration of war, if the subject were presented. Mr. Flood made the same remark in regard to the House—that he was sure that they would vote against such a declaration. They both expressed themselves as believing that the *Lusitania* case did not justify a resort to hostilities and that they felt sure the country did not regard the matter as one that would justify war. I asked them to put their views in writing, that I might be sure to submit them accurately and they said they would, but as they may not have time to send me the letter this evening, I am writing you the substance of their conversation from memory.

With assurances [etc.] W. J. BRYAN

763.72/1849d

The Secretary of State to President Wilson

WASHINGTON, *June 5, 1915.*

MY DEAR MR. PRESIDENT: The fact that the note to Germany has not yet been completed encourages me to trespass upon your time for a moment to present again three matters which, to my mind, are necessary to insure us against war with Germany—

First, A reference to the plan embodied in our thirty treaties— the principle of which has been accepted by Germany. Her mention of arbitration opens the way and makes the suggestion easy, if it does not in fact compel the suggestion. It will ensure a peaceful settlement of this controversy. And we can not forget that this peace plan for investigation in all cases was endorsed by the Senate and is now in force with Great Britain, France, and Russia.

Second, Steps to prevent passenger ships from carrying ammunition. This is referred to by Germany. Action ought, in my judgment, to be taken before the reply is sent.

Third, Before we send another note to Germany I think we should make a renewed protest to Great Britain against interference with our trade with neutrals. These three propositions have been under consideration before. The first was decided upon—that is the idea was to be given to the public and communicated to Germany, but you were dissuaded by some thing that you heard. The second is thought by the Attorney General to be possible—and even if it could not be accomplished as a matter of fact the same end could be reached almost as well by advice such as was given to Americans in Mexico. The third suggestion was about to be carried out but you were dissuaded by a message from Mr. House.

I beg to renew the suggestions most urgently believing as I do, that without them the note as you outlined it at cabinet meeting would be likely to cause a rupture of diplomatic relations and this might rush us into war in spite of anything we could do. If the initiative were with us I would not fear war, for I am sure you do not want it, but when the note is sent it is Germany's next move—if the note causes her to act in an unfriendly way it may cause conditions here that will increase the difficulties of our position. This may be our last chance to speak for peace, for it will be much harder to propose investigation after some unfriendly act than now.

Pardon me for presenting these suggestions so earnestly but I am sure that the sober judgment of the people will not sustain any word or act that provokes war—they will support you if war comes but they will do all in their power to prevent war, and I fully share their desire and purpose in this respect.

With assurances [etc.]   W. J. BRYAN

763.72/1849½

President Wilson to the Secretary of State

WASHINGTON, *5 June, 1915.*

MY DEAR MR. SECRETARY: I hope that you realize how hard it goes with me to differ with you in judgment about such grave matters as we are now handling. You always have such weight of reason, as well as such high motives, behind what you urge that it is with deep misgiving that I turn from what you press upon me.

I am inclined to think that we ought to take steps, as you suggest, to prevent our citizens from travelling on ships carrying munitions of war, and I shall seek to find the legal way to do it. I fear that, whatever it may be best to do about that, it is clearly impossible to act before the new note goes to Germany.

I am sorry to say that, study as I may the way to do it without hopelessly weakening our protest, I cannot find a way to embody in our note the principle of long discussion of a very simple state of facts; and I think that our object with England can be gained better by not sending a note in connection with this one than by sending it; and, after all, it is our object and the relief of our trade that we wish to accomplish.

I recast the note last night. I hope you will think a little better of it.

I would be very much obliged if you would go over it for substance, making any suggestions that may occur to you, and that you will ask Mr. Lansing to go over it for form and validity of statement and claim.

With the warmest regard, and with a very solemn and by no means self-confident sense of deep responsibility.

Cordially and faithfully yours,

WOODROW WILSON

763.72/1862½

The Counselor for the Department of State (Lansing) to the Secretary of State

[WASHINGTON,] *June 5, 1915.*

DEAR MR. SECRETARY: I have received the draft of the note to Germany, prepared by the President,[96] and also your statement of his

---

[96] For this draft, embodying Mr. Lansing's suggested changes, see p. 441; for text of the note as sent, see *Foreign Relations,* 1915, supp., p. 436.

request that I should go over the note for form and validity of statement and claim.

This note is of such grave importance to this country that I do not feel I can comply with the President's request properly at the Department, or within a short time. I desire to take the draft home with me and study it tonight and tomorrow, unless the President is desirous that it should be sent tomorrow. I think, in justice to myself, as well as to my duty to you, that I should have this time for consideration of the matters submitted to me by the President.

Faithfully yours,

ROBERT LANSING

763.72/1854½

President Wilson to the Secretary of State

WASHINGTON, 7 June, 1915.

MY DEAR MR. SECRETARY: This expression of the views of Senator Martin and Representative Flood has made a deep impression on me, and I have no doubt echoes a great part of public opinion.[97] I wish with all my heart that I saw a way to carry out the double wish of our people, to maintain a firm front in respect of what we demand of Germany and yet do nothing that might by any possibility involve us in the war.

Faithfully yours,

W. W.

763.72/1780½

President Wilson to the Counselor for the Department of State (Lansing)

WASHINGTON, June 7, 1915.

MY DEAR LANSING: Thank you for letting me see this.[98] I have no doubt that it interprets a very large element of opinion in the country, but I do not think that anything that we are doing would exclude temperate action.

Faithfully yours,

WOODROW WILSON

---

[97] See letter of June 4, 1915, from the Secretary of State to President Wilson, p. 436.

[98] Mr. Lansing had forwarded to President Wilson a telegram from Mr. Daniel F. Kellogg, of New York, in which arbitration of the *Lusitania* case was suggested and in which it was stated that "people here would be strongly adverse to any government action that would make war possible on any grounds that have been disclosed to date." (File No. 763.72/1779½.)

763.72/1866½

The Counselor for the Department of State (Lansing) to the
Secretary of the Treasury (McAdoo)

[WASHINGTON,] *June 7, 1915.*

DEAR MR. SECRETARY: I enclose a paragraph embodying your oral suggestion made this evening which might find a place in the note to Germany.

I am not entirely convinced that it is expedient, but it is certainly worthy of careful consideration as it leaves the door open for further discussion and it will be Germany's responsibility if it is closed.

Cordially yours,

[File copy not signed]

[Enclosure]

Proposed Paragraph for Insertion in Note to Germany

The Government of the U. S. nevertheless realizes that a belligerent ought not to be deprived of the use of the submarine in its efforts to interrupt commerce with the enemy provided the operations of the submarine do not jeopardize human life or result in the indiscriminate destruction of neutral property. The Govt. of the U. S. is willing, therefore, to consider any suggestion, which the German Imperial Government may see fit to make, looking toward a modification of the existing rules of international law governing naval warfare applicable to the use of submarines which will efficiently safeguard the lives of persons and neutral property on merchant vessels which are intercepted on the high seas.

763.72/1865½

The Counselor for the Department of State (Lansing) to the
Secretary of State

[WASHINGTON,] *June 7, 1915.*

DEAR MR. SECRETARY: I enclose herewith the President's draft of a note to Germany with suggested changes indicated by underlining and parentheses.[99] The underlined portions indicate new matter or changed phraseology, and portions within parentheses indicate suggested omissions. I enclose also a memorandum [1] on certain of the suggestions which require explanation.

Faithfully yours,

ROBERT LANSING

---

[99] Actually, brackets were used by Mr. Lansing rather than parentheses. For text of the note as sent, see *Foreign Relations*, 1915, supp., p. 436.
[1] Not printed.

THE WORLD WAR: PERIOD OF AMERICAN NEUTRALITY 441

[Enclosure]

Draft Instruction to the Ambassador in Germany (Gerard)

You are instructed to deliver textually the following note to the Minister of Foreign Affairs.

In compliance with Your Excellency's request I did not fail to transmit to my Government immediately upon their receipt your note of May 28th [2] in reply to my note of May 15th [*13th*][3] and your supplementary note of June 1st [4] setting forth the conclusions so far as reached by the Imperial German Government concerning the attacks on the American steamers *Cushing* and *Gulflight*. I am now instructed by my Government to communicate the following in reply:

[Allow me to acknowledge the receipt of your note of the twenty-eighth of May, transmitted through the Honourable James W. Gerard, Ambassador of the United States of America near the Imperial German Government, in answer to the note I had the honour to address to the Imperial German Government on the thirteenth of May on behalf of the Government of the United States, and also the receipt of your supplementary note of the first of June communicating the conclusions of the Imperial German Government, so far as arrived at, concerning the attacks on the steamers *Cushing* and *Gulflight*.]

The Government of the United States notes with gratification the full recognition by the Imperial German Government, in discussing the cases of these two steamers, of the principle of the freedom of all parts of the open sea to neutral ships and the frank willingness of the Imperial German Government to acknowledge and meet its liability where the fact of attack upon neutral ships "which have not been guilty of any hostile act" by German [those in control of its] aircraft or vessels of war is satisfactorily established; and the Government of the United States will in due [of] course lay before the Imperial German Government, as it requests, full information concerning the attack on the steamer *Cushing*.

The Government of the United States cannot turn away from the discussion of these cases without again very earnestly calling the attention of the Imperial German Government to the fact, that its attempt [the policy of the Imperial German Government in seeking] to establish a war zone upon the high seas which neutral vessels are warned that they will enter at their peril, itself constitutes a very grave and [quite] unprecedented infringement upon the freedom of the seas and the rights of neutral nations and their citizens,

---

[2] *Foreign Relations*, 1915, supp., p. 419.
[3] *Ibid.*, p. 393.
[4] *Ibid.*, p. 431.

and, [is sure] if persisted in, will [to] continue to be fruitful of fatal and tragical mistakes such as these of the *Gulflight* and *Cushing*. This Government [It] therefore urges upon the Imperial German Government the necessity for a reconsideration of the whole situation. The submarine attack upon the steamer *Gulflight* resulted not merely in damage to the vessel but also in the loss of the lives [life] of two of her seamen, and for [such] loss of life in such circumstances no adequate compensation is possible. The freedom of the seas, for which the Imperial German Government is contending, cannot be vindicated by [a] violations of that freedom on the part of that great Government [itself].

With regard to the sinking [case] of the steamer *Falaba*, by [upon] which an American citizen lost his life, the Government of the United States is surprised to find the Imperial German Government contending that an effort on the part of a merchantman to escape capture and secure assistance alters the obligation of the officer seeking to make the capture in respect of the safety of the lives of those on board the merchantman although the vessel had ceased her attempt to escape when torpedoed. These are not new circumstances. They have been in the minds of statesmen and of international jurists [lawyers] throughout the development of naval warfare, and the Government of the United States does not understand that they have ever been held to alter the principles of humanity upon which it has insisted. Nothing but actual forcible resistance or continued efforts to escape by flight when ordered to stop for the purpose of visit on the part of the merchantman has ever been held to forfeit the lives of her passengers or crew. The Government of the United States, however, does not understand that the Imperial German Government is [as] seeking in this case to relieve itself of liability but only intends to set [as setting] forth the circumstances which led the commander of the submarine to allow himself to be hurried into the course which he took.

Your Excellency's note, in discussing the loss of American lives resulting from the sinking of [on] the steamship *Lusitania*, adverts [speaks] at some length to [of] certain information which the Imperial German Government has received with regard to the character and outfit of that vessel, and [which] Your Excellency expresses the fear that this information [fears] may not have been brought to the attention of the Government of the United States. It is asserted in the note that [speaks of] the *Lusitania* was undoubtedly [as having been] equipped with masked guns, supplied with trained gunners and special ammunition, transporting troops from Canada, carrying a cargo not permitted under the laws of the United States to a vessel also carrying passengers, and serving, in virtual effect, as an auxiliary to the [armed] naval forces of Great Britain. Fortunately these are matters concerning which the Government of the United States is in a position to give the Imperial German Government authoritative information. Of the [Such] facts asserted in Your Excellency's note, if true, the Government of the United States would have been [is] bound to take official cognizance [of] in performing its recognized duty as a neutral power and in enforcing its national laws. It was its duty to see to it that the *Lusitania* was not armed for offensive action, that she was not serving as a transport, that she did not carry a cargo prohibited by the statutes [laws] of the United States, and that, if in fact she was a naval vessel [in the service of the navy] of Great Britain, she should not receive clearance [papers] as a merchantman; and of course it performed that duty and enforced its statutes with scrupulous vigilance through its regularly constituted officials. It is able, therefore, to assure the Imperial German Government that it has been misinformed.

Whatever may be the contentions of the Imperial German Government regarding the carriage of contraband of war on board the *Lusitania* or regarding the explosion of that material by the torpedo, it need only be said that these contentions are irrelevant to the question of the legality of the methods used by the German naval authorities in sinking the vessel.

But the sinking of these [this] passenger ships involves principles of humanity which throw into the background any special circumstances of detail that may be thought to affect [have affected] the case, principles which lift it, as the Imperial German Government will no doubt be quick to recognize and acknowledge, out of the class of ordinary subjects of diplomatic discussion [diplomacy] or of international controversy [obligation]. Whatever be the other facts, the principal fact is that a great steamer, primarily and chiefly a conveyance for passengers, and carrying more than a thousand souls who had no part or lot in the conduct of the war, was torpedoed and sunk [sent to the bottom] without so much as a challenge or a warning, and that men, women, and children were sent to their death in circumstances unparalleled in modern warfare. The fact that more than one hundred American citizens were among those who perished makes it the duty of the Government of the United States to speak of these things and once more, with solemn emphasis, to call the attention of the Imperial German Government to the grave responsibility which the Government of the United States conceives that it has [it to have] incurred in this tragic occurrence. [Only her actual resistance to capture or refusal to stop when ordered to do so for the purpose of visit could have afforded the commander of the submarine any justification for so much as putting the lives of those on board the ship in jeopardy. This principle the Government of the United States understands the explicit instructions issued on August 3, 1914, by [of] the Imperial German Admiralty to its commanders at sea to have recognized and embodied, as do the naval codes of all other nations, and upon it every traveller and seaman had a right to depend.] [5]

[The Government of the United States cannot too often or too earnestly draw the attention of the Imperial German Government back to this, its chief and only contention] [5a] and to the indisputable principle upon which that responsibility [it] rests. The Government of the United States [It conceives that it] is contending for something much greater than mere rights of property or privileges of commerce. It is contending for nothing less high and sacred than the rights of humanity, which every government [nation] honours itself in respecting and which no government [nation] can with honour resign on behalf of those under its care and authority. No case could more vividly or thoroughly demonstrate than does this case of the *Lusitania* the overwhelming argument against the use of submarines against merchantmen where visit and search are impracticable and where the humane rules [principles] of international law are impossible of application. Only her actual resistance to capture or refusal to stop when ordered to do so for the purpose of visit could have afforded the commander of the submarine any justification for so much as putting the lives of those on board the ship in jeopardy. This principle the Government of the United States understands the explicit instructions issued on August 3, 1914, by [of] the Imperial German Admiralty to its commanders at sea to have recognized and embodied, as do the naval codes of all other nations, and upon it every traveller and seaman had a right to depend. It is upon this principle of humanity as well as of law founded upon this principle that the United States must stand and stand without compromise or abatement of its rights.

The Government of the United States is happy to observe that Your Excellency's note closes with the intimation that the Imperial German Government is willing, now as before, to accept the good offices of the United States in an attempt to come to an understanding with the Government of Great Britain by which the character and conditions of the war upon the sea may be changed. The Government of the United States would consider it a privilege thus to serve its friends and the world. It stands ready at any time to convey to either government any intimation or suggestion the other

---

[5] A marginal notation to the two preceding sentences reads, "Transferred to page 10." See line 15 of the following paragraph.

[5a] Apparently this was included in the marginal notation as part of the matter to be transferred to page 10 of the draft, but was not transferred.

may be willing to have it convey and cordially invites the Imperial German Government to make use of its services in this way at its convenience. The whole world is concerned in anything that may bring about even a partial accommodation of interests or in any way mitigate the terrors of the present distressing conflict.

[In the meantime, whatever arrangement [action] may happily be made [taken as] between the parties to the war, and whatever may in the opinion of the Imperial German Government have been the provocation or the circumstantial justification for the past acts of its commanders at sea, the Government of the United States confidently looks to see the justice and humanity of the Government of Germany vindicated in all cases where Americans have been wronged or their rights as neutrals invaded.]

The Government of the United States therefore very earnestly and very solemnly renews the representations of its note transmitted to the German Imperial Government on the fifteenth [of the thirteenth] of May, and relies in these representations [not only] upon the principles of humanity and the universally recognized understandings of international law [but also upon the explicit covenants of the treaty of 1828 between the United States and the Kingdom of Prussia.] [6]

763.72/1854a

The Secretary of State to President Wilson

WASHINGTON, *June 7, 1915.*

MY DEAR MR. PRESIDENT: I am sending you the suggestions made by Mr. Lansing in the form of a re-draft of the note,[7] together with a letter from Mr. Lansing [7] explaining the changes so that the re-draft can be intelligently read. While I have expressed to you orally and in former communications my views as to the line that should be followed, I feel that I owe it to you to offer some suggestions in regard to the text as you desire it to be. In the paragraph beginning near the top of page 3,[8] you use the *Cushing* and *Gulflight* incidents as a justification for condemning the establishment of a war zone. It seems to me that, in view of the fact that we accept the offer made by the German Government and accept apologies and reparation in case of attack of neutral vessels by mistake, it is an unnecessary enlargement of our demand which really weakens the demand itself. Our interest in the war zone ceases to be acute if the right for which we ask, namely, that time will be allowed for

---

[6] Hunter Miller (ed.), *Treaties and Other International Acts of the United States of America*, vol. 3, p. 427.
[7] *Supra.*
[8] See p. 441, last paragraph.

passengers to escape, is recognized. While there is force in the suggestion that they should avoid the setting apart of a zone because mistakes are liable to occur, still, what we are really demanding of them is that everywhere, whether in any particular zone or upon the seas generally, they shall not sink a merchantman without giving the crew and passengers time to escape.

Second: the sentence beginning near the bottom of the third page and concluding on the second line of the fourth page [9] states that there is no adequate compensation for the lives of the two seamen lost on the *Gulflight*. I suggest that that sentence raises a question which is nowhere answered in the note. If there can be no adequate compensation for the loss of life of these two seamen, how are we to settle this particular case? Would it not be well to indicate the manner in which this claim can be adjusted? Do you mean that although a pecuniary compensation is accepted, it cannot be adequate for the loss of life? This would indicate that in this particular case damages will be accepted—the vessel having been attacked without intention. If, however, you mean that money cannot be accepted in such cases, then what other compensation have you in mind? The punishment of the officer or the physical punishment of the government responsible for it? It would, in my judgment, be unfortunate to raise an inquiry upon the subject and then leave it a matter of doubt as to what would be acceptable or to leave the impression that nothing whatever can be done to atone for this mistake.

Third: the next sentence following, that is the sentence beginning on the second line of the fourth page,[10] would seem to be not only a surplusage, but a surplusage that is calculated to offend. It evidently refers to the argument which is made by Germans not in their notes to us, but in their interviews in favor of the freedom of the seas, and, it seems to me, that it detracts from the dignity of the paper to turn aside from the main discussion to answer an argument that is not involved in the controversy. I think that in discussing the *Falaba*, some attention should be paid to the assertion that the failure to give sufficient time for the passengers and crew to escape was due to the alleged fact that "suspicious steamers were hurrying to the aid of the *Falaba*." This statement raises two questions, one of law and one of fact. In the first place we do not have any other evidence except that contained in this note that suspicious steamers were hurrying to the rescue, but if that is a fact and a material fact, it cannot be overlooked. The second point raised is whether if it were true it would be a justification for the sinking of the vessel. I feel sure that there must be precedents on this point and I have asked Mr. Lansing to

---

[9] See p. 442, 1. 5 (sentence beginning, "The submarine attack").
[10] See p. 442, 1.8 (sentence beginning, "The freedom of the seas").

investigate. I would not feel like answering from intuition and I could not answer it on information without knowing what the precedents are. It seems to me that many cases of this kind must have arisen during the operation of the rules in regard to prizes. It must often have occurred that vessels have hurried to the rescue of a prize ship before the passengers and crew could have been taken off. What is the rule in such a case? Must the attacking vessel withdraw and leave the prize ship or is it justified in sinking the prize ship, crew and all? If a merchantman, instead of stopping when ordered to stop, continued its efforts to escape, it can be sunk. Its refusal to stop changes to that extent the character of the vessel. Does the effort of another vessel to rescue it have the same effect as a continued effort to escape, or must the attacking vessel withdraw, if it sees a vessel of superior force approaching before it is able to rescue the passengers?

I am inclined to think that the use of the phrase "is surprised to find" [11] might be softened by the use of some milder phrase like "the United States is sure that upon more complete investigation" or that "upon more complete consideration, the Imperial German Government will not contend etc.," or something like that.

In the discussion of the *Lusitania* on pages six and seven [12] the note speaks as if our statement of the facts foreclosed further discussion. I do not understand that either side has a right to assert a statement of facts and then act upon the theory that there can be no further dispute. We think that the facts assumed to be true by the German Government are in fact erroneous, but the real facts are the things that must decide, not the facts as assumed by either side. And right here, it seems to me, is not only an opening for the suggestion which I have had the honor to submit to you, but a condition that really requires the thing suggested. If, in our reply, we say, as the note seems to say, "all of these things alleged or assumed by you to be facts and upon which you acted are without foundation, and, therefore, there is nothing further for you to do but to accept our view of the law as applied to the facts as we state them," we shall, it seems to me, foreclose any further discussion of the facts and make ourselves the final judges. We would not, however, regard Germany as justified in saying to us "we have investigated this matter and we regret to inform you that all the facts upon which you rested your claim are erroneous, and therefore, we expect you to withdraw the claim." Would it not be proper here to say something like this: "We have stated the facts as we believe them to exist and this statement, if true, would seem to remove the grounds upon which Germany bases her

[11] See p. 442, l. 14.
[12] See pp. 442–444.

departure from the rules covering prizes. If she is satisfied that these assumed facts are erroneous, we feel sure that she will be pleased to acknowledge that a grave mistake was made. If, on the contrary, she feels that she has reason to question the facts as we have stated them, we respectfully suggest joint investigation in order that the true facts may be arrived at, since the real facts must determine the principle to be applied." I think that if you are inclined to favor such a statement, it would be still further emphasized by the suggestion that the treaties which we have made with thirty countries, the principle of which Germany has approved, would indicate a means by which these facts might be arrived at.

I agree with Mr. Lansing in the reference which he makes in Section k, page 3 of his explanations to the Treaty of 1828.[13] It does not seem to apply in this case. I do not agree with Mr. Lansing, however, in his view of the words "with honor" in the third line on page ten.[14] I think a softer word would be better, for instance, "no Government is justified in resigning"—"with honor" might be regarded as offensive. I do not agree with him either in advising the omission of the paragraph covering the first half of page twelve[15]— I believe that is a very important part of your statement and not only adds strength to it, but indicates that the note is written in the language of a friend.

I think the reference to our willingness to be the means of bringing the two governments together on some concessions is a very important part of the note. The only trouble is that the first part of the note will, in my judgment, make it unnecessary as it now stands, for Great Britain to make any concessions. If we undertake the task of protecting her passenger ships from submarines she will not have as much of an incentive as she otherwise would to agree upon concessions that would be valuable to neutrals. The effect of what you say to Germany is more than counterbalanced by the encouragement which is given to Great Britain not to make any concessions at all, that is to refuse the concessions which are so important to our welfare. In saying that Great Britain will be encouraged to refuse concessions, I am only saying that she, like other belligerent nations, will view the matter from the standpoint of her own interests and not from our unbiased point of view.

It is not pertinent to this discussion of this note to reiterate what I have said in regard to the wisdom of making at the same time representations to Great Britain in regard to the interference with our ships, but I will venture to repeat that I believe the reception of this

---

[13] The reference is apparently to Mr. Lansing's memorandum of explanations, not printed.
[14] See p. 444, l. 14.
[15] See p. 445, first paragraph.

note and the action likely to follow would be much more favorable to us if, before the note was sent, you announced that, pending negotiations with Germany as to the use of submarines and without any surrender of any of our rights, you felt impelled to refuse clearance to belligerent ships carrying American passengers and to refuse clearance to American passenger ships carrying ammunition. I believe that the moral effect of such an announcement, coupled with the suggestion in regard to investigation, would, without in the least subtracting from the strength of the note, relieve the tension, deny to the jingoes foundation for their alarming statements and win the approval of our people, who, while firm in insisting upon the respect for our rights, will be quick to recognize the christian forbearance exhibited at a time when the exigencies of war make it difficult, if not impossible, for Germany to consider this question upon its merits and apart from its connection with the war in which she is engaged.

With assurance [etc.]   [File copy not signed]

763.72/1863½

The Counselor for the Department of State (*Lansing*) to the Secretary of State

[WASHINGTON,] *June 7, 1915.*

DEAR MR. SECRETARY: I have read over carefully your letter to the President [16] in regard to the redraft of the note to Germany, and, in compliance with your request, I offer the following comments:

In the paragraph beginning near the top of page 3, to which you refer, it seems to me that there is a measure of justice in your criticism, in that if the German Government agrees to in the future observe the practice of visiting vessels and removing the crews and passengers before sinking them, the question of war zone becomes of far less importance.

I think your comment upon the sentence relative to "adequate compensation" for the lives of two seamen lost on the *Gulflight* is well taken. It would be advisable to express just the sort of amends we expect, or else omit any reference to their death, in view of what we have said about the acceptance of liability by Germany.

In regard to your third comment, I agree with you that it would be well to change the latter part of the sentence, to which you refer. To my mind, it does not comport with diplomatic expression, and I am not at all sure how it would be rendered into German. It might needlessly offend the German Government. In any event, it is doubtful whether its force in the argument warrants the possible view which may be taken of it.

---

[16] *Supra.*

Your fourth comment, which begins in the fifth line from the bottom of page 2,[17] I regret to say I cannot agree with.

I have had careful search made of the authorities in relation to the right of destroying enemy merchant vessels and I find none which justifies such destruction without first removing the crew and papers. The approach of a superior naval force is a ground for destruction of the vessel but not of the crew. I append an extract from Oppenheim, vol. 2, which is the most comprehensive and concise statement of the law.

In the War of 1812 we instructed our naval vessels to destroy prizes, and over 70 were burned. The practice was followed in the Crimean War, in the Civil War by the Confederates, in the Franco-Prussian War and the Russo-Japanese War. In all these cases the persons on board were removed before the vessels were destroyed.

I do not think that the approach of suspicious vessels to a captured vessel can in any way warrant the destroying of the vessel with persons on board. It justifies possibly the destruction of the vessel, but not the destruction of life.

A defense of this sort, so far as it is applied to the taking of human life, cannot be justly urged.

The fact of the approach of other vessels, even if true, is therefore entirely irrelevant.

Your fifth comment, which is in the last paragraph on page 3, I agree with.[18]

Your sixth comment in regard to the *Lusitania*, beginning at the bottom of page 3 and running over onto page 4,[19] I also regret to disagree with, in that I do not think that if all the facts alleged by the German Government in its note were true, that they would be relevant to the real question at issue, which is a question of right. While I fully appreciate the decided advantage it would be to leave open a door of discussion as to the facts in the case, I cannot bring myself to admit that the facts are pertinent and entitled to investigation. The only question which might be considered as possible of investigation would be whether or not the *Lusitania* was an auxiliary of the British navy, but that appears to me so manifestly contradicted by the presence of passengers on board and the vessel clearing on its regular trade route, that it offers slender excuse for an inquiry.

I believe, my dear Mr. Secretary, that the foregoing comments cover those which you made in your letter, to which you directed my particular attention.

Faithfully yours,

ROBERT LANSING

---

[17] See p. 446, par. 2, sentence beginning, "I think that in discussing the *Falaba*."
[18] See p. 447, par. 1.
[19] See p. 447, par. 2.

[Enclosure]

Extract From L. Oppenheim, "International Law"[20]

The *Règlement international des prises maritimes* of the Institute of International Law enumerates in Sec. 50 five cases in which destruction of the capture is allowed—namely (1) when the condition of the vessel and the weather make it impossible to keep the prize afloat; (2) when the vessel navigates so slowly that she cannot follow the captor and is therefore exposed to an easy recapture by the enemy; (3) when the approach of a superior enemy force creates the fear that the prize might be recaptured by the enemy; (4) when the captor cannot spare a prize crew; (5) when the port of adjudication to which the prize might be taken is too far from the spot where the capture was made. Be that as it may, in every case of destruction of the vessel the captor must remove crew, ship papers, and, if possible, the cargo, before the destruction of the prize, and must afterwards send crew, papers, and cargo to a port of a Prize Court for the purpose of satisfying the latter that both the capture and the destruction were lawful.

763.72/1867½

The Secretary of State ad interim to President Wilson

WASHINGTON, *June 15, 1915.*

DEAR MR. PRESIDENT: I enclose a memorandum which the British Ambassador handed me yesterday, requesting copies of sworn declarations of the United States customs or other officers who examined the *Lusitania* prior to her departure from New York, for the use of the British Government in connection with the *Lusitania* inquiry. I am informed by the Treasury Department that the reports of the Collector at New York are in your hands.[21] I therefore venture to ask if you perceive any objection to having copies of the Collector's whole report, or certain portions of it, made and sent to the Ambassador, in compliance with his request. It may be that the Collector's report is in such shape that it would be more convenient to ask the Treasury Department to obtain sworn statements of the customs officers, covering the particular points mentioned by the Ambassador in his memorandum.

Very sincerely yours,

ROBERT LANSING

---

[20] Second edition (London and New York, 1912), vol. II, p. 244.
[21] See p. 428.

[Enclosure]

Memorandum by the British Ambassador (*Spring Rice*)

Is there any objection to communicating to the British Government for use in connection with the *Lusitania* enquiry copies of sworn declarations of U. S. customs or other officials who examined the vessel prior to departure from New York, describing precise nature of their inspection and stating whether or not there were any guns on board and whether or not the vessel carried any explosives. [*?*]

WASHINGTON, *June 14, 1915.*

763.72/1868½

President Wilson to the Secretary of State ad interim

WASHINGTON, *June 16, 1915.*

MY DEAR MR. SECRETARY: I think that perhaps it would not be wise to send the Collector's report concerning the *Lusitania* to Great Britain for the use of the Court of Inquiry, and that it would be better to ask the Treasury Department to supply the British Ambassador with sworn statements of the customs officers covering the particular points mentioned by him in his memorandum.

In haste

Cordially and sincerely yours,

WOODROW WILSON

763.72/1961½

President Wilson to the Secretary of State

WASHINGTON, *2 July, 1915.*

MY DEAR MR. SECRETARY: These suggestions of Gerard [22] seem to me entirely unwise, or, at the least, impossible of acceptance, as, I dare say, they seem to you. But if you have any thought that something might be done, I would be very much indebted to you if you would indicate it.

Faithfully Yours,

W. W.

---

[22] See *Foreign Relations*, 1915, supp., p. 453.

763.72/1918 : Telegram

The Secretary of State to President Wilson [23]

WASHINGTON, *July 7, 1915.*

In view of the usual delay in communicating with Berlin I considered an immediate answer to Gerard regarding preliminary negotiations should be sent at once. I, therefore, sent the following telegram: [24]

"July 6, 1915. 7 P.M. Amembassy, Berlin. 1915. The suggestion[s] contained in your 2543 [25] and 2544 [26] are receiving attentive consideration. The belief in Germany as reported in your 2544 regarding the resignation of Mr. Bryan is entirely erroneous. Mr. Bryan is not endeavoring to influence public opinion against this Government, and he will support the President. As far as one can judge, the country is almost unanimous in its hearty support of the President. We do not think it advisable at present to enter negotiations on the subject of the German reply. The position of the United States was fully set forth in its instruction to you of June 9th,[27] and we do not feel that the principles upon which this statement [*Government*] stands can be properly the subject of preliminary negotiations. Lansing."

You will perceive that this telegram permits a change of attitude if it seems desirable to you to have Gerard negotiate on the subject. My personal opinion is that Gerard, judging from his previous expressions favoring the German proposals, ought not to be given any latitude in the negotiations if you consider it wise to proceed with them. I am afraid that the principle for which we contend would be sacrificed by him in order to reach a compromise to which Germany would agree. To recede on any of our assertions of principle ought not, in my opinion, to be considered. If Germany would admit the correctness of the principle asserted by this Government, a negotiation of its application to present conditions might be advisable.

ROBERT LANSING

763.72/1962½ : Telegram

President Wilson to the Secretary of State

WINDSOR, VT., *July 7, 1915.*
[Received 5:15 p. m.]

Papers received. Am I right in supposing that message from Vienna [28] is merely gratuitous advice from the Austrian Government as to our duty as neutrals?

---

[23] Then at Cornish, N. H.
[24] Printed in *Foreign Relations*, 1915, supp., p. 462.
[25] *Ibid.*, p. 459.
[26] *Ibid.*, p. 460.
[27] *Ibid.*, p. 436.
[28] *Ibid.*, p. 790.

In regard to the message from Gerard [29] I would suggest if your own judgment coincides that we instruct him [30] to convey unofficially to the Imperial Government our determination not to yield or compromise in any way our rights as neutrals or prestige of our citizens but our hearty willingness to exercise our good offices with regard to effecting any arrangements which will open the sea to common use with as little danger as possible to non-belligerents, keeping these two things entirely distinct, namely, our rights, which we cannot abate, and our services as friends of all parties. We will discuss anything that it is reasonable and practicable to discuss except the curtailment of our clear and established rights.

WOODROW WILSON

763.72/1963½

President Wilson to the Secretary of State

9 JULY, 1915.

MY DEAR MR. SECRETARY: I learn to-day from the representative of the Associated Press who accompanied me up here that the German note was delivered to Gerard late last evening. I assume, therefore, that it will be in our hands, and in mine here, by Monday or Tuesday. I shall take a little while to mull over it before returning to Washington to confer with you about it.

May I not suggest that while I am getting my ideas straightened out about it and meditating the necessary reply you will yourself sketch what you think should be said in answer? We can then immediately get our minds together when we meet. Perhaps you would be kind enough to let me have a memorandum of your thought for a reply. You will at once, I take it, see what my own position will necessarily be when you see the note itself.

Faithfully Yours,

W. W.

763.72/1965½ : Telegram

President Wilson to Mr. J. P. Tumulty (Secretary to the President)

WINDSOR, VT., *July 11, 1915—9:19 p. m.*

According to our telephone conversation shall not expect Secretary of State to come here without previous consultation with me as to the best plan for conference.

WOODROW WILSON

---

[29] *Foreign Relations*, 1915, supp., p. 460.
[30] For the instruction, see telegram No. 1918, July 8, 1915, to the Ambassador in Germany, *ibid.*, p. 462.

763.72/1965½

The Secretary of State to President Wilson

WASHINGTON, *July 12, 1915.*

MY DEAR MR. PRESIDENT: Mr. Tumulty has just sent me your telegram to him of the 11th, 9:19 P. M. I have felt that it was unfortunate that the newspapers gathered the impression that I was to hasten to Cornish to consult with you in regard to the German note.[31] The reporters evidently misunderstood Mr. Tumulty as to the possibility of my visiting you. My own impression has been that it would be unwise, unless it would very materially lengthen your holiday. It would give, I fear, a bad impression to the country as to the situation and, furthermore, in view of our foreign relations, I do not think that it would be well for both of us to be absent from Washington at the same time.

Faithfully yours,

ROBERT LANSING

763.72/1967½

President Wilson to the Secretary of State

13 JULY, 1915.

MY DEAR MR. SECRETARY: I have of course been giving a great deal of thought to the German note since I received the official text of it. According to my suggestion in my last letter, I am now writing to tell you how the reply lies in my mind in outline.

But, first, certain questions:

Do you think it worth while to take notice of and refute their arguments about the arming of merchantmen destroying the difference between public and private vessels; about this, that, and the other alleged utterance of English ministers or order of the English Government having made their recent course necessary and justifiable; etc., etc., or do you think we had better just speak, and briefly at that, to the merits of the case, in bulk, as they present it,—for example as follows:

1. We cannot discuss special arrangements whereby a few vessels may enjoy the rights all are entitled to, nor admit that such arrangements would be in any way adequate to meet the contentions of this Government.

2. We are not merely contending for the rights of Americans to cross the seas as they will without fear of deliberate breaches of international law, but conceive ourselves as speaking for the rights of

---

[31] For the German note of July 8, 1915, see *ibid.*, p. 463.

neutrals everywhere, rights in which the whole world is interested
and which every nation must wish to see kept inviolable.

3. These rights the Imperial German Government itself recognizes
in theory, professes itself anxious to see safeguarded, and is surely
ready to admit as quite as vital to itself, both now and in the years
to come, as to any other nation.

4. Violations of neutral rights and of the general obligations of
international law by the Government of Great Britain we of course
cannot discuss with the German Government; but will discuss with
the British Government, so far as they affect the rights of Americans.
We will, moreover, as already intimated to the German Government,
be glad to be the means of conveying any suggestions as to modifications of methods of warfare which any one of the belligerents may
wish conveyed to the others.

5. We note with interest the fact that in the more recent operations
of German submarines it has been feasible to keep within the limits
and restrictions of international practice and to act upon the general
principles upon which we have insisted. We can see no reason, therefore, why there is not opened a way of immediate agreement between
the two governments and of such action as will sufficiently safeguard
all legitimate interests and enable the German Admiralty to return
to the practice long established and fully recognized in their own
instructions already more than once referred to.

I am not selecting words; I am merely trying to outline an argument. What do you think of it?

And what do you think ought to be the concluding terms of demand, that will bring the correspondence to a definite issue? Two
things are plain to me, in themselves inconsistent, viz. that our people
want this thing handled in a way that will bring about a definite
settlement without endless correspondence, and that they will also
expect us not to hasten an issue or so conduct the correspondence as
to make an unfriendly issue inevitable.

I shall await your own suggestions with the greatest interest.
When I have had a chance to see them and reflect upon them, I will
confer with you in person, preferably in Washington where we will
have all the documents we wish at hand, and all the other persons
we might wish to consult with regard to particular phases of this
important matter.

With warm regard,
     Faithfully Yours,

[File copy not signed]

763.72/1966½

President Wilson to the Secretary of State

14 JULY, 1915.

MY DEAR MR. SECRETARY: I fully understood your feeling about this,[32] or thought I did, instinctively, but for once allowed myself to credit what the newspapers contained, under the impression that somehow our currents had got short-circuited. Please never feel that it is necessary to explain. I knew that you would understand my telegram. You evidently have understood it.

Faithfully Yours,

W. W.

763.72/1969½a

The Secretary of State to President Wilson

WASHINGTON, *July 14, 1915.*

MY DEAR MR. PRESIDENT: I have been making a number of notes on the German reply of the 8th in an endeavor to crystallize my thoughts as to the answer which should be made. I am loath to send you these notes in their present shape as I think that you would find them more useful in a digested form.

The impression which I have gained from careful reading and re-reading of the German note is that the thought of "home consumption" entered largely into its composition, while at the same time the German Government failed to appreciate public temper in this country. I think that considerable allowance should be made for the sarcastic tone of certain phrases because written for German readers and to meet the public demand in Germany.

We are to an extent bound to respond to a similar chord in this country. It would be easy to understand American public opinion if the press accurately reflected it. But I am not sure in my own mind that it does. As I read the state of mind of the vast majority of the people it is that they do not want war, that no war spirit exists, but at the same time they want the Government not to recede a step from its position but to compel Germany to submit to our demands. Of course this attitude, if I read it aright, is most difficult to meet. To carry out both ideas is well nigh impossible. Of course I do not feel that public opinion should dictate the Government's action but it is well to consider it.

---

[32] See letter of July 12, 1915, from the Secretary of State to President Wilson, p. 455.

As to the reply itself I feel that the German note's comments on the action of Great Britain can be dismissed with a statement that they are irrelevant to the subject at issue. That will dispose of nearly half of the note. In the next place I think that we can refuse to discuss a *modus vivendi* for the future until the general principles involved have been considered and the *Lusitania* matter satisfactorily adjusted so far as it is possible. The setting aside of these two subjects in our reply will materially shorten it, and I believe that brevity will impress the German Government with the earnestness of our purpose to insist on our rights (an impression which I have sometimes felt they did not have) and will also cause a feeling in this country that this Government does not intend to prolong the controversy indefinitely. I think in the present state of the discussion a concise and direct statement will be most effective.

As I reached this point your letter to me of the 13th arrived. After reading it I have decided to enclose my undigested notes [33] calling particular attention to Note 13.

I will go over your letter with care and send you any comments which may suggest themselves. I think that you will find on examining the enclosed notes our minds have worked in much the same way.

In order that I may not forward to you at Cornish further memoranda, which might arrive after your departure, can you indicate to me about the time you expect to return here?

I am [etc.]   ROBERT LANSING

763.72/1967½

The Secretary of State to President Wilson

WASHINGTON, *July 15, 1915.*

MY DEAR MR. PRESIDENT: *In re* your letter of the 13th as to an outline for a reply to the German note may I offer the following comments:

I do not think that it is at all essential to refute the German allegation that the *Lusitania* was to all intents a public ship; at the same time it presents an argument which to the average man appears to have considerable force, and, if it is not met, it may be thought that it could not be answered. There is always danger, I think, in omitting reference to an assertion, since it may be construed into an admission. You will see that my Note 6 (July 11th) [34] deals with the question.

Your paragraphs numbered 1, 2 and 3 seem to me to treat the *modus vivendi* proposed by Germany in just the right way, and put

---

[33] Not printed.
[34] Not printed; enclosed with Secretary Lansing's letter of July 14, *supra.*

the subject on the ground of principle, which is a higher ground than the one I suggested and, therefore, a better one.

Paragraph 4, I think, presents the exact way to deal with the charges made against Great Britain. The subject should be stated to be irrelevant to the issue as well as improper for discussion with Germany. The last sentence in the paragraph might possibly obtain greater emphasis by being placed at the end of our answer and show a friendly disposition.

Paragraph 5 might be used in the answer, to emphasize our disappointment that the German Government does not in its note agree to do the very thing it has been doing for the past two months. Possibly this could be used at the beginning in complaining that the rights of Americans are not acknowledged.

I think that you will find that the view of public sentiment contained in the next to the last paragraph in your letter was identical with that expressed in the first part of my letter of yesterday. I am sure the people do not want war with Germany, and I am equally sure that they want the Government to insist firmly on its rights. As you say, the two things are "inconsistent." How they can be brought into harmony is the chief problem.

This brings up the question, which you ask, as to "the concluding terms of demand." Frankly I am not prepared yet to answer that question. I would prefer to wait until the note is drafted in a tentative form and see what demands would be consistent and appropriate. Of course the demands we make will be the most difficult part of the note. Is it possible to be firm and at the same time to compromise?

I think that in formulating the demands the possible consequences must be considered with the greatest care. In case of a flat refusal what will happen? In case of counter proposals what then? Should the demands be so worded as to admit of only "Yes" or "No" as an answer, or should a loophole be given for counter proposals? Can we take a course which will permit further correspondence? These are the questions which are running through my mind and I have not as yet been able to answer them. I wish more time to consider them.

I am now working on a tentative draft, which will put my ideas in a more concrete form than the Notes which I sent you.

Not being sure whether you kept a copy of your letter of the 13th I am returning it to you so that this letter will be intelligible. I have retained a copy.

Faithfully yours,

ROBERT LANSING

763.72/1981½

The Solicitor for the Department of State (Johnson) to the Secretary of State

[WASHINGTON,] *July 16, 1915.*

DEAR MR. SECRETARY: It is devoutly desirable that the *Lusitania* affair be brought to an end as quickly as possible, having regard for the rights and duties of the United States.

There is danger that it may drag along and finally "peter out" leaving the issue deadlocked; in which case there will be many clamoring to know why we do not hold Germany to accountability.

War between the United States and Germany is not to be thought of now, for the reason, if no other, that such a war could not be conducted at this time.

Severance of diplomatic relations would "get us nothing," except criticism from our opponents for producing that situation, without our having the countervailing benefit of an aroused national spirit.

The attitude of "not speaking" is one that provokes no enthusiasm and is difficult to maintain with credit.

Moreover in that event we would have to acquiesce in the Orders in Council and decrees of Great Britain and the Allies with reference to trade to Europe and submit our commerce to be sifted, doled out and manipulated to serve European politics.

I submit some notes on the late German note.

JOHNSON

[Enclosure]

Notes by the Solicitor for the Department of State (Johnson) on the Second German Note in the "Lusitania" Correspondence

[WASHINGTON,] *July 16, 1915.*

There will hardly be two opinions whether the United States is to insist that Germany reprobate the destruction of the lives of American citizens through the sinking of the *Lusitania* by its submarine.

But presupposing this is done—may the United States, without compromise or surrender of the principle, in its essence, for which it has contended, consider proposals for arrangements for setting aside a certain number of vessels for the carriage of passengers in European waters, the same to be free from molestation and danger from war craft?

"The Government of the United States is, of course, not oblivious to the great changes which have occurred in the conditions and means of naval warfare since the rules hitherto governing legal blockade were formulated. It might be ready to admit that the old form of 'close' blockade with its cordon of ships in the immediate offing of the blockaded ports is no longer practicable in face of an enemy possessing the means and opportunity to make an effective defense by the use of submarines, mines and air craft; but it can hardly be maintained that, whatever form of effective blockade may be made use of, it is impossible to conform at least to the spirit and principles of the established rules of war. If the necessities of the case should seem to render it imperative that the cordon of blockading vessels be extended across the approaches to any neighboring neutral port or country, it would seem clear that it would still be easily practicable to comply with the well-recognized and reasonable prohibition of international law against the blockading of neutral ports by according free admission and exit to all lawful traffic with neutral ports through the blockading cordon. Such procedure need not conflict in any respect with the rights of the belligerent maintaining the blockade since the right would remain with the blockading vessels to visit and search all ships either entering or leaving the neutral territory which they were in fact, but not of right, investing." (Note of the United States to the British Government of March 30,[35] relating to the British Order in Council of March 11th.)

I interpret these expressions as indicative of a disposition on the part of the United States Government, in view of the recent great changes in the means of warfare, to admit reasonable modifications in the application, in practice, of the established rules of international usage, when the essence of the right of belligerent and neutral, respectively, will be preserved.

Presumably, the view of the author of the paragraph just quoted comprehended the right of Great Britain to establish and maintain a blockade of German ports and an appreciation that rigid compliance with the established and recognized form and manner of blockade would not be insisted on, if to do so the right of blockade would be lost; provided always, and of course, that the substance of the right of the neutral is preserved.

Moreover Great Britain has insisted that the established mode of visit and search of merchant ships on the high seas can no longer be followed on account of the danger to the searching ship from attack by German submarine war craft while such visit and search is taking place, and has insisted upon taking neutral ships wherever found in European waters to British or allied ports, and there detaining them while search for contraband or illicit goods goes on; her contention being that she should not be expected to forego the substantial right of visit and search, which she would have to do, she says, if she pursued the practice in that matter hitherto known to international usage.

The right of a belligerent to overtake and destroy, in so far as neutrals are concerned, enemy merchant ships carrying contraband

---

[35] Printed in full in *Foreign Relations*, 1915, supp., p. 152.

or munitions of war is to be admitted. (Personally I abhor the whole conception of war which comprehends war on private owned merchant ships, when flying the flag of the enemy, except in the case of munitions and supplies of war, which latter I think may well be summarily dispatched wherever met with.) But we are dealing with a situation where one belligerent insists that its substantial right to overtake and destroy enemy ships carrying munitions of war with which to attack it, is not to be defeated entirely by the presence on such ship of neutral passengers.

It is hardly correct to say that the neutral has the right, unlimited, of traveling on merchant ships of belligerents carrying contraband and munitions of war. A neutral does not have the right to afford, by his presence, protection to such a ship or its cargo, as we see from the admitted principle by which he is required to abandon the ship when overtaken by the enemy—if afforded opportunity to do so with reasonable safety; his right consists in the opportunity to leave the ship in safety before it is sunk. His presence affords no legal protection to the ship or its cargo.

The concurring right of the belligerent to take and destroy enemy ships with their cargoes, and the right of those found aboard to be taken off before the ship is destroyed, may coexist where naval warfare is conducted by the ordinary ships of war; but, it seems, this is not the case where the submarine is employed in the pursuit of enemy merchantmen.

I pass up any discussion of what should be made, or may perhaps finally become, the accepted rule of international law respecting the operation of submarines as relating to merchant ships.

The question arises shall consideration be given to this change in the instrumentalities of naval warfare, or shall we contend for the right of our nationals to use any and all ships, including those flying the flag of Germany's enemy and carrying arms and munitions of war, thereby, in a measure at least, extending protection to the ship and its cargo except when overtaken by an ordinary warship which is able to destroy the ship and at the same time furnish means of escape to those on board.

It should not be overlooked that the protection insisted on for the American traveler on a British ship from New York to Liverpool may also be demanded for the American citizen on a British merchantman loaded at Liverpool and bound for Havre with a full cargo of arms and ammunition destined for immediate delivery to the troops of the allies in the trenches.

Is it of the essence of the right of an American citizen to travel in European waters that he be allowed to take passage on any and all of the ships of the belligerents, whatever may be their cargo or destination? I hardly think so. If abundant facilities are furnished for the safe conveyance of our people in European waters within the zone of hostilities, it seems to me there would be no ground for complaint on the part of any American citizens who might prefer a ship of the enemy carrying munitions of war into the zone of hostilities.

Bearing in mind the views which have been expressed in the correspondence with Great Britain respecting consideration to be given to the momentous changes in the conditions and means of warfare, I am impressed with the idea that if Germany will reprobate the destruction of innocent lives through the attack of its submarine upon the *Lusitania* and the circumstances of its sinking, we should not close the door to the consideration of proposals, if reasonable and practicable, for setting aside an adequate number of ships upon which our people may take passage and travel unmolested in European waters, those ships not to carry mixed cargoes of babies and bullets.

JOHNSON

763.72/1940

The Secretary of State to President Wilson

WASHINGTON, *July 21, 1915.*

MY DEAR MR. PRESIDENT: I have been through the draft of the reply to the German note and enclose a copy with my suggestions.[36]

There were two things which I thought ought to be in the reply, namely, reference to the *Lusitania* and a closing paragraph disavowing responsibility on our part for the consequences if Germany should continue her illegal practices.[37] While I think both of these ought to be presented to the German Government, American public opinion will, I am sure, be better satisfied. The last paragraph may seem a little too vigorous, as it undoubtedly contains a veiled (rather thinly veiled) threat, but it is no more than we have already said in other notes. I am confident that it would make a very good impression in this country, and of course we cannot ignore the effect of the reply here, and I do not believe that it would increase German irritation.

The reply has two primary ideas, the illegality of retaliatory acts by a belligerent and the possibility of using submarines in accordance with the rules of maritime war.

---

[36] A draft prepared by the President on July 19; not printed. For text of the note as sent, see *Foreign Relations*, 1915, supp., p. 480.
[37] Secretary Lansing's proposed concluding paragraph read: "In the event that this situation should unhappily arise the heavy responsibility would rest upon the Imperial Government for the inevitable consequences. The people and Government of the United States are determined to maintain their just rights and will adopt the steps necessary to insure their respect by all nations."

You will see that I suggest the transposition of paragraph 6 [38] on page 6 (I have numbered the paragraphs for reference) to page 5 immediately preceding paragraph 4. This, I believe, will give a more logical treatment of the subjects.

Analyzed the subjects are as follows:

Par. 1. Dissatisfaction.
" 2. Admission of principles.
" 3. Exemption from principles.
" 6. Possibility of conformity.
" 4. The *Lusitania*.
" 5. Suggested *modus vivendi*.
" 7. Freedom of the seas.
" 8. Agreement between belligerents.
" 9. Observance of neutral rights.
" 10. Responsibility for consequences of violation.

I have followed my previous practice of putting suggested omissions in brackets and underscoring suggested insertions.

I hope that a final draft may be determined upon today, if possible, for I believe that it should go forward as soon as possible in order to put an end to newspaper speculations which have a tendency to affect public opinion and prevent impartial judgment when the note is actually published.

Faithfully yours,

ROBERT LANSING

_____

763.72/1940

President Wilson to the Secretary of State

WASHINGTON, *21 July, 1915.*

DEAR MR. SECRETARY: Thank you for this draft. I have gone over it and am glad to accept practically all of your suggestions.

I have taken the liberty of omitting, however, the last paragraph. It has the tone of an ultimatum, and does not seem to me in fact to add to the meaning of the document as a whole,—the manifest meaning of it. I do not think that we need add a sting.

I shall be away from the house for a couple of hours, but will get into communication with you so soon as I get back.

Faithfully Yours,

W. W.

_____

[38] See the order of paragraphs below.

763.72/1940 : Telegram

The Vice President (Marshall) to the Secretary of State

INDIANAPOLIS, IND., *July 24, 1915—10:28 a. m.*

[Received 11:41 a. m.]

Congratulations.[39] You have said it. Follow with note to England defining the American idea and we are impregnable.

THOS. R. MARSHALL

462.11 Se 8/39

The Secretary of State to President Wilson

WASHINGTON, *August 7, 1915.*

MY DEAR MR. PRESIDENT: I enclose, for your consideration, a draft of reply [40] to the German note on the *Frye* case,[41] which has been prepared by Mr. Chandler P. Anderson. He also submitted with the draft a memorandum on the case which explains certain features of the draft.

It seems to me that the proposed reply is excellent and takes a very consistent attitude on the questions in dispute. It furthermore introduces the principle of arbitration which, if once adopted, may be extended to other subjects of difference.

I am also enclosing a printed copy of the German note on the *Frye* case.

Faithfully yours,

ROBERT LANSING

[Enclosure]

Memorandum by Mr. Chandler P. Anderson on the "Frye" Case [42]

WASHINGTON, *August 5, 1915.*

There is a special purpose in the answer I have drafted in the *Frye* case which requires a few words of explanation.

Apart from the advisability of settling by arbitration the questions at issue in this case, it is to be hoped that this resort to arbitration will make easier the adoption of similar action in dealing with the differences between the two Governments about submarine warfare against merchant ships. In that case, however, it would be absolutely essen-

---

[39] i. e., on the note to Germany of July 21, 1915, printed in *Foreign Relations*, 1915, supp., p. 480.

[40] Not printed; for the reply as sent, see *ibid.*, p. 504.

[41] *Ibid.*, p. 493.

[42] Filed separately under file No. 462.11 Se 8/39½.

tial for the purposes of the United States Government that Germany should suspend her illegal operations pending the arbitral award, and it is anticipated that Germany will refuse to do this unless in our negotiations with Great Britain about their violation of our neutral trade rights, we insist that they also discontinue their unlawful practices pending arbitration. The present case gives an opportunity to ask Germany what its position is on this point, and it is for the purpose of getting a statement of Germany's position that the last clause of this note has been framed in the form of an inquiry.

If it becomes necessary for the United States to express its own views on this point, my suggestion as to the position we should take is that in cases involving the destruction of life, the action complained of must not be repeated pending a legal inquiry as to its illegality, but that in cases involving merely the loss of property, which can be measured by money damages, a *modus vivendi* should be arranged on a basis which will avoid so far as possible destruction of property pending the decision of the arbitral tribunal.

This rule would apply equally in our dispute with Great Britain about unlawful restraints of trade, and in our dispute with Germany in the present case, and it draws the essential distinction between these cases and the *Lusitania* Case so that if arbitration is offered there, we can insist, pending the decision of the tribunal, that there shall be no repetition of the course of action complained of while it is under judicial investigation.

If it be found that Germany is unwilling to adopt this course, then it will be necessary for the United States Government to consider whether it is possible to submit to arbitration our differences with Germany.

CHANDLER P. ANDERSON

462.11 Se 8/40½

President Wilson to the Secretary of State

9 AUGUST, 1915.

MY DEAR MR. SECRETARY: I approve of this note, though I must say that I do so with a little hesitation.

My hesitation is due to the very thing Mr. Anderson points out in his memorandum: that the principle of arbitration may be a little too acceptable to the German Government and may lead to the proposal from them that the matter of the *Lusitania* also be so submitted, and I do not think that public opinion in this country will stand for that at present.

Faithfully Yours,

W. W.

841.857 Ar 1/89a

The Secretary of State to President Wilson

WASHINGTON, *August 20, 1915.*

MY DEAR MR. PRESIDENT: The torpedoing of the *Arabic* [43] has created a crisis of the most serious nature. The vessel was outward bound from Liverpool. There could, therefore, be no pretext that the cargo consisted of munitions of war, which was so strongly urged in the case of the *Lusitania.* From our advices up to the present time the submarine attacked without warning. There were from fifteen to twenty Americans on board. Whether any of these were lost is still uncertain. I do not see, however, that that materially affects the case. From the official accounts received the attack seems to have been wanton and from a military point of view needless.

In the newspaper accounts there are two facts stated, which, if true, may have some bearing on the case.

First, the *Arabic* was under convoy up to a few moments before she was attacked. Of course it is not required to visit a ship under convoy. If the convoying vessels were still near enough to offer protection the question arises as to whether the submarine was legally bound to visit the *Arabic*, that is, compel her to stop and give time for the persons on board to reach a place of safety. This is discounted, however, by the official statement that rescue ships did not arrive for four hours.

Second, in one statement by a survivor it appears that the persons on the *Arabic* were, at the time when the torpedo struck, watching another vessel, the *Dunsley*, which was evidently being attacked by a submarine as her boats were being launched. The important part of the statement is that "the *Arabic* was making toward the *Dunsley* when the streak of a torpedo" was seen. The point is just this. Can the Germans claim, with any show of reason, that they feared that the *Arabic* intended to ram the submarine or drive it away? I don't think that it is a very strong argument but it may be raised in defense of the attack without warning.

Until we have full reports I do not wish to express any opinion, but it seems to me that it would be well to have some plan of action in mind in case no real excuse can be urged and the act of the submarine is shown to have been wanton and inhuman.

I proceed on the assumption that we do not want to enter the war, and that the American people do not wish it but are greatly incensed over this last submarine outrage. Outside of the newspapers everybody I have met, official and civilian alike, take the position that the declarations in our notes are so strong that we must act, that other-

---

[43] See *Foreign Relations,* 1915, supp., pp. 516 ff.

wise it will be said that our words have been mere "bluff", and that it would place the United States in a humiliating position to temporize.

It is the attitude of the public mind which makes the situation especially difficult, but I do not think that it can be ignored without inviting widespread criticism. To satisfy public opinion something must be done at once to show the intense earnestness of the Government to maintain the rights of Americans and to show that we view the situation as most grave and critical. Probably the easiest way to do this would be to send out notice for an immediate meeting of the Cabinet and to let it be known that the cabinet is summoned to consider this case. I believe that would convey to the public the impression desired, and would not have a bad effect on the German Government.

Meanwhile the possible course of action could be carefully considered and a definite policy determined in case the official reports confirm the newspaper accounts.

Faithfully yours,

ROBERT LANSING

841.857 Ar 1/89½

President Wilson to the Secretary of State

WASHINGTON, *21 August, 1915.*

MY DEAR MR. SECRETARY: I have your letter about the *Arabic,* and find myself in substantial agreement with it.

I do not think that an immediate summons of the Cabinet would be wise. We should first know all the facts. So soon as they are known we ought of course to find the views of our colleagues. Haste in the matter would be likely to give the country the wrong impression, I fear with regard to our frame of mind.

Faithfully Yours,

W. W.

841.857 Ar 1/90½

Mr. Rudolph Forster (Executive Clerk to the President) to the Secretary of State

WASHINGTON, *August 21, 1915.*

DEAR MR. LANSING: Mr. Tumulty has asked me to send you a copy of a note which he dictated over the telephone this morning.

Sincerely yours,

RUDOLPH FORSTER

[Enclosure]

Mr. J. P. Tumulty (Secretary to the President) to President Wilson

AVON, N. J., *August 21, 1915.*

MY DEAR GOVERNOR: I intended to return to Washington immediately upon receipt of the news of the sinking of the *Arabic* but upon second thought determined to remain here until Sunday afternoon. Realizing the seriousness of the situation, I thought that it would be wise to leave you free. My time here, however, is occupied in considering the issue raised by the sinking of this ship. My mind is clear as to the following:

1. The people are very calm and apparently are unmoved by this new situation. But they have an unfaltering confidence in the President and are willing to follow him wherever he may wish to go.
2. There is no jingoistic sentiment among the people.
3. Radical action is not demanded (by radical action I mean a declaration of war and a severance of all relations with Germany).
4. There is, however, a universal demand for the recall of von Bernstorff and the withdrawal of Gerard. If no radical action is intended, the latter course should follow very speedily after an ascertainment of all the facts in the matter. The very heart of action of this kind lies in the speed and the expedition in which it is carried out and done.

J. P. TUMULTY

462.11 Se 8/41½

Mr. Chandler P. Anderson to the Secretary of State

AUGUST 23, 1915.

I had my interview with Bernstorff this evening and am returning tonight to Newport for a few days going back to York Harbor on Thursday with Harriet.

I told Bernstorff as I suggested to you over the telephone on Sunday about the possibilities in the last paragraph in the *Frye* note if they would agree not to repeat the acts complained of pending arbitration, pointing out that the same arrangement in the *Lusitania* case would deprive Great Britain of the only views they have ever advanced in defense of their so-called blockade which in turn is the only excuse Germany has for its submarine attacks on merchant vessels. He saw at once that they could throw the entire responsibility for illegal interference with American rights upon G. B. by adopting this course and if G. B. did not adopt the same course our relations to the situation would be on a different basis. He is turning the matter over in his mind and is going to prepare a cable to his Government which he will show to you when he comes to Washington as he intends to do as soon as he gets authority to deal with the situation which he has cabled for. He is somewhat embarrassed by the facts that he cannot make any suggestions to his Government without disclosing them to the Dept.

I made it clear to him of course that I was not speaking for you or the Department.

Let me know if you want me in Washington.

Faithfully yours,

C[HANDLER] P. A[NDERSON]

841.857 Ar 1/90½a

The Secretary of State to President Wilson

WASHINGTON, *August 24, 1915.*

MY DEAR MR. PRESIDENT: In view of the situation created by the torpedoing of the *Arabic* and the danger of being involved in war with Germany in case we should sever diplomatic relations, which appears probable, I have been considering the general effect of a state of war between this country and Germany upon the part we desire to play when negotiations for peace may seem practicable.

The position which we have hoped to occupy, was that of a mutual friend to the belligerents, who would act as intermediary in opening negotiations and as a restraint upon either party in making oppressive demands.

As the war has progressed I have become more and more convinced that we are losing constantly the friendship of both parties and that we would have little influence upon either in bringing about negotiations or in moulding the terms of peace. It would take but little to eliminate us entirely in the final settlement.

So far as Germany is concerned, I think that we have lost irretrievably any influence we may have possessed over her Government, and that our participation in any way in the restoration of peace would be resented.

As to the Allies, I believe that their distorted views as to our attitude, which is certainly misunderstood in Great Britain, would deprive us of influence with them.

Now, on the assumption that we sever diplomatic intercourse with the German Government, which responds by a declaration of war, the consequences internationally would seem to be the complete restoration of friendship and confidence with the Allies and the necessary recognition of the United States as a party to the peace negotiations. We would be in a position to influence the Allies, if they should be victorious, to be lenient in their demands and to regain a part of the good will of Germany by being a generous enemy. If, on the other hand, Germany should triumph, we would be included in any settlement made, and Germany would be deprived of the free hand she would otherwise have in dealing with us after she had overcome her European adversaries.

If the foregoing views are sound, it would appear that our usefulness in the restoration of peace would certainly not be lessened by a state of war between this country and Germany, and it might even be increased.

I have endeavored to analyze the situation impartially from the standpoint of our international relations and not from the standpoint of domestic policy. As to the latter standpoint my ideas are less definite. I do not know what effect war would have upon the American people. Of one thing though I am convinced, it will not arouse very much enthusiasm, however it may be approved by the American people other than those of German birth or descent. Beyond this I do not wish at the present time to express an opinion.

Faithfully yours,

ROBERT LANSING

841.857 Ar 1/91½

President Wilson to the Secretary of State

WASHINGTON, *26 August, 1915.*

MY DEAR MR. SECRETARY: I very much appreciated your letter setting forth the pros and cons of the effect of hostilities with Germany. I find that it runs along very much the same lines as my own thought.

Faithfully Yours,

W. W.

841.857 Ar 1/91½a

The Secretary of State to President Wilson

WASHINGTON, *August 26, 1915.*

MY DEAR MR. PRESIDENT: Count Bernstorff at my request called upon me this morning. I informed him that I wished to see him about the proposed wireless code message which he desired us to send for him to his Government.[44] I pointed out to him the objectionable feature of making any reference to the *Arabic* in connection with negotiations; that the *Arabic* could not be considered in the same way as the *Lusitania* in view of what had passed between the Governments since the latter vessel was sunk; that he must appreciate that the torpedoing of the *Arabic* might interrupt further negotiations, since a condition of their continuance was the cessation of de-

---

[44] *Foreign Relations*, 1915, supp., p. 525.

stroying passenger vessels without warning and opportunity to reach a place of safety.

The Ambassador replied that he realized the situation had changed and that he would take the proposed wireless message and rewrite it. As soon as he sends it to me in revised form I will send it to you.

I then asked the Ambassador what the statement of his Government, which he had telegraphed to me and had made public,[45] meant in regard to instructions to submarine officers, that I would like to know what those instructions are.

He replied that he had not been told but supposed they referred to warnings and opportunities to leave ships attacked.

I asked him, if such instructions had been given, how there could be any doubt about their violation in the case of the *Arabic?*

He said that the facts seemed uncertain and he hoped to have an explanation from his Government.

To this I answered that we had received evidence from Americans on board the *Arabic* showing the vessel was torpedoed and that a German submarine had shelled the *Dunsley* and was seen by the survivors of that vessel after the *Arabic* foundered, and that there was practically no doubt at all but that the vessel was intentionally attacked without warning. I said to him that to advance any excuse of mistake by the submarine commander would be absurd and would irritate rather than relieve the situation.

He asked me if we were willing to await a report of the affair from Berlin, because he felt sure there was some explanation.

I replied that I could not see how any explanation could be given which would be satisfactory; and that our experience in awaiting reports of submarine attacks was not encouraging. I then pointed out the case of the *Orduna*, in which we had waited for a report for a month without reply. The Ambassador seemed greatly surprised and said that he could not understand it.

I said that any considerable delay could not be thought of, that, while the public feeling here was less demonstrative than it had been after the sinking of the *Lusitania*, I believed it to be far more intense.

He said that he realized this, but hoped that some time would be given so that his Government might have opportunity to make reparation if its officer was at fault.

This was the substance of our conversation.

The Ambassador seemed to be worried over the situation and was, for him, in a very serious mood. He is, however, optimistic that the affair can be amicably arranged. I did not indicate to him that I shared his optimism but rather tried to give him the impression that I considered the situation most critical and that Germany would

---

[45] *Foreign Relations*, 1915, supp., p. 524.

have to act quickly to avoid the consequences of the torpedoing of the *Arabic*, even if it were possible to do so.

Faithfully yours,

ROBERT LANSING

763.72/2139½

President Wilson to the Secretary of State [46]

WASHINGTON, *27 August, 1915.*

MY DEAR MR. SECRETARY: It does not seem to me that the Ambassador states our position fully enough here, and I should very much dread seeing his Government misled. Our point is, not merely that no passenger ships should be attacked without warning, but that care should be taken to make adequate provision for safe-guarding the lives of non-combatants. Mere warning on a stormy sea, mere putting of passengers and crew into open boats, might be as brutal as giving them no warning at all. "Without warning and provision for the safety of the lives of non-combatants", if he would accept the phraseology, would cover my point.

Faithfully Yours,

W. W.

763.72/2140½a

The Secretary of State to President Wilson [47]

WASHINGTON, *August 27, 1915.*

MY DEAR MR. PRESIDENT: I had a conversation this morning with the German Ambassador in which I told him of the objectionable feature of his proposed wireless message to Berlin. He appeared to appreciate the force of the objection and I accordingly returned him his letter of yesterday with the draft of message. I have now received another letter with a revise of the message.

If this meets with your approval please return it at once so that it can go forward to Berlin. I think that it practically eliminates the objectionable features of his former dispatch although, of course, he has in it the sentence—" . . . which would put the burden on England to refrain from unlawful blockade pending negotiations." I think, however, he is entitled to express this view which is his own.

Faithfully yours,

ROBERT LANSING

---

[46] This paper bears the notation: "Telegram of Amb. taken by him at 10 a m Aug 27/15 for revision RL."
[47] A notation attached to this paper reads: "Dear Mr. Sec'y: Thank you. I am willing that this should go forward. W. W."

111.33/98b

The Secretary of State to Colonel E. M. House

WASHINGTON, *August 28, 1915.*

MY DEAR COLONEL HOUSE:

.   .   .   .

You will have seen in the papers the general statement that Mr. Polk had been offered the position of Counsellor for the Department. How this became public I cannot imagine, and I was afraid it might embarrass Mr. Polk with Mayor Mitchel,[47a] who desired the matter to be kept secret for the present. As you doubtless know Mr. Polk has accepted the appointment and I am now only awaiting the assent of Mayor Mitchel to announce formally the appointment.

The German situation is much more favorable than it has been. There is a decided tendency on the part of the German Government to reach an amicable settlement. Of course we shall recede in no way from our position in regard to warnings, and provision for the safety of passengers and crews on vessels torpedoed. There is evidently a controversy between the Foreign Office and the Admiralty in Berlin. The attitude of the Foreign Office is one of [compliance with] our demands. Whether von Jagow, who is supported by the Chancellor, can succeed over the influence exerted by von Tirpitz and the Emperor is still in doubt, but the prospects seem good.

I will write you in regard to the Mexican situation in a few days, when I think that we will know more about it than we do at present.

With warm regards [etc.]   ROBERT LANSING

———————

763.72/2142½a

The Secretary of State to President Wilson

WASHINGTON, *September 2, 1915.*

MY DEAR MR. PRESIDENT: I have just received the following telegram from Mr. Bryan:

"Please accept for yourself, and convey to the President my hearty congratulations upon the successful settlement of the submarine controversy."

I have also received from David R. Francis, Esquire,[48] the following:

"Germany's conceding our contention is great diplomatic achievement for America and merits hearty congratulations which are sincerely tendered."

———————

[47a] Mayor of New York City.
[48] Former Governor of Missouri; former Secretary of the Interior; appointed Ambassador to Russia Mar. 6, 1916.

I have received other communications of a similar nature but these two, I think, would be of particular interest to you.

Faithfully yours,

ROBERT LANSING

841.857 Ar 1/51

The Secretary of State to President Wilson

WASHINGTON, *September 4, 1915.*

MY DEAR MR. PRESIDENT: I have just received a letter from the German Ambassador, a copy of which I enclose to you.[49]

I do not feel that we should wait very long for an explanation in regard to the *Arabic* and I am inclined to answer the Ambassador to that effect. What would be your impression of letting him know that the attitude of the German Government might be stated hypothetically on the evidence which we have received from the survivors of the *Arabic* and the persons who were on board the *Dunsley?* This, of course, would be based on the fact that the German Admiralty is not in receipt of a report within a short time.

I will not reply to Count von Bernstorff until I hear from you as to your wishes.

Faithfully yours,

ROBERT LANSING

841.857/32½

President Wilson to the Secretary of State

WASHINGTON, *7 September, 1915.*

MY DEAR MR. SECRETARY: The sinking of the *Hesperian* [49a] has for the time arrested everything, and therefore an answer to the enclosed [50] is perhaps too much belated to be of any use to you. But this is clear, that we should let the German Government know that it was not wise to wait too long to state their attitude and the course they intend to pursue with regard to the sinking of the *Arabic.*

However, we shall not be certain of anything until we hear all the facts about the *Hesperian.*

Faithfully Yours,

W. W.

---

[49] *Foreign Relations,* 1915, supp., p. 533.
[49a] For correspondence previously printed regarding the *Hesperian,* see *ibid.,* pp. 533–556 *passim,* and p. 607.
[50] Note of Sept. 3, 1915, from the German Ambassador, *ibid.,* p. 533.

841.857/28

The Secretary of State to President Wilson

WASHINGTON, *September 9, 1915.*

MY DEAR MR. PRESIDENT: I enclose to you three letters which I have received today from the German Ambassador, and to which I have made no reply.[51] Please return them at your earliest convenience.

Faithfully yours,

ROBERT LANSING

[Enclosure]

The German Ambassador (*Bernstorff*) to the Secretary of State

CEDARHURST, N. Y., *September 8, 1915.*
[Received September 9.]

MY DEAR MR. SECRETARY: I have just received the following wireless message from Berlin:

"According to information available here it seems highly improbable that *Hesperian* was torpedoed. Much more likely boat ran on mine. Foreign Office."

I remain [etc.]   J. BERNSTORFF

763.72/2106

The Secretary of State to President Wilson

WASHINGTON, *September 9, 1915.*

MY DEAR MR. PRESIDENT: I enclose you a telegram which has just been received from Ambassador Page, in London, which, as you see, is of a strictly confidential nature.[52]

I confess that it conveys to me an impression that the British Government and British public are desirous of having us "pull their chestnuts out of the fire".

As I assume this telegram is intended for you especially, I wish you would indicate, if you will be so good, what answer, if any, should be made to it.

Faithfully yours,

ROBERT LANSING

---

[51] Two of these letters are printed in *Foreign Relations*, 1915, supp., pp. 538, 540; the third is printed *infra.*
[52] *Foreign Relations*, 1915, supp., p. 537.

841.857/30½

President Wilson to the Secretary of State

WASHINGTON, *10 September, 1915.*

MY DEAR MR. SECRETARY: The only present comment necessary on these letters,[53] obviously meant to be reassuring, is that my original error in speaking of "unarmed" vessels when I should have said "unresisting" is now rising up to embarrass us, for which I am very sorry.

The reply about the *Arabic,* if correctly outlined in the newspapers this morning, is not very promising of a fulfilment of what Bernstorff indicates as the attitude of his government in these letters.

Faithfully Yours,

W. W.

763.72/2140½

President Wilson to the Secretary of State

WASHINGTON, *10 September, 1915.*

MY DEAR MR. SECRETARY: I do not think any answer to this despatch is necessary.[54]

It is no doubt useful to know what opinion is on the other side of the water. After while even Englishmen will begin to understand (I wonder if they really ever will?) that what we are guided by is our sense of what is just and right and not our sensibility as regards what other nations think about us.

Faithfully Yours,

W. W.

841.857 Ar 1/62

The Secretary of State to President Wilson

WASHINGTON, *September 11, 1915.*

MY DEAR MR. PRESIDENT: I have received a note from the German Ambassador dated the 9th,[55] asking me whether I wish to discuss with him the *Arabic* case. I have not replied to the note as I thought it well to have an understanding as to what our course is to be before I see Bernstorff, if I do see him at all, on this matter. I am sending you in another letter a rather full discussion of the *Arabic* case and my views as to the probable course we will have to adopt.

---

[53] See Secretary Lansing's letter of Sept. 9, 1915, to President Wilson, p. 476 (file No. 841.857/28).
[54] See footnote 52, p. 476.
[55] Not printed.

The Ambassador added in his letter the following:

"As you know I also have instructions to discuss our answer to your last *Lusitania* note with you as soon as you consider the *Arabic* incident closed."

Faithfully yours,

ROBERT LANSING

841.857 Ar 1/89

The Secretary of State to President Wilson

WASHINGTON, *September 11, 1915.*

MY DEAR MR. PRESIDENT: I have been through the German note on the *Arabic* case [56] and also the affidavits which we have received from London and Liverpool given by survivors of the *Arabic* and of the *Dunsley*.[56a]

I consider that the German note is most unsatisfactory; that in fact we are back where we were before Count von Bernstorff communicated to us the German admission of principle in submarine warfare.

From the evidence I think that the following facts are conclusively established:

(1) The *Arabic* was never nearer the *Dunsley* than two miles;

(2) The *Arabic* was pursuing a zig-zag course, which is a customary maneuver when the presence of a submarine is suspected.

This method of avoidance must have been known to the submarine commander so that the changes of course by the *Arabic* could not have been mistaken by the commander as an attempt to ram, though the *Arabic* might have been headed for him at one or more times during her approach to the *Dunsley*.

(3) The submarine, on observing the approach of the *Arabic*, submerged;

(4) The submarine was never seen by any person on board the *Arabic*. If it had been seen, the presumption would be that the *Arabic*, being at least a mile or more away, would have turned from and not toward the submarine, as the *Arabic* carried no armament.

(5) The torpedo was not seen by persons on board the *Arabic* until it was about two hundred yards away from the vessel. There was evidently no time to swing the vessel to any considerable extent after the torpedo was seen. Yet the torpedo appears to have struck the *Arabic* almost at right angles, not far from the vessel's beam. Judging the location of the submarine by the direction from which the torpedo came, the submarine commander could not, at the time the torpedo was released, have had the slightest reason to suppose that the *Arabic* was attempting to ram his vessel.

---

[56] *Foreign Relations*, 1915, supp., p. 539.
[56a] See telegram No. 2680, Aug. 23, 1915, from the Ambassador in Great Britain, *ibid.*, p. 518; also telegram No. 2186, Sept. 14, 1915, to the Ambassador in Germany, *ibid.*, p. 547.

(6) The unavoidable conclusion seems to be that the submarine commander did not believe the *Arabic* was attempting to attack him, but that he wantonly torpedoed the vessel without warning and with utter disregard for the lives of persons on board.

I would submit the following comments on the German note:

The statements as to what occurred do not purport to be by the commander of the submarine. Every allegation might easily be constructed from the press reports of the incident. The only fact alleged which appears to be solely within the knowledge of the officers of the submarine, is the alleged attack in the Irish sea on August 14th, five days before the *Arabic* was sunk, and this may have been reported to the German Admiralty before the *Arabic* incident occurred.

The question arises—Did the submarine commander make any report? If he did, why does the note fail to say so, and why does it not give the language of the report as to the facts?

Reference is made to the instructions issued to the Commander of the submarine. Why is not the language of the instructions given?

The failure to admit liability for indemnity for the lives of American citizens lost amounts to a justification of the commander. If the commander is justified in drawing such a conclusion, as it is alleged in the note the commander of the submarine did draw from the facts in this case, then the lives of persons on board merchant ships are in as great danger as they were before the instructions were issued.

The note proposes to submit the question of liability to The Hague for arbitration, expressly withholding the question of the legality of submarine warfare in general.

The whole tenor of the note is a cold and uncompromising declaration that the commanders of submarines have practically a free hand though bound, technically, by some general form of instructions, and that if they make mistakes, however unwarranted, their Government will support them. It seems to me that we must reach a conclusion that the Bernstorff statement of principle is valueless and cannot be relied upon as a protective measure.

If the foregoing analysis of the evidence as to the facts is true, and the comments on the German note are justified, it would seem as if a course which this Government might pursue is to inform the Berlin Government that the note is highly unsatisfactory both in its declarations and in its tone, and a demand that the act of the submarine commander who torpedoed the *Arabic*, being deliberately unfriendly, be disavowed, that the officer be punished for his wanton and illegal conduct, and that a formal declaration be made that the sinking of the *Arabic* was contrary to the instructions issued to submarine commanders, of which instructions this Government was notified by the German Ambassador here.

If the foregoing course is not adopted, I see no alternative other than to announce that the German note is entirely unacceptable as an explanation of the conduct of the submarine commander, and that as the German Government supports the commander, this Government must consider that the German attitude is one of deliberate unfriendliness and, therefore, the United States must sever diplomatic relations with Germany.

I regret very much that the present situation has arisen which seems to preclude further negotiations, as continued discussion of this subject would, I believe, be contrary to the dignity of the United States and would invite general criticism from the American people. I further think that we should reach a decision promptly.

Faithfully yours,

ROBERT LANSING

841.857 Ar 1/91½b

The Secretary of State to President Wilson

WASHINGTON, *September 13, 1915.*

MY DEAR MR. PRESIDENT: The interview with the German Ambassador on the *Arabic* case took place at noon today. I believe that he fully appreciates the gravity of the situation and is very anxious about the outcome. I also believe that he will do anything in his power to have his Government take the steps necessary to change the situation.

We discussed the German note on the *Arabic* and I pointed out to him very explicitly the objectionable features which made it impossible for us to reply to it in its present form. I told him that the attack upon the *Arabic* and the unconditional support of the submarine commander's conduct by his Government made the Ambassador's acceptance of the principle insisted upon by the United States as valueless. He replied that he understood perfectly that such must be our feeling; that he had done all he could to prevent such a crisis as the present; and that he was greatly disappointed at what had occurred. He said that all the information which his Government had, of course, was the report of the submarine commander and that he wished they might know of the evidence which we possessed, and which I had read to him. I told him that in view of the critical state of affairs the Government was disposed to transmit for him a cipher message to his Government in order that he might explain fully the situation, and that we would send to Ambassador Gerard, at von Bernstorff's request, a summary of the evidence which we had in regard to the *Arabic*.

I pointed out to him at the same time that the *Arabic* note did not disclose that any report had been received from the submarine commander, and if the statements were based on such a report I thought that his Government should so inform us.

I said that the instructions to the submarine commander had never been revealed to us except in the most general terms, and, therefore, we did not know what discretionary powers had been conferred upon the commander.

The Ambassador seemed particularly grateful for our willingness to transmit a message for him and said that he would impress upon his Government the seriousness of the present situation.

I also said that such a mistake as was made by the officer who attacked the *Arabic* made this Government very doubtful as to the efficacy of the instructions.

He said that he realized that that must be so and that he was very much distressed at what had happened; that he was not sure that he could accomplish what was desired; but that he would use every effort to do so.

I also said to him that I thought the German Government should broaden its declaration so as to include all merchant vessels and not be limited to passenger steamers; that in the past the practice of the German submarines has been to warn freight vessels and I could not see why an exception should be made in their case as to the general principle, since some of these freighters might have American citizens in their crews. He replied that he would do what he could to obtain such an extension of the principle which his Government had announced.

We also spoke of the matter of arbitration and I said to him that I thought it was valueless at the present time to discuss it because I considered the evidence was so clear in the case of the *Arabic* that we could not arbitrate the justification of the submarine commander and that the only question left was the amount of indemnity; that I thought his Government should admit that the mistake was without justification and disavow the act of the officer; and that it would then be a proper time to discuss whether or not we could arbitrate the amount of indemnity which Germany should pay.

The whole attitude of the Ambassador was conciliatory and an evidence of willingness to do anything to avoid a rupture between the two Governments. I think I may say he was extremely "docile". There was none of the aggressiveness which he has shown on other occasions. He seemed to be much depressed, and doubtful as to what he could accomplish with his Government.

He did not mention his desire to have an audience with you and I did not think it worth while to inform him that at the present it would be impossible for you to see him.

Faithfully yours,

ROBERT LANSING

841.857 Ar 1/103½

Colonel E. M. House to President Wilson

NEW YORK, *September 26, 1915.*

DEAR GOVERNOR: Bernstorff came to see me very promptly this morning. He said he had an intimation from Washington, indirectly through Tumulty, that you wanted him to hasten the *Arabic* matter and to see Lansing when he passes through New York before he reaches Washington.

This is what he would like to know.

(1) Do you want anything done before he sees Lansing? He reiterates that what he can do now is to give additional assurances directly from his government that no passenger vessel will be torpedoed in the future without notice, and that the ship will have the benefit of the doubt.

(2) They are willing to submit the *Arabic* case to an international commission and accept the principle of indemnity for the loss of life. If this is not satisfactory, he will take the question up with his government as to some form of disavowal based upon American evidence. But if his government makes the disavowal they would want to refer the question of reparation to the Hague.

(3) If you decide a disavowal must be made, do you want him to make an effort at once, or would you prefer that he wait until after he consults Lansing?

I have told him I thought I could get him this information by Tuesday morning.[57]

Your devoted,

E. M. HOUSE

841.857 Ar 1/104½

President Wilson to the Secretary of State

WASHINGTON, *30 September, 1915.*

MY DEAR MR. SECRETARY: I enclose for your information a letter from House, which explains itself.[58]

I replied that I was willing to wait until Bernstorff could see you in New York on Saturday,[59] and that when he did see you I thought

[57] September 28.
[58] *Supra.*
[59] October 2.

it best that he should take it for granted that we would have to insist upon a disavowal of the action of the submarine commander in sinking the *Arabic*. I said that I did not think that public opinion in this country would be in the least satisfied with anything short of that.

You will know better than I can as yet just what line to take with the Ambassador when you see him.

I hope that you have had a real and a very refreshing rest. We shall all be mighty glad to see you back. Polk has been doing finely.

Faithfully Yours,

WOODROW WILSON

841.857 Ar 1/105½

The German Ambassador (Bernstorff) to the Secretary of State

CEDARHURST, N. Y., *October 2, 1915.*

MY DEAR MR. SECRETARY: Prompted by the desire to reach a satisfactory agreement with regard to the *Arabic* incident my Government has given me the following instructions:

The orders issued by His Majesty the Emperor to the commanders of the German submarines—of which I notified you on a previous occasion—have been made so stringent that the recurrence of incidents similar to the *Arabic* case is considered out of the question.

According to the report of Commander Schneider of the submarine that sank the *Arabic* and his affidavit as well as those of his men, Commander Schneider was convinced that the *Arabic* intended to ram the submarine, and he evidently had every reason to be so convinced. On the other hand, the Imperial Government does not doubt the good faith of the affidavits of the British officers of the *Arabic*, according to which the *Arabic* did not intend to ram the submarine. The attack of the submarine, therefore, was undertaken against the instructions issued to the commander. The Imperial Government regrets this and has notified Commander Schneider accordingly.

As you know, my Government does not recognize the liability of paying indemnity for the American lives, which to its deep regret have been lost on the *Arabic*.

However, in a spirit of conciliation and friendship for the United States my Government will be prepared to pay an indemnity, about the amount of which I am authorized to negotiate with you.

I am [etc.] J. BERNSTORFF

763.72/2236½

The German Ambassador (Bernstorff) to the Secretary of State

CEDARHURST, N. Y., *October 2, 1915.*

MY DEAR MR. SECRETARY: With regard to our conversation about the *Arabic* incident this morning I beg to say that according to my instructions the report of Commander Schneider of our submarine and the German affidavits have been sent to you through the American Embassy in Berlin. If you should not have received them, I will be glad to send you a copy.

In this same envelope I have pleasure in sending you my tentative letter about the *Lusitania* incident.

I remain [etc.]   J. BERNSTORFF

[Enclosure]

Tentative Letter From the German Ambassador (Bernstorff) to the Secretary of State [60]

CEDARHURST, N. Y., *October 2, 1915.*

MY DEAR MR. SECRETARY: Prompted by the desire to reach an amicable understanding about the *Lusitania* incident my Government has given me the following instructions:

The attack on the *Lusitania* formed part of the reprisals enacted by my Government against Great Britain on account of her unlawful starvation policy. In our opinion such reprisals were amply justified by the inhuman British warfare. At that time the Imperial Government had not yet issued the instructions which now regulate our submarine warfare and according to which the *Arabic* case was settled. Even then, however, it was not the intention of the Imperial Government that our reprisals should lead to the loss of the lives of non-combatants. My Government has, therefore, on previous occasions expressed its deep regret that American lives should have been lost on the *Lusitania.*

As you know, the Imperial government does not acknowledge any liability to grant an indemnity in the matter. However, in a spirit of friendship and conciliation the Imperial Government is prepared to submit the question of liability to pay indemnity to the Hague Tribunal.

In your note of July 21st concerning the *Lusitania* incident [61] the Government of the United States invited the practical cooperation of the Imperial German Government in contending for the principle of the freedom of the seas, and you added that this great object could

---

[60] Filed separately under file No. 763.72/2235½.
[61] *Foreign Relations,* 1915, supp., p. 480.

in some way be accomplished before the present war ends. I am instructed to say that the Imperial Government will at all times gladly cooperate with the Government of the United States for the purpose of accomplishing this great common object.

I remain [etc.] J. BERNSTORFF

841.857 Ar 1/106½

Memorandum by the Secretary of State of an Interview With the German Ambassador (Bernstorff), October 5, 1915, 10:30 a. m.

The German Ambassador called at my request in regard to the note which he had submitted to me, dated October 2d, concerning the *Arabic* case.[62]

I informed the Ambassador that when he handed me the note in New York on the 2d that as I then told him I was not prepared to comment upon it, although I congratulated him on having influenced his Government to secure an amicable settlement of the controversy. I also told him that after digesting the note I had submitted it to the President, without comment, and that he had reached substantially the same conclusion as I—namely, that it was not satisfactory in its present form.

The Ambassador asked me in what particulars it was not satisfactory. I pointed out to him that in the third (3) paragraph the German Government appeared to support entirely the commander of the submarine in the conviction which he had reached as to the purpose of the *Arabic* to ram the submarine. I told him that in view of the fact that the note stated that the attack of the submarine was against the instructions issued to the commander, this assertion appeared to be contradictory.

The Ambassador replied that he was willing to omit that from the note.

I also said that it was very unsatisfactory that the note failed to frankly disavow the act; that there was no question but that the language was open to the interpretation of the disavowal. The Ambassador said that that was his intention and I then asked him why he had not stated it in the note. He said he thought that he possibly could do so.

In regard to the last paragraph, relating to the payment of indemnity, I said to him that the note offered to pay an indemnity as an act of grace and that this Government could not accept it on that basis, for they considered there was a legal right to an indemnity. I suggested, however, that a controversy on this point could be avoided by a change of language.

[62] *Ante*, p. 483.

The changes which I proposed I indicated on the note of October 2d, in lead pencil.[63]

The Ambassador said that he was not sure whether his instructions would permit him to go as far as these changes, but that he would go back to the Embassy and examine the instructions, and if they were broad enough he would make the changes proposed and would send me a new note within an hour.

When he left I was convinced that he would meet the wishes of this Government as he assured me his instructions were of the broadest character.

ROBERT LANSING

838.51/438½

The Secretary of State to Colonel E. M. House

WASHINGTON, *October 6, 1915.*

MY DEAR COLONEL HOUSE:

You will have seen by the morning papers the successful outcome of the negotiations regarding the *Arabic*. Last Saturday, when I saw the German Ambassador, I felt a measure of discouragement on account of the note which he then handed me. I told him, however, I would take the matter up with the President. I did so and the President agreed with me that we could not accept a note of that sort. After reaching this decision I asked Count von Bernstorff to call upon me at the Department, which he did on Tuesday, and the published note is the result of our conference on that day.

I hope I can see you in a few days in regard to the South American matter,[64] in which the President is so much interested, and concerning which I am not as familiar as I wish I was. I have no doubt that a talk with you would help very much.

With warm regards [etc.]

ROBERT LANSING

462.11 Se 8/48

The Secretary of State to President Wilson

WASHINGTON, *October 8, 1915.*

MY DEAR MR. PRESIDENT: I enclose an instruction to our Ambassador at Berlin relative to the *William P. Frye* case.[65] It is in response

---

[63] For the resulting text of the note dated Oct. 5, 1915, see *Foreign Relations, 1915,* supp., p. 560.

[64] Negotiations for a pan-American treaty. See vol. II, pp. 471 ff.

[65] For the instruction as sent, see *Foreign Relations, 1915,* supp., p. 570.

to the German note on the subject dated September 19—the original of which I also enclose.[66]

You will perceive that we accept the proposal for a joint commission of experts to fix the amount of indemnity and also agree to submit to arbitration the controversy as to the interpretation of the Treaty of 1828. As the submission to arbitration will be by *compromis* it will be necessary to lay it before the Senate for their consent. For this reason I am troubling you with the matter.

I believe the course proposed in the telegram to be advisable, as it will close the interchange of notes on the subject.

Faithfully yours,

ROBERT LANSING

462.11 Se 8/53½

President Wilson to the Secretary of State

WASHINGTON, *12 October, 1915.*

MY DEAR MR. SECRETARY: I entirely approve of this.

I notice that there is nothing in the despatch to intimate to the Imperial Government that the submission to arbitration will need, so far as we are concerned, the consent of the Senate. Would it not be well to instruct the Ambassador to give this information to the Berlin Foreign Office?

Faithfully Yours,

W. W.

763.72/2237½

Colonel E. M. House to the Secretary of State

NEW YORK, *October 30, 1915.*
[Received November 1.]

DEAR MR. LANSING: Bernstorff has just called. He says his Government believe that the concessions they made in regard to submarine warfare, were largely for the purpose of getting us to maintain the doctrine of the freedom of the seas, and he wonders if this is not a propitious time for something to be done, either by them or by us.

I told him that what we all wanted was success and not a mere agitation for political or other reasons. That it might be very inadvisable to discuss this doctrine at this time, or to openly advocate it. I strongly advised against his Government pushing it at all for the reason that it would probably harden public opinion in England

[66] *Ibid.*, p. 551.

against it and make it more difficult of accomplishment when the right moment comes.

He tells me that he hopes to see you on Monday or Tuesday of next week, and I thought it well for you to know of our conversation.

Sincerely yours,

E. M. HOUSE

763.72/2269a

The Secretary of State to President Wilson

WASHINGTON, *November 2, 1915.*

MY DEAR MR. PRESIDENT: I had a talk this morning with Ambassador Bernstorff in regard to the *Lusitania* matter. He is evidently far less hopeful of a settlement satisfactory to this Government of that case than of the *Arabic* case. I think I can understand this attitude in view of the telegrams which we have received from Berlin, and which you have undoubtedly seen, as to the disapproval of his Government of his action in admitting as much as he did. I believe he has been told by his Government that his conduct of that matter was not satisfactory. For that reason I did not feel that I could insist as strongly as I otherwise could that the German Government should admit the wrong and pay indemnity without the intervention of arbitration.

At the time that the Ambassador delivered to me the note which settled the *Arabic* question he also handed me for consideration a draft of a note in regard to the *Lusitania*.[67] He again produced this draft and said that he felt sure that was as far as his Government could go in the matter. I told him that I would consider the draft further but that in its present form it would be unacceptable to this Government. I will, in a day or two, send you the draft with notes and suggestions as to what, it seems to me, would be satisfactory. The Ambassador said that any suggestions I might have he would have to refer to Berlin as he did not feel he was authorized to accept them without instructions.

I pointed out to him (the Ambassador) that in view of the fact that they had under their naval instructions ceased to attack passenger vessels I could see no practical reason why they should insist that the attack on the *Lusitania* was justifiable; that there might be a sentimental reason for this insistence in view of the natural dislike which a Government had to admit a wrongful act and that I realized the public opinion in Germany might criticise such an admission. I told him further that I was willing to go as far as possible to relieve that situation but that we also had to deal with public opin-

---

[67] See p. 484.

ion in this country and that in the case of the *Lusitania* it was not a sentimental matter at all but a practical matter and that I thought his Government should admit liability for the loss of life. He said that he was convinced his Government would not make such an admission and that some other method would have to be found to determine liability. I also said to him that I thought the matter should be settled because we had already been extremely patient in the matter. He replied that if we insisted upon an admission of liability he did not believe it could be settled. I said that I regretted very much to have him say that as I felt that the question must be settled and very soon.

He left me with the understanding that I would go over the draft and communicate with him in a few days.

Faithfully yours,

ROBERT LANSING

763.72/2269b

The Secretary of State to President Wilson

WASHINGTON, *November 11, 1915.*

MY DEAR MR. PRESIDENT: I submit for your consideration a proposed formula in the *Lusitania* case which, if it meets with your approval, I will discuss orally with the German Ambassador.

You will observe that I have not used the word "disavow" in the formula as I am convinced that the German Government will not be willing to use the word in view of the great dissatisfaction expressed in regard to its use in the settlement of the *Arabic* case. I believe, however, that the last paragraph of the formula may be interpreted as a disavowal and if we can obtain the assent of the German Government to that paragraph it will be interpreted generally as a formal disavowal.

I would like your views in this matter at your earliest convenience as I wish to renew my conversations with the Ambassador as soon as possible.

Faithfully yours,

ROBERT LANSING

[Enclosure]

Formula Proposed by the Secretary of State in the "Lusitania" Case

The sinking of the British Steamship *Lusitania* was in pursuance of a policy of retaliation against the enemies of Germany.

Retaliatory measures by a belligerent against an enemy are essentially acts in contravention of the recognized rules of warfare.

Citizens of the United States on the *Lusitania* were justified in the belief that the recognized rules of warfare would be applied in the event that the steamship was intercepted by a German war vessel.

The sinking of the *Lusitania* being in violation of the international rules of naval warfare the act was illegal and so far as the lives of citizens of the United States are concerned imposed upon the German Government liability therefor.

The German Government, having in its instructions to its naval officers issued subsequent to the event shown its recognition that the sinking of the *Lusitania* was contrary to the rules of naval warfare and to the principles of humanity, expresses profound regret that citizens of the United States suffered by reason of the act of its naval authorities in sinking the *Lusitania*, declares it to have been in contravention of international law, and offers to make reparation for the lives of citizens of the United States which were lost, by the payment of a suitable indemnity.

NOVEMBER 11, 1915.

763.72/2269½

President Wilson to the Secretary of State

WASHINGTON, *17 November, 1915.*

MY DEAR MR. SECRETARY: I believe that neither you nor I are satisfied with this formula, but I think that it is probably the best that can be drawn, and I hope that you will press it upon the German Imperial Government. I have kept it in the hope that I could suggest something more satisfactory, but I have not been able to formulate anything that pleased me at all.

Faithfully Yours,

W. W.

763.72/2270½

Memorandum by the Secretary of State of an Interview With the German Ambassador (Bernstorff)

[WASHINGTON,] *November 17, 1915.*

The German Ambassador called upon me this afternoon at the Department at my request. I told him that it seemed necessary that the *Lusitania* case should be settled if possible within a very short time—that the recent sinking of the *Ancona*, although acknowledged by Austria to have been done by her submarine, had aroused deep feeling in this country; that the peculiar thing was that in spite of the Austrian admission the blame was falling upon Germany as being the dominant power in the Central Alliance.

The Ambassador said that he realized that that was so and that when I had last seen him I told him I would endeavor to have some suggestions which he might consider.

I told him that I had prepared a formula which seemed to me possible and that I had avoided the use of the word—"disavow"—and substituted in its place an acknowledgement of illegality. I then handed him the paper which is hereto annexed.[68] He read it through and said that he would submit it to his Government, as he had no authority to go beyond the proposed letter which he had sent me at the time of the settlement of the *Arabic* case.

We further discussed the general situation in this country in regard to submarine warfare. I told him that I hoped this matter could be settled satisfactorily to this Government before the assembling of Congress, as the present resentment of public opinion in this country might cause a serious situation of affairs if the matter was discussed in Congress; that it was even possible that Congress, with whom the power rested, might declare war. He replied that he appreciated the seriousness of the present situation but that he could do no more than submit the formula to his Government; that he considered the great difficulty lay in the admission of liability for the lives of Americans on a British vessel, which they had denied.

I pointed out to him that in view of the changed policy of the German Government and its return to the recognized rules of warfare in the conduct of its submarine activities it would amount to a practical final settlement of the controversy, and that I earnestly hoped he would be able to accomplish this. I further said to him that I realized the difficulty of the German Government in dealing with public opinion in Germany, but that I thought the time was especially opportune on account of our recent note to Great Britain.[69]

He answered me that he was in entire accord as to the advantage of urging a settlement at this time, both on account of the note to England, and on account of the approaching assembling of Congress.

He left me with the understanding that he would immediately send the formula to his Government and ask for instructions.

ROBERT LANSING

763.72/2270½a

The Secretary of State to President Wilson

WASHINGTON, *November 19, 1915.*

MY DEAR MR. PRESIDENT: I am afraid that we are coming to an *impasse* in the matter of the *Lusitania.* Day before yesterday I had a conversation with the German Ambassador and submitted to him

---

[68] The formula proposed by the Secretary of State, p. 489.
[69] *Foreign Relations*, 1915, supp., p. 578.

the possible formula which his Government might employ. He said that he would send it to his Government as his instructions were not broad enough to assent or dissent, but that he was doubtful of his Government admitting any liability for the lives of Americans lost on board of a British vessel.

Of course, if Germany takes this position and we do not recede from our position, which we cannot do, there is a deadlock which no further diplomatic exchanges would affect, exchanges which, in my opinion, it would be unwise and improper to continue.

From two or three sources, which have been heretofore reliable, I have reports that the German Ambassador has indicated that it is his plan or that of his Government to prolong discussion of the question until the American people had forgotten it and this Government had let it drop.

Whether these reports are true or not I think that delay would cause wide criticism of the Administration as being supine and ready to go any lengths in order to avoid a direct issue with Germany.

Assuming that Germany fails to act promptly on the formula which we have suggested or refuses to acknowledge liability for the loss of American lives on the *Lusitania*, I believe that a situation will arise which will call for definite and firm action on our part and that action should be taken without delay. In order to do this our policy should be determined in advance. It seems to me that we have two courses to pursue. First. To sever diplomatic relations by withdrawing Gerard and by handing Bernstorff his passports. Second. By laying the facts before Congress and stating that, as further negotiations will be useless, it will be necessary to act, and that, as the action which may be necessary may be of nature involving the question of war or peace, the matter is laid before the branch of the Government charged with power to declare war.

Probably the first method is the simplest and less liable to commit the Government to drastic action. On the other hand the second method would impress the public, I believe, with the fact that the Administration desired the representatives, supposed to be nearest the people, to determine a question which may precipitate war.

From the selfish standpoint of politics I think that the people generally are very much dissatisfied with a continuance of negotiations, that, if our demands are not acceded to, they desire action in asserting our rights, and that if there is further delay, they will turn against the Administration. I believe the pro-German vote in this country is irrevocably lost to us and that, no matter what we do now, we can never win back any part of it. If this view is correct, we ought not from the political standpoint lose the support of the Americans hostile to Germany. And I am afraid that we will do so if we are not rigid in our attitude on the *Lusitania* case. The people have, I think, been patient and considerate in view of the fact that nearly seven months have passed since the vessel was torpedoed. They do not reason out the causes which compelled delay and I doubt if it could be explained satisfactorily to them. At any rate I notice a growing spirit of complaint at what they consider inaction by the Government. The country newspapers as well as letters coming in voice this increasing dissatisfaction.

I should like, therefore, an indication of your views on this subject in order that I may regulate my conversations with Count von Bernstorff accordingly and may be prepared to act promptly if action becomes necessary.

Faithfully yours,

ROBERT LANSING

763.72/2271½

President Wilson to the Secretary of State

WASHINGTON, *21 November, 1915.*

MY DEAR MR. SECRETARY: I am quite clear that the position we should take, in conversations with the German Ambassador and in all future dealings with his government in regard to the matters in controversy between us, is

First, that the matter of the *Lusitania* is just as important and just as acute now as it was the day the news of her sinking arrived, and that a failure to secure a satisfactory settlement will disclose the same questions of future action that then lay in the background;

Second, that we now know, as a result of the various communications that have passed between that government and this, that the commander of the submarine which sank the *Lusitania* acted contrary to the instructions which had been given by the Imperial German Admiralty; and

Third, that we should regard a failure to settle this question in the same frank way that the sinking of the *Arabic* was settled would be little less than a repudiation of the assurances then given us and seem to lead back to the very crisis in our relations that was then so happily avoided.

I think the Ambassador cannot be too explicit with his government in this matter.

Is there anyone representing Austria here whom we could get to understand the seriousness of the *Ancona* affair? Or do you feel that you know enough of the facts?

Faithfully Yours,

W. W.

865.857 An 2/75a

The Secretary of State to President Wilson

WASHINGTON, *November 22, 1915.*

MY DEAR MR. PRESIDENT: I enclose a memorandum [70] of the information which we have in regard to the *Ancona* case.[71] It seems to me that it is very unsatisfactory as to detail and definiteness. We have made other inquiries in regard to the case both at Vienna and Rome which I hope will throw more light on the subject.

The Austro-Hungarian affairs in this country are in the hands of the Chargé, Baron Zwiedinek, and we can communicate with him whenever the time seems opportune.

I also enclose an editorial from the New York *Evening Mail* [70] which seems to me is very sensible and shows that some of the papers at least understand the difficulties which the Department has to face in a case of this sort.

Faithfully yours,

ROBERT LANSING

865.857 An 2/75½

President Wilson to the Secretary of State

WASHINGTON, *24 November, 1915.*

MY DEAR MR. SECRETARY: This information is, as you say, most unsatisfactorily incomplete and inconclusive. I sincerely hope that we can get a complete account of the case from the two points of view of Rome and Vienna, through our Ambassadors, at an early date. I think the public are growing uneasy because of our apparent inaction in what seems a very aggravated case.

Faithfully Yours,

W. W.

763.72/2322½

President Wilson to the Secretary of State

WASHINGTON, *24 November, 1915.*

MY DEAR MR. SECRETARY: Here are two recent letters from Mr. House which I am sure will interest you.[72] Bernstorff evidently wants to use House as a channel of unofficial communication with us.

---

[70] Not printed.
[71] For correspondence previously printed concerning the *Ancona* case, see *Foreign Relations*, 1915, supp., pp. 611–658, *passim*.
[72] Not enclosed with file copy of this letter.

I would be very much obliged to you if you would return the letters with your comments on them.

Faithfully Yours,

W. W.

763.72/2322½

The Secretary of State to President Wilson

WASHINGTON, *November 24, 1915.*

MY DEAR MR. PRESIDENT: Thank you for letting me see the two letters from Colonel House, which I herewith return.

I tried to impress upon Bernstorff when I saw him the necessity of a speedy settlement of the *Lusitania* case. I have heard nothing from him since that conversation and shall write him today urging him to act in the matter. Something must be done before Congress assembles or else I am afraid we will have some embarrassing requests for the correspondence.

I think the time is very opportune for us to press compliance with our demands, with the success for the Teutonic arms in the Balkans and the wavering neutrality of Roumania and Greece the German Government could ill afford to have any sort of a break with this Government on account of the moral effect it would have.

In regard to the discussion relative to peace, I think that there is a possibility that it might work out along the lines suggested but there are so many problems connected with it—such as boundaries, colonial possessions and indemnities, that I hardly like to express an opinion until it takes more definite form.

In regard to the two questions which Colonel House asks in his second letter [73] relative to the removal of certain persons connected with the Embassies and Consular Service of Germany and Austria-Hungary, I feel that the time is very near when some such step should be taken. As you know, we have been collecting and marshalling, as far as possible, the evidence which we have against the various individuals. While the proofs are not conclusive I think there is sufficient for action but I would prefer to submit to you the memorandum on the subject before any decision is reached.

In regard to severing diplomatic relations with Austria on account of the *Ancona*, you know how incomplete our information is. I hope that we may shortly have something definite from Vienna and from Rome also.

I am attending the Army-Navy football game in New York on Saturday and will remain over Sunday. Colonel House has been

---

[73] See Charles Seymour, *The Intimate Papers of Colonel House*, vol. II, p. 47.

good enough to invite Mrs. Lansing and myself to luncheon Sunday, so I will have an opportunity to discuss these questions with him at length.

Faithfully yours,

[File copy not signed]

763.72/2322c

The Secretary of State to the German Ambassador (Bernstorff)

WASHINGTON, *November 24, 1915.*

MY DEAR MR. AMBASSADOR: I have not heard from you since our conversation in regard to the *Lusitania* case. I hope that you have been able to accomplish something. It is imperative that we should reach a speedy settlement of this controversy for the reasons which I stated to you when we talked the matter over. I hope that a conclusion may be reached within a very few days.

I am [etc.]   ROBERT LANSING

763.72/2323½

The German Ambassador (Bernstorff) to the Secretary of State

J. No. A 7615   WASHINGTON, *November 25, 1915.*

MY DEAR MR. SECRETARY: In answer to your favor of 24th inst. I beg to say that I wrote a confidential report to my Government directly after our last conversation. However, as you know, I have no other means for confidential communications to my Government than the mail, so that certainly several weeks will elapse before I shall be able to renew the confidential discussion on the *Lusitania* question with you. As you will kindly remember, I gave you our proposals for a solution of the question nearly two months ago, whilst I have had your counter proposals only since a few days.

Whatever the decision of my Government may be, I feel bound to tell you, as my personal opinion, that my Government will not be prepared to make any further concessions. Permit me to recapitulate in a few words the course of the negotiations as far as I have been intrusted with them. When the first official notes on the *Lusitania* question had been exchanged and had created a tension which made war between our two countries probable, I considered it my duty without instructions from my Government to ask the President to grant me an audience, because I hoped, that I might be able to restore the usual friendly relations between our two Governments. The President at that time kindly outlined his policy to me and on this basis I recommended with all possible emphasis to my Government the policy which has since been adopted. I took up the matter, because the President showed me a common ground on which we could meet, viz. his policy of "the freedom of the seas". Besides, the President left no doubt in my mind, that if we gave binding assurances for the future, the past would cause no more friction. As far as I am concerned, I have fully carried out the work I undertook. We have given binding assurances for the future and have adhered strictly to them. In so doing we have been seriously hampered in our reprisals against the British blockade, which you yourself have publicly denounced as illegal. The effect has been that the blockade has not yet been relaxed, but in the contrary tightened, e. g. by the abolishment of the parcel post to Germany. I can not recognize that the *Ancona* incident has in any way changed the state of affairs, because 1) we are not responsible for it, and 2) the captain of the *Ancona* did not stop when warned. If he had acted according to the rules of maritime warfare, I am convinced that the commander of the Austrian-Hungarian submarine would have let the *Ancona* go on to her destination unmolested.

You expressed the opinion to me, that the note you wrote to the British Government with regard to the blockade [75] might have the influence to induce my Government to make further concessions. Personally I do not believe that my Government will share this view till the action you took against Great Britain has had some effect. My Government has always declared its intention to recognize the declaration of London as binding, if our enemies would do the same. But as long as the latter increase their illegal methods instead of relaxing them, my Government will hardly be inclined to make any further concessions. Public opinion in Germany would not understand such concessions without any equivalent. I am afraid that if the case of the *Lusitania* is now pressed too much on my Government, the effect will be contrary to the one you desire. By such pressure my Government might be led to consider that the policy of concessions to the United States for the purpose of obtaining the great and common object of the "freedom of the sea" was wrong and that it would be better to return to a policy of severe reprisals against Great Britain's illegal blockade.

I am [etc.]   J. BERNSTORFF

865.857 An 2/75½a

The Secretary of State to President Wilson

WASHINGTON, *December 3, 1915.*

MY DEAR MR. PRESIDENT: I enclose a draft for an instruction to Ambassador Penfield in regard to the *Ancona* case.[76] We have no

---

[75] *Foreign Relations*, 1915, supp., p. 578.
[76] For text of the note as sent, see *ibid.*, p. 623.

further information on the subject than that which I have already submitted to you. The essential fact, that the vessel was shelled and torpedoed while persons were still on board—one of whom, at least, is an American—is amply proven.

Faithfully yours,

ROBERT LANSING

865.857 An 2/76½

President Wilson to the Secretary of State

WASHINGTON, *5 December, 1915.*

MY DEAR MR. SECRETARY: This is a peremptory note, but I see no other course open to us.

I understand that Penfield has asked for a fuller statement of the facts from the government at Vienna, but that so far they have not furnished him with any more than we already had. Can we say that we have the Austrian official version of what happened?

Faithfully Yours,

W. W.

763.72/2327½a

The Secretary of State to the German Ambassador (Bernstorff)

WASHINGTON, *December 15, 1915.*

MY DEAR MR. AMBASSADOR: I have been hoping to hear from you in regard to the *Lusitania* affair. I feel that continued delay in reaching an agreement in this matter may precipitate a situation which both of us would seriously regret. I trust that you can give me an indication as to the attitude of your Government upon the formula which we considered sometime ago.

I am [etc.] ROBERT LANSING

763.72/2327¾ : Telegram

The German Ambassador (Bernstorff) to the Secretary of State

NEW YORK, *December 16, 1915—10:07 a. m.*
[Received 10:15 a. m.]

Your letter followed me here where I have urgent business for a day. I am sending one more wireless to Berlin. It is really not our fault if the events of the last weeks postponed a solution of the older question.

J. BERNSTORFF

865.857 An 2/71

The Secretary of State to President Wilson

WASHINGTON, *December 17, 1915.*

MY DEAR MR. PRESIDENT: I send you herewith the text of the Austrian reply in the *Ancona* case.[77] My own view is that it is a special pleading consisting of technicalities and quibbles. I believe it would be a mistake to reply to it in detail and that the best course is to send a short and firm note, avoiding argument of legal points and discussion of facts. We can rest the whole case on the Admiralty's admission that the vessel was torpedoed while she was standing still and while people were on board. It seems to me that it would be most unwise to elaborate in our reply.

I realize that such a course may invite serious consequences and yet I do not see how we can consistently recede from our position or enter into any correspondence, such as the Austrian Government appears to be desirous of doing.

I will prepare at once a draft reply, possibly I can send it to you tonight, for I think our answer should go within two or three days.

Faithfully yours,

ROBERT LANSING

865.857 An 2/71

The Secretary of State to President Wilson

WASHINGTON, *December 17, 1915.*

MY DEAR MR. PRESIDENT: I send you a draft of a proposed reply to the Austrian note.[78] I have studied the note with care and feel that we should avoid the pitfall of further correspondence. The essential fact is admitted by the Austrian Admiralty; the principles of law and humanity cannot be debated. I feel that it would be contrary to our dignity to continue a discussion of this sort. I realize that the proposed reply is practically an ultimatum and I feel fully the responsibility of sending it. But what other course is open to us if we wish to maintain our self-respect as a Government? It is a crisis which seems unavoidable.

If there is any other way of treating the Austrian note I would be very glad to be instructed, but discussion of the subjects treated in the note seems to me impossible in view of the position we have taken.

---

[77] *Foreign Relations,* 1915, supp., p. 638.
[78] Secretary Lansing's draft was not sent, but, instead, a substitute written by President Wilson. For text of the note as sent, see *ibid.,* p. 647.

I am sorry to trouble you with this at the present time, but I feel
that we should reply to the note very promptly and especially so if
we do not intend to continue to discuss the case.

Faithfully yours,

ROBERT LANSING

[Enclosure]

Draft Telegram to the Ambassador in Austria-Hungary (Penfield)

You are instructed to address a note to the Austro-Hungarian
Minister of Foreign Affairs, textually as follows:

"The Government of the United States has received the note of
your Excellency relative to the sinking of the *Ancona*, which was
delivered at Vienna on December fifteenth, nineteen-fifteen, and
transmitted to Washington, and has given the note very careful
consideration.

"The admission in the report of the Austro-Hungarian Admiralty
which was transmitted to this Government by the Austro-Hungarian
Chargé d'Affaires at Washington that the *Ancona* was torpedoed
after her engines had stopped and when passengers were still on
board is a sufficient fact alone to condemn the officer responsible for
the sinking of the vessel as having wilfully violated the recognized
law of nations and those humane principles which a belligerent
should observe in the conduct of hostile operations. The details of
the sinking of the vessel; the witnesses corroborating the Admiralty's
report; the number of Americans killed and injured, are not essential
to the establishment of the guilt of the commander. The fact is that
citizens of the United States were killed, injured, or put in jeopardy
by the commander's lawless act.

"The rules of international law and the principles of humanity,
which were so grossly violated by the commander of the submarine,
have been too generally recognized and too manifest from the standpoint of right and justice to admit of debate. The Government of
the United States therefore has no other course but to hold the
Austro-Hungarian Government responsible for the admitted conduct
of the commander of the submarine. As this Government holds these
views as to the illegality of the act and the responsibility therefor,
the Imperial and Royal Government must realize that the Government of the United States cannot further discuss the admitted circumstances of the case or the established law and principle violated
by the commander. The Government of the United States can only
repeat the demands which it made in its note of December sixth,
nineteen-fifteen, sincerely hoping that with the foregoing explanation
of its position the Imperial and Royal Government will perceive the
justice of those demands and comply with them in the same spirit
of frankness and regard for good relations with which they were
made."

865.857 An 2/93½

Memorandum by the Secretary of State of a Conversation With the Austro-Hungarian Chargé (Zwiedinek), December 18, 1915

Baron Zwiedinek called this morning for the purpose, apparently, of finding out what the attitude of this Government was to be in regard to the Austrian reply.

He asked me first what impression the reply had made upon this Government and I told him it had made a very bad impression; that I considered it to be more or less frivolous and I was surprised that the Austrian Government supposed for a moment that such a reply would be acceptable to the United States.

He seemed much disturbed at what I said and entered into an argument to show that there might be a question as to the rule of international law when a merchant vessel sought to escape from an enemy even though she subsequently ceased the attempt. I told him that I could not conceive of such a technicality as that being a subject of discussion and that if the Austrian Government sought to advance it I feared that it would irritate rather than help the situation. I went on to say that ever since there had been naval warfare a vessel, unarmed, which was attacked by a warship sought to escape, but that I did not see that the warship obtained the right to destroy people on board after the vessel had practically surrendered. I likened the case to the flight of troops who were finally compelled to surrender and that I thought the murderous attack upon a vessel at rest was very similar to the indefensible slaughter of prisoners.

Baron Zwiedinek replied that he regretted I held to that view and he still thought that there was argument in the idea that a vessel lost its immunity by seeking to escape. I told him that I thought he would gain nothing by a further discussion of a question which entered into the views as to what was humane when, apparently, we differed so radically as to a belligerent's obligation. He asked me if I did not think we would discuss such questions as that. I told him no, that the only thing that would remove the present crisis would be for Austria to comply at once with our demands; that otherwise I feared the consequences; and that I felt that the blame would be entirely upon his Government.

The Baron suggested as a possible basis of settlement that his Government should promise not to repeat the offense complained of in the case of the *Ancona* and that the questions relative to that case be left for further negotiation. He said that he made this tentatively and without instructions from his Government. In reply I said that it did not seem to me to offer a possible basis for settlement. He then asked me if I would take it under consideration, and I replied that of course I would be willing to do that and would let him know my decision in regard to his suggestion.

Baron Zwiedinek showed very much emotion and left my room with the understanding that if I had anything further to say I would ask him to come again to the Department.

ROBERT LANSING

763.72/2328½

The German Ambassador (Bernstorff) to the Secretary of State

J. No. A 8326   WASHINGTON, *December 20, 1915.*

MY DEAR MR. SECRETARY: With reference to previous correspondence I beg to inform you that according to a wireless message I received today, my Government has mailed explicit instructions to me which it hopes will lead to an amicable settlement of the *Lusitania* case.

I remain [etc.]   J. BERNSTORFF

763.72/2328½

The Secretary of State to the German Ambassador (Bernstorff)

WASHINGTON, *December 20, 1915.*

MY DEAR MR. AMBASSADOR: I have received your letter of today telling me that your Government had mailed to you explicit instructions in the *Lusitania* case.

It is to be regretted that these instructions were not telegraphed as the time occupied in transit by the mails may seriously affect the negotiation. The protracted delay in the settlement of this controversy, though due to unavoidable causes, is unfortunate and makes it increasingly difficult to adjust our differences.

I am convinced that you realize, as I do, that the tension in this matter is growing every day, that American public opinion is become more bitter and that this state of affairs cannot continue much longer without the gravest consequences. I fear that a delay of two weeks will be serious and a satisfactory adjustment will be well-nigh impossible then.

In order to avoid a situation, which would make the task of negotiating extremely difficult, might I suggest that your Government repeat the instructions mailed, by telegraph, in order that we may take up the case immediately? In order to make this course possible I am willing that the instructions be sent in cipher through our Embassy at Berlin and this Department, and you may so advise your Government if you agree with me as to the advisability of proceeding with a consideration of the case without further delay.

I am [etc.]   ROBERT LANSING

865.857 An 2/94½

Memorandum by the Secretary of State of a Conversation With the Austro-Hungarian Chargé (Zwiedinek), December 21, 1915 [79]

Baron Zwiedinek called and said he had received two telegrams from his Government which he desired to communicate to me. He then read the telegrams, copies of which are annexed. In commenting on them he said he felt very hopeful that his Government would be able to find a satisfactory way to meet the desires of the United States; that he knew they were anxious to preserve friendly relations. I said to him that he must realize that we had taken a position from which we could not recede. He said he knew that; that he thought it was possible that the Austrian Government would be willing to acknowledge that our attitude as to the principle involved should be accepted and that he thought that the difficulty would lie in our demand for the punishment of the commander. I told him it seemed to me that the Commander not only was bound by his instructions, but also by the law and principles of humanity, and that if he violated these he was as guilty as if he had violated his instructions. He replied that if his Government had held a different view as to the principle involved which they now held and had issued instructions in accordance with their former view, that the Commander would certainly not be to blame for following such instructions.

To this I said: "Either the Commander is guilty, or your Government is guilty. If your Government desires to take the responsibility they should frankly say so, exonerating the Commander, but they should assume his guilt." He replied that that was a very difficult thing for a Government to do. I said I realized that but it seemed to me the only alternative and if it did assume such responsibility it would be necessary for the Austrian Government to apologize, in addition to denouncing the act and offering to indemnify the sufferers.

He said that he would take the matter up immediately with his Government and hoped that they could reach a satisfactory conclusion. He also said that he was very sorry that they had not received his telegrams before they answered our first note, because he thought it would have made a difference in the tone of their reply.

He also asked me what I thought of the advisability of the Austrian Government recalling Consul General von Nuber,[80] as he realized that his presence caused the present newspaper attacks upon him. I told him I thought it would be a way to remove one of the

---

[79] Copy transmitted to President Wilson on the same day.
[80] See pp. 83–88.

difficulties which we had to face in order to preserve good relations, and doubtless it would be expedient to have him recalled. He said he realized that even if the facts were not proven against von Nuber, which he knew they could not do, at the same time if he was under suspicion he would not be useful as a Consular officer and that he thought he would advise his Government to recall him.

ROBERT LANSING

[Enclosure 1—Telegram]

The Austro-Hungarian Minister of Foreign Affairs (Burian) to the Austro-Hungarian Chargé (Zwiedinek)

We thoroughly appreciate the interpretation given by Mr. Lansing to the American note on the *Ancona* case and trust that an accurate knowledge of the entire conditions under which the sinking of steamer took place will corroborate the Secretary of State in his opinion on the chivalrous spirit of our navy. A detailed statement we are preparing and for which any details which Mr. Lansing could place before us would be most valuable will contain authentical and important information about the behaviour both of the commander of the submarine and of the crew of the *Ancona*. We hope it will show Mr. Lansing that his idea about the spirit of our navy has not been erroneous and that the officer commanding the submarine did everything in his power to combine the necessities of warfare with the duties of humanity.

BURIAN

[Enclosure 2—Telegram]

The Austro-Hungarian Minister of Foreign Affairs (Burian) to the Austro-Hungarian Chargé (Zwiedinek)

You should tell the Secretary of State that always anxious to insure the practice of firm principles of humanity and wishing to conform to the averred rules of international law we quite agree with the United States Government that all consequences to be drawn from the *Ancona* case depend on the *quaestio facti* viz on authentical and exact information how the sinking of the steamer took place. A statement containing this information and based on reports of the Austro-Hungarian admiralty will be handed over to Mr. Penfield in a few days in answer to his letter of the 1 inst.

BURIAN

865.857 An 2/88 : Telegram

The Ambassador in Austria-Hungary (Penfield) to the Secretary of State

VIENNA, *December 23, 1915—6 p. m.*
[Received December 24—2:30 p. m.]

1049. From informal conversation with a responsible official of the Ministry of Foreign Affairs I am inclined to anticipate that the Austro-Hungarian reply to our last *Ancona* note will again contend that the American demands are based on inaccurate and insufficient evidence. Feeling in responsible quarters opposed to rupture of diplomatic relations. Should a settlement through diplomatic channels prove impossible it is probable that suggestion will be made that the dispute be submitted to arbitration. In an interview published today the Hungarian Premier, Tisza, says that the dispute must be amicably settled in a few days satisfactory to both parties which can only be accomplished through correspondence between the two Governments. Article by jurist, Dr. Lammasch, was excluded from the *Freie Presse* of the 19th by the Government but appearing in both morning and evening editions today may indicate views of the Government undergoing change. He says that the sources of our information are open to question especially since our contentions are in such sharp conflict with Austro-Hungarian Admiralty's report. He recalls the Dogger Bank incident between Great Britain and Russia and suggests that the present difficulty with the United States be settled by recourse to a similar arbitral board. Ministry of Foreign Affairs informally advise me that their reply to our last note will be delivered early next week.

PENFIELD

865.857 An 2/95½

President Wilson to the Secretary of State

HOT SPRINGS, VA., *24 December, 1915.*

MY DEAR MR. SECRETARY: I am not sure whether I am encouraged or not by this,[81] but I am clear that you said the right things to the Baron and that it was very wise to make him see the position of the United States without any penumbra about the edges of the statement.

Cordially and faithfully Yours,

WOODROW WILSON

---

[81] Memorandum by the Secretary of State, Dec. 21, 1915, p. 503.

865.857 An 2/95½a

The Secretary of State to President Wilson

WASHINGTON, *December 24, 1915.*

MY DEAR MR. PRESIDENT: The Austrian Chargé has just called and handed me a telegram which he received from his Government yesterday. I enclose you a copy.

Wishing you and Mrs. Wilson a very happy Christmas believe me [etc.]

ROBERT LANSING

[Enclosure—Telegram]

The Austro-Hungarian Minister of Foreign Affairs (*Burian*) to the Austro-Hungarian Chargé (*Zwiedinek*)

American note handed over to me 21st inst. Tell Secretary of State that the answer we are preparing shall be guided by the same concern for good relations between both countries as mentioned by Federal Government. In consequence of the Christmas holidays our answer cannot be expected before next week.

BURIAN

865.857 An 2/96½

President Wilson to the Secretary of State

HOT SPRINGS, VA., *26 December, 1915.*

MY DEAR MR. SECRETARY: This is encouraging as to the spirit of the Austro-Hungarian government, but I fear they are preparing to contest the facts with us, and the inferences to be drawn from them.

Faithfully Yours,

WOODROW WILSON

865.857 An 2/97½

President Wilson to the Secretary of State

HOT SPRINGS, VA., *27 December, 1915.*

MY DEAR MR. SECRETARY: I have read this with misgivings.[82] We certainly do not wish to be drawn into a correspondence with the Austro-Hungarian government; but, if they propose arbitration, how can we refuse to consider that? To do so would be contrary to all

---

[82] Telegram No. 1049, Dec. 23, 1915, from the Ambassador in Austria-Hungary, p. 505.

our traditions and would place us in a very difficult position to justify in the opinion of the rest of the world, do you not think so?

Faithfully Yours,

WOODROW WILSON

865.857 An 2/110a

The Secretary of State to President Wilson

WASHINGTON, *December 28, 1915.*

MY DEAR MR. PRESIDENT: As a matter of precaution I think that we should consider what action should be taken in case Austria fails to meet our demands or refuses to do so.

The severance of diplomatic relations, under normal conditions, would not be considered an act of war but merely an expression of disfavor. Under present conditions, however, I feel convinced that that course would be looked upon as hostile by Austria, and would result in war.

If my surmise is correct and war is the inevitable consequence of breaking off relations, should the Government take that action without consulting Congress, the war-making power?

I know from information which has been received from various quarters that the conduct of the Administration, if war results from the stand we have taken in the *Ancona* case, will be attacked on the ground that Congress alone has power to declare war and that the Executive exceeds his power if he brings about a situation which must eventuate in war. Perhaps this would be an unjustifiable criticism, and yet there seems to be a measure of reason in it on account of the constitutional provision. In fact I am not at all certain in my own mind that it is not a sound position.

It might be avoided by laying the papers in the case before Congress with an address dealing with the situation and showing that, while the dignity of the United States precludes continued relations with Austria, the Administration realizes that the severance of relations would in all probability bring about a state of war, and that, therefore, in view of the power conferred on Congress, the papers are presented to it before such action is taken in order to obtain its approval and to avoid any charge of infringement upon the constitutional rights of the Legislative by the Executive.

I do not say that I consider this the best course to pursue, but it has the merit of placing the responsibility where it legally belongs, although the conduct of the negotiations created a situation which seems to offer no other solution than the breaking off of diplomatic relations.

In submitting the foregoing I do so only because it seems to me that possibly the future action should be considered carefully and a decision reached before the time arrives to act.

Faithfully yours,

ROBERT LANSING

763.72/2337½a

The Secretary of State to the German Ambassador (Bernstorff)

WASHINGTON, *December 29, 1915.*

DEAR MR. AMBASSADOR: The *Lusitania* case is causing me anxiety because of the continued suspension of the negotiation. I am loath to make a formal representation to your Government on the subject, as it might cause you embarrassment, but I feel that the time is very near when I will have to do so.

I hope, therefore, that you, who appreciate that this state of inaction can not continue much longer, will endeavor to impress your Government with the expediency of reaching a speedy settlement.

I am [etc.]   ROBERT LANSING

763.72/2338½

The German Ambassador (Bernstorff) to the Secretary of State

J. No. A 8578   WASHINGTON, *December 29, 1915.*

MY DEAR MR. SECRETARY: In answer of your favor of to-day I beg to say that since our last conversation I have taken the greatest possible trouble to get instructions from my Government regarding the *Lusitania* case. Many of my reports and probably also of my telegrams have, in violation of international law, been detained by our enemies. I did, however, receive a wireless message in code last Monday evening, which passed through the State Department and which informed me that a cipher telegram containing instructions had been given to Mr. Gerard on Monday. It should, therefore, if not detained by our enemies, have been delivered to the State Department yesterday or latest to-day.

I remain [etc.]   J. BERNSTORFF

865.857 An 2/110½

President Wilson to the Secretary of State

HOT SPRINGS, VA., *29 December, 1915.*

MY DEAR MR. SECRETARY: I have your letter of yesterday about our relations with Austria-Hungary.

What new elements in the case make you feel now, what, I remember, you did not feel at the outset of this matter, that a breach of diplomatic relations would <u>probably</u>, rather than possibly, mean war? I do not now recall any new influences that have recently come into the field, and I would very much like to know what has made this impression on your mind.

You may of course be right. All along there has been reason to fear that such might be the outcome. And I quite agree with you that we ought to think our course out very frankly and carefully, blinking nothing.

I do not think that it would be wise in any case to lay the matter publicly before Congress. The most that I could do would be to consult with the leaders on the hill. To lay the matter publicly before Congress would in effect be to announce that we expected war and might be the means of hastening it.

There are some wise and experienced men on the Senate Committee on Foreign Relations and it is quite possible that we might get useful guidance from them. For myself I do not doubt the constitutional powers of the Executive in this connection; but power is a different matter from wise policy.

Your answer to some of the questions I raised or suggested in my last brief note to you on the news from Vienna will necessarily form a part and a very fundamental part of our discussion of the whole situation. If the Imperial and Royal Government thinks that it can put a very different face upon the *Ancona* case by representations which it thinks us bound in fairness to it to consider, how can we refuse to discuss the matter with them until all the world is convinced that rock bottom has been reached?

Cordially and faithfully Yours,

WOODROW WILSON

865.857 An 2/95 : Telegram

The Ambassador in Austria-Hungary (Penfield) to the Secretary of State

VIENNA, *December 29, 1915—5 p. m.*
[Received December 30—2:45 p. m.]

1063. Austro-Hungarian answer [83] to second *Ancona* note [84] received at 4:30 this afternoon. It is communication upwards of 3,000 words. Will require all night to translate and encipher.

Note is practical compliance with our demands. It acknowledges culpability of submarine commander who it states has been punished. Will pay indemnities under certain conditions, but specifically leaves

---

[83] *Foreign Relations*, 1915, supp., p. 655.
[84] *Ibid.*, p. 647.

question of future conduct of submarine warfare for further discussion. Reciprocal desire for maintenance of good relations is expressed.

PENFIELD

865.857 An 2/95

The Secretary of State to President Wilson

WASHINGTON, December 30, 1915.

MY DEAR MR. PRESIDENT: I enclose a copy of a telegram which has just been received from Vienna under date of the 29th.[85] I assume that by tomorrow or next day we will receive the full text of the note.

From the summary given by Mr. Penfield it would seem as if the *Ancona* case offered possibilities of solution.

Faithfully yours,

ROBERT LANSING

865.857 An 2/111½

President Wilson to the Secretary of State

HOT SPRINGS, VA., 31 December, 1915.

MY DEAR MR. SECRETARY: This does indeed afford us something more than a ray of hope for a satisfactory settlement, and my mind is, at any rate for the time being, much relieved.

Faithfully Yours,

WOODROW WILSON

763.72/2339½

Memorandum by the Secretary of State of a Conversation With the German Ambassador (Bernstorff), December 31, 1915

The German Ambassador called upon me and handed me the annexed paper, which is the substance of a telegram which he had received from Berlin. He said that this did not complete his instructions in the matter as the telegram said—"to be continued."

The Ambassador said that he appreciated this was going over the ground which we had traversed many times, but he thought that while his Government suggested arbitration he had received an intimation that they would like to know the reasons why we were unwilling to submit the case to arbitration. He added that he believed that his Government, if a fairly good case could be made out against arbitration, would follow the course which had been adopted apparently by Austria in their *Ancona* case.

---

[85] *Supra.*

I answered him that we had discussed the illegality of retaliatory measures by a belligerent and that so far as the legal point of view was concerned I could not see that there was anything to arbitrate. In addition to this I called his attention to the next to the last paragraph in the German reply in the *Frye* case, dated November 29, 1915,[86] wherein they specifically stated that persons on board a vessel about to be sunk should be placed in safety. The Ambassador seemed surprised at this statement of his Government and said— "Have they gone as far as that?" I said—"Yes, that is their language and of course it applies as well to belligerent merchant ships as to neutral merchant ships engaged in contraband trade because the only legal ground for sinking a neutral vessel would be its temporary belligerent character."

He said he would communicate with his Government at once in regard to the matter and see if they would not follow out a course which they had so plainly set forth as to the illegality of retaliatory measures, and as to the duties imposed upon the commander of a submarine in sinking a merchant vessel.

He said he was hopeful that we could reach an agreement along these lines.

ROBERT LANSING

[Enclosure]

The German Foreign Office to the German Embassy [87]

The German submarine war against England's commerce at sea, as announced on February 4, 1915,[87a] is conducted in retaliation of England's inhuman war against Germany's commercial and industrial life. It is an acknowledged rule of international law that retaliation may be employed against acts committed in contravention of the law of nations. Germany is enacting such a retaliation, for it is England's endeavor to cut off all imports from Germany by preventing even legal commerce of the neutrals with her and thereby subjecting the German population to starvation. In answer to these acts Germany is making efforts to destroy England's commerce at sea, at least as far as it is carried on by enemy vessels.

The question whether neutral interests may in any way be injured by retaliatory measures should, in this instance, be answered in the affirmative. The neutrals by allowing the crippling of their commerce with Germany contrary to international law which is an estab-

---

[86] *Foreign Relations*, 1915, supp., p. 644.
[87] This paper bears the notation: "The substance of a telegram recd from Berlin. Handed me by German Amb. Dec. 31/15. RL."
[87a] See *Foreign Relations*, 1915, supp., p. 96.

lished fact, cannot object to the retaliatory steps of Germany for reasons of neutrality. Besides, the German measures, announced in time, are such that neutrals easily could have avoided harmful consequences by not using enemy vessels employed in commerce with England. If Germany has notwithstanding limited her submarine warfare, this was done in view of her long standing friendship with the United States and in the expectation that the steps taken by the American Government in the meantime aiming at the restoration of the freedom of the seas would be successful.

As Germany cannot see a violation of international law in her course of action, she does not consider herself obliged to pay indemnity for damages caused by it, although she sincerely regrets the death of American citizens who were passengers on board the *Lusitania*. In view of the amicable relations between our two countries the German Government is however ready to have differences of opinion settled through international arbitration—a way always warmly recommended by the United States—and therefore to submit to the Court of Arbitration at the Hague the question, whether and to which extent Germany is obliged to pay indemnity for the death of American citizens caused by the sinking of the *Lusitania*. The sentence of the Court should in no way be taken as deciding the question whether or not the German submarine war is justified according to international law, but it would be a means to settle definitively the regrettable *Lusitania* incident.

841.857 P 43/46 : Telegram

President Wilson to the Secretary of State

HOT SPRINGS, VA., *January 2, 1916.*
[Received 10 : 30 p. m.]

Are we sufficiently informed as to the facts in the case of the *Persia* to form a judgment and plan for a course of action? I would very much like your candid advice as to whether you think it best that I should return to Washington at once. I would suggest a message like the following to Penfield:

"Having just received the reply of the Austro-Hungarian Government in the matter of the *Ancona* and having formed a most favorable impression of the friendly and reasonable attitude of the Government and of the probability of an amicable and satisfactory settlement, we are the more deeply disturbed by the news that reaches us of the destruction of the steamship *Persia*. Please make immediate inquiry at the Foreign Office concerning the facts, express the grave solicitude of this Government and seek assurances of early and very serious action on the part of the Austro-Hungarian Government in the case, in the spirit and upon the principles so frankly set forth in its last note to us concerning the *Ancona*".[88]

WILSON

841.857 L 97/124½

The Secretary of State to President Wilson

WASHINGTON, *January 7, 1916.*

MY DEAR MR. PRESIDENT: The German Ambassador has just called upon me and stated that he was instructed by his Government to say, in the first place, that they had heard through the press reports of the sinking of the *Persia* and that they had no information whatsoever in regard to it.

He then handed me a communication which he was also instructed to deliver,[89] setting forth the attitude of the German Government in regard to submarine warfare in the Mediterranean. At his request I am making public this statement.

The Ambassador then handed me a communication in regard to the *Lusitania* case, which he said his Government wished to be considered confidential unless it was satisfactory to this Government, when it could be embodied in a more formal document. I enclose the communication, together with one marked "strictly confidential" relating to arbitration of questions of fact in connection with submarine warfare.[90]

I have not studied the proposed reply of Germany in regard to the *Lusitania* with sufficient care to express a final opinion. There is lacking any recognition of liability since the indemnity which they proposed to pay is, in fact, on the basis of comity and not on the basis of right—at least that is my view at present. If in any way the agreement to pay the indemnity can be construed into a recognition of liability it would seem as if a final settlement of the case was very near.

I also enclose for your information an extract from the reply of the German Government in the *Frye* case,[91] which has a direct bearing on submarine warfare in general and must be read, I think, with these other communications. In view of that declaration I do not see why the German Government is not willing to definitely admit liability in the *Lusitania* case.

---

[88] This message was sent Jan. 3, 1916, 10 a. m. ; see *Foreign Relations*, 1916, supp., p. 143.

[89] *Ibid.*, p. 144.

[90] Latter not printed.

[91] *Foreign Relations*, 1915, supp., p. 644. (For the extract referred to, see *ibid.*, p. 645, first paragraph.)

The German Ambassador desires that the reply in the *Frye* case should be made public and, as I could see no reason to withhold it, I agreed to do so.

I hope that I may soon receive your views in regard to the communication relative to the *Lusitania* as I think the negotiation, if it is to be continued, should be pressed to speedy settlement.

Faithfully yours,

ROBERT LANSING

[Enclosure]

The German Embassy to the Department of State

The German submarine war against England's commerce at sea, as announced on February 4, 1915, is conducted in retaliation of England's inhuman war against Germany's commercial and industrial life. It is an acknowledged rule of international law that retaliation may be employed against acts committed in contravention of the law of nations. Germany is enacting such a retaliation, for it is England's endeavor to cut off all imports from Germany by preventing even legal commerce of the neutrals with her and thereby subjecting the German population to starvation.

In answer to these acts Germany is making efforts to destroy England's commerce at sea, at least as far as it is carried on by enemy vessels.

The question whether neutral interests may in any way be injured by retaliatory measures should, in this instance, be answered in the affirmative. The neutrals by allowing the crippling of their commerce with Germany contrary to international law which is an established fact cannot object to the retaliatory steps of Germany for reasons of neutrality. Besides, the German measures, announced in time, are such that neutrals easily could have avoided harmful consequences by not using enemy vessels employed in commerce with England. If Germany has notwithstanding limited her submarine warfare, this was done in view of her long standing friendship with the United States and in the expectation that the steps taken by the American Government in the meantime aiming at the restoration of the freedom of the seas would be successful.

The German Government, on the other hand, recognizes from the course which the negotiations so far have taken, the difficulty to reconcile in principle the American and the German point of view, as the interests and legal aspects of the neutrals and belligerents naturally do not agree in this point and as the illegality of the English course of procedure can hardly be recognized in the United States as fully as it is in Germany. A perpetuation of this difference of opinion, however, would not tend to further the amicable relations between the United States and Germany which have never been disturbed and the continuation of which is so sincerely desired by both Governments. Actuated by this spirit the Imperial Government again expresses its deep regret at the death of American citizens caused by the sinking of the *Lusitania* and, in order to settle this question amicably, declares its readiness to pay indemnity for the losses inflicted.

865.857 An 2/112½a : Telegram

The Secretary of State to Colonel E. M. House

WASHINGTON, *January 7, 1916—6 p. m.*

No. 1. Second *Ancona* note from Austria made splendid impression.[92] Sinking of *Persia* caused note to be forgotten and created utmost indignation. Strong feeling that something must be done by Administration but as there is no evidence as to how ship was sunk no plan of action settled on yet. German and Austrian Governments deny knowledge. Austrian representative here much disturbed and assures us that his Government would repudiate act if it is found to have been Austrian submarine. Senate has begun discussion of foreign affairs. Strong feeling expressed because of English attitude but no embargo can pass nor is any action by Congress probable unless with President's approval. Republicans standing by President. Protest sent to England on seizure of mails on neutral ships. Still great complaint of interference with our trade by Great Britain.

LANSING

841.857 L 97/125½

President Wilson to the Secretary of State

WASHINGTON, *10 January, 1916.*

MY DEAR MR. SECRETARY: I have tried hard to find something in this note about the *Lusitania*[93] out of which a satisfactory answer to our demands could be made, but must admit that I have failed. It is a concession of grace, and not at all of right.

And yet I do not see that it would be essentially out of tune with it if the Imperial Government were to say that, even while it was arguing and without abatement insisting on the necessity for retaliation and even the right to retaliate, it was not willing to make that necessity an excuse for abbreviating the rights of neutrals or for unnecessarily imperiling the lives of non-combatants, and that, there-

---

[92] *Foreign Relations*, 1915, supp., p. 655.
[93] *Ante*, p. 514.

fore, while wishing to make very plain the imperative grounds for its recent policy, it was ready to recognize very frankly the justice of the contentions of the United States with regard to the rights of American citizens and assume the responsibility which she (the Imp. Gov.) had incurred by the incidental ignoring of those rights on the occasion referred to.

She could in this wise put Great Britain more obviously in the wrong as compared with herself, by showing that she, in contrast with Great Britain, was willing to make good for the damage done neutrals.

I understand you had a conference with Bernstorff to-day. Do you think from the present aspect of the situation that a suggestion such as I have outlined would set the settlement a step forward, or not?

Faithfully Yours,

W. W.

841.857 L 97/126½

Memorandum by the Secretary of State of a Conversation With the German Ambassador (Bernstorff)

[WASHINGTON,] *January 10, 1916.*

The German Ambassador called this morning and read me a wireless dispatch which he had received from his Government,[94] a copy of which he handed me, upon the understanding that it would be treated as strictly confidential.

After I had made a few comments on the dispatch I referred directly to the *Lusitania* case and said that I feared that the proposed note, copy of which he had given me, would not be satisfactory; that the question of indemnity was only important so far as it was an admission of liability; and that as I read his draft of the note the indemnity was given as an act of grace and not because Germany was liable for illegal conduct. I told him that I thought it was necessary that Germany should admit liability frankly as that would amount to a disavowal, and disavowal in some form we must have.

He replied that they had great difficulty on account of Great Britain's continuance of her illegal blockade and that the German public, and many in the Government were not willing to abandon the policy of reprisals.

I told him that I did not see that that was at all necessary; that while there might be justification for retaliation against Great Britain, that retaliation was necessarily illegal conduct in a strict

---

[94] *Infra.*

sense and that all it was necessary to do was to admit that it was illegal and that insofar as neutrals were concerned it imposed liability on the German Government. I said to him that that was the same course we were taking with regard to Great Britain—that Great Britain's interruption of trade to Germany was admittedly retaliatory and that it, therefore, was illegal and so far as neutrals were concerned it imposed liability on Great Britain; and that I could not see how we could treat the matter differently with the two Governments.

He told me he would at once communicate these views to his Government in the hope that a course might be found which would meet our views.

ROBERT LANSING

841.857 L 97/126½

The German Foreign Office to the German Embassy [95]

We have modified submarine war, waged in retaliation against illegal English starvation policy, to meet American wishes. Result was that submarine war lost considerably in efficiency. This was done in consideration of valued friendly relations which Germany desires continued with America. In return we expected that U. S. Government would contend with us for freedom of seas and obtain from England reestablishment of legitimate neutral trade with Germany. The United States on November fifth sent note to England [96] to which apparently no reply has been made, at any rate no concessions obtained from England. Instead, British Government recently published White Paper enumerating all measures which tend to cut off Germany from legitimate commerce and to control neutrals. American Note which was very much to the point exposed the illegality of these measures.

Since August last and, even before Germany modified submarine war, if incidents happened they were regrettable mistakes for which due reparation has been made. Germany showed good will by making concessions seriously affecting efficiency of submarine war. England has conceded nothing but instead boasts of more and more success in strangling Germany. We therefore may expect and should be grateful if America at last takes energetic steps to establish real freedom of seas.

---

[95] This paper bears the notation: "Handed me by German Amb. Jany 10/16 RL."

[96] Apparently the note of Oct. 21, 1915, *Foreign Relations*, 1915, supp., p. 578.

841.857 L 97/126½

The Secretary of State to President Wilson

WASHINGTON, *January 11, 1916.*

MY DEAR MR. PRESIDENT: I have your comment upon the proposed reply of the German Government in the Lusitania case. With your views I entirely agree.

Yesterday I had an interview with Count von Bernstorff, of which I enclose a memorandum which was made immediately after I talked with him.[97] You will perceive that I took very much the line of approach which you suggest in your letter.

Faithfully yours,

ROBERT LANSING

841.857 L 97/126½a : Telegram

The Secretary of State to Colonel E. M. House

WASHINGTON, *January 11, 1916—6 p. m.*

No. 2. *Lusitania* case progressing. Satisfactory settlement probable. Germany apparently believes if case settled it will leave only matters with Great Britain unsettled and some action will be necessary.

[File copy not signed]

841.857 L 97/127½a : Telegram

The Secretary of State to Colonel E. M. House

WASHINGTON, *January 19, 1916—6 p. m.*

No. 3. German Foreign Office apparently has come to no decision on *Lusitania*. Strongly urged to meet our views by some of their people on ground that such action would in the end cause public sentiment to turn against England. Favorable action seems probable. British Ambassador thinks his country can make no further material concessions and expects a deadlock. Draft of English note in answer to our note to England[98] now in hands of France for revision. In view of probable settlement with Germany resentment in Congress centering on England. Mexican situation causing trouble in Congress.

LANSING

---

[97] *Ante,* p. 516.
[98] Note of Oct. 21, 1915, *Foreign Relations,* 1915, supp., p. 578.

841.857 L 97/128½

The German Ambassador (Bernstorff) to the Secretary of State

J. No. A 530   WASHINGTON, *January 22, 1916.*

MY DEAR MR. SECRETARY: I beg to thank you for your note of January 21st [99] by which you kindly transmitted to me a cipher message from the German Foreign Office concerning the *Lusitania* case.

As it is too late to trouble you this afternoon I beg to submit to you confidentially the two enclosed drafts of memoranda, which are both based on the instructions I received to-day. I sincerely hope that one of the two will prove satisfactory to you and that we may at last settle this old case.

I should be very much obliged to you, if you would kindly let me know by telephone when I may have the pleasure of discussing the matter with you on Monday.

Believe me [etc.]   J. BERNSTORFF

[Enclosure 1]

Draft Memorandum From the German Embassy to the Department of State

A

The German submarine war against England's commerce at sea, as announced on February 4, 1915, is conducted in retaliation of England's inhuman war against Germany's commercial and industrial life. It is an acknowledged rule of international law that retaliation may be employed against acts committed in contravention of the law of nations. Germany is enacting such a retaliation, for it is England's endeavor to cut off all imports from Germany by preventing even legal commerce of the neutrals with her and thereby subjecting the German population to starvation. In answer to these acts Germany is making efforts to destroy England's commerce at sea, at least as far as it is carried on by enemy vessels. If Germany has notwithstanding limited her submarine warfare this was done in view of her long standing friendship with the United States and in the expectation that the steps taken by the American Government in the meantime aiming at the restoration of the freedom of the seas would be successful.

The German Government, on the other hand, recognizes from the course which the negotiations so far have taken the difficulty to reconcile in principle the American and the German point of view, as the interests and legal aspects of the neutrals and belligerents natur-

_____
[99] Not printed.

ally do not agree in this point and as the illegality of the English course of procedure can hardly be recognized in the United States as fully as it is in Germany. A perpetuation of this difference of opinion, however, would not tend to further the amicable relations between the United States and Germany which have never been disturbed and the continuation of which is so sincerely desired by both Governments. Actuated by this spirit the Imperial Government again expresses its deep regret at the death of American citizens caused by the sinking of the *Lusitania* and, in order to settle this question amicably, declares its readiness to pay indemnity for the losses inflicted.

[Enclosure 2]

Draft Memorandum from the German Embassy to the Department of State

B

The attack on the *Lusitania* formed part of the reprisals enacted by the Imperial Government against Great Britain on account of her illegal starvation policy. According to the German opinion such reprisals were amply justified by the inhuman British warfare. At that time the Imperial Government had not yet issued the instructions which now regulate the German submarine warfare and according to which the *Arabic* case was settled. These instructions were issued with regard to the friendship of many years' standing between Germany and the United States and in expectation that the steps the American Government has undertaken in the meantime to reestablish the freedom of the seas would be successful. Even before these instructions were issued it was, however, not the intention of the Imperial Government that our reprisals should lead to the loss of the lives of noncombattants. My Government has, therefore, on previous occasions expressed its deep regret that American lives should have been lost on the *Lusitania*.

As for the question whether the Imperial Government is obliged to grant an indemnity in this case, it appears from the negotiations which have hitherto taken place that a further accentuation of the difference of opinion which has arisen on this point would not been [*be*] apt to promote the friendly relations between Germany and the United States which both Governments have at heart and which so far have never been troubled. In a spirit of friendship and conciliation, therefore, the Imperial Government in order to settle definitely the *Lusitania* incident, declare themselves willing to grant an indemnity for the lives of American citizens which were lost by the sinking of the boat.

841.857 L 97/128½

The Secretary of State to President Wilson

WASHINGTON, *January 24, 1916.*

MY DEAR MR. PRESIDENT: I received late Saturday night a letter from Count Bernstorff enclosing two drafts of memoranda in the *Lusitania* case. Copies of these papers I am sending you.

Neither of the drafts seems to me to be at all satisfactory. There is no acknowledgement of the illegality of the sinking of the *Lusitania* and no admission of liability for the indemnity offered. The proposed memoranda are no improvement over the last one which the Ambassador submitted. They come no nearer meeting our demands. The offer of indemnity is based on good will; it is an act of grace and not a matter of right.

I shall not see the Ambassador until I have your opinion of this last effort to settle the controversy, but, when I do, I am disposed to tell him very frankly that further conversations will be useless as they do not appear to bring us any nearer together, and that there seems to be no other course but to make a formal demand upon the German Government for admission of illegal conduct by the submarine commander and of liability for the lives of citizens of the United States destroyed by the sinking of the vessel.

It does not seem to me to be in accord with the dignity of this Government to continue these informal negotiations which have become purely dilatory and offer no possible middle ground for an agreement.

Of course if we take this step and Germany fails to comply with our demands it will mean that we will have to send Bernstorff home or announce that we will do so unless full satisfaction is given within a definite time. While I dislike this course I see no alternative. We have delayed bringing this matter to a direct issue as long as we can. I had hoped a satisfactory settlement through delay. With more or less justice there has been increasingly severe public criticism of the policy pursued by the Government. If I felt that all would come right in the end I would be indifferent to public comment, but in view of these drafts of memoranda I am convinced that further delay will accomplish no good purpose and will only add to the belief that we are not insisting on compliance as we should.

It is possible that a demand, which the German Government understands to be inflexible, will accomplish more than our informal negotiations have accomplished. I do not think that they want a diplomatic break, and, if they are convinced that compliance is the only way to avoid it, they may submit. In any event I see no other course which we can honorably take.

I would like to see you as early today as possible or else talk with you over the telephone, in order that I may arrange an interview with Count Bernstorff as he requests.

Faithfully yours,

ROBERT LANSING

841.857 L 97/129½

President Wilson to the Secretary of State

WASHINGTON, *24 January, 1916.*

MY DEAR MR. SECRETARY: I do not see wherein this memorandum differs from that previously submitted and which we declared unsatisfactory. I entirely agree with you that we cannot accept it as a recognition of our rights. It is only a concession as of grace.

You will remember the despatch [1] I sent you from House, in which he asks that we take no steps against Germany until we receive the letter which he was to send by a steamer leaving England last Wednesday, the nineteenth of January. I have not the least idea what that letter contains, but I do not think that it would be prudent to take any steps towards a diplomatic break before we know what is in it.

I hope, therefore, that you will until then only see Bernstorff and let him know that the reply he has submitted is not satisfactory and seems to close conversations unless his government can see its way to a change of attitude, and then feel your way for a few days. House's letter ought to reach us by the twenty-seventh. I assume it will come in the pouch from London.

Or would it be practicable and wise to put Bernstorff off until then?

Faithfully Yours,

W. W.

763.72/2355½

President Wilson to the Secretary of State

WASHINGTON, *25 January, 1916.*

MY DEAR MR. SECRETARY: Do you not think that it would be wise to post Gerard pretty fully in this matter. I think that House ought to know the full facts, but I do not like to go over Gerard's head and tell House and not him. House, according to this despatch,[2] will be in Berlin to-day and it is of the utmost importance, of course, that he

---

[1] No copy found in Department files.
[2] Telegram No. 3375, Jan. 21, 1916, from the Ambassador in Germany, *Foreign Relations.* 1916, supp., p. 148.

be fully posted. It might be well to instruct Gerard specifically to tell House everything, though I suppose he would do so in any case.

Faithfully Yours,

W. W.

841.857 L 97/130½

The Secretary of State to President Wilson

WASHINGTON, *January 25, 1916.*

MY DEAR MR. PRESIDENT: I enclose a memorandum of a conference with the German Ambassador, which took place this afternoon. In accordance with our understanding this morning you will see that I have delayed matters in a measure and, at the same time, have practically broken off our informal conversations—though I am to see him tomorrow morning.

Faithfully yours,

ROBERT LANSING

[Enclosure]

Memorandum by the Secretary of State of a Conference With the German Ambassador (Bernstorff), January 25, 1916

I said to the Ambassador that I had considered very carefully the two memoranda which he had sent me Saturday night, and that I regretted to say that neither of them was at all satisfactory; that I could not see any material change from the memorandum which he had previously submitted on the subject. He replied that he thought they differed in the fact that they left out the portion which related to a warning of American citizens. I told him I considered that non-essential; that the essential omission was the frank admission on the part of Germany that the sinking of the *Lusitania,* being an act of reprisal, was an illegal act; and that while it might be justified in regard to enemies, it could not be justified in regard to neutrals; that their rights were violated and that the violation of rights imposed upon the German Government the liability of which the outward manifestation was the payment of a reasonable indemnity.

The Ambassador said that they had offered to pay the indemnity and he thought it might be concluded from that that they recognized that a right had been invaded, and that, therefore, there was liability.

I told him I did not read the memoranda in that way; that the language indicated that the payment of an indemnity would be an

THE LANSING PAPERS, 1914–1920, VOLUME I

act of grace on the part of Germany, growing out of her desire to preserve the friendship of the United States; that when Italians were massacred by a mob in New Orleans the United States had paid a considerable indemnity but had denied obligation to do so and, therefore, had denied liability for the wrong.[3]

The Ambassador asked me what I desired him to do. I said that in view of the circumstances I could see no good reason for continuing our informal conversations on the subject, unless his Government frankly admitted the illegality of the submarine commander's conduct and also admitted liability for the American lives lost. He replied that he was convinced his Government would not be willing to consent to such admissions in view of the fact that it would be turning black into white, as they had always denied the wrong and the liability. I answered him that he evidently, then, had reached the same conclusion—that further informal negotiations would be useless.

The Ambassador seemed greatly perturbed and sat for several moments considering the situation. He finally said:—"And what would be your course in case my Government will not accede to these terms, which seem harsh?"

I replied:—"I see no other course, Mr. Ambassador, except to break off diplomatic relations."

The Ambassador said:—"I do not see how the matter could stop with the breaking off of diplomatic relations. It would go further than that."

I replied:—"Doubtless you are correct in this view. I have given the matter most earnest consideration and have discussed it with the President, and I can assure you we do not hesitate to assume responsibility for what may occur in case your Government refuses to accede to our just demands. You know that we have striven to arrange this controversy amicably and for that reason I submitted to you a formula which I thought would, to an extent at least, harmonize the attitude of your Government with mine. I feel that we have gone as far as we can in accordance with the dignity and honor of the United States."

The Ambassador took the copies of the memorandum which he had been holding in his hand and started to make certain changes in them. I said to him that I thought it would be as well if he would take them to the Embassy and prepare a memorandum meeting our views, with the understanding that it might be possible to induce his Government to adopt it, and that I would see him tomorrow morning at 11:45. He replied that he would do so, but that he doubted very

---

[3] See *Foreign Relations*, 1891, pp. 658–728.

much if his Government could be induced to admit the wrong conduct of the submarine commander; or that it was liable for the death of the Americans on board the *Lusitania.*

ROBERT LANSING

841.857 L 97/131½

Memorandum by the Secretary of State of a Conversation With the German Ambassador (*Bernstorff*), *January 26, 1916*

The German Ambassador called at 11:45 this morning and handed me a memorandum which he proposed to communicate to his Government for their approval. In the memorandum was the admission of liability of the German Government for the lives of American citizens lost on the *Lusitania* but no admission of the illegality of the act of the submarine commander in sinking the vessel.

After reading the memorandum I told the Ambassador that I did not think it would be satisfactory but that I would submit it to the President if he so desired. He asked me in what particulars I would have it changed. I told him in the particular as to the admission of illegality so far as neutrals were concerned. He then made several changes in the memorandum and after we went over them together he dictated them to Mr. Sweet. The result was the annexed memorandum which the Ambassador will send today to Berlin for the approval of his Government.[4]

Over the telephone I read the proposed memorandum to the President who said that he thought if Bernstorff could obtain that our demands would have been fully met.

I then telephoned the German Ambassador that the President considered the memorandum satisfactory and that I hoped he could secure it.

ROBERT LANSING

763.72/13402b : Telegram

The Secretary of State to the Ambassador in Germany (*Gerard*)

WASHINGTON, *January 26, 1916—5 p. m.*

2645. For the Ambassador and Colonel House:

On the 22d the German Ambassador submitted two tentative drafts of a memorandum in the *Lusitania* case by which the German Government repeated its regret that Americans were killed by the justifiable retaliatory act of its submarine commander and offered, out of regard for the friendship of the two countries, to pay an indemnity.

---

[4] Quoted in telegram, *infra.*

On the 25th I had an interview with Count von Bernstorff and told him that both drafts were unsatisfactory; that the act of the submarine commander, being retaliatory, was admittedly illegal and though it might be justified against an enemy it could not be justified against neutrals. I told him that this Government would be satisfied with nothing less than an admission of the wrongful conduct of the submarine commander and an admission of liability for the lives of American citizens lost by his act. He replied that he was sure his Government could not go as far as that as they had denied liability. He asked me what would be our course in case Germany could not meet our demands. I replied that I saw no other course except to break off diplomatic relations, to which he answered that he thought it would go further than that in case we followed that course. I told him that was probably correct but that I had discussed the matter fully with the President and that we would not hesitate to assume responsibility for the consequences. He stated that he would think the matter over and see me again today.

At noon today the German Ambassador called and after discussing the matter he submitted the following memorandum which he is sending to his Government for their approval.

"The German submarine war against England's commerce at sea, as announced on February 4, 1915, is conducted in retaliation of England's inhuman war against Germany's commercial and industrial life. It is generally recognized as justifiable that retaliation may be employed against acts committed in contravention of the law of nations. Germany is enacting such retaliation because it is England's endeavor to cut off all imports from Germany by preventing even legal commerce of neutrals with her and thereby subjecting the German population to starvation. In answer to these acts Germany is making efforts to destroy England's commerce at sea, at least as far as it is carried on by enemy vessels. If Germany has notwithstanding limited her submarine warfare this was done in view of her long-standing friendship with the United States and in view of the fact that the sinking of the *Lusitania* caused the death of citizens of the United States. Thereby the German retaliation affected neutrals, which was not the intention as retaliation becomes an illegal act if applied to other than enemy subjects.

The Imperial Government, having, subsequent to the event, issued to its naval officers the new instructions which are now prevailing, expresses profound regret that citizens of the United States suffered by the sinking of the *Lusitania* and, recognizing the illegality of causing their death, and admitting liability therefor, offers to make reparation for the lives of the citizens of the United States who were lost by the payment of a suitable indemnity.

In the note of the American Government, July 21,⁶ concerning the *Lusitania* incident, the Government of the United States invited the practical cooperation of the Imperial German Government in con-

---

⁶ *Foreign Relations*, 1915, supp., p. 480.

tending for the principle of the freedom of the seas, and added that this great object could, in some way be accomplished before the present war ends. The Imperial Government will at all times gladly cooperate with the Government of the United States for the purpose of accomplishing this common great object."

If the German Government can agree to the above memorandum I believe that the *Lusitania* case will be satisfactorily ended. The memorandum was read to the President and received his approval.

LANSING

841.857 L 97/131½

Draft Note From the Secretary of State to the German Ambassador (Bernstorff), Proposed in Case of Entire Failure of Informal Negotiations

EXCELLENCY: The informal conversations which I have had with your Excellency relating to the sinking of the British steamship *Lusitania* by a German submarine, through which a large number of citizens of the United States lost their lives, have, I regret to say, failed in their purpose although conducted in the most amicable spirit and with a sincere effort on my part to remove as far as possible those differences which prevented a settlement of the controversy.

After careful consideration of the present state of the discussion my Government has with great reluctance reached the conclusion that a continuance of these conversations would not be justified, since the only result would be further delay without reasonable prospect of a satisfactory settlement of the dispute.

In view of the failure to reach an agreement informally but one course remains, if we are to preserve the friendly relations between our Governments, and that is a frank presentation of its demands by the Government of the United States and an equally frank compliance by the Imperial German Government.

The Government of the United States, therefore, must very respectfully insist that the Imperial German Government declare

(1) That the sinking of the *Lusitania* by a German submarine, being an act admitted to be in retaliation for alleged illegal conduct by an enemy, was itself, so far as it affected neutrals, illegal and in violation of the accepted rules of civilized warfare;

(2) That, as citizens of the United States, who were neutral noncombatants, lost their lives in consequence of this illegal act of the German naval authorities, the Imperial German Government admit liability for the lives lost and agree to pay a just indemnity therefor; and

(3) That the officer of the German Navy responsible for the sinking of the *Lusitania*, will be punished for having committed a lawless and inhumane act in thus causing the death of citizens of the United States.

In order to avoid any misapprehension which may possibly exist I wish to state to your Excellency that the demands, upon which my Government is constrained to insist, cannot be withdrawn or changed in substance without abandoning those principles of international law and humanity for which it has from the beginning of this controversy contended, and that, firmly convinced of the righteousness of these principles, it cannot now abandon them.

The Government of the United States, believing that in presenting these demands it is fully justified by the law of nations and by the humane sentiment of civilization, expresses the earnest hope that the Imperial German Government will realize that it does so in the same spirit of friendship and with the same regard for the amicable relations of the two countries, which it has manifested in the informal negotiations which have been in progress during the past three months. My Government has sought with patience and confidently expected to obtain a settlement of the controversy which would give due recognition to the rights of the United States and its citizens. The admissions of principle contained in the assurances of your Government of September 1, 1915,[7] in the statement in the German note of November 29, 1915,[8] in regard to the steamer *William P. Frye*, and in the declaration as to submarine warfare received January 7th,[9] justified this hope and expectation. The Government of the United States found further encouragement in the fact that your Excellency's Government by declaring that the sinking of the *Lusitania* was in retaliation for alleged breaches of international law by Great Britain admitted substantially that the act of the commander of the submarine was illegal. I have not failed to point out repeatedly to your Excellency that an act of admitted illegality is unjustifiable where it impairs neutral rights and imposes upon the perpetrator a full measure of liability, whatever justification may be urged for it as an act of retaliation against persons of enemy nationality. As this assertion has remained practically unchallenged my Government has patiently and hopefully awaited its acceptance by the Imperial Government and an acknowledgment of liability for the illegal and culpable conduct of its officer. But it seems now that the patience of the Government of the United States was in vain, and its hope unwarranted.

I need not impress upon your Excellency the critical stage which the controversy has reached, as I know that you appreciate as fully as I do, that a direct issue can no longer be avoided. My Government, while it views this situation with the gravest concern and would

---

[7] *Foreign Relations*, 1915, supp., p. 530.
[8] *Ibid.*, p. 644.
[9] *Ibid.*, 1916, supp., p. 144.

deplore a severance of those relations with your Government which have always been characterized by sincerity and cordiality, cannot recede from the position which it has taken, or lessen the demands which it has made.

The Government of the United States feels that the time has come when it should know whether the Imperial German Government purposes to recognize the justice of the contention of the United States and is willing to rectify as far as possible the wrongs done to its citizens. After the very full exchange of views which have taken place, the Government of the United States does not consider the subject is open to further discussion; and it, therefore, requests that the Imperial Government reply categorically to the demands which have been presented and that in doing so it bear in mind that upon it rests the responsibility for the future relations between the two countries, which the Government of the United States most earnestly and sincerely desires should continue to be inspired by cordial friendship and esteem and by a due regard for the rights of their respective citizens and subjects.

JANUARY 26, 1916

763.72/2364

The Secretary of State to President Wilson [10]

WASHINGTON, *January 31, 1916.*

MY DEAR MR. PRESIDENT: I enclose flimsies of two telegrams— numbers 4006 [*3406*][11] and 4008 [*3408*],[11] received from Berlin, relative to the *Lusitania* case.

I call your particular attention to number 4008 [*3408*] because the suggestion made by Gerard, in which he says that "Colonel House concurs" is, to my mind, exactly in line with the memoranda which we have received from Count Bernstorff. I am very much afraid that Gerard, and possibly House, do not appreciate the real point at issue—namely, that the German Government should admit the wrongdoing of the submarine commander who torpedoed the vessel. I am also afraid that they have held out hopes to Zimmermann that a declaration such as is suggested would be acceptable to you. It shows the danger of attempting to negotiate at two ends of the line.

Do you wish to suggest a reply to Gerard or shall I prepare one, explaining the point at issue, so that he may disabuse Zimmermann of the idea that the suggested declaration would be acceptable.

---

[10] Addressed to reach the President at Kansas City, Mo., February 2, 1916.
[11] *Foreign Relations*, 1916, supp., p. 153.

I congratulate you upon the splendid reception you are receiving from the people whom you have addressed in behalf of preparedness.

Faithfully yours,

[File copy not signed]

P. S. Please telegraph me an answer. I enclose also copy of a telegram which I have just sent Gerard.[12]

763.72/2364 : Telegram

The Secretary of State to the Ambassador in Germany (Gerard)

WASHINGTON, *January 31, 1916—10 a. m.*

2661. Your 4008 [*3408*].[13] Offer no encouragement that the suggested statement would be at all acceptable. It has already been several times submitted to this Government. Will advise you later.

LANSING

763.72/2389½ : Telegram

President Wilson to the Secretary of State

KANSAS CITY, MO., *February 2, 1916—7 : 07 p. m.*

[Received 10 : 30 p. m.]

Your letter of January 31st received. Please frame and send message you suggest explaining the point at issue.

WOODROW WILSON

763.72/2390½ : Telegram

President Wilson to the Secretary of State

TERRE HAUTE, IND., *February 3, 1916—4 : 22 p. m.*

[Received 6 : 45 p. m.]

Please hold message suggested yesterday until I can see you or if it has been sent send word to await further instructions. Will explain when I reach Washington.

WOODROW WILSON

763.72/2611

The Secretary of State to President Wilson

WASHINGTON, *February 4, 1916.*

MY DEAR MR. PRESIDENT: The German Ambassador has just called upon me and left the enclosed memorandum [14] which he gave me to

---

[12] *Infra.*
[13] *Foreign Relations*, 1916, supp., p. 153.
[14] *Ibid.*, p. 157.

understand was as far as his Government possibly could go in complying with our requests.

I have only analyzed the memorandum very hastily. In the first place I think it may be drawn from it that the German Government recognizes that retaliatory acts are not lawful, though justifiable; in the second place, it declares that "retaliation must not aim at other than enemy subjects", which means, I think, that it is unlawful so far as neutrals are concerned; and in the third place, the German Government assumes liability for the death of citizens of the United States as a result of the sinking of the *Lusitania*. It comes so near meeting all our demands that I wish to study it with care to see if it cannot be considered acceptable.

Of course the word *illegal* and the word *illegality* are omitted, but if we do accept this settlement I believe we could state our understanding of the language in order to show in our acceptance that we consider there is a direct admission of wrong.

Faithfully yours,

ROBERT LANSING

763.72/2611

The Secretary of State to President Wilson

WASHINGTON, *February 8, 1916.*

MY DEAR MR. PRESIDENT: The German Ambassador called upon me at half-past four this afternoon and I talked with him about the suggested changes in his memorandum. He said he would like very much to make the changes himself without consulting his Government, but that he had been so attacked by his enemies at home that he did not dare to do so. He agreed to at once advise Berlin of the changes sought and was satisfied that they would accede to them. He seemed to think there was no doubt about it. I am not at all sure that I share his optimism as I fear they may seek to modify their statements in some way.

It will, therefore, be a few days before anything further can be done, as I assume the Ambassador will not be able to send a telegram until tomorrow morning.

Faithfully yours,

ROBERT LANSING

763.72/2392½

The Secretary of State to President Wilson

WASHINGTON, *February 16, 1916.*

MY DEAR MR. PRESIDENT: The German Ambassador called on me this noon and left a letter embodying his Government's reply to our official note of July 21st, 1915, a copy of which I herewith enclose.[15]

I told the Ambassador that I would take the matter under consideration, and would give him no opinion on the subject at the present time.

You will perceive that substantially all our suggestions have been accepted, except the change of the last phrase in paragraph 2 which reads—"as retaliation should be confined to enemy subjects". Our suggestion, you will recall, was—"as retaliation must not prevent the exercise of rights of other than enemy subjects." I am not at all sure whether the difference of phraseology is a substantial one.

In view of the recent manifesto from Berlin in regard to armed merchant vessels [16] I do not see how we can now accept this answer as a settlement of the *Lusitania* case. The German Government was fully advised as to our attitude in regard to the legal right to arm merchant vessels. It was, at the time it gave its three several assurances, with full knowledge of the British Admiralty orders to their merchant vessels, yet they gave those assurances without qualification and they became an essential basis for a settlement of the difficulty. The recent declaration, in which it is stated that armed merchant vessels will be treated as auxiliary cruisers is, therefore, contradictory of their former position and would appear to nullify the assurances which they have given.

I believe it would be well for me to see the German Ambassador again, or else write him a note saying that in view of the recent change of policy by his Government the part of the settlement relating to the future conduct of submarine warfare has been materially changed and will require further consideration by this Government before it can accept as satisfactory the enclosed reply.

Faithfully yours,

ROBERT LANSING

763.72/2393½

President Wilson to the Secretary of State

WASHINGTON, *16 February, 1916.*

MY DEAR MR. SECRETARY: I have no hesitation in saying that, but for the recent announcement of the Central Powers as to the treatment to which they purpose subjecting armed merchantmen and those which they presume to be armed, it would clearly be our duty in the circumstances to accept the accompanying note as satisfactory. But that announcement inevitably throws doubt upon the

---

[15] *Foreign Relations,* 1916, supp., p. 171; the original is now filed under file No. 763.72/2392½. For the American note of July 21, 1915, see *ibid.,* 1915, supp., p. 480.

[16] *Ibid.,* 1916, supp., p. 163.

whole future, and makes it necessary that we should think the situation out afresh.

I would suggest that you have a frank conversation with the German Ambassador [17] and point out to him just our difficulty—the difficulty of interpreting their recent assurances in the light of their new and dangerous policy, and of understanding that new policy in view of the fact that all the circumstances upon which they base their adoption of it were known to them at the time of the *Arabic* note.

I doubt whether it would be wise to address a note to him. I think that it would be best, all things considered, to make the interchange of explanations oral only, for the present.

Faithfully Yours,

W. W.

763.72/2483½

The Secretary of State to the German Ambassador (Bernstorff)

WASHINGTON, *February 19, 1916.*

MY DEAR MR. AMBASSADOR: I desire to call your attention to the enclosed clipping which appeared in the *Washington Post* of Friday, February 18th, and seems to have been sent out by the International News Service. The particular portion of the article to which I desire to call your attention is the last two paragraphs in which the quotation marks indicate that the statement was made by an official of your Embassy.

As this statement appears to imply a lack of good faith on the part of this Government in the settlement of the *Lusitania* case, I would like to be advised as to the authenticity of the statement and also as to the official who is responsible for it.

I am [etc.] ROBERT LANSING

[Enclosure]

Clipping From the "Washington Post," February 18, 1916

The suggestion was made last night in diplomatic circles that the present attitude of the United States on the *Lusitania* controversy and the whole question of submarine warfare is based on political expediency. There are three reasons influencing the administration in its changed course, according to this diplomatic opinion. These are:

1. If Germany can be induced to consent to embody in her reply to the *Lusitania* note the assurances for the future conduct of submarine warfare he demands, President Wilson may claim a diplomatic victory.

---

[17] For a report of this conversation, see *ibid.*, p. 172.

2. If Germany insists on confining the *Lusitania* controversy strictly to the facts of that issue alone, negotiations can be drawn out until after the election next November.

3. The speech of Elihu Root, at the Republican State convention in New York, attacking the administration, has influenced the President to put on a bold front against the central empires.

Meantime negotiations looking to a settlement of the case have come to an abrupt halt. For the first time in the nine months that have elapsed since the dispatch, May 13, 1915, of the first *Lusitania* note officials of the German embassy have felt justified in assuming a frankly dilatory attitude.

One of these officials expressed the embassy's viewpoint as follows:

"Until today Germany has supposed that the United States was sincerely anxious to settle the *Lusitania* case with the least possible delay. Now, however, it is apparent that this is not the situation.

"The United States has taken the view that an immediate settlement would be a favor to Germany. Quite the reverse is true. Indefinite postponement would put Germany in the tenth heaven of delight. The United States, now that it has made its position clear, can count on all the delay imaginable, so far as Germany is concerned."

763.72/2485½

The German Ambassador (Bernstorff) to the Secretary of State

J. No. A 1225   WASHINGTON, *February 22, 1916.*

MY DEAR MR. SECRETARY: In answer to your letter of 19th inst. I beg to say that no member of this Embassy gave any statement to the International News Service concerning the *Lusitania* incident. The contents of the statement, which I return herewith,[18] are so entirely in contradiction with the policy of my Government that the alleged interview can only have been fabricated for some mischievous purpose.

I never give any interview myself and never allow statements to be made by any member of this Embassy except under express instruction from my Government. In the latter case the statements are given out in writing. I have, notwithstanding, to my great surprise, during the last days read in some of the anti-German newspapers of this country, that I had been blamed by officials of the State Department for having published information which should have remained confidential. You know that some of my instructions, regarding the *Lusitania* question, were given to American correspondents in Berlin before I had received them. This was not my fault, and I had nothing to do with it. As far as I am concerned, I have

---

[18] *Supra.*

never given any newspaper men any information which they had not received from other sides before they spoke to me. I do not deny that I have tried to explain to correspondents such information as they already possessed. This I consider perfectly legitimate as long as the system prevails that newspaper men are at liberty to follow diplomats by day and night and attack us whenever they please. At the present time I can see no other reason for such attacks by the above mentioned anti-German newspapers than the desire to discredit my work, because they know that I have done and I am still doing all I possibly can to bring about an amicable settlement of the various questions pending between the United States and Germany.

Believe me [etc.]   J. BERNSTORFF

763.72/2623

The Secretary of State to President Wilson

WASHINGTON, *March 8, 1916.*

MY DEAR MR. PRESIDENT: I enclose a memorandum which was handed to me by the German Ambassador this morning,[19] and which contains more or less a historical review of the submarine warfare question, directing particular attention to the shortcomings of Great Britain.

You will note that the Ambassador expresses a desire to give the memorandum publicity and I could not well object to his doing so, as it does not directly affect our negotiations with Germany. I would, however, call your attention to the last paragraph which indicates to me that the memorandum was prepared with the idea of making an appeal to the American people. Please return the memorandum with any suggestions you have as to what treatment we should give it.

Faithfully yours,

ROBERT LANSING

763.72/2635½

President Wilson to the Secretary of State

WASHINGTON, *8 March, 1916.*

MY DEAR MR. SECRETARY: In view of the wording of the last paragraph of this communication, it is evident to me that it is intended not as in any proper sense a memorandum for the information of this Government but as an appeal to American public opinion, and, for my own part, I resent being made use of in this way.

---

[19] *Foreign Relations,* 1916, supp., p. 198.

Do you not think that it would be well to ask the German Ambassador why, since it is addressed to the American people and makes no reference whatever to a desire to inform the Government of the United States of the subject matter of its contents, it was handed to this Government at all?

Faithfully Yours,

W. W.

_____

763.72/2623

The Secretary of State to President Wilson

WASHINGTON, *March 24, 1916.*

MY DEAR MR. PRESIDENT: I submit a draft of a letter to the German Ambassador which follows, I believe, your views as to the attitude we should take in regard to the memorandum which he delivered on March 8th,[20] and which was given to the press on the same day.

I should like to send this letter as soon as possible.[21]

Faithfully yours,

ROBERT LANSING

[Enclosure]

Draft Note to the German Ambassador (Bernstorff)

MY DEAR MR. AMBASSADOR: On account of absence from Washington I have delayed commenting on the Memorandum explanatory of "the U-Boat question", which you handed me on March 8th. Meanwhile the memo has received the careful consideration of the President and myself and he directs me to call your attention particularly to the wording of the last paragraph which escaped my attention during our conversation on the 8th, when it was agreed that it should be made public. Upon consideration however the Govt. is constrained to the belief that it was the intention of the Imperial Government to appeal to the American people and to submit the case before the bar of public opinion, rather than to this Government. This belief is confirmed by your earnest desire to furnish the Memorandum to the press for publication immediately upon its delivery.

This unusual, if not unprecedented, procedure, which gives the impression of having been adopted for the purpose of securing popular support in the United States for the German position without regard to the attitude of this Government, cannot be passed over without comment, especially as it was employed in relation to a

_____

[20] *Foreign Relations,* 1916, supp., p. 198.
[21] Apparently the proposed letter was not sent.

subject, which, at the time, was being considered by the Congress of the United States.

As the subject of the Memorandum was a matter of diplomatic discussion between the two Governments, the Government of the United States must express its disapproval of the course of the Imperial Government in appealing directly to the American people in support of its position on a pending question between the two Governments. Not only does this Government disapprove this action but it resents the delivery to it by your Excellency as the diplomatic representative of Germany of a document which on its face is intended to influence public opinion in the United States and possibly to arouse directly or indirectly opposition in the Congress to the policy of the President in dealing with the question of submarine warfare.

I am reluctant to believe that your Govt. fully considered the consequences before permitting you to become the medium of transmitting this appeal to the people of the United States though in form addressed to this Government. Without exceeding the bounds of diplomatic propriety this Government cannot permit a diplomatic representative to address the people of this country through the press or otherwise on a controversy pending between the Government of the United States and the Government which he represents.

I would be wanting in duty to my Government and in justice to yours, if I did not thus candidly state the unfavorable impression which has been made by the Memorandum of March 8th and by the way in which it was laid before the American public.

851.857 Su 8/54a

The Secretary of State to President Wilson

WASHINGTON, *March 27, 1916.*

MY DEAR MR. PRESIDENT: All the information which we are receiving in regard to the sinking of the *Sussex* in the English Channel, by which several Americans were injured and some undoubtedly killed, indicates that the vessel was torpedoed by a German submarine.[22] If this information is corroborated as the investigation proceeds it will present a very serious situation in our relations with Germany. I think we should determine what course should be taken in the event that the evidence points very strongly to the culpability of the Germans.

Every effort undoubtedly will be made by the Allies to prove that the vessel was torpedoed, and I believe that they will make a

---

[22] For correspondence previously printed concerning the *Sussex*, see *Foreign Relations*, 1916, supp., pp. 214–268.

strong case, judging from the telegrams we have thus far received. On the other hand, I feel sure that the German Government will deny the charge and assert that a floating mine of English origin caused the disaster. There will be thus a flat contradiction of statements as to the facts.

I do not believe that the Government can remain inactive because of this contradictory evidence. There will be a strong demand that something should be done and, personally, I would be disposed to view such a demand as justifiable.

The argument which will meet with general favor will be that the sinking of the *Sussex* is similar to that of the sinking of other vessels in the last few days, and is a direct result of the greater activity of submarines, in accordance with the new German policy which went into effect March first; and that even if the evidence of torpedoing was absent the presumption raised by the announced policy of Germany and the submarine attacks of the past ten days makes it almost certain that the vessel was torpedoed.

Assuming that Germany will fail to establish conclusively the innocence of her submarine commanders I do not see how we can avoid taking some decisive step. We can no longer temporize in the matter of submarine warfare when Americans are being killed, wounded, or endangered by the illegal and inhuman conduct of the Germans.

Of one thing I am firmly convinced and that is that the time for writing notes discussing the subject has passed. Whatever we determine to do must be in the line of action and it must indicate in no uncertain terms that the present method of submarine warfare can no longer be tolerated.

Proceeding on the assumption that the *Sussex* was torpedoed the action which seems to me the most practicable would be to demand the immediate recall of Count Bernstorff and the severance of diplomatic relations with Germany. This action might be made conditional upon the German Government unequivocally admitting the illegality of submarine warfare in general, paying a just indemnity for the Americans killed and injured, and guaranteeing that the present method of warfare will cease. Such a conditional admission would be in the nature of an ultimatum which could very properly include a time limit at the expiration of which, in case of failure to comply with the conditions, Count von Bernstorff could be given his passports.

I realize that this action is drastic but I believe that to be patient longer would be misconstrued both at home and abroad. We have already shown in the case of the *Lusitania* an earnest desire to avoid trouble with Germany and now, after ten months of negotiations and on the eve of an amicable settlement, Germany has renewed the method of warfare against which we so strongly protested. In these circumstances I do not see how we can avoid the issue and remain inactive. The honor of the United States and the duty of the Government to its citizens require firm and decisive action.

While I have advanced these views on an assumption as to the sinking of the *Sussex* I think that the assumption will be justified. Doubtless the German Government would view the breaking off of diplomatic relations as an unfriendly act and might possibly go so far as to declare war against the United States, yet, with the probable consequences fully in mind, I can see no other course open to us. The case arises at a most unfortunate time in view of the state of our Mexican affairs and also in view of the proposed treaty which is receiving the consideration of the Danish Government. If we could, consistently with the dignity of the United States and our duty as a Government, delay action I would favor delay, but, in view of all the facts, if the assumption of German responsibility is established, I do not believe a long delay is possible.

Faithfully yours,

ROBERT LANSING

851.857 Su 8/54½

President Wilson to the Secretary of State

WASHINGTON, *30 March, 1916.*

MY DEAR MR. SECRETARY: I have your letter of the twenty-seventh in which you state your preliminary impressions about the *Sussex* Case. My impressions are not quite the same. The proof that the disaster was caused by a torpedo seems to me by no means satisfactory or conclusive. And, if it was caused by a torpedo, there are many particulars to be considered about the course we should pursue as well as the principle of it. The steps we take and the way we take them will, it seems to me, be of the essence of the matter if we are to keep clearly and indisputably within the lines we have already set ourselves.

But in this, as in other matters referred to in the papers I am now sending back to you, a personal conference is much the best means of reaching conclusions. We must have one very soon.

Faithfully Yours,

W. W.

851.857 Su 8/54½a

Draft Instructions to the Ambassador in Germany (Gerard) [23]

You are instructed to deliver to the Secretary of Foreign Affairs a note reading as follows:

On March 24, 1916, at two-fifty p. m. the unarmed steamer *Sussex*, with three hundred and fifty to four hundred passengers on board, among whom were a number of American citizens, was torpedoed in the English Channel en route from Folkestone to Dieppe. Eighty of the passengers, which consisted of non-combatants of all ages and sexes, were killed or injured.

A searching and impartial investigation by officers of the United States has established conclusively that the vessel was torpedoed without warning or summons to surrender, and that the torpedo was launched by a German submarine.

The attack upon the *Sussex*, like the attacks made upon the *Englishman*, *Manchester Engineer*, *Eagle Point* and other steamers of belligerent and neutral nationalities, was contrary to the rules of civilized warfare and in violation of those principles of humanity which enlightened nations respect in conducting hostile operations on the high seas.

The Government of the United States has been forced to the conclusion, by evidence of the most convincing character, either that the explicit assurances heretofore given to it by the Imperial Government as to the employment of undersea craft in intercepting enemy and neutral commerce have been violated by German submarine commanders with the knowledge and acquiescence of the Imperial Government, or that that Government in recently issuing orders to its submarines to renew their activities did so with the intention of ignoring the assurances given.

Whichever of these alternatives is the fact is immaterial, for in either case the Imperial Government has, through its naval authorities, broken its solemn pledge to the Government of the United States and resorted to a method of warfare which invites the condemnation of the civilized world. The Government and the people of the United States have viewed with abhorrence this policy of wanton and indiscriminate slaughter of helpless men, women and children traversing the high seas in the enjoyment of their recognized rights, and it justly resents the breach of faith, of which the Imperial Government is guilty in thus renewing an inhuman and illegal practice which it had expressly agreed to abandon.

For a century the tendency of the nations has been to ameliorate the human suffering which is the inevitable consequence of war. By treaties, by declarations, and by common usage non-combatants have been more and more protected in their lives and property from the horrors incidental to conflicts between nations. The spirit of modern civilization revolts against needless cruelty and the wanton destruction of human life. The present conduct of submarine warfare by Germany is hostile to this spirit; it is a reversion to that barbarism which took no thought for human life and which caused the innocent

---

[23] This paper bears the notation: "Original handed to Prest for his consideration 2:30 pm April 6/16. RL." See also footnote 34, p. 546.

and defenseless to suffer even more grievously than those who bore arms.

In its first note in regard to the sinking of the *Lusitania*,[24] the Government of the United States expressed the opinion that it was impossible for a submarine to conduct operations against the commerce of an enemy and conform to the laws of naval warfare and to the principles of humanity. The Government of the United States, though subject to the greatest provocation to adopt severe measures against the Government which had permitted and which defended the lawless act of its submarine commander, conducted its negotiations with a restraint and patience which evinced its earnest desire to obtain by amicable means a settlement which would make amends for the past and guarantee humane conduct for the future. As the negotiations progressed, the Government of the United States became increasingly hopeful that the Imperial Government would recognize the illegality of the sinking of the *Lusitania* and prevent a repetition of the outrage by its submarine commanders. The recent operations of German submarines, which have been carried on with the same brutal indifference to the right of life as was exhibited in the case of the *Lusitania*, has destroyed this hope and proved that the patience and restraint of the Government of the United States have been in vain, while the moderation shown appears to have been misconstrued by the Imperial Government.

The opinion, which the Government of the United States expressed in the note, to which reference has been made, as to the impossibility of legally and humanely employing submarines as commerce destroyers, has become a settled conviction. The course, upon which Germany has now entered, can no longer be tolerated, and a Government, which permits such practices, is no longer entitled to continue its intercourse with other Governments which regard the rules of international law and the principles of humanity as binding upon all belligerents.

In view of the manifest intention of the Imperial Government to continue this lawless and inhuman method of warfare it becomes, therefore, my solemn duty to inform your Excellency that the Government of the United States is compelled to sever diplomatic relations with the Imperial German Government until such time as that Government shall announce its purpose to discontinue and shall actually discontinue the employment of submarines against commercial vessels of belligerent as well as of neutral nationality.

I am, therefore, instructed to request my passports and directed to depart from Germany without delay; and I am further instructed to announce to your Excellency that the German Ambassador at Washington will forthwith be handed his passports and requested to take his immediate departure from the United States.[25]

In view of the manifest purpose of the Imperial Government to prosecute relentlessly submarine warfare against commercial vessels, without regard to legal right or the dictates of humanity, the Government of the United States is compelled to announce its intention

---

[24] Note of May 13, 1915, *Foreign Relations*, 1915, supp., p. 393.
[25] The paragraph which follows is appended, apparently intended as an alternative to the penultimate paragraph of the draft instructions.

to sever diplomatic relations with Germany unless the Imperial Government declares unconditionally that it will abandon its purpose and no longer employ its submarines against vessels of commerce.

851.857 Su 8/54½a

The Secretary of State to President Wilson

WASHINGTON, *April 10, 1916.*

MY DEAR MR. PRESIDENT: I enclose a suggested insertion in the draft of instructions to the American Ambassador at Berlin, which I handed to you at the White House on the 6th instant.[26]

The suggestion is due to Mr. Gerard's telegram #3713 of April 6th.[27] I have just this moment received another telegram from Mr. Gerard [28] saying that he expected to receive today the German reply in the *Sussex* case. I am, however, sending forward this suggestion for insertion because I assume the German answer will deny the presence of one of their submarines in the vicinity of the *Sussex* at the time she was wrecked—which will not materially affect our position as I see it.

I also enclose a flimsy of Mr. Gerard's 3713 and also a statement of the facts in the case of the *Sussex* based on the evidence which we now have in hand. My idea is that this statement should accompany the proposed instructions, together with the evidence upon which it is based.[29]

In case that course is followed it will be necessary to insert on page one of the draft of instructions a parenthetical clause at the end of the third paragraph, reading: "(A statement of the facts in the case is enclosed.)"

In spite of the dispatches we are receiving from Berlin I am still of the same opinion which I have by letter and orally expressed to you—that the course of action of this Government should be decided upon as soon as possible.

Faithfully yours,

ROBERT LANSING

[Enclosure]

Suggested Insertion at the Beginning of Draft Instructions to the Ambassador in Germany (Gerard)

I did not fail to transmit immediately by telegraph to my Government your Excellency's note of the 5th instant [30] in regard to the

---

[26] *Supra.*
[27] *Foreign Relations,* 1916, supp., p. 225.
[28] Not printed.
[29] For text of statement as sent, see *Foreign Relations,* 1916, supp., p. 234.
[30] *Ibid.,* p. 225.

disastrous explosion, which on March 24th wrecked the French steamship *Sussex* in the English Channel. I have now the honor to deliver, under instructions from my Government the following reply to your Excellency:

The Government of the United States, after careful consideration of the Imperial Government's note of April 5, 1916, regrets to state that it appears from the statements and requests contained in the note that the Imperial Government fails to appreciate the gravity of the situation which has resulted not alone from the attack on the *Sussex* but from the submarine warfare as waged by the German naval authorities, which without apparent discrimination has been directed against neutral merchant vessels as well as those of Germany's enemies.

If the *Sussex* had been an isolated case, the Government of the United States might consider that the officer responsible for the deed had wilfully violated his orders and that the ends of justice would be satisfied by imposing upon him an adequate punishment and by a formal disavowal of the act by the Imperial Government. But the *Sussex* is not an isolated case, though the attack was so utterly indefensible and caused a loss of life so appalling that it stands forth today as one of the most terrible examples of the inhumanity of submarine warfare as it is now being waged by Germany.

Even if the *Sussex* was torpedoed by mistake or in deliberate disobedience of orders, the fact remains that the act is in accord with the spirit manifested by the German naval authorities in their general policy and practice of submarine warfare. In view of this fact no apology, no disavowal, no admission of wrongdoing, no punishment of a guilty officer, and no payment of indemnity will satisfy the Government of the United States. Furthermore, the question of submarine warfare, which has for so many months been under discussion, is no longer debatable. The evidence of the determined purpose of the Imperial Government in the employment of submarines against peaceable merchant vessels is too certain and too plain to require explanation, and it is too manifestly lawless to admit of argument.

Thoroughly convinced that the attack on the *Sussex* was directly due to the German policy, though there may possibly have been a technical violation of orders by the commander of the submarine who torpedoed the vessel, the Government of the United States, while communicating to the Imperial Government the facts in the case of the *Sussex*, is constrained to go further and to announce the course of action which it has determined to follow and the reasons for such action.

763.72/2648½

Memorandum by the Secretary of State of a Conversation With the German Ambassador (Bernstorff), April 10, 1916, 3 p. m.

B   I did not come to see you the last days because I thought you had no information, but today I hear that you had received information and I wanted to ask if I could be of any service. Anything I could do in the matter would be pleased to do.

L   Not yet. As I understand it Mr. Gerard was to receive the note today.

B   I understood it had come, but I only got a telegram that he would get it.

L   No, we have not received it. We had a preliminary but not the full text.

B   Do they ask for more information?

L   They would like the details.

B   Then at the present moment there is nothing to be done?

L   We are simply collecting the evidence—that is all.

B   I wanted to keep in touch with the matter and if there is anything I can do you know I certainly want to do all I can. * * *[31] My Government is in a serious political situation in parliament so I do not know whether they have settled down to do anything definite in the matter. * * *

L   I realize there must be political considerations.

B   (The Ambassador talked further about the parliamentary situation, but his speech was too rapid and broken for me to understand.)

L   No, there is nothing at present. We are still awaiting certain information.

B   May I ask if you have any definite proof—considered definite?

L   Not yet; though we are expecting fuller reports than summaries of evidence. I expected we would have it today but I understand the *St Paul* did not sail until last Wednesday.

B   Then, generally speaking, at the present moment there is nothing definite.

L   Yes, I mean by definite we have gotten certain summaries of evidence but I always prefer to have the documents as far as possible.

B   At the present moment nothing can be done.

L   I do not think there is anything to say at all in regard to the situation.

B   I do not want to "butt in" but I want to help. * * * I asked them to give me such information as they could, and besides, I told

---

[31] This form of punctuation appears at intervals in the original.

them that the situation was grave. I did that on my own initiative and I would have waited until I heard more from Berlin. * * *

L   I consider the situation as grave as it has been.

B   I cannot judge from what I hear whether anything has been proved in contradiction. Of course— * * *

L   Of course I have given no expression of opinion and would not until I collected what evidence we could get in regard to the matter.

B   During the past week I had a pleasant conversation with Mr. Polk in regard to the commercial situation.

L   * * * I myself do not handle those matters * * *

B   If there is anything I can do, if you will advise me, I would like to help if I can. You know I never made matters worse, so if I can do anything to help I will be glad to do it.

L   All right. Thank you for coming.

851.857 Su 8/56½ : Telegram

The German Secretary of State for Foreign Affairs (Jagow) to the German Ambassador (Bernstorff) [32]

[Translation]

BERLIN, *April 11, 1916.*
[Received Tuckerton, N. J., April 13—10:27 p. m.]

No. 130. For your information. Reply regarding *Sussex*, other cases handed Gerard Monday night. Careful investigation shows that no German submarine responsible for attack on *Sussex*, but are willing to examine any evidence American Government may have and in case disagreement suggest mixed commission of inquiry in accordance with article 3 of Hague Convention, 1907,[33] consequences of which we naturally shall naturally [*sic*] assume. This ought to be considered sufficient proof of our *bona fides*. Steamers *Englishman, Eagle Point, Berwindvale* all ran away regardless of warning but only destroyed after crew saved in life boats. Investigation about *Manchester Engineer* so far without result, more details requested. Germany willing to conduct submarine warfare with due regard to neutral rights. We naturally stand by our assurances given America and have issued such precise instructions regarding this matter that according [to] human foresight errors are excluded. Should any mistakes happen contrary to expectation we are willing to remedy them in every way. Germany in face of daily increasing

---

[32] This paper bears the notation: "This wireless was delivered to German Amb. am April 14/16 RL."

[33] Malloy, *Treaties*, 1776–1909, vol. II, p. 2220 (Part III).

violations of international law by England cannot give up submarine war altogether but regrets that England apparently succeeds in luring a few American citizens also for [apparent omission] freight ships in war zone as you know are not immune by our promise, and thus tries to cause a break with America. Our *bona fides* cannot be doubted since Chancellor second time announced before whole world Germany ready to conclude peace and pointed out only defensive aims. Our opponents however sneeringly refuse our outstretched hand and are still preaching Germany's lasting military and economical annihilation.

JAGOW

851.857 Su 8/55½a

The Secretary of State to President Wilson

WASHINGTON, *April 12, 1916.*

MY DEAR MR. PRESIDENT: I am very heartily in accord with the proposed redraft of an instruction to Ambassador Gerard, (though I have suggested certain alterations in the text which do not change the spirit or sense), except as to one thing and that is the closing part which defines our action.[34]

It seems to me to say that we must sever relations unless Germany ceases her submarine practices weakens the communication very much. The impression I get is this, that we say we will wait and see if you sink another vessel with Americans on board. If you do we will recall our Ambassador. Why should we postpone to the happening of another outrage action which I feel will do much to prevent such

---

[34] Redraft not printed; for the note as sent, see *Foreign Relations*, 1916, supp., p. 232.

The concluding portion of President Wilson's redraft read as follows:

"Unless the Imperial Government should now immediately declare its intention to abandon its present practices of submarine warfare and return to a scrupulous observance of the practices clearly prescribed by the law of nations, the Government of the United States can have no choice but to sever diplomatic relations with the German Empire altogether."

Secretary Lansing's proposed conclusion read:

"It [the Government of the United States] can have no choice but to sever diplomatic relations with the German Empire until such time as the Imperial Government shall declare its purpose to abandon and shall abandon its present practices of submarine warfare, return to a scrupulous observance of the rules of naval warfare prescribed by the law of nations, and agree to make amends so far as is possible for the deaths and injuries suffered by citizens of the United States through the wanton attacks of German naval commanders on vessels of commerce.

"I have the honor to inform your Excellency that I am further instructed to request my passports and to depart from the German Empire as soon as possible, and to state that the Imperial German Ambassador at Washington will be requested to take his immediate departure for the United States."

outrage? It impresses me we are actually endangering the lives of our citizens by such a course.

I do not see that we gain anything strategically by postponing an action which I believe, and I think you agree with me, we will have to take in the end.

On the other hand, I think that vigorous and uncompromising action will be far more effective and may accomplish the purpose we desire. I am afraid that the ending as it reads will be construed as indefinite as to time and as giving an opening for discussion.

I have taken the liberty to put down the ending, which I would very much prefer. If they intend to submit at all they will have time to do so before his passports are handed to Gerard. If they do not intend to give up their practices, we are far better off than if we waited till they killed some more Americans.

Of course there is another way and that is to fix a time limit for a favorable answer, say, forty-eight hours; but to me that seems more offensive and more like an ultimatum than to break off diplomatic relations without delay or opportunity for parley.

I feel strongly in favor of the action I have proposed, as I think that it would have a profound effect on Germany, on this country and on other neutral nations.

Faithfully yours,

ROBERT LANSING

851.857 Su 8/57½

The German Ambassador (Bernstorff) to Colonel E. M. House [35]

WASHINGTON, *April 14, 1916.*

MY DEAR COLONEL HOUSE: With regard to our last confidential conversation I beg to add the following remarks based upon instructions just received from Berlin.

[Here follows, almost verbatim, telegram No. 130, April 11, from the German Secretary of State for Foreign Affairs to the German Ambassador, printed on page 545.] My Government entirely shares your wish to bring about peace and hopes that the relations between the United States and Germany will remain so friendly that both Governments can work together for the purpose of achieving this object so desirable in the interest of humanity and of all nations.

The foregoing statements as I said before, are entirely based on instructions from my Government. For my own part, I venture to suggest that it might be advisable to refrain from a further exchange of official notes, the publication of which always causes irritation.

---

[35] This paper bears the notation: "This has just come from B. and may interest you. E. M. H."

At your suggestion, I called on Mr. Lansing the other day and put myself at his disposal in case he wished me to take up any phase of the matter. Experience has proved, again in the question of exportation of dyestuffs from Berlin, that we always obtain better results if I take up matters confidentially with my Government. Otherwise, they do not, in Berlin, get the right impression of the state of affairs in this country.

I shall give myself the pleasure of calling on you the next time I visit New York which will probably be during the Easter Holidays.

I remain [etc.]   J. BERNSTORFF

851.857 Su 8/58½

The French Ambassador (Jusserand) to the Secretary of State

WASHINGTON, *April 14, 1916.*

MY DEAR MR. SECRETARY: I send you herewith a translation of a telegr[am] just received.

My Gov^t asks that, for the time being, no publicity be given to such information in it which is not public as yet.

Believe me [etc.]   JUSSERAND

You may have noticed that yesterday's papers (e. g. the *N. Y. Times*) had a telegr[am] from Berlin stating that the Prussian order "Pour le Mérite" had been conferred on "Lieut. Otto Steinbrinck, the commander of a submarine."

[Enclosure—Telegram—Translation]

A German submarine has been sunk by an Anglo-French naval force in the English Channel, on the 5th inst. It has been possible to save the officers and crew.

The answers made by the prisoners when examined have fully confirmed the information in our possession in accordance with which the author of the torpedoing of the *Sussex*, on March 24th, was the German submarine *U. B. 18*. This vessel was under command of Lt. Commander Steinbrinck.

The same *U. B. 18* had sunk near Havre, on March 22nd, the English freighter *Kelvin-Vank* and the Swedish one *Kanik*.

851.857 Su 8/81b

The Secretary of State to President Wilson

WASHINGTON, *April 15, 1916.*

MY DEAR MR. PRESIDENT: Yesterday afternoon the French Ambassador called upon me and left me the enclosed clipping from the

New York Times [36] in which it is stated that it was announced at Berlin on April 12th that Lieutenant Steinbrinck had received the Prussian Order of Merit in recognition of his exceptional merit in military and naval matters, and that he was the commander of a submarine. Undoubtedly this officer was the commander of the submarine which torpedoed the *Sussex*, and the decoration was conferred apparently after it was known that he was charged with this offense.

I do not think that this can be used in any way at the present time, but I think you should know the attitude of the German Government in regard to the incident.

Kindly return the papers after reading them.

Faithfully yours,

ROBERT LANSING

763.72/2580a

The Secretary of State to President Wilson

WASHINGTON, *April 15, 1916.*

MY DEAR MR. PRESIDENT: I have been going over the ending of the instruction to Gerard in the submarine matter and I am more and more convinced that the formula which you propose in your redraft, beginning—"Unless the Imperial Government should now, etc.", raises some serious objections.[37]

In the first place, the phrase—"return to a scrupulous observance of the principles clearly prescribed by the law of nations"—offers an opportunity to raise the question as to what are the clearly prescribed principles. As you know, these are not very well defined except as to visit and search. In addition to this, the whole question of the treatment of armed and unarmed merchantmen will be raised. There is a decided difference of opinion as to the conversion of a merchant vessel into a warship. I am afraid if we employ that language that we will be involved, unavoidably, in a discussion of that question, which I assume we both wish to avoid. Any phrase which raises a reasonable difference of opinion invites discussion, and the word "immediately" would be nullified.

If we are to follow, substantially, the language of the redraft, I would suggest its amendment as follows:

"Unless the Imperial Government immediately declares that it abandons its present method of submarine warfare against passenger

[36] Not printed.
[37] See footnote 34, p. 546.

and freight-carrying vessels, the Government of the United States can have no choice but to sever diplomatic relations with the German Empire."

I am always at your service to discuss this matter, when you desire to do so.

Faithfully yours,

ROBERT LANSING

851.857 Su 8/82½

The Secretary of State to President Wilson

WASHINGTON, *April 15, 1916.*

MY DEAR MR. PRESIDENT: I have been through the affidavits which were taken in France in the case of the *Sussex,* and also some that were taken in England.[38]   They do not add materially to our fund of knowledge in regard to the case, although they do furnish three additional witnesses who saw the wake of the torpedo as it approached the vessel.

I am enclosing a redraft of the statement of facts, giving the authorities.[39]

Faithfully yours,

ROBERT LANSING

851.857 Su 8/83½

President Wilson to the Secretary of State

WASHINGTON, *17 April, 1916.*

MY DEAR MR. SECRETARY: Thank you for letting me see this statement of fact which is to accompany our communication to the Imperial German Government.   It seems to me quite complete enough.

I understood you to say that the affidavits received by mail will necessitate only one or two alterations of detail in the statement.

Faithfully Yours,

W. W.

---

[38] For text of these affidavits, see *Diplomatic Correspondence With Belligerent Governments Relating to Neutral Rights and Duties* (Washington, Government Printing Office, 1916), vol. III, pp. 251 ff.

[39] For the statement as sent, see *Foreign Relations,* 1916, supp., p. 234.

851.857 Su 8/81½

President Wilson to the Secretary of State

WASHINGTON, *17 April, 1916.*

MY DEAR MR. SECRETARY: Circumstances of this sort are of course very disturbing;[40] but I did not know that we had learned the name of the submarine which attacked the *Sussex.*

Faithfully Yours,

W. W.

_____

763.72/2596½

President Wilson to the Secretary of State

WASHINGTON, *17 April, 1916.*

MY DEAR MR. SECRETARY: Here is the draft of our communication to the Imperial German Government as I think it should go to Berlin.[41]

I have gone over it again and again, and believe now that it is sound at every point. I will see you tomorrow and agree with you as to the exact time at which it shall be sent. Will you not, in the meantime have it put in code and made ready to send?

May I not add this earnest caution? So soon as copies of your suggested revision of this paper were made at the State Department (or was it only a single copy,—the one I am now returning with my own final handling of it?) the newspapers became aware of its contents. Will you not use extraordinary precautions in having this final draft copied and make it absolutely safe against the newspaper men both in the transcription and in the coding? This seems to me of the essence of wisdom just at this juncture. I hope that you will make absolutely sure how it is handled and by whom, and hold each individual to the strictest responsibility, upon pain of immediate dismissal. The draft you sent me was undoubtedly given out from the Department (I mean the substance of it), for no one here saw it in the form in which I had written it or in your first redraft except myself.

Faithfully Yours,

W. W.

_____

[40] See letter from the Secretary of State to President Wilson, Apr. 15, 1916, p. 548.
[41] *Foreign Relations,* 1916, supp., p. 232.

851.857 Su 8/85½

The French Ambassador (Jusserand) to the Secretary of State

WASHINGTON, *April 18, 1916.*

MY DEAR MR. SECRETARY: When I last saw you and we talked abᵗ the *Sussex,* you asked me how the crew of one German submarine may have known what had been done by that of another.

I put the question to my Govᵗ. The explanation is that the crew captured by us navigated a submarine having the same base as the *U. B. 18.* They were there between the 25th and 29th of March and met during that period the sailors who had torpedoed the *Sussex.* The official text of the interrogatory is being sent me by mail.

Believe me [etc.]   JUSSERAND

763.72/2649½

Memorandum by the Secretary of State of a Conversation With the German Ambassador (Bernstorff), April 18, 1916

B   My Government wants me to talk over with you once more the submarine question, and the instruction which I have received. I thought it would be better if I would give you confidentially a copy of the telegram.[42] I had the telegram Friday but I had to put it in order. * * *[43]

L   No, I noticed that the note did not suggest arbitration.

B   It suggested a commission of inquiry. Have you anything to tell me today?

L   Well hardly today. I think I will be able to tomorrow. The facts in the case appear to us to be conclusive.

B   The facts of the *Sussex* case? I have had no information except what they told me.

L   Of course there is one very disquieting thing that runs through the note that was sent. There are five cases presented. In two of these cases they do not seem to know whether the steamer torpedoed was the one torpedoed or not. They do not seem to know what steamers they have torpedoed, which seems to me a serious situation because they seem to be torpedoing anything, regardless of whether an armed vessel or an unarmed vessel, or neutral.

B   A neutral vessel, according to instructions, is not supposed to be attacked.

L   We have received reports from various capitals of neutral countries, of vessels attacked.

B   Without warning?

---

[42] *Infra.*
[43] This form of punctuation appears in the original.

L Without any warning at all. Some they say were probably destroyed by hitting a mine, some they state were torpedoed. Of course we have not all the details.

B It was because of advocating this general attack that von Tirpitz was compelled to resign. The instructions are very plain that the naval authorities have given that neutral vessels must not be attacked.

L It seems to me very strange they cannot control their commanders. They torpedoed one neutral ship when it was not even going to an English port. That is a report from Madrid; and furthermore it appears that about half the people on board the *Sussex* were neutrals.

B Of course they constantly report from London that such and such a ship was torpedoed without warning.

L I am not referring to the London reports but to those of neutrals.

B I don't understand it.

L They seem to torpedo a vessel and find out her nationality afterward, which is a dangerous proceeding.

B It certainly is.

L That is what makes the situation serious. It is a menace to the safety of Americans when they torpedo a vessel without Americans on board, if Americans had a right to travel on them.

B (This concerned the real intention of his Government in regard to submarine blockade as to routes of safety and neutral vessels, and closes—"but everything else is regarded as blockaded and any ships that do not regard the blockade will be sunk.")

L I cannot understand the actions of the submarine commanders unless the Government has no control over them. Of course some of our reports are very full as to certain vessels, and the evidence comes in slowly on others. We made a special effort on the *Sussex* case because that was one of the most harrowing, so we made a special effort to collect our evidence as rapidly as we could and the evidence which we have is perfectly conclusive as to the facts. We shall make out a full statement of the facts as established by the evidence and it will be found, I think, that everything substantially in the note of April 10th from your Government [44] corroborates the facts, except as to the sketch.

B And that you have sent?

L No we have not, but it will be sent.

B (Asks if there is anything he can do)

L I do not think there is at present. I think I will be able to communicate with you more definitely tomorrow.

---

[44] *Foreign Relations*, 1916, supp., p. 227.

B   I would like to help because I have been worried. We could manage it better here. You know I have used every effort to preserve friendly relations.

L   I appreciate your efforts.

B   I do not want trouble and I am absolutely certain that my Government does not want trouble though I say this without instructions. They have to meet public opinion over there which is very strong for submarine war.

L   I think I appreciate the position. I understand and appreciate the difficulties all Governments have in dealing with public opinion.

B   Certainly my Government does not want trouble.

L   We shall have to wait until tomorrow. I can then talk more freely.

B   Will you be good enough to let me know?

L   Yes, good bye.

763.72/2650½ : Telegram

The German Foreign Office to the German Embassy [45]

J. No. A 2813/16

We are now conducting submarine war absolutely in accordance with general principles of International Law. Only exception is commerce war against enemy freight ships in English war-zone. This is only aimed at destruction of ships but we try to save human lives as far as possible. This retaliatory step against English starvation policy does not touch interests of neutrals as neutral passengers on enemy freight ships manifestly try to render futile German war measure and as neutral members of crew are brought into relation of dependents on state whose flag ship flies; consequently both neutral passengers and crew on enemy freight ships lose neutral character. We, therefore, never gave any promises regarding enemy freight ships in war-zone.

Instructions to submarine commanders regarding their proceeding and observance of all our assurances are so precise that according to human foresight errors are excluded and certainly not more possible than in ordinary naval war; furthermore submarine commanders are instructed not to attack ships when in doubt. A ruthless submarine war would certainly have greatly increased loss in enemy ships; for this reason alone all doubts whether our instructions are meant seriously and strictly carried out bona fide are without foundation.

---

[45] This paper bears the notation: "Handed me by German Amb., April 18/16 4 pm RL."

We have modified submarine war to maintain friendly relations with America sacrificing important military advantages and in contradiction to excited public opinion here.

We, therefore, trust that American Government will appreciate this and not put forward new demands which might bring us into an impossible situation.

In order to correct errors apparently existing in American press I state that we have not suggested arbitration *Sussex* case but commission of inquiry to establish facts which are different.

763.72/2652½

Memorandum by the Secretary of State of a Conversation With the German Ambassador (Bernstorff), April 20, 1916

L Good morning.

B Good morning, Sir. You handed me a copy of the note yesterday,[46] and in the present state of affairs of course my chief object is to find a way how this break can be avoided, because I hope it can be avoided. My idea is to find a way out of it, but of course I had to telegraph my Government that this Government seemed to offer little opportunity for settlement. If it means the entire stopping of the use of submarines, I am afraid that it cannot be arranged.

L You will recall that we said in the first *Lusitania* note[47] that we thought it was impossible to use submarines in a really humane way and that later, in our note of July 21,[48] we said that the way submarine warfare had been conducted for the past two months showed that it was possible and therefore we hoped that course would be pursued. Then we had the sinking of the *Arabic* right on top of that, which was another great disaster. Our position is that, if submarine warfare had been conducted in that way, that possibly there would have been no further question raised. But it has not. It has been conducted in the most indiscriminate way and we cannot help but believe that it is ruthless. In those conditions submarine warfare should stop against commercial vessels, unless visit and search is observed.

B That, of course, is impossible. Germany cannot abandon submarine warfare. No government could come out and say—"We give up the use of submarines." They would have to resign.

L What possible methods in the use of submarines, that are effective from a belligerent standpoint, can be suggested which will comply with the law?

---

[46] Note of Apr. 18, 1916, on the *Sussex* case, *Foreign Relations*, 1916, supp., p. 232.
[47] Note of May 13, 1915, *ibid.*, 1915, supp., p. 393.
[48] *Ibid.*, p. 480.

B   I had always supposed that warning was to be given.

L   We do not consider that the people on board—the non-combatants on board the vessels—are in a place of safety when put into an open boat a hundred miles from land. It might be calm there, but in the two days it would take them to reach land there might be a severe storm. That is one of the grounds of complaint.

B   That, of course, speaking of neutral vessels—

L   The fact that we do not have Americans on these vessels does not remove the menace to American lives. The sinking of neutral vessels shows that Americans cannot travel with safety on neutral vessels even. That is the serious part of it and I do not know how your Government can modify submarine warfare and make it effective and at the same time obey the law and the dictates of humanity.

B   Humanity. Of course war is never humane.

L   "Humanity" is a relative expression when used with "war" but the whole tendency in the growth of international law in regard to warfare in the past 125 years has been to relieve non-combatants of needless suffering.

B   Of course I think it would be an ideal state of affairs, but our enemies violate all the rules and you insist on their being applied to Germany.

L   One deals with life; the other with property.

B   Yes.

L   The German method seems reckless to me. It is as if a man who has a very dim vision should go out on the street with a revolver in search of an enemy and should see the outline of a figure and should immediately fire on him and injure him seriously and then go up and apologize and say he made a mistake. I do not think that would excuse him. That seems to be the course pursued by your submarine commanders—they fire first and inquire afterwards.

B   I myself cannot at all explain how it comes that so many neutral vessels have been attacked. I have not the slightest evidence. I do not know anything about it from our communications.

L   Of course we are gradually collecting the evidence. We have not in all the cases but we have in certain ones. The *Tubantia*, for example, seems to have been torpedoed by a German torpedo—a Schwartzkopf.

B   She was at anchor.

L   No. I do not think she had let her anchor down but she was preparing to anchor. She was at rest.

B   Yes, I know. And then there was a Spanish vessel which—

L   Of course there is this, Mr. Ambassador, that any discussion of the submarine and its present method of attack cannot go on indefinitely.

B   What was your idea to prevent the break—that we should for the time being stop?

L   I think the only way is to declare an abandonment and then if the German Government desires to discuss a method of renewal—

B   An absolute abandonment, to my mind, is impossible. It might be possible to announce stopping for a time for discussion and giving the reason plainly for the purpose of quieting our public opinion, that might be possible.

L   I understand that you are speaking entirely without instructions.

B   I am not at all instructed. I am speaking to you purely from my desire to prevent a break.

L   In view of our note I would not want to say that that would be satisfactory, but if it was made—

B   I am only trying to see what can be done because a declaration to my Government to absolutely abandon submarine warfare would make a break absolutely necessary. To abandon it would mean the overthrow of the Chancellor.

L   Probably you would get a more radical man. I realize that.

B   So the question is what we can do.

L   There would have to be a complete abandonment first and then if the German Government desires to discuss the matter—

B   I want to do what I can, because I am perfectly convinced they do not want to break; quite apart from the sentimental side I think they do not want a break. A break would prolong the war. It would last for years.

L   We do not any of us want to prolong the war.

B   That is exactly why I want to get out of this present difficulty. From the present state of affairs it looks as if the end is coming and if now there was a break and the United States was brought into the war it would prolong it. It would cause new complications.

L   New complications?

B   New economic difficulties.

L   I think that would be Germany's problem. The only possible course is an abandonment of submarine warfare, whether limited or not would depend on the terms. I would want to see an abandonment first and then possibly a discussion could follow as to how submarine warfare can be conducted within the rules of international law and entire safety of noncombatants, because, of course, in my viewpoint that is the chief question of international law in regard to attacks by belligerents on enemy's commerce.

B   Then I am to understand that you do not recognize the law of retaliation?

L   We do not recognize retaliation when it affects the rights of neutrals.

B   The British retaliate by stopping all commerce to Germany.

L   It is a very different thing. The right to life is an inherent right, which man has from birth; the right of property is a purely legal right.

B   Only in this case, England's methods affect the lives of non-combatants of Germany.

L   Not neutrals.

B   No, but it affects non-combatants.

L   Does it affect their lives? I thought from the statements which have been made that Germany was not suffering from want of food.

B   But they are trying to starve them. You do not stop England but insist we must stop our retaliation.

L   But you must appreciate that we care more for the lives of our people than we do for the property.

B   We have the same difficulty—our people are getting to care more for lives. That is the whole difficulty—we are dealing with a warlike population.

L   I realize that. I appreciate that you have great difficulty with your public.

B   If you and I were to have the say in settling the case it would be an easy matter, because one can discuss the matter without heat.

L   I realize that. It makes it very difficult, but I do not think there is any other course. That certainly may be an impossible course for your Government to pursue, yet I see no other way, and I think I am as anxious to preserve peace as anyone.

B   I wanted to find out what I could do, because I do not see how they can do it though they might do it temporarily. I am sure that in the first place they would say they believed in the submarine entirely and that secondly the rules of international law must be modified by conditions. Your idea is that the submarine cannot be used if it does comply with the rules.

L   That is true. My view is that certain instruments of war are not proper to use under certain conditions, and that is the viewpoint that has largely been held in regard to the submarine as a commerce destroyer. You can not and do not know the nationality of the boat attacking. It attacks without being seen and so avoid[s] responsibility. It gives every opportunity to kill indiscriminately and recklessly.

B   I perfectly agree with you that sinking without warning would have to stop entirely, sinking without warning is an international offense, and that is why I thought possibly my Government might give up the retaliation, but I do not think it would be possible to say we would give up submarine warfare. I do not think we would do it.

L   And if they should now sink another vessel it would be very serious—that is the way I look at the situation.

B   And if they continue the submarine warfare and an instance should happen directly after the break of diplomatic relations, if that should come, it would be still more serious.

L   That is logical.

B   That is why I look at it so seriously.

L   I do not feel that breaking off of diplomatic relations necessarily means war.

B   I do not say it myself but I do not see how it can be avoided. If we refuse it will be because we are to continue submarine warfare and then something might happen which would mean war.   I came to see if something could not be done.

L   I am very much obliged to you for coming in, Sir.

B   Good bye, Mr. Secretary.

L   Good bye.

851.857 Su 8/86½

The French Ambassador (Jusserand) to the Secretary of State

WASHINGTON, *April 20, 1916.*

MY DEAR MR. SECRETARY: Here are some more particulars just received from my Government concerning the torpedoing of the *Sussex* and the way we happened to be able to ascertain who was the author of this shocking deed.

Lieut. Commander Cayrol of our staff was entrusted with the care of examining the crew of the German submarine *U. B. 26* captured by us on April 5.   He has summed up, under oath, before the judge, the information he thus gathered.   The chief points are:

Four German submarines and not more were cruising in the English Channel toward the end of March, viz., the *U. B. 18*, the *U. B. 19*, the *U. B. 26* (the one we captured) and the *U. B. 29*.

It was expressly acknowledged that the *U. B. 18* was at sea [on the 22nd March and returned to Bruges on the 25th][49] the day after the torpedoing of the *Sussex;* and that during this cruise, the same submarine had torpedoed three ships, two of which were in the Havre roads.   As for the third, no explanation could be secured.

We know, however, that the steamers *Kanning* and *Kelving Bank* were torpedoed in the Havre roads between the 22nd and 23rd; and that the *Sussex* met the same fate on the 24th.

On the 24th of March, the *U. B. 26* and the *U. B. 29* were at Bruges and the *U. B. 19* had failed up to then to torpedo any boat.

---

[49] Corrected on the basis of a letter from the French Ambassador, Apr. 21, 1916 (file No. 851.857 Su 8/87½).

Put together these statements make it clear that, on the 24th of March, the only German submarine present in the English Channel was the *U. B. 18* and that this submarine torpedoed three ships, two of which are confessedly known by name, and the third cannot be but the *Sussex*.

The *U. B. 26*, now captured, had remained at Bruges from the 22nd to the 30th of March and during the five last days of her stay was there at the same time as the *U. B. 18*. The crews talked together about their experiences.

All prisoners examined state that the officer in command of the *U. B. 18* is the same Steinbrinck recently decorated by the Emperor for his numerous torpedoings.

Believe me [etc.]   JUSSERAND

Though there is no specific mention as to this in the telegr[am] I received today, I suppose that it is better not to make public those numbers of boats etc., until they choose to do so on the other side.

J.

763.72/2656½ : Telegram

The Ambassador in Germany (Gerard) to the Secretary of State

BERLIN, *April 24, 1916—5 p. m.*
[Received April 26.]

3797. Please deliver the following cipher message to Colonel House.

My impression after long conversation with Chancellor is that he is inclined to send note agreeing that Germany will not attack without previous warning, etc., unarmed passenger liners, according to arrangement merchant vessels. Note also to express regret for *Sussex*, offer to pay indemnity and punish commander. Wish I had details as to whether this, or what would [be?] satisfactory [to?] President. Perhaps word "unarmed" could be left out and no reference then made to armed passenger and merchant ship question by either side. If Germany now adds merchant [ships?] as demanded in note is that not enough? Our note does not specifically refer to armed ships. [apparent omission]

GERARD

763.72/2634½

President Wilson to the Secretary of State

WASHINGTON, *24 April, 1916.*

MY DEAR MR. SECRETARY: I have looked this memorandum through with a good deal of care, and think that it covers the whole question comprehensively and with great clearness.[50]

---

[50] Memorandum on the status of armed merchant vessels, made public Apr. 27, 1916, *Foreign Relations*, 1916, supp., p. 244.

I take it that paragraph #13, on page 9,[51] is the one which really defines what we must maintain to be the law with regard to the particular question raised in the German orders of February last with regard to armed merchantmen. It shows that they have left out some of the most necessary elements of their case, namely, orders to attack in all circumstances, right to prize money, and liability to discipline if orders are not carried out.

Is it not law, and might it not be well to bring sharply out, that vessels bound on normal errands of trade are never transformed into war vessels by attacking everything that threatens them on their way, when the purpose is protection?

Faithfully Yours,

W. W.

763.72/2653½

The Secretary of State to President Wilson

WASHINGTON, *April 25, 1916.*

MY DEAR MR. PRESIDENT: In view of the press despatches which are coming from Berlin—although we have received nothing of an official nature indicating the course which the German Government will pursue—I am convinced that there will be an attempt to compromise in the declaration, if they do make any declaration in regard to the abandonment of submarine warfare. Any conditions which they may advance will undoubtedly be based upon their position as to armed and unarmed merchant vessels.

It would seem to me a decided strategic advantage to have made known clearly our position in regard to armed vessels before Germany presents her reply. To do that it will be necessary for us to make public in some way the memorandum which I sent you Monday morning, and which you returned to me with your general approval. It could be done by a formal statement issued from the Department; by sending the memorandum to the various belligerents; or by sending it to the Committees on Foreign Relations and Foreign Affairs in Congress. If it seems advisable to you to do this it seems to me that the time to do it is at once, before we receive Germany's reply.

Faithfully yours,

ROBERT LANSING

P. S. Since writing the foregoing Mr. Polk has just handed me the enclosed memorandum of a conversation over the telephone with Colonel House this afternoon.

---

[51] i. e., par. No. 12, *ibid.,* p. 248.

69471—vol. I—39——36

[Enclosure]

Memorandum by the Counselor for the Department of State (Polk)

[WASHINGTON,] *April 25, 1916.*

Colonel House called me up this afternoon shortly after four and said he had just had a conversation with the German Ambassador who had heard from his Government. His Government is most anxious to avoid a break and asked him what was the best course to pursue. They also asked him what was meant by "illegal method of submarine warfare". These two questions will be answered by the Ambassador without going to the Department of State.

His Government also wanted to know if they gave up submarine warfare what the United States would do about the blockade.

Colonel House advised him to tell his Government not to send a note suggesting a compromise, and, above all, not to raise any question in regard to the blockade. He stated the only safe course to pursue would be to advise the German Government to agree to discontinue submarine warfare pending negotiations.

This the Ambassador said he would do at once, and also said he would warn them not to send anything in the nature of a note. In regard to the Blockade, Colonel House pointed out that our relations, as far as Great Britain is concerned, are quite different from our relations with Germany; that war with Germany would be possible, whereas, war with Great Britain was more or less out of the question. This the Ambassador said he understood.

Colonel House thought it advisable to issue at the earliest possible moment the memorandum on armed merchant vessels, a copy of which he had seen. He suggested that it be issued tonight for the morning papers, but I told him in the absence of the President that was impossible. He urged that the matter be presented to the President with the suggestion that the memorandum be given out not later than in time for the afternoon papers Wednesday.

He suggested one or two changes in the wording of the memorandum. These changes have been called to your attention and have been made.

763.72/2630

The Secretary of State to President Wilson

WASHINGTON, *April 26, 1916.*

MY DEAR MR. PRESIDENT: I enclose a proposed telegram to Mr. Gerard.[52] While I am not disposed to unduly press the German Government for an answer to our note, I feel that we should let that

_____

[52] For the telegram as sent, see *Foreign Relations*, 1916, supp., p. 252.

Government know that we are becoming impatient at the delay, which would seem to indicate that they intend to avoid a frank declaration. I also thought it would be well to furnish Gerard with our idea as to the rules which should govern the conduct of naval operations against merchant vessels.

I would be very much pleased for any changes or suggestions which you may desire to make, and also your views as to the advisability of sending a telegram like the enclosed.

Faithfully yours,

ROBERT LANSING

763.72/2649

The Secretary of State to President Wilson

WASHINGTON, *May 5, 1916.*

MY DEAR MR. PRESIDENT: I enclose herewith Gerard's report of his interview with the Kaiser.[53] It seems to me that taken altogether he handled the matter very well and assumed a position very much in accord with this Government. He does not mention whether or not he used the definite rules which were sent him, as to visit and search, and I have therefore wired to ask whether he brought them to the attention of the Secretary of Foreign Affairs before the German note was delivered to him. I think it is important we should know this before drafting any answer or deciding what course should be taken.

Faithfully yours,

ROBERT LANSING

763.72/2654

The Secretary of State to President Wilson

WASHINGTON, *May 6, 1916.*

MY DEAR MR. PRESIDENT: I enclose the official text of the German reply [54] together with a memorandum on one point in the note which seems to me of special importance and one which should receive careful consideration.

The more I study the reply the less I like it. It has all the elements of the "gold brick" swindle with a decidedly insolent tone. I think that we should take time to scrutinize the document and give no indication as to whether it is acceptable or unacceptable until we weigh every portion with care. The first impression is bad; the

[53] *Ibid.,* p. 253.
[54] Note of May 4, 1916, *ibid.,* p. 257.

second, good; and the third unsatisfactory. At least that is the way
my mind has been impressed thus far. But my final judgment I am
not ready to give, without further study.

Faithfully yours,

ROBERT LANSING

[Enclosure]

*Memorandum on the New Orders to Submarines as Contained in the
German Note of May 4, 1916*

[WASHINGTON,] *May 5, 1916.*

The German Government in its note states that it has decided "to
make a further concession, adapting methods of submarine war to
the interests of neutrals." (See page 6)[55]

The extent of this new concession is to be determined by comparison of the orders which "the German submarine forces have
had" (See page 3)[56] and the order which the German Government
"notifies the Government of the United States that the German naval
forces have received." (See page 12)[57]

PREVIOUS ORDERS	NEW ORDERS
To conduct the submarine warfare in accordance with the general principles of visit and search and the destruction of merchant vessels recognized by international law, the sole exception being the conduct of warfare against enemy trade carried on enemy freight ships encountered in the war zone surrounding Great Britain.	In accordance with the general principles of visit and search and the destruction of merchant vessels recognized by international law, such vessels both within and without the area declared a naval war zone shall not be sunk without warning and without saving human lives unless the ships attempt to escape or offer resistance.

First: It is noticeable that the essential difference between these
orders is that the new orders eliminate the war zone and place the
same restrictions upon submarine warfare in all parts of the high
seas as were in force previously outside the war zone.

Second: The new orders recite a portion of the established rules
by asserting that the immunity from being sunk without warning
and without saving human lives is lost if the ships attempt to escape
or offer resistance. The phrase "offer resistance" is significant since
it indicates that <u>armed</u> vessels possessing power of resistance are
included in the general term "merchant vessels" covered by the order.

Third: In the previous orders the same restrictions on submarine
warfare were in force as to all merchant vessels, both within and

---

[55] *Foreign Relations,* 1916, supp., p. 258, first paragraph.
[56] *Ibid.,* p. 257, last paragraph.
[57] *Ibid.,* p. 259, sixth paragraph.

without the war zone, except as to "enemy freight ships encountered in the war zone." By these orders enemy passenger ships and all neutral ships were entitled to be visited and searched.

Fourth: It would appear that the only additional limitation placed upon submarine warfare beyond those previously in force is that "enemy freight ships encountered in the war zone" will be accorded the same treatment as that accorded to passenger ships and neutral ships in all parts of the high seas and as that accorded to such freighters if outside the war zone. It would appear, therefore, that enemy freight ships are the only beneficiaries under the new orders. It is not apparent how this is "a further concession", as asserted "to the interests of neutrals."

Fifth: The United States' complaints have been chiefly directed against the methods employed in attacking passenger vessels. If these attacks are "in accordance with the general principles of visit and search and the destruction of merchant vessels recognized by international law", as interpreted by the German Government and applied by the German naval forces, then the new orders offer no change in the methods which the United States demands should be abandoned.

Sixth: Unless the German Government states frankly that the rule as to visit and search will be applied in the customary manner and that it will not be interpreted as it has been by the German submarine forces under their previous orders, the new orders in no way lessen the danger to life or restore to neutrals their just rights on the high seas.

Seventh: In view of the similarity of the previous orders and the new orders, and the way that the previous orders have been carried out, the new orders do not constitute a declaration of abandonment of the present methods of warfare.

763.72/2654

The Secretary of State to President Wilson

WASHINGTON, *May 8, 1916.*

MY DEAR MR. PRESIDENT: After returning home last evening I took your draft of an answer to the German note and went over it with considerable care.[53] I found on reading it that the same impression I had when we discussed it last evening remained with me— namely, that it expressed satisfaction and gratification, which do not appeal to me. While I think our note should be polite I feel we should omit any expression of relief on having avoided a break with

---

[53] This draft not found in Department files; for the answer as sent, see *ibid.*, p. 263.

Germany. I also thought the note was longer than was necessary and that it should be limited as far as possible.

With these ideas in mind I made another draft of an answer which I am enclosing,[59] together with your original draft. If final decision can be reached early today I will have Gerard instructed to deliver the note and at the same time have it given to the press for publication tomorrow morning. I hope this can be done, for I feel we should delay as little as possible in the matter.

Faithfully yours,

ROBERT LANSING

763.72/2662

President Wilson to the Secretary of State

WASHINGTON, *8 May, 1916.*

MY DEAR MR. SECRETARY: You are probably right about cutting out all "satisfaction", and I am quite content to have the note go as you have amended it. I am returning it so that it may be sent at once.

In haste,

Faithfully Yours,

W. W.

763.72/2654

The Secretary of State to President Wilson

WASHINGTON, *May 8, 1916.*

MY DEAR MR. PRESIDENT: I enclose for your consideration a suggested comment on the German reply, which, if you think advisable, I might give to the press.

In the event that we send a note to Gerard today, would you think it well to give out the comment at the same time that we give out the text of our instruction?

In regard to the Commissioners for the Board of Investigation under our Treaty with Great Britain,[60] I find that they are the following:

United States Commissioners—
　　Judge George Gray, of Delaware,
　　Mr. Domicio da Gama, *Brazilian Ambassador to the United States.*

---

[59] Not printed; this draft is almost identical with the answer as sent.
[60] Treaty for the Advancement of Peace, Malloy, *Treaties,* 1910–1923, vol. III, p. 2642.

British Commissioners—
    Viscount James Bryce,
    Mr. Maxim Koveleski, *Member of Counsel [Council] of Russian Empire.*
Joint Commissioner—
    Mr. Fridtjof Nansen, Norway.

    Faithfully yours,

ROBERT LANSING

[Enclosure]

Proposed Statement for the Press [61]

The greater part of the German answer is devoted to matters which this Government cannot discuss with the German Government. The only questions of right which can be discussed with that Government are those arising out of its action or out of our own, and in no event those questions which are the subject of diplomatic exchanges between the United States and any other country.

The essence of the answer is that Germany yields to our representations with regard to the rights of merchant ships and noncombatants on the high seas and engages to observe the recognized rules of international law governing naval warfare in using her submarines against merchant ships. So long as she lives up to this altered policy we can have no reason to quarrel with her on that score, though the losses resulting from the violations of American rights by German submarine commanders operating under the former policy will have to be settled.

While our differences with Great Britain cannot form a subject of discussion with Germany it should be stated that in our dealings with the British Government we are acting, as we are unquestionably bound to act in view of the explicit treaty engagements with that Government. We have treaty obligations as to the manner in which matters in dispute between the two governments are handled. We offered to assume mutually similar obligations with Germany, but the offer was declined. When, however, the subject in dispute is a continuing menace to American lives it is doubtful whether such obligations apply unless the menace is removed during the pendency of the proceedings.

---

[61] A notation by President Wilson dated May 8, 1916, reads: "Dear Mr. Secretary Excuse pencil. This seems to me all right. I hope you will issue it. W. W." (File No. 763.72/2662½.)

The statement was given to the press at 8:45 p. m., May 8, 1916.

763.72/2754a

The Secretary of State to President Wilson

WASHINGTON, *May 10, 1916.*

MY DEAR MR. PRESIDENT: In the submarine controversy we will unavoidably be forced to meet a situation which will arise, if it has not already arisen, and to determine on a course of action.

The problem is this: A German submarine torpedoes, without conforming in any way to the rules of international law, a merchant vessel of the enemy, which has no Americans on board. No American life is directly endangered by this lawless act, but how did the German submarine commander know that? Is it to be supposed that he considered the matter at all? Did he not simply take a chance?

Now, if the attack is made without definite knowledge as to the nationality of the persons on board, then the action of the submarine commander as a part of a general policy, becomes a serious menace to Americans traveling on merchant ships within the sphere of submarine activity. Though in the particular case cited our rights are not directly affected, they are affected indirectly by making their exercise hazardous.

In our "*Sussex* note" we took a position based on humanity and insisted on respect for neutral rights in general. The rights of all non-combatants are impaired by the conduct referred to. Are we or are we not to consider a sudden attack by a submarine a violation of the assumed pledge of the German Government to comply with the rules of naval warfare even though no American life is immediately endangered?

My own impression is that we will have great difficulty in explaining our position, if we do not resent every lawless attack on a merchant ship whether Americans are or are not among the passengers or crews. On the other hand, I realize that public opinion in this country would not support drastic action unless Americans were killed or imperiled by the submarine warfare. It is to me a very difficult problem to solve, and I would be gratified if you would advise the policy to be followed.

Faithfully yours,

ROBERT LANSING

763.72/2755

President Wilson to the Secretary of State

WASHINGTON, *17 May, 1916.*

MY DEAR MR. SECRETARY: I have thought a great deal about the questions you here put,—both before and since you sent me this letter.

Undoubtedly there is an awkward quandary here, but I think we would not be justified in assuming the general representation of neutral rights in this matter, whether our own citizens are affected or not.

If Germany should show a purpose to return to the practices we have objected to by attacking ships again without warning, I think we would be justified in making pointed inquiries of her as to the facts in any given case, even if no Americans were on board; but we would not be justified in acting, unless her reply to those inquiries indicated a departure from the policy she has now agreed to follow.

At any rate, this is my present judgment.

Faithfully Yours,

W. W.

763.72/2869 : Telegram

The Ambassador in Germany (Gerard) to the Secretary of State

BERLIN, *September 14, 1916—12 noon.*
[Received September 15—1: 50 p. m.]

4338. In general conversation with Von Jagow recently he said that the offensive in the Somme could not continue without the great supply of shells from America. He also said that recently a German submarine submerged in the Channel had to allow 41 ships to pass and that he was sure that each ship was full of ammunition and soldiers but probably had some American [?] also on board and therefore the submarine did not torpedo without warning. He seemed quite bitter.

GERARD

763.72/2926b

The Secretary of State to President Wilson

WASHINGTON, *September 21, 1916.*

MY DEAR MR. PRESIDENT: There are two matters in connection with our foreign affairs which I understand are being industriously used by the Republicans in their attacks against you. I believe that some steps should be taken to correct the misconception which I feel exists among certain of our people in regard to these subjects.

The first of these is our failure to protest against the German invasion of Belgium. As to that, there is no difficulty, I believe, in making it perfectly clear why we did not protest and why we should not have protested. It is only a question of the best method of giving publicity to our explanation. Possibly it might be done by you either in a letter or in an address.

The second subject is more difficult to deal with. It is the delay which has occurred in the *Lusitania* case. Of course, there are reasons for our deliberation which cannot be made public, chief of these being the fact that in the summer of 1915 there was a strong element in the German Government which considered war with the United States desirable, and this powerful faction, headed by Tirpitz, was not subdued by their opponents until last winter. I am not at all satisfied in my own mind how to meet this complaint, which is being successfully used, as I am informed, in certain parts of the country by the opponents of the Administration. It is possible that I could see Bernstorff and take up the settlement of the case along the lines agreed upon last winter, which were interrupted by the declaration of February 10 as to Germany's attitude in dealing with armed merchant vessels.[62] Whether anything could be accomplished along this line at the present time I am not sure, as I presume the German Government, or at least its representatives in this country, would be disposed to delay a settlement on account of the approaching election. Nevertheless, it might be worth while attempting it in order to remove the charge that we were simply letting matters drift. Of course, another way would be to make a public statement of the whole negotiations, but to make it effective would require, I fear, the disclosing of much of the confidential negotiations which have taken place. Doubtless we would be justified in doing this, but at the same time it might cause very considerable resentment on the part of the German Government.

I lay these matters before you, as I consider them of very great importance at the present time. May I have your judgment as to what should be done in regard to them?

Very sincerely yours,

ROBERT LANSING

763.72/2926½

President Wilson to the Secretary of State

WEST END, N. J., *29 September, 1916.*

MY DEAR MR. SECRETARY: I think the matter of protesting against the invasion of Belgium has been made sufficiently plain to our public.

As for the other matter, it might be well to take up a settlement of the *Lusitania* outrage with Bernstorff if he thinks it can be settled now without soon widening into the ancient difficulty. Let me warn you that negotiation at the present time is very dangerous because it affords the German Government an opportunity to play into the hands of the German mischief makers on this side of the water

---

[62] *Foreign Relations*, 1916, supp., p. 163.

and supply them with campaign material by all sorts of false impressions. Please go very slowly in this critical matter. The atmosphere of the moment is a most unfavourable one for the handling of things of this kind . . .

Please keep me informed of any conversations you may have with him, and take no step without my advice.

At present I hope that the Department will confine itself as much as possible to routine matters. We should ourselves no doubt be unconsciously influenced by political considerations and that would be most unfair to the country.

With sincere regard,

Faithfully Yours,

W. W.

P. S.   Please be patient in awaiting replies to your communications from this distracting place.

W. W.

763.72/2926½

The Secretary of State to President Wilson

WASHINGTON, *October 2, 1916.*

MY DEAR MR. PRESIDENT: I have your letter of the 29th ultimo in regard to closing the *Lusitania* case.

I believe that I am fully alive to the danger of any negotiations regarding this delicate subject at the present time. When I wrote you about the matter on September 21st, I am afraid that I was impelled more or less by the indignation which I felt at the caustic criticism of the opposition press and speakers. Of course it is unwise to be so influenced although it is human. I am now in a different frame of mind and doubt the wisdom of taking up the matter until after election although, if a settlement was reached which would satisfy the public, it would be of decided political advantage. Appreciating the danger of taking any steps in the matter I shall not act without your explicit direction.

I do not think that the matter requires any further informal negotiations with Bernstorff. A settlement would be reached if we replied that his letter of February 16th [63] was satisfactory. In order that you may refresh your memory on the subject I enclose a copy of his letter.

I am doubtful, however, if this would be expedient just at present because the terms of the settlement would be gone over with a fine-toothed comb, and the criticisms which would undoubtedly be made might later be employed by the German Government. Probably it is

---

[63] *Ibid.*, p. 171.

better to endure the criticism of delay on our part than to start anew a public discussion of the case, which might embarrass us in the event that submarine warfare is renewed.

I am sorry to trouble you at this time with matters of this sort, and will endeavor to spare you in the future from their consideration, as I appreciate how fully your time is occupied with other subjects, as it ought to be when so much is at stake for the welfare of this country.

Faithfully yours,

ROBERT LANSING

763.72/2927½

President Wilson to the Secretary of State

EN ROUTE, *October 6, 1916.*
[Received October 9.]

MY DEAR MR. SECRETARY: I have your letters of October second.[63a] Pray do not think that you are troubling me unnecessarily about anything that is in your mind.

I am heartily glad that you agree with me about the necessity of holding things in their unstable equilibrium for the present. I feel that we might introduce more elements of disturbance than we remove.

Thank you for sending me a copy to remind me of the contents of von Bernstorff's last letter about the *Lusitania.* It will enable me to freshen my thought for it when we return to the discussion.

Always

Cordially and sincerely yours,

WOODROW WILSON

123 G 31/65a

The Secretary of State to President Wilson

WASHINGTON, *October 16, 1916.*

MY DEAR MR. PRESIDENT: I have been thinking over the matter of your summoning Gerard to Shadow Lawn for an interview, which you will remember we discussed last Tuesday. I gained the impression that you considered it expedient not to summon him at once and delay possibly seeing him until after election.

After considering the matter I have reached the conclusion that a long delay before seeing him would be misconstrued by the people and would in any event serve no good purpose. It might be thought that you were too busy with the political campaign to give attention to an Ambassador who had returned from a principal belligerent

[63a] *Ante,* pp. 320 and 571.

power and was in possession of valuable information. Such an impression, however unwarranted, would be, I think, unfortunate. Of course I realize that delay in seeing Gerard was advisable in order to dispel the idea that he was the bearer of a special message from Germany or was called home because of a possible crisis in the submarine matter. I think, however, that the delay in summoning him to you which has already taken place has accomplished that purpose, and that further delay would be unwise.

At this time, when every little thing is subject to partisan scrutiny and criticism, I feel that we should give more heed to a matter of this sort than we would under normal conditions.

Faithfully yours,

ROBERT LANSING

763.72/3060½

Memorandum by Colonel E. M. House of a Conversation With the German Ambassador (Bernstorff), November 20, 1916 [64]

I told the Ambassador that we were on the ragged edge and brought to his mind the fact that no more notes could be exchanged: that the next move was to break diplomatic relations. He appreciates this and will urge his Government again to be more careful. He said they would make an apology and reparation for the *Marina* and that it would be forthcoming tomorrow or next day.

I told him the President would move for peace at the first opportunity. He said that peace was on the floor waiting to be picked up. He does not believe a belligerent government could refuse to parley, particularly since Germany is willing to evacuate both France and Belgium and any refusal to negotiate would be an admission that they would continue the war for conquest.

The Ambassador seems thoroughly alive to the danger of the situation and what the participation of this country in the war would mean and I think he will do everything possible to prevent it.

841.857 M 331/42

The Secretary of State to President Wilson

WASHINGTON, *November 22, 1916.*

MY DEAR MR. PRESIDENT: I enclose the report of our Consul at Cork, Mr. Frost, dated November 1st,[65] in the case of the *Marina,* to which is attached the affidavits of the American citizens who were

---

[64] This paper bears the notation: "Handed me by Mr. Polk, Nov. 23/16 RL."
[65] Not printed.

on board the vessel. I also enclose the report of the Consul dated November 2d on the same subject.[66]

It seems to me to be a case in which, from the facts sworn to, there appears to be little possible defense. Even the excuse that the vessel was laden with contraband for Great Britain is absent, in the fact that she was on her homeward voyage and practically in ballast.

I have been considering in my own mind whether it is possible for us to avoid taking definite action in the case in accordance with our *Sussex* note. I do not feel, however, that I wish to express an opinion at present, although I consider the situation very grave.

Faithfully yours,

ROBERT LANSING

763.72/3059½

The German Ambassador (Bernstorff) to Colonel E. M. House [67]

WASHINGTON, *November 23, 1916.*

MY DEAR COLONEL HOUSE: On Tuesday I sent a long cable to Berlin as I promised you.

There is no intention on the part of my Government to make any change in the principle of submarine warfare. I am, therefore, sure, that Berlin will be prepared to make all necessary reparation for the mistakes in the *Arabia* and *Marina* cases. If these two ships were really not—as the submarine commanders believed them to be—armed transport ships, they certainly came very near it.

I hope the whole question of "armed merchantmen" will not be brought up, but that we can limit the discussion to "armed transports" so that a long controversy is avoided, and I do hope that the President will be satisfied, if my Government goes as far as it can.

I shall call on Mr. Lansing as soon as I receive definite information. If you wish to see me on this subject, please wire or phone and I will come over to New York immediately for a few hours.

What do you think of Lord Derby's speech? [68] It seems to confirm my opinion, that the Allies could not and would not refuse to talk, and that is all they are to be asked to do. Whether the negotiations would lead to peace, is, of course, quite a different matter, but I am confident that they would.

Yours very sincerely,

J. BERNSTORFF

---

[66] Not printed.
[67] This paper bears the notation: "Copy of letter given me by Polk—Nov. 28/16 RL."
[68] British Under Secretary of State for War.

841.857/256½

The Secretary of State to President Wilson

WASHINGTON, *December 8, 1916.*

MY DEAR MR. PRESIDENT: The information which we now have regarding the *Marina, Arabia,* and other vessels sunk during the past two months seems to me to create a very serious situation in the submarine matter. We took a very definite stand in the *Sussex* case declaring that we could not continue diplomatic relations with a government which attacked merchant vessels without warning. Germany has done this and attempts to defend her submarine commanders on the ground of mistake, a defense which I do not see how we can accept without receding from our position that there can be no such things as mistakes when American lives are lost or put in jeopardy as a result of the acts of submarine commanders. If we do take that position, and I do not see how we can avoid it, and if we live up to our *Sussex* declaration, as I feel we are honorably bound to do, what course remains other than to reject the explanations offered and announce that we have no alternative but to break off diplomatic relations?

I feel that a crisis has come in the submarine matter which ought to be met promptly and squarely. We ought not to let the matter drift along with Germany continuing at intervals to sink vessels on which Americans have taken passage. The longer we delay the more frequent I believe will be these outrages and the less regard will Germany give to our declaration in the *Sussex* case. Delay, in my opinion, will accomplish no ultimate good, as there seems to be a very definite determination on the part of the German Government to make submarine warfare more effective by pursuing more reckless methods, which I am convinced will increase as more submarines are launched.

It is with increasing anxiety that I have seen the progress of events, hoping that in some way the issue might be avoided, for I realize fully how serious a step it will be to sever our relations with Germany. I do not think that we can longer avoid facing the situation with firmness and definitely deciding whether our declaration in the *Sussex* case will be carried out or abandoned.

The facts, on which the foregoing statements are made, are given in the enclosed memoranda.[69] The *Marina* and *Arabia* cases are dealt with more fully than those included in the list entitled "Ves-

---

[69] Not found in Department files.

sels carrying American Citizens sunk by Submarines", which is a continuation of the list dated November 13, 1916, previously sent you. I would in the list call special attention to the *Chemung*, the *Palermo*, and the *John Lambert*.

I am also sending to you a copy of a letter dated today which I have just received from the German Ambassador.

Faithfully yours,

ROBERT LANSING

[Enclosure]

The German Ambassador (Bernstorff) to the Secretary of State

J. No. A 8230 WASHINGTON, *December 8, 1916.*

MY DEAR MR. SECRETARY: Late yesterday evening I received from Berlin the information about the *Arabia*, which had already reached you through Mr. Grew and had been published yesterday. I, therefore, need not trouble you today for the purpose of transmitting the information I received.

With reference, however, to our last conversation, I beg to repeat, that my Government has instructed me to put myself at your disposal in view of a speedy and satisfactory settlement of the *Marina* and *Arabia* cases. I should, therefore, be very much obliged, if you would kindly let me know confidentially as soon as you have reliable evidence concerning the two cases. My Government has received very little information on these matters, as the state of war makes communication very difficult, and is, therefore, prepared to draw its conclusions from any confidential information you may transmit to me.

I remain [etc.] J. BERNSTORFF

763.72/3105a

The Secretary of State to President Wilson

WASHINGTON, *January 3, 1917.*

MY DEAR MR. PRESIDENT: I am sending you a statement made by Mr. Arthur Page to Mr. Harrison, of this Department, and also confidential reports on the *U–53* and the German submarine activities, which are furnished by the office of Naval Intelligence.

It will oblige me if you will return these to me after you have read them.

Faithfully yours,

ROBERT LANSING

[Enclosure 1]

Mr. Leland Harrison to the Secretary of State [70]

[WASHINGTON,] *January 3, 1917.*

DEAR MR. SECRETARY: Mr. Arthur Page of the *World's Work*, who recently returned from Europe, has told me that the peace proposal of December 12th last [70a] was not the first effort of Germany to make peace at this time. Mr. Page said that during November he had seen Mr. Hoover of the Belgian Relief Committee and that Mr. Hoover had told him that sometime in October the Germans had asked him to present certain proposals of peace to the British Government, which he had refused to do. Mr. Page also said that during his visit to Paris he had heard from reliable sources that Germany had endeavored to sound out France as regards peace and had also approached Russia, which had caused considerable anxiety in French circles and which had no doubt led to the resignation of Sturmer.[71] Mr. Page spoke of the efforts made by Germany with Russia and France as a matter of general knowledge, but in the case of Great Britain his information was definite as it had come direct from Mr. Hoover.

L. HARRISON

[Enclosure 2]

Reports on the "U-53" and German Submarine Activities, Furnished by the Office of Naval Intelligence

SECRET REPORT: THE "U-53"

It seems that the boat that accompanied the *U-53* did not get close to American waters and that Commander Rose with his *53* sunk the ships off the Newfoundland Coast. The report of three submarines there was due to his painting out his number *53* and substituting other numbers. He did this on four separate occasions and finally came into Germany under the number *61*.

Commander Rose's report of his adventures close to American waters filed with the German Admiralty teems with praise of the Americans. Their fairness and the sporting instinct of his American naval colleagues. His treatment by the authorities and the generous welcome extended him not only by German-Americans but all of Americans is the theme of his report. He has declared that

---

[70] Filed separately under file No. 763.72119/408½.
[70a] See *Foreign Relations*, 1916, supp., pp. 85–97.
[71] Russian Minister of the Interior.

the zone of his recent operations is a most lucrative one and suggests that more boats be sent and of larger tonnage and better carrying proportions to remain out longer under their own fuel.

Secret Report: German U-Boat Activities

Several U-boat commanders emphasize that if the *Marina* was shot at and sunk either by artillery fire or torpedo without warning the Commander violated his strict orders. They all deplore the fact that warning must be given for they declare that every third boat stopped is not only sailing under a false flag but has also masked batteries and that although keeping off the regulation 5,000 meters, they do, in hailing and stopping a ship risk the safety of their boat and the lives of the crew. They are most vehement in denunciation of this regulation and they are discussing the advisability of petitioning the Kaiser to rescind this order.

One Commander said "They expect us to sink 40 or 50,000 enemy tonnage each time we go out and yet in rough weather when we cannot guarantee the safety of the passengers and crew of enemy vessels after they would take to the boats, we are, under existing orders, compelled to let the ships go by even they are carrying the most deadly munitions". The same officer said that he had been close to British waters for 20 days at about the same time that the *Marina* was sunk and while he sighted 35 ships of the enemy, he was on account of the rough weather and high seas, forced to let them pass because no ships boat could live in such seas.

U-boat commanders emphatically declare that if Garrach sunk the *Marina* he did so in absolute violation of his strict orders and will be punished therefor. At the same time they express their disgust at the existence of such orders and believe that the Admiralty in limiting their activities to meet the wishes of the United States is demonstrating a weakness that is most damaging to their cause. They similarly believe that this order will be rescinded and that in the very near future they will be given a free hand in the exercise of their own discretion as to what action to take against enemy's ships regardless of the nationality of the passengers and crew.

It is the general opinion among German Naval Officers that President Wilson will not break with Germany under any condition, being afraid of them. That the landing of the *U-53* was an object lesson to him that he would speedily learn. Many of them are bitter enemies of America and pretend to believe that their submarines could cripple us. It is not known to what extent these wild expressions reflect the ideas of their superiors but the fact is that these young chaps are pretty cocky at present.

An Army officer of high rank said that a general U–boat warfare in opposition to the declared wishes of the United States must be inaugurated eventually to enable Germany to win the war. He too is of the opinion that high officers of the Army are one in that belief and that the Kaiser and his advisers must meet these wishes sooner or later for the Navy is also in harmony with extensive submarine warfare ideas. Another army officer of high rank is of the same belief.

The matter of a general U–boat warfare is now before the Kaiser and he is giving it his earnest attention. Great pressure is being brought upon him from all sides.

763.72/3106½

President Wilson to the Secretary of State

WASHINGTON, *4 January, 1917.*

MY DEAR MR. SECRETARY: Let me thank you for the enclosed,[72] which I return for your files. The information about the U–boats makes painfully interesting reading.

Faithfully Yours,

W. W.

763.72111/4443

The Secretary of State to President Wilson

WASHINGTON, *January 12, 1917.*

MY DEAR MR. PRESIDENT: I enclose to you a copy of a letter from the German Ambassador dated January 10th,[73] transmitting a memorandum upon the subject of armed merchant ships. His letter also requests an appointment to discuss the matter after I have had an opportunity to examine the memorandum.

I conceive that this memorandum is sent at the present time for the purpose of laying the groundwork for excuse in beginning a more drastic submarine campaign. Before seeing the Ambassador, therefore, I would like very much to have your views upon the memorandum, and the policy which should be taken in treating with him on the subject.

Faithfully yours,

ROBERT LANSING

---

[72] *Supra.*
[73] *Foreign Relations,* 1917, supp. 1, p. 82.

763.72111/4420

The Secretary of State to President Wilson

WASHINGTON, *January 17, 1917.*

MY DEAR MR. PRESIDENT: I am sending you a confidential report from Ambassador Page at London (No. 5568, January 5, 1917)[74] dealing with the question of armed merchant vessels, which I think that you will read with as much interest as I have, since it not only presents the British point of view but brings out very clearly the difficulties which enter into the problem.

I do not think that we can long delay determining upon a very definite policy in this matter, particularly in view of the fact that a renewal of submarine activities seems imminent. The trouble is there are reasonable arguments on both sides of the question which lead to conclusions utterly irreconcilable. I can see no common ground for compromise; in that lies the chief difficulty of our situation. It seems to me, however, that the position of this Government ought to be settled and a definite statement prepared which could be issued promptly at the proper time, as doubtless the question will soon become acute.

I enclose for your information in this connection our public statement of September, 1914,[75] and March, 1916,[76] dealing with this subject.

As I am taking up the question from the politic as well as the legal point of view I would be greatly obliged for any comments on Mr. Page's report and also for any suggestions on the general subject.

Faithfully yours,

ROBERT LANSING

763.72111/4441

The Secretary of State to President Wilson

WASHINGTON, *January 23, 1917.*

MY DEAR MR. PRESIDENT: I call your special attention to this telegram received this morning from Berlin,[77] which appears to me to create a very serious situation, if Mr. Gerard is accurate in his presumptions—which sound to me very reasonable.

Faithfully yours,

ROBERT LANSING

---

[74] *Foreign Relations,* 1917, supp. 1, p. 546.
[75] *Ibid.,* 1914, supp., p. 611.
[76] *Ibid.,* 1916, supp., p. 244.
[77] Telegram No. 4912, Jan. 21, 1917, from the Ambassador in Germany, *ibid.,* 1917, supp. 1, p. 91.

763.72111/4469½

President Wilson to the Secretary of State

WASHINGTON, *24 January, 1917.*

MY DEAR MR. SECRETARY: It is only too probable that Gerard's conjectures in this matter are well founded. I wonder if you have come to any fixed conclusion in your own mind as to whether the recent practices of the British in regard to the arming of their merchantmen force upon us an alteration of our own position in that matter.

Faithfully Yours,

W. W.

———

763.72111/4470½

President Wilson to the Secretary of State

WASHINGTON, *31 January, 1917.*

MY DEAR MR. SECRETARY: This is, to my mind, quite the most puzzling and difficult question we have had to deal with.[78] It is becoming pretty clear to me that the British are going beyond the spirit, at any rate, of the principles hitherto settled in regard to this matter and that the method in which their ship captains are instructed to use their guns has in many instances gone beyond what could legitimately be called defense. It appears that they have more than once attacked. The question is more whether their guns have been used only for defense than whether they exceed in calibre what would reasonably constitute armament for defense and whether their being mounted in the bow is a presumption that they are to be used for offense. I would be glad to know the progress of your own thought in this matter.

Faithfully Yours,

W. W.

———

763.72/3179

The Secretary of State to President Wilson[79]

WASHINGTON, *January 31, 1917.*

MY DEAR MR. PRESIDENT: I am convinced from our telegrams from Gerard as well as from the press statements which I am confidentially advised emanate from the German Embassy that the German Government intends to renew unrestricted submarine warfare in the near future. If this conviction is correct, we are going to face a serious

---

[78] i. e., the activities of armed merchant ships.

[79] This paper bears the notation: "I was writing this letter when the German Amb. brought in the German declaration of this date, so the letter was never finished. Robert Lansing." For the German declaration referred to, see *Foreign Relations*, 1917, supp. 1, p. 97.

situation. If Germany adopts that policy every possibility of con-versations regarding peace will in my opinion vanish and we will have to take some radical step which will be considered as unneutral.

The question is what can we do to prevent this crisis? After con-sidering the matter from various angles I feel that further pleas and advice will have little effect because the German Government seems to hold the opinion that we will in no event take a strong position but will submit, while protesting, to any submarine policy which they may adopt. I think that this is most unfortunate because it will encourage them to act with ruthlessness and if they do act peace will be further away than ever.

In view of this state of affairs and of the danger which seems imminent I believe that the wisest course is to adopt a firm and uncompromising position as to the right of merchant vessels to arm for defense, and [80]

763.72111/4443

The Secretary of State to President Wilson [81]

WASHINGTON, *January 31, 1917.*

MY DEAR MR. PRESIDENT: I enclose in compliance with your request of January 24th, supplemented by your letter of today, a memoran-dum of views on the subject of armed merchant vessels. From the standpoint of abstract right as well [as] of accepted legal rules I am convinced that the conclusions reached are just and should control our policy in dealing with this vexed and dangerous question.

Of course the whole matter boiled down is this: Since a belligerent has the right to capture or destroy private owned merchant ships of enemy register, such ships are entitled to defend themselves from certain loss to their owners, and their treatment as public ships because they carry an armament adequate to protect them from destruction can find no warrant in the rules of naval warfare or in justice.

I feel that we ought without delay to reach a very definite con-clusion as to this matter because everything indicates the intention

[80] See footnote 79, p. 581.
[81] A memorandum attached to this paper reads: "Dear Mr. President: Please read immediately Enclosure E and accompanying memoranda, and the postscript to my letter. Faithfully yours Robert Lansing Jany 31, 1917." For the Ger-man Ambassador's communication referred to as "Enclosure E," see *Foreign Relations*, 1917, supp. 1, p. 97.

A second memorandum reads: "These papers the President handed back to me after a conference at the White House (Jany 31, 1917, 8:45-10:30 p m). The German note of Jany 31st with 2 memoranda were the subject of discussion and its receipt made the subject of the letter and memorandum on armed merchant ships unnecessary of consideration. The President, however, indicated that he was in doubt as to the soundness of the memorandum of the 30th. Robert Lansing. 2/1/17."

of the German authorities to treat all armed merchant vessels as ships of war. The press is industriously circulating this view and I understand it is getting its material from the German Embassy. Gerard's reports all point the same way; and the memorandum sent me by the German Ambassador on January 10th (Enclosure B)[82] makes it very evident that the stage is being set for a new act on the part of his Government. In fact everything is being done to prepare the American public for a more vigorous submarine war on commerce.

If we let the German memorandum go unanswered it will be alleged that we have accepted their interpretation of our declaration of March 25, 1916 (Enclosure C),[83] and that we are, therefore, *particeps criminis*. Nothing we can say later will remove the impression on our own people that though fully warned we permitted Germany to proceed in her announced purpose of treating armed merchant vessels as warships. For that reason I deem it essential that a very definite attitude should be at once reached.

Furthermore, if the German Government carries out her manifest plan to renew ruthless submarine attacks I believe that the consequences will be irreparable so far as peace is concerned. Not only will the Entente powers be so enraged as to refuse to consider any overtures, but, if we with previous knowledge fail to do all we can to prevent it, your influence over them, I fear, will be seriously impaired, and the very hope of peace will be extinguished.

I believe this is a time to state to Germany frankly and with the greatest firmness our views and to impress them with the possibility of an actual break in our relations if they attempt to carry forward their plan. In dealing with that Government our greatest success has come when they saw we would not recede or compromise. I think this is a time to adopt that course. If we do not, we may expect, in my opinion, a critical situation especially if American citizens are killed or imperiled.

You may see, Mr. President, from what I have written that I am greatly agitated over the present state of affairs. I am indeed more anxious than I have been since the *Sussex* affair. In many ways this is even a greater crisis as so much depends on nothing being done which will prevent the movement toward peace, and that movement will, I am firmly convinced, come to an end if submarine war of a reckless sort is renewed by Germany.

---

[82] *Foreign Relations*, 1917, supp. 1, p. 82.
[83] *Ibid.*, 1916, supp., p. 244.

I enclose also for your consideration a report of the Neutrality Board on this subject (Enclosure D)[84] which is referred to in my memorandum (Enclosure A).[85]

Faithfully yours,

ROBERT LANSING

P. S. Since writing the foregoing the German Ambassador has been to see me and has left me a communication accompanied by two memoranda (Enclosure E),[86] which shows the prognostications were right, and we are face to face with the gravest crisis presented since the war began. I think that as soon as you have read these papers we should have a conference to determine the course to be taken.

R. L.

[Enclosure]

Memorandum on Armed Merchantmen

[WASHINGTON,] *January 30, 1917.*

At present the condition of armed merchantmen may be stated as follows:

(1) There is a tendency to increase the size of guns up to six inches on vessels coming to American ports.

(2) The number of guns, in some cases, has also been increased from one to two on the stern. No guns have as yet been placed on the bow.

(3) Naval gunners and officers, both of the Naval Reserve, have been put in charge of guns in many cases.

(4) These men are reported as being paid by the steamship companies, but in a few cases it appears that the gunners are paid a shilling a week extra by the British Government.

(5) Instructions have been issued for the guidance of merchantmen by the French Government, and perhaps by other governments, to "open fire as soon as the submarine is fairly within range," or, if near by, to "try and ram it." There have come to the Department's notice reports of half a dozen instances in which armed merchantmen have fired at submarines on sight. Two or three of these vessels have subsequently come to American ports.

(6) At a conference held at the London Foreign Office, December 10, 1916, it was agreed to arm all British, French, Russian, and Italian merchant ships with from two to four guns (according to the size of the vessel) of six-inch caliber or less, and to place them in charge of men and one to three officers, as the case might require.

[84] Not printed.
[85] *Infra.*
[86] *Foreign Relations*, 1917, supp. 1, p. 97.

The Department's memorandum of September, 1914,[87] states that a merchant vessel of belligerent nationality may carry an armament and ammunition for the sole purpose of defense without acquiring the character of a ship of war; that the presence of an armament and ammunition on board a merchant vessel "creates a presumption that the armament is for offensive purposes," but this presumption may be overcome by contrary evidence; that evidence sufficient to overcome this presumption might be, by way of illustration, that the guns are under six inches, few in number, mounted on the stern of the ship, manned by usual crew, and that the vessel follows its regular trade route, and carries the usual quantity of fuel and supplies, and the usual character of passengers; and that the conversion of a merchant ship into a ship of war is a question of fact to be established by evidence of the intention as to the use of the vessel.

The memorandum of March 25, 1916,[88] states that a neutral government may proceed upon the presumption that

"an armed merchant vessel of belligerent nationality is armed for aggression, while a belligerent should proceed on the presumption that the vessel is armed for protection. Both of these presumptions may be overcome by evidence—the first by secondary or collateral evidence, since the fact to be established is negative in character";

that

"A belligerent warship is any vessel which, under commission or orders of its government imposing penalties or entitling it to prize money, is armed for the purpose of seeking and capturing or destroying enemy property or hostile neutral property on the seas,"

the size of the vessel, strength of armament, and its defensive or offensive force being immaterial; that armed belligerent merchantmen which are under commission or orders to attack in all circumstances enemy naval vessels, are to receive prize money for such service, and are liable to a penalty for failure to obey the orders given, lose their status as peaceful merchant vessels, and are to a

"limited extent incorporated in the naval forces of their government, even though it is not their sole occupation to conduct hostile operations;"

that such vessels engaged

"intermittently in commerce and . . . in pursuing and attacking enemy naval craft, possess a status tainted with a hostile purpose which it can now throw aside or assume at will."

---

[87] Memorandum on the status of armed merchant vessels, *ibid.*, 1914, supp., p. 611.

[88] *Ibid.*, 1916, supp., p. 244.

and should, therefore,

"be considered as an armed public vessel and receive the treatment of a warship by an enemy and by neutrals";

that as to offensive and defensive operations of merchant vessels,

"The attacking vessel must display its colors before exercising belligerent rights";

that

"When a belligerent warship meets a merchantman on the high seas which is known to be enemy-owned, and attempts to capture the vessel, the latter may exercise its right of self-protection either by flight or by resistance";

that

"it has become the established practice for warships to give merchant vessels an opportunity to surrender or submit to visit and search before attempting to seize them by force";

that

"If, however, before a summons to surrender is given, a merchantman of belligerent nationality, aware of the approach of an enemy warship, uses its armament to keep the enemy at a distance, or after it has been summoned to surrender, it resists or flees, the warship may properly exercise force to compel surrender";

and that

"A merchantman entitled to exercise the right of self-protection may do so when certain of attack by an enemy warship; otherwise the exercise of the right would be so restricted as to render it ineffectual."

As the present or proposed "defensive" character of merchant vessels enjoying the hospitality of United States ports or transporting American citizens on the seas shows a tendency to increase in point of government control, skilled personnel, and strength of armament, it is important to determine, if possible, the extent to which the increase may be carried without endangering the neutrality of the United States or limiting the protection to be accorded American citizens traversing the seas on armed merchant ships.

It may add to clearness of discussion to consider the classes of cases likely to arise when a warship and an armed merchant ship meet at sea.

(1) A warship (*a*) sends up colors, and (*b*) signals a merchantman to stop, and the merchantman flees and fires—this is not offensive action, because the enemy nationality and the intention of the warship are known.

(2) The merchantman makes no reply, the warship fires blank shots, and the merchantman flees and fires—not offensive action.

(3) The warship then fires solid shot until merchantman is halted, and merchantman returns fire—not offensive action.

(4) If, before (1), a merchant vessel is certain of enemy-character warship and then fires—not offensive action, because presence of enemy warship presumes attack.

(5) If, after (1) (*a*) and before (1) (*b*) merchantman fires—not offensive action.

(6) If, before (1), a warship chases a merchantman and latter fires—not offensive action, because chase by warship presumes attack.

These cover roughly all the classes of cases which might occur. From them it is evident that while it may be difficult to define "offensive" or "defensive" action in general terms, it is not difficult to determine which action has been taken in a specific case. This is because of the assumption which naturally comes to the mind that the presence of a battleship of known enemy nationality presages peaceful or forcible capture.

Perhaps it may be said generally that "offensive action" means action that is initiated by one ship against another, or is provocative of action in defense by the other. Such offensive action may be by direct attack, as by gunfire, ramming, etc., or it may be by signalling, chasing, etc. It is conceded that an enemy merchantman may interpose for self-protection against capture all the resistance in its power. The best method of defense may be to use force immediately upon the appearance of a warship. The mere appearance of a warship provokes resistance, but this is not offensive action. When the warship is a submarine, the best, if not the only time to resist is when it appears on the surface. It is no fault of the merchantman that a submarine can not safely expose itself to the resistance which merchantmen may legally make, or comply with the usual methods of visit and search, conveying to port, and placing persons in safety.

If a merchantman may resist capture or destruction, what is to govern the size, strength, or efficiency of her armament? The character of the craft she has to resist. It is out of the question for a vessel of the size and build of a merchant vessel to carry arms sufficient to keep off a battleship. Perhaps in the old days this was possible, for we read of merchantmen resisting and overpowering their assailants. If, however, this were possible today, it would be logically and legally correct for merchantmen to carry the armament of a warship. The number, size, and emplacement of the guns, therefore, is immaterial so long as they bear some relation to the vessel which it is purposed to resist. If this is so, then clearly a merchantman may carry sufficient armament to resist a thinly-armored submarine. If she may carry guns, she must be allowed skillful gunners under officers of experience. Otherwise, her guns may be practically useless.

Suppose the belligerent government sought to control or direct the merchant ship through commissions or other orders to her officers to act as a part of the armed forces of the state, or through paid naval officers of the state in control of the vessel instead of merchant officers, or through penalties imposed or prizes offered to induce hostile conduct. The flying of a naval flag might be confirmatory of this condition. What effect would the presence of these elements have on the character of the vessel? They would make the vessel a fighting arm of the state. Theoretically, all of these elements might be present, and the vessel be used nevertheless as a commerce-carrier for profit, its fighting qualities being reserved for self-protection. Carried to the extreme limit, we might have a battleship engaged solely in peaceful commerce. What, then, can be the distinction between peaceful and aggressive ships? It is, as the United States has stated, really a matter of intention—an intention to seek out and hunt down war vessels of the enemy or merchant vessels of enemy nationality.

As a practical matter, however, there must be some rule to prevent neutrals being imposed upon by a change of intention after leaving port. The assurance of the belligerent does this in part, and this is supplemented by investigation of each case. The use of a battleship, for example, as a commerce-carrier would be so liable to abuse, and the very extraordinary and unnecessary preparations for the use of force, considering the surface strength of submarines, or converted cruisers, if they were the only enemy craft to be feared, would so arouse suspicions as to her intentions, that whatever her theoretical status might be, it would be difficult to believe, and the enemy could never be brought to believe, that such a vessel was not a ship intended for aggressive purposes. Moreover, being in the service, control, and direction of the state, she might well be regarded as a military arm of the state, and therefore indistinguishable from the class of public armed ships generally subject to attack without warning by the enemy. She would indeed fall within the rules agreed upon by the Second Hague Conference regarding the conversion of ships. According to the Hague Convention No. 7 of 1907,[89] a merchantman is converted into a warship if the vessel is "placed under the direct authority, immediate control, and responsibility of the power whose flag it flies." (Art. 1.) She "must bear the external marks which distinguish warships of their nationality" (Art. 2), have a "commander . . . in the service of the state and duly commissioned by competent authorities" (Art. 3), have a "crew . . . subject to military discipline." (Art. 4), "observe in its

---

[89] For text of convention, see *The Second International Peace Conference, Held at The Hague From June 15 to October 18, 1907*, Senate Document No. 444, 60th Cong., 1st sess., p. 161.

operations the laws and customs of wars" (Art. 5), and "must as soon as possible be announced in the list of warships" (Art. 6.). These criteria have no binding force, as the Convention is not in effect, but they are important as indicating an agreement of nations on what constitutes a conversion of merchant ships into warships.

Suppose that the belligerent government own, control, and operate merchant ships. This may be done so long as they submit to treatment accorded to merchant ships in foreign ports. The Brazilian Lloyd ships are of this class, being operated as government ships by the Minister of Finance of Brazil. If such a vessel mounts arms for defense, she does not necessarily become a public fighting ship. A government-owned merchant ship is, it is true, under the "direct authority, immediate control, and responsibility" of the government, as provided in Hague Convention No. 7; the officers and crew are in the service of the state; the captain is no doubt duly commissioned, but as a merchant captain instead of a naval officer; the crew are not under military discipline; the vessel does not observe the laws and customs of war, because it does not engage in war; the vessel is not listed in the roster of warships, and does not carry a naval flag.

These distinctions, however, as to kind of officers, kind of discipline, kind of laws observed, kind of roster of ships, kind of flag—are of minor importance. For a vessel may be in fact a fighting arm of the state without any of them, and a peaceful commercial vessel with them all. The test is more fundamental. It is in the real purpose and use of the vessel. These distinctions are merely *prima facie* indications of the purpose and use. If, however, the purpose and use are peaceful, it will be hardly necessary for the vessel to have naval officers and marines, military discipline, naval commissions, a name on the roster of the fleet, or a naval flag. Nevertheless, as these criteria have hitherto by long custom been limited to fighting ships, their presence in connection with merchant vessels arouses at once inquiry as to the use to be made of such vessels. While the best evidence of that purpose and use will be the formal statement of the government controlling the vessel, and the past actions of the vessel itself, yet, if either should belie the fact, the neutral would be criticizable for having harbored such a ship. It is proper, if not necessary, therefore, for the neutral to be on the side of safety, and to refuse to recognize a vessel as a peaceful ship which has any of the usual characteristics of a naval vessel, or which has acted as an aggressive ship, notwithstanding the assurance of its government to the contrary or the evidence of prior peaceful conduct. Assurances may be regarded as binding the government that gives them to liability for breaches thereof to the extent of offsetting any claim by the enemy that the vessels violating the assurances have used American ports as bases of operations. But allowance into port as a peaceful ship would be notice to travelers that the United States would protect them in case of attack without warning.

It would seem, therefore, the part of wisdom for a neutral, for the purpose of maintaining its neutrality or of not giving a strained interpretation to the protection of neutrals on board, to regard merchantmen, whether private ships or government-owned, as peaceful commercial ships, regardless of the size, number, or emplacement of the guns up to what might be reasonably regarded as sufficient to resist successfully the kind of enemy vessel which will probably be met at sea, but arbitrarily to regard a vessel on the naval list, or carrying a commission or orders of a government authorizing the unlimited use of force, officers on board in the naval service and in the pay of the government, or a naval flag, as a warship, because these elements are unnecessary to a ship's peaceful and commercial purposes, or even to such resistance as she might possibly make against the enemy. Even a naval crew or naval gunners in the service and pay of the government do not change the character of the vessel if they are not given absolute control of the guns or ship, and act solely as expert gunners under officers in the service and pay of the owners of the vessel. Furthermore, former naval officers or men of naval experience in charge of these men, but not in the active service and pay of the government, in no way affect the character of the vessel.

SUMMARY. (1) The following vessels should be treated as warships:

(a) Vessels under government commissions or orders to use force without restraint;
(b) Vessels with officers in the service and pay of the government;
(c) Vessels carrying a naval flag;
(d) Vessels named on the naval list.

Such vessels, being warships, may be attacked without warning, and the United States Government is not responsible for the protection of life and property on board, the decision of C. J. Marshall to the contrary notwithstanding.

(2) Other armed vessels should be treated as merchantmen, so long as they leave port under an assurance of their government that they are not to operate aggressively, and so long as there is no reason to doubt their faithful compliance with the assurance. To avoid criticism by the other belligerent, and possible claims for unneutral conduct, as well as to preserve friendly relations with him by restraining excessive armament, it would be wise, however, as a matter of policy, to place a limit on the number of guns, on their size, and on the number of men and officers serving them. A reasonable maximum limit of armament for defensive purposes under present con-

ditions would, it is believed, be the following: four guns of six inches or less caliber, placed anywhere on the ship, with an officer for each gun, and a number of men for each gun equal to the caliber in inches, the officers and men not to be members of the regular military forces detached for temporary duty, but still in the service and pay of the government, though they may be members of the reserve. This strength of armament has been recommended by the Joint State and Navy Neutrality Board as the "reasonable minimum" which a merchant vessel might carry for self-defence, but it is believed that for the guidance of the Government in view of present conditions of naval warfare, and in order not to give the impression of opening the doors to excessive armament, the Board's "reasonable minimum" would appropriately serve as a conservative maximum armament for peaceful belligerent merchant vessels.

763.72/3312a

The Secretary of State to President Wilson

WASHINGTON, *February 2, 1917.*

MY DEAR MR. PRESIDENT: I send you some thoughts [90] on Germany's broken promise and the crime of submarine warfare, which I put down in writing last evening. These express my real views, which of course are given no publicity.

Faithfully yours,

ROBERT LANSING

763.72/3312b

The Secretary of State to President Wilson

WASHINGTON, *February 2, 1917.*

MY DEAR MR. PRESIDENT: I have been considering deeply and I believe without emotion the present crisis and just what course should be taken. The results are as follows:

I am firmly convinced that we must without taking any preliminary step break off diplomatic relations by sending Bernstorff and his suite home and by recalling Gerard and closing our Embassy at Berlin.

The next step is less clear and requires very careful thought before it is adopted. There seem to be two courses open to us.

First: To follow the severance of diplomatic relations by announcing to Congress this action with a statement that this Government must consider Germany to be an international outlaw, and that it

---

[90] There are no enclosures with the file copy of this letter; the reference is probably to the following document.

would be necessary to warn Americans to keep away from the seas infested by its piratical craft.

Second: To follow up the severance of relations by announcing to Congress this action with a statement that Germany has forfeited every consideration by reason of her breach of faith, that the full criminality of her previous acts is revived and that no other honorable course remains but for this country to employ every resource which it possesses to punish the guilty nation and to make it impotent to commit in the future crimes against humanity.

The first course has certain advantages in that, while we would not be at war, we would be in a position to do certain things which we cannot do now consistently with strict neutrality. Furthermore it would give time for consideration as to the advisable steps to be taken afterward for I feel convinced that Germany will not declare war on the breaking off intercourse. As to the suggested warning of Americans, we could do it with propriety if we declare Germany outlaw, something which could not be done as long as we treated her as a friend. It has this disadvantage, which requires very careful consideration and may make it inadvisable, namely, that it will accomplish the very purpose which Germany sought a year ago by keeping American ships and citizens from going to Great Britain and her allies. So that it would result in Germany obtaining by threat of lawless action what she was unable to obtain through friendly negotiation.

The second course has these advantages. It amounts to a frank declaration that an outlaw Government is an enemy of mankind, and will show that the present military oligarchy must be eliminated for the sake of civilization and the future peace of the world. It will influence other neutrals far more than the less vigorous course and will, in my opinion, induce them to follow such action, which I do not think they will do unless they are certain we are willing to go the limit. It will leave us some friends after the war. It will do more to end the war than anything that can be done. It will give this country a prominent place in the peace negotiations which will prevent unjust treatment of the Central Powers and will be decidedly for their interests. It will give tremendous moral weight to the cause of human liberty and the suppression of Absolutism. It will remove all charge of weakness of policy and satisfy, I believe, our own people. (This latter advantage is not of great importance but the benefit of popular support is not to be ignored.)

In brief these are my views as to the two courses open to us if severance of diplomatic relations takes place.[90a]

Faithfully yours,

ROBERT LANSING

[90a] For correspondence previously printed regarding the severance of diplomatic relations with Germany, see *Foreign Relations*, 1917, supp. 1, pp. 106-112.

763.72/3207

The Secretary of State to President Wilson

WASHINGTON, *February 5, 1917.*

MY DEAR MR. PRESIDENT: The enclosed telegram has just been received from Minister Gonzales, at Habana.[91] I would like to know your wishes in the reply I am to make to this dispatch. I think we should consider very seriously requesting the Cuban Government to remove the German Consuls and breaking off relations, in view of the proximity of Cuba to this country and to our West Indian possessions.

Faithfully yours,

ROBERT LANSING

763.72/3203

The Secretary of State to President Wilson

WASHINGTON, *February 5, 1917.*

MY DEAR MR. PRESIDENT: In connection with my letter of today's date regarding severance of relations with Germany by Cuba, I enclose a copy of a telegram from Panama asking instructions, as I read it, as to whether German Consular Officers there should be recalled.[92] It seems to me that on account of the proximity to the Panama Canal, Panama should remove the German Consuls and break off relations with Germany. I would like to know your wishes in order that I may make a reply to this despatch.

Faithfully yours,

ROBERT LANSING

763.72/3312c

The Secretary of State to President Wilson

WASHINGTON, *February 5, 1917.*

DEAR MR. PRESIDENT: The British Ambassador called upon Mr. Phillips [92a] this morning and asked that you be advised privately that he had received a message from the Duke of Devonshire, Governor-General of Canada, expressing, not only on his own behalf but on behalf of both parties and the people of Canada, the intensity of their feeling of admiration for the course which you have taken.

Apparently it is the policy of the British Government to suppress to a considerable extent the press reports of the tremendous enthusi-

---

[91] *Ibid.,* p. 221.
[92] *Ibid.*
[92a] William Phillips, Assistant Secretary of State.

asm in the British Empire, not only in Government circles but in all classes of society including the labor element, fearing that the outburst of enthusiasm, which has in fact occurred, if advertised too much, might not be desirable from the point of view of this country. Sir Cecil Spring Rice therefore has informed the Duke of Devonshire that his message to you is being communicated unofficially through me.

With assurances [etc.]   ROBERT LANSING

763.72/3312½

President Wilson to the Secretary of State

WASHINGTON, *6 February, 1917.*

MY DEAR MR. SECRETARY: I am glad that the British authorities are showing this kind of good taste and good judgment.

I wonder if there is any need of my making personal acknowledgment? Perhaps it would be best for the Department to make acknowledgment for me.

Faithfully Yours,

W. W.

763.72/3314½

President Wilson to the Secretary of State

WASHINGTON, *6 February, 1917.*

MY DEAR MR. SECRETARY: I entirely agree with this suggestion so far as Panama is concerned.[93]

In the case of Cuba I have this question in my mind: might not such action on her part be used as an excuse by Germany for an early attack upon her, or the seizure of a naval base there, on the pretext that Cuba was in effect hostile? It might be to Germany's advantage, in other words, to declare war on Cuba (or make it without declaring it) before taking action against us. A base for her submarines on this side the sea would be most convenient. What do you think?

Faithfully Yours,

W. W.

---

[93] See p. 593 (file No. 763.72/3203).

763.72/3236 : Telegram

The Ambassador in Italy (Page) to the Secretary of State

ROME, *February 6, 1917—1 p. m.*
[Received 6 p. m.]

827. My telegram 800.[94] From the same source I learned day before President's move severing relations a message to President was prepared by Vatican declaring in effect Germany's attitude not unexpected in "well balanced circles" since England is attempting Germany's political destruction, adding that President holds in his hands decision of peace or war in his power to forbid exportation from America of money, food, munitions. Memorandum declares this conformable to perfect neutrality and adds otherwise war will proceed more frightfully than ever, but if President would embargo exports peace will certainly ensue to immortal glory America and benefit of humanity. Intention was to request me to forward memorandum as direct message.

NELSON PAGE

195.91/274

Memorandum by the Secretary of State on the Sailing of American Ships for European Ports

The Government cannot give advice to private persons as to whether or not their merchant vessels should sail on voyages to European ports by which they would be compelled to pass through waters delimited in the declaration issued by the German Government on January 31, 1917.[95]

It, however, asserts that the rights of American vessels to traverse all parts of the high seas are the same now as they were prior to the issuance of the German declaration, and that a neutral merchant vessel may, if its owners believe that it is liable to be unlawfully attacked, take any necessary measures to prevent or resist such attack.

[WASHINGTON,] *February 6, 1917.*

The foregoing statement, to be communicated to the Departments of War, Navy, Treasury and Commerce in the form of a confidential memorandum for their guidance and as a basis for replies to letters of inquiry to the Department of State, I read over the telephone to the President at 6:45 p. m. February 6, 1917, who authorized its use as above stated.

[94] *Foreign Relations,* 1917, supp. 1, p. 22.
[95] *Ibid.,* p. 101.

763.72/3314½

Memorandum by the Secretary of State

[WASHINGTON,] *February 7, 1917.*

Saw the Cuban Minister and advised him that it would be unwise for Cuba to break off diplomatic relations with Germany. He said that he would so advise his Govt

ROBERT LANSING

763.72/3355½

The Secretary of State to President Wilson

WASHINGTON, *February 10, 1917.*

MY DEAR MR. PRESIDENT: Thank you for letting me see Colonel House's letter of the 8th [96] with Professor Hays' [*Hayes'?*] memorandum on armed neutrality, which I herewith return.[97]

Colonel House's information from Cardeza [98] confirms our reports as to the Austrian situation.

Phillips had a long talk last evening with Tarnowski.[98a] The latter said that his Government is most anxious to avoid breaking off relations and hoped that we could find some subject for conversations. I think this can be done, as Austria last spring complained of the illegal attacks of French submarines and we can ask an explanation of their attitude then and now, thus providing a reasonable basis for discussion.

If we could meanwhile persuade the Entente Governments to so modify their peace terms that Austria would not feel that they meant the dismemberment of that Empire, I believe something might be done to lessen Austrian dependence on Germany. If any means could be found to weaken their alliance, it would be a decided step toward peace. Of course this is a hope rather than an expectation, but I think that it is worth trying, since we know the desperate internal situation of Austria and also because from now on our intercourse with Austria's representative here will not be under the influence of the German Ambassador.

If these suggestions meet with your approval I would like to know it in order that the machinery may be set in motion.

Faithfully yours,

ROBERT LANSING

---

[96] See Charles Seymour, *The Intimate Papers of Colonel House,* vol. II, p. 448.

[97] The President had written on February 9: "I think you will be interested to read this letter from House and the accompanying memorandum. Please let me have them back when you have read them." (File No. 763.72/3355½.) There are no enclosures with file copy of this letter.

[98] Secretary to Ambassador Penfield in Austria-Hungary.

[98a] For correspondence previously printed concerning the position of the Austro-Hungarian Ambassador designate, Count Tarnowski, see *Foreign Relations,* 1916, supp., pp. 798–807, and *ibid.,* 1917, supp. 1, pp. 38, 112, 143, 169, 177, 178–179, 186, 188, 193, 594–598.

763.72/3262½

The Secretary of State to President Wilson

WASHINGTON, *February 12, 1917.*

MY DEAR MR. PRESIDENT: Mr. Polk reported to me that the Swiss Minister on Saturday called at the Department and in my absence saw him. The Minister said he had received a reply to a suggestion which he had made that he might do something here to prevent war between this country and Germany.[99] He stated in substance what is contained in the enclosed memorandum,[1] and Mr. Polk said he would submit the matter to me.

I told Mr. Polk Sunday morning when he told me of the interview that I wished to have the statement in writing and until then would make no comment. He saw the Minister and as a result Sunday night I received the enclosed note and memorandum.

Prior to seeing Mr. Polk the newspapers were informed that Germany had taken steps to open a discussion with the United States as to means for preventing war. Both Mr. Polk and I denied this Saturday afternoon but it appeared under prominent headlines in all the Sunday papers. When the Swiss Minister was asked if he had given this out he denied having done so, and no one in the State Department knew of the interview of the Minister with Mr. Polk, except Mr. Polk and I. There seems to be one conclusion as to the source of the newspaper reports and that is the German Embassy which is in constant communication with the press.

As to the memorandum of the Swiss Minister I think that there is little to say. Of course we cannot for a moment consider negotiations either formal or informal unless the German Government ceases its present ruthless methods and returns to the *status quo ante* the proclamation of January 31st, and that the memorandum declares they cannot do. Of course they knew that we would not accept such a condition as appears in the memorandum and, when it was sent, they knew that there could only be a refusal to an overture on that basis.

I believe that the purpose of this movement had nothing to do with an actual desire to open negotiations, but was intended for public consumption in this country and as an aid to those who are endeavoring to stir up opposition to the Government's continuing to take a firm and unyielding attitude toward the present ruthless conduct of Germany. The wording of the memorandum, the publicity given the idea that the German Government was ready to negotiate before we knew it, and the extension of the statement in the press

---

[99] For correspondence previously printed concerning this peace move, see *ibid.,* pp. 125, 126, 129, 136–137, 139–141.

[1] *Ibid.,* p. 126.

beyond the exact language of the memoranda, all indicate the design of embarrassing this Government by putting it in the light of refusing to consider overtures of arrangement voluntarily offered by Germany. It is apparently done to convey the impression that Germany is willing to do anything to prevent war but that you are not willing to listen to them, being determined to go forward. The attempt is to throw the responsibility on you in case hostilities cannot be averted.

I am convinced that the whole scheme was hatched here in Washington, and that not only Bernstorff had much to do with it but also I am ashamed to say that I believe that he has been assisted by certain Americans who are antagonistic to your policy and who will go to almost any lengths in order to force you to recede from the firm position which you have taken. I have heard in the last few days some things which have aroused my intense indignation against certain people and which, if true—and the evidence seems very strong, smacks of treason. I do not wish to write of these matters but will tell you when I see you.

It seems to me that the only answer which can be made to the memorandum is to say that no discussion or negotiation can take place except upon the condition precedent that the proclamation of January 31st be annulled; and that, when that has been done, this Government is prepared to consider any subjects which the German Government desires to propose for discussion. I also think that the memorandum and our answer should then be made public, in order that the people may have no erroneous impression as to the character of the German overture, and we may counteract the effect which has possibly resulted from the insidious statements published by the Germans here and those who are aiding them to arouse opposition to the Government.

Faithfully yours,

ROBERT LANSING

763.72/3264½

President Wilson to the Secretary of State

WASHINGTON, *12 February, 1917.*

MY DEAR MR. SECRETARY: I am obliged to concur in your conclusions with regard to this matter. I suggest that you reply to the Swiss Minister in the following sense:

I am requested by the President to say to you, in acknowledging the memorandum which you were kind enough to send me on the eleventh instant, that the Government of the United States would gladly discuss with the German Government any questions it might propose for discussion were it to withdraw its proclamation of the thirty-first of January, in which, suddenly and without previous intimation of any kind, it cancelled the assurances which it had given this Government on the fourth of May last, but that it does not feel that it can enter into any discussion with the German Government concerning the policy of submarine warfare against neutrals which it is now pursuing unless and until the German Government renews its assurances of the fourth of May and acts upon the assurance.

Faithfully Yours,

W. W.

763.72/3353½

The President of the American Peace Society (George W. Kirchwey) to the Secretary of State

NEW YORK, *February 12, 1917.*

MY DEAR MR. SECRETARY: I take pleasure in complying with your request to submit to you a statement of my connection with recent unofficial efforts to bring about such modifications of the German submarine warfare as might lead to a restoration of friendly relations between our government and that of Germany.

Believing that the action of the German Government in promulgating the new submarine policy was due, in some measure at least, to its failure to understand the attitude and policy of our government and people, and fearing that the action of the President in severing diplomatic relations would be interpreted by the German Government and people in the usual sense, as a mere preliminary to an act or declaration of war on our part, or as indicating that we, as a people, had gone over to the "war party," it seemed to me that it might be useful to remove such misconceptions if they existed.

I had no thought of playing any part in the situation when I arrived in Washington, Sunday morning, Feb. 4, but circumstances quickly placed me in a position where, as it appeared to me, I could not refuse to accept the responsibility of taking action along the lines above indicated.

A German newspaper correspondent, Dr. George Barthelme,[2] representing the Cologne *Gazette*, who had called on me for the purpose of securing an interview with Mr. William J. Bryan, was induced to abandon that purpose and to prepare in its stead a dispatch which might have the effect of enlightening the German people and Government as to the attitude and purpose of the American Government and people. He gladly accepted the task and later in the day submitted the matter to me for criticism and correction. I rewrote it in large part, the matter marked in the enclosed copy of the dispatch having been written by my hand,[3] and all the rest, with the

[2] Washington correspondent of the *Kölnische Zeitung.*
[3] Enclosure 1, the paragraph beginning "First thing necessary," p. 602.

exception of the opening and closing paragraphs, having been suggested by me.

As the wireless via Sayville was no longer open to Dr. Barthelme, I undertook to see Secretary Daniels with a view to having the embargo lifted, and accordingly did so on the following day (Tuesday morning, Feb. 6). The Secretary heard me with apparent interest and read the dispatch with care, after which he called Admiral Benson into conference with us and submitted the dispatch to him. Both officials expressed their satisfaction with the tone and substance of the paper but suggested a few changes in phraseology and the elimination of some matter which Dr. Barthelme had quoted from Mr. Bryan's published "Statement to the American People" (Feb. 4.). The changes suggested seemed to me wise and on the same evening the corrected dispatch was submitted to Admiral Benson. The enclosed copy (marked No. 1) represents this final form of the dispatch as it was submitted by Dr. Barthelme for transmission to his newspaper. I learned subsequently from Admiral Benson that before passing it he made a further change in the first sentence. (Probably deleting the two words "almost implored", to which I had previously taken exception).

It may be proper for me to add that I took the action above outlined without consultation with anyone except as stated, and in particular that Mr. William J. Bryan had no part in nor any knowledge of the affair. It is true I obtained from him a formal note of introduction to Secretary Daniels, but without giving him any information as to my purpose except that I desired to see the Secretary in order to ascertain whether the wireless service via Sayville was still available for the transmission of regular newspaper dispatches to Germany.

In the meantime I had sought and obtained, Sunday afternoon, February 4th, an interview with Count von Bernstorff, in order to secure as trustworthy information as possible as to the probable effect of the severance of diplomatic relations between the German and American Governments on the question of peace or war between the two countries. As President of the American Peace Society it seemed to me of the utmost importance to secure such information in order that the Society might be in a position to act promptly and intelligently in an effort to secure united, prudent and patriotic action by the numerous and influential peace organizations of the country in the crisis confronting the nation, and especially to forestall any unwise, precipitate action by any pacifist groups that we might be able to influence.

As I feared would be the case, Count von Bernstorff took the view that the severance of diplomatic relations between the two countries made war inevitable. He was of the opinion that the German Government and people could put no other construction on the President's act. I urged the contrary view, that unless the Imperial Government was bent on war with the United States (which, he assured me, was not the case) it might still be possible to avert that calamity by inducing the German Government, even at the last moment, to modify its program of submarine warfare in such a way as to make it acceptable to our government. Finally the Count accepted my view of the situation and referred me to Dr. Paul Ritter, the Swiss Minister, to whom the interests of Germany had been committed.

I was unable to secure an interview with Dr. Ritter until Tuesday morning, Feb. 6, when the opportunity was afforded me of laying the matter before him. I found that Count von Bernstorff had already enlisted his interest in the cause and that Dr. Ritter was quite willing, in the interest of his own government and people, who were, as he pointed out, vitally concerned in the avoidance of war between the two great powers, as well as in the general interests of peace and good will, to make an effort to secure the good offices of his government to that end.

At his suggestion I drafted a note embodying my views, as they had been expressed to him and previously to Count von Bernstorff, as to the attitude of the Government and people of the United States and as to the steps that might be taken by the Imperial German Government to avoid war between the two countries.

This note, a copy of which I enclose (marked No. 2) I submitted to Dr. Ritter, and it was, as I am informed, made the subject of a conference on the same day (Tuesday, February 6) by Dr. Ritter, Count von Bernstorff and Dr. Barthelme, and approved by them. I am also informed that it was somewhat condensed and, possibly, otherwise altered for transmission, but that its substance and effect were carefully preserved, and that it was then transmitted to the Swiss Government on the evening of that day.

I desire to add that in this, as in the matter of the newspaper dispatch, I acted solely on my own initiative and without consultation with anyone, save that I reported from time to time to Mr. Arthur Deerin Call, the Secretary of the American Peace Society. In particular I wish to state that Mr. William J. Bryan had no cognizance of my plans or proceedings and to my personal knowledge had no communication, direct or indirect, with Count von Bernstorff or Dr. Ritter.

Meanwhile, Tuesday afternoon, I had made several efforts to see you, but the Cabinet meeting and subsequent conferences in which you were engaged made it impossible for me to do so. However, in the evening I saw Secretary Baker at the War Department and gave him a full account of my activities as well as of the motives that had inspired them—of all of which, I am happy to say, he expressed complete approval. The following morning (February 7) I had the pleasure of seeing you and of submitting a resumé of the matter.

I know that you do not need any assurance from me that in all the proceedings above recounted I have had no aim but to serve the highest interests of our country—its honor and dignity as well as its peace—and to further, as far as it might lie in my power to do so, the aims and policy of the President and of your high office.

With sincere appreciation of the opportunity you have afforded me of submitting this detailed statement of my efforts in this crisis of our national life, I have [etc.]

GEORGE W. KIRCHWEY

[Enclosure 1—Telegram]

Mr. George Barthelme to the "Kölnische Zeitung"

FEBRUARY 5, 1917.

From high sources whose identity I cannot disclose I am urged, (almost implored), to convey to the German people and government the idea that the message [3a] must not be construed as indicating any desire on the part of the government or people for war with Germany. Strongest attention is called to the following passage:

"I refuse to believe that it is the intention to do in fact, what they warned us they will feel at liberty to do. Only an overt act can make me believe it even now."

Further the following sentence:

"If this inveterate confidence should unhappily prove unfounded, I shall take the liberty of coming again before Congress to ask authority to use any means necessary for the protection of our seamen and people."

These passages widely construed, first, as expression of confidence that some way out might be found; second, as not containing any war threat, notwithstanding language used. General opinion is that the President could do nothing else but sever relations to make good his former note. It is now up to Germany to provide an opening.

First thing necessary, avoid everything which makes maintenance friendly relations impossible, particularly refrain from destruction American ships; then make clear misunderstood terms of German note, that no unrestricted submarine warfare contemplated but only a blockade confined within narrowest limits compatible with neces-

---

[3a] i. e., President Wilson's message to Congress, Feb. 3, 1917, *Foreign Relations,* 1917, supp. 1, p. 109.

sary military aims; even within those limits greatest care taken not to interfere with innocent American commerce and every precaution taken to limit destruction of neutral ships carrying contraband and of enemy vessels to ship and cargo, safeguarding wherever possible lives of passengers and crews, as was the recent practice. Then propose joint commission for negotiation of code governing blockade and submarine warfare generally, such offer inducing delay and made as a special token of ancient friendship of the two countries. Then consider possibilities provided in Hensley resolution [4] for calling conference of the powers, which possibilities would be closed by hasty action. Furnish some explanation about sailing of only four especially marked American ships. This would remove extremely bitter impression created by this wholly incomprehensible proviso hurting national pride as nothing else.

My informants assure me in the most emphatic manner that the country is not for war; will be for war only when forced into it by an overt act on part of Germany, only certain very small circle are clamoring for hostilities, but huge majority praying for peace with honor.

I feel it my solemn duty to inform you about these sentiments and opinions entertained by men of the highest standing, noblest character, responsible position, loftiest ideals and thoroughly good will. Should you deem it advisable to exert influence of our great paper, do so to find way out of situation not yet unavoidably pregnant with gravest possibilities. I honestly believe country just anxiously waiting for one more good word.

GEORGE BARTHELME

[Enclosure 2—Telegram]

Draft Message From the Swiss Minister (Ritter) to the Swiss Federal Political Department

FEBRUARY 6, 1917.

With the approval of Count Bernstorff, I urgently recommend immediate transmittal of following to Imperial German Government.

American public opinion strongly supports President in his actions and sentiments but strongly averse to war, which however will inevitably result from serious overt act. Tension will relax as time elapses without such act. Such forbearance coupled with reasonable modifications of announced blockade would afford American Government welcome opportunity to restore friendly relations. Slight modifications already announced have produced good effect. New announce-

---

[4] See *Congressional Record*, 64th Cong., 1st sess., vol. 53, p. 9143.

ment should make clear that no unrestricted submarine warfare contemplated but only blockade confined within narrowest limits compatible with necessary military aims and even within those limits greatest care taken not to interfere with innocent American commerce and every precaution taken to limit destruction of neutral ships carrying contraband and enemy vessels to ship and cargo, safeguarding wherever possible lives of passengers and crews. Not impossible that constructive proposals allowing time to elapse and demonstrating sincerity and reasonableness of Imperial Government might prove acceptable—as that the two governments institute a joint commission, perhaps in conference with other neutral powers affected, for negotiation of a code governing blockade and submarine warfare generally, or suggestion for a conference of powers authorized in Naval Appropriation bill (1916).

Extreme gravity of situation would seem to warrant earnest representations to above effect to Imperial German Government.

763.72/3313½a

The Secretary of State to President Wilson

WASHINGTON, *February 13, 1917.*

MY DEAR MR. PRESIDENT: From a newspaper correspondent who is I believe reliable comes the information that he has found in visiting the Entente Embassies here a change of sentiment in the last day or two as to the desire that this country should be drawn into the war. It now seems, according to this informant, that they are as anxious now to have us keep out as a few days ago they were anxious to have us come in. The conclusion drawn from his conversation with various members of the Embassies was that they had decided that they did not want this Government to take part in the peace negotiations because we would be too lenient with Germany.

I do not know what was said to him and I only give you his opinion as of interest without attempting to value it.

There is, however, this: You may recall that last spring, when the *Sussex* affair was being discussed, I said that I could see a possible reason for Germany's wish to have us in the war as her antagonist if she was convinced that she would be defeated or could not win, and that was, that when the peace was negotiated we would be a generous enemy and favor moderate terms, so that she would be protected from the hatred of the Allies.

The present viewpoint of the Embassies would seem to be the complement of that idea.

Faithfully yours,

ROBERT LANSING

763.72/3315

The Secretary of State to President Wilson

WASHINGTON, *February 14, 1917.*

MY DEAR MR. PRESIDENT: I send you a letter [5] which has just been received from the Sun Company, of Philadelphia relative to the arming of their vessels in English ports, with the aid of the British Government. Since the letter was received the Company has telephoned that the British Government is willing to supply the guns, provided our Government does not object.

This raises a new problem in the matter of arming merchant vessels. I would not favor allowing them to receive guns without our consent, and, at the same time, I am very doubtful as to whether we should give consent. This is but one additional perplexity to the many which are presented by the existing situation.

I think it would be well if you could arrange to let me see you sometime tomorrow (Thursday) in order that certain of these questions may be answered in accordance with the policy which you have in mind. If you can arrange this will you please let me know by telephone? [6]

Faithfully yours,

ROBERT LANSING

763.72111/4527½

The Secretary of State to President Wilson

WASHINGTON, *February 14, 1917.*

MY DEAR MR. PRESIDENT: I have received the enclosed letter of the 13th from Senator Stone transmitting a resolution introduced by Senator Saulsbury in regard to the use of our ports by belligerent warships.

Senator Saulsbury called to see me yesterday morning and showed me the proposed resolution asking my views in regard to it. I told him that of course I could not endorse the resolution, but that under certain conditions it might be useful.

He asked me if it would embarrass the Government if it was introduced. I told him I did not think it would if it was referred without debate to the Foreign Relations Committee. He said that he intended to do that.

I repeated to him that he must not consider anything I had said as endorsing the resolution or approving its introduction. He said that he understood that.

---

[5] Not printed.
[6] The President replied on February 15: "I shall be very glad to discuss this delicate matter with you this afternoon at 2.30, if you can come over to the House at that time." (File No. 763.72/3314½.)

I took this course because I saw that the Senator was very desirous to introduce the resolution, and I thought that it could be better handled if it was referred to the Committee as it could then be suppressed or held without action for the time being.

Senator Stone's letter will have to be answered, however, and I should like to have your instructions before reply.

Faithfully yours,

ROBERT LANSING

[Enclosure]

The Chairman of the Senate Committee on Foreign Relations (Stone) to the Secretary of State [7]

[WASHINGTON,] *February 13, 1917.*

DEAR MR. SECRETARY: At the request of Senator Saulsbury, I have directed the Clerk of this Committee to forward you, for any comment you might care to make thereon, his Resolution presented this morning; copy of which is herewith enclosed.

Sincerely yours,

WM. J. STONE

[Subenclosure]

An Act to Discourage the Violation of International Law Upon the High Seas [8]

Whenever a state of war exists between two or more nations with whom the United States are at peace and one or more of the belligerents shall upon the high seas enter upon, engage in or permit a course of warfare or use a method not justified or warranted by the laws of war as generally accepted or as construed by this Government, the ports, harbors and waters of the United States may, as freely as in time of universal peace, be resorted to, used and frequented by the warships or other vessels of any other belligerent, however armed, for the possible purpose of capturing, destroying, resisting or escaping from any vessel of the belligerent or belligerents engaged in such unwarranted course of warfare, or using such illegal methods.

Provided, before the ports, harbors and waters of the United States may be so resorted to, used and frequented, the President shall by proclamation declare that proper occasion has arisen therefor under the terms of this act.

---

[7] Filed separately under file No. 763.72111/4520½.
[8] Senate bill 8236, 64th Cong., 2d sess.

763.72111/4527½

President Wilson to the Secretary of State

WASHINGTON, *15 February, 1917.*

MY DEAR MR. SECRETARY: The proclamation by the President here contemplated would, in effect, be a proclamation of outlawry against the naval representatives of a Government with which this Government would be at peace, and would beyond all doubt be considered so unfriendly an act as virtually to amount to a declaration of war. To vest such a power in the President would, therefore, be in fact (whatever the theory or intention of the Act) to depute to him the power to declare war. That would clearly be unconstitutional, virtually if not technically, and I think very much better and more direct ways of bringing on war would be preferable to this.

I would be glad if you would let Senator Stone have a copy of this letter when you reply to his inquiry.

Faithfully Yours,

WOODROW WILSON

763.72111/4520½

The Secretary of State to the Chairman of the Senate Committee on Foreign Relations (Stone)

WASHINGTON, *February 15, 1917.*

MY DEAR MR. SENATOR: I received yesterday your letter of the 13th enclosing a copy of the resolution introduced by Senator Saulsbury, which I herewith return.[9]

I at once submitted the resolution to the President as by its terms it conferred unusual powers upon him. This afternoon I received a letter from him, a copy of which I herewith enclose.[10]

In view of the very definite views expressed by the President I do not think it necessary or of value for me to make any comment.

Very sincerely yours,

ROBERT LANSING

763.72/3352½

The Secretary of State to the Secretary of the Treasury (McAdoo)

WASHINGTON, *February 17, 1917.*

MY DEAR MR. SECRETARY: Referring to your letter of the 12th [11] concerning the arming of merchant vessels in which a friend, whom you quote, asserts that arming is a belligerent right and therefore

---

[9] *Ante*, p. 606.
[10] *Supra.*
[11] Not printed.

not proper for a neutral, I wish to point out that there are and have been two distinct reasons for merchant vessels carrying guns.

In the first place a merchant vessel on the high seas is without the protection of its government from lawless acts, it is, therefore, entitled to protect itself from pirates or other marauders, and may of course arm for that purpose. I do not see that it makes any difference whether a state of war or a state of peace exists so far as this right of defense is concerned.

In the second place a merchant vessel of belligerent nationality has a right to resist attack because enemy private property on the high seas may be by the laws of war seized and confiscated. To arm and resist are therefore legitimate as long as private property is not exempt from capture.

The arming of American merchant vessels falls under the first right. The United States is at peace. American vessels cannot arm to resist the exercise of a recognized belligerent right, but they can arm to resist illegal acts by a belligerent ship or any other ship. It is merely carrying out the general principle of self-defense due to the unprotected condition of a merchant vessel on the high seas.

Faithfully yours,

ROBERT LANSING

763.72/3351½

The Counselor for the Department of State (Polk) to the Secretary of State

[WASHINGTON,] *February 17, 1917.*

MY DEAR MR. SECRETARY: The Swiss Minister called yesterday and among other matters he brought up the subject himself of the suggestion he made on Saturday, February 10, on behalf of Germany, for a discussion of ways and means of avoiding war. He said he had seen the stories in the papers that Germany had repudiated any such overtures and wished you to be assured and, through you, the President, that he never would have brought up the subject if he had not received specific instructions from his Government to do so at the request of the German Minister in Berne. He stated that he read me his instructions from the actual telegram. He also wished to assure you that he had nothing whatever to do with the publication of this proposal; that Draper, the Associated Press correspondent, brought him the statement Saturday afternoon and as soon as he found that the press had the statement he came down here at once to carry out his instructions. It had been his intention to wait two or three days before coming down.

F. L. P[OLK]

763.72/3353½

The Secretary of State to President Wilson

WASHINGTON, *February 17, 1917.*

MY DEAR MR. PRESIDENT: I send you a letter which I have received from Doctor Kirchwey,[12] and which I thought you would find of interest in connection with the activities of the pacifists. Will you please return it after you have read it?

Faithfully yours,

ROBERT LANSING

763.72/3354½

President Wilson to the Secretary of State

WASHINGTON, *19 February, 1917.*

MY DEAR MR. SECRETARY: I have always had a good opinion of Professor Kirchwey and have no reason to doubt that he did what he did in this instance with the best intentions, but it was certainly a most extraordinary performance, take it in all its aspects.

Faithfully Yours,

W. W.

763.72/3468½

The Secretary of State to President Wilson [13]

WASHINGTON, *February 21, 1917.*

MY DEAR MR. PRESIDENT: I enclose a memorandum which I have prepared on the subject of arming merchant vessels, with particular reference to the question of supplying guns and trained men to American vessels visiting the "danger zone." The memorandum also includes a brief reference to the conflict of right, duty and expediency which it seems to me must be considered in determining upon a definite policy.

Faithfully yours,

ROBERT LANSING

---

[12] *Ante,* p. 599.
[13] This paper bears the notation: "The Prest said to me that I did not include [in] the memo. a course of action. I told him that I had not intended to do so, that I wished to lay before him my conception of the principles involved and the questions which were raised in my mind by the situation, but that the question of right policy lay with him. RL Feby 22/17."

[Enclosure]

Memorandum by the Secretary of State on the Arming of Merchant Vessels

[WASHINGTON,] *February 20, 1917.*

The arming of merchant vessels of belligerent nationality and the arming of merchant vessels of neutral nationality rest upon two different principles.

A belligerent merchant vessel's right to carry an armament and to employ it in resisting attack by an enemy ship arises primarily from the fact that a merchant vessel and its cargo are under the recognized rules of naval warfare proper prize of an enemy who may seize and confiscate them. As the vessel is not under the direct protection of the armed forces of its government when traversing the high seas, it may rightfully defend itself from seizure and thus attempt to prevent its owner from suffering a total loss by reason of its capture. If the rule as to private property on the high seas was the same as that applicable to private property on land so that it would be immune from confiscation without just indemnity, it is probable that forcible resistance would be declared to be illegal; but as long as the present rule of prize exists the right of defense can not justly be denied to a belligerent merchant vessel.

A neutral merchant vessel's right to carry and use an armament arises primarily from two facts, first, the defenseless character of a commercial vessel, and second, that, as a rule, there is no protection furnished by a government to its merchant vessels on the high seas against piracy or any other form of lawlessness imperiling human life. It is manifestly impossible for a government to give full protection to its merchant marine in all parts of the globe and, therefore, its merchant vessels are warranted in being prepared against lawless attacks and in resisting lawless assailants. It is the same primitive law of self-defense that justifies an individual in arming and defending himself from a highwayman in a region which is known to be without police protection.

Neutral property on the high seas is by the laws of naval warfare immune from confiscation by a belligerent unless it has through the voluntary act of the owner become tainted with enemy character. Against the exercise of the belligerent right of visit and search to determine the character of its cargo a neutral merchant vessel has no right to resist by force, since if it is engaged in innocent trade it cannot lawfully be seized and confiscated. If, however, a neutral merchant vessel is attacked by methods which ignore the rule of visit and search, the immunity of innocent cargoes, and the safety of human life, it possesses the right of self-defense whether the lawless attack is made by a public or a private ship. The essential element of this right of defense is the duty, as well as the right, to protect human life, the protection of the property being incidental and subordinate to the more important object. As to the loss of innocent neutral property, whether it be vessels or cargoes, there is an adequate remedy through the enforcement by diplomatic or judicial processes of indemnities.

If an illegal attack is made upon a neutral merchant vessel under the direct order of a belligerent government, the primitive right of defense ought not by reason of that fact to be annulled or abridged. To deny the right of resistance in such circumstances would amount to legalizing illegality and to subordinating neutral right of safety to life on the high seas to the arbitrary will of belligerents.

If the orders issued by a belligerent government to its naval vessels are flagrantly in violation of the laws of naval warfare which give protection to the lives of neutrals traversing the high seas in neutral bottoms (not to mention belligerent merchantmen) and if, by notifying neutral governments that "all ships within" a certain portion of the high seas "will be sunk," the threat is made that neutral ships and cargo will be destroyed without regard for the safety of the persons on board the vessels, there would seem to be no valid reason for a neutral government to refuse to allow its merchant vessels to carry armaments and to use them to defend themselves from the lawless attacks threatened. To compel a merchant vessel to proceed on its voyage without means of defense, when it is notorious that the laws of naval warfare protective of human life will be disregarded by a belligerent, would come near to making the neutral government an accessory in the crime and in any event encourage the offending government to continue with free hand its reprehensible practices. It would seem to be the duty of a neutral government to give full sanction to and to advise its merchant vessels to arm and resist illegal attacks of such nature.

With the right of a neutral merchant vessel to arm and to use its armament to protect the lives of the persons on board if lawlessly attacked, the question arises as to the duty of a neutral government to provide the guns and gun crews necessary to equip its merchant vessels for defense against the announced illegal purposes of a belligerent.

This question viewed from the standpoint of abstract right offers little difficulty as there can be no doubt but that a government should defend, if it is able, its merchant vessels on the high seas from all forms of outlawry and particularly so if the lives of the persons on the vessels are imperiled. The practical means would be to furnish an armament and trained men to man it. Such a course would be based on the same principle as convoy except that the vessel would be subject to the belligerent right of visit and search. However, if a belligerent government gave notice which in effect amounted to a declaration that the right of visit and search would not be exercised, the very presence of a belligerent armed vessel would be a menace to human life, and warrant the use of an armament to ward off attack.

From the standpoint of expediency the question can be less readily answered. A belligerent government having announced its purpose to employ lawless methods of attack against all vessels regardless of nationality or of the safety of the persons on board, might consider resistance by an armament furnished by a neutral government and served by gunners from its navy to be a hostile act amounting to a *casus belli*. It would certainly entail a certain measure of danger of creating a state of war between the neutral and the belligerent.

On the other hand if the purpose of the announced policy of lawlessness is to prevent by threats as well as by force neutral vessels from entering a certain zone on the high seas which they have a right to traverse in safety, the failure to provide arms and trained men for defense would accomplish that purpose, if unarmed vessels should refrain from entering the zone on account of fear of the threats made and especially if they could not obtain an efficient armament from other sources than the government.

Where the duty of a neutral government lies in such circumstances is not entirely clear. The right to aid its merchant vessels to protect the lives of the persons on board while traversing the high seas seems certain, but if the exercise of the right is a menace to the peace of the nation ought the right to be exercised? If refraining from the exercise of the right encourages lawlessness and accomplishes the purpose of the lawbreaker ought it not to be exercised? If the failure to exercise the right increases the peril to human life and prevents neutrals from entering certain portions of the high seas through fear of lawless attacks should the neutral government exercise its right if by so doing it will lessen the peril and remove the fear of travelers?

In dealing with a situation in which a neutral government's obligations are manifestly complex and conflicting it is necessary to have in mind the maintenance of rights, the national honor and prestige, the future consequences of resistance or of non-resistance to lawless acts from the domestic as well as the foreign standpoint, the probability of a state of war resulting in any event, whatever policy is adopted, the effect of a severance of diplomatic relations upon the probable outcome, the expediency of awaiting an actual loss of life before acting, the effect of delay of action upon domestic popular support, the effect of immediate action upon the public mind, the effect of non-action upon the commerce and industry of the neutral, these and other subjects shoud be carefully considered and weighed before a policy is determined upon.

ROBERT LANSING

763.72/3468½a

The Secretary of State to President Wilson

WASHINGTON, *March 6, 1917.*

MY DEAR MR. PRESIDENT: As I told you this afternoon I have been studying the statute of 1819 (now Section 4295 of the Revised Statutes, copy enclosed) which has been suggested as a possible restriction upon the arming of merchant vessels proceeding to the German "danger zone", and I am firmly convinced that it in no way restricts the power to arm against submarine attacks or affects the status of the vessel so armed.

In analyzing the statute I find the following reasons which are more or less technical for its not being applicable to the pending question:

1st. In excepting an armed public ship from attack by a merchant vessel, the ship excepted is that "of some nation in amity with the United States". It is significant that the customary words "peace and amity" are not used, only the word "amity". I would define "amity" to be "in friendly relations with". When diplomatic relations have been severed I do not think that it can be said that "friendly relations" exist or a state of "amity" exists. We are still at peace but not in amity with Germany.

2d. The law applies to "the commander and crew" of a merchant vessel. It would not apply to arms or an armed guard put on board such vessel by the Government, if that policy is determined upon.

3d. The statute is clearly an enabling act and not a prohibiting act. That is, it defines what a merchant vessel may do in case of aggression by a foreign private vessel, but it does not prohibit it from any act in relation to a foreign public ship. If it had a right to resist lawless conduct by a public ship prior to the passage of the statute, that right remained unimpaired.

4th. The act being without any provision for a penalty is effective [*ineffective?*] and could not be enforced even if it could be construed as prohibitive. The absence of a penalty clause seems conclusive evidence that it is an enabling act and permissive in nature. If it was prohibitive there would be a penalty fixed.

Furthermore the statute when incorporated in the Revised Statutes was placed under the title of "piracy" and pertained, I assume, to the right to resist pirates. I do not consider that submarines can be so classed although their acts might be considered piratical. It is another form of lawlessness endangering life which is involved and to which the statute in question in no way applies. While a cursory reading of the provisions might raise a doubt as to the right of armed defense against a public ship, a study of the terms and purpose of the statute removes the doubt as entirely inapplicable to an illegal submarine attack.

In view, however, of the fact that the section of the Revised Statutes falls under the title of Piracy it is possible that private citizens may hesitate to arm their merchant vessels. It would not be at all unnatural if there was a measure of hesitancy.

There are two ways to meet this state of affairs. First, to issue a public statement declaring that the statute of 1819 does not apply to present conditions and that a merchant vessel has the right to arm and resist illegal attacks by submarines. Second, for the Government to furnish guns and gun crews to merchant vessels sailing for the German "danger zone", which would remove any doubt of violation of a statute.

The first way has the disadvantage of placing the guns under the control of the master of a merchant vessel, who might not act with the discretion of a naval officer in using them. Furthermore, as the guns and ammunition can only be obtained from the Navy Department, the furnishing of the armament would appear to give official authorization to the merchant vessel to use it, and in no way relieve the Government of responsibility for its use.

The second way has the advantage of placing the armament under the control of naval gunners who could be given explicit orders as to its use. It would undoubtedly be far more efficient to have the guns handled in this way than under the direction of an inexperienced commander of a merchantman.

As to the propriety of furnishing naval guns and naval gunners to merchant vessels I have no doubt. On February 10, 1916, the German Government declared that it would consider armed merchant vessels to be public warships and not entitled to the treatment of private vessels of commerce. In view of this declaration I can not see that it will give Germany any greater justification for lawless attack if the guns are directly operated by order of the Government than she would have if the ship's crew handled the armament under the captain's orders. It might be well, if it is decided to use naval guns and naval gunners, to direct particular attention to the German declaration.

As I pointed out in a memorandum submitted to you on February 22d,[14] the employment of naval guns and gun crews would be in the nature of an armed guard to protect American lives, and would be based on the general principle of convoy, though differing in this, that the guard being on the vessel the belligerent right of visit and search would not be waived. In the present case, however, the German Government has announced its intention not to exercise

[14] *Supra.*

the right and to sink all vessels on sight, so that a government armed vessel would have the indubitable right to use its armament on the approach of a German submarine. As the purpose of the arming would be to protect live [*life?*] and not the cargo I do not see that the presence of contraband on board would affect the case. If the German submarines visited and searched the vessels the use of an armament by a vessel with or without contraband would be unjustified, but the declaration of a purpose not to observe the law, thereby imperilling life, removes any responsibility of the vessel to surrender or of the Government, which has armed it, to guaranty the innocent character of the cargo.

It seems to me that there is no more impropriety in placing armed guards on an American merchant vessel to preserve the lives of the persons on board than there is to land guns and blue jackets to protect the lives of American citizens on foreign soil when they are in danger of lawless attack. I do not know but the present case is even stronger because the sea is common to all nations and not subject to the sovereignty of any one nation. In fact the legal fiction that "an American vessel is American territory" might be applied. In that case the resistance of lawless acts would be like guarding the border from outlaws.

My own belief is that we would be in a stronger and more defensible position legally and accomplish better results if we frankly declared it to be our duty to place on every American merchant vessel sailing for the "danger zone" a naval guard with an armament sufficient to protect it from submarine attack, and that this practice would be followed regardless of the character of the cargo so long as the German Government menaced American lives by declining to exercise the right of visit and search and by attacking indiscriminately all vessels without regard to the safety of the persons on board.

Faithfully yours,

ROBERT LANSING

[Enclosure]

Commerce and Navigation: Regulations for the Suppression of Piracy [15]

CH. 8. SEC. 4295. The commander and crew of any merchant vessel of the United States, owned wholly, or in part, by a citizen thereof, may oppose and defend against any aggression, search, restraint, depredation or seizure, which shall be attempted upon such vessel, or upon any other vessel so owned, by the commander or crew of any

---

[15] Rev. Stat. 829.

armed vessel whatsoever, not being a public armed vessel of some nation in amity with the United States, and may subdue and capture the same; and may also retake any vessel so owned which may have been captured by the commander or crew of any such armed vessel, and send the same into any port of the United States.

———

763.72/3469½

The Secretary of State to President Wilson

WASHINGTON, *March 8, 1917.*

MY DEAR MR. PRESIDENT: I enclose a telegram which I have just received from Honorable Richard Olney,[16] and which I thought you might like to see.

Faithfully yours,

ROBERT LANSING

[Enclosure—Telegram]

Mr. Richard Olney to the Secretary of State

BOSTON, MASS., *March 8, 1917—1:10 p. m.*

Entirely concise [*concur*] in your view that nothing in the statutes cited impairs the President's constructional [*constitutional*] right and duty to safeguard the lives and property of American citizens by providing American merchant ships with guns and other instrumentalities required to enable them to defend themselves against lawless and hostile attack.

RICHARD OLNEY

———

763.72/3469½a

The Secretary of State to President Wilson

WASHINGTON, *March 8, 1917.*

MY DEAR MR. PRESIDENT: I know that you are giving constant and anxious thought to the course of action we should take in regard to arming merchant vessels, but I feel it my duty to express to you my personal views on the subject knowing that you will understand my motives in doing so.

It seems to me that we must proceed upon one of two hypotheses and should regulate our policy accordingly. These hypotheses are that we will ultimately be at war with Germany or that we will continue the present state of unfriendly peace.

———

[16] Secretary of State, 1895–97.

As to the second hypothesis I can see no satisfactory outcome. Suppose we continue as we are, then Germany will have gained all she seeks by preventing American vessels from visiting the waters of the "danger zone" and meanwhile our people will become more and more incensed at German activities and intrigues until they turn against our own Government for failure to act under the greatest provocation. If delay in action is in the expectation or hope that Germany will declare war upon this country and relieve us of that grave responsibility, I am convinced that both expectation and hope will be vain unless we do something very definite which may be interpreted to be a *casus belli*. I think the German Government will be entirely satisfied to let the present situation continue and will do everything possible to avoid hostilities, feeling that by so doing this Government will be seriously embarrassed and placed in a very undesirable position before the American people. But can we afford to let matters stand as they are? If we do, what possibility is there for an improvement in conditions by continued inaction? I confess that I can see nothing to gain by a continuance of this situation so satisfactory to Germany and so unsatisfactory to us. I have considered the matter very carefully and endeavored to construct some result which will warrant a continuance, but I have failed.

Feeling the present state of affairs is hopeless for ultimate peace and being convinced of the impossibility of founding a policy on the hypothesis that we can remain at peace, it seems to me that we ought to proceed on the theory that we will in a short time be openly at war with Germany. If we assume that hypothesis our course is largely a matter of expediency taking chiefly into account what actions will appeal most strongly to the sense of justice and right of the American people and will most firmly unite them in support of the Government. I think that to be of first consideration at the present time.

My own belief is that prompt and vigorous action will do more than anything else to crystallize public support and unite the people behind the Government. As I read the public mind there is an impatient desire to go forward. The people will follow readily and whole-heartedly if a policy of action is adopted and pressed with vigor. I am firmly convinced that expediency as well as duty lies in action.

In view of the conclusion, which I have reached—and reached reluctantly in view of the great issue at stake—, I think that our merchant vessels should be sent out under armed guards, that announcement of this policy should be made immediately and the guns and men placed on the vessels as soon as possible.

I would not advise this course if I could see any possible benefit from delay, but I do not. On the contrary I think that delay is causing a wrong impression of the Government among the people, which, in view of the certainty of war at no distant day, ought to be avoided.

It is with hesitation I have written this letter, because I know that you are devoting your time to this greatest question of your Administration, but I felt that I would be derelict in my duty not to state frankly my views to you.

Faithfully yours,

ROBERT LANSING

763.72/3470½

Mrs. Edith Bolling Wilson to the Secretary of State

[WASHINGTON, *March 9, 1917*.]

MY DEAR MR. SECRETARY: Mr. Wilson asks me to send you these papers, just received from the Secretary of the Navy—and ask if you will be kind enough to read them as soon as possible, and advise him which program you deem wise to follow.

He would be very much pleased if you could let him know in time to enable him to issue the orders today.

Cordially yours,

EDITH BOLLING WILSON

[Enclosure]

The Secretary of the Navy (Daniels) to President Wilson

WASHINGTON, *March 9, 1917.*

DEAR MR. PRESIDENT: Admiral Benson went over to New York last night to confer with Admiral Usher, Mr. Franklin [17] and others looking to carrying out the policy desired. The important question now seems to be which is the best policy to be adopted to carry into effect the arming of ships. There were three different methods outlined in the memorandum submitted to you yesterday. Briefly summarized, they are:

Policy No. 1.

Replies to the German threat to sink neutral vessels in designated zones of the high seas by assuming all German submarines on the high seas are attacking United States vessels and that merchant vessels of the United States consequently may fire upon German submarines wherever they are met on the high seas.

Policy No. 2.

Replies to the German threat to sink neutral vessels in designated zones of the high seas by assuming that all German submarines within

---

[17] P. A. S. Franklin, vice president of the International Mercantile Marine Co.

those zones are attacking U. S. vessels and that consequently merchant vessels of the United States may fire upon German submarines wherever they are met within those zones, but that merchant vessels must grant to German submarines the right of visit and search in all other areas of the high seas.

Policy No. 3.

Replies to the German threat to sink neutral vessels in designated zones of the high seas by continuing to recognize the rights of German submarines to visit and search American merchant vessels, but authorizes those vessels to resist by force certain named unlawful acts of submarines.

I am enclosing redrafted copies of the memorandum submitted to you yesterday giving in detail the three separate policies suggested.[18] Policy No. one denies the right of German submarines to search and seizure, and if ships carrying contraband are to have guns and naval crews on board will it not be necessary to deny search and seizure? Otherwise, practically no goods could be transported and the orders from abroad could not be filled. Would not this practically tie up American ships from going through the barred zone? To be sure this would deny the belligerent right of Germany to visit and search anywhere on the high seas. This would, of course, be a departure from international law and usage. Germany and the world might say that, demanding observance of international law, we had ourselves failed to observe it. Of course, our answer would be that Germany's note that it would sink without warning justified our action. This would be sufficient answer, undoubtedly, if in your message to Congress you had not expressed the doubt that Germany would be guilty of that unprecedented act. I am calling your attention to what is involved in Policy No. 1 before you determine upon which course should be pursued.

Admiral Benson is strongly of the opinion that the first thing to be done would be to notify Germany that, in view of the declaration that she intends to sink our ships without warning in a certain zone, it is our purpose to arm our ships for protection. He believes if this information is imparted it is barely possible that Germany might not carry out her threat. If we deny the right of visit, Germany would declare that to be a warlike act, and that we were responsible for bringing on war. It is entirely probable that the next step would be war. If we must enter it to protect our rights and the lives of our people, I have felt we ought to do nothing to put the responsibility for this step upon our Government.

---

[18] No copies of these papers found in Department files.

Last night I conferred with Admiral Palmer about the crews to man the guns. He has taken action, and sends this note which I thought you would like to read. It is as follows:

Confidential   March 9, 1917.
    From: Bureau of Navigation.
    To: Operations.
    Subject: Arming merchant vessels with Naval gun crews and a
        Naval Officer.

Before any action is taken the Secretary should know that the presence of U. S. sailors (and an officer) on merchant ships will probably be considered an act of war from the German viewpoint.

That it is most probable that a German submarine, knowing an American merchant vessel is armed, and has armed forces of the U. S. on board, for the definite and sole purpose of resisting attack of submarines, will attack without warning.

That the master of the merchant vessel and the Naval officer will believe the German submarine will attack without warning, and therefore, for the safety of the vessel, passengers, U. S. sailors and crew, they will fire at the submarine on sight.

The Secretary should be fully informed on this subject before final steps are taken to place 50 U. S. sailors and officers on armed merchant vessels.

                (Signed)   Leigh C. Palmer

Admiral Benson is to telephone me how soon ships could leave and whether action can be taken without publicity. My own opinion is that it would be impossible to take the action without our own people knowing it for these reasons:

1. Passengers would not go on these ships unless they knew they were armed and had competent gun crews. Their families and friends would know they were going and publicity would be certain.

2. Shippers and all their employees would be busy loading the cargo, and this could not be kept secret.

3. The sending of the gun crew—40 or 50 on the larger ships— would be known on the ships or stations from which they are taken, and experience has shown how impossible such movements are to be confined to service channels.

The question arises, too, whether it would not be wisest to state that you had reached the conclusion that you had a right to arm the ships and would do so, making no statement as to the time or the method. I cannot resist the feeling that this would be the best course and meet public approval. If Germany wants war, she will try to sink in any event. If she wishes to avert war with us, there would be time to modify her orders to Naval commanders so they would not commit the overt act.

Admiral Benson will return this afternoon and I will send you tonight or tomorrow morning a statement from him after his talk with Mr. Franklin. It will take five days, after notice that ships are to be armed, for one to sail, and until I hear from you I will give no orders to arm them, but will have guns and crews ready for immediate action.

I suggest whether, when we undertake to arm the ships, it will not be necessary to secure some co-operation with the English or French to whose shores the ships are destined. The information comes to us that when a ship leaves New York, its route and time of arrival are cabled to the Admiralty and it is met and convoyed into port by destroyers or other craft through a lane traversed all the time by Naval craft. Suppose we send out an armed merchant ship, ought we not to secure some such convoy or protection when she nears port in the barred zone? This is a big question but is one that we probably must face. The English also on this side know when a ship is coming into an American port and keep ships over here to afford protection. Certain French and English Naval officers here have suggested to officers in our service that some character of co-operation would be necessary. Naturally they would expect us to patrol and convoy their ships coming into our ports if they protect and convoy our ships going into their ports. Such co-operation would be easy if we were at war with Germany, but as we are not at war, would not such co-operation make us regarded as an ally of the entente powers? The protection of our ships and their reaching ports in safety raises so many difficult questions, and the consequences are so grave, that I am trying to present them to you before the final order to arm is given, though, of course, they have been present in your mind during the whole controversy.

Sincerely yours,

JOSEPHUS DANIELS

763.72/3470½

The Secretary of State to President Wilson

WASHINGTON, *March 9, 1917.*

MY DEAR MR. PRESIDENT: I return herewith the papers from the Navy Department in regard to the arming of merchant vessels, which Mrs. Wilson was good enough to send me this morning.

As you know from my letters of the 6th and 8th I strongly advocate placing an "armed guard" on an American merchant vessel proceeding to the German "danger zone". I think that that policy would remove all question of constitutional right and executive power. It appears from the papers submitted that this method has not been considered in the three policies suggested by Secretary Daniels on which the three sets of regulations are based.[20] It would seem, however, that they could readily be adapted to such a change.

---

[20] Not printed; for the regulations as issued, see *infra.*

After going over the policies stated and the regulations proposed I think that Policy No. 2 is the best from a legal standpoint, although it does not cover cases of illegal attack outside the zone. It is evident that to permit the people on board of a vessel to be placed in open boats at so great a distance from land as they would be if captured outside the zone would as seriously imperil their lives as if attacked without visit within the zone. I think it best to adopt Policy No. 2, with instructions allowing the armed guard to resist illegal attack outside the zone. In no circumstances would I favor No. 3.

In regard to the Regulations (or if issued to an armed Guard, Instructions) I do not feel competent to pass judgment upon them, but believe that with a definite policy adopted they can be worked out by the naval experts so as to be efficient and consistent with the policy. I think that it would be well to omit such positive statements as Regulation No. 2 (page 2). They would only serve to cause controversy. In Regulation No. 4 (page 3) I have also indicated a little more latitude to the armed guard.

I agree with Secretary Daniels that it is not practicable to proceed with this matter secretly, furthermore I do not think that it is politic to do so. My own view is that a public statement of the policy should be made very soon, tomorrow morning if possible, but the regulations (or instructions) should remain secret for the present. I enclose a suggestion for a public statement.[21] In no event would I indicate that we had any choice of policies or that the protection is to be limited to the barred zones.

It is with very real gratification that I learn of your determination to adopt this course. It is so consistent with all you have said and so entirely right that I know it will meet with the approval of the American people.

Faithfully yours,

ROBERT LANSING

763.72/3576½

The Secretary of the Navy (Daniels) to the Secretary of State

WASHINGTON, *March 11, 1917.*

DEAR MR. SECRETARY: Enclosed are tentative regulations drawn up for the government of the Armed Guard to be placed on merchant ships. Will you be good enough to suggest any changes, additions or omissions that you think will be wise? We wish to send

---

[21] For text of statement as issued, see announcement to foreign embassies and legations at Washington, *Foreign Relations*, 1917, supp. 1, p. 171.

these instructions out on Monday.   I will be glad to call to go over this matter if you desire.

Sincerely,

JOSEPHUS DANIELS

Please return enclosed with your suggestions.

[Enclosure]

Regulations Governing the Conduct of American Merchant Vessels on Which Armed Guards Have Been Placed

1. Armed Guards on American merchant vessels are for the sole purpose of defense against the unlawful acts of the submarines of Germany or of any nation following the policy announced by Germany in her note of January 31, 1917.[22]   Neither the Armed Guards nor their arms can be used for any other purpose.

2. The announced policy of Germany, in her note of January 31, 1917, to sink all vessels that enter certain areas of the high seas, has led the Government of the United States to authorize Armed Guards on merchant vessels to resist any and all attempts of the submarines of Germany or of any nation following the policy announced by Germany in her note of January 31st, to put that policy into practice.

3. It shall be lawful for the Armed Guard on any American merchant vessel to fire upon any submarine of Germany or of any nation following the policy of Germany announced in her note of January 31, 1917, that attempts to approach, or lies within 4,000 yards of the commercial route of the vessel sighting the submarine, if the submarine is sighted within the zone proscribed by Germany.

4. No Armed Guard on any American merchant vessel shall fire at any submarine that lies more than 4,000 yards from the commercial route of the vessel sighting the submarine, except that the submarine shall have fired first.

5. No Armed Guard on any American merchant vessel shall take any offensive action against any submarine of Germany or of any nation following the policy of Germany announced in her note of January 31, 1917, on the high seas outside of the zones proscribed by Germany, unless the submarine is guilty of an unlawful act that jeopardizes the vessel, her passengers, or crew, or unless the submarine is submerged.

6. No Armed Guard on an American merchant vessel shall attack a submarine that is retiring or attempting to retire either within or without the zone proscribed by Germany, unless it may be reasonably presumed to be manoeuvering for renewal of attack.

---

[22] *Ibid.*, p. 97.

7. In all cases not herein specifically excepted the Armed Guard on American merchant vessels shall be governed by the principles of established international law and the treaties and conventions to which the Government of the United States is a party.

8. American merchant vessels are forbidden to pursue or search out the submarines of any nation or to engage in any aggressive warfare against them.

9. American merchant vessels shall make every effort compatible with the safety of the merchant vessel to save the lives of the crew of any submarine that may be sunk, or that submits, or is in distress.

10. American merchant vessels shall make every effort to avoid the submarines of Germany and of any nation following the policy of Germany announced in her note of January 31, 1917, while in the zones proscribed by Germany.

11. American merchant vessels shall display the American colors continuously at sea.

12. American merchant vessels should communicate with the Commandant of the Naval District before leaving a United States port to make sure of the latest information.

13. The safety of American merchant vessels requires that they obey all instructions of vessels of war of the United States.

On Sighting a Submarine in the Proscribed Zones

14. If a submarine is sighted beyond torpedo range, bring submarine abaft the beam and keep her there. If submarine attempts to close, bring her astern and proceed at highest possible speed.

15. If submarine is sighted close aboard forward of the beam, the greatest safety lies in changing course directly toward the submarine.

16. If submarine is sighted close aboard abaft the beam, the greatest safety lies in turning away from the submarine and proceeding at highest speed.

On Opening Fire in Defense Against the Unlawful Acts of Submarines

17. Hoist national colors before first shot is fired.

18. Once it has been decided to open fire, do not submit to the gun fire of a submarine so long as the armed guard can continue to fire.

19. Send all persons except bridge force and the armed guard below decks while vessel is under fire.

20. Watch out for torpedoes and maneuver to avoid them. If unable to avoid them, maneuver so that they will strike a glancing blow.

THE ARMED GUARD

21. The Armed Guard is commanded by the Senior Naval Officer on board. He shall have exclusive control over the military functions of the Armed Guard and shall be responsible for the execution of all the regulations given herein governing the employment of the Armed Guard.

22. The military discipline of the Armed Guard shall be administered by the naval officer commanding the Armed Guard.

23. The Armed Guard shall be subject to the orders of the Master of the merchant vessel as to matters of non-military character, but the members of the Armed Guard shall not be required to perform any ship duties except their military duty, and these shall be performed invariably under the direction of the officer commanding the Armed Guard.

24. The decision as to opening fire or ceasing fire upon any submarine shall reside exclusively with the naval officer commanding the Armed Guard.

25. The enlisted personnel of the Armed Guard shall be quartered and messed together on board both in port and at sea, at the expense of the owners of the vessel, on which the Armed Guard is serving, in a manner satisfactory to the naval officer commanding the Armed Guard.

26. The naval officer commanding the Armed Guard shall take precedence next after the Master, except that he shall not be eligible for succession to the command of the ship. He shall be quartered and messed on board both at sea and in port, at the expense of the owners of the vessel on which he is serving, and in a manner appropriate to his precedence next after the Master.

27. The Master of the merchant vessel shall, on request of the commander of the Armed Guard, detail members of the crew to handle ammunition, clear decks, and otherwise supplement the service of the gun.

28. The naval officer commanding the Armed Guard shall be responsible for:—

(a) The condition of the battery and its appurtenances.

(b) The training of the guns' crews and spotters, including members of the ship's force detailed by the Master to assist in the service of the guns.

(c) The readiness of the ship's battery at night.

(d) The readiness of the Armed Guard to perform its duties at all times.

(e) The continuous lookout near each gun by a member of the Armed Guard.

(f) The making of all reports required by the Navy Department.

JOSEPHUS DANIELS
Secretary of the Navy
MARCH 13, 1917.

711.622/5

The Secretary of State to President Wilson

WASHINGTON, *March 16* [*17?*], *1917.*
MY DEAR MR. PRESIDENT: Doctor Ritter has been very persistent in asking us for a reply to his note of February 10th [23] in relation to an interpretative protocol suggested by the German Government in relation to Article 23 of the Treaty of 1799,[24] which was revived and continued by our treaty with Prussia in 1828.[25]

If it meets with your approval I propose to send him the following note in answer to his communication.[26]

Faithfully yours,

ROBERT LANSING

763.72/3577½a

The Secretary of State to President Wilson

WASHINGTON, *March 19, 1917.*
MY DEAR MR. PRESIDENT: After considering carefully our conversation this morning I wish to say that I am in entire agreement with you that the recent attacks by submarines on American vessels do not materially affect the international situation so far as constituting a reason for declaring that a state of war exists between this country and Germany. I think that these incidents, however, show very plainly that the German Government intends to carry out its announced policy without regard to consequences and to make no exception in the case of American vessels. It will, therefore, be only a question of time before we are forced to recognize these outrages as hostile acts which will amount to an announcement that a state of war exists.

I firmly believe that war will come within a short time whatever we may do, because the German Government seems to be relentless in pursuing its methods of warfare against neutral ships. It will not be

---

[23] *Foreign Relations*, 1918, supp. 2, p. 160.
[24] Miller, *Treaties*, vol. 2, p. 433.
[25] *Ibid.*, vol. 3, p. 427.
[26] Draft note not printed. President Wilson replied: "I have made certain alterations in this paper, but am glad to approve it as altered. W. W." (File No. 711.622/13½.) For the note as sent, see *Foreign Relations*, 1918, supp. 2, p. 162.

many days, if past experience indicates the future, before an engagement will take place between one of our guarded steamships and a submarine. Whether that event will cause Germany to declare war or will cause us to recognize a state of war I do not know, but I do not think that we can successfully maintain the fiction that peace exists.

With the conviction that war is bound to come—and I have come to this conviction with the greatest reluctance and with an earnest desire to avoid it—the question seems to me to be whether or not the greatest good will be accomplished by waiting until some other events have taken place before we enter the conflict, or by entering now.

The advantage of delay would seem to be that in some future submarine attack on an American vessel the armed guard would with gun fire sink or drive off the submarine and by so doing induce the German Government to declare war upon us. If there is any other advantage I have been unable to imagine it. I am also convinced in my own mind that the German Government will not declare war in any circumstances. Why should it? It will prefer to continue to wage war on us, as it is today, and at the same time keep our hands tied by our admitted neutrality. It can do everything practical to injure us and prevent us from doing many things to injure Germany. It would seem most unreasonable to expect the German Government to increase its difficulties by declaring the United States an enemy.

The advantages of our immediate participation in the war appear to me to [be] based largely upon the premise that war is inevitable. Of course if that premise is wrong what I say is open to question. I should add two other premises, the truth of which seem to me well established. They are that the Entente Allies represent the principle of Democracy, and the Central Powers, the principle of Autocracy, and that it is for the welfare of mankind and for the establishment of peace in the world that Democracy should succeed.

In the first place it would encourage and strengthen the new democratic government of Russia, which we ought to encourage and with which we ought to sympathize. If we delay, conditions may change and the opportune moment when our friendship would be useful may be lost. I believe that the Russian Government founded on its hatred of absolutism and therefore of the German Government would be materially benefited by feeling that this republic was arrayed against the same enemy of liberalism.

In the second place it would put heart into the democratic element in Germany, who are already beginning to speak boldly and show their teeth at their rulers. Possibly delay would not affect to a very great degree the movement, but I believe it would hasten the time when the German people assert themselves and repudiate the military oligarchy in control of the Empire.

In the third place it would give moral support to the Entente Powers already encouraged by recent military successes and add to the discouragement of the Teutonic Allies, which would result in the advancement of Democracy and in shortening the war. The present seems to be an especially propitious time to exert this influence on the conflict.

In the fourth place the American people, feeling, I am sure, that war is bound to come, are becoming restive and bitterly critical of what they believe to be an attempt to avoid the unavoidable. If there is a possibility of keeping out of the war, this attitude of the public mind would affect me not at all, but convinced as I am that we will in spite of all we may do become participants, I can see no object in adopting a course which will deprive us of a certain measure of enthusiastic support which speedy action will bring.

In the fifth place I believe that our future influence in world affairs, in which we can no longer refuse to play our part, will be materially increased by prompt, vigorous and definite action in favor of Democracy and against Absolutism. This would be first shown in the peace negotiations and in the general readjustment of international relations. It is my belief that the longer we delay in declaring against the military absolutism which menaces the rule of liberty and justice in the world, so much the less will be our influence in the days when Germany will need a merciful and unselfish foe.

I have written my views with great frankness, as I am sure you would wish me to do, and I trust that you will understand my views are in no way influenced by any bitterness of feeling toward Germany or by any conscious emotion awakened by recent events. I have tried to view the situation coldly, dispassionately and justly.

Faithfully yours,

ROBERT LANSING

763.72/3528

The Secretary of State to Colonel E. M. House

WASHINGTON, *March 19, 1917.*

MY DEAR COLONEL: I enclose you a copy of a strictly confidential dispatch received from Copenhagen under date of March 16th.[27]

[27] This read in part as follows: "Since Bernstorff's return, German officials insist that the Carranza note was a legitimate precaution. Bernstorff officially takes this view, though he personally is trying for peace. German Legation here believes that military party will go to extreme lengths, in spite of moderate attitude of Foreign Office. Zimmermann still believes in a Japanese alliance. Egan." (File No. 763.72/3528.)

Of course it is all nonsense about Bernstorff denying the Carranza note.[28] The effort seems to be to obtain knowledge of the source of our information. That the German Government will not get.

. . . .

I trust that Mrs. Lansing and I will be able to be with you next Saturday night, but the sudden turn of events as a result of the sinking of three American vessels may interfere with our plans.

I have just returned from a conference with the President. He is disposed not to summon Congress as a result of the sinking of these vessels. He feels that all he could ask would be powers to do what he is already doing. I suggested that he might call them to consider declaring war, and urged the present was the psychological moment in view of the Russian revolution and the anti-Prussian spirit in Germany, and that to throw our moral influence in the scale at this time would aid the Russian liberals and might even cause revolution in Germany. He indicated to me the fear he had of the queries and investigations of a Congress which could not be depended upon because of the out-and-out pacifists and the other group of men like Senator Stone.

If you agree with me that we should act now, will you not please put your shoulder to the wheel?

Faithfully yours,

ROBERT LANSING

763.72/3579½

Colonel E. M. House to the Secretary of State

DEAR MR. SECRETARY: Thank you for your letter of yesterday with its enclosure.

In regard to the Egan despatch, I think we ought to do everything possible to discredit Zimmermann whose influence seems to be wholly anti American. Suppose we let the matter rest until you come on Saturday when we can talk it over. There are some things I can tell you about the matter that perhaps have not reached you.

I wrote the President very strongly yesterday along the lines you suggested through Frank Polk. I find that many thoughtful people believe that the President would do better not to call Congress before the sixteenth if he would proceed as rapidly as possible towards preparing the country for war.

There is so much to be done and so little time in which to do it that it might be prudent not to declare war until we have more nearly gotten ready. Haste in this direction is what I believe is most to be desired. If the President would outline such a policy to you and to

[28] See *Foreign Relations*, 1917, supp. 1, p. 147.

the Army and Navy Departments and let it be known what was being done, it would satisfy public opinion and be more effective than if actual war was declared before having taken the necessary precautions.

I hope nothing will prevent your coming on Saturday for we not only have invited some twenty odd people to meet Mrs. Lansing and you, but I am anxious to have a talk which we can do better here than in Washington.

Sincerely yours,

E. M. HOUSE

NEW YORK, *March 20, 1917.*
    [Received March 21.]

763.72/3593a

The Secretary of State to President Wilson

WASHINGTON, *March 26, 1917.*

MY DEAR MR. PRESIDENT: I would like to make a statement to the press, which would be in substance like the enclosed. There is much misapprehension on this subject and it seems to me the public should have [it] brought clearly to their attention.

I talked the matter over with Colonel House on Saturday and he thought such a statement would be very helpful.

Faithfully yours,

ROBERT LANSING

[Enclosure]

Proposed Statement to the Press

There seems to be a tendency in certain quarters, judging from newspaper reports, to show dissatisfaction with the President because he does not declare his position in regard to Germany or direct hostile acts against her. Some of these people criticize through ignorance and some in an effort to commit the Government before Congress meets next Monday.

Everyone who indulges in criticism of this character knows or ought to know that the power to declare war rests with Congress alone and that it would be highly improper for the President to say anything or do anything which infringes upon this constitutional power of Congress.

The course of silence which the President is following is the only one consistent with his office. The American people ought to understand that and not be influenced by radical partisans who assert that President Wilson is undecided because he refuses to declare his purpose or to authorize an act of war against Germany. They want him to usurp the powers of Congress and are trying to force him to do so.

The people should not tolerate criticism of this sort.

763.72/3759b

The Secretary of State to President Wilson

WASHINGTON, *March 26, 1917.*

MY DEAR MR. PRESIDENT: There is a policy which it seems to me should be determined upon without delay as preliminary arrangements will have to be made to carry it out. It is presented by the question, If a declaration of war against Germany or if a declaration of the existence of a state of war is resolved by the Congress, what ought the Governments of Cuba and Panama to do?

It seems to me that we cannot permit Cuba to become a place of refuge for enemy aliens. It would give them great facilities for plots and intrigues not only against this country but against the peace of Cuba. I have in mind the possibility of submarine bases, the organization of reservists, the use of cables, etc., which would be to my mind very serious and possibly disastrous. In addition to this, if Cuba remained neutral, we could not use her ports for our war vessels and that might result in a renewal of the rebellious activities in the Island, which would be abetted by the Germans there. To prevent this situation there seems to me but one policy to adopt and that is to have the Cuban Government follow our action with similar action.

Both the Minister here and Minister Desvernine [29] have stated that they will do whatever we wish them to do. But we ought to be prepared to tell them exactly what we want.

The Panama situation is not so easy to handle as the Government is less amenable. I feel, however, that it would be perilous to permit Germans to be at liberty to go and come so near to the Canal. It would be almost essential to have the Germans expelled from the Republic. Furthermore, the laws of neutrality would seriously embarrass our people. These conditions could only be avoided by Panama entering the war, if we become a party.

I think that I can influence the Panama Government to do whatever we wish in the matter, but it will take a little time and requires preliminary work to accomplish it.

---

[29] Pablo Desvernine, Cuban Secretary of State.

Please advise me at your earliest convenience as to your wishes, because delay may cause embarrassment and possibly a dangerous situation.

Faithfully yours,

ROBERT LANSING

763.72/3759¾

President Wilson to the Secretary of State

WASHINGTON, *27 March, 1917.*

MY DEAR MR. SECRETARY: It is clear to me that the only thing we can prudently do is to urge both Cuba and Panama to do just what we do.

In case Cuba follows our lead it will be necessary, I take it for granted, to give her our military protection as fully as we give it to Porto Rico and St. Thomas. I hope that you will get the negotiations in course as soon as possible, but that you will first confer with Baker and Daniels about the practical consequences and our ability to handle them.

Faithfully Yours,

W. W.

701.6311/270a

The Secretary of State to President Wilson

WASHINGTON, *March 27, 1917.*

MY DEAR MR. PRESIDENT: Count Tarnowski called at my house last evening by appointment and discussed his situation here.[30] He asked for the appointment on account of having received a communication from Count Czernin.[30a] After talking the matter over and sympathizing with him in the embarrassment of his Government and also of himself in the present situation, I requested him to give me a transcript of Count Czernin's dispatch which he had read to me. This he did and I enclose to you a copy. I told him that I would lay the matter before you and would endeavor to give him an answer today or tomorrow. Will you please advise me what I should say to Count Tarnowski?

Faithfully yours,

ROBERT LANSING

---

[30] See footnote 98a, p. 596.
[30a] President of the Austro-Hungarian Council of Ministers, and Minister for Foreign Affairs.

[Enclosure]

The Austro-Hungarian Ambassador Designate (Tarnowski) to the Secretary of State

WASHINGTON, *March 26, 1917.*

MY DEAR MR. SECRETARY OF STATE: You expressed the wish in the course of the conversation we just had that I should outline for your personal information the substance of my communications to make use of such a written pro-memoria when submitting the matter to the President tomorrow.

I had the honor of informing you of the following:

"Count Czernin has instructed me to draw in a most friendly spirit Your Excellency's attention to the fact that the long delay of my reception by the President renders his position extremely difficult, the public opinion in Austria-Hungary resenting it already, and if this feeling has not until now become evident it is only due to the censure [*censorship*] of the press.

My Chief thinks to have shown his desire for the maintenance of the diplomatic relations between the Monarchy and the United States and he believes this desire to be shared by Your Excellency but he must ask not to be placed in too difficult position.

Besides Mr. Penfield's situation is also growing very difficult as the public opinion begins to lose faith in his good will."

Having been instructed to deliver the above communication orally only, and having written this for Your Excellency's convenience, I need not ask you to consider my letter as strictly confidential.

Very sincerely yours,

TARNOWSKI

701.6311/271

President Wilson to the Secretary of State

WASHINGTON, *27 March, 1917.*

MY DEAR MR. SECRETARY: This is certainly a most delicate and embarrassing situation, but I see only one thing we can do. There is no choice in the circumstances but to say to Count Tarnowski that the explicit acceptance and avowal by his Government of the policy which led to our breach of diplomatic relations with Germany (before the policy had been put into operation) makes it impossible, to our sincere regret, that I should receive him.

This announcement to him (I think it should not until absolutely necessary be made public) can of course be made in the most friendly spirit; and he can be told that we will relieve the embarrassment at Vienna by recalling Mr. Penfield so soon as he (Tarnowski) has heard from his Government and received its instructions.

All of this, I take it for granted, will be at once communicated to Mr. Penfield and he will be told to hold himself in readiness to receive instructions as to himself, pending Vienna's reply to Tarnowski.

In any case Penfield should express again to Count Czernin our deep regret that the Austro-Hungarian Government should have felt itself obliged to join Germany in its sub-marine policy and so interrupt relations which we had hoped might remain friendly in form as well as in fact. In short, he ought to make it plain to Count Czernin that we are acting without feeling in this matter, and merely on principle.

Faithfully yours,

W. W.

763.72/3761½

President Wilson to the Secretary of State

WASHINGTON, *1 April, 1917.*

MY DEAR MR. SECRETARY: This is the passage in my address [30b] which should give form to the Resolution of which we were speaking over the 'phone this evening:

"I advise that the Congress declare the recent course of the Imperial German Government to be in fact nothing less than war against the government and people of the United States; that it formally accept the status of belligerent which has thus been thrust upon it; and that it take immediate steps not only to put the country in a more thorough state of defense but also to exert all its power and employ all its resources to bring the Government of the German Empire to terms and end the war."

I would be very much obliged if you would be kind enough to have the Resolution drawn in the sense of these words.

I am putting this in writing rather than give it to you orally over the 'phone because I know you will wish to have before you just the language I am to use.

Faithfully Yours,

W. W.

[30b] For text of the address, see *Foreign Relations*, 1917, supp. 1, p. 195.

763.72/3760¾

Draft of Joint Resolution To Be Introduced in Congress, April 2, 1917 [31]

Whereas, The recent course [acts] of the Imperial German Government is [are] in fact nothing less than [acts of] [32] war against the Government and people of the United States,

Resolved, by the Senate and House of Representatives of the United States of America in Congress Assembled, That the state of belligerency [war] between the United States and the Imperial German Government which has thus been thrust upon the United States is hereby formally declared; and

That the President be, and he is hereby authorized [and directed] to take immediate steps not only to put the country in a thorough state of defense, but also to exert all of its power and employ all of its resources to carry on war against the Imperial German Government and to bring the conflict to a successful termination.

763.72/3761½a

The Secretary of State to President Wilson

WASHINGTON, *April 3, 1917.*

MY DEAR MR. PRESIDENT: I send you a tentative draft of a proclamation of which I spoke to you yesterday afternoon and which, it seems to me, should be issued immediately upon the passage of the Joint Resolution which I assume Congress will adopt.

Will you please advise me whether this meets with your wishes in order that we may prepare the proclamation so that it will issue without delay?

Faithfully yours,

ROBERT LANSING

[Enclosure]

Draft of Proclamation To Be Issued by the President

WHEREAS the Congress of the United States in the exercise of the constitutional authority vested in them have resolved, by joint resolution of the Senate and House of Representatives bearing date this

---

[31] Bracketed words represent amendments. This paper bears the notation: "Thus amended after talks April 2, 1917, with Senators Swanson and Knox and Rep. Flood. Original approved by President April 2, 11.30 am. Amendments approved by President April 2, 5 pm RL." For text of the resolution as introduced, see *Foreign Relations*, 1917, supp. 1, p. 195.

[32] This bracketed expression is apparently intended to replace the phrase "nothing less than," which has been crossed out in the original.

day "That the state of war between the United States and the Imperial German Government which has thus been thrust upon the United States is hereby declared":

Now, THEREFORE, I, WOODROW WILSON, President of the United States of America, do hereby proclaim the same to all whom it may concern; and I do specially direct all officers, civil or military, of the United States that they exercise vigilance and zeal in the discharge of the duties incident to such a state of war; and I do, moreover, earnestly appeal to all American citizens that they, in loyal devotion to their country dedicated from its foundation to the principles of liberty and justice, uphold the laws of the land, and give undivided and willing support to those measures which may be adopted by the constitutional authorities in prosecuting the war to a successful issue and in obtaining a secure and just peace.

IN TESTIMONY WHEREOF—

763.72/3761½b

The Secretary of State to Colonel E. M. House

WASHINGTON, *April 4, 1917.*

MY DEAR COLONEL: I send you a letter [33] which I received sometime ago from William J. Curtis one of the senior members of the firm of Sullivan & Cromwell who is, as you probably know, a very sincere Democrat and an ardent supporter of the President. I thought you would be interested in reading it but have not felt that I could send it to the President. What do you think?

It is needless to say how gratifying it is to see with what unanimous approval and enthusiasm the President's message has been received throughout the country. I believe it to be one of the greatest, if not the greatest state paper issued by a President of the United States. As you may imagine, I was personally gratified to see the President's attitude in regard to democracy as essential for a permanent peace in this world. You know how earnestly I have supported that thesis for the past four months. On every occasion when opportunity has offered I have urged it upon the President and endeavored to wean him away from a peace based upon force. Fortunately the recent Russian revolution relieved the Entente Powers of inconsistency in their attitude of waging a war in the interest of human liberty. I think it has worked out most splendidly.

Will you please return Mr. Curtis' letter after you have read it?

Faithfully yours,

ROBERT LANSING

---

[33] Not enclosed with file copy of this letter.

763.72/3761½c

The Secretary of State to President Wilson

WASHINGTON, *April 4, 1917.*

MY DEAR MR. PRESIDENT: I send you a draft of a proclamation combining the one prepared by me and the one suggested by the Attorney General.[34]

Frankly I do not like the idea of one proclamation because the two original proclamations are addressed to different classes, the one citizens; the other, aliens.

As a matter of preference I would issue the proclamation of the state of war at once on the adoption of the resolution by Congress and let the one dealing with enemy aliens issue on the next day. It seems to me that the force gained by a short proclamation such as the one addressed to the American people is lost by appending statutory provisions and regulations governing aliens.

I have, with this idea of two proclamations in mind, re-drafted the first part of the proclamation suggested by the Attorney General to fit the circumstance of the previous issuance of a proclamation declaring a state of war.

As soon as you can return the papers indicating which course you desire to follow we will prepare the same for signature.

Faithfully yours,

ROBERT LANSING

763.72/3762¾

President Wilson to the Secretary of State

WASHINGTON, *4 April, 1917.*

MY DEAR MR. SECRETARY: I think that two proclamations would be a mistake. They would make the impression that we had several agencies at work and did not know how to do the thing in right cooperation, or, else, that we were a little rattled and were firing proclamations in volleys!

The Single proclamation seems to me admirably constructed and I hope that you will have it perfected so soon as the Congress has acted, and published immediately.

I would be obliged if you would cooperate with the Attorney-General in the matter. He must act upon the proclamation through his Marshals and act as promptly as possible. He may wish to send copies at once to these officers.

Faithfully Yours,

W. W.

---

[34] Draft not printed; for the proclamation as issued, see *Foreign Relations,* 1918, supp. 2, p. 165.

763.72/3762½a

The Secretary of State to President Wilson

WASHINGTON, *April 4, 1917.*

MY DEAR MR. PRESIDENT: I send you the proclamation combining the proclamation prepared by this Department and the one prepared by the Department of Justice. I have countersigned it and it is ready for your signature immediately upon your approval of the Joint Resolution of the Senate and House which I assume will be given sometime tomorrow. I have, however, left the date of the proclamation a blank not knowing when the Congressional action would take place. As soon as you have approved the resolution and signed the proclamation will you return it to this Department and we will at once make it public.

Faithfully yours,

ROBERT LANSING

763.72/3798½

Colonel E. M. House to the Secretary of State

DEAR MR. LANSING:

.   .   .   .

In reply of yours of April 4th, I believe I would show Mr. W. J. Curtis' letter to the President if a favorable opportunity presents itself. It is in line with what I have been saying to him.

One of the best parts of the President's address was his statement in regard to democracy being essential to permanent peace and I know you are gratified beyond measure to have your idea brought to the fore so prominently at this time.

I am sorry I did not have a chance to talk with you and hope for better luck next time.

Sincerely yours,

E. M. HOUSE

NEW YORK, *April 5, 1917.*

[Received April 6.]

CORRESPONDENCE BETWEEN THE SECRETARY OF STATE AND AMERICAN AMBASSADORS IN EUROPE

AUSTRIA-HUNGARY

763.72/2251½

The Ambassador in Austria-Hungary (Penfield) to the Secretary of State

VIENNA, *November 4, 1915.*
[Received November 23.]

MY DEAR MR. SECRETARY: Pursuant to your request for frequent confidential and personal letters dealing with the general war situation in Austria-Hungary, not to be made part of the Embassy records, I beg to hand you the following communication dealing with topics that I would hardly feel like discussing in an official capacity. I shall try to send something by each pouch, and you may rest assured that it will be my endeavor only to write you upon matters that in my judgment have an illuminating value:

The return of Dr. Dumba excited little public attention. In one or two unimportant journals there were eulogiums of him as a fine type of devoted servant who had been sacrificed as a sop to an enemy country of Austria. Barring the bald announcement of his arrival in Vienna the influential newspapers said nothing, probably acting under orders of the Government.

It is within my knowledge that Dr. Dumba had a hearty reception at the Foreign Office, and that in a limited circle of Austrian society he is looked upon as a martyr.

It was widely printed in the Continental press as well as in *The London Times* that the Emperor had conferred upon the returned Ambassador an order carrying with it the dignity of Ritter (knighthood.) This was not the fact. Had the Monarch wished to mark his approval of the Ambassador's conduct he would probably have conferred a Countship or at least a Barony on him. To be a Ritter has little significance in this land of aristocratic rule, as it is the rank given usually to successful manufacturers and merchants, and to small functionaries. Dr. Dumba had an audience lasting nearly an hour with the Emperor a day or two after his return to the capital.

Dr. Dumba is not much in Vienna, because of his interest in a small castle thirty miles west of the capital, purchased just before he went to Washington. This he is now furnishing with a view of spending his time in the country.

In a discreet manner I have sounded certain officials of the Foreign Office with reference to Austria-Hungary's representative at Washington, and informally said that I could see a benefit coming from the early sending of an Austrian or Hungarian of high standing and ability as Dr. Dumba's successor—in no more effective manner could the proclaimed desire for a continuance of good relations be proven. My judgment seemed to meet approval.

But a day or two since the Secretary of Embassy in conversation with an Under-Secretary of the Foreign Office was given to understand that to send an Ambassador to Washington, so long as private communication with his Minister in Vienna was impossible, would be worse than useless. The Foreign Office believes it has a bona fide grievance against the American Government, preventing the Teutonic representatives from telegraphing by wireless in secret to their Governments, while the Entente representatives have every facility of peace times.

It requires little prescience to see that Turkey in Europe is to be the great theatre of war this winter, eclipsing probably all other "fronts" in dramatic if not in political interest. The entrance of Bulgaria into the conflict it is claimed opens the way to Constantinople for the Austro-German armies. Indeed, I have the opinion of a leading statesman of Serbia, stated with tears in his eyes and brought to Vienna by a Balkan diplomatist of importance, that the tardiness of the Allies in sending assistance to Serbia would have no other outcome than the crushing of his country—and this meant a free road to the Bosporus.

As I write the prediction is freely made that Nish, Serbia's city of second size and for a time the national capital, will be conquered by the Germanic armies within the next few days. In all human probability Belgrade has been permanently removed from Serbian rule, and will hereafter be administered from Vienna as a city of Austria-Hungary.

Why did Bulgaria, the racial and constitutional enemy of Turkey, enter the lists as the ally of Germany and Austria?

The answer is simple. England announced months ago that an Entente victory meant that Constantinople would be given to Russia. Every Bulgarian with whom I have talked has stoutly maintained that his country preferred to have Turkey in command at the Golden Horn and Dardanelles. Russia was not wanted at any price, not with the practical certainty of the eventual absorption of Bulgaria by

Russia once she was established in Constantinople. Besides, in Bulgarian opinion, Russia's setback was a serious one, from which there was no evidence that she could rally. Germany was victorious. And the King of Bulgaria was a German prince, be it remembered.

.   .   .   .

It is common knowledge, further, that a contributing influence in shaping Bulgaria's decision to join the Central Powers was the pessimistic articles in the London press, and especially in *The Times* regarding Britain's real position in the war. German agents gave a wide dissemination to the opinions of *The Times* and *The Daily Mail* through influential Bulgarian newspapers. These are the most potent reasons why Bulgaria joined a combination that included the arch enemy of his country, the Ottoman Empire.

Bulgaria is today in the fullest possible prominence and popularity in Vienna as the loyal friend of Austria. The Bulgarian Minister has been sought out in his modest apartment and made to take his place as the visible exponent of the new alliance. He speaks at public gatherings and seems to enjoy his sudden recognition as a diplomatist of importance. Yesterday the Bulgarian Minister of Finance and several colleagues from Sofia, who are visiting Vienna, were entertained at luncheon by the Baron Burian, who for the first time since he has been Minister for Foreign Affairs emerged from his domestic privacy to honor Austria's new friends. The German Ambassador assisted at the function, but the name of the Turkish Ambassador is not in the list of those breaking bread with the distinguished Bulgarians at the board of the Austro-Hungarian Minister for Foreign Affairs. The Emperor Francis Joseph has decorated all the members of the Bulgarian traveling party.

I feel that I should advise you of the understanding in military circles of the significance and potentialities of the Germanic "drive" through Serbia. This I can do most easily by relating the statement of a group of young German officers passing through Vienna a few days since on their way to join their commands in Serbia.

"We are en route to Constantinople," said one of them, "and in all probability shall be there by the middle of December. A few weeks after we see the Golden Horn it is our programme to go on to Egypt—we shall certainly be in Cairo by Spring. The military railway is practically completed through Palestine to the Suez Canal, and a German-Austrian-Turkish expedition can not be turned back."

While this statement had the frankness of a holiday-maker announcing his itinerary, it probably is the programme of the Germanic Empires and their Allies, and the Egyptian feature is assumedly the outcome of *pourparlers* in Berlin between the German general staff and the Ottoman statesmen who made the pilgrimage to the capital of William II a few months since.

It has long been known that the German Kaiser covets control of Palestine and the Holy Land, as a fruitful field for German colonization, an impulse for expansion that is denied to him in the Western Hemisphere by the detested Monroe Doctrine.

If the German Kaiser has the empire-building ambition with which he is credited, it is but reasonable to believe that he could supply a son to rule over the Turks, besides placing another on the throne founded by Mehemet Ali.

But does not King Ferdinand see himself in triumphal progress at the Kaiser's right hand to Stamboul to wear an imperial diadem? This is the belief of sapient persons in Vienna, and the Bulgarians have no hesitation in saying that this is to be a reward for espousing Austria's and Germany's cause at the psychological moment.

But Napoleon, who may be the Kaiser's model in world-conquering, gave thrones to his own kin before considering the claims of others, be it remembered.

I have [etc.]   FREDERIC C. PENFIELD

763.72/2252½

The Ambassador in Austria-Hungary (Penfield) to the Secretary of State

VIENNA, *November 11, 1915.*
[Received November 29.]

MY DEAR MR. SECRETARY: In both Austria and Hungary the Third War Loan closed a few days since, and it was successful to a remarkable degree. The aggregate figures as semi-officially announced are 5,500,000,000 crowns, which sum in ordinary times would be more than a billion dollars. The first loan, made when the Russians occupied the most of Galicia and were well through the Carpathians, was not very successful. The second loan, occurring a few weeks after Italy entered the fray, was but moderately successful. But this new loan, to run fifteen years and netting the holder about six and one-quarter per cent, has been a veritable triumph in financing.

Great corporations and firms and municipalities subscribed liberally. The Archduke Friedrich appears on the subscribers' list for 12,000,000 crowns, and his brother Archduke Eugen is down for 2,000,000 crowns. The Wiener Bank Verein claims to have placed a tenth of the loan with its clients.

If one could know the inside facts it might be discovered that the loan's success is more apparent than real, especially when intelligent Austrians assure one that perhaps half the gross amount has been arrived at by hypothecating every form of obligation having pecuniary value, including government pensions, public bonds of lower interest, and even certificates of the first and second war loans netting lesser revenue. It is well known that a goodly part of the loan was subscribed on what Americans would recognize as the "margin" plan. But, with all these deductions, the third loan is an unqualified success.

Probably two-thirds of the gross sum realized has already been spent, as it must have been by a Government whose direct war cost is stated to be $7,000,000 a day, and whose cash-box was practically empty when the war began.

From this time forward the war must be a test of resources quite as much as a trial of military strength, I feel. There are several raw materials of which Austria-Hungary is absolutely destitute, and were it not for Holland, Sweden and Denmark there would be little possibility of getting another pound of such vital requisites as cotton, copper or rubber. Bohemian cotton mills, those not already closed, have for months been running on half time, and were it not for the accommodating neutral neighbors of Germany and Austria all the factories would have closed many months ago. I hear of an enterprising speculator who last week succeeded in getting twenty carloads of crude rubber through from Holland and cleaned up a small fortune therefrom.

The Austrian Government has issued an appeal to the public to take all gold and silver jewelry, plate and other articles made of these metals to the mints for conversion into coin or bars. The necessity of strengthening the gold reserve and meeting payments abroad for goods for military purposes is given as the reason for the appeal. Persons who surrender gold or silver will receive full payment in bank notes as well as certificates of honor, it is stated.

By way of showing existing conditions at Fiume I extract these pertinent sentences from a letter of Consul Chase to me under date of the 5th instant:

"The Croatian authorities have placed an embargo on foodstuffs of every kind being taken out of that province. This affects Fiume very seriously, as much of the vegetable and garden truck used was brought from near-by Croatian places. It makes more serious the question of food supplies for Fiume. One paper advocates seriously the use of wooden shoes, especially for children, owing to the shortage of leather. In Fiume the question of the war seems to be partly forgotten and to have given way to the one great question of food. It seems the sole live topic of constant street discussion. This is the result of conditions, not theories. The city has been unable to procure over one-fifth of the grain promised long ago by the Government. At a meeting of the City Council the director of the gas plant reported that he would soon have to suspend unless arrangements were promptly made for more coal and other prime necessities. Gas is much used for heating, cooking and lighting. The director of the civic hospital at the same meeting demanded that an increase in the sum for the daily feeding and care of the inmates be provided or the hospital would have to be closed. Another member of the Council urged the importance of procuring potatoes before the price became too high."

This picture of conditions in a city at the beginning of winter forebodes great misery through scarcity of staples of existence before the cold season is half over. And what Consul Chase writes of Fiume must be true of Trieste and probably of every city and town in the Monarchy.

To one possessing adequate means the matter of existing in Vienna has thus far presented no very serious problem. But one has to exist in keeping with the possibilities of this war time, and not as he might prefer to live. There are scores of essential articles that cannot be had at any price, and nearly every obtainable article of food has doubled or even quadrupled in cost. Meats cost generally a dollar a pound, while pork and ham is even more expensive. And on two days in each week it is forbidden to purchase meat. Fish is practically unobtainable. The price of butter and eggs is practically prohibitive. Milk has decreased in purity and doubled in cost. Coal and coke have correspondingly advanced in cost.

As I have said, these conditions may be met by persons of means, but the masses can be in no position to purchase articles of food having these inflated values. Great self-denial has to be practiced on all sides by the millions, and the wonder is that poor people can find ways of existing. Yet the proletariat seems to do so, and without complaining. How much longer the people can go on living under these conditions I know not.

In this connection I think I may be permitted to tell a little of how my wife and I manage to live in this capital rent by conditions of war. More than a year since, perceiving that the conflict was to be a long and bitter one, we decided to guard against possibilities by having our own milk, butter, fowls and eggs. Being Catholics, we had, before hostilities began, been generous to an order of Sisters having a convent ten or fifteen miles out of Vienna. When it was seen that the war was to be a terrible one, these good souls were glad to lend us the small farm connected with their institution. There we installed a Tyrolean cow and a hundred hens, and the Embassy has had the products of these to a bountiful extent. Recently we have added forty live turkeys to our holdings—and famine can gain no foothold in our modest home. An attendant goes daily back and forth, and Vienna society has enjoyed many a laugh over the Ambassador's neutral cow and hens. Just now I am getting a thousand litres of gasoline from Roumania by favor of the Roumanian

Minister in Vienna. There are practically no private motors in commission in the capital, and none in the diplomatic service save those of our Embassy. Our wheat flour comes from Bucharest by the slowest imaginable train, through the personal influence of our colleagues in that capital.

Naturally members of this Embassy, as well as of the Embassy in Berlin, are living in a beleaguered land shut off by sea power and blockade from a good part of the world. There are many necessary things, perhaps not essential to actually keeping alive, that we want and should have. Certain articles not too bulky we used to get through from London, but that medium seems harshly to have been cut off. If the war runs a few months longer the Department, it seems to me, must consider plans for getting certain supplies if not succor to its diplomatic and consular servants loyally performing a burdensome duty in the Central Empires without complaining.

I have [etc.]   FREDERIC C. PENFIELD

763.72/2329½

The Ambassador in Austria-Hungary (Penfield) to the Secretary of State

VIENNA, *November 25, 1915.*
[Received December 17.]

MY DEAR MR. SECRETARY: In conversation a few days since with Baron Burián at the Ministry of Foreign Affairs I asked how "things were going," and inquired if there was any information in connection with the war that he could give me. He had just returned from a three days' conference in Berlin with Bethmann-Hollweg and Foreign Affairs Minister von Jagow.

"Extremely well in one way and not well in another," was His Excellency's reply. Then he explained at length that the Austro-German armies were carrying everything before them and that the Teutonic Powers were clearly victorious and that their present success should by right be recognized and made final. But instead of England and France admitting this, their responsible statesmen announce with unmistakable determination that they will continue the struggle until the last drop of blood of their people and the last coin is exhausted.

"This," admitted Baron Burián, "has no other meaning than a long war and a bitter one."

From no functionary of the Austro-Hungarian Government had I heard a statement half so discouraging to the prediction that peace was actually in sight. Only a few days prior to this conversation I had been visited by an American journalist, who has gained a place in the forefront of the correspondents as one behind the scenes at the German capital, and this writer reported that many people in Germany believed the war was practically over, with the crushing of Serbia and the securing of undisputed communication with Constantinople. This journalist claimed that in Berlin the opinion was held by many that the war would end by New Year's day.

When I read the speeches of Briand, Asquith and Bonar Law— and from my own judgment perceive that henceforth the conflict must be one of resources—I incline to the opinion that it will be a triumph of civilization if the war is concluded by New Year's day, 1917. And I pray that I may achieve no success as a prophet, for I wish the slaughter might end this day.

"One thing may be said," explained Baron Burián, "and that is that Austria-Hungary is popular with its war prisoners." The Minister mentioned the Russians in support of his assertion, of whom it is known that many thousands of these subjects of the Czar are so pleased with their captors that they want to marry and accept Austro-Hungarian allegiance as soon as the war ends. It may truthfully be said that this Monarchy is taking good care of its prisoners. During the past year delegates of the Embassy have on various occasions visited the camps at which the British, French and Italian civil internees and the Italian military prisoners are confined, without finding many things to ask for change or improvement in. Few complaints, with the exception of a lack of blankets and clothing, were communicated to the Embassy visitors and most of them were trivial and generally aimed at over-zealous officials who are inclined to show personal enmity to the peoples at war with Austria-Hungary.

I pretend to no military acumen and in no way am I in the confidence of the Teutonic Powers as to their military plans and aspirations. But, on the other hand, I feel that I understand natural and political conditions in the Near East and the Orient. As you are aware, my books upon Eastern countries have long been recognized as standard works.

In Vienna we listen to much talk of Germany's programme for invading Egypt, with the assistance of Austria-Hungary and Turkey, even eventually for wresting India from Britain's control. I have been told in detail by more than one person what the German Kaiser's plans are for sending an irresistible German-Austro-Turkish expedition through Palestine to the Suez Canal and thence to Cairo. Young officers from Berlin, passing through Vienna, have stated nonchalantly that they are en route to the Egyptian capital by way of Constantinople, and later that they expect to take part in the conquest of India itself.

To my mind this can be but the gabble of shallow persons, for without ships Germany couldn't capture India in a thousand years, and it is my modest belief that if members of the proposed Egyptian Expedition cross the Suez Canal in any numbers, and get to Cairo, that it will be as prisoners of war.

The talk about Egypt and India, in my judgment, is designed to conceal a programme much simpler of accomplishment, but if successfully accomplished one that will have an influence in India and elsewhere in Asia of stupendous importance. Briefly, I mean the stoppage of the Canal, the effect of which would be to create consternation throughout Ceylon and India, and if continued for any considerable period would probably be responsible for uprisings and revolts throughout Britain's possessions in the Far East, for it would be considered as tangible evidence that England was defeated in the war, perhaps had lost everything. India's 300,000,000 people are none too easily held in control even now, according to news from Bombay and Calcutta.

It may be Germany's programme to use her long-range ordnance from a point five or eight miles east of the Canal, with the result of causing the high banks between the Bitter Lakes and the Suez terminus to fall in and thereby block traffic indefinitely, and of making every steamer traversing the water-way a target for German gunners—meaning that a vessel obliged to proceed in the narrow channel could scarcely hope to successfully run the gauntlet.

I feel that you will forgive me for recording my simple opinion of what the real spring campaign of Germany and her allies is to be. If it becomes a serious movement against Egypt, I venture to predict that Lord Kitchener will be found in command on the west side of the Suez Canal.

Dr. Dumba has gone to his country estate a short way out of Vienna and will probably pass much of his time there. While his return to Vienna could not be regarded by anyone as an event of importance, he managed to engender additional dislike of America with his reports of official injustices from the Government and the snubs visited upon his wife and himself by society.

I think I should mention some of the difficulties we experience in getting world news in Vienna, especially news having an American importance. Nothing is printed in Austrian journals that could have an embarrassing effect upon the Teutonic Powers, nothing whatever. The censorship is a rigorous and super-partisan one, and the entry of foreign journals into the country is banned. No British or French information and little American news is published unless it possesses something damaging to the countries cited. I get the London *Times* over Holland, and the Paris *Herald* in a letter through the courtesy of Minister Stovall at Berne, but these publications are at least five days old when reaching Vienna, and frequently do not come at all.

Hence there are many events like the Dumba incident and the torpedoing of the *Ancona*, concerning which the Embassy is sublimely ignorant until information is received in the shape of a State Department instruction. I want to assure you that the Embassy staff is in touch with business practically all the time, and there is never delay in acting upon instructions. Taking account of the difference in time, it requires practically two days for a Department telegram to reach Vienna.

I am [etc.] FREDERIC C. PENFIELD

763.72/2347½

President Wilson to the Secretary of State

WASHINGTON, *5 December, 1915.*

MY DEAR MR. SECRETARY: This is a most interesting letter,[1] and it seems to me that many very significant inferences may be drawn from it as to the state of affairs in the Central Monarchies!

Faithfully Yours,

W. W.

763.72/2348½

The Ambassador in Austria-Hungary (Penfield) to the Secretary of State

VIENNA, *December 9, 1915.*
[Received December 29.]

MY DEAR MR. SECRETARY: At this time when American finance has become the world's bulwark; when German, French and even British exchange on New York has fallen to the lowest figures known, the occasion seems opportune to advise you of the present contrast between American credit and Austrian credit.

In normal times the dollar's parity in Austrian currency is about 4 crowns and 93 hellers. Today it is 7 crowns and 25 hellers. Stated simply this means that the American dollar enjoys a premium of practically 47 per cent.

The depreciation of Austria's money is a sore subject with officialdom, and many are the theories and conjectures brought forward to explain it. Most people say that the exchange on America is purely a matter of supply and demand, and let it go at that. I have no aptitude for finance, but my training makes me confident that the

---

[1] *Ante,* p. 642.

fall in the world's estimate of Austria's paper money is that it has but a small gold reserve to back it up, and this reserve is growing less with the efflux of every day. I have not seen a gold coin in circulation in Austria for years.

When the war began it was a fact that Austria-Hungary was in a bad way financially, as a sequel of two neighboring Balkan wars that had had a paralysing effect on business.

This paper currency of Austria, lacking adequate support in the bullion vaults, cannot have much purchasing power outside the Monarchy, naturally. Hence the Government and individuals are compelled to pay in gold or its equivalent for everything purchased abroad. Throughout the period of the war vast quantities of fibres, metals and foodstuffs have been purchased in neutral countries, and of course everything has to be paid for in gold. This means an unceasing drain, and this is my explanation of why the paper money of Austria-Hungary has lost its standing.

I have it on fair authority that financial officials of the Austro-Hungarian Government have been assigned the task of studying the creation of new monopolies to increase the public revenue immediately the war ceases, with instructions to obtain data from governments where the sale of matches and salt are monopolies. In addition to the intention of dealing with these requisites for the benefit of the public exchequer, the Austro-Hungarian Government is contemplating a monopoly in illuminating and lubricating oils. At the present time the refiners in Austria-Hungary have to pay a tax of 13 crowns per 100 kilogrammes on oils with a specific gravity lighter than .880. It is said that there is to be an increase in the selling price of cigars, cigarettes and tobacco—the Government's present monopoly, and that spirits and beer will shortly be made to yield greater revenue than at present.

At the outbreak of the war certain tax measures were inaugurated, such as an extra charge of two hellers upon the publisher's price per copy of an extra newspaper issue, and ten hellers on every prescription compounded at a chemist's shop. These taxes have created a vast amount of irritation, to say the least, by a public condemning them as trivial and unworthy of a great Power.

With the Serbian King in flight and what remains of his Government moving weekly from one place of safety to another, the inquiry of the hour in Vienna is "What is to be the future of Serbia?" Some argue that it will either be attached to the Austro-Hungarian Monarchy or at least be governed from Vienna. The wiseacres agree that Germany cannot want it; hence it must become Austrian, they argue.

An American medical man who visited certain prison camps in Hungary recently asked why Serbians were given liberties denied to

Russian prisoners, and was told by the officer in charge that it was because in a few months Serbia would be a part of Francis Joseph's Monarchy and it was wise to secure the good will even of men who now are prisoners.

Many people in Vienna pretend to believe that Serbia has ceased to exist as a political entity, for of course the country can have no other destiny than becoming a part of or a vassal of Austria-Hungary.

No one capable of dispassionately weighing cause and effect can believe this for a moment, for in all probability when the smoke of war is dispelled and the Peace Congress has finished its work Serbia will still be found on the map of Europe. But it will probably be a Serbia decreased in area, and under a dynasty unrelated to the house of Kara-Georgévitch, of which King Peter is the head. I cannot venture to predict who will be called to the throne, but with half an eye one can see that a German prince or Austrian archduke could hardly find the job an agreeable one.

There is some ground for believing that Belgrade and a strip of Danubian territory may be kept by Austria-Hungary for the sake of political glory, notwithstanding that in the anxious days immediately preceding Francis Joseph's declaration of war against Serbia his ambassadors at St. Petersburg and London declared "officially and solemnly" that their Government had no desire for territorial gain in Serbia and that it would not touch the existence of the Kingdom And it likewise is a fact that four days prior to the declaration of war against Serbia Count Berchtold, then Austro-Hungarian Minister for Foreign Affairs, emphatically assured the Russian Chargé d'Affaires in Vienna that his Government would not claim Serbian territory, that the Monarchy entertained no thought of conquest in punishing the people who inspired the assassination of Archduke Francis Ferdinand.

That was a year and a half ago and much water has flown [sic] beneath the bridges of Vienna since the words were uttered. But in all likelihood there can be no important change in the Government's intentions.

Naturally Bulgaria will expect territorial reward for her timely assistance to Germany and Austria-Hungary, and will want a goodly slice of Serbia. She will certainly demand Macedonia.

The greatest difficulty of governing Austria-Hungary in normal times is the presence of many discordant races, with more trouble coming from the Southern Slavs than all the other races combined, unless it be from the Czechs in Bohemia. It can scarcely be believed, consequently, that Austria-Hungary would wish to incorporate a purely Slav nation in its national family. But this Monarchy is sure to have a voice in the administration of Serbia, and probably a dominant voice in choosing its ruler, in my opinion.

The man in the street asks with some pertinence why Austria-Hungary feels that it must go further with its debilitating conflict, when the declared purpose of going to war was solely the punishment of Serbia. A land having at the outset of the conflict but four million people, of whom at least a quarter must be dead, to say nothing of the devastated country with its population bleeding and homeless, would seem to have received all the "punishment" it could stand.

Since these speculative remarks on the future of Serbia were drafted, I have been visited by Count Berchtold, whom I induced to express his opinions on the subject. He is firm in his judgment that for Austria-Hungary to have a dominant voice in administering Serbia would tend to subdue the rebellious spirit of the Southern Slavs dwelling in Hungary, Bosnia and Herzegovina, inasmuch as the race might then be controlled at its source, and further propaganda could not be spread among the kinsfolk of Serbians in Hungary. Count Berchtold states his belief that when the war is ended there will be fewer small Governments in Europe.

I am [etc.]   FREDERIC C. PENFIELD

763.72/2329½

The Secretary of State to the Ambassador in Austria-Hungary (Penfield)

WASHINGTON, *January 13, 1916.*

MY DEAR MR. PENFIELD: I have read with very great interest your confidential letter of November 25th. The remarks of Baron Burián show that he appreciates the spirit which dominates England and France, and I have noted with interest your opinion of the German program in regard to the Suez Canal.

I have given directions that the *New York Times*, The New York *World*, and the *Springfield Republican*, shall hereafter be sent to you in the pouch, in order that you may the more easily keep in touch with the situation in this country as it appears in the press.

I hope that you will continue to write me from time to time whenever you have matters of interest which you prefer to report to me confidentially rather than by dispatch.

Very truly yours,

ROBERT LANSING

874.001 F 37/44½

The Ambassador in Austria-Hungary (Penfield) to the Secretary of State

VIENNA, *February 21, 1916.*

MY DEAR MR. SECRETARY: King Ferdinand of Bulgaria has been in Vienna just a week today. His Apostolic Majesty Francis Joseph had made this astute Balkan ruler an honorary Field Marshal, and etiquette demanded that he come to thank in person the venerable ruler of Austria-Hungary.

I learn by underground wireless that the visitation had more to it than the ceremonious giving of thanks for the Marshal's baton, very much more. Only on the day of the visitor's arrival was he the guest of the Emperor. The rest of the time he has been at the Vienna palace of his brother, Prince Philip of Saxe-Coburg and Gotha. The function at Schönbrunn was of the conventional character, with the usual *dejeuner*, and the usual court officials present. The conventional decorations were conferred back and forth, the town was beflagged, and everything bore the impress of perfunctoriness.

I am assured however that the event lacked the usual attractive character of a royal visitation, and there was no warmth or enthusiasm observable anywhere in official circles.

Ferdinand has never been liked by Austrians, who believe that his shrewdness at times borders on sharpness of practice. Certain Vienna grandees claim that Ferdinand has always bested the Government of Francis Joseph, and that he is so shifty in his opinions and character as to be called the "Weathercock of Balkan diplomacy."

The real purpose of the King's visit is the parceling of Servia, and I have been favored from a dependable quarter with information as to Ferdinand's programme—which is to help himself to two-thirds of the conquered country, permitting Austria-Hungary to possess the Danubian section with a hinterland amounting approximately to practically a third of King Peter's former territory. The Sandjak of Novi Bazaar also falls to Austria-Hungary by the programme agreed in principle between the Ballplatz and the visiting sovereign. When in the *pourparlers* it was hinted that Ferdinand was hoping to receive a share greater than had been expected, Ferdinand's negotiators insisted that had Bulgaria not entered the war at the psychological moment Serbia would not have been conquered. And, besides, as the German Emperor was waiving his rights in the parceling of the conquered soil, Ferdinand, likewise a German prince, felt a moral right to any portion that Kaiser William might have been entitled to.

It looks as if Ferdinand's scheme for apportioning Servia will prevail.

Another mission of the Bulgarian ruler in Vienna presumably was the propitiation at long range of the Pope. It was the solemn promise of Ferdinand to his first wife on her deathbed that the Crown Prince Boris should be brought up in the Roman Catholic faith. The star of Russia in those days loomed brightly over the Balkans, and Ferdinand shocked the Catholic world by causing his heir to embrace the Orthodox faith, and especially did he shock the Holy Father and His Apostolic Majesty Francis Joseph, and all of his wife's powerful relatives.

During his sojourn in Vienna Ferdinand had the Papal Nuncio (a newly-created Cardinal, soon to return to Rome) celebrate a private mass for him, and rewarded this ecclesiastico-diplomatic personage by giving him a high Bulgarian order set in brilliants. Sapient persons claim to perceive signs that Boris's conversion from the religion of Russia may be looked for at no distant time, and further that a consort for the heir to the Bulgarian throne may be sought among the Archduchesses of Austria, of whom there are eight or ten charming girls in sight with no takers.

It was an unfortunate circumstance that a sister of Ferdinand's deceased wife is the Archduchess Zita, now the Crown Princess of Austria-Hungary. It is court gossip that from the heir to the Hapsburg crown and his consort the visiting monarch had a reception not remarkable for its cordiality.

. . . .

I am favored with advance information that the Austro-Hungarian Government has decided to immediately repatriate 10,000 Russian war prisoners whose homes are in that part of Russia now under the military rule of Germany and Austria. The purpose of this is to conserve the food of Austria, and to return these men to their homes in time to plant crops for the coming season.

It was most kind of you to order three newspapers to be sent to me through the State Department pouch. One of them—the *Springfield Republican*—has never come. Hence I am wondering if you would let me substitute the New York *Sun*, daily and Sunday, for the *Springfield Republican*?

I am [etc.]   FREDERIC C. PENFIELD

763.72/2664½

The Ambassador in Austria-Hungary (*Penfield*) *to the Secretary of State*

VIENNA, *April 15, 1916.*
[Received May 8.]

MY DEAR MR. SECRETARY: Probably there is not one person in the Dual Monarchy who is not heartily sick of the war and wishes for an early peace.

On all sides one now hears expressions bearing out the above statement, as well as the inquiry "How much longer can Austria-Hungary continue in the war?" That is the eternal question asked thousands of times daily.

Persons influenced by skepticism profess to believe that the resources of the Monarchy can last but another six months.

On the other hand I have the opinion of a member of the Hungarian Cabinet, reaching me second-handed, that Austria-Hungary can stand two years more of war before reaching final exhaustion. This oracle's optimism is doubtless colored by officialism and the fact that Hungary is always in a better material position than Austria.

Taking the mean of the many predictions reaching me it would be my prediction that Austria-Hungary can go through another twelve months on the resources of men, food and money at her command, but not longer.

Throughout the Monarchy every essential commodity is decreasing in supply with an attendant increase in price of everything required by humanity. The practice of economy months since assumed an acute form. The country is supposed to have no cotton or copper, and we now hear of an alarming shortage of sugar, beer, butter and all fats. Having in mind that the Monarchy is essentially agricultural, I have maintained in all reports to the Department that the people cannot be starved. But it is a very different matter for the Empire-Kingdom to be in a condition to indefinitely carry on war with all its special requirements and great waste.

The above brief statements sufficiently explain the popular wish for an early peace. But how it may be brought about no one has the temerity to announce. Baron Burian, the Minister for Foreign Affairs, started last night for Berlin for a conference with Bethmann-Hollweg. Although the object of the journey is not explained, the newspapers surmise that it may be in connection with the pacific attitude expressed in Mr. Asquith's recent speech.

It is common knowledge that the coffers of the Dual Monarchy are practically empty. At the present moment the plans for the Fourth War Loan are being groomed by the press, preparatory to formal announcement in a few days.

American exchange is ruling at 7 crowns and 85 hellers, meaning that for a draft on New York one receives in local currency practically the equivalent of $1.50 for the dollars.

It is estimated that this season's crops will have an acreage of but 70 per cent. of normal. And it is admitted that fields tilled by women, children and Russian and Servian war prisoners do not yield as bountifully as when worked by native men whose occupation has never been other than farming. There are few cattle and horses in the country, and consequently little manure for the properties of small farmers. Farming utensils have long been uncared for, and factories usually producing agricultural machinery are occupied with war munitions.

There is no longer talk of Austria-Hungary receiving an indemnity from any of her foes. Hitherto it was the mode to predict that Austria-Hungary would recoup the cost of the war by the indemnities received.

It seems more than rumor that Austria-Hungary means to weld conquered Montenegro and the Belgrade section of Serbia into the Hungarian government of the Monarchy. This would be a political step of decided merit, as it would unify under a single control most of the so-called "Sud-Slavs" a race believing it has political grievances and whose untiring agitation has ever been baneful. The assassination of the Archduke Franz Ferdinand at Sarajevo was claimed by many as directly traceable to the machinations of the "Sud-Slavs."

I am [etc.]   FREDERIC C. PENFIELD

763.72/2803½

The Ambassador in Austria-Hungary (Penfield) to the Secretary of State

VIENNA, *June 3, 1916.*
[Received June 19.]

MY DEAR MR. SECRETARY: I feel I should write you of the Austrian opinion on the subject of bringing the war to a close, a theme that a fortnight ago dominated the speech of almost every human being in the Habsburg capital. All seemingly wanted peace, while many believed it was certain to come in a few months and through the efforts of President Wilson.

Newspapers rang with these opinions, and the man in the café was as certain of early peace as the man in the street. That was immediately following the President's North Carolina speech.[2]

---

[2] For the text of President Wilson's remarks at Charlotte, N. C., May 20, 1916, see the *New York Times*, May 21, 1916.

Day by day I have seen the idea contract until the Austrian official now is far from certain that the Monarchy of Francis Joseph wants the war to end before some of the issues of the vast struggle have been settled in a way making a recurrence of strife impossible for generations.

There seem to be four reasons for this reaction of judgment, and are:

Firstly, the Fourth War Loan of Austria-Hungary recently closed succeeded beyond expectation, giving encouragement for fresh borrowing.

Secondly, the forces of the Monarchy are having such success on the Italian front and on Italian soil that many Austrians want to go on until the Archduke Eugen's armies are in Verona and on the plain of Venice and hated Italy is humbled.

Thirdly, the triumph this week of Germany over the British fleet in the North Sea gives color to the belief that the Central Powers in the not distant future may practically dictate terms of peace without submitting to mediation.

Fourthly, in certain circles there is growing fear that our President may not be the best mediator to bring benefit to a Monarchy peopled by a congeries of nationalities as is Austria-Hungary with its nine or ten different races. Many persons have been circulating the report that more than once President Wilson has stated his belief that it was the inherent right of every race to govern itself, and that this belief might conflict with the interests of a Monarch ruling Austrians, Hungarians, Bohemians, Slavs, Croats, and various other races. Some debaters of the peace proposal pretend that the King of Spain, half Habsburg and a Roman Catholic, and for the most part reared in Vienna, might give the Dual Monarchy a larger measure of advantage than the well-intentioned American President.

I know that some members of the Imperial Family, near relations of the King of Spain, are doing their utmost to eventually have the Archduchess Christina's son officiate as sole mediator; and failing this, then as joint mediator with America's Chief Executive. There seems to be but little real sentiment in favor of the Pope as a co-arbitrator. Austrians revere the Holy Father but prefer as peacemaker a potentate whose influence is more than spiritual.

It is widely published here that the President recently told the Peace League that each people should have the right to choose the form of its Constitution; and that small States, like the Great Powers, should be entitled to have their sovereignty and integrity respected. This may not be pleasing reading to a people conquering Montenegro, Albania, and a portion of Serbia in the present war.

A newspaper before me states that the number of orphans in Hungary caused by the war now exceeds 400,000, that misery is everywhere growing there, while the cry for peace is becoming louder. These statements only show that the masses of poor—the man with the hoe and the widow with numberless children to feed—want peace, and want it quickly. They care not through whose instrumentality it comes so long as it arrives in time to keep them from perishing.

I am informed from good sources that Germany is far more desirous of early peace than is class-ruled Austria-Hungary.

These rambling observations I am aware can have but little value, and are only sent in the performance of what I deem a duty—to advise you frankly of the current state of opinion in Vienna.

I am [etc.]   FREDERIC C. PENFIELD

701.6311/224½

The Ambassador in Austria-Hungary (Penfield) to the Secretary of State

VIENNA, *June 15, 1916.*
[Received July 5.]

MY DEAR MR. SECRETARY: As so many meddlers are showing a disposition to become interested in the subject of Austria-Hungary's representation at Washington, I want to repeat to you what I have said in a formal despatch—that this Government has no thought of sending an Ambassador at this time, and probably will take no action in that direction until the war is over. Baron Burian repeated this opinion to me but a few days since, after certain journalists had sought to interview him on the strength of a hint from Copenhagen that somebody in the Danish capital was arranging to have Austria-Hungary send a new Ambassador to the United States. The Minister for Foreign Affairs spoke approvingly of the service being rendered by the Austro-Hungarian Chargé, and smilingly added "It would not be easy at this time for us to get an Ambassador over to your country."

A foolish news message went forth from Vienna recently—a "Wireless Press despatch," whatever that means—to the effect that the Austro-Hungarian Government had "administered a rebuff" to me for attempting to intervene on behalf of two Czech ladies of Prague, Miss Masaryk and Mme. Benes, who have been imprisoned in Vienna for many months awaiting trial by the military authorities for treason. Of course I have "intervened" in no manner, nor been "rebuffed" in any degree. In fact I know of Mme. Benes only through the news despatch spoken of.

When I showed Baron Burian a clipping from *The London Times* he said it was mischievous and had absolutely no foundation of fact. He then volunteered the opinion that the case against Miss Masaryk was probably not serious, perhaps nothing more than that in her possession were found incriminating letters and documents left by her father when he fled the country. "Anyway," said he, "the affair has not the making of a Cavell case." His remarks gave the distinct idea that he looked upon the Miss Masaryk case as of minor importance, and this I learned and gathered without asking a question.

I am informed that the prisons contain many persons whom the Government for reasons serious or trivial object to having their liberty. Hence these unfortunates are not promptly brought to trial.

.   .   .   .

I am [etc.]   FREDERIC C. PENFIELD

763.72/2804½

President Wilson to the Secretary of State

WASHINGTON, *21 June, 1916.*

MY DEAR MR. SECRETARY: Thank you very much for having let me see the enclosed very interesting letter.[3] I dare say that it is now very much out of date because of the Russian successes and of the altered aspect of the fight in the North Sea.

Faithfully Yours,

W. W.

763.72/2832½

The Ambassador in Austria-Hungary (Penfield) to the Secretary of State

VIENNA, *July 3, 1916.*
[Received July 19.]

MY DEAR MR. SECRETARY: After studying conditions and circumstances recently developed by the war, I decide to take the risk of predicting, but only to you, that the chances are more than even that Roumania will this summer enter the conflict and on the side of the Entente.

From a person highly placed in Roumanian diplomacy I am assured that this is probable, and from an Austrian military expert I learn that the step is regarded by high officials of his Government as more than likely to ensue. If it comes to pass it will leave this Monarchy with an enemy on every foot of boundary with the exception of the small frontiers where Austria adjoins Switzerland and Germany. The unfortunate plight of the Monarchy of the Habsburgs with Roumania added to the list of enemies would then be more than obvious.

---

[3] *Ante,* p. 655.

Roumania has always sympathized with the Entente, but the desire to enter the lists was held in check during the months when the Austro-German armies were conquering Serbia and the Austro-Hungarian forces taking possession of Montenegro.

Now, with the irresistible advance of Russia into the Bukovina and the capitulation of Greece to the demands of the Entente Powers, the desire to participate in the struggle has had recrudescence, and the reports from Bucharest are that nothing short of a miracle can keep Roumania out of the war—most Roumanians believe that the psychological moment is near. The Roumanian King, it is known, is doing his utmost to have his country remain neutral.

It is Roumania's ambition to restore Transylvania to its former place in the Roumanian Kingdom. A year ago the report was current that the Emperor Francis Joseph had said that he would give no part of that region to Roumania as a peace inducement, and that Roumania could never by force take a meter of soil from him.

By the sale of cereals and other essentials to Germany and Austria, at enormous profit, Roumania's finances at present are in a position of enviable solvency.

I am [etc.]   FREDERIC C. PENFIELD

763.72/2833½

President Wilson to the Secretary of State

WASHINGTON, *27 July, 1916.*

MY DEAR MR. SECRETARY: Thank you for letting me see this letter from Penfield. He always says something that it is useful to keep in mind.

Faithfully yours,

W. W.

763.72/2834½

The Ambassador in Austria-Hungary (Penfield) to the Secretary of State

VIENNA, *August 1, 1916.*
[Received August 21.]

MY DEAR MR. SECRETARY: A month ago I advised you that the chances seemed to favor Roumania's entering the war when the psychological moment arrives, unless the Russian advance can be checked. Today the prospect of having Roumania as an additional enemy is the dominating topic in the capital, and it is good opinion that Austria-Hungary is decidedly menaced by the danger of having a new foe. The Austrian press seems already to be preparing the people for the possibility of this new phase of the world conflict.

The fear of Roumania as a combatant grows with each admission of new advances by Russia in Galicia and Bukovina. It is concrete fact that Russia has undisputed possession of 4,000 square miles of Austrian territory, and it is reported from Petrograd that the Czar will in a few days pay an official visit to Czernowitz, the capital of his "newly-acquired province of Bukovina." These utterances day by day increase the belief that astute Roumania will decide to come in with the "winner." In this connection it must not be forgotten that fifteen months ago Russia held three times as much Austrian soil as she now does, and that she was driven back to her own country.

Three days since Baron Burian told me that it was his judgment that when the Roumanians became certain that Russia was to be victorious over his country, Roumania would then come in. The Minister described the Roumanians as opportunists, who would strike at the moment when they believed they could secure territorial reward.

Yesterday I was visited by your friend Professor Lammasch, who volunteered the statement that the people of Roumania had much reason for disliking the Hungarians, as a consequence of the Hungarian Premier's long persecution of their compatriots dwelling in Hungary. Professor Lammasch said that Count Tisza's injustice to Roumanians had been harsh enough to almost decide the Roumanian Government to enter the fray.

Among military men the idea is growing that the Emperor Francis Joseph's next foe will be Roumania.

Considerable feeling is coming to the surface against the Bulgarian Government, since Austria-Hungary's request for troops to help combat the Russian advance in Galicia and Bukovina was denied. Thus far the press is silent on the subject, but individuals are expressing the opinion that King Ferdinand has again duped Austria.

If you could find time to glance at my despatch No. 1821,[4] dealing with "Austria-Hungary after Two Years of War," I would be pleased. Very great care did I take to present only reliable information and justified opinions in this strictly impartial report. It seems full of "meat."

I am [etc.]   FREDERIC C. PENFIELD

---

[4] Not printed.

872.142/63½

The Ambassador in Austria-Hungary (Penfield) to the Secretary of State

VIENNA, *September 2, 1916.*

[Received September 25.]

MY DEAR MR. SECRETARY: Being aware of your keen interest in the work of the American Red Cross, I feel warranted in departing from my strict official duty by writing you briefly on the subject of the American relief in Serbia.

Yesterday and the day before I had long conversations with Dr. Edward W. Ryan, a man prominently identified with the American Red Cross, and who has just returned from a lengthy journey in the interior of Serbia undertaken as chief distributor of flour and other staple foods contributed by American generosity.

Dr. Ryan assured me that there is now no necessity for sending food into Serbia, as the year's crops are so phenomenally abundant that grain is actually being shipped from Serbia into Austria-Hungary, leaving a sufficient supply for the needy of Serbia. He found willing recipients of American food everywhere, but he insists that there was no actual need for it.

Ryan I regard to be honest to the point of not readily making friends with persons whose knowledge of Serbian conditions is gained from newspapers. He knows Serbia thoroughly, speaks some of the language, and has the confidence of all grades of people there. He told me that it was his judgment that it would be more honest to relieve distress in the cities of America than to continue to send supplies and money to Serbia, where these are not really needed.

Dr. Ryan is making a detailed report on his visit to Serbia to your Mr. Ernest P. Bicknell, which to me is not half as convincing as what he has told me verbally.

For months whenever the Embassy has negotiated with the Ministry of Foreign Affairs in Vienna for the visits of Americans intent upon relieving distress and hunger in that portion of Serbia under Austro-Hungarian military control, we have always been assured that outside food was not required.

On the other hand, it is a fact admitting of no dispute, that this Monarchy's conquered territory in Montenegro and Northern Albania is filled with peoples suffering almost to starvation.

This information I write in confidence that my motives will not be misunderstood.

I am [etc.]

FREDERIC C. PENFIELD

763.72/2932½

The Ambassador in Austria-Hungary (Penfield) to the Secretary of State

VIENNA, *September 23, 1916.*

MY DEAR MR. SECRETARY: The announcement that the national taxes were at once to be increased so as to produce 750,000,000 kronen for the "service of the debt" on the four war loans already issued, was a blow surprising enough to render thinking Austrians almost insensible. The public had fallen into the way of regarding the war debt and its interest obligations as matters to be taken care of by coming generations or as a burden of which the Dual Monarchy was to be relieved perhaps by magic or the alchemy of old. Incidents of the new revenue schedule are an increase of 80 per cent. on land taxes, and of between 60 and 70 per cent. upon industrial enterprises.

Instructed from official headquarters, important journals are beginning to hint at the prospect of yet another chance to financially assist the Government at an alluring rate of interest. In all likelihood it will be found difficult to make this Fifth War Loan "go." But the patriotism of the people will be played upon with all the ingenuity of accomplished promoters. A fair sum may be realized, but probably nothing like the Fourth Loan, exploited before the great Russian and Italian drives had set in.

Meanwhile the currency of the realm is falling to the lowest value in history. At the moment American money commands a premium approaching 70 per cent., and it is good opinion that the premium will go to 100.

Two days after the announcement of the increased taxation, Roumania's declaration of war filled the cup of despondency to overflowing. The war proclamation angered the Austro-Hungarians almost as much as Italy's intervention had done.

I have dispassionately observed the gradual change in the public mood, from exaltation when the Central Powers were progressing in Poland a year ago and forcing Russia from Galicia, to the current state of mind describable by no other words than utter and complete despair. The masses are thoroughly tired of the war and would welcome peace in any form that took but a reasonable amount of territory from them. The people this week have been slightly roused from their despondency by the Austro-German-Bulgar victories over the Roumanians in the Dobrudja, but this for a day or two only.

Threatened with disaster by the Russian advance and with the Czar's armies almost at the gates of Lemberg, by the victorious progress of the Italians, whose cannon on the Carso are heard in

Trieste, and finally attacked in Transylvania by Roumania, Austria-Hungary's situation is nothing short of desperate.

I am just informed by the American Consul at Trieste that the Italian bombardment has destroyed the aqueduct supplying the city, and that ancient wells and cisterns are being resorted to for water. Should the only seaport of Austria fall to the enemy, it will be a hard matter for the Government to longer keep from the public the true condition of affairs. Italian journals state that General Cadorna's forces are certain to be in Trieste in a future not distant.

The fact that Hindenburg, aided by Mackensen, had been placed in supreme control of the armies of Austria-Hungary, and that nearly every commanding office in the forces of this Monarchy had been turned over to the Germans, has had a discouraging effect on every class of humanity. It was naturally a blow to the morale of the troops not easily to be rectified. There are stories of Hungarian regiments refusing to longer fight on the Italian front, when Russia and Roumania were attacking their own land.

A military expert tells me that Germany's chief purpose now is to save Austria-Hungary from catastrophe, and to this end hundreds of thousands of Germans have in the last month been poured upon the southeastern front and into the Balkans, and that a subordinate purpose is to prevent a rupture of rail communication with Constantinople.

Austria's food supply is being so rigidly conserved that the people have now three meatless days each week, with other days when fats of every sort and butter are forbidden. At best the remaining days are but half-portion ones. Because the army has commandeered two-thirds of the cows, there is a milk and butter famine in the land. The pinch this winter must be severe, and the fear is that March will find the people reduced to straits of real desperation. In all communications to the Department I have consistently maintained that starvation could not come to a Monarchy possessing the grain field of Hungary and Moravia.

Foreign newspapers are making much of the statement that in this Monarchy millions are reduced to eating horseflesh. As in Germany, poor people in Austria-Hungary have always consumed much horseflesh, but not half as much as at present. The price is half that of beef or mutton, and the article is claimed not to be unwholesome. The Government forces horseflesh shops to plainly advertise their character and to sell no other meat.

No less accentuated is the pinch arrived at in finding recruits for the army. Old men, boys, and men who have hitherto been pronounced medically unfit for service, are being called up. In my judgment such soldiers can do little actual fighting. Bear in mind that the Monarchy possesses various racial classes now considered too

dangerous to be sent into the field, like the Czechs, Bosnians, Herze-
govinians, and those of Italian blood. Even pulpit utterances seem
charged with teachings preparing the people for an outcome of the
war very different from what was expected a year ago.

In the Austrian division of the realm, where public speech is
unknown and any newspaper is little else but a governmental bul-
letin, one is only told *sotto voce* of the dark outlook. But in Hungary, where the Parliament is open and the press not so completely
gagged, existing conditions are discussed freely enough to make an
alien wonder if it is not criminal to advertise the plight that Austria-
Hungary is in after twenty-six months of fighting.

I am [etc.]   FREDERIC C. PENFIELD

GERMANY

763.72/2272½

The Ambassador in Germany (Gerard) to the Secretary of State

BERLIN, *October 25*[, *1915.*]

MY DEAR MR. SECRETARY: I was wrongly informed about Dumba—
he was not ennobled.

I had a long interview (over one hour) today with the Kaiser
alone. I am supposed by rule here not to inform anyone of what
he said—otherwise he will not receive me again or talk confidentially.
The audience took place at Potsdam—had a special car going down &
Royal carriage at station. Several ministers went down also to
present their letters of credence.

An article yesterday in Socialist paper *Vorwaerts* is rather bitter
about a new news service organized by the Government with the
avowed purpose of influence [*influencing*] elections after the war.
The *Vorwaerts* complains that this is a violation of the "truce" between Socialists & Gov't for the period of the war.

Much rejoicing quietly over the Balkan situation—I think they
have the King of Greece solidly on their side—here.

Having much trouble now to get British prisoners clothed in
German camps. It is a delicate matter to handle. Visited one camp
myself and had all prisoners about 1800 lined up with all the clothes
& blankets they possessed for my inspection.

.   .   .   .

Disturbances at Chemnitz continue—strongest measures taken &
military on guard. There seems more objection to high prices than
to being killed in the war.

The Germans are very bitter against our Embassy in Petrograd.
Also at the loan in America—& especially at the attendant banquets
to the loan commissioners—must say these banquets are not very
neutral.

I hope we are getting ready for defence—If these people win we are next on the list—in some part of South or Central America which is the same thing.

Yours ever

J. W. G[ERARD]

763.72/2274½

The Ambassador in Germany (Gerard) to the Secretary of State

BERLIN[, *November 1, 1915?*].

MY DEAR MR. SECRETARY:

. . . .

I and the staff are much obliged for your telegram permitting us to take vacations & allowing me to go home—I am afraid that unless the President or you wish particularly to see me that I had better stick here—we have very heavy work & the English would not understand it if I left. I am having a hard fight now to get the British prisoners clothed for the winter.

I think before the winter is out that we shall be on meat & butter cards as well as bread—already on two days a week meat cannot be sold and on three days pork cannot be sold.

However the effort to starve Germany out will fail. Unbroken military successes are reported: the Greek Minister (who is a son of Theotokis one of the Greek Cabinet) [said?] that Greece will never join the allies.

They are not yet taking men over 45 here & claim that they have plenty of men left. The actual losses to date are about 850,000 killed & three hundred and fifty thousand crippled. I have known cases of men being wounded & going back four and even five times. There is still absolute confidence in the result & I cannot see, myself, how Germany can be beaten.

I thought for a time that Bernstorff might be repudiated on the *Arabic* note,[5] but finally the matter was settled & a note sent me by von Jagow last week which I cabled you.[6] The trouble was that the Germans thought Bernstorff's note stated too boldly that in a conflict of evidence between the crews of the *Arabic* & the German submarine, he found for the *Arabic*.

I am afraid that after this war the Navy party will be all for attacking the U. S. A. in order to show the Navy is worth something—get revenge for the loans & export of arms, a slice of Mexico or S. America & money. And if Germany is successful in the war the country & army will agree to this raid.

---

[5] *Foreign Relations*, 1915, supp., p. 560.
[6] *Ibid.*, p. 603.

The Germans are incensed at Brand Whitlock *re* the Cavell case & are looking for an excuse to attack him & demand his recall. So if he is attacked you will know the reason.

The Foreign Office, particularly von Jagow & Zimmermann seem now much stronger with the Emperor, a good thing for peaceful relations: as both are reasonable men who do not let personal feelings or mob clamors run away with them.

.   .   .   .   .   .

Some German-Americans, including one Viereck either the editor of the *Vaterland* or a relation are talking of starting a club here which will be American (?) & declare against President etc.

This project will fail.

No great news this week.

Said that Germany gave 2 or 5 milliards & promises to Bulgaria.

> Yours ever
>
> J. W. GERARD

Just talked to a man who has talked yesterday to Tisza (Hungarian Premier).

Serbs wished for peace if they could keep their territorial integrity.

This was refused.

Italians rumored here to have asked peace. Answered that Austria is to have a free hand in dealing with them. Austria will not include Italy in any peace negotiations.

Austria is to get Tripoli & Malta if things go German way.

763.72/2275½

The Ambassador in Germany (Gerard) to the Secretary of State

> BERLIN, *November 9, 1915.*
> [Received November 23.]

DEAR MR. SECRETARY: Kirk duly arrived here.[7]

There have been uneasy movements among the people in Leipzig, a great industrial center, and the *Volkszeitung*, a Socialist paper there, has been put under permanent preventive censorship.

All these movements start with the question of the price of food.

The Prussian Junkers, however, are really benefiting by the war. They get, even with a high "stop price", three times as much as formerly for their agricultural products and pay only a small sum, 60 pfennigs daily, for the prisoners of war who now work their fields. They may in addition have to pay the keep of the prisoners, but that is very small. Camp commanders are allowed 66 pfennigs per head per diem.

---

[7] Alexander C. Kirk, secretary of embassy.

Some of the prison camps are still very bad. I visited one of these at Wittenberg yesterday.

There is much talk of peace and the shares of the Hamburg America Line and the shares of the Hamburg South America Line have risen enormously in price, from I think 56 to 140 in one case. This may be caused by an advantageous sale of some shares of the Holland America Line or by promise of a subsidy or by hopes of peace.

There is no question but that every man under 45 that can drag a rifle has been impressed for the Army, with the possible exception of men working in railways, munitions, etc.

Yesterday I noticed many women working on the road bed of the railway.

The new Peruvian Minister is named von der Heyde; his father was a German.

The Greek Minister still thinks Greece will stay out of the war. His father is one of the Zaimis cabinet.

The Germans are very glad to get rid of Brand Whitlock—they have been looking for an excuse for some time.

The dyestuff and other chemical manufacturers are getting quite scared about possible American competition. I hope the Democrats will give protection to these new industries and will also enact some "anti-dumping" legislation.

The German cities are adding to the general weight of debt by incurring large debts for war purposes, such as relief of soldiers' families, etc.

I have a shooting tract ¾ of an hour by motor from the door. On it there is a village which gives an index of the number in war and the killed. Inhabitants, 600. In war, 60. Killed, 8. Prisoners, 3. 1 only badly wounded, others all recovering and going back.

The former Turkish Ambassador who is against the Young Turks is living here. He is afraid to go back and also the Germans are keeping him in stock in case the Young Turks go out of power— also possibly to stir up trouble in Egypt as his wife is a daughter of one of the Khedives.

Yours ever

J. W. GERARD

611.626/½

The Ambassador in Germany (Gerard) to the Secretary of State

BERLIN, *November 22, 1915.*

DEAR MR. SECRETARY: I think that the dye stuff and chemical manufacturers here are getting worried over possible action by Congress in protecting new American factories in these lines either by raising the tariff or enacting anti-dumping legislation.

Follows a copy of a letter from C. von Weinberg, who, with his brother, controls the Cassella Company, one of the great dye stuff companies of Germany, which, together with five other companies, form the "Trust".

> Waldfried bei Frankfurt a. M.
> November 18th, 1915.

"My dear Ambassador,

In my last letter I told you that my people in the United States were trying to form a corporation to which our colors might be sent for distribution. Now today I have got a cable saying they have finally succeeded and that all American agents of the German color works have agreed to have their shipments addressed to the 'Republic Trading Corporation.'

Now this difficulty being removed I hope that there will be soon found a way to release the suffering American textile-industry.

> I remain, dear Excellency,
> very sincerely yours,
>
> (signed)   C. v. Weinberg."

Note Congressman Metz represents one of these companies, the "Hoechst", in America.

This letter would seem to imply that the German dye stuff manufacturers find that the embargo on the export of their goods will not compel the United States either to send in cotton or go to war with Great Britain and that the creation of a protected industry in America is a possibility to be faced.

Personally I hope to see the industry created and protected in America so that we can be independent of Germany in future, but if you desire German dye stuffs and can pass them through the English blockade, a mere intimation of coming protective legislation will, I think, induce the Germans to lift the present embargo.

Weinberg, the writer of the letter, is a personal acquaintance of mine.

The Germans claim that they defeated the English near Bagdad and drove them back forty kilometers.

Many intelligent rich persons here are expressing the fear that after this war the Socialist high price system, governmental seizure of food, control of raw materials, etc., will be continued and also that the owners of large landed estates will be compelled to subdivide them.

There are rumors which I don't believe that a new party is in process of formation which will really be a new incarnation of the Social-Democratic party, but which operating under a different name will be free from the disadvantages the Socialists now labor under, such as the mere burden of the name of Socialist.

Von Wiegand [8] just back from the Italian-Austrian front reports Italians will probably soon take Goerz and if then they take the mountain San Michele will force the whole Austrian line back. He calculates Austrian losses 80000 Italian 300000.

About twelve million Germans have to date been called to colors or work in factories for munitions.

Yours ever

J. W. GERARD

Nov. 23, 1915.

Reichstag meets Nov. 30th will probably pass law authorizing Government to call to colors men 18 to 50, both inclusive.

Would like to take advantage of your offer of vacation to U. S. but can't leave the English. They are not too well treated and naturally want three rooms and a bath and meals from Delmonicos— it's in the blood.

A prominent German-American banker has just now come in to tell me he was today fired from the board of directors of the big General Electric Co. because he was an American citizen. He is going to move to America—he says the hate against Americans is intense. Defense!!

763.72/2341½

The Ambassador in Germany (Gerard) to the Secretary of State

BERLIN, *November 30, 1915.*

[Received December 17.]

MY DEAR MR. SECRETARY: The enclosed statement of a Socialist and translation of an article from a Socialist paper may interest you.[9] . . .

My Greek colleague still thinks Greece will remain neutral.

Red Cross Doctor Schmitt just in from Servia says Belgrade was completely plundered.

Having lots of difficulty getting the Germans to give the English prisoners clothes. Camps usually good—found one bad one at Wittenberg, fierce dogs used on prisoners, etc.

Got out some beet seed for you—like pulling teeth, but Germans are beginning to see their embargo will not force us to go to war with England.

Hate of Americans worse than ever.

Germans are not resentful when I fight to get things for English prisoners, they only say they hope our Ambassadors are doing the same for Germans.

---

[8] Karl von Wiegand, Berlin correspondent of the New York *World.*
[9] Neither printed.

Much disappointment Dr. Snoddy's mission not yet permitted to work in Russia.

There was quite a Socialist demonstration in Unter den Linden last Sunday about noon. About 2000 or 3000 crying "Down with arms"—"Give us Peace" etc. Quickly handled by Police & many arrests.

Zimmermann just lunched here—says at Reichstag opening today, Hellferich, Treasurer, may possibly make a speech. Chancellor will wait until he sees how sentiment is & then cut loose, probably in about 10 days.

Yours ever

JAMES W. GERARD

763.72/2342½

The Ambassador in Germany (Gerard) to the Secretary of State

BERLIN, *December 2, 1915.*
[Received December 17.]

MY DEAR MR. SECRETARY: I have just received your personal letter of Nov 12th.[10] Thank you for what you say about my work.

Of course I should like a vacation but as I have written you the English would be sure to criticize. Meanwhile I have a shooting place which I can reach in ¾ hour from the door by auto—eat some lunch on the way down and murder pheasants and roebuck one or two afternoons a week. This keeps me in fair condition.

Night before last, while taking a walk, I ran into quite a demonstration—very quiet people—I asked several men why they were demonstrating—two or three refused to answer—finally one said "We have enough of this silly war and days without meat." I said where are you going—he said "Wherever they drive us"—There were several thousands in the demonstration. All night a lot of mounted police were outside this embassy—whether they feared a demonstration here or against the Chancellor, whose palace is across the square, I don't know. At any rate there was no crowd in the Wilhelmplatz that night. Last Sunday, as I had already written you, there was another demonstration on Unter den Linden.

The people are undoubtedly getting a little restless and the food question brings the war home to them. Probably there will soon (3 mos.) be a shortage of coffee—the Germans are great coffee drinkers, especially in the middle classes. And great eaters—as one of my brothers said "it is not true that the Germans eat all the time—they eat all the time with exception of five times a day when they take

---

[10] Not printed.

their meals." Any cutting off of food is resented by every German. Personally I think the country can hold out.

Gus. Roeder of the New York *World* is here to write on the industrial and general situation: I think you will find his reports excellent—he is a great observer.

Hans Winterfeldt, a German American (American citizen born in Germany) has just come in to tell me he is resigning from 20 directorates and leaving the country—he is being driven out solely on account of his citizenship. He was managing director of the National Bank of Germany, director of the General Electric Co., etc. This shows how the international hate has attacked business men, usually rather liberal.

Maximilian Harden gives a lecture Monday next. He has a great following & if allowed will say something about peace.

Yours ever

J. W. GERARD

763.72/2343½

The Ambassador in Germany (Gerard) to the Secretary of State

BERLIN, *December 7, 1915.*
[Received December 21.]

MY DEAR MR. SECRETARY: All of a sudden the people are beginning to talk peace. The Reichstag members, all now in town, are bolder, and many not Socialists are talking peace. These joining with the Socialists (but not openly) will force the Chancellor to make some statement about peace and as to what Germany is fighting for. The Chancellor will follow the sentiment of the Reichstag whatever it is on the day he makes his speech. That will be before this reaches you. Quiet meetings of Reichstag members are being held.

Butter is scarce; women rush the shops.

The copper roof on a new building near here is being taken off.

.   .   .   .

Hindenburg is out with an interview saying it is not yet time to make peace—that France wants Alsace-Lorraine & England will not make peace. This is Government order to try to stop peace movements in Reichstag and elsewhere.

I suspect Germans and Japanese of getting together.

Yours ever

J. W. GERARD

763.72/2344½

The Ambassador in Germany (Gerard) to the Secretary of State

BERLIN, *December 14, 1915.*
[Received December 29.]

DEAR MR. SECRETARY: I think the German Press has received orders to step softly on the von Papen–Boy-Ed recall.[11] The greatest danger now lies in Austria, and over the *Ancona* note.[12] Here there is a large body of manufacturers, ship-owners, etc. who at the last moment declare themselves against war with the U. S. A. and use their influence to that end. But in Austria with no such interests to help toward peace . . . almost anything may happen. However, pressure from here may be brought to bear.

Von Jagow claims that, in the case of both diplomats and military and naval attachés, the nation to which they are accredited has the right, without assigning reasons, to reject them, but that once accepted the reasons must be given which have made them *personae non gratae*, if their recall is asked. I think Germany will not send successors to von Papen and Boy-Ed even with safe-conduct; whether they will ask the recall of our attachés is another question, not yet decided.

Von Jagow also tells me confidentially that Rintelen was sent to America to buy up the product of the Dupont Powder Company, and that if he did anything else, he exceeded his instructions.

The night of the day of the peace interpellation in Reichstag a call was issued by placards for a meeting on Unter den Linden, but the police surrounded Unter den Linden in force and the meeting was impossible. I walked through the lines, but found very small crowds outside. Most of the men are in the war and the Socialists are terrorized. I was present in the Reichstag; there was quite a row. The Socialist, Scheidemann, made a quite moderate speech, the Chancellor answered, and then the majority endeavored to close the debate. The Socialists made a big row, and finally the majority gave way, and Landsberger was allowed to speak again for the Socialists. He made a very reasonable speech, saying that the Socialists would not allow Alsace-Lorraine (where only 11 per cent of the population was French) to go back to France. He also said "the Disunited States of Europe were making war to make a place for the United States of America."

Shop-people, etc., in Berlin with whom I have talked are getting sick of the war.

.   .   .   .   .   .

---

[11] See *ante*, pp. 83–93, and *Foreign Relations*, 1915, supp., pp. 939–941, 947 ff.
[12] *Ibid.*, p. 623.

I hear rumors that Germany is trying, through its Minister in China, to come to an understanding with Japan and Russia.

The banks are sending circulars to all safety-deposit boxes and are trying to get all holders to give up their gold.

I expect newspaper attacks etc., here on this Embassy and on me, in retaliation, as it were, for the recall of Von Papen and Boy-Ed.

The hate of Americans grows. An American clergyman has just told me the German church body has refused to receive an American church deputation and has written a very bitter letter.

Von Jagow has told me no new military attaché will be sent to America. The naval people have not yet decided.

If safe conduct is offered Germany for new attachés the German Government will be in rather an awkward position, if they ask recall of our attachés here.

Yours ever

J. W. GERARD

763.72/2345½

The Ambassador in Germany (Gerard) to the Secretary of State

BERLIN [, *December 20, 1915?*].

[Received January 4, 1916.]

MY DEAR MR. SECRETARY: The Chancellor sent for me early Saturday morning. He complained again bitterly that he could not communicate in cipher with Bernstorff. He said, How can I arrange, as I wish to, in a friendly way, the *Ancona* and *Lusitania* cases, if I cannot communicate with my Ambassador. He said, Why does the United States Government not allow me to communicate in cipher? I said the German Foreign Office tried to get me to ask for a free pass to America for the notorious Rintelen, saying he was going on charitable work for Belgium; perhaps the American Government thinks you want to communicate with people like that. He then changed the subject and spoke of the feeling against Germany in America, and said that after the war there would be bad feeling here against America. I said that that idea had been expressed by a great many Germans and German newspapers, and that I had heard privately from a great many Americans that if Germany intended to make war on America after this war that perhaps we had better go in now. He then became very amiable and said war with America would be ridiculous. He asked why public opinion in America was so against Germany. I said things like the Cavell case made a bad impression in America and that I knew the Kaiser even was against the *Lusitania* torpedoing. He said, how about the *Baralong*.

I said I didn't know, but first, there is no doubt about the fact that Miss Cavell was shot, and second, that Miss Cavell was a woman, and the crew of the German submarine men. I then took up in detail questions of treatment of British prisoners and said it could not go on, and we talked over this. He kept calling me "his dearest Ambassador," and I think he is worried over the *Ancona* note.

Speaking of the *Baralong* case,—I think Senator (State) Isaac Barth, of Albuquerque, New Mexico, can tell something interesting about this. As I remember it, he told me in Berlin that in Liverpool he met some of the crew of the *Nicosian* who claimed they saw the submarine which sank the *Arabic* in turn and in sight of the *Arabic* (or its place of disappearance) sunk by an English boat which at first flew the American flag and had the American colors or arms on a large board hung over the side; as the submarine which sank the *Arabic* finally turned up, the story of the *Nicosian's* crew evidently had to be changed.

. . . .

Dr. Ohnesorg, U. S. N., and Osborne back from inspecting camps report bad conditions; they were not allowed (contrary to our treaty) to talk out of hearing of camp officers to the prisoners in Limburg Camp. These prisoners are 2000 Irish, and the reason, of course, for the refusal of the usual permission is that the Germans through the notorious Sir Roger Casement have been trying to seduce the Irish, and do not want the soldier prisoners to tell us about it. I have learned through other sources that the Germans seduced about 30 Irish. I told von Jagow what I had learned and asked what the Germans had done with these victims,—whether they were in the German army; he said, no, most had been sent to Ireland to raise hell there. I suppose they were landed from submarine; they may be dynamiting in America.

. . . .

I think there will be a stormy attack by Germans soon on West front with Turks in it. Also Zeppelin on London.

Yours ever

J. W. G[ERARD]

———

763.72/2346½

The Ambassador in Germany (Gerard) to the Secretary of State

BERLIN, *December 28, 1915.*
[Received January 13, 1916.]

MY DEAR MR. SECRETARY: I am very glad to hear Colonel House is coming over. There are many things I want to tell the President and you but which I do not dare commit to paper.

. . . .

My impression is that the Austrians will eventually give in, owing to pressure from here, on the *Ancona* business and I have already cabled you I thought the present a good time to force the settlement of the *Lusitania* question. I think the German Government will allow Ford or any of his angels to come here but the Peace Ark seems pretty well wrecked.

Provincial and small newspapers are much more bitter against America than the larger ones. I shall try to get and enclose herewith a very bitter article in the Cologne *People's Gazette* (not the Cologne *Gazette*) an organ of the Catholic party.

I am sending by the courier the general economic view you requested.

Von Jagow told me the other day that he thought the feeling here against America so bitter that eventually war would be inevitable. Today he seems more optimistic. Possibly a question of digestion. The Kaiser is laid up—only a boil on the neck.

Yours ever

J. W. G[ERARD]

763.72/2356½

The Ambassador in Germany (Gerard) to the Secretary of State

BERLIN, *January 3, 1916.*

[Received January 17.]

DEAR MR. SECRETARY: We are getting vague and conflicting reports in the newspapers here about the sinking of the *Persia*. There seems to be no end to this business. Perhaps it is best to have the inevitable come now. The hate of America has so grown under careful governmental fostering that I am quite sure that we will be the first attacked after the war. So that if it is to come, it had better come now when with a certain fleet we would start with command of the seas, making it impossible for agitators, dynamiters, and spies to be sent to Mexico and South America and into the U. S. A. through Canada and Mexico. From the highest to the lowest I get intimations that at the first chance America will be attacked.

Nothing new has occurred since my last letter. There is still a spirit of confidence in ultimate success, amply justified, it would seem, by the military situation.

A lot of dyestuff mysteriously left Germany, in spite of the embargo, lately, and got to Holland, billed to America, where it remains, awaiting a permit from the British. Perhaps the Germans are getting worried about the possible building-up of the industry at home. The profits of the German dye-stuff "trust" are certainly great enough to tempt the trust to do anything to keep the monopoly. Hardly a company pays less than 24 percent dividends.

New Year's Day, on invitation of the Commandant of Ruhleben, where 4000–5000 English civilians are interned, the entire Embassy attended a Christmas pantomime given by the prisoners. Very well done; costumes and scenery all made in the camp. Yesterday the Commandant and the second and their wives all lunched here. All this helps on prison questions.

The Kaiser still laid up with a boil on his neck.

J. W. G[ERARD]

611.626½

The Secretary of State to the Ambassador in Germany (Gerard)

WASHINGTON, *January 11, 1916.*

DEAR MR. GERARD : I have read with considerable interest your personal and confidential communication of November 22d, 1915 and have sought to ascertain the real situation as to dye-stuffs and chemicals in this country before I made reply.

It seems to me that the manufacturers of dyestuffs and chemicals in Germany have every reason to fear legislation here. The situation is becoming so difficult for the manufacturers in the United States and so many different classes are being affected by the shortage of dyes and chemicals that legislation protecting these industries will receive every favorable consideration. Many Democrats feel that the Government should take immediate steps towards protecting people who were willing to invest money in plants to help meet the emergency. The output of dyes by the first of the year shows, I am informed, an increase of about six hundred per cent.

With best wishes [etc.]   ROBERT LANSING

763.72/2470½

The Ambassador in Germany (Gerard) to the Secretary of State

BERLIN, *February 8, 1916.*
[Received February 23.]

MY DEAR MR. SECRETARY : I was very glad to see Colonel House in Berlin, for many reasons and especially that the President and you may get his view of the situation here. He had long talks with the Chancellor, von Jagow, and Zimmermann and also met Dr. Solf, the Colonial Minister, von Gwinner, head of the Deutsche Bank, Gutmann of the Dresdner Bank, and Dr. Rathenau, head of the General Electrical Company and many corporations, who is now engaged with the General Staff in providing raw materials for Germany.

I think Zimmermann hollered at the Colonel—he certainly tried to scare me.

Morgenthau was here a day. I took him to see von Jagow, and through some Germans he met Zimmermann. Of course having a political talk with Zimmermann was technically an invasion of my bailiwick, but I welcome anything that might clear the situation.

Von Jagow said that Germany had never given any guarantees about submarine war, but had only stated that certain orders had been given to submarine commanders. He said Germany reserved the right to alter these orders—at any time.

Morgenthau says that Zimmermann asked him if the German-Americans would not rise in rebellion in case of war.

The enclosed from the [London] *Times* of February 6th [*4th*] [13] confirms one thing stated to me in a certain interview, which interview has doubtless been related by now by my brother-in-law, Marcus Daly, to the President.

I think the Germans are getting short of copper and nickel, especially the latter. Copper lighting rods of churches have been taken and an effort was made to take the brass reading desk in the American church and the fittings in the Japanese Embassy.

I think from underground rumors that the Germans and the propagandists will endeavor to embroil us with Japan.

.   .   .   .

There was a well-defined report that Germany would issue a manifesto stating that enemy merchant ships would be fired on without notice and this because of orders alleged to have been found on British ships ordering merchant ships to fire on submarines at sight.

The Chancellor told me Germany was ready for peace—but that all his emissaries had met with a cold reception in the allied countries of France England & Russia.

The other enclosure [14] shows a slight concession to the Socialists & the general regulation as it stood might interest Labor Leaders, of intelligence, like Gompers.

> Yours ever

> J. W. G[ERARD]

---

[13] Not printed; quotes the Cologne *Gazette* to the effect that the war is one between governments of lawyers at London, Paris, and Rome, and governments of national kings at Berlin, Vienna, Budapest, and Sofia.

[14] Not printed; an article from the *Berliner Tageblatt* of February 8, 1916, reporting that the Prussian Ministry of Railways was no longer prohibiting railway employees from taking part in Socialist Party activities.

763.72/2471½

The Ambassador in Germany (Gerard) to the Secretary of State

BERLIN, *February 16, 1916.*
[Received March 6.]

DEAR MR. SECRETARY: No great news this week. By this mail you get copies of the Memo regarding armed merchant ships.[15]

There is a fight against the Chancellor—started in the home of the Junkers, the Prussian Chamber. The powerful liberal papers are jumping hard on the disturbers and the Chancellor hit back quite hard. These Junkers are demanding unlimited submarine war and are stirred up by von Tirpitz. It is one of their last kicks; as soon a real suffrage will have to be introduced in Prussia. The Chancellor foreshadowed this in opening this Prussian Chamber; *hinc illae lachrymae.*

The visit of Colonel House here was undoubtedly, from this end, a success; and I am glad that he can give the President and you a fresh and impartial view. After nearly three years my judgment is probably warped.

March 1st we go on a milk and butter card regime. I have put the Polish question (food) up to Zimmermann, and asked informally if proper guarantees against the direct or indirect taking of food and money from Poland will be stopped, if relief is sent; no answer yet.

Yours ever

J. W. G[ERARD]

763.72/2473½

The Ambassador in Germany (Gerard) to the Secretary of State

BERLIN, *February 29, 1916.*

DEAR MR. SECRETARY: I had the grippe, went to Partenkirchen for a few days, but the first night in country air since July 1914 was too much for me and filled me with such energy that I tried skiing, fell down and broke my collar-bone,—came to Berlin and can sit at my desk but am very uncomfortable.

I think Germany was about to offer to sink no merchant ships without notice and putting crews etc. in safety, if England would disarm merchant ships, but now, since the President's letter to Stone,[16] both the Chancellor and von Jagow say they are convinced that America has a secret understanding with England and that nothing can be arranged.

---

[15] See *Foreign Relations*, 1916, supp., p. 187.
[16] *Ibid.*, p. 177.

It is claimed by the Foreign Office here that you said to von Zwiedenek that you approved of Germany's recent memorandum *re.* disarming merchant ships.[17]

Captain Persius points out in to-day's *Tageblatt* that it is not submarines alone that are now, without notice, going to sink armed merchant ships, but cruisers etc. will take a hand.

It is reported that the Kaiser went to Wilhelmshafen to warn submarine commanders to be careful. It is reported that submarines will hunt in pairs, one standing ready to torpedo while the other warns. It is also reported that the German losses at Verdun are small as artillery fire annihilated enemy first. I think an attack will be made now in another part of the front.

Germany has forbidden the import of many articles of luxury; this is to keep exchange more normal and keep gold in the country. This will continue after the war—probably.

Yours ever

J. W. G[ERARD]

763.72/2551½

The Ambassador in Germany (Gerard) to the Secretary of State

BERLIN, *March 7, 1916.*

[Received March 23.]

MY DEAR MR. SECRETARY: Some newspaper men just in from Verdun report the Germans saving men,—losses small,—going at it with artillery, probably over 1000 guns, and making a slow and almost irresistible push. Some military attachés think there may be a strong attack somewhere else on the front.

This Verdun attack was undoubtedly made to keep Roumania out.

I think the food question here is getting very serious, but before they are starved out they will starve six million Belgians, eleven million Russians and Poles, and two million prisoners: so that after all this starvation business is not practical.

There was a Grand Council of War last week at Charleville to determine whether von Tirpitz's proposition, to start an unlimited submarine blockade of England, should be started or not,—i. e. sink all ships, enemy and neutral, at sight. Falkenhayn was for this, the Chancellor against, and von Tirpitz lost. The decision, of course, was made by the Emperor.

Great advertising efforts are being made on the question of the Fourth War Loan. It will, of course, be announced as successful.

---

[17] *Ibid.*, p. 163.

There are undoubtedly two submarine parties in Germany and, if the President loses out, there may be an unlimited blockade of England.

I think Germany, as at present advised, is willing, if merchant ships are disarmed, to agree to sink no boats whatever without warning and without putting passengers and crew in safety. The Admiralty approves of this.

Von Wiegand publishes an article in the *Lokal Anzeiger* on America in which he makes some statements no loyal American should make just now.

As B. Franklin said: "We must all hang together or we shall hang separately."

Yours ever

J. W. G[ERARD]

763.72/2552½

The Ambassador in Germany (Gerard) to the Secretary of State

BERLIN, *March 14, 1916.*
[Received April 4.]

MY DEAR MR. SECRETARY: As I cabled you, I read your Zwiedenek memorandum [18] to von Jagow. He said it was too long to remember and asked for a copy. Government people here are convinced that you were in favor of the German side of the armed merchantmen controversy but say that the President came home from a trip and ordered you to switch. I don't think however they are going to start any controversy with you on the matter.

The "illness" of von Tirpitz is announced. I think it means his resignation, and have just so cabled you, although it is possible that his resignation may never be publicly announced.

For one thing—the K————. and army people began to think it was a bad principle to introduce to have any officer or official appealing to cheap newspapers and the "man in the street" in a conflict with superior authority.

I heard that at Charleville conference both the Chancellor and von Jagow said they would resign if von Tirpitz's policy of unlimited submarine war on England was adopted.

Verdun is still being attacked and will be anyway until the 22nd. when the subscriptions to the War Loan close.

The Catholic or Centrum party is very much against the U. S. A., and the President. It is said the cause for this is that the Catholics in America are against the President's Mexican policy.

---

[18] *Foreign Relations*, 1916, supp., p. 202.

The food question becoming really acute—the village people are about starving in some sections and are not as well off as the people in the big towns; it being the policy to keep the people in the cities as satisfied as possible in order to prevent riots, demonstrations, etc.

Some Germans have asked me if the sending of a German Colonel House to America would be agreeable to the President. Probably the Envoy would be Solf, and he could informally talk to President and prominent people. How about this? If sent he would require a safe conduct from England and France.

I hear the submarines now are mostly engaged in mine laying, at the Thames mouth, etc.

Yours ever

J. W. G[ERARD]

763.72/2553½

The Ambassador in Germany (Gerard) to the Secretary of State

BERLIN, *March 20, 1916.*
[Received April 8.]

MY DEAR MR. SECRETARY: Events are beginning to march. At first von Tirpitz's "illness" was announced, then came his resignation.

Yesterday was his birthday and a demonstration was expected, there were many police out, but I could see no demonstrators. The row may come in the Reichstag.

There are two sources of danger. First—A failure at Verdun and the new food regulations may make people ready to accept Tirpitz's guarantee that if he is allowed his way the war can be won and ended. He has a large following already who favor this plan. Second—There are some Reichstag members and others who think the Tirpitz people can never be re[con]ciled unless there is a new Chancellor.

The Chancellor sent for me Friday. I did not get his particular point, if he had any. I have cabled a summary of the conversation.[19]

In addition I assured him the President did not want war with Germany. I told him of Root's and Roosevelt's speeches and said that of the three parties in America the President and the Democrats alone stand for peace.

I think the Chancellor wants to keep peace with America and also wishes to make a general peace. He talked or rather I talked, a little about terms. He still wants to hang on to Belgium but I think will give most of it up—but is fixed for an indemnity from

---

[19] *Ibid.*, p. 207.

France. The loss of life here is affecting everyone, the Chancellor is a very good man, and I think honestly desires an honorable peace.

Potatoes are restricted, from to-day, 10 pounds per. head in 12 days—not much—bacon and lard practically not to be had, butter only in small quantities and meat out of reach of the poor.

I told the Chancellor I thought a great source of danger to the good relations of Germany and U. S. A. was in Mexico, that if we had trouble there, had to raise a large army and roused the military spirit at home, that the President might find it hard to hold the people. This struck him as a new view as most Germans think that Mexican troubles are to their advantage, and I am sure Villa's attacks are "made in Germany".

I shall not come home, both the Chancellor and von Jagow have begged me not to go.

The enclosed [21] about a Japanese book may interest those members of Congress who are against preparedness.

Just heard that a Dane who sold 1,000,000 tons of manganese, which he had in Brazil, to Levino & Co. of Philadelphia for U. S. Steel Co., was arrested here and in jail three days. The charge was that the Manganese was used in steel which was used for munitions against Germany.

Enclosed is a speech made in Prussian Landtag by a socialist.[21]

Yours

J. W. G[ERARD]

_____

763.72/2615½

President Wilson to the Secretary of State

WASHINGTON, *7 April, 1916.*

MY DEAR MR. SECRETARY: Thank you for letting me see the enclosed.[22]

It is probably too late now to answer Gerard's question about the advisability of sending a special representative of the German Government here (a "German Colonel House"), but if there should be a renewal of the suggestion or Gerard should for any reason remind us of it I think we should say that we would of course welcome any messenger of friendly counsel the Emperor might think it desirable to send,—without indicating any judgment or desire of our own about the matter.

Faithfully Yours,

W. W.

_____

[21] Not printed.
[22] *Ante,* p. 680.

763.72/2663½

The Ambassador in Germany (Gerard) to the Secretary of State

[BERLIN,] *April 11, 1916.*
[Received April 25.]

MY DEAR MR. SECRETARY: The recent sessions of the Reichstag have been lively. Liebknecht caused a row on several occasions. Once by interrupting the Chancellor to imply that the Germans were not free, next to deny that the Germans had not wished the war, and another time by calling attention to the attempts of the Germans to induce Mohammedan and Irish prisoners of war to desert to the German arms. The Irish being attacked through the notorious Sir Roger Casement. Liebknecht finally enraged the Government by calling out that the loan subscription was a swindle.

.   .   .   .

This cry in America that German babies have not sufficient milk is all rot. Enclosed is a report of one of our Doctors on the subject.[23] The cry is only raised to get a hole in the British blockade.

The Germans probably will take Verdun in the end. They are going at it carefully, and an imitation of each French position or trench they wish to take—planned from airmens' and spies' reports—is constructed behind the German lines and the German soldiers practise at taking it until they are judged letter perfect and are put to work to capture the original.

It is said the Germans have developed a submarine periscope so small as to be almost invisible and which works up and down so that only at intervals for a second does it appear above the water. Also it is said the wireless vibrations by means of copper plates at each end are transmitted through the boat, and every member of the crew learns the wireless code, and no matter when working can catch the vibrations.

Sussex and other four ships' note just received—[24] that we treat by cable—I think Germany is now determined to keep peace with America as the plain people are convinced that otherwise the war will be lengthened, a contingency abhorrent to all.

Yours ever

J. W. G[ERARD]

---

[23] Not enclosed. An added notation reads: "Enclosures go in letter to President."
[24] *Foreign Relations*, 1916, supp., p. 227.

763.72/2757½

The Ambassador in Germany (*Gerard*) *to the Secretary of State*

BERLIN, *May 10, 1916.*

MY DEAR MR. SECRETARY: They say that the Apache Indians have the biggest backbones but they have nothing on the President and you.

You know the story of the coon and Colonel Scott, who aimed at a racoon in a tree; the coon said, "Air you in airnest, Colonel Scott?" "I air," said the Colonel. "Then I'll come down," said the wise racoon.

.   .   .   .

I delivered the last American Note to von Jagow to-day.[25] He said they probably would not answer, and then engaged me in gossipy conversation.

These people want peace and will gladly accept the President as mediator.

.   .   .   .

If they get good and sick of war here, perhaps they may not feel like revenge after all,—but there is an ever present danger we must prepare for.

The fact that you gave detailed instructions as to leaving etc.— which they undoubtedly learned, with their wonderful spy system— helped a settlement.

The Chancellor and I became great friends as a result of my stay at the Hauptquartier. . . . The Government published a certificate in the *Official Gazette* to the effect that I was their fairhaired boy, etc.—very nice of them. I really think they recognize that the propaganda was an awful failure and want to inaugurate the era of good feeling.

I did not go to the front at the Hauptquartier as reported. I had enough to do in Charleville, but did witness the splendid relief work being done by the Americans who are feeding 2,200,000 of the population of Northern France. The Americans told me that 50,000 of the inhabitants of Lille, Roubaix, Tourcoing are being sent under circumstances of great barbarity to work in the fields in small villages. I spoke to the Chancellor and he promised to remedy this.

Germans say they will take Verdun. A military treaty with Sweden is reported; a large Swedish Military Commission is now here, receiving much attention.

While at Charleville, in connection with American work, I asked, at one village, to see the German Army stores so as to convince

---

[25] *Foreign Relations*, 1916, supp., p. 263.

myself that the German Army was not using the stores from America. I saw that one-half the stores came from Holland.

Please show this to Colonel House.

Yours ever,

JAMES W. GERARD

763.72/2759½

The Ambassador in Germany (Gerard) to the Secretary of State

[BERLIN,] *May 17, 1916.*

[Received June 6.]

MY DEAR MR. SECRETARY:

. . . .

The food question is getting very serious. We are to go, in a few days, on a meat ration of less than half a pound a week. For a long time the poor have had no meat—a chicken costs 20 Marks or so, and a goose 30—and living has become fearfully expensive. The Germans foolishly killed most of their pigs early in the war, and also exported sugar to keep up the price of the Mark, but now they are practically without fat, and sugar is getting low. Delbrück, Minister of the Interior, is being bounced for this. We are on rations for nearly everything. The Germans however will last, somehow, and the harvest so far promises to be extra fine. Rye, which is the principal crop, is harvested about July 15th. The German military situation seems very strong, there are plenty of soldiers to be seen in the towns and cities, and Germany is by no means down to her last man. All our military experts tell me the ammunition supply is plentiful. But the psychological moment for a peace proposal, as far as this country is concerned, is here.

I do not think the meat supply can be bettered here for a long time, butter sugar and fat very short. The new harvest and grain from Roumania will keep the population alive, but how long these meat eaters will stand being vegetarians is another question. Personally I do not believe any serious uprising will occur. The Government is too strong and the people too well disciplined. Nevertheless there have been serious riots (food) in Leipzig recently. In the workingmen's part of the city no one is allowed on the streets after 8 PM, and in other parts, after 9 PM. These riots are sporadic, caused by the food question and are leaderless.

I am sorry Taft jumps off with lead in the matter of getting hospital supplies to Germany through the British blockade. See my cables to Department running back six or seven months or more on this question.[26]

Yours ever

J. W. G[ERARD]

763.72/2760½

The Ambassador in Germany (Gerard) to the Secretary of State

[BERLIN,] *May 24, 1916.*

[Received June 6.]

MY DEAR MR. SECRETARY: Yesterday I had a talk with the Chancellor. The occasion was the Polish Relief question which I shall now take up direct with Helfferich who, as I predicted, is the new Minister of the Interior and Vice Chancellor. He is a very business like man and did much for the favorable settlement of our last crisis.

The Chancellor seemed rather downcast yesterday, without apparent cause. He says that Germany from now on will have two months of hardship on the food question but that after that things will be all right. The crops as I have seen on my shooting place are magnificent and the rye harvest will probably begin even before July 15th.

Mrs. Gerard has just returned from a week in Buda Pest with her sister. The Hungarians are once more gay and confident. The Italians their hereditary foes are being driven back and on the Russian front there seems to be a sort of tacit truce of God—no fighting and visiting in trenches etc—on terms of great friendliness. Food is plentiful.

At the races here last Sunday there was an absolutely record crowd and more money bet than on any previous day in German racing history. The cheaper field and stands were so full of soldiers that the crowd seemed grey, which goes to show that the last man is not at the front.

State Socialism makes advances ever here. A proposition is now mooted to compel the young men who are earning large wages to save a part thereof.

On the *Sussex* question—I got my Spanish Colleague, who has orders to ask about the punishment of the Commander to say at the Foreign Office, after he had once been refused any information, that I had heard that the people at large in America believed the Commander has received "Pour le Merite". Von Jagow said that he was sure that this was not so, but that he did not know the name of the Commander, and that it was not "usual" to tell what punishment

---

[26] See *Foreign Relations*, 1916, supp., pp. 941 ff.

had been given. So that I suppose the matter will rest, unless I get orders to formally ask about the punishment.

The German military people and ruling "Squire" (Junker) class are furious at the settlement with America, and abuse America, the President and me indiscriminately.

Any thing the President says about peace is prominently placed in the newspapers. See to-day's enclosed paper giving the President's speech at Charlotte—no time to translate it.[27]

Yours ever

J. W. G[ERARD]

763.72/2761½

The Ambassador in Germany (Gerard) to the Secretary of State

BERLIN, *May 31, 1916.*
[Received June 19.]

MY DEAR MR. SECRETARY: Enclosed is copy of debate in Reichstag yesterday,[28] in which Stresemann applauded by all except Socialists said that Germany threw away Wilson as a peace-maker. However the Government is pleased with President's peace talk as it keeps the people amused over food and U boat crisis.

U boat crisis will come up again, when Pan-Germanists and Conservatives demand a reckless U boat war because we have done nothing against England.

Von Jagow much attacked in his own (Junker) crowd for general weakness and may have to go unless Kaiser thinks Parliament is become too interfering.

On Polish Relief. Germany feels that England should not complicate case by asking Germany for Guarantees about feeding territory not under German control—viz that part of Poland under Austrian occupation, Servia, Montenegro, and Albania. Also the army of occupation, Germans say of about 150,000, must get their food in Poland. Especially as the army planted most of the crop, as in Northern France where I myself saw soldiers tilling the fields with army horses.

Hardins' paper has been confiscated again.

JAMES W. GERARD

---

[27] For the text of President Wilson's remarks at Charlotte, N. C., May 20, 1916, see the *New York Times*, May 21, 1916.
[28] Not printed.

763.72/2796½

The Ambassador in Germany (Gerard) to the Secretary of State

BERLIN, *June 7, 1916.*
[Received June 19.]

MY DEAR MR. SECRETARY:

.   .   .   .

The debates in the Reichstag have been quite interesting yesterday and the day before. The Chancellor irritated by the anonymous attacks on him in pamphlets etc. made a fine defense. In the course of the debate allusions were made to President Wilson and the U boat question. Summaries enclosed.[29] The U boat question may break loose again any day.

I do not think that either Austria or Germany wishes President Wilson to lay down any peace conditions, there may possibly be a Congress after the Peace Congress but meanwhile all parties here feel that America has nothing to do with peace conditions. America can bring the parties together but that is all. The speech about the rights of small peoples has, I hear, made the Austrians furious as Austria is made up of many Nationalities and the Germans say that if the rights of small peoples and peoples choosing their own Sovereignty is to be discussed that the Irish question, the Indian question and the Boer question, the Egyptian question and many others involving the Allies must be discussed. I think that generally there is a big change in public opinion and the Germans are beginning to realize that the President is for peace with Germany.

The Germans expect that by September preparations will be finished and that the Suez Canal will be cannonaded, bombed and mined so that it will dry up, and then the Indian-Afghan troubles will begin. The crops are fine and the food question will soon be solved.

Yours ever

J. W. G[ERARD]

────────────

763.72/2798½

The Ambassador in Germany (Gerard) to the Secretary of State

BERLIN, *June 14, 1916.*
[Received June 26.]

MY DEAR MR. SECRETARY:

.   .   .   .

The president's peace talks carried over the dangerous moment after the submarine submission. Von Jagow told me that President

───────
[29] Not printed.

and you must not think because of debates in Reichstag that President is not welcome as mediator.

Crops look well.

The Break in Austro-Russian line is reported to have been caused by wholesale desertions of Ruthenian troops to Russians.

The editor of the *National Zeitung* responsible for the fake interview with me has been "fired" from that paper which has published a notice to that effect.

Yours ever

J. W. G[ERARD]

763.72/2800½

The Ambassador in Germany (Gerard) to the Secretary of State

BERLIN, *June 21, 1916.*

[Received July 5.]

MY DEAR MR. SECRETARY: Great Admiral von Koester made a speech implying that reckless submarine war should be taken up and England thus defeated. He is retired but is head of the Navy League, a concern backed by the Government, possessing a million members and much political influence.

.   .   .   .

The U. boat question will probably come up again, say in three months, unless we get in serious trouble in Mexico, when it will come up sooner.

.   .   .   .

Letters, codes etc. for Bernstorff and individuals are sent to America as follows. The letters are photographed on a reduced scale so that a letter a foot square appears as an inch and a half square. These little prints are put in layers of a shoe heel of a travelling American or elsewhere, book cover, hat band, etc., and then rephotographed and enlarged in America. Also messengers travel steerage and put things in the mattress of a fellow passenger and go back to the ship after landing in New York and collect the stuff.

A German friend just returned from Austria says the feeling there against America very strong on account of the Dumba incident.

Yesterday I was told by a German that the German army already had aeroplanes which develop 300 H. P., and would soon have some of 1000 H. P.

Serious riots in Munich, Leipzig & Dresden.

Yours ever

J. W. G[ERARD]

763.72/2801½

The Ambassador in Germany (Gerard) to the Secretary of State

BERLIN, *July 18, 1916.*

MY DEAR MR. SECRETARY: A committee called the National Committee for an Honorable Peace has been formed. Prince Wedel is head. Most of the people are friends of the Chancellor and of the three real heads one is an editor of the *Frankfurter Zeitung* which is the Chancellor's organ. On August 1st. fifty speakers of this Committee will begin to speak, probably the opposition will come in their meetings and try to speak or break up the meetings.

The *Lokal-Anzeiger* also a government organ prints an editorial to the effect that Germany may take up reckless submarine war again. Great numbers of U. boats are being built and in Sept. operations will be on a big scale, though the Chancellor will try to keep them to cruiser warfare.

The prisoner question on all sides is growing acute. The Germans sent me a note today threatening stern reprisals if the alleged bad treatment of their prisoners in Russia does not stop.

We can no longer talk to prisoners alone. Von Jägow told me that after the visit of Madame Sasenoff, or Samsenoff, to a Russian prisoners camp, there was almost a riot, but the real reason is that the Germans have much to conceal. The prison food now is a starvation ration.

Two Irishmen were shot recently at Limburg. How I found this out I cannot tell.

The Alliance of the Six, really organizations fostered by Big Iron Business in Westphalia, is very active for annexation. They want to get the French iron mines and coal, and so control the iron business of the Continent and perhaps Europe.

The new Mexican Minister, Zuburan, has been here some time and has not called on me in accordance with invariable custom.

I think if Mexican question is not settled hard, now, that later The United States will have to fight Germany, secretly through Mexico.

Yours ever

J. W. G[ERARD]

763.72/2802½

The Ambassador in Germany (Gerard) to the Secretary of State

BERLIN, *July 25, 1916.*
[Received August 14.]

MY DEAR MR. SECRETARY: A man from Syria passed through here recently and gave me most interesting accounts of the state of affairs there. The Turks are oppressing the Arabians and the revolt of the Grand Sherif of Mecca may have great effects in this war. This man says the English are building two railroads from Suez into the desert and the Germo-Turks are building toward the canal from the North. For the canal attack there are at present principally Austrian troops assembled. The Turks are beginning to take Greeks from the Coast cities into the interior of Asia Minor and are oppressing the Syrian Arabian Cities, such as Beirut where thousands are dying of starvation. At the Islahje-Aleppo R. R. head 30 Turkish soldiers a day die from Cholera. The Germans by their precautions escape. He passed 147 German auto. trucks in the Cilician mountains bound for Bagdad. Also saw the British prisoners from Kut el Amara, who are dying of dysentery, being compelled to walk in the hot sun from Kut. He thinks the English and the Grand Sherif will transfer the title of head of the religion from the Sultan at Constantinople to either the Sultan of Egypt or some new Sultan to be established as an Arabian Sultan, perhaps at Bagdad if the Russians and English take it, or at Mecca, and he considers this movement of Arabians against Turks may assume great proportions.

There is still talk here of a resumption of reckless submarine war which question is complicated and involved in the eternal efforts of the Conservatives to get the Chancellor out.

The recognition of the "merchant submarine" has made a very good impression here.

The plain people are eager for peace but those interested in carrying on the war have the upper hand.

The Harvest is good, is now being garnered and, as I have always said, there is no question of starving Germany out.

A number of navy and (which is significant) army officers visited von Tirpitz, lately, in his Black Forest Retreat and gave him a testimonial.

There is prospect that what is called here a "Burg Frieden" (Peace of the City) will be declared between the Chancellor and the principal Conservative newspapers.

One of the American Correspondents back from Verdun says that a corps Commander said his corps took no prisoners.

I think many of the Hungarians are for peace. I get this from Andrassy's son in law who is also a member of the lower house. Tisza however is still in full control.

Prince Leopold['s] stags (he is brother in law of Kaiser) have destroyed vegetables of the plain people (as in the days of William Rufus) and people dare write letters, and Liberal papers dare publish them complaining of these depredations.

Yours ever

J. W. G[ERARD]

763.72/2836½

The Ambassador in Germany (Gerard) to the Secretary of State

BERLIN, *August 8, 1916.*

[Received August 21.]

MY DEAR MR. SECRETARY: Count Andrassy, leader of the opposition to Tisza in Hungary, has been here for some time. He lunched with us one day and I had a talk with him in German (Oswald Villard please note). Andrassy is rather old and tired but his wife is full of energy and ambition and pushes him on. Andrassy's father, Prime Minister, was originally a great friend of Germany.

It is possible that Andrassy through German influence may be made Minister of Foreign Affairs instead of Burian. This is to be the first step in a German *Coup d'État* to take place on the death of Francis Joseph—the throne successor to be given Austria alone, and Prince Eitel Fritz, the Kaiser's favorite son, to be King of Hungary with possibly a Czech kingdom in Bohemia.

Andrassy had an audience with the Kaiser here. Andrassy is apparently a friend of America and is also for peace.

Tirpitz is out with a statement practically demanding war with America. I am surprised that the newspapers were allowed to publish it. If it was not allowed to go out of here it should be published in America.

Germany will probably come out with a strong note about Poland, refusing help and saying harvest sufficient. This is not true as to food for babies who cannot live on rye and wheat, but need condensed milk.

The treatment of prisoners is going from bad to worse. The Chancellor and Foreign Office can do nothing against the Military.

. . . .

Hoover, Professor Kellogg, and I are all very much discouraged about Polish and other relief questions. The Germans are getting more and more disagreeable about these matters, even tho' they are for the benefit of Germany. Warwick Greene, of the Rockefeller Foundation, being a new arrival is more hopeful but that will soon wear off.

The trial and execution of Captain Fryatt was a bad bit of work. I am glad to say I suspected some railroading would be done and covered this Embassy well by sending Two notes to F. O. demanding date of trial and right to name an advocate.

. . . The Germans are getting a blacklist of their own. One Barthmann an American who sells American shoes in Germany wanted to get his pass stamped to go to America, and permission to come back, and was told that would only be done if the Chamber of

Commerce (*Handels-Kammer*) consents. You see the connection, no American goods for Germany.

The Jews here are almost on the edge of being "pogrommed". There is great prejudice against them, especially in naval and military circles, because they have been industrious and have made money. Officers openly talk of repudiating the war loan which they say would only mean a loss for the Jews.

.   .   .   .

How about sending me a letter of Credence to the King of Bavaria? Our Ministers used to be accredited there. There is no legal objection, as I am named Ambassador to Germany, a place which does not exist, either politically or geographically. [*sic*]

I have talked with Zimmermann about it, and he said there was no objection to the letters to those German Govts. to which our Ministers had been formerly accredited. It was merely a matter of friendliness and courtesy. As the Centrum or Catholic party holds the balance of power, is unfriendly to America and centers in Bavaria, I should like to meet Bavarians etc. on a proper footing.

The Germans say they have new and horrible inventions which will end the war soon.

.   .   .   .

There was no office copy accompanying the letter from the President to the Emperor, concerning Poland,[30] and so I could not know exactly how it was couched. I have rumors that instead of being headed "Great and Good Friend" as has been the custom in the past, it was headed "Your Majesty", and this has caused quite some feeling. I suggest immediate investigation.

> Yours ever
>
> J. W. G[ERARD]

763.72/2837½

The Ambassador in Germany (Gerard) to the Secretary of State

> BERLIN, *August 16, 1916.*
> [Received August 29.]

MY DEAR MR. SECRETARY: The Chancellor and von Jagow have been in Vienna. Von Jagow told me only on current business, but this was a diplomatic statement. I believe they went to settle the fate of Poland. I hear Prussia wants an independent Poland and Austria wants to make it part of the Austrian Empire. In any event I think Prussia will secure the organizing of the army which will soon be raised. A Pole told me two days ago that the peasants were coddled

----

[30] *Foreign Relations,* 1916, supp., p. 903.

by Russia, whose motto in Poland was "divide et impera", and that they will violently resent being drafted into the Prussian army.

The bitter attacks on the Chancellor continue. At a recent meeting in Bavaria resolutions even passed that the first objective of the war was to get rid of the Chancellor and the second to "clean out the Anglophile Foreign Office", which prevented Germany from resorting to "reckless" methods for the swift winning of the war.

As a son-in-law of a high official told me to-day the break between the military and navy on one side and the Civil Government on the other has widened into almost Civil war. The same man told me that the K————. had lately become quite apathetic and lets events take their course.

.   .   .   .

The harvest is very good, but does not provide fat, and as yet, meat. But the starving out business I have always said was an "iridescent dream".

New men, 80,000 in this vicinity alone, are being called to the colors.

Everyone here is getting more on razor edge, prisoners are treated more roughly and get worse food, there is a total failure of any Central Government. Bavaria is getting restless and dissatisfied, this will not amount to anything definite but is a sign of the times.

I went to Herringsdorf for a few days swimming. At a concert in the evening a man recited a poem he said he had written about "having bled enough", and was violently applauded. Quite a contrast to the days when the best actors in Germany were not ashamed to spout the "hymn of hate".

The military use the censorship even against papers friendly to the Chancellor and Germans certainly can hate each other as thoroughly and scientifically as they do most other nations. Dr. Taylor thinks that in peace times someone fed this nation too much meat.

The newspapers are rather preparing the people for the entry of Roumania but personally and knowing little about the situation I do not think that Roumania will march.

> Yours ever
>
> J. W. G[ERARD]

763.72/2838½

The Ambassador in Germany (Gerard) to the Secretary of State

> BERLIN, *August 23, 1916.*
>
> [Received September 7.]

MY DEAR MR. SECRETARY: I have asked our Embassy, London, to ask British not to publish any camp reports from here for the present. Owing to many circumstances the German nerves are very sensitive just now.

Professor Stein, a school friend of Tisza's and Burian's, who was recently in Austria, saw Burian and says Burian is ready and even anxious to make an arbitration treaty with America and also send an Ambassador in Dumba's place to Washington. I only send this as news, as it is all out of my jurisdiction. Prof. Stein owns a magazine here and was for peace with America last April. He says that tomorrow or next day there will be an interpellation in the Hungarian Chamber about sending an Ambassador to America. "Timeo Danaos et dona ferentes."

The National Liberals will probably unite with the Conservatives and demand a strong hold on Belgium, if not actual possession of that country, as one of the objects of the war.

. . . .

This Union of National Liberals and Conservatives is dangerous and may mean a resumption of submarine reckless war.

. . . .

Yours ever

J. W. G[ERARD]

763.72/2928½

The Ambassador in Germany (Gerard) to the Secretary of State

BERLIN, *August 30, 1916.*
[Received September 11.]

MY DEAR MR. SECRETARY: The entry of Roumania took every one by surprise. Beldiman the Roumanian Minister here was visiting the reigning Prince of Hohenzollern Sigmaringen, brother of the Roumanian King, and apparently knew nothing of even the danger of a break.

Today Hindenburg is named Chief of the General Staff, and his chief of Staff, Ludendorff, is made Quartermaster General. Falkenhayn, former Chief of Staff is bounced without even excuse of a diplomatic illness. This is all a great concession to popular opinion. I do not know where Hindenburg stands with reference to America, but have heard that he is a reasonable man. Of course here the Army has as much to say in Foreign affairs as the Foreign Office, if not more. When I was at the Great General Headquarters, Falkenhayn, although I know him did not call on me, and dodged me, even not appearing at Kaiser's table when I lunched there. From all this I judge he was against America on the submarine question. I have also heard that at this time when Helfferich was talking before the Kaiser, in favor of peace with America, that Falkenhayn interrupted him, but was told by the Kaiser to "stick to his last" or words to that effect.

These people here are now nervous and unstrung and actually believe that America will now enter the war against them. You cannot conceive of the general breakdown of nerves among this people.

I have heard lately of men as old as 47 being taken for the Army.

In the Foreign Office waiting room the other day I was talking to Count Moltke, the Danish Minister, who is violently pro-German. I noticed that he had with him a sort of report about the action of the Danish Parliament concerning the sale of the islands to America, which he was evidently waiting to give to Zimmermann.

Zimmermann has now gone on a vacation, his place being temporarily taken by von Treutler, Prussian Minister to Bavaria, who since the commencement of the war has been with the Kaiser. I judge this means the Kaiser is looking personally into matters at the Foreign Office. Von Treutler is, I think, against the resumption of reckless submarine war, he is lunching with me today. . . .

Yours ever

J. W. G[ERARD]

763.72/2929½

The Ambassador in Germany (Gerard) to the Secretary of State

BERLIN, *September 13, 1916.*
[Received October 2.]

MY DEAR MR. SECRETARY: In general conversation with von Jagow, recently, he said that the offensive on the Somme could not continue without the great supply of shells from America. He also said that recently a German submarine submerged in the Channel had to allow 41 ships to pass, and that he was sure that each ship was full of ammunition and soldiers but probably had some protecting Angels on board, and therefore the submarine did not torpedo without warning. He seemed quite bitter.

The wife of von Wiegand the *World* Correspondent was recently attacked in the street. . . . Two stenographers from this Embassy were recently slapped on coming out of a theatre because they were speaking English.

Reventlow's paper was recently suppressed and Reventlow forbidden to write without special permission. This is a good sign from the Chancellor.

Old Dr. Hale was recently given a special trip to the West front, was allowed to talk to the Crown Prince etc.

Yours ever

J. W. G[ERARD]

763.72/3107½

The Ambassador in Germany (Gerard) to the Secretary of State

BERLIN, *January 3, 1917.*
[Received January 22.]

MY DEAR MR. SECRETARY: The weather is most depressing. Dark and rain every day. All hands seem cross. Zimmermann, I think finds it much more difficult to be the responsible first than the criticising second. It is not as easy as it looked to him.

The Kaiser, I hear direct, stated the other day that he did not expect peace now, that the English would try a great offensive in the Spring and would fail.

Hoover writes me that the Germans are violating all the pledges in Belgium. He expects a year of great difficulties.

I hear this confirmed on the best authority and that even the German official who is supposed to see that food is not sent from Belgium to Germany, in violation of Germany's pledges, sends out butter to his family.

I hear on the best authority that there is an absolute reign of terror in Belgium. Sudden and arbitrary arrests etc. I think the Germans want to see all foreign diplomats out of Bucharest and Brussels . . .

.   .   .   .

The greatest danger *re* submarine war is that unthinking persons in the United States may start a crusade against the President's policy, encourage the Germans in the belief that we are divided and lead them to resume reckless acts in that belief. The continuance of a strong front is the best way to keep the peace.

Both Zimmermann and the Chancellor asked me about Bernstorff and, returning good for evil, I said that he was O. K., on very good terms with the government, well liked, and that no one could do better. One of his kind friends sent Zimmermann the "Sketch" bathing picture.

The Germans will do nothing about Belgium. The deportation was a military measure, demanded by Ludendorff, who constantly fears a British landing on the Belgian coast.

.   .   .   .

The food situation grows worse. Potato cards must now be presented in restaurants and hotels. I doubt if the potatoes can last beyond April. There is food in Rumania but much will go to troops, Austrians and Turks, and railways are so used by troops etc. that it is doubtful if any food from there can reach Germany for months.

All apartment houses in Berlin are closed at nine and lights in halls extinguished. Theatres close at ten and cinos. There is want of coal due to lack of transportation.

Yours ever

J. W. G[ERARD]

123 G 31/51½

The Ambassador in Germany (Gerard) to the Secretary of State

BERLIN, *January 9, 1917.*

[Received January 29.]

MY DEAR MR. SECRETARY: Pursuant to orders I have been jollying them here. Last Saturday the American Association of Commerce and Trade gave me a banquet at the Hotel Adlon. Every place possible was occupied and many distinguished and influential Germans were present. Such as Helfferich, Solf, Professor Delbrück, Dernburg, Gutmann, Gwinner, von Holtzendorff, Prince Isenburg, Meyer Gerhardt, the Vice President of the Reichstag, etc., the proprietors and editors of the best newspapers, etc. I enclose a list of guests [31] but the menu adorned with my picture I do not send out of modesty—besides, it is too large.

Remarks, all I think "safe", were made by Mr. Wolf, head of the association, Helfferich, von Gwinner, Zimmermann, (who came in late) and me.

Yesterday the Chancellor sent for me to congratulate me and thank me. So you see orders are obeyed.

I brought with me, or there has been sent me, about 370,000 marks for charitable purposes—quite welcome.

Of course the Pan German and anti Chancellor papers attacked the dinner. But it is my business to be with the Chancellor—whom I like anyway.

Our Consul received a letter from Belgians who say they are made to work and are beaten with guns and badly treated in Germany.

No chance at present of Germany either stating peace terms or sending back the stolen Belgians.

At Dr. Solf's house last Sunday night, a Duke of Mecklenburg Schwerin (not the reigning one) tackled me quite offensively about the President and the sale of war supplies. It is hard to keep the temper but as this individual abused the Kaiser as well perhaps he is not all there.

.   .   .   .

Germany wants a peace conference in order to make a separate peace, on good terms to them, with France and Russia. Then she

---

[31] Not printed.

hopes to finish England by submarines, then, later, take the scalp of Japan, Russia, and Japan [*sic*] separately. The Allies ought to remember what Ben Franklin said about hanging together or separately. I get the above scheme from very good authority.

Yours ever

J. W. G[ERARD]

763.72/3173½

The Ambassador in Germany (Gerard) to the Secretary of State

BERLIN, *January 16, 1917.*

[Received February 6.]

DEAR MR. SECRETARY: The nearer I get to the situation the more I consider the President's peace note an exceedingly wise move. It has made it difficult for the Terrorists here to start anything which will bring Germany in conflict with the U. S. The Chancellor, Zimmermann, Stumm; have all ridiculed the idea that Germany will go back on her *Sussex* pledges; but if she does, then the peace note makes it easier for America to enter the war on the Allies side with a clear conscience and the knowledge on the part of the people at home that the President did everything possible to keep us out of the mess.

Our love feast here and its advertisement all over Germany has also helped matters.

While the Chancellor, *et al*, have all stated to me that they would not name Germany's peace terms, even in confidence, to the President, I believe that they will eventually do so, if they really want peace.

Everything points to a coming crisis in the matter of food, how serious it will be even the officials themselves do not know, as there is much concealed food and much smuggling over the various frontiers. In some parts of Germany, the country police or *gens d'armes* are searching the farmhouses thrice weekly.

I have secured permission to visit and inspect the enslaved Belgians, have named as inspectors all the members of our staff speaking French, but as yet have not received the passes.

My wife, just returned from a weeks visit to her sister in Hungary, reports a great desire for peace and that the persons who a year ago said that the President could have nothing to do with peace or negotiations, now say he is the only possible mediator. This comes from high government circles there.

Yours ever

J. W. G[ERARD]

123 G 31/52½

President Wilson to the Secretary of State

WASHINGTON, *31 January, 1917.*

MY DEAR MR. SECRETARY: Allow me to return Mr. Gerard's letter with my thanks.[32]

It is odd how his information seems never to point to any conclusions whatever; but in spite of that his letters are worth reading and do leave a certain impression.

Faithfully Yours,

W. W.

GREAT BRITAIN

763.72/1671

The Ambassador in Great Britain (Page) to the Secretary of State

LONDON, *April 8, 1915.*
[Received April 21.]

MY DEAR MR. SECRETARY: I take the liberty to report to you the following very remarkable coincidence. Your first long Note to the British Government reached us by cable in cipher on the 24th of December,[33] which was the day before a week's holiday—ten days' holiday in fact—for they make much of Christmas here and everything is suspended for at least ten days. Your last Note to the British Government [34] was received in cable the day before the Easter holiday, which is the other great holiday in English life. Under normal conditions everybody leaves London, official people and all, for nearly a fortnight during these two holidays; and most of all the principal papers skip an issue for about half the days in these holidays.

Of course we shall never send many more long notes, and of course it could never happen again that any one of them would come just on the eve of one of the two long holidays, so that there is no use in our making a note guarding against a repetition of these unfortunate dates, and I merely report this to you as one of the curiosities of life and as an explanation of the apparently unusual length of time that had to elapse before publication. The Englishmen take their holidays very seriously.

But the publication of this last Note, as you have of course been informed, came off all very well, and it has had an excellent reception from the Press. I have not yet had any discussion of it officially because Sir Edward Grey has gone off to rest a little to keep from

---

[32] Letter of Jan. 9, 1917, from the Ambassador in Germany, p. 698.
[33] Apparently the cable of Dec. 26, 1914, *Foreign Relations*, 1914, supp., p. 372.
[34] *Ibid.*, 1915, supp., p. 152.

breaking down, but I have just heard this morning that the Prime Minister remarked that as a lawyer he regarded it as a very able document, and he thought that the stress was laid on exactly the right places.

I do take the liberty, however, to make the following suggestion, that, in case of any future long notes, you might consider the propriety of sending them by mail. They would really reach me practically as soon as they can be made ready by cable. When you count the time required to put them in cipher, to translate out of the cipher and to secure corrections, I believe that we would gain time, and of course we would save expense, by sending them by the pouch, unless of course there was some special reason for wishing to save possibly a day. I should like an expression of opinion from you regarding this method of transmission of any answer, provided it is a long answer, that the British Government may give to your last Note. If we say nothing about the despatch of the Note, the newspaper people will of course have no reason to be inquisitive.

With my congratulations on the continued good feeling between this Government and our own, which was never better at any period since the war began than it is now,

I remain [etc.]   WALTER H. PAGE

763.72/1979½ : Telegram

The Ambassador in Great Britain (Page) to the Secretary of State

LONDON, *July 15, 1915—11 a. m.*
[Received 4:15 p. m.]

2462. I interpret thoughtful and responsible opinion here as follows and send it as in the past for your information. Germany reckons on American unpreparedness for war and hopes that pro-German sentiment can prevent munitions from going to the Allies, arguing that if pro-German sentiment fail the United States cannot fight and therefore the risk of insulting us is negligible since as a neutral her enemies obtain help from us through their command of the seas and as an enemy we could do no more harm than we now do.

The feeling seems to be that Germany can never be persuaded to give us a satisfactory answer and that if we do not take effective action of some sort we shall lose the confidence and respect of the Allies and in time have to face Germany alone; that if democracy as represented by the United States yield, its standing in the world will be gone for an indefinite time and its advocates weakened in every country.

Men here point out the similarity of Germany's dealing with the United States to her dealing with England, always by evasion, and they point to England's mistake in hoping to avoid war and not equipping an army 10 years ago. They say that unless German military power is crushed by the crushing of the professional military party all the world will be terrorized and that we must range out effectively against this menace without delay or suffer ultimately whatever the outcome of the present struggle may be.

I think this opinion is practically universal here among thoughtful men. They are saddened by it but regard it as practically certain that we cannot escape; that the Germans will continue assassination and incendiarism in the United States and will sooner or later destroy more American travelers.

British opinion has great and growing confidence in the President himself but seems to show a doubt about the virility and courage of American public opinion attributing to it a timidity arising from failure to grasp the scope of the issues involved in the struggle and the effect of its outcome on the United States.

AMERICAN AMBASSADOR

---

123 P 14/48a : Telegram

The Secretary of State to the Ambassador in Great Britain (*Page*)

WASHINGTON, *October 25, 1915—4 p. m.*

Rumors through representatives of the press that you intend to resign have been brought to the attention of the President and have been denied by him and by me. The rumors persist and are causing both of us much anxiety although we can not believe them to have any foundation.

In view of their repetition we thought it advisable to inform you and to tell you how earnestly we hope that there is no foundation at all for the setting afloat of such rumors. I trust that you can set our minds at rest.

LANSING

---

123 P 14/48½a : Telegram

The Secretary of State to the Ambassador in Great Britain (*Page*)

WASHINGTON, *October 29, 1915.*

The President and I are very much gratified with your personal and confidential telegram October 26th,[35] and are relieved to hear that the rumors were entire fabrication. Your continued and helpful service is greatly needed in London.

LANSING

· · · · · · ·

---

[35] Not found in Department files.

865.857 An 2/112½ : Telegram

The Ambassador in Great Britain (Page) to the Secretary of State

LONDON, *January 3, 1916—6 p. m.*
[Received January 4—8:26 a. m.]

3500. The Washington correspondents of the most important London papers report that the last Austrian note on the *Ancona* [36] would have been acceptable if the *Persia* had not been sunk. This opinion, the sinking of the *Persia*, and the [lack of] a settlement [of the] *Lusitania* provoke unfavorable comment on the administration in every London newspaper today. Following are a few [specimen] comments:

The *Morning Post* says: "We have long ago relinquished all expectation that neutral nations would effectually intervene in respect of repeated outrages of the law of nations," and "at the same time it must be said that their position in this regard is singularly inconsistent with their pleadings addressed to the allied belligerents that they may be allowed to trade with the enemy."

The *Times* says: "The Germans and Austrians can have no objection against engaging in further diplomatic correspondence with President Wilson to any extent and to congratulating each other upon the 'refreshing and delightfully pungent irony' with which they answer the 'clumsy tone' of his efforts. Why after all the Germans may argue should the killing of a single American in the *Persia* do more than that of a hundred Americans in the *Lusitania* and of the many Americans killed in other ships."

The *Daily Telegraph* says: "The interchange of notes has now plainly reached and passed the point of farce and no spirited nation can long endure that condition of affairs."

The *Standard* says: "If President Wilson thinks it worth while to continue argle-bargling with the governments of Germany and Austria when the crimes of the *Yasaka Maru*, the *Ville de la Ciotat* and the *Persia* have been committed while the note promising redress for that of the *Ancona*—with the tongue of course in the cheek—was on its way to him, that is his concern." And the *Standard* says of the Austrian note: "If the United States will accept this it will accept anything."

The *Pall Mall Gazette* says: "Berlin and Vienna we dare say are quite prepared to work upon a commercial tariff in their slaughter of American citizens so long as Washington is content to put a price upon them, and to declare the honor of the United States satisfied by a receipt upon the 'butcher's bill'," and "The proverbial fly upon the wheel does as much to influence locomotion as the diplomatic pen can effect in the restraint of German deviltry," and "It is for the American people to decide whether their national prestige and dignity can be assuaged upon this mercantile basis. But we cannot forget that when President Wilson took up his pen upon the destruction of the *Lusitania* he announced himself with considerable emphasis as the champion of reason, justice and humanity upon the high seas. After

---

[36] *Foreign Relations*, 1915, supp., p. 655.

half a year's correspondence with the Central Empires he must be painfully conscious of the entire futility of his performances in that capacity."

The *Westminster Gazette* says: "The German warlords apparently take a cynical pleasure in apologizing to the American Government one day and proving to their own people the next day that their apology was humbug."

Public opinion both official and unofficial is expressed by these newspaper comments with far greater restraint than it is expressed in private conversations. Ridicule of the administration runs [through] the programs of the theaters; it inspires hundreds of [cartoons]; it is a staple of conversation at private dinners and in the clubs. The [most] serious class of Englishmen including the best friends of the United States feel that the administration's reliance on notes has reduced our Government to a third or fourth rate power. There is even talk of spheres of German influence in the United States as in China.

No Government could fall lower in English opinion than we shall fall if more notes are sent to Austria or to Germany. The only way to keep any shred of English respect is the immediate dismissal without more parleying of every German and Austrian official at Washington. Nobody here believes that such an act would provoke war.

I can do no real service by mincing matters. [My previous telegrams] and letters have been purposely restrained as this one [is]. We have now come to the parting of the ways. If English respect be worth preserving at all, it can be preserved only by immediate action. Any other course than immediate [severing] of diplomatic relations with both Germany and Austria will deepen the English opinion into a conviction [that the administration was insincere] when it sent the *Lusitania* notes and that its notes and protests need not be taken seriously on any subject.

And English opinion is Allied opinion. The Italian Ambassador said to me—"What has happened? The United States of today is not the United States [I knew] 15 years ago when I lived in [Washington]." French officers and members of the Government who come here express themselves even more strongly than do the British.

The English newspapers today publish translations of ridicule of the United States from German papers.

Steamers to the United States are still held up at Liverpool presumably because of submarine activity in the Irish Sea.

AM[ERICAN] EMBASSY

763.72/2481½ : Telegram

The Ambassador in Great Britain (Page) to the Secretary of State

LONDON, *February 17, 1916—9:48 p. m.*
[Received 9 : 55 p. m.]

3783. To the President: Because of the ever-increasing public feeling against the administration the British Government has ordered the censor to suppress as far as he prudently can unfavorable comment on our Government. The *Lusitania* controversy, since it has been continued so long and especially since it is now used by the Germans in their revived submarine program, has brought British opinion of the Administration to [a] point where a turn in its tide can be made only by prompt action. My loyalty to you therefore would not be absolute if I shrank from respectfully sending my solemn conviction of our duty and opportunity.

If you immediately refuse without further parley to yield a jot or tittle of your original *Lusitania* notes and at once sever diplomatic relations with Germany and follow this action by a rigid embargo against the Central Powers you will quickly end the war. Economic measures are all that are necessary. German credit will collapse. The [wavering] Allies, if there be such, will be kept in line. Sweden, Roumania, Greece and other European neutrals will resist further German influences and some of them will join the Allies. The German propaganda throughout the world will be stopped. The moral weight of the United States will be the deciding force in bringing an early peace for which you will receive immortal credit even from the people of Germany. I do not [believe] we should have to fire a gun or risk a man.

This action moreover will settle the whole question of securing permanent peace. It will bring to our side the full and grateful loyalty of the whole British Empire, the British Fleet and all the Allies. The great English-speaking nations without [any] formal alliance will control the conditions of permanent peace. The Japanese threat [will be silenced]. The saving of human life and treasure will be [incalculable]. Germany can honorably give in with good grace since all the world will be [against her] and the internal pressure of her bankrupt and blockaded people will hasten her decision.

Such action would also bring the Administration in line with the sympathies of our people.

On the other hand if we settle the *Lusitania* controversy by any compromise of your original demands or permit it to drag on longer we can have no part in ending the war. [Allied] opinion will run so strongly against the administration that no [censorship] nor other friendly act of any Allied government can stem the onrushing European distrust of our Government.

Longer delay or any other plan will bring us only a thankless, [opulent] and dangerous isolation. The *Lusitania* is the turning point and the time for action is come.

AM[ERICAN] EMBASSY

763.72/2481½

The Secretary of State to President Wilson

WASHINGTON, *February 18, 1916.*

MY DEAR MR. PRESIDENT: You are perfectly right in what you stated to me over the telephone in regard to the message from London which I handed you this morning.[37] It is undoubtedly the expression of the Ambassador.

. . . I am relieved to find that it is not the expression of Colonel House, as I was unable to see any consistency between this dispatch and the dispatches which he had been sending previously.

I am enclosing herewith a memorandum of the conversation which I had yesterday noon with the German Ambassador.[38]

Faithfully yours,

ROBERT LANSING

763.72/2637½ : Telegram

The Ambassador in Great Britain (Page) to the Secretary of State

LONDON, *March 26, 1916—4 p. m.*
[Received 8 : 15 p. m.]

4032. For the President only. Thoughtful men here in public and private life agree on two propositions.

First. That a break in American-German diplomatic relations would quickly end the war. This is, in English opinion, the one practical and effective move to bring an early peace, to save perhaps a million lives and [incalculable] suffering.

Second. Nobody believes that a diplomatic break would lead to war between the United States and Germany. It would be merely such a threat of war as would convince the Germans that their cause is lost. For commercial and financial reasons after the war they will not provoke open hostilities. [Kitchener] holds these two opinions and openly expresses them.

---

[37] *Supra.*
[38] *Foreign Relations,* 1916, supp., p. 172.

A third proposition would [follow,] namely, that such a breach of diplomatic relations would prepare a practical basis for an enduring peace which it will be exceedingly difficult otherwise to arrange. And this is the only plan whereby the moral influence of the United States can be exerted for peace.

AM[ERICAN] AMBASSADOR

763.72/2689½ : Telegram

The Ambassador in Great Britain (Page) to the Secretary of State

LONDON, May 6, 1916—12 noon.

[Received 3:35 p. m.]

4256. For the President and the Secretary only. Newspaper comment and private opinion here regard the German note [39] as only [another] effort to prolong discussion, to embroil our Government and Great Britain and to evade the issue. [The expectation] of our friends here, as far as I can gather [it,] is of an immediate break. Else they will consider that we have yielded to evasion.

AMERICAN AMBASSADOR

763.72/2694½ : Telegram

The Ambassador in Great Britain (Page) to the Secretary of State

LONDON, May 6, 1916—2 p. m.

[Received 6 p. m.]

4260. For the President and the Secretary only. [I hear] through credible channels that the recent secret session of the House of Commons brought out the feeling that the total fighting manhood of Great Britain was necessary to prevent the war ending as a [stalemate.] Universal conscription has given renewed confidence.

The belief is widespread here that the Germans are renewing or will renew efforts for peace on a [stalemate] basis which universal conscription will enable the Allies to reject. Economic pressure is also more and more relied on to bring a real Ally victory. Kitchener told Squier, our military attaché, that without American aid the war will last another year and that with aid it would end in an Ally victory within 6 months.

AM[ERICAN] EMBASSY

---

[39] *Ibid.*, p. 257.

763.72/2895½

Memorandum by the Ambassador in Great Britain (Page)[40]

NOTES TOWARD AN EXPLANATION OF THE BRITISH FEELING TOWARD THE
UNITED STATES

Of recent years and particularly during the first year of the present Administration, the British feeling toward the United States was most cordial. At the time of the repeal of the tolls clause of the Panama Act the admiration and friendliness of the whole British public, governmental and private, reached the highest point in our history. In considering the change that has since taken place, it is well to bear this cordiality in mind as a starting point.

When the war began this attitude at first remained unchanged. The hope of many persons that our Government would protest against the German invasion of Belgium caused some feeling of disappointment at our inaction; but thinking men did not generally share it, and this criticism would have been forgotten if it had stood alone. Many persons have continued to share and to express disappointment on this score who really had some other criticism to make of us. It has been a convenient vent for feeling aroused by other incidents.

The unusually high regard in which the President and hence our Government were held at the beginning of the war was, to a degree, new. The British had of course for many years held our people in high esteem, but they had not as a rule so favorably regarded the Government at Washington—especially its conduct of foreign relations. They had looked upon the Government, certainly during most recent administrations, as ignorant of European affairs, indifferent to conventional methods and usages, and somewhat "touchy". When I first got to London, I found evidence of this feeling even in the very friendly atmosphere of that time. But, when the Panama tolls incident was closed, our Government as well as our people came into the highest measure of British esteem.

The war began. Our neutral attitude was of course expected and was approved. To this day no considerable body of British opinion has expected us to come into the war. But we at once interfered, as they regarded it,—or tried to interfere—by insisting on the Declaration of London,[40a] which no Great Power but the United States (I think) had ratified and which the British House of Lords had rejected. That Declaration they think would have given the victory to Germany. Our repeated and vigorous insistence on its adoption aroused distrust of our good judgment and even of our friendly

---

[40] This paper bears the notation: "Rec'd. from Ambassador W. H. Page Sept. 25/16 RL."
[40a] *Foreign Relations*, 1909, p. 318.

attitude. Thus we started out somewhat unfortunately so far as British feeling towards us was concerned. Their Government foresaw danger of difficulties with us and signed Mr. Bryan's Peace Treaty—to refer disputes to a Commission. They had no particular respect for the philosophy of this Treaty, but they were eager to take every precaution against trouble.

When they developed their naval policy, we entered protests against

(1) Such actions as we regarded as contrary to the best precedents, i. e. to international law. We thus asserted neutral rights and made our position clear.

(2) Injuries done to our trade and interests. We thus laid the foundation for claims.

So much for our legal and doctrinal position. With these protests the British made no quarrel. They replied to them in their own way and they are quite willing to leave doctrines and damages to competent tribunals which will be set up after the war—without any disturbance of good relations. These protests produced no real ill will.

Then we began a long series of specific requests and complaints, in which, (I observe, after the manner of most governments) we give few facts but repeat the substance of Protests already made. The effect of many of these was to nag them—as if we wished to pick a quarrel. They came to look upon the Department of State as a sort of Bureau of Complaints. Some of our informal requests they have granted and many they have declined. They have granted and declined them according to their notion of the degree of harm they would do to their military cause. Lord Grey and the whole civil part of the Government have always shown great courtesy and a willingness, often a great eagerness to meet our wishes.

Our trade advisers bureau hears *ex parte* commercial complaints day in and day out, month in and month out, as its business is to do; and this bureau does not verify statements made to it. I dare say it cannot verify them with its present force of men. Commercial men themselves come, their lawyers come, Senators and Representatives come. Some complaints are, of course, of real injuries for which we must hold the British Government responsible. But many others are based on "rights" that do not exist and on statements that are not true. These create an atmosphere of suspicion, and this Bureau has drawn conclusions about the British Government's methods and purposes that are unwarranted. It writes instructions to me that have confirmed the British impression that our State Department lends itself, with too little discrimination, to complaint-bearers. A constant flow of such complaints and protests changes international trust and respect and forbearance into an evergrowing distrust and misunderstanding. Thus both we and the English are more or less forced to lose the proper perspective of our history and the proper perspective of this present upheaval of the world; and we lose the great vision of the ultimate triumph of international good will and of democracy.

I venture to suggest such a change in this Bureau as will enable it independently to verify the facts presented it, and as will require it to embody verified facts in its instructions. With facts, I could accomplish very much more, for the mere repetition of former Protests does not compel attention.

We, very properly, act most carefully to gain and to keep the good will of South America. But our routine trade controversies with Great Britain are—in many cases—so conducted as to cause an increasing irritation of the best friend and best customer we have in the world.

Since the safety and order of the world depend on the sympathetic understanding of the English-speaking nations (and on nothing else); since we are the larger of those nations, having nearly three out of every five English-speaking white men in the world, and are potentially the richer and the stronger and are the more free; and since the British will come out of this war so chastened and for the first time willing to accept our leadership if they feel that they can depend on our leadership and larger vision; and since England and her Allies will have overcome the strongest and most arrogant military absolutism that ever existed and will have prepared the way for such a spread of democracy and of free institutions as has not taken place since our Republic was founded; and since we have for the first time a chance to make a sort of moral conquest of the British by a just sympathy and forbearance,—it is a pity to lose the great vision of the world's advancement under our leadership and to imperil the natural development of the human race by a series of trivial trade disputes, which become important only because our handling of them shows a lack of moral sympathy. The strongest force in the world— or that has ever been in the world—would be the underlying sympathy and unity of aim of the English-speaking nations. This is now put in grave jeopardy by a trade-bureau and by the system whereby it is permitted to work.

So much for continuous irritating complaints—"causes" that go no further to establish any principle than we had gone before.

The German activity in the United States caused British wonder, then surprise and finally a doubt whether we are any longer a nation and not a mere aggregation of different races and groups of people. They fear that we have lost our national consciousness and unity and, therefore, our national character. They do not publicly discuss our retention of the German Ambassador since this is none of their business. But they say that no other diplomatic officer in civilized history has been so tolerated under less provocation. They ask themselves, "Suppose a British Ambassador at Washington had been the centre of such activity, would he have been retained?" They do not believe that our Government is pro German in deliberate intention, but they do believe that it has become the victim of German bluff and bluster—of the bluff, for instance, that if we should dismiss the German Ambassador we should provoke war, and they fear that we provoke future wars by our patience in dealing with him.

The impression has become general both in private and official circles that the President expects to be consulted when arrangements for peace are undertaken and perhaps that he will offer mediation on his own initiative. The British read the President's acts and utterances by the light of this impression and misconstrue them to fit their idea of his intentions. This notion was unintentionally deepened and spread by House's visits especially his last visit—of course without House's knowledge. He was spoken of almost every day in the newspapers as the President's Special Envoy. They expected him to have some special word or proposal; and when he had none, they proceeded to settle by gossip just why he had come; and they concluded that he had come to elicit an invitation to mediate. This is the impression which, I think, almost every member of the Government, except Lord Grey, has, and which the public surely have. They take all sorts of occasions, as Kitchener and Grey and Bryce took in conversations that have been reported to the President, to point out that there is no precedent for belligerents to call in a neutral when they discuss peace. There is some sensitiveness, too, about a Special Envoy conferring with the German Government and then coming to confer with the Governments of the Allies. They wonder what he said to the Germans. These results, I am sure House does not know. Any Special Envoy would have had the same effect,—to cause a peace-suspicion of our Government, and a suspicion of meddling.

The British have concluded that our Government does not understand the moral meaning of their struggle against a destructive military autocracy. Few of them want (or expect) our military help, but they all want some token of our understanding. They doubt our appreciation of the necessity of English-speaking sympathy, or [our] national unity, our national aims, our national virility. They doubt whether we keep our old vision of the necessary supremacy of democracy as the only safeguard against predatory absolutism. They have not expected us to abandon neutrality. But, since they are fighting for the preservation of free government, they are disappointed that our Government seems to them to make no moral distinction between them and the enemies of free government. They feel that the moral judgment of practically the whole civilized world is on their side except only the Government of the United States. They wonder whether our Government will show in the future a trustworthy character in world affairs. The British, therefore, though they are sincerely desirous of keeping our good will, show an increasing indifference to our actions and opinions. Witness the blacklist.

Thus we are fast drifting into an estrangement really against the deep-lying wishes of the people of both countries; and, if the war lasts long enough, there will be danger of the coming of definite ill will between the Governments of the two most friendly peoples on earth.

Yet we have never had an Administration more willing to keep on the friendliest terms, nor has there ever been a British Government more eager for our sympathy. A part of this friendly wish is an enlightened selfishness—they will need our help in the future as they have not needed it in the past; but most of it is unselfish— is the result of kinship in blood, in aims, and in ideals. If we shape our actions with a view to the long future, we can now do what we will in conjunction with the British Empire. We can become the leader of the English-speaking world in preventing wars of aggression. But they will grant leadership only if it be founded on sympathy.

As the Germans have to be driven into understanding, the British have to be led. The keynote of successful diplomacy with them is an intelligent and courteous sympathy. You cannot move them merely by protests and notes. And in many ways, they are very slow—the result, I imagine of their carrying a heavy burden of mediaeval baggage, in thought and ways. But in dealing with them their slowness must not be mistaken for malice. And they are more appreciative of friendliness and courtesy and forbearance and sympathy, I verily believe, than any other people that ever lived. For this reason they are hurt and irritated by the accusation, worked up in a part of the American press, that the British Government uses the information that its censors acquire for the personal profit of British traders and manufacturers and that it is preparing a commercial war against the United States. I have seen no facts to support such an accusation.

(1) I venture to suggest that in all future Protests and complaints we ascertain the facts by independent inquiry, and put all the facts on the table. No world is so full of suspicion or so careless in handling evidence as the commercial world.

(2) I venture to suggest that we go over the whole list of differences and disputes to see if there be not some items on which we can

yield, without in the least yielding any principle, and other items about which we can ask a similar yielding by the British Government.   If I had authority to undertake such a negotiation, under the President's direction and guidance, I believe a great change could be wrought in the present dangerous tension.

I believe, too, that these recommendations, if they were undertaken by us, would produce reciprocal action by the British Government.   The gravest danger in our relations comes not from large differences on important principles but from mistakes in the method and in misunderstandings that grow out of ignorance of facts and out of suspicions of purposes.

SEPTEMBER 15, 1916.

763.72111/4468

The Ambassador in Great Britain (Page) to the Secretary of State

LONDON, *January 7, 1917.*
[Received January 22.]

DEAR MR. SECRETARY: As I telegraphed you, I am sure there was no need to show to the Foreign Office the two personal statements that you made to the newspapers.[41]   They were both telegraphed to all the principal London newspapers, and they had, therefore been read here; and everybody here regarded them as a purely domestic episode.   They caused no confusion in the British mind.   To have taken them up with any officer of the Government would have seemed somewhat forced.   The whole incident did not the slightest harm here nor did it cause the slightest confusion.

I am much worried about the irritation that the British way of dealing with our ships is causing and the very much greater irritation that will be caused if they continue their stupid and shortsighted actions.   I am constantly discussing this subject both with Mr. Balfour and Lord Robert Cecil, Minister of Blockade, trying to get them to adopt some other plan of action.

Their aim, tho' they have never publicly explained it, is perfectly simple.   The German submarines sink so many European neutral ships, all which serve this Kingdom by bringing food or something else here, that the owners of these ships naturally wish to get them out of European waters.   Hence they are willing, and even eager, to get hauling to do in safer waters.   Naturally they are purchasable or charterable to American companies.   Just as naturally the British wish them to stay this side the Atlantic and they seek methods of discouraging them to go over our side.

---

[41] *Foreign Relations*, 1916, supp., p. 106.

But they have hit upon what I regard as the worst possible methods. They take ship by ship and try to find some discouragement to it. With one it is the so-called bunker agreement. With another it is a possible former part-ownership by Germans. With another it is something else. Now these devices and excuses and straining of mere coal-supply contracts wouldn't hold for a day in any court of justice— certainly most of them would not. And they have, besides, the enormous incidental disadvantage of annoying American shippers and ship companies. All this I repeat to them over and over again. They know it is all true, but they don't quickly see what other way to do it.

The interference with our rights and the infinite annoyance to us is not a part of their aims, and they regret it. "But", they ask, "what can we do?"

Well, I'm trying to help them answer that question. "First", I say, "that isn't my task. I don't care what you do, if only you will not contravene our rights. Then, as a preliminary, make a clean, clear, frank statement of your problem. You have not yet informed our Government why you do these things. Make a clear, frank statement." They are doing that now, and I expect it in a few days. Such a statement has now gone to Sir C. Spring-Rice. But that only clears the way—and doesn't yet remove the difficulty.

Then, I have said to them: "If you object to American companies' buying or chartering Scandinavian ships, why don't you buy or charter them yourself? Or, if you need shipping bad enough (and they do) why don't you try to charter ships belonging to other European countries? It's all a matter of price—unfortunately, for you, of very high prices. But by such means as these you will keep from doing violence to American rights and keep from the inevitable irritation of the American shipping-world, the American public and the American Government. Call in your big practical shipping men and ask them for plans."

The new Government has created a new Cabinet portfolio—the Ministry of Shipping, and the Minister is Sir Joseph Maclay, a big Liverpool ship-man. At my suggestion, Mr. Balfour is now arranging a meeting with himself of Sir Jos. Maclay, Ld Rob't Cecil & myself.

I have at least got this far with them—to show them that their present small method will cause an increasing trouble with us. I come back to this with every turn of every conversation.

They are quite sincere in their protestations that the last thing they want is another subject of controversy with us. What they want is to keep as many ships as possible on this side the Atlantic to serve their ever-growing needs. "All right," say I, "we have no objection to that, provided only that you do not interfere with American rights." It's the submarine trouble—the most damaging and threatening blow that the Germans have dealt them. That's what staggers them.

I'll report what progress I make towards inducing them to change their present foolish plan. I have ask^d them in the meantime to give us no more provocation—with what result remains to be seen. I am demanding, too, the setting-right of the breaches of our rights that they have already committed.

Yours very sincerely,

WALTER H. PAGE

763.72119/404 : Telegram

The Ambassador in Great Britain (Page) to the Secretary of State

LONDON, *January 20, 1917—1 p. m.*

[Received 8:50 p. m.]

5514. The following is of immediate importance to the President.

Since there has been an apparent delay in delivering your speech to the Senate [42] I venture respectfully to offer a comment on the phraseology in the sentence about "Peace without victory." My experience of the state of mind in this country makes me fear that unless you define your use of the word "Victory" it will be misconstrued as an effort directly to influence the result of the present war, and even as an interference on behalf of Germany since you took no step while the Germans were gaining military advantages. Any phrase which now appears to the Allies to interfere just when they hope to gain a striking military advantage is enough [to] provoke a storm of criticism that may greatly lessen your influence hereafter. Nothing can now stop the war before the almost imminent great campaign in France for which every preparation has been made. There is a general expectation here that after that peace may soon come.

[If?] instead of "Peace without victory" you should amplify your statement in some manner such as "Peace without conquest" or "People of either side" your speech will have the greatest good effect. Your words as they stand may be construed here as a sort of denial of Balfour's letter and possibly even as an unfriendly interference in the war at its most critical moment.

The sentiments you express are the noblest utterance since the war began, and, with an explanatory modification of this passage, the

---

[42] Delivered January 22, 1917; for text, see *Foreign Relations*, 1917, supp. 1, p. 24.

speech guaranteed greatly [to] further the cause you plead, enhance your influence, and fix you at the front of the movement for securing permanent peace.

PAGE

---

123 P 14/54a : Telegram

The Secretary of State to the Ambassador in Great Britain (*Page*)

WASHINGTON, *February 5, 1917—4 p. m.*

4395. Under extreme pressure of present situation President has been unable to consider your communications in regard to your resignation.[43] He desired me to inform you that he hopes that at the present time you will not press to be relieved from service, that he realizes that he is asking you to make a personal sacrifice but believes that you will appreciate the importance in the crisis which has developed that no change should be made. I hardly need to add my personal hope that you will put aside for the present any thought of resigning your post.

LANSING

---

123 P 14/55 : Telegram

The Ambassador in Great Britain (*Page*) *to the Secretary of State*

LONDON, *February 6, 1917—12 noon.*
[Received 4:20 p. m.]

5611. Your 4395, February 5, 4 p. m. At any sacrifice I am happy to serve here until after the end of the war and I am making my arrangements to stay for this period.

I have no wish to be relieved from service since the President wishes me to remain; and I beg you to do me the favor of expressing personally to him my grateful appreciation of this fresh proof of his confidence which I hope I can continue to justify. I also thank you heartily for the evidence of your sympathetic approval.

PAGE

---

⁴³ Not found in Department files.

ITALY

763.72/1391

The Ambassador in Italy (Page) to the Secretary of State

ROME, *December 25, 1914.*
[Received January 14, 1915.]

MY DEAR MR. SECRETARY: As you will have seen by my telegrams, I have for some time past been closely occupied in endeavouring to relieve the situation here touching the interference with our commerce with Italy, Switzerland and, to some extent, with other countries to the eastward, also.   The situation of our commercial relations can be said to be almost deplorable.   As my telegrams have shown, the Embassy is in receipt continually of complaints from American representatives in Italy and from Italian business houses as well, of the frustration of their efforts to carry through deals of great importance and value, and in these complaints unite persons who assure me, and I believe truly, that they are endeavoring to secure orders for the Italian Government and in some cases actually as their representative. This obstruction takes the form of interference with telegrams and of other means of impeding trade, and I confess that my efforts to get the matter solved does not meet with the success which I could wish. The Royal Decree promulgated in Italy on the 13th of November, prohibiting the exportation of many important lines of goods, including cotton, hemp, leather, rubber, oil, et cetera, has been a great obstruction as Italian shipping lines are inclined to refuse to accept bills of lading, even into Italy, where they think the goods may be subsequently sold outside and much more so where the bills of lading are through bills of lading for houses in Switzerland.   Switzerland itself has suffered greatly from this stoppage of articles of vital necessity to her, and has addressed, I am informed, a strong note to the Italian Government, and, as instructed by you, I have rendered such assistance as I properly and judiciously could, by personal interviews with the Italian Minister for Foreign Affairs, and by using such arguments as I thought might prevail.

It has not been easy to place the exact responsibility for this state of affairs.   Italy declares that she is compelled to prevent the reexportation of these articles under the provisions of the Royal Decree above mentioned; because otherwise England and France,—more particularly the former,—threaten to cut off articles of vital necessity to Italy.

My English colleague seems to think this reason thus assigned is pushed far beyond its proper application.   But it would seem that Italy must have some ground for her attitude in as much as the action of England and France in holding up her ships and preventing the importation of the articles specified in the Decree as prohibited from re-exportation, has caused great feeling among the people of Italy and is undoubtedly at the bottom of the change of sentiment which has been going on for some time. This change of sentiment has lately become quite marked. At first it was almost insensible; but within the last two or three weeks, the mental attitude of the people here and, to some extent I believe that of the Government, has undergone a decided change, and the change is, so far as I can judge, extending to other neutral and hitherto friendly countries as well.

This judgment is based on the expressions of such representatives of those countries as I have seen, or on press reports from them, and these countries include Switzerland, the Scandinavian countries and Greece.

Newspapers here which have been all along almost enthusiastically friendly to the Allies, are now changing their attitude to one of sharp criticism. A very important paper, the *Giornale d'Italia* has had several articles protesting most earnestly against the action of the Allies in holding up Italian ships, and suggestions are made that the Allies are not actuated only by their fear of their enemies being helped through the arrival of these cargoes; but are no less afraid of their friends being helped.

It is said that some of these articles are written by persons very close to those in authority and at least express their views.

The arrival of former Chancellor Prince von Bülow to take the place of Herr von Flotow as German Ambassador has of course caused great comment in Italy as well as outside and rumors regarding the reason for the change vary all the way from the simple statement that he is known to be one of the ablest and most experienced statesmen in Germany, to the suggestion that he has come for the purpose of proposing terms to Italy so advantageous that she will espouse the side of the allied Emperors.

There seems to be nothing in the latter idea, and I question if the intervention of any single person, however able he may be, will influence Italy's course greatly. It looks as though she had taken her course and proposed to follow it, with the single idea of furthering her interests. For the present this seems to be along the line of strengthening her position of neutrality, at the same time that she provides for future eventualities by increasing and thoroughly equipping her army. For the present, certainly, the people appear much calmer than they were a month ago, and the Government seems to have acted with great wisdom in securing the confidence of the people who now seem willing to await the Government's decision.

One constantly hears references to some possible movement in the Spring,—the date usually given being the last of March. This may be due in part to the reported instruction by the Government that schools shall endeavor to compress the whole session's work into the time between now and the middle of March and to the extension of the Moratorium to that date.

I think that the attitude of England and France in holding up ships in the Mediterranean is regarded as an attempt on their part to force the hand of the Government, and I am sensible of a certain feeling of resentment because of this attitude.

There appears to be what I might term a growing idea that the time may come when other countries, and our country and Italy are often mentioned together in this connection,—may have to follow the course which the Scandinavian countries have pursued, of banding together to see that their commerce as Neutrals, shall not be interfered with.

Another very interesting matter is the recent appointment by England of an Ambassador to the Holy See in the person of Sir Henry Howard. This is said to be only a Special Embassy; but it is in the line with what some think is a strong effort on the part of the Vatican to strengthen itself with a view to the internationalization of its present status in Italy. At the time of the first Hague Conference, when the Vatican desired representation there, Italy interposed her objection, as you will recall, and it was supported by England in the first place, and afterwards by other Powers. It is now thought by some that the Vatican is taking steps to be represented in the Peace Congress, or whatever the conference may be, to be called when the time comes to close this war, and it is said that the relations between the Vatican and France are more amicable than they have been since the time of the separation. I am not sufficiently informed to have an opinion of any value on this subject; but I give the matter as I have heard it discussed, feeling that it is one of much interest.

The subject upon which I have a much clearer opinion is that which I have already emphasized,—that the attitude of England and France towards the commerce of Italy and other neutral countries on the High Seas, is affecting adversely the sentiment of the people here, and that the present situation appears to me to be one fraught with real danger to the continuance of the warmth of sentiment which has hitherto existed here towards those Allies. Switzerland particularly has suffered greatly in consequence of this interference; but Italy has suffered enough to make a marked change in the feeling of many people with whom I come in contact.

I cannot close this letter this Christmas evening without wishing you, and all those whom you have so faithfully and ably represented, every happiness and good in the coming new year.

Believe me [etc.]   THOS. NELSON PAGE

763.72/1643

The Ambassador in Italy (Page) to the Secretary of State

ROME, *March 17, 1915.*
[Received April 8.]

MY DEAR MR. SECRETARY: For some time past, as you will see by the papers, and as I have telegraphed you, there has been much talk here of Italy's coming to an agreement with Austria through the negotiations of Prince von Bülow, the German Ambassador, by which Austria will cede to Italy the Trentino and a further region lying along the northern Italian border, and perhaps other territory, comprising enough to satisfy Italy, and keep her from going to war against her.

This came about just at the moment when it was announced through the Greek press that the allied fleets were half way through the Dardanelles and that Greece was going to join them. Evidently Bülow made a great effort and succeeded in stemming this sudden rush which might have resulted in throwing both Greece and Italy into the scale against the Central Empires. As it transpired that the Dardanelles were still unforced and that Greece had not gone into the war, and in fact was no longer controlled by Venizelos; but by a government friendly to Germany or at least to peace—Austria,—whatever she might have done in the other contingency,—refused to accede to the plan which it is said was proposed to her, and appears to have ended by offering to cede only a small portion of the Trentino, and simply to hand this over to Germany, as it were, in trust for Italy, to be given to the latter only at the close of the war, and meantime to be held as a pledge for Italy's good conduct.

In view of this there has been, as I telegraphed you today,[44] a sudden smoothing down of matters here, and no one appears to think that Italy will move if she moves at all, before the end of April.

Undoubtedly things have suddenly quieted here, and a sort of apathy appears to have set in after the state of suppressed excitement which existed here a week ago.

I do not know when she will move; but I feel measureably sure that if she does so, she is not going to set a given date for it; but will move without warning. This is what she did at the time of the Libyan war, and I feel pretty sure that she will do the same thing this time also.

Bulgaria still appears to me to hold the key to the situation, as she holds Greece in check, and should Greece move Italy will hardly

---

[44] *Foreign Relations*, 1915, supp., p. 20.

remain quiet. The fact is that up to this time, Italy and Greece alike have been afraid that Germany and Austria were still sufficiently strong to mass forces which would, to use a phrase that I have heard used again and again, "treat them precisely as Belgium has been treated".

An interesting thing came to my notice yesterday. I heard, through private sources, that Germany is bitterly hostile to America and that although this hostility has been intensified by America's refusing to accede to her demand that no munitions of war et cetera should be sold to the belligerents opposed to her, this was not the beginning of it, and that she hated America because America had stood in the way of certain plans which she had with regard to Mexico last year.

You will recall that last year during the Huerta regime, we heard that a large number of the discarded rifles of the model of 1890–91 were about to be sold by the Italian government, ostensibly to be shipped to Bremen; but destined in fact for Mexico. I succeeded in getting the Marquis San Giuliano to prevent the shipment of these arms, although it seems some Ninety Thousand Dollars had been paid "on account" of the purchase of these rifles, and the arms are still held here in Italy, where the representatives of a number of governments have been trying, ineffectually, to buy them.

Since the account given me yesterday of the feeling in Germany against us, and of the part that Germany's aspirations about Mexico played in that, I have put two and two together. And there has also come to me what, from time to time, persons have said to me, that after the war is over, we shall probably have to look out for Germany on one side and Japan on the other.

From time to time people say to me that the time must soon come when America will have to take a hand and do something towards making peace. Some of them evidently mean only in the way of tenders of good offices; others, however, mean in the way of going in as the ally of the Allies,—for no one here imagines that we could go in on the other side. I think that, should the time come, as well it may come, when the tender of good offices may appear proper and even necessary, the neutral powers would be likely to give at least a moral support to such a tender. This I judge from the expressions of representatives of some of the neutral powers who talk to me now in a very friendly spirit.

I enclose as a bit of interesting gossip here the translation of a news item [45] which appeared two or three days ago in the *Corriere della Sera*, the most important newspaper in Italy. From it you will see that there are rumours in circulation that Mr. Bellamy

---

[45] Not printed.

Storer,[46] who you will observe is mentioned here, not as an "ex" Ambassador, but as an Ambassador at present, is suggested as being interested in a mediation to be arranged between Benedict XV and the President in favor of a Treaty of Peace whenever events shall enable such a step to be taken.

I was called on a day or two before this notice appeared by a newspaper correspondent who informed me that the rumour was rife here that Mr. Storer is to be appointed as the representative of America to the Holy See. I informed him that I knew nothing whatever about the matter; but hardly thought it probable. I have also heard since then from an Ecclesiastic, who is a personal friend of mine, that his information is that Mr. Storer is working with this in view. It is not for me to offer advice unless it shall be requested; but I think it will not be considered improper for me to say that since I came here to Rome, no facts have come to my knowledge which would make it appear necessary from this end of the line to have in Rome an additional representative to the one accredited to the Quirinal.

Believe me [etc.]   THOS. NELSON PAGE

763.72119/88½

The Secretary of State to the Ambassador in Italy (Page)

WASHINGTON, *July 30, 1915.*

MY DEAR MR. AMBASSADOR: I received your letter of the 30th ultimo [47] and appreciate very much your congratulations upon my appointment as Secretary.

.   .   .   .

I hope you will continue to write me personally and confidentially in this way, as it is just the sort of information we require here to interpret the policies of the Italian Government and to comprehend the actual political situation in Italy.

We are here in a peculiar situation in our relations to Germany. The American people, I believe, do not desire war with Germany; in fact, there is no war spirit in the country. On the other hand they have been most desirous that the Government should take a firm stand in regard to the submarine warfare conducted by the Imperial Navy. They do not seem to appreciate what a firm stand means and to what it may lead. Of course, these two attitudes of the public mind are inconsistent, indeed they are almost paradoxical. It was with full recognition of the mental attitude of the American people that the

---

[46] Ambassador to Austria-Hungary, 1902-6.
[47] Not printed.

recent note to Germany was drafted. I hope and believe that war may be avoided because of the change which has taken place in the German method of submarine attack. If, however, there should be another passenger ship sunk with Americans on board, a sentiment in this country would result which would be very difficult to check.

There is another agency operating against a radical and rigid attitude toward Germany, and that is the general public feeling against Great Britain on account of her so called blockade and the interruption of trade between neutral countries. This offsets to an extent the feeling against Germany or, at least, keeps the balance of sentiment more or less equal. It is not equal for two reasons: one is, the preponderance of American sympathy is with the Allies, and, in the second place, the illegal acts of Germany cause loss of life while the illegal acts of Great Britain cause loss of property. This, briefly, is the situation here and whatever I should say further would be purely speculative.

Thanking you for your letter [etc.]   ROBERT LANSING

763.72/2141½

The Ambassador in Italy (Page) to the Secretary of State

ROME, *August 21, 1915.*

MY DEAR MR. SECRETARY: Before this reaches you Italy will probably be at open war with Turkey, as she has substantially been in fact for some little time, though no declaration of war has yet been made, so far as is known here. It would be more proper to say, perhaps, that Turkey is at war with Italy, as Italy has committed no act of war against Turkey. Whether this will change in any way the situation in the Balkans remains to be seen. The fact is that the Balkan muddle is so great that no one appears to know what the final result there will be. It is only known that Italy and the other Powers of the Quadruplice are doing what they can to bring them into concert; a thing so difficult as to seem quite impossible. The Balkan Powers have all been tremendously staggered by the Russian situation, and even though Venizelos should resume the reins of Government in Greece, it is hardly expected that he will move at present to have Greece enter the lists. There is much talk of Roumania coming in with Russia, but few expect her to do so unless Russia shall prove able to recover and make head against Germany in the south, which so far there is no sign of her being able to do. Bulgaria presents a somewhat different situation, and is so important to the Allies that they must be doing everything in their power by promises and whatever means are at their disposal to induce Bulgaria to join them. If they could induce her to do this it would probably settle Turkey's fate in a very short time, as she is generally believed to be very short of all means of defence and to be dependent on Germany by way of Bulgaria for nearly everything. Essad Pashá who seems to be the strongest man in Turkey is absolutely pro-German and is sustained, it appears, not only by the Turks, but by a strong German force, who seem to have the upper hand in Constantinople; in fact at this moment Constantinople is quite a German stronghold.

While it is said that Russia was promised possession of Constantinople and the Dardanelles, and undoubtedly has looked forward to this, and while France is believed to have been acquiescent in this plan, so far as I can find out, none of the other Powers, either among the Allies or in the Eastern Mediterranean have been desirous of such a disposition of this apple of discord on which they all look with longing eyes.

I myself feel that the most probable solution of the whole matter will be that in the end Constantinople will be left in the hands of the Porte with a modest hinterland and the city and the Straits will be neutralized and put under the protection of the Powers; otherwise it will almost certainly prove, what I have said, an apple of discord, and no one knows what difficulties will arise over it at the close of the present immense war.

I feel very much pleased at having secured the release of the several Italians, American citizens, born after their father's naturalization, and I am now urging on Baron Sonnino the necessity of obviating all possibility of friction between our two countries by entering into a Convention of Naturalization. Confidentially, I think I can say that he is entirely at one with me in regard to the importance of doing this, and I am hopeful of being able to carry it through. He tells me that he is trying to find some basis on which the matter can be arranged to the mutual satisfaction of us both, without undertaking to change the law of Italy, which is in a way fundamental. Several of these young men have not yet been found, but are being searched for, he informs me, and will be he thinks released, when found. This also is my opinion. One difficulty in these cases is, that these young fellows come over here and pass themselves off as Italians, until they are put in the Army. However, this does not affect the principle.

Please accept my cordial thanks for your kind letter which I received on yesterday. It is a great pleasure to me to be kept informed as to what is going on at home.

We are all looking forward with great interest and more than that to the next step at home, after the reported sinking of the *Arabic*. I am happy to feel that the matter is in such capable hands, and feel assured that the wisest possible thing will be done. Whatever that may prove to be, all that I have and am is at the service of the President.

With cordial regards [etc.]   THOS. NELSON PAGE

763.72/2142½

The Ambassador in Italy (Page) to the Secretary of State

ROME, *August 31, 1915.*
[Received September 27.]

MY DEAR MR. SECRETARY: The present situation, on the outside, in Italy is about the same as it was when last I wrote you. The successes of the German and Austrian forces against Russia have progressed so rapidly and with so little interruption, except for the failure to capture Riga, that it has cast a sort of gloom over the representatives of the other side; though they speak of it and I think consider it only a temporary advantage for the allied Empires. It is recognized however as having the immediate serious effect of prolonging the war and of turning the Balkan States, certainly for the present, from any idea that they may have had of joining the Quadruplice Allies. Saturday afternoon I went with Mrs. Page down to Fiuggi, a summer place in the mountains some forty five or fifty miles from Rome, where both the French and Russian Ambassadors were staying, and the Chilean and Brazilian Ministers as well as the Belgian Minister, and I had an opportunity of seeing more of these colleagues than one has in Rome.

The first two were undoubtedly much depressed by the news from Russia but both of them spoke with confidence of the final outcome and I believe expressed their real conviction, the importance of which consists in its being a reflection of the feeling in their respective countries. One of the most serious results of the German success in that region is the effect on the Balkan States alluded to. It looks at present as though Bulgaria had reached an agreement with Turkey by which in consideration of concessions made her by the latter she will permit munitions of war and other things as well to pass through her borders to Turkey. If she does it will probably mean that Germany will send a strong force to Constantinople to aid the Turks. This will of course bring Bulgaria into the war on their side. In such event it would scarcely seem possible that Greece and Roumania would abstain from joining the Allies.

One thing on which all here appear united is the necessity of the Allies sending a sufficient force immediately to capture Constantinople. Greece I understand holds the view that the only way to effect this will be to overawe Bulgaria and push for Constantinople from that side. Should Bulgaria however side actively with Germany, Austria, and Turkey and should Germany aid her with a strong force it will be no easier to capture Constantinople from that side than by way of the Dardanelles. However it seems that France is unquestionably sending troops to the Dardanelles and Italy is certainly sending troops south though where they go afterwards I have not yet learned.

I had a long talk this morning with the Minister for Foreign Affairs . . . He thinks that the United States would exert a great moral influence if she declared war on Germany—in consequence of Germany's attitude and acts at sea against us—and that she would have a very important part to play when it comes to making peace. He thinks that this influence would be of great importance even if she never sent a ship or a regiment to Europe as the United States would be the coolest member of the peace congress and her views would probably be less influenced by passion than those of other members of the congress just out of a violent war. I told him that I did not believe either our Government or any important element among our people wished to go to war or would go to war except on necessity. In expressing this opinion I of course gave him to understand that I had no authority and that I was not speaking officially. I added that the breaking off of relations was contingent upon the future result of the steps now being taken between the two governments. He expressed the view that should the Government of the United States be limited as I appeared to think at most to breaking off relations, the moral effect of this step would be greatly increased if the United States should strengthen her military and naval power. In this action he felt that she might have a great moral effect. He spoke very earnestly and I feel sure, as I said, that he speaks his convictions.

I see from the press that we have had a repetition after a century and a third of the Plattsburg address. Mr. Roosevelt's speech, except for the openness with which it was delivered, presents a curious parallel with the anonymous address which Major Armstrong circulated through Washington's camp at Plattsburg [*Newburgh*] one hundred and thirty odd years ago. I think the prompt action reported in the papers touching the matter seems to have had an excellent effect and if, as the papers say, the stand taken by the President proves effective without a war, not all the speeches which Mr. Roosevelt and his adherents can make will have any effect.

SEPTEMBER 1, 1915.

Since writing the foregoing I have had a talk with the Under Secretary Comm. de Martino who has a minister's rank (and who is one of the most important men in the Ministry for Foreign Affairs, his title being Chief of the Cabinet of the Ministry for Foreign Affairs) on the matter as to which I have telegraphed you to-day: [48] the embargo on the sale of arms to a belligerent. He, I found, confirmed what I already believed to be the fact, that Italy placed an embargo on the exportation of arms and munitions of war last autumn as she did on the exportation of many other important commodities, but this was solely because she needed these things herself and de Martino mentioned the fact that the sale of arms by a neutral to belligerents was entirely in accord with the principles of International Law and covered by the rules of the Hague Convention.

I have also telegraphed you to-day, simply that you might be informed about it, as to what is the view taken of the resumé of the German reply to our Note which has appeared in the press.[49] The general opinion of public men which is reflected in a way in the press is that Germany has not really made the concessions which at first sight her Note appears to make and while she says she will give warning she does not say that she will undertake to secure the personal safety of the ship's company. Of course the Note itself may clear up this point. A further criticism here is that underneath it all is a condition that the United States should pledge herself to secure from England a loosening of the blockade. There is in fact a pretty general idea here that Germany knows that her submarine policy has not proved successful and has aroused more resentment on the part of neutrals than it was worth. I incline to this opinion myself but frankly admit that I am not sufficiently informed to have an entirely clear opinion on this point. On one point which I have alluded to above I find my conviction much strengthened as time passes and this is that Germany will come after us the first time she has an opportunity to do so. Many things which have come to my knowledge, small things, point to what seems to me a very firmly lodged intention on her part to put the Monroe Doctrine to the test at the earliest possible moment.

Italy does not seem to be making any very great progress in her invasion of the region beyond the Austrian frontier, though her progress appears to have been fairly steady and she is said to have conquered the first line of Austrian defenses, which of course would be right on the border, and to be making steady progress against the second line after which there is the third line, the most difficult of all to capture. Her losses are not known; but I believe them to have been fairly heavy and have heard them reckoned as high as twenty seven thousand. I was interested to hear the Russian Ambassador, who is a very clever man, say to-day when I saw him for a moment,

---

[48] *Foreign Relations*, 1915, supp., p. 802.
[49] This telegram of Ambassador Page is not printed. For the American note, see *ibid.*, p. 480, and for the German Ambassador's reply, *ibid.*, p. 530.

that the Italians, he thought, should confine activity to the Austrian frontier, especially in the Isonzo region, with the view to threatening Vienna rather than to send Italian troops to the Dardanelles, where, according to his view England should mass sufficient troops to bring that enterprise to a successful conclusion. I wondered how far this view, which I feel was sincere, was based on the traditional politics which center about the Dardanelles and the eastern Mediterranean.

.   .   .   .

Believe me [etc.]   THOS. NELSON PAGE

_____

211.65 C 38/151½

The Ambassador in Italy (Page) to the Secretary of State

ROME, *October 5, 1915.*
[Received October 25.]

MY DEAR MR. SECRETARY: As you know I recently took advantage of a slackening up of work here which demanded my personal presence at Rome to pay a visit to northern Italy, partly, perhaps I should say mainly, to recuperate from the heat and depression of the late Roman summer, and partly to see northern Italy and form my own judgment as to how things are going. We passed through the war zone where there appear a countless number of soldiers and also a much larger number of men not yet called under arms than I had imagined there were.

.   .   .   .

With regard to the general European situation I find that the Ambassadors of the allied powers seem somewhat encouraged by the very latest developments. Russia's apparent ability to begin to make a stand, and even in some sections to proceed to a counter-offensive movement, is undoubtedly having an effect on the Balkan States, though it is too early yet to know the extent of this. Greece is at this moment apparently balancing herself; but it looks as though she were more than glad to have the allied powers go in through Salonica, and she must recognize that if Germany and Austria win she herself will be sacrificed to Bulgaria, so that her only hope of maintaining herself even in her present position is to secure the victory of the Allies and stand in with them. I feel sure that her protest against the landing of the allied troops at Salonica was only *pro forma* and that she was more than glad to see it done.

In Italy three classes are just being called out, probably with a view to having on hand ready for work as many men as possible should the Germans and Austrians undertake a descent on Italy. Austria still holds her second line of defense which gives her a great advantage not only for defense but also in the event of an offensive movement. So far Italy is not at war with Germany; but I do not see how she can keep out of war if the general war continues. Believe me [etc.] THOS. NELSON PAGE

868.00/75½

The Ambassador in Italy (Page) to the Secretary of State

ROME, *October 8, 1915.*
[Received October 25.]

MY DEAR MR. SECRETARY: By this same pouch you will receive a letter from me written two days ago in which, among other things, I spoke of the situation in Greece.[50]

Although that situation has changed so unexpectedly and apparently so radically since that letter was written, I am letting it go, as it at least shows what were the views here at that time held, not only by myself; but by the English and Russian Ambassadors here.

The *bouleversement* in Greece was a complete surprise to everyone here. Unless it is intended simply as a means to secure better terms from the Allies than Greece had yet been able to obtain, it undoubtedly creates an even more serious situation in the Balkans and consequently in the general conduct of the war, than previously existed, and might almost be said to have brought the war to a crisis. I cannot help thinking, however, from what I know of the efforts which Greece has been making to secure from the Allies terms greatly beyond anything they have been willing hitherto to concede, that her real aim is to wring from their necessities concessions that may include a considerable part of the twelve islands now held by Italy; as much of Macedonia as possible and even possibly Constantinople.

This looks fanciful; but it certainly has been in the Greek mind. Of course the action of the King and of those with him may be based on their apprehension of the Central Empires and Bulgaria in alliance, and their belief that the latter are the prevailing power in the Balkans. I cannot help thinking, however, that no matter what happens, Greece's interest is with the Allies, inasmuch as should the others win, Bulgaria must become the dominant Balkan State and Greece must inevitably become subordinate to her, if not subject to her.

There is a rumor in circulation that the three Kings in the Balkan States have got together in a sort of personal league with a view to increasing the influence and power of the Royal houses in those States. This if proved would of course indicate that they are doing so under the protection of Germany. If the story be true, and if true it would explain a good deal,—they might be commended to read

---

[50] *Supra.*

some of the Chronicles in the Old Testament, which are among the most vivid histories of what happens to Kings who enter into such leagues.

In any event, I cannot but think that the only chance that Greece has to carry out her aspirations is to side with the Allies, either openly or secretly.

Believe me [etc.]   THOS. NELSON PAGE

763.72/2325½

The Ambassador in Italy (Page) to the Secretary of State

ROME, *December 4, 1915.*
[Received December 27.]

MY DEAR MR. SECRETARY: I have at last closed up and am sending forward in this pouch my report on the *Ancona* tragedy, together with the sworn statements and other official documents which we obtained, and the substance of which I had already telegraphed from day to day, as the information reached me. . . .

.   .   .   .

The Balkan situation changes so rapidly these days that one hardly dares to form an opinion on what would generally be taken as a sound basis. The present storm-center is Greece, and if one place is more uncertain than another, Greece would seem to be that.

For example, day before yesterday afternoon, the Minister for Foreign Affairs, in his opening declaration to the Chamber on its reconvening, declared that Greece had given satisfactory assurances to the Quadruple Alliance that she was going to stand by her engagements with them, and he seems to be assured that such residuum of difficulties as still remained would, without doubt, be readily disposed of.

This appeared satisfactory enough, especially coming from a man like Sonnino of whom the story is told that von Buelow said he had bad luck in Italy as when he came back as Ambassador to a country where every one talked about everything he found himself confronted by the only man who never said a word about anything.

The very next morning after Sonnino's declaration, however, the Athens despatches declared that Greece had rejected all the proposals of the Quadruplice and was apparently nearer to attacking them than she had ever been before. This I understand the Greek Minister here has denied to the Italian Government and has declared to be without a word of truth in it.

What the truth is, I would not like to undertake to say; but I think this much may be affirmed with assurance, that Greece is going to do just the thing which she believes will be most for her interest, and her policy will follow the lead of the successes which take place about her. This at present would seem to give Germany the best chance of getting her aid. It is possible, however, that if England, France and Italy can make show enough to hold her in check until they get sufficient forces on hand, she may remain neutral. From present indications, it looks as though these powers were not going to push troops much further on the Greek side and might feel relieved to get those that they have there now safe back to Salonica, while Italy is, according to report, preparing the way for a big expedition into Albania. She is supposed to have already sent fifty or sixty thousand men over to Valona, and it is said that engineers and road-makers are busily at work building roads into Albania now.

The Adriatic is, however, at this moment, swarming with sub-marines and I understand the difficulties of supplying her troops are very great. I expect, though, to see Italy make a strong push to get an abiding foot-hold on the eastern shore of the Adriatic, and this was one of the plain intimations in Sonnino's speech.

I know that the newspapers have given you substantially the whole of this speech, and I sent you a brief summary of the principal points made by him; but I am going to send a translation of the entire speech for the Department files, as it relates to Italy's permanent policy along certain lines.

The speech was especially strong in its declaration as to Italy's determination to fight the war through to the end alongside of her Allies and make no separate peace. This was a direct denial of inti-mations which have been going the rounds *sub rosa* in certain quar-ters and which had in fact aroused the apprehensions of some of her Allies. This apprehension,—and it might also be termed a belief, and certainly a suspicion,—seems to have been based on Italy's not having declared war against Germany.

A curious thing about the speech is that the only reference to Germany in it is one to Germany's having broken off diplomatic relations with Italy on her declaring war on Germany's Ally. I feel pretty certain that she will keep out of war with Germany so long as she can.

There has been a sort of under-current latterly which from time to time seems more apparent than at others, critical of the present government for having plunged Italy into war precipitately, and having misread the signs.

This I understand to be the position of the opponents of the present Government, headed, it is said, by those very near to the former Premier. Sonnino's speech seems to have been a sort of answer to this. The other side, however, say that Time will justify their view.

It would appear, therefore, that the present Government must fight
the thing through, or they will be held responsible for the failure.
The divergence, although not apparent on the surface, is very wide;
but the present Government are undoubtedly most patriotic and apparently determined, as I rather think they must be.

Believe me [etc.]   THOS. NELSON PAGE

763.72/2326½

The Ambassador in Italy (Page) to the Secretary of State

ROME, *December 4, 1915.*

MY DEAR MR. SECRETARY: I observe that I have left out one matter which I meant to speak of. It relates to the President's sound
policy of "Preparedness". I have it borne in on me more and more
all of the time that we not only are not in Mr. B's idyllic condition
"of a country at peace without an enemy in the world"; but in fact
we have not a friend in the world,—unless possibly it be Switzerland.
And further, that when this war is over, we are going to find it out
promptly. One has only to read the English press which reflects the
English opinion to see how deep is the feeling against us in England,
in spite of all we have done for her. She considers that we have been
inspired solely by selfish motives in whatever our people have done
for her, and she resents tremendously our determination to maintain
the freedom of the seas, and not less our apparent success in availing
ourselves of such freedom.

On the other hand, Germany unquestionably, according to all that
I hear, and I hear a good deal,—though it comes mainly in frag-
ments,—is bitterly hostile to us and intends, when this war is over,
to make us answer for what she terms our unneutrality and aid to
England.

They talk openly of making America pay their expenses of war
because of America's furnishing England with the means to prolong
the struggle,—at least openly enough for it to come to my ears from
sundry directions. Whether it shall be immediately after the war,
or whether some time shall elapse before she finds it convenient to
attack us,—it is coming as certainly as she remains intact herself,
and unless I am mistaken it will come very soon after she gets the
Allied powers off her hands. They envy our condition and believe
sincerely that we shall not be able to put up any fight against them,—
so I say: *Evviva* Mr. Wilson's policy of preparedness.

I give you this as my opinion for whatever it is worth, and will
only say that I myself have arrived at it from causes which seemed
to admit of no other conclusion.

Believe me [etc.]   THOS. NELSON PAGE

763.72/2340½

President Wilson to the Secretary of State

HOT SPRINGS, VA., *29 December, 1915.*

MY DEAR MR. SECRETARY: Thank you very much for letting me read these letters from our Ambassador at Rome.[51] His letters are singularly lacking in definiteness of impression, and yet, taken as wholes, they do serve to give one something of the atmosphere of the court at which he is living and of the politics that is stirring Europe just now.

I do not think he states the feeling of animosity towards the United States with entire accuracy or with a full knowledge of all the elements involved; but I fear that in the main he is right.

Cordially and faithfully Yours,

WOODROW WILSON

763.72/2413½

The Ambassador in Italy (Page) to the Secretary of State

ROME, *February 9, 1916.*

MY DEAR MR. SECRETARY: The political situation here seems, for the moment, about what it has been for some time past. It is possible, however, that two or three things which are promised, may produce some changes, though no one appears to know precisely what form these will take. The two most likely factors among those referred to are the visit of M. Briand, who is expected to arrive to-morrow with a suite of several members of the cabinet and a general or two for the purpose,—according to the press,—of bringing about a closer political harmony among the Allies than has hitherto existed. The other thing is the re-convening of the Chamber, which is set for the 1st of March, the date fixed at the time of its adjournment.

There was talk some little time ago of calling the Chamber in session, even before this date; but the apparent danger of the crisis which existed at that time passed away. Undoubtedly, however, the meeting of the Chamber will bring the Government face to face with the discussion of questions which may make their position somewhat difficult, and which I doubt not they will be glad to have obviated.

The men at the head of the Government, however, are strong men as well as men of experience in parliamentary life, and if they work in harmony, they may be able, by forcing a vote of direct confidence based on the conduct of the war, to secure the substantial majority, as they did during the last session.

---

[51] i. e., the two preceding documents.

Although, as you know, the constituency of the Chamber did not contain a Salandra majority, the Government has hitherto been able always to have a substantial majority at its back, and it is not likely that in the present state of affairs any considerable part of the Chamber will undertake to do directly what would be equivalent to swapping horses in the midst of the stream.

There appear from time to time strong undercurrents of criticism of the Government made up of the most part of a number of subsidiary currents, all counter to the Government; but yet unwilling to fuse their forces in front of the manifest danger of overthrowing a Government without a better one to put in its place.

The victory of the Austrians in the western Balkan States and the complete collapse of Montenegro following that of Servia, has been a tremendous blow to the pride of Italy and has occasioned a very real danger to what Italy has hoped for her unquestioned control of the Adriatic.

As I stated in my last letter,[52] it was in a way fortunate for the Government that the failure to succor Montenegro resulted in such criticism in the English press and, to a less extent, in the French press. No country in the world is more sensitive to criticism than Italy and the Italian press was quick to respond, reflecting the resentment which this criticism caused throughout Italy.

Another cause contributed at the same time to arouse resentment here against England,—the sudden increase of freight rates for sea traffic from England to Italy, from which resulted a coal famine that threatened for a time to be disastrous, and an increase in prices of other necessary commodities. There was danger, indeed, of having to shut down important manufactures and of stopping important railway trains. Hard coal went up to 225 lire a ton, which is in the neighbourhood of forty dollars, and soft coal was somewhat less; but still high enough to make even an Ambassador shiver.

The feeling manifested over this throughout Italy has led to the English government's undertaking some remedial regulations and the English press seems to have felt it opportune to change the tone of criticism, to one of what, to judge from the quotations therefrom in the Italian press at present, is almost adulatory.

Undoubtedly, these things have served to emphasize divergencies between the Allies, and while the Governments have worked in entire accord, one gets echoes of much criticism among those who have no official responsibility to temper their expressions.

I hear, and I believe it to be true, that Briand's visit here is partly with the design of soothing asperities which, although not publicly

---

[52] Not printed.

expressed, are in private life hinted at, as well as to help formulate an accordant plan of political action hereafter.

One rumor, possibly it is more than a rumor, is that there is to be a French head to the inter-allied commission which is said to be in process of formation, with its headquarters at Paris, and that this is because of a view held by the other allies that England has the *materiel;* but so far as [*has*] not developed men to direct its application in the most effective manner.

I give this report as throwing a light on the views held here by some whose opinions are usually considered of value.

It is possible that the arrival of Briand may bring out facts which will clear up some of the obscurities at present existing to which I have referred.

Believe me [etc.]   THOS. NELSON PAGE

711.00/15½

The Ambassador in Italy (Page) to the Secretary of State

ROME, *March 18, 1916.*
[Received April 8.]

MY DEAR MR. SECRETARY: I have been so outdone by the persistent, senseless and groundless criticisms of the President's foreign policy that I have felt moved to write a paper as a sort of challenge to all, and especially to the leaders who are at the back of the campaign of criticisms and depreciation. I, of course, however, do not feel at liberty to publish anything relating to politics without submitting it to you with a view to knowing whether such a publication meets with your approbation or whether you think it in any event might not be inappropriate for me to publish it. I accordingly am availing myself of an opportunity to send by the pouch leaving to-day a paper[53] which I have written along the line suggested and I hope you will not think I am imposing on you too much in asking you to look it over at your leisure and if you think it proper to send it to Colonel House to whom I have written on the subject. I may add that I have also written to the President a letter setting out my views, though he, of course, knows nothing of the contents of this paper. Perhaps, it might be published without my name, though I am always ready to stand for anything that I write for publication. If you think there is no objection to it in the main, but that certain parts of it had better be eliminated, this course will be entirely satisfactory to me, as will be, indeed, whatever course you and House think proper in dealing with it.

[53] Not printed.

I feel that my pen may be of some service to the President in certain directions if I can use it. I recognize, of course, that I have to be very careful; but the fact seems so clear to me that the President's foreign policy has been not only not what his enemies proclaim it to have been; but really just the opposite to what they say, that I cannot but think it proper to set forth the facts as they are. A Minister of one of the neutral European countries said to me not later than yesterday that he felt that American diplomacy to-day was on the highest level that it had ever reached, and when I spoke of the soundness of the President's notes he said, "Yes, in the future we shall be citing your President's notes as the highest authority on the principles which they cover". My own opinion is that the way to wage this coming campaign is not to go in any sense on the defensive; but to make an offensive campaign and put the cavilers and the critics on the defensive. If this is done I believe that the verdict of the American people this year will be what I know the verdict of Posterity will be, that the foreign policy of this administration will be held to have been not only sound but brilliant. I hope you will allow me to add my tribute of respect to your own part in this sound, able, and brilliant policy.

Believe me [etc.]   THOS. NELSON PAGE

763.72/2651½

Colonel E. M. House to the Secretary of State

DEAR MR. LANSING: I know you are pleased with the action taken yesterday in the submarine controversy.[54] I feel sure it will meet the approval of the best opinion of the country.

I have not had time yet to read Mr. Page's article which you sent me, but I shall do so in a day or two.

I have a feeling that it may not be in the best of taste for an Ambassador to write complimentary articles concerning the Administration under which he is serving and is a part.

When Mr. Page comes we might take this up with him in person.

Sincerely yours,

E. M. HOUSE

NEW YORK, April 20, 1916.
[Received April 21.]

---

[54] See Foreign Relations, 1916, supp., p. 232.

763.72/2830½

The Ambassador in Italy (Page) to the Secretary of State

ROME, *August 14, 1916.*
[Received September 6.]

MY DEAR MR. SECRETARY: I am sending you by this pouch a despatch of to-day's date [55] transmitting copies (translations) of the two Decrees promulgated last Friday by the Royal Regent here, relating to the confiscation of the property of subjects of countries at war with Italy or with her Allies, and to the prohibition of all dealings on the part of Italians everywhere and of others in Italy or her colonies with such subjects.

As I have stated in the despatch, I took up the matter of the blacklist which, it seems indicated in the Decrees, is about to be put forth, in conformity with the action already taken by England, pursuant to the Paris Conference,—I mean took it up quite informally, in the hope of forestalling such action here so far as relates to Americans, and I pointed out as clearly as I could how friendly our people at large are at present towards Italians, and the almost inevitable consequences of disturbing our present friendly relations if action shall be taken which we consider invasive of our rights.

I received the impression, from what the Minister said, that while no black-list has so far been made out, and there is certainly no desire on their part to do anything which might be considered as affecting our rights, the Paris Conference, which was agreed to by the participants therein, provided for measures whose object is to cut off all dealings with the countries at war with the Allies.

Baron Sonnino said that they had in mind the prevention of dealing on the part of Italians with these subjects. As I have already telegraphed you, in my telegram of the 11th instant, No. 683 [55] and in my telegram of to-day's date, No. 688,[56] these Decrees have been generally considered as having the purpose of drawing from Germany a declaration of war.

It seems now to be thought that Germany, for tactical reasons, will probably not make such a declaration and that Italy will have to take the initiative in this matter. Her Allies are undoubtedly pressing her with much urgency to take this step and I understand that it is accepted that while the two countries have been for some time substantially in a state of war with each other, and possibly no very great change will ensue from the formal declaration,—a declaration will solve certain difficulties which the Allies consider of much importance.

---

[55] Not printed.
[56] *Foreign Relations*, 1916, supp., p. 40.

I find a very strong feeling, and a growing feeling here now, that the Allies have now got the longer end of the lever and must win.

We are forwarding by this pouch a report from our Consul at Venice [58] which shows that the recent air-raid on the night of the 9th instant caused more destruction in Venice than has appeared in the press here. The destruction of the church of Santa Maria Formosa was enlarged on in all the papers here; but no mention was made of the destruction of a great cotton-mill there, or of the sinking of the British submarine in the basin of the Arsenal.

No mention has been made here of the heavy losses which it must have cost Italy to make the very decided and important advance which she has made above the Isonzo. No casualty lists are published here. The losses must have been very heavy; but the gains are considered here to be of the utmost importance.

I find in some quarters, reasonably conservative generally, the belief that the way is being rapidly opened to cut off Triest from Austria. In any event, it looks as though Italy had made a very important advance. Moreover, it has had a decided effect on public opinion.

I have not sent any information in regard to the sinking of the fine Italian dreadnaught, *Leonardo da Vinci* at Taranto at the mouth of the harbor, from some cause which has not so far been explained. I knew that the information would be sent by the naval attaché here, and nothing so far as I know has ever been said about it in the press here. There is talk of being able to raise the boat and at least save the imperishable part of its equipment; but it hardly seems likely to be possible.

Believe me [etc.]   THOS. NELSON PAGE

763.72/2831½

The Ambassador in Italy (Page) to the Secretary of State

ROME, *August 28, 1916.*

MY DEAR MR. SECRETARY: As I have telegraphed you,[59] events appear to be moving a bit in this quarter of the world, and I judge from the good spirits of my colleagues the French and Russian Ambassadors whom I see at Fiuggi where we, as well as some of the Ministers are,—a couple of hours run out of Rome,—that they consider the movement both very important and very favorable to them. Italy has just declared war on Germany after having failed to get Germany to declare war on her, and according to the reports here, not only in the

---

[58] Not printed.
[59] *Foreign Relations*, 1916, supp., p. 47.

newspaper "extras" this morning; but in official circles,—though they do not seem prepared at the Foreign Office to guarantee the fact,—Roumania has also declared war on Austria-Hungary. This act has been expected on her part for some time; but it was not believed that she would take the step until a few days later. However, it seems to be thought that the Allies have come to some sort of an arrangement with Italy and with Roumania also which has brought both of these countries to take the step which the Allies have been pushing them towards so long.

According to rumour, another movement of importance is in the air and apparently imminent: It is said that there is expectation in circles usually well informed that Bulgaria will soon be induced to make a separate peace. If so, I fancy that it will mean that some sort of assurance will have been given to her, guaranteeing to her a considerable part of what she went to war for.

Greece, for the present, seems to be regarded by the Allies as almost a negligible quantity. She has been forced by the Allies to demobilize and since their apprehension that she might attack them in the rear should they move forward against Bulgaria, has been relieved, they appear to pay little attention to her. I understand that it is thought that at the approaching election Venizelos will have a slight majority, though the army and the pro-German element are bitterly hostile to him at present. However, his chances appear to be improving and if he comes into power, Greece may be able to make better terms with the Allies than appear probable at present.

On the whole, the Allies appear to feel that they are in a much more promising situation than they were a short time since.

.   .   .   .   .   .

I am much interested in the American news; though it is exasperating to find it so stale when it arrives, I read it with avidity. It all depends, it seems to me, on whether you can carry New York by a sufficient majority to bring Connecticut and New Jersey along also.

I have just written the President a long letter containing a suggestion which I hope he may find practical. Mr. Lincoln did it and Mr. Roosevelt did it also in a different way, and I do not see why he himself may not make an appeal in the form of a letter directly to the people, setting forth simply what his Administration has accomplished.

However, you will all know better than I what is necessary to do, and the way to do it.

Believe me [etc.]

THOS. NELSON PAGE

811.00/18½

The Ambassador in Italy (Page) to the Secretary of State

ROME, *November 25, 1916.*

[Received December 20.]

My Dear Mr. Secretary: By the time this reaches you, the election will have become a thing of the past; but news reaches here so slowly that it will be still crisp to us even then. It is only to-day that I heard indirectly that Mr. Hughes has telegraphed his congratulations to the President. No paper has come later than the 30th of October and only one letter has arrived written since the 7th of November.

So, we are all waiting eagerly to get the American papers telling how the various States have gone. In any event, it is sufficient for me to know that Americanism, sheer and clear, has triumphed over all the other sorts and conditions, whether diluted or undiluted.

What a triumph it has been for Americanism and Democracy, and what a great triumph it has been for the President as the representative of both. I hardly know which to admire most,—the ability or the dignity with which he conducted this campaign. In fact, I think they are so closely connected that they must be taken together.

. . . .

Moreover, I feel that there is a distinct feeling of relief in those parts of Europe with which I may be said to be in touch, even to a limited extent, that the policy of the American Government as heretofore presented, will not be substituted by an unknown policy, preceded by a period of several months in which the unknown must have over-shadowed that which, although known, might be said to have been repudiated.

I have received personal congratulations from any number of my colleagues, the most interesting of which, to me, were those of the Japanese Ambassador, who took the trouble to write a note expressing his personal congratulations. . . . I have received congratulations from both the British and the Russian Ambassadors, as well as from the representatives of the Government here.

I desire to express to you personally my high appreciation of the able manner with which the foreign relations of our Government have been conducted during these last two years of stress and storm. I do not believe that greater problems were ever presented to any Government or conducted with greater skill and success than those which have been presented to this Administration, and which you have borne so great a part in solving.

I believe that from now on European Governments will recognize the power of the Administration as being much greater than it has been esteemed by them, certainly for the last year. The whole tone of the press has changed, especially of the London press, and I feel sure that a considerable part of the attitude exhibited by this press toward America in the past, was due to the attitude of their correspondents in America who have always had an attitude, not only critical towards America; but actually hostile to all American opinion which was not subservient to England.

I have been following with much care the reports of the various conferences or meetings or whatever they are termed, which have been going on between the representatives of the allied countries and have felt it opportune to keep in mind here the danger which Italy might have to face hereafter, of finding herself greatly hampered if she should bind herself now by the sort of pacts which the newspapers state are the object of these inter-ally conferences. Only this morning I had an opportunity to bring to the attention of the Minister for Foreign Affairs certain published reports of work that is going on to render the economical relations between Italy and her Allies ever closer and closer, and I asked him how far these combinations were expected to go,—all in a perfectly unofficial way, of course,—and he assured me that there was not the slightest intention of entering into any obligation which would bind them, beyond the period of the war, and he seemed to agree with me in thinking that conventions dealing with economic questions were likely to have to yield to the economic conditions themselves and that the people of a country were not likely to submit to anything that was manifestly against their interests in such matters. In other words, that economic laws would prevail over whatever attempt might be made to traverse them.

There is great interest here in what our Government will do regarding the two most recent moves on the part of the Central Powers—the sinking of the British hospital-ships and the deportation of the civil population of Belgium into Germany. It does not appear yet to have been definitely established that the *Britannic* was sunk by a torpedo, though it looks as though this were the cause. She was a great ship and by far the most wonderful thing in the shape of a hospital that I ever saw. I was taken over her last winter when she was at Naples and was shown her hospital equipment from top to bottom,—I rather think with a view to showing me that she was not armed in any way whatever, or indeed used for any other purpose than that of a floating hospital.

As the Greek situation is too complicated and too changeable,—though the change always seems to be from bad to worse,—for one to give any definite opinion upon it, I will not cumber this letter with it.

The death of the old Emperor of Austria has been received here with the sentiment which might well have been expected. The press has given the expected report of his relation to Italy, with references to the suffering which Italy endured under his rule or administration. The people at large were glad to have that which is considered the most terrible thing to which mortality is subject, visited upon him. The thoughtful accept the inevitable without knowing precisely whether his death will produce any change whatever and if so what the effect will be. It is apparently not thought that there will be any great change in the military conduct of the war; but there seems to be an idea that the young Emperor may fall more under the influence of the Emperor of Germany than the old Emperor was.

I know too little of the internal affairs of Austria to have an opinion on this subject. I rather think, however, that this new Emperor will follow the course of the old one until he gets well seated in the saddle and that then he will wish to choose his own road and gait and personally I look for some change in the Austrian relation to the present situation, though I would not be rash enough to say what form it will take.

Believe me [etc.]   THOS. NELSON PAGE

811.00/19½

President Wilson to the Secretary of State

WASHINGTON, *26 December, 1916.*

MY DEAR MR. SECRETARY: I have read this letter with a great deal of interest. Mr. Page had written me one in which he said many of the same things, but this letter is fuller and more definite and contains some items that are quite significant.

Faithfully Yours,

W. W.

763.72119/308½

The Ambassador in Italy (Page) to the Secretary of State

ROME, *December 29, 1916.*
[Received January 17, 1917.]

MY DEAR MR. SECRETARY: Matters seem to be moving so in these days that it is difficult to keep up with them, and it would be unwise to prognosticate anything. As you know, the President's circular note to the belligerents [60] created here as elsewhere a great sensation, and still makes a strong impression not only on the public mind but on the minds of the men in the government. The very first reception was one of questioning, then came within twenty-four hours a mass

---

[60] *Foreign Relations,* 1916, supp., p. 97.

of curiously vehement criticism—so vehement in fact that it had a tone of insincerity—and I feel sure that it was responsive to a cue given the press. I have just written the President a letter giving an account of my interview with the Minister of Foreign Affairs who is I think the ablest man in the Government and has the gift of calmness—not the commonest gift here. I have a conviction that the criticism of the note was first for home consumption—to prevent the opposition, which is secretly stronger than it appears, from running away with the situation; and secondly, was for the Allies. In fact, I tend to believe that the reception accorded the note was by concert among the Allies—all of whom having just passed through Ministerial crises or peril of such, felt it necessary to withhold from their people any belief that peace is possible in the present situation. The Italian criticism followed almost exactly the French criticism. Along with the attack on the President's note went reports of desperate conditions in Germany and Austria-Hungary. The British here are always talking of this—and I think delude themselves and thereby hurt themselves. I cannot however get out of my mind the impression that this last note, whether sent at the right time or not according to the views here, was timely enough to serve—and that it marks the beginning of a movement that will bring peace eventually if it be followed up.

The day the note came—the 20th.—I tried again and again to get an appointment with the Minister of Foreign Affairs, but he was at the Chamber that day and at seven o'clock I called without avail to see if I could not get a chance to see him. And as I could not do so I saw his chief Secretary and told him that I had a very important document and would call next morning at ten. When I saw Sonnino next morning he undoubtedly felt the importance of the note, though he thought the moment unpropitious for its success. I however left no doubt on his mind as to the earnestness behind it—and it still continues the chief subject of discussion here. The vehement criticism of it is probably due as I say to apprehension that the opposition might use it as a weapon against the Government. A short time back there was quite a recrudescence of the Giolitti opposition. The violence has, however, begun to show signs of having spent itself and I have thought it timely to bring attention back to the note itself from the mass of adverse criticism directed against it, and so I have just given out a statement calling attention to several glaring errors in the criticism—especially that which has stated that the note assumed that both sides are fighting for the same objects—naturally, I expressed no opinion myself but simply asked that the note be taken and read itself and judged on its own merits. I think that it is known by the thinking that the note must bring the result it was intended to bring—though the time when that result comes may be somewhat deferred. Privately men tell me that it was just what ought to have been done—so we will have to wait and see. The Czar's address just out is thought by those I have talked with to mean that Russia feels it necessary to show activity in order to get Constantinople. It also outlines what Russia is fighting for.

I am sending and would like the President to see a short paper which I wrote over a month ago and came near sending before.[61] You will see if you care to look at it that my reasoning led me to conclusions not unlike those which you must have reached about the same time. The term "a just and durable peace" has a certain effect here and may well be emphasized.

Believe me [etc.]   THOS. NELSON PAGE

763.72119/307½

The Ambassador in Italy (Page) to the Secretary of State

ROME, *December 29, 1916.*
[Received January 18, 1917.]

MY DEAR MR. SECRETARY: I telegraphed you two or three days ago of a curious report brought to me of the Vatican's suggestion about America's power to make peace.[62] I did not, however, telegraph the whole story, but I want you to have it just as I got it.

My informant is a man of high character and I feel sure that what was said to him was intended for my ears, even though he was not sent directly to me. He said that he had been sent for to go over there and on arrival was told by Cardinal Gasparri, the papal secretary of state, that America had it in her power to make peace within twenty-four hours if she wished to do so. He said: "How does Your Eminence mean?" and the cardinal said: "Simply by acting as a neutral in fact as well as in theory". He then went into a little discussion as to two kinds of neutrality, one a neutrality which followed the strict letter of the law, the other a neutrality which followed the spirit of the law. The first, he said, was the neutrality which America was following, but if instead of this she would follow the spirit of the law, as Spain had done and would stop all trading whatever with the Allies in as much as she could not trade with the Central Empires, the war would come to an immediate end and peace would be concluded. My informant suggested that for America to do this might be considered by the Allies at this stage as a hostile act. To this the cardinal replied substantially that gov-

---

[61] Not printed.
[62] Telegram not printed.

ernments could always find ways in which to meet such difficulties and that it would be easy for the United States, in as much as she was always having questions arise between her and Japan, to bring one of these questions to a point at which she might proclaim to the world that she could no longer send munitions and food supplies, etc., to foreign countries because she must reserve them for her own possible imperative use. Thus she would obviate the danger to which my informant alluded and at the same time need have no apprehension that Japan would wish to engage in war with her, and the question with Japan could be settled afterwards without serious trouble.

The story is so curious that I feel that the President and you will be interested to know it. I have no doubt, however, of the accuracy of the report made to me.

Believe me [etc.]   THOS. NELSON PAGE

811.00/20½

The Ambassador in Italy (Page) to the Secretary of State

ROME, *January 7, 1917.*
[Received January 31.]

MY DEAR MR. SECRETARY: Without undertaking at this time to go into the question of the reception here of the President's recent note to all the belligerent governments,[63] which I am dealing with in another letter, there is one point as to which I desire to direct your particular attention, and which I think has had a certain effect, in moulding the opinion here.

This is the attitude towards the Administration on the part of a considerable number of what may be termed the American Colonies in this and other European capitals. I do not refer to Americans abroad who are engaged in business; and who for the most part preserve their American loyalty; but rather to those who may be termed residents of foreign capitals, whether permanent or temporary, and whose desire is to be distinguished by the native population as quite distinct from the other Americans who are here, either as visitors or in business.

The attitude of this class, which claims to be American and only anti-Wilson and his Administration, would not be worth mentioning, but for the fact that it is taken here as an example of the American general attitude, and the exaggerated criticism of this class is taken as an expression of true American feeling; and that the deduction that the President's action represents rather his personal views than

---

[63] *Foreign Relations,* 1916, supp., p. 97.

the views of the American people, is found even among some connected with the Government.

For example, I was informed by an important Italian some days ago that the chief secretary of one of the cabinet ministers here,—Scialoia, who has charge of the war propaganda here,—stated to him that President Wilson was not supported by the American people and did not have the country at his back in his action. But, said my informant, how do you know this? And the secretary replied that he had been so informed by a very well known American, Mr. . . ., when he was in Rome only a short time since. And I myself was told by an Italian only this morning, in reply to my suggestion that I had been surprised at the extremely erroneous view which had been taken of the President's note by the Italians here, that one of the principal causes was the almost universal criticism of the President for his action by the American colony in Rome, who have given the impression that Mr. Wilson is not supported by the American people and has acted in a purely personal way.

These people, said my informant, have created, in the minds of the Italians, the idea that the President's notes carry little weight in America or elsewhere, and the natural inference is drawn by the Italians and the French that if Americans, who are assumed to know their own country, state such things about the Administration, they must be well-founded.

At least this is what the people who hear what these unpatriotic Americans say, deduce from their attitude.

Wherever I have run across the trail of these unpatriotic Americans, I have taken occasion to express myself in unmistakable terms, and I think that in time the Italians will find out the emptiness of their declarations; but meantime, they undoubtedly cause a certain amount of misunderstanding and mischief, and it is a pity that they should be permitted, while sheltering themselves under American passports, to act in so mischievous a way.

The consequences of this un-Americanism abroad, are very widely different from any consequences that anything which they might say at home could possibly have.

Before closing on this point, I wish to say that there are of course any number of absolutely loyal Americans in Rome as in other European capitals who reflect honor on our country, as they appreciate the honor of being Americans, and I only wish that there were some way in which the un-American element with whose personal opinion I am not concerned; but whose actions causes me much concern, might be segregated from the true Americans.

Believe me [etc.]   THOS. NELSON PAGE

763.72/3169½

The Ambassador in Italy (Page) to the Secretary of State

ROME, *January 15, 1917.*
[Received January 31.]

MY DEAR MR. SECRETARY: As I am having an opportunity to send by special messenger Mr. Thomson, Vice Consul at Salonika, who is on his way home for service in the Department of State, a letter which I can make more confidential than I could through the open mail, I am writing this with a view to having you read it and show it to the President also, should he have time to read it.

I wrote fully some days ago as to the effect here of the President's note of December 18th [64] and the reasons why I thought it was received by the press as it was, and I also wrote of the Conference here of the Premiers of the Allies with other representatives.

Since then, the Allies' note [65] in reply to the President's has been published and the press has been very full of it, with comments which, naturally enough perhaps, are entirely eulogistic of it. They have also been commenting in quite an opposite tone upon the Notes which the Central Empires have sent upon the receipt of the Allies' note referred to.

The unmeasured praise of the Allies' note contained in the press is reflected in some quarters here; but on the other hand, there is a subcurrent of criticism which holds that they have gone so much further than they can establish it practically that it was perhaps unwise to do so. Although it has been very difficult to learn with any precision what occurred in the Conference here, I have heard on what I believe to be good authority that in the Conference Lloyd George took the leading part in laying down the principles on which the Conference should proceed to base its decision; that in fact he did most of the talking and presented his ideas with great vigor and positiveness; but in a very general form, and that then Baron Sonnino would take up the various matters and in a calm and cogent way, show just what was practical and what was not, according to his view,—presenting both facts and figures in a way which generally resulted in the conference adopting his views, and that Briand sided with him.

In this way, it appears, that Baron Sonnino gave whatever there was of friendliness of form to the Note to the President in which he was sustained by Briand.

I have heard further that Russia was so to speak in opposition to the others nearly all the time and no one seems to know here just what

---

[64] *Foreign Relations*, 1916, supp., p. 97.
[65] *Ibid.*, 1917, supp. 1, p. 6.

Russia is doing or possibly even what she can do. It is said that it was not until Sunday afternoon,—the last day of the Conference, that the Conference came to anything like accord. Finally, however, an accord was reached and according to the press the accord is very close and complete. Sonnino seems to have made a deep impression upon his colleagues and has undoubtedly strengthened himself very much with the Italians who have been sensible of this impression and are much flattered by it. This, however, does not necessarily mean that an attack will not be made on the Ministry when the Chamber re-assembles on the 21st instant, as it is almost certain will occur, unless some victory shall be obtained by Italy in the meantime. Sonnino, however, is likely to remain.

My own view of the Note of the Allies to the President is that how-ever friendly the phrases may be which it contains, and however much it may be praised, it could scarcely have been less,—what shall I say, positive,—had they already won the decisive battle which they are only hoping to win.

It contains an answer quite complete and perhaps even more than complete, to the President's inquiry as to the purposes with which the Allies are conducting the war; but it contains also, as I read it, two quite distinct affirmations, one that the Allies propose to deal with the map of Europe to suit themselves; the other that when they shall have done this, they may be ready to hear anything that the United States may have to say on the question of a future League for Peace.

I do not think that there is much question as to the large part which England has had in the substance of the Note. At least for the present, however, the people seem ready to keep on. The tug will come in the Spring.

It is a singular circumstance that immediately on the heels of this very comprehensive declaration of intentions with regard to the disposition of Europe, things should suddenly be tightened up here. Nearly all the necessaries of life seem suddenly to have become scarcer or at least difficult to obtain them here and there is such an absence of fuel that railroad trains are being taken off; coal and coke are being corralled by the Government and I have had to apply, as an Ambassador, to the Foreign Office to obtain the privilege of paying 300 lire a ton for coal. I confess that I do not understand why they should at the very moment in which apparently everything is scarcer than ever before, talk as though they were on the way to Berlin and Vienna. They all seem to think here that Austria is in a terrible plight and that Germany also is in the most straitened circumstances. You will know far more of the truth of these things than I can learn here, where only one side is ever permitted to be told.

I have been much struck in these last weeks by the open attempt made in the press to secure some sort of league, formal or informal, of what they call the Latin American peoples or nations. Some time ago, whenever the newspapers mentioned the South American countries, they always spoke of the "little South American Republics." They now speak of the "Great South American countries" of [or?] the "Great Latin American countries" etc. and the press is full of praise of "Latin America", with suggestions of its spiritual nearness to the Latin civilization of Europe.

Efforts have been made, with more or less success, to create what they call the Latin Union, taking in Italy, France, Spain and the South American Republics. There was a great meeting in Lyons quite a time back in which this idea was advanced and since then any number of associations in which the name of Latin Race appears, have been and continue to be formed, or at least promoted.

Meanwhile, I find among my "Latin American" colleagues two sentiments which appear to me to have considerable influence with them, one the apprehension that the Monroe Doctrine may be abandoned and their countries thus be placed at the mercy of European cupidity; the other that the United States may become so powerful as to overshadow them, if not menace their liberty. The two are quite diverse if not antagonistic and yet undoubtedly they feel both of these things to be a menace.

Moreover, it is equally an undoubted fact that there is an effort over here in Europe to draw these South American countries into closer relations with Europe and divide them from the United States. The newspapers contain not infrequent references to the fact that all the Latin countries are Roman Catholic and have similar ideals et cetera. On this subject, however, I will write further another time.

Meanwhile, I will only say that although at the present moment the President's plan for hastening peace appears to have failed of execution at any time in the near future, I personally feel that the step which he has taken, has brought peace unquestionably nearer than it was before, and that it will play its part in the consummation of that which he desires.

I would greatly like to see him when the time comes, as I believe it will come before very long, for him to take another step or point attention to the one already taken, place distinctly in the foreground his suggestion that the peace at which he aims is a peace that shall be both just and durable.

Believe me [etc.]   THOS. NELSON PAGE

763.72/3170½

The Ambassador in Italy (Page) to the Secretary of State

ROME, *January 22, 1917.*

[Received February 14.]

MY DEAR MR. SECRETARY: Night before last I was called on by a gentleman who had received from the Vatican a very interesting memorandum in regard to the views of the latter on the Allies' note to the President in reply to his note of December 18th, although more specifically it related to Mr. Balfour's note of explanation and endorsement of the Allies' note.[66] The substance of this memorandum I sent you in a confidential telegram yesterday morning[67] and I am writing you this so that you may show it to the President. I gave the substance of the memorandum in my telegram, but there were one or two interesting things mentioned by the gentleman in question which were not in the written memorandum. This memorandum was first written out and given him, but the next morning he was recalled and was given permission to copy the memorandum, but had to leave the original, as indeed he had been told he must do, when it was first handed to him. He was told that Poincaré when Minister in 1912 promised Russia, in consideration of her support in France, that she should have Constantinople and the Straits, and that after Poincaré was elected President, he confirmed this promise in writing. Also that when in the autumn of 1914 the conference of the Allies took place in London at the time, I think it was, when England secured the promise from the Allies that no one would make a separate peace but that all would stand together to the end, Russia presented Poincaré's written engagement,—that she should have Constantinople and the Straits,—and England had to yield to secure her engagement not to make a separate peace.

I have read in the press in the last few days that the Vatican got the Spanish Ambassador in Washington to call on the President and assure him of the Vatican's entire sympathy with his recent move to ascertain the terms of the Allies in the hope of leading eventually to peace, yet at the same time the press here has been commenting constantly on the Pope's entire abstention from any reference to the President's step in the allocution which the former made here the day before Christmas and his failure in such a discourse to refer to the President has been generally accepted as evidence that he did not approve of the President's step. On the side many have drawn the inference therefrom that the Pope is working with Spain to be, if possible, selected as the arbiter when the peace conference shall

[66] For Mr. Balfour's note, see *Foreign Relations*, 1917, supp. 1, p. 17.
[67] Telegram No. 800, Jan. 21, 1917, *ibid.*, p. 22.

assemble; but in any event to be recognized and have a seat in that conference. I have given you the information which has come to me, not because I do not appreciate the futility of the curiously antiquated sort of intriguing diplomacy which it exemplifies, but because I think it shows very clearly that the Vatican is working with all its power for Austria. The contention set forth in the memorandum which came to me and which I telegraphed you is undoubtedly true; the handing over to Russia of all the provinces therein listed with the cession of Constantinople and the Dardanelles will undoubtedly give her tremendous, if not overwhelming, power in Europe and make her very strong in the Orient. The whole tone of this memorandum, however, is against England and, incidentally, her allies, who accede to this programme. It was said, indeed, in the memorandum that England does not dare to present the true program which she has in mind to Europe and therefore has violently protested against the cruelty of the Turks against the Armenians, et cetera.

The gentleman told me that the Vatican keeps, he believes, absolutely informed of every move that is made in the whole field of present diplomacy and he believes that the Vatican knows just what terms Germany and Austria would be willing to make peace on. I am sure that the Vatican used certain influences during the last electoral campaign in America, on account of the President's attitude with regard to Mexico, to withdraw from the President the support of representatives of the church in America.

The newspapers here are filled all the time with stories of the troubled conditions existing in Germany and Austria. Thoughtful men, however, who are not swayed by prejudice think that Germany can hardly be starved out, but the very general impression is that Austria is in a very bad way indeed. I myself, remembering the days of my childhood in the South, am skeptical as to the people's being forced to yield because of the scarcity of even the necessaries of life.

I have written the foregoing to you, not only for yourself, but thinking this the most confidential way to have it reach the President.

Believe me [etc.]   THOS. NELSON PAGE

763.72/3171½

The Ambassador in Italy (Page) to President Wilson

ROME, *January 22, 1917.*

MY DEAR MR. PRESIDENT: I have written a letter to the Secretary Mr. Lansing by this pouch which it may interest you to see and I will not repeat anything that I have said in that letter.

The unknown quantity in the present problem, here at least, seems to be Russia. No one here appears to know just what is going on

there. The Russians themselves say that Russia is getting ready for
a great move and that she will be able to save Roumania; that the
change will take place very soon, et cetera. They also declare that
Russia is absolutely determined to carry the war through to com·
plete victory. I am sensible myself that there at least seems to be,
not only considerable ignorance here among the representatives of
the other Allies as to what Russia is doing or can do; but also some
anxiety on this point. According to what we read and hear here, the
Russian cabinet appears to be in a constant state of change, or
"crisis", as they say here. Ministers succeed Ministers with startling
rapidity, without any one here knowing precisely why. One thing,
however, appears reasonably certain, that Russia has recently been
on the verge of making some sort of separate accommodation, if not
actually a separate peace, and the whole matter of the Dardanelles
and Constantinople has come out in consequence of this fact. As my
telegram of yesterday stated,[68] Russia seems to be in a fair way of
getting from the other Allies a hand sufficiently free to give her a very
preponderant position as regards, not only Eastern and Southeastern
Europe; but even the Orient itself. I draw from this the conclusion
that it was necessary to make large concessions to Russia, either to
secure her continued co-operation or to make it appear worth while
to her to face the conditions in which she finds herself and to put
forth extraordinary efforts.

There seems a general impression here that Germany may be in
a bad way, economically, but that Austria is certainly in an exceedingly bad way. I incline to the opinion that the Memorandum to
which I have referred in my letter to Mr. Lansing, was brought to
my attention because of the untoward condition in which Austria-
Hungary is at present and the apprehension that Russia may become
absolutely preponderant in Southeastern Europe.

As you will have heard, the recent Conference here of the Prime
Ministers of the Allies, excepting that of Russia,—with their leading
military representatives, besides deciding on an answer to your Note,
decided also to create a mobile army the size of which is set at anywhere from three-quarters of a million to a million men, composed
of forces of all the Allies to be used wherever occasion demands.
In pursuance of this, considerable numbers of French troops have
been coming into Italy,—whether for use in the Balkans or for use
in Italy along her northern battle front, I have not so far been able
to ascertain. Some say one thing, some another. It was, however,
in consequence of this proposed mobile army, no less perhaps than
in consequence of the alleged increase of German Austrian forces
along the Swiss northern and western frontier, that Switzerland

---

[68] *Foreign Relations*, 1917, supp. 1, p. 22.

the other day decided to mobilize the greater part of her troops. The press here, as in the other Allied countries, makes the claim that this mobilization is entirely against Germany and Austria, while I see the latter say it is against the Allies. I think it may be said with certainty that it is not against the Allies solely that Switzerland has mobilized. I know that the Swiss Government made representations to the Allies that the step was not taken with any hostile intent against them. It was taken to protect Switzerland's neutrality from aggression on either side. This is the real fact and I understand that Switzerland now feels pretty well assured that neither side in the great combat will undertake to do that which will fling the whole weight of her force, which although small by modern reckoning, is pretty compact,—against them.

I learn from the best authority here that Switzerland at present, although very short of supplies, has sufficient for her immediate needs. A short time ago there was a great discussion among the Allies as to whether Switzerland should be permitted to export anything into Germany, which she imported, and that England was for excluding her right to export anything whatever. She was obliged, however, to yield to the extent of permitting the exportation of what is called here "agrume", that is, fruits such as oranges, lemons, citron, etc. and possibly certain vegetables such as onions, inasmuch as Sicily and Southern Italy, where these fruits are the principal staple of production and export, absolutely demanded it, and Italy herself stated that it was necessary to make this concession.

Switzerland, as you know, has been a great producer of condensed milk, cheese, butter, etc. and I learn that there is great apprehension lest, owing to the inability to get a continuance of imports of winter feed for the cattle, they will have to be killed, in sufficient numbers at least to injure seriously this source of her supply.

I have been much troubled recently to find how far Italy has appeared to think it necessary to yield to what I cannot but think is a sort of dictatorship on the part of England with regard to certain very important necessaries of life here for which Italy is entirely dependent on importations, such as coal, grain, steel, etc. There is a very apparent propaganda in progress and not a great deal that is American escapes the interference on the part of these British propagandists in one way or another, the general method being that which dates back to the earliest days of Rome, of whispers that these American representatives have Austrian connections and are really working not in Italy's interest.

I took the matter up informally with the Minister of Foreign Affairs. He, however, gave me to understand that, with regard to the particular articles as to which I approached him,—coal, grain, steel,—

Italy had no choice. It was a matter of necessity for her to fix prices in order to secure a guarantee of the quantities of these staples necessary for her existence. My contention with him was that America could not compete if the prices were that at which they were fixed; but that if she were left to take her chance of finding a market, she would bring coal, etc. to Italy. The Minister said that this was a war measure and was necessary for the reasons he gave me, as otherwise the war could not continue; but he said it would not be continued after the war.

The text of your address of this afternoon before the Senate [69] arrived here in sufficient time to have it put in proper shape to deliver, according to instructions, this evening at the hour of its delivery in Washington, and I have made an appointment with the Minister of Foreign Affairs for that purpose. At the same time I am having to-day careful translation made from English into Italian, so that if necessary I may send it with the English text for publication in the press here.

Your Note of the 18th of December [70] suffered very much I think from the somewhat inexact translation made here at the Foreign Office, and I attribute a part of the virulence of attack made on it here in the press, to this translation.

I do not, however, mean to attribute too large a part of this attack to this cause, for I feel sure that the cue came from the outside and I believe that it was given because there was a serious apprehension that the suggestion of Peace might weaken the power of the Allied countries.

The position that was allowed to be taken that you had declared the two sides to be of similar merit was so manifestly without foundation that I feel very well assured that no representative of any Government who read your note, really believed what the press declared.

I think it quite possible that at the very beginning some of them suspected that Germany had asked you to intervene in some way; but certainly they were soon disillusioned and I do not think that this view was ever entertained by Baron Sonnino. A certain amount of mischief has resulted from the efforts of certain American busybodies who have undertaken a sort of propaganda to create in the minds of representatives of the Allies as well as in the public mind, the impression that you and your administration speak rather for a fraction than for the whole of the American people. Even the complete reversal of their prophecy that you would not be re-elected, has not entirely failed to stop them and there is so much

---

[69] *Foreign Relations,* 1917, supp. 1, p. 24.
[70] *Ibid.,* 1916, supp., p. 97.

ignorance here as to America that their propaganda is at times really mischievous.

Immediately after your Note came out, I heard from one of the Ministries here a reference to the impression which had been made by the impertinent activities of the man who in Paris is the sort of head and front of this propaganda and more recently the press has occasionally had a reference to the opinion of Americans of standing who are critical of the position which you have set forth in your note.

I cannot close this without expressing to you the enormous interest which your address before the Senate set for this afternoon has for me. It is a very high note which you have struck. I do not see how it could be higher. I shall await with breathless interest its effect. I do not mean its immediate reception; but its subsequent influence on the present world conflict and its consequences. Whether the world is ready for it or not remains to be seen. In any event, it is nearer to a declaration of the principle of right, based on the highest ethical foundation, than anything that I remember in any State paper, of which I have knowledge.

Believe me [etc.] THOS. NELSON PAGE

763.72/3350½

The Ambassador in Italy (Page) to the Secretary of State

ROME, *February 17, 1917.*
[Received March 15.]

MY DEAR MR. SECRETARY: I wrote two days ago and sent by private hand to Paris to Judge Gerard a long confidential letter to the President about the situation here. I have, however, just had a conversation with Baron Sonnino, which I think well worth reporting . . .

Sonnino seems very firm in his conviction that the requisitioning of the German interned ships would have an enormous effect in Germany in discouraging the Germans in the prosecution of their submarine campaign and eventually in the prosecution of the war. He even appears to think that it will have a greater effect than if we were to declare war out of hand.

He used the illustration of a man with a pistol in his hand being able to intimidate a robber whom he is not certain of hitting, whereas if he has fired and has not hit or wounded him seriously, the robber may not be stopped. "Why not let the Germans declare war?", he asked. Naturally, he said that he preferred that we should go into the war; but to do this there must be clear grounds for coming in and until we shall be satisfied on this point, he evidently thinks that the requisitioning of the interned ships will be a tremendous aid to the Allied cause. Further, he thinks that it may be followed by Brazil. He was so earnest about this that I have just telegraphed you.[71] Rodd, the English Ambassador, as I telegraphed, also holds this view. There is a great and apparently growing apprehension here that the "push" which will begin as soon as the weather permits, will be a tremendous fight and cause tremendous slaughter. It is thought that the chief weight of the German attack will be thrown against the Italian front, which is almost the only part of the line in which they have not exerted their full force hitherto and both sides appear to be making changes with a view to meeting the brunt of the other's attack. There is a rumor of dissensions between Cadorna and the Duc d'Aosta, who commands the third army, and there is talk of the Duc d'Aosta coming to Rome to take the place of the Duke of Genoa as the King's regent. There was talk a short time since of the Duc d'Abruzzi taking this place; but that passed and I do not know what truth there is in this last story either.

The Germans and Austrians are thought here to be prosecuting their submarine warfare with the greatest activity possible. I hear to-day that two big Italian ships have just been sunk, one a grain ship sunk two days ago off the coast of Spain, the other a passenger ship sunk near Malta. Of the latter ship three boats have been picked up or have landed; but three others are still missing.

The Chinese Minister called to-day to make inquiry as to the facts of the American four-masted schooner *Lyman M. Law*, [sunk] five or six days ago near the coast of Sardinia. He says that his government has instructed him to keep it informed as to the facts incident to the sinking of all ships whatever; that his government is deeply interested in this matter and desires to keep in touch with the United States and to know at the earliest moment possible what our action is in this great crisis. He called my attention to a denial in one of the Roman papers of yesterday evening of a suggestion which had appeared in the Paris correspondence of that paper, saying that the energetic protest of the Pekin government against the German submarine blockade was the result of a suggestion on the part of another government, (viz. ourselves). The correction denies completely this suggestion and declares that the action of China was the result of the spontaneous, energetic, and generous decision of the Chinese government itself.

The crew of the above mentioned schooner, *Lyman M. Law* are to land to-day at Civitavecchia which is in the Rome district, and our Consul, Mr. Tredwell, has gone there to receive them and to get

---

[71] Telegram not printed.

their sworn statements. The sworn statement of the captain has already been telegraphed by him.

I am sending this letter about things which may already have come to a crisis long before this reaches you. It is not thought here that Germany could withdraw from the position which she has assumed and therefore it is believed that we shall soon be at war with her.

The newspapers contain reports of the effects of the German propaganda in Mexico and Cuba, and the results of the propaganda in Mexico as reported,—that is the prohibition on the export of supplies to any of the Allied countries, is so in accord with the repeated suggestions which have come to me from Vatican sources as to how the President might stop the war, i. e., by taking a similar step, that taken in connection with certain other things, I feel pretty sure that the influence of the Vatican has also been exerted on Carranza. . . .

I have been asked by the writer of the pamphlet entitled *Pace giusta e durata* to send a half dozen copies for him to various peace advocates in America. He mentioned the Department of State and Mr. Bryan and I am accordingly going to send these, although I have not had an opportunity to read them. It is printed by the Vatican press and from a little glance which I have taken into it, it seems to be quite anti-Ally. I do not think, however, that it is likely to hurt or affect either you or Mr. Bryan in any views which you hold.

It is not thought here that the Germans will or perhaps can retire from the position which they have assumed, as the propaganda in favor of the submarine policy has had a great success among the German people, and they are really buoyed up by the belief that they may win out or possibly will win out within three or four months and to withdraw now might almost bring on something like a revolution. It is believed, however, that in a few months they will be in a different frame of mind. This is the opinion, as I gather it, of Baron Sonnino himself. Accordingly, it is believed here that we shall soon be at war, and it is rather expected that if we go to war, we shall do something remarkable immediately.

Believe me [etc.]   THOS. NELSON PAGE

763.72/3578½

The Ambassador in Italy (Page) to the Secretary of State

ROME, *March 20, 1917.*
[Received April 11.]

MY DEAR MR. SECRETARY: Mrs. Heiberg, the wife of our late Military Attaché, Major Elvin R. Heiberg, is leaving Rome this evening with her two children, returning to Washington, and will be escorted by Mr. Roger C. Tredwell, our Consul here, who goes home on leave. Accordingly I avail myself of this opportunity to write you a confidential letter.

The internal situation here seems about the same as for some time past, except that through apprehension or through the actual sinking of merchant ships by German and Austrian submarines, the lines have been much more closely drawn of late in every way, and this has caused pressure enough to make itself felt in many new directions; for example, bread tickets have just begun to be issued here, the sale of sweets and articles which require sugar are forbidden from the first of next month; the consumption of meat is regulated, etc.

All this has naturally an effect on the spirit and temper of the people at large. So far as appears on the surface, however, everything seems to be going along as smoothly as ever; the Government appears to have everything well in hand, and it is only from whispers caught here and there that one finds the existence of the feeling that lies underneath. I would say that the people at large, partly from necessity, but mainly I think because they are really hopeful of a favorable issue of the war, are willing to undergo any reasonable sacrifices to give the ruling authorities the opportunity to carry out their plans, and have steeled themselves to the sacrifices which may be entailed by the great struggle that is expected to take place now almost immediately.

The Government was, as I telegraphed you duly,[72] sustained in the Chamber on Saturday evening by a vote of confidence of 369 to 43.

The fact still stands, however, that the majority is composed of elements held together rather by not knowing what better to do than by any desire to sustain this especial Government.

The situation in Russia and the situation in France are still involved in some mystery, and their effect on Italy will only be known hereafter. For one thing, unless the situation becomes too exigent, Italy will take much pride in being able to show the world that she has a more ordered policy and a more steadfast position than some of the other Allied countries. Baron Sonnino is undoubtedly the master spirit of the Government, and has strengthened himself greatly in the public esteem by his consistent and firm policy united with the moderation of his language as compared to that of some of the other Cabinet leaders.

I am struck by a certain influence which the memory and reputation of Cavour seem to have on the procedure here and indeed on the spirit in which matters are dealt with.

---

[72] Telegram not printed.

One of the serious elements in the present situation is the depreciation in the currency here.   The exchange at present has risen to about
7.86 as against 5.18—the normal exchange.   The press is full of discussion about this and all sorts of nostrums are proposed to rectify
this trouble, with certain suggestions which certainly are sound if
they could be adopted.   Naturally these last are related to the fundamental principle of supply and demand.

One trouble is that the rise in exchange is felt throughout Italy in
every class and in every direction, and the entire economic situation
is affected by it, and unless relieved it may affect disastrously in time
even the prosecution of the war.

Out of this situation has arisen apparently a strong desire on the
part of those responsible for the future conduct of the Government
to get into new relations which may aid in relieving the press existing through the other old relations, and I have had several important
people interested in finance come to me to ask if some assistance could
not be rendered from America in solving this serious problem.   The
suggestion made is that it might be found of mutual interest if Italian
financiers might be brought into direct relations with American
financial circles.   Among those who have come to me is the head of the
Bank of Italy, greatest of the Italian banks.   I have told him to
give me a memorandum of the whole situation, and when this is done
I will be able to inform you as to what is wanted, and to learn whether
what they want will probably interest America sufficiently to justify
my reporting the same to you.

One result of the present situation is that Italy finds herself
almost completely in the power of England, who has been mainly
financing her, and who not unnaturally perhaps has taken measures
which many Italians consider far more for England's interest, at
least immediate interest, than for that of Italy.   In fact, there is
much grumbling over England's control of matters, of great, if not
of vital importance, to Italy.   An example of this was England's
recent orders against the importation of articles from abroad, which
include articles of Italian production whose exportation is of great
importance to Italy.   For example: fruits, wine, silk, carved stone,
wood, etc.

England seems—on the insistence of the Italian Government, which
in turn was pressed by Sicily and Calabria who live by the sale of
their fruits, to have bought up the fruit crop of Italy for distribution in France, where a part of it is as I understand to be resold,
and a part given to the British soldiers.   But the problem of silk
and other articles still remains and causes great dissatisfaction here,
and I understand in France also.   In this connection it seems not

out of place to mention a fact that was told me the other day by General Ricciotti Garibaldi.

He says that he was in London a few months back and attended a dinner at which a number of important persons were invited to meet him, and in the course of the conversation he asked how the Allies were going to pay their debts when the war was over. On this point, an Englishman, whom he spoke of as a man of great importance and wealth, worth he said about forty million dollars, said: "Why, we will make America (The United States) pay for them". "How will you do this?" asked General Garibaldi. "Why", said the other, "England will at the close of the war control all of the markets of the world, and if necessary we will put an ad valorem tax of 100 per cent which will have the effect of making America pay the debts."

This is chiefly of interest to me as showing a point of view which undoubtedly is very extensively held. Happily, as I said to General Garibaldi, we are pretty good at building tariff walls ourselves if occasion demands.

I am [etc.]   THOS. NELSON PAGE

763.72119/558½

The Ambassador in Italy (Page) to the Secretary of State

ROME, *March 20, 1917.*
[Received April 7.]

MY DEAR MR. SECRETARY: I am going to ask that you deliver this personally to the President.

A matter that has interested me greatly of late is the secret work of the Vatican relative to us and to the European belligerents. I have from time to time sent you telegrams referring to what has been going on as far as it has been brought to my notice. You will find from my telegram no. 800 [73] and those following, that a gentleman came to me from the Vatican, that is from the Cardinal Secretary of State, Gasparri, with a suggestion of a way for the President to stop the war immediately by preventing the exportation of munitions of war and other supplies to any of the belligerents. It was full of praise of the President's fine idealism. When it was suggested by the gentleman who came to me that this might be regarded as an unfriendly act by the Allies, the reply was that we were always having questions arise between us and Japan, and that Governments could always arrange such matters, and we could make it appear that we

---

[73] *Foreign Relations,* 1917, supp. 1, p. 22.

thought it necessary in view of all this to reserve our products for ourselves.

Soon after that, the same gentleman came again, having been sent for to [sic] the Vatican, and presented the same ideas, rather more urgently and with rather less praise for the President. And this time it referred to our difficulties with Mexico as well as with Japan, and spoke of us in rather more positive terms.

The next time an actual message was written out, but not signed, for me to send to the President. I, however, declined to send such a message from the Vatican directly to our Government, but I later sent you for your information the substance of what had been told me.

Now again has come another, which my informant spoke of as another "Delenda est Carthago". It declares that

"in well-balanced political circles of this Capital the following considerations are advanced:

"The position of President Wilson relative to the belligerent powers is not sustained from the point of view of International Law. It would have been much more logical and magnificently fine if he had really vindicated complete freedom of the seas, or the right of American citizens to trade with both groups of belligerents, carrying them not contraband of war but those products which on the basis of the Hague Conference do not constitute contraband of war. In this case the action of President Wilson would have been consonant with International Law, and he would have been followed by all the neutrals, and his figure in the history of the world would have towered gigantically.

"But now his position is not logical, because on one hand he says that he defends freedom of the seas while in reality he not only does not defend it, but yields to England's injunctions not to navigate to the Central Empires; therefore in reality he is not neutral."

You will observe the entirely different tone of this from former communications. At the same time there has appeared in a Jesuit journal published in Florence, a long article, signed "Catholicus," on the neutrality of the Pope, in which the Pope is declared to be the only true neutral, and that there is a manifest desire to abase his neutrality to the level of a cleverly calculated policy of interest,—to that indeed of many neutral states—"as to cite a classical example of selfishness, the United States who, have used their vaunted neutrality to gain millions and billions to the rhythmic beat of preparing ammunition which were used to scatter broadcast death and destruction throughout Europe—the sort of neutrality which no one has forbidden, no one has spoken against, and against whose base bargaining no one has lifted his voice in protest."

This and more is contained in this article, which is evidently intended to help secure for His Holiness that which is the prime wish of the Vatican—the internationalization of the law of guarantee which at present is the work of Italy alone, and as a first step towards this a seat in the peace congress when it shall assemble.

I am [etc.]   THOS. NELSON PAGE

TURKEY

867.00/797½

The Ambassador in Turkey (Morgenthau) to the Secretary of State

CONSTANTINOPLE, *November 4, 1915.*
[Received December 1.]

MY DEAR MR. LANSING: In compliance with your cable,[74] I shall send you frequent confidential and personal letters concerning the general conditions here . . . I take it for granted that you want me to write very frankly and unreservedly.

At the present time, conditions here are extremely precarious. The Sultan is absolutely powerless. He has to simply affix his signature to whatever Iradés are submitted to him. The Grand Vezier never exercised much power, and now that he has turned over his portfolio of Minister for Foreign Affairs to Halil, he has become merely ornamental. The real governing force in this country is in the hands of the Committee of the Union and Progress Party, consisting of about forty members, of whom the following nine are the leading spirits: Dr. Nazim, Chairman of the Committee; Midhat Chukri, General Secretary; Talaat, Minister of Interior; Enver, Minister of War; Djemal, Minister of Marine and Commander-in-Chief of the 4th Army; Ayoub Sabir (now prisoner of war at Malta); Halil, Minister for Foreign Affairs; Hadji Adil Bey, President of the Chamber of Deputies; Beha-ed-lin Chakir.

The real power is exercised by the entire forty or a majority thereof, which is changeable and therefore never definitely fixed. Whenever anyone of the men assumes too much authority, as has occurred several times recently, the majority combine against him and no matter how important his position may be, he is compelled to obey the orders of the Committee and abandon all efforts to become the supreme ruler. This is where their government distinctly differs from the Boss Rule in the United States, and it is intensely interesting to observe its development.

All the important and even some unimportant questions are submitted to this Committee for its consideration. The Committee has

---

[74] Not printed.

at present absolute control of the army, navy and civil government of the country. They have removed many governors of interior vilayets who would not obey their orders. They also completely control the Chamber of Deputies, whose members are absolutely selected by them and the people have no choice but to go through the formality of electing the candidates of the Committee. In the Senate the majority are independent of them, as Senatorship is a position for life and most senators were elected by Kiamil Pasha and appointed by Abdul Hamid in 1908. Recently, when Senator Ahmed Riza Bey, an ex-Union and Progress man, wanted to champion the cause of the Armenians and questioned their treatment and also wanted to interpellate the Cabinet on the question of the control of the sale and distribution of food supply and the title of "Conqueror" conferred upon the Sultan, I was informed that Talaat sent word to him that if he really wanted to benefit the Armenians, he had better stop his agitation; for, if he continued it, he, Talaat, would publish statements about the Armenians that would incite the Turkish population against them and they would thereupon fare worse than before. From other sources it is stated that the Cabinet promised to modify their attitude towards the Armenians if Ahmed Riza and his friends would agree not to interpellate the Government. This Ahmed Riza and his friends did.

The Committee of Union and Progress have very few actual followers among the people of the Empire. They have some adherents in Constantinople and Smyrna and a few other centers. They rule through the fact that they are in possession of most of the offices and the army, and are so exercising their power that they have frightened almost everyone into submission. They have reinstated the spy system so prevalent under Abdul Hamid. By their treatment of the Armenians, they have so cowed the people that they have succeeded for the time being in suppressing all opposition to them, and they are so determined to retain possession of the government, that they will not hesitate to use any means that will enable them to do so. The only members of the Cabinet, and I believe of the inner Committee, that had any decent standing or possessed any property prior to the Revolution, were the Grand Vezier and perhaps Halil Bey. When I arrived here two years ago, only one of these nine was a member of Cabinet: that was Talaat. The Cabinet then had amongst its members Djavid Bey, a Deunmé, as Minister of Finance; Oscan Effendi, an Armenian, as Minister of Posts and Telegraphs; Mahmoud Pasha, a Circassian, as Minister of Marine, Bustany Effendi, a Christian Arab, as Minister of Commerce and Agriculture. But at the time Turkey entered the war a year ago, all these men resigned because they could not assent to the war, and the

Union and Progress men themselves did not want in the Cabinet anyone except most faithful adherents of the Committee. There is no opposition party in existence. The press is carefully censored and must obey the wishes of the Union and Progress Party. The people have absolutely no part in the government and therefore their opinions and wishes are totally disregarded and only the good of the party is considered. They have gradually filled the various posts with the trusted and leading members of the Union and Progress Committee and are continually strengthening themselves. Last year Enver was made Minister of War, and a little later Djemal was made Minister of Marine; Talaat, besides being Minister of Interior, acted and is still acting as Minister of Finance; Chukri, the Minister of Public Instruction, took also charge of the Ministry of Posts and Telegraphs after the resignation of Oscan; only last week Halil was given the Ministry for Foreign Affairs and Hadji Adil, former General Secretary of the Committee and ex-Governor General of Adrianople, was made President of the Chamber of Deputies. It is expected here that shortly either Enver or Talaat will be made Grand Vezier. It is a personal government and not one of policy, but unfortunately no one of them has full power, and as there are so many of them attempting to exercise power, absolute confusion and anarchy is resulting therefrom. The most glaring instance of this fact is Djemal Pasha, who at the beginning of the war was Minister of Marine and now is Commander of the 4th Army and has established himself as absolute dictator in Palestine and Syria. Repeatedly, when I have asked Enver to do something for me in that district, he told me that he would recommend it to Djemal and if he had no objection thereto, my request would be granted. I have begged Enver several times to order it done, and he said that he could not do so as military reasons might exist which would justify Djemal to object thereto.

At present the clique in power feel that they have succeeded in abrogating, without bloodshed or fighting, the Capitulations and thereby freed themselves from the control of the six Powers; that they have been able with their own resources (except five million pounds borrowed from Germany) to put an army of over one million men into the field and to successfully defend themselves against the four big nations arrayed against them. They claim with pride that they are the nation that have shown that the English fleet was not unconquerable, and that the Russians, who have for generations held the big stick over them, are unable to carry out their threat to punish them. They have devised a method by which they could put this tremendous army into the field with practically no cash expenditure. They pay some of their soldiers the ridiculous sum of 20 cents a month, and even from that they deduct a share for taxes, etc., while others get neither pay nor food. They have requisitioned, without paying for it, a great part of the materials and articles that they required (and even things they did not require) to dress and feed part of their army, and thus demonstrated how to conduct a war almost without cost to the Government.

These men seven years ago were looked upon as a set of irresponsible revolutionists and adventurers, and have now usurped and maintain this tremendous power; you can therefore readily understand that they have become dizzy from success. From a desperate band playing a desperate game, they have become the allies and friends of two of the important nations of the world and are convinced that they have been of greater service to their allies than their allies have been to them. They claim, and justly so, that they have compelled England and France to employ 500,000 troops to try and force the Dardanelles and to use a tremendous fleet, sacrifice numerous ships and spend millions of pounds worth of ammunition, all of which greatly diminished their power to defeat the Germans. They feel at present that they have successfully kept the great Powers at bay and are very proud of the achievement.

. . . They have been very much influenced by the Germans who have used them to create this tremendous diversion against the English and French, and who are still thinking and scheming to create uprisings of the Moslem populations in Egypt, India and Persia.

At the present moment, the authorities would be very glad to have this war end. They begin to realize that economically they have injured their country tremendously through these high-handed, indiscriminate and mismanaged requisitions. They have destroyed the producing and earning power of their country. Thousands of farmers were deprived of all their animals. The authorities foolishly did not even leave them single pairs of cattle so that the farmers could have a beginning for new herds. They have drawn from the fields the male population and thereby destroyed their agricultural communities. They have annihilated or displaced at least two thirds of the Armenian population and thereby deprived themselves of a very intelligent and useful race. They have used the railroads almost exclusively for military purposes and the ordinary roads have become so unsafe that the little that has been produced cannot be brought to markets. All the products that used to be exported are at their places of production and selling at considerably less than their usual prices; this particularly applies to tobacco, opium, silk and figs.

I have given you the conclusions first, as I would have done in a first interview with you, and am going to write you special letters

on some of the different topics, such as the effects of the abrogation
of the Capitulations; the present conduct of their courts of justice
and the management of prisons; public debt and internal financial
conditions; the educational institutions and the new regulations under
which they will probably be compelled to administer them; the Armenian atrocities; the management of the sale of food, bread, meat
and other foodstuffs; the diplomatic representatives here, their influence or lack of influence with the authorities; the evils resulting from
an invisible and irresponsible government as now conducted here,
etc. etc.

With my kindest personal regards [etc.]   H. MORGENTHAU

867.00/798½

The Ambassador in Turkey (Morgenthau) to the Secretary of State

CONSTANTINOPLE, *November 18, 1915.*
[Received January 12, 1916.]

MY DEAR MR. LANSING: In August 1914, when the general war
broke out, this country was in a most unprepared condition. The
Treasury was empty and the salaries of the officials were in arrears
for three to four months. Notwithstanding this, the authorities immediately commenced to mobilize and did so with great energy and
determination, requisitioning all the material they needed for the
army without paying for same. The British, French and Russian
diplomatic representatives in Constantinople were making every effort and all kinds of promises to induce Turkey to remain neutral;
while the German Ambassador was answering all arguments advanced by the Entente and urging the Turks to join them in the
conflict. He made particularly good use of the fact that the English
had deprived Turkey of her two great ships. As the money to pay
for the same had been secured through the most extraordinary efforts
and deprivations of the Turkish community, it was easy to encourage
anti-English feeling. The stronger and more determined the Entente Powers were in their requests for Turkey to remain neutral,
the more convinced the Turks became that the Germans were right
in saying that the Entente nations were afraid of them.

Up to the end of October, the majority of the Cabinet were opposed to war; but Talaat and Enver had committed the nation to
espouse the cause of the Germans. There is no doubt that when
Admiral Souchon of the *Goeben* bombarded Odessa, only Talaat
and Enver of the Cabinet knew what was going to happen. Almost
all the prominent Turks felt that their country had not yet sufficiently recovered from the losses of her last two wars to enter into
another one; but I believe that many of the prominent Turkish

officials felt that if they did not thoroughly prepare themselves, they would be made the scapegoat of the contest and would be divided up amongst the various countries. Unfortunately England, France, Russia and Italy had already selected the portions of the Empire which they expected to acquire or control; while Germany appeared disinterested and had, by a fictitious sale, put the *Goeben* and the *Breslau* at the disposal of the Turks and promised to assist them to reconquer Egypt and make a loan to enable them to meet their expenses, if they joined forces with them.

Shortly after Turkey entered the War, Enver went to the Caucasus and took command of the army. As you know, he was defeated by the Russians and the loss of the Turks were [*was*] enormous. This was greatly due to the assistance rendered to the Russians by the Armenian volunteers who also caused the failure of the Turkish expedition in Azerbaijan. This made a deep impression upon Enver and Talaat and produced in them a great enmity against the Armenians.

For the first days after his return to Constantinople, Enver was greatly depressed and very retiring, until he saw that his defeat was not held up against him. He returned just at a time when the entire population, and a great many of the officials, were very much alarmed at the possible forcing of the Dardanelles by the combined fleets. They had already made all arrangements for leaving the Capital and, as I informed the Department at that time, trains were kept ready at the stations to move the Sultan and the Ambassadors of their Allies and other members of the Porte to Esgui Shehir, where two hundred buildings had been requisitioned for their occupation. All the men who were to go had already received their tickets. Enver took advantage of their depression and conferred with Liman von Sanders and determined that they would concentrate their entire forces in the defense of the Dardanelles. He reassured the doubting ones and gave positive orders that the Government should not be removed from Constantinople. As the Sultan and also the German and Austrian Ambassadors had also opposed the removal, Enver's action promptly rehabilitated him; and when they successfully repulsed their enemies at the straits early in the spring, their courage arose, and the crowd—that was trembling with fear and had practically abandoned all hopes of retaining Constantinople and had even pleaded for safety zones which should be exempted from bombardment when the fleet would enter the harbor,— gradually dropped its terror and changed into a self-reliant, and later on defiant, nation. It is almost impossible, without going into details, to portray the contrast between the fear stricken, almost discouraged set of men that were trying to govern here in the spring of 1914, with an empty treasury, and restricted by the Capitulations to an 11% duty, with post offices in the hands of foreigners, their navy under the control of the British naval mission, their army in such a chaotic state that they were urging the Germans to send them a military mission to whip them into shape, Foreign Inspectors General arriving to supervise the Armenian districts in order to satisfy demands made by outside people on behalf of the Armenians,—and the same set of men now thoroughly entrenched in the important posts of the Government, feeling that they are absolutely in control, and that they have successfully prevented their enemies from invading their large seaport towns and have almost succeeded to secure for their country recognition that they are still an important Power.

These men are absolutely intoxicated with their apparent success and are already beginning to completely underestimate the assistance that the Germans have rendered them. They are very touchy on that point and want no one to give the Germans any credit for the defense of the Dardanelles. There has already developed considerable feeling between the Turks and the Germans. The diplomatic corps of the Germans and Austrians are extremely cautious not to offend the Turks and really fear that if they went too far with any demands, it might create trouble between them. All the prominent Turkish officials emphatically object to Germany's bringing an army into Turkey. They do not say so openly but I know that they fear that if the Germans ever come here, they will not leave the country again. As it is, the Germans are now gradually making a bloodless occupation of this country. For the last three months, almost every day, 30 to 40 German soldiers or ammunition manufacturers, engineers, etc. have been arriving here. Many of them are being sent further inland. I have been reliably informed by one of the members of the German Embassy that all the military stations south of Aleppo are under control of the Germans.

It was after the futile attempt of the English and French to force the Dardanelles on March 18th, that the Turkish authorities became convinced of the almost impregnability of the Dardanelles and began to develop the plan of exterminating the Armenians to punish them for their alleged perfidy towards the Turks in November and December 1914 at the Caucasus boundary. And as they could not reach the guilty ones, they punished all those that were left, irrespective of age or sex; and as Enver put it, they had no time to discriminate and settle this matter, while war was pending, in a "platonic" way, but had to resort to drastic measures, no matter who might be hurt thereby.

Enver has told me repeatedly that he warned the Armenian Patriarch that if the Armenians made any attack on the Turks or rendered any assistance to the Russians while this war was pending, he will be compelled to use extreme measures against them. Quite recently, when I was discussing the Armenian Question with Halil Bey, the new Minister for Foreign Affairs, he told me that he had warned the Armenian deputy Vartkes that if the Dashnaguist Committee would take any independent action and attack the Turkish troops, then, in self-defense, the Ottoman Commander would not only dispose of the Armenians on the frontier but of all that were on the rear of the army. Halil Bey deplored the tragic results as well as the excesses and violations committed in the matter, and said that he desired to tell me the point of view of the Sublime Porte not as a justification of those results, but as an explanation which any one who would judge this matter should take into consideration as attenuating [*extenuating*] circumstances of the action of the Ottoman Government.

· · · · · · · ·

With my kindest personal regards [etc.] H. MORGENTHAU

867.00/799½

The Ambassador in Turkey (Morgenthau) to the Secretary of State

CONSTANTINOPLE, *December 1, 1915.*
[Received January 17, 1916.]

MY DEAR MR. LANSING: Since I wrote you last (November 18th), I cabled that Enver Pasha, the Minister of War, had asked me to communicate to the President through you that better peace terms could be secured by the Entente Powers if arranged for, before the complete annihilation of Servia and the invasion of Egypt.[75] He had a long talk with me about the matter and wanted me to inform the President that this was a most opportune time for him to offer his good offices.

I did not cable at once, as I felt that it was simply his own idea and not backed either by his entire Government or by any of their Allies. Two days later, while I was with the Austrian Ambassador, the latter asked me what I had done about the matter and told me that Enver had reported our conversation to him and given him to understand that I would communicate with the President. The Austrian Ambassador informed me that he knew absolutely nothing officially of the wishes of his Government, but that he individually felt convinced that Austria was not disinclined to entertain negotiations for peace.

---

[75] Apparently the reference is to the cable of Nov. 3, 1915, printed in *Foreign Relations*, 1915, supp., p. 67.

After I received your answer that the matter had been submitted to the President, I called on the Minister of War and informed him thereof and asked him whether the suggestion he made had emanated from him alone or who else stood sponsor for it. He replied that it was entirely his idea but he felt convinced that he had expressed the feeling of all the Central Powers. He then informed me that he was about to meet Falkenhayn and others at some convenient place. (I have since ascertained that they met at Ossova, the boundary line of Roumania and Bulgaria). He stated that now that Servia had been almost completely destroyed and was in the hands of the central Powers, they would consider at this conference the details of the invasion of Egypt and what big guns and artillerists and other equipments were needed by the Turks and are to be furnished by Germany and Austria. He told me he would talk to Falkenhayn and get an expression from him what Germany's views are as to peace negotiations.

I have since had several talks with the new German Ambassador, Graf von Metternich, and he also has talked to me about the possibilities of peace. Among other things he stated that England ought to be ready to talk peace as they have not lost any territory and have established their supremacy of the seas, annexed Cyprus and Egypt, have a foothold at Gallipoli and are in possession of part of Mesopotamia and all the German colonies excepting one in China. From my conversations with him I gathered that Germany is quite willing to talk peace.

To-day Enver Pasha took lunch with me at the Embassy, and we had a long talk about the peace matter. He reported to me what had taken place at Ossova and stated that Falkenhayn did not favor that Germany should state her peace conditions at present, as he feared it would be taken as a sign of weakness, but that Germany would willingly consider any proposition made by England, in other words, they wanted England to state her conditions first.

I told Enver that this was impossible and that the only probable way by which the two sides could make a start in the peace negotiations would be if both of them simultaneously present their proposed terms to the President of the United States and have him then and there inform the other what those terms are. Both parties would have to obligate themselves that their demands would be a bona fide statement of what they expected to accomplish and not an exaggerated one with a view to compromising. He thought well of the idea and agreed to telegraph Falkenhayn about it. He would have preferred to have me telegraph the President and request him to make the suggestion to the German and British Ambassadors in Washington. I declined to do this, as I deemed it unwise to take any steps until Germany had assented to the proposition.

Enver informed me that they had agreed upon all the plans and details of their Egyptian campaign and had also discussed various other matters. He told me that his brother was in command of some troops that were approaching Egypt from the West, and had already taken 100 prisoners. He said Falkenhayn felt sure that by next August they will have completed the defeat of the Allies. They expect to annihilate the Russian army first and then make a determined attack on the West front. He felt quite positive that in a short time they would drive the English out of Mesopotamia. He told me that his forces there were about four times as large as the British.

I have felt that if I could in some shape be instrumental to hasten peace, my conduct would have the approval of the President and yourself. I do not intend to take any definite steps in the matter without telegraphing you. Enver started this matter and I am trying to twist it into something tangible before cabling further to you. It seems to me that both factions would be willing to make peace if they could do so without jeopardizing their standing in their respective countries and without sacrificing their pride. I told Enver that when people wish to submit a matter to an appellate court, it is customary for both factions to simultaneously submit their statements of facts and briefs.

I believe that although the authorities in this country are of the opinion that they are going to succeed, still they realize the necessity of an early peace to prevent conditions from reaching in the immediate future such a desperate state as may cause internal difficulties and lead to revolution, which would displace the men that are now in authority. As I wrote you before, these men are willing to do almost anything to retain their power.

Their financial condition is worse than ever, and they realize the danger of possible bankruptcy. Their revenues which formerly were about twenty-eight million pounds Turkish, will be diminished to about fifteen millions. On their import duties alone, they lose four million pounds, as all their harbors are blockaded and only very few foreign articles were brought in via Dedeagadj during 1915.

Of the forty-five million pounds worth of merchandise that were usually imported into Turkey, twenty-four millions came from countries with whom they are now at war; and that portion of the remaining twenty-one millions which came from the United States, Switzerland, Holland, and other neutral countries, has also been largely reduced.

Their collections for internal taxes have also been considerably curtailed through their destruction of the Armenians in Turkey and the reduction of the income tax owing to the diminished incomes of the population. The large receipts from taxes on sheep, camels, buffaloes, horses, etc., have been greatly affected on account of so many of the animals having been requisitioned for military purposes.

The finances of the country were assisted by the proceeds of their exports which have usually been about twenty-four million Turkish pounds annually. Of this amount, about fifteen millions were sent to countries with which they are now at war; of the rest about one and a half million used to reach America according to Turkish statistics. Owing to the fact that all their ports are closed, there has practically been no exports. As a result all the people employed in raising export articles are in a terrible condition because the little that they have sold was disposed of at one third of its value and below cost of production. As you probably have noticed from our communications, we have been unable to obtain for them permission to export their figs. Within the last few weeks some Austrian and German merchants have purchased some wool and mohair.

Their railroads have been used almost exclusively for military purposes. This has left the crops where they were raised and has caused a large increase in prices of all products in the larger cities. Here in Constantinople, nearly everything is from three to ten times as expensive as in normal times. Petroleum, which used to cost 17½ piasters or 70 cents per tin, is now selling for 140 piasters or $5.60 a tin. Sugar, which used to cost 10 cents an öke, is now selling at from 80 cents to one dollar an öke, and even then very difficult to secure. Strange to say, even vegetables, which are raised in the immediate neighborhood of Constantinople, have all increased from 100 to 200%. This is due to the fact that none come from the outlying districts and many of the vegetable growers are in the army and their farms are neglected. Next year conditions will be still worse.

The deportation of the Armenians has caused great economic damage. The sections where they have been deported from are in a terrible plight because they had been depending on the Armenians for all skilled work; and the sections where the surviving Armenians have been moved to are in similar predicament because they have had so many additional consumers thrown upon them and their resources have not been increased as these poor people have come there without funds and without clothing and are really a charge upon the communities where they now are.

I doubt if any other country is in as bad an economic condition as Turkey is at present. In Constantinople merchants are simply eating up their capital and very often it is not their own but belongs to their creditors. Nearly all the prosperous foreigners of the belligerent and neutral countries have left Turkey. This has greatly diminished the money in circulation here, as these people were the ones that patronized the stores, restaurants, tailoring establishments etc. Their absence is very noticeable.

Since the last few weeks all the gold has disappeared from circulation. The Government has issued paper money or so-called Treasury Bonds which, having no gold reserve back of them, have caused hoarding of gold, and while two months ago gold was circulating freely, at present everything is paid with paper money.

The Turkish authorities are still continuing their efforts to make everything Turkish. I do not know whether you are aware that they have taken possession of nearly all public utilities for which concessions had been given to citizens of the belligerent countries. I refer to the Water Works, the Docks, the Telephone, the Railroads, Lighthouses. All the foreign employees have been dismissed from the services of these concerns, and many of them have left the country.

Some months ago the authorities compelled everyone throughout the city to remove all signs in any foreign language, so that to-day it is difficult, if not almost impossible, for a foreigner (and many natives) to locate the various shops. This week they ordered the street railway lines to remove from their cars all Roman lettered signs of the names of the places to which they go. The Railroad Company, in order to enable the people who do not read Turkish to distinguish their different cars, has adopted a system of signs of which I enclose you a sketch.[76]

They have also compelled all Ottoman corporations to keep their books in Turkish. The Director of the Tram Lines and the Electric Light Company, who is a Belgian, said it is utterly impossible for him to conduct his business that way and consulted me about it. I advised him to keep two sets of books, one in Turkish and one in French.

Last week Mr. Rosenthal, representing the largest ammunition factory in Austria, lost the agency, although he was an Austrian, because the officials here insisted that they would transact business only with a Turk, and the agency was given to a friend of one of the high officials. I am writing you these few instances to show you the trend here.

With my very best personal regards [etc.]   H. MORGENTHAU

---

[76] Not printed.

762.67/⅜

The Ambassador in Turkey (Morgenthau) to the Secretary of State

CONSTANTINOPLE, *December 22, 1915.*

SIR: In the interview I had with the Minister for Foreign Affairs on the 20th instant, His Excellency informed me that an Ottoman delegation was going to Berlin to conclude negotiations and sign four Conventions between Germany and Turkey. The instruments to be signed are a Consular Convention, a Convention for judicial protection and assistance, an Extradition Convention, and one concerning Institutions. The Minister told me that there already is an accord between the two Governments on the main points and that the most essential feature of this accord consists in the fact that the whole matter is settled on a basis of reciprocal treatment of the subjects of the contracting parties residing respectively in the territory of the other party. Thus Germany has, according to Halil Bey, agreed in principle to the suppression of German Consular Courts in Turkey. This in itself, if it is unconditional, will naturally be construed by the Sublime Porte as a tacit acquiescence by Germany in the abrogation of Capitulations. The Minister thinks that in about one month the German and Ottoman delegates will be able to agree on the text of these Conventions. He hopes that after the matter has been concluded with Germany, the Sublime Porte will be able to make similar conventions with the other Governments including the United States.

I learn from reliable sources that Turkey, as an ally that has rendered most valuable service to Germany, expects to and may obtain from Germany more liberal terms than any other power would concede to Turkey. On the other hand it is stated that at this juncture and without endangering her own interests Germany can afford to be liberal towards Turkey, as at the end of the war, if Germany wins, she will have such a preponderating position in this country that she will practically govern Turkey, in which case any concessions she now makes to Turkey may eventually mean concessions made to Germany herself. If on the other hand the other allies win they will extort from Turkey such terms that all the capitulations, will be re-established with revisions and additions. Germany will then avail herself of the benefits of the most favored nation clause, losing nothing by the concessions she may now make to her ally. The German Embassy has not concealed the fact that it considers these days as a transitory period. I may here mention the Turco-German treaty of Commerce of 1890 in which Germany made several concessions to Turkey and in this way appeared as Turkey's best friend. But as none of the other powers had signed and exchanged such treaties the liberal provisions of the treaty never went into effect, as the German Embassy benefited by the most favored nation clause.

In this connection I must mention a most significant feature in the Germano-Turkish relations. All the Ottoman Departments, except the Grand Vizirate, the Sheikhul-Islamate, the Department of the Evcaf and the Foreign Office, will hereafter have German advisers. It appears that in parliamentary circles there was some feeling against this measure. It is stated that at the Union and Progress party meeting both Talaat Bey and Halil Bey defended the measure by admitting that it is now demonstrated that those at the head of affairs were unable to properly administer the Government and the finances of the country and that they needed foreign expert assistance to carry on the work. The appointment of foreign technical advisers is not an innovation. Without mentioning the German military mission and all the German officers, I can state that a German is now acting as adviser to the Department of Public Instruction. Between 1908 and 1914 the Finance Office has had French advisers, the Navy Department as well as the Department of Justice have had British advisers. The Customs administration had Sir Richard Crawford who at one time acted also as adviser to the Finance Office. Those who acted hitherto did not in reality make their presence felt, except perhaps Sir Richard Crawford. They were looked upon more as ornaments and a luxury than as real factors in the Government machinery. Will it be the same with the Germans who will soon be appointed? The time is not ripe for me to express an opinion. But I can state for the information of the Department that both in diplomatic and Turkish circles there is a difference of opinion about the matter. While some think that this is a repetition of the old practice and that the new German advisers will shortly after their appointment be treated like their "unlistened to" predecessors, others think that this new step is one that has been imposed on Turkey by Germany and that the new advisers will play an important part in advancing German interests in this country.

I have [etc.]   H. MORGENTHAU

763.72/2931½

The Ambassador in Turkey (Elkus) to the Secretary of State

CONSTANTINOPLE, *September 15, 1916.*
[Received October 9.]

DEAR MR. SECRETARY: I arrived here September 11th and on my way spent several days in Berlin and had an opportunity of estimating the sentiments and feelings of people there because I had been to Berlin several times before and know a number of people;

being familiar with the language and knowing the people they talk with me more freely than they would publicly.

First: Food. As you probably know there are two no meat days in Germany, and bread, meat, eggs, sugar, coffee, soap, et cetera, are distributed upon cards as are articles of clothing. Coffee, sugar and milk are very difficult to obtain. The coffee is very poor; a substitute for it that is used consists of roasted bread and some kinds of beans. The absence of this is very much felt. There is no real milk to be had, only skimmed milk. The Government allows one egg per person per week, one-eighth or $\frac{1}{4}$ pound of meat per person per week; a similar allowance of skimmed milk; practically no sugar and a very small quantity of butter per person per week. Potatoes and bread such as it is are fairly plentiful and while filling, the people find them absolutely unsatisfying. The middle classes and the poor people talk of nothing but food and when they speak frankly as they did to me in their homes they said that they were always hungry. When talking publicly these same people will say how plentifully they are fed and indeed how much healthier they now are because they eat so much less meat. Statistics which were given to me by some of the bank and government officials apparently show that food supplies after the gathering of this harvest will be sufficient. It is claimed that this harvest is a very abundant one and more than thirty per cent. larger than the harvest of last year. I learned, however, from unofficial sources that while the harvest is in excess of that of last year, that the harvest of 1915 was far below the average and that this year's harvest is still below the average yield. You know what statistics are and anyhow the mass of the people do not believe that there is going to be any great improvement in food supplies; in fact, it is unofficially rumored that after October first there will be three no meat days and that there will be no milk at all except for children and invalids.

I was also told unofficially that there was a great increase in tuberculosis cases because of the lack of sufficient proper food. Although the open-air restaurants are full of people who at first sight seem to be not only well but happy, yet it needs but little close inspection to see the marked depression underlying all. Almost all of the faces are pale and denote bad or insufficient food and the great loss of bulk in the men and women is noticeable. This is claimed to be a sign of increased or improved health and it may be so.

These conditions to which I have thus briefly referred and which struck me forcibly because of the great contrast between the situation now as I saw it and when I was in Berlin a few years ago cannot be underestimated. From my interviews and conversations with numerous people it already appears to have sapped the courage and the nerve of the people. It seems that the rich, especially those with country estates, do not suffer as much as the medium class and the poor, as apparently, also, there is some favoritism.

Second. Peace. Along with the universal talk of food the subject of importance discussed is peace. When they talk frankly with you the people say they want peace at almost any price or on any terms. While they will not say it openly they seem to think the end is going to be very disastrous especially since the entry of Roumania into the war. There is of course the conflict between the military element and the business element. A leading business man, whose brother is a well known merchant and an American citizen of high standing in America, told me that the universal sentiment of the business men in Germany was for immediate peace on any terms which would preserve a part if not the whole of Germany's self-respect.

Third. Feeling about America. There is still a great dislike of America and Americans which is based on three grounds: First, supplying ammunition to the Allies; second, the stopping of the submarine warfare and three, permitting England to interfere with the neutral mails, et cetera. But despite all this they all look to President Wilson as the only commanding figure in the world who will be able to bring about peace. Mr. Gerard told me, and it is rumored and talked about among the people that because of the dissatisfaction with the present administration in Germany that the present Chancellor will be succeeded by von Tirpitz or Falkenhayn. Von Tirpitz is still demanding the resumption of submarine warfare and in case of his selection it would mean the resumption of that kind of warfare. One official said in my presence that one submarine saw forty one English or French ships carrying ammunition crossing the English channel and that because each one of these ships had hired a few Americans to travel on them for safety's sake, the submarine did not dare to interfere. Mr. Gerard told me that he believed that Germany was so disappointed about the war and conditions that they would replace von Bethmann-Hollweg by von Tirpitz or some one like him and begin a new submarine warfare. But two or three business men told me, with strict injunctions as to secrecy, that this was all bluff and that the business men and general public would not submit to any such proposition; that they were fast being ruined and did not propose to allow the military to ruin them entirely as they had substantially ruined the country itself. The newspapers unfriendly to the President contained statements when I was in Berlin unwillingly admitting that his election now seemed certain because of his magnificent work in settling the railroad strike and because of his other works of public importance.

Fourth. Settlement of war. The editor, a man named Stein, of one of the leading papers of Berlin called upon me and said that he had proposed to Mr. Gerard with the authority of the Austrian Government officials that if the United States would indicate its willingness to sign the Treaty of arbitration which Austria had rejected before the war, that Austria would signify at once its acceptance of the Treaty. Of course I referred this gentleman to Mr. Gerard and told him that I had nothing to say about the matter and preferred not to listen to him. But Mr. Gerard sent him back to me after he had seen him. Mr. Gerard told me that he had talked over the matter in full with Mr. Stein, and that he did not believe that he had any authority to make the statements which he did from either the Austrian or German Governments, although he was a man of high standing and great influence in Berlin. Mr. Gerard asked me to tell Mr. Penfield what Stein had told him and me, as Mr. Stein said he was going to Vienna to confer with Mr. Penfield about the matter. Accordingly when I was in Vienna I informed Mr. Penfield of the substance of the conversation. Mr. Gerard said to me that he had told Mr. Stein that it was absurd for the United States to now enter into a Treaty with Austria, which would permit the resumption of the submarine warfare and require the United States to wait one year after complaint to arbitrate the matter. Mr. Stein told me then that he was authorized by Austria and Germany to say that they would waive all provisions of arbitration in so far as they applied to submarine warfare or to any event causing loss of life. He claimed to Mr. Gerard and myself that the reason that Austria should be approached first was because the Austrian Parliament would not have to be consulted. That the Austrian Government officials could enter into the Treaty at once while if the matter were submitted to Germany first it would have to be submitted to the Reichstag. Mr. Gerard asked me particularly to write this fully to you so that I could give you my impressions after talking with Stein. Of course I did not know Mr. Stein before I was in Berlin and know nothing of his standing except what I heard. He claims to have the only newspaper which has been a supporter of the President and that is borne out by the statements in his paper which I read while in Berlin, in which he wrote, with reference to the arrival of the *Deutschland*, that if it had not been for President Wilson's absolute neutrality the *Deutschland* would not have been allowed to land. Mr. Gerard seems to think possibly Stein might be the unofficial representative of German officials and that this proposition is made in this way so that if unaccepted or the results are displeasing the officials can disown Mr. Stein and his authority. Mr. Gerard told Mr. Stein that while he would send the statement to Washington he did not see how anything could be done based upon such unofficial communications. Mr. Penfield, to whom I told the substance of this conversation said that he knew Mr. Stein and that he was a man of position and standing but doubted if he had any real authority and that he would propose to him if he came to Vienna to have the Minister for Foreign Affairs sanction his proposition before anything further was done. I told Professor Stein in the presence of Mr. Gerard and upon Mr. Gerard's invitation that the only way it seemed to us that the President could properly act would be if the parties accepted the President's invitation which he made in writing at the outbreak of the war when he offered to do anything he could to bring about peace then or thereafter if requested, but that the communication must be made through the appropriate authorities. Mr. Stein is an enthusiast, anxious to figure as a leader in the peace movement, and probably has a little authority for what he says.

Mr. Gerard is carrying on the work of the Embassy exceedingly well and although he is included in the dislike of Americans, which is natural, yet I believe he is very well liked by the officials from what I saw and heard and the interests of America are well represented by him.

Fifth. Newspaper articles. I gave a written interview to two newspapers in Berlin and one in Vienna. In Berlin I gave an interview to the *Vossische Zeitung* and the *Lokal Anzeiger;* they were substantially the same and after being written and submitted to me I gave them to Mr. Gerard and obtained his approval before publication. The one at Vienna appeared in the *Neue Freie Presse* and was substantially the same; they were also in writing and carefully revised. These interviews have been quoted by the Turkish newspapers with approval. I have declined to be interviewed here by the newspapers until after I have been received by the Sultan. Editorials referring to these will be sent to the Department through Mr. Philip.[77]

Sixth. Turkey. Naturally I know little or nothing about conditions in Turkey except what I have heard and some information I received in Berlin from an Ottoman subject which is strictly confidential. This man had just left Turkey and was on his way to either Switzerland or Denmark and he had travelled through Asia Minor recently. He told me that, although the Government had announced an exceptionally good harvest and therefore no need of outside food supplies, the harvest was the worst in thirty-five years and that great suffering would ensue this winter unless there was help from America or from other countries. He said that Roumania until her entry into the war supplied fifteen carloads of flour per day for Turkey. Herr von

---

[77] Hoffman Philip, counselor of embassy.

Jagow said to Mr. Gerard and myself when we visited him officially and when Mr. Gerard brought up the question of the German Government helping the American authorities in Constantinople to obtain permission from Turkey to send food into Turkey, that the Turks were suspicious of all German authorities' and interference and resented it. I am told by Mr. Philip that this is true.

This is a rather rambling and hastily prepared statement of my impressions which I hope may be of some service to you. As I become better informed of the situation here I will write you again.

With regards [etc.] ABRAM I. ELKUS

763.72/2934½

The Ambassador in Turkey (Elkus) to the Secretary of State

CONSTANTINOPLE, *September 26, 1916.*

[Received October 24.]

DEAR MR. SECRETARY: I would like to add to the observations contained in my letter of the fourteenth [*fifteenth*] certain notes on conditions as I found them in Vienna. In this city, though the general impression gained (for reasons hereinafter stated) is less depressing than in Berlin, the actual situation is much worse. Food is much more expensive, meat one dollar a pound, sugar beyond reach of the poor, as is butter—flour and bread difficult to obtain (on some days one is met by the statement in poorer-class restaurants that "today we have received no allotment of bread and therefore can serve none with meals"). It is now impossible to obtain a really satisfying meal even in a cheap, third-rate restaurant under seventy five cents. The currency has depreciated until a krone is worth only half of what it formerly was. Yet salaries have not increased, and salaried people find their financial resources cut in two. Commodities not classified as food: clothes, shoes, et cetera, now cost twice and three times as much as before the war. Even carfares have been increased more than ten percent. I was assured the condition of the poor is lamentable in the extreme.

Meanwhile the prospects for an increase of food supplies are very bad. Austria never has sufficient food to feed itself, and always imports food from Hungary. This year Hungarian as well as Austrian crops have been particularly bad. Therefore, while Austria faces an unusual food stringency, Hungary is not in a position to supply the deficit. This matter was recently the subject of acrimonious argument in the Hungarian parliament; where it was asserted that Hungary had food enough only for itself, and would, under no circumstances, send any to Austria. Budapest at present has plenty of food (this information comes from a reliable source), although prices are very high. But I was assured that there would be "trouble" (meaning political disturbances) if any attempt were made to send food from Hungary in quantities to Austria. The feeling of Hungarians in general toward Austria is bitter, because it is claimed that the Austrians have pushed the Hungarians into all the most difficult positions on the front but have done little or no real fighting themselves. Naturally the Austrians reciprocate Hungarian animosity. However this is a traditional feud, and need not be given too much weight in figuring political consequences.

These are the reasons why conditions are actually worse in Vienna and Austria than in Germany. The reasons why the general feeling in Vienna seems better than in Germany are as follows:

1. The Austrian and more particularly the Viennese temperament is more cheerful than that of the Germans. Even hard times fail seriously to affect Viennese light-heartedness.

2. The upper and middle classes, who parade the main streets and fill the cafés have really more reason to be cheerful than the people in a corresponding station of life in Germany.

   a. Government food regulations are not strictly enforced as in Germany. Bread, meat, sugar cards are now in use, theoretically limiting individual consumption of these commodities. But as a matter of fact people of means can purchase any thing they want at exorbitant prices. Some families keep a servant to do nothing else all day, but stand at various food stations and purchase supplies. Thus well-to-do households really have almost all the luxuries. Even the three meatless days are not adhered to with absolute strictness.

   b. Many well-to-do families have no one at the front and therefore do not fear that they will be affected by the frightful loss of life. There has been tremendous favoritism in recruiting. Money and influence keep a large percentage of the rich out of danger, in sinecures. So while the age limit for drafting men has been advanced almost to the middle period of life, many young men are seen about town (often in uniform) who have never done active duty. This, in spite of the fact, that the streets are full of convalescent officers and soldiers limping along on canes. A new call had just been issued for recruits, when I was in Vienna, and a great many of the well-to-do men feared that, because the supply of human material without "protection" (the Austrian word for "pull") had been exhausted, they would not be able any longer to avoid service.

To return to the food situation. Owing to government favoritism which permits the well-to-do to purchase as much as they can pay for, the prospects are that the eventual pinch will be felt more keenly in Austria than in Germany. The German authorities, by enforcement of food-consumption restrictions, no doubt are enabled to hoard supplies for the future. The Austrians meantime are living beyond their income, consuming their capital. This is, of course, even more true of Turkey, where the whole Empire is being denuded of cattle and grain to feed Constantinople and the army. When there are no more herds of sheep and cows left to be driven down to the Golden Horn and no more grain to be sent to the capital's markets, Constantinople will be facing starvation. That is the general opinion here. To a very much more limited extent similar conditions exist in Austria and Vienna.

Here, from a confidential personal source, I am told that the Germans have told the Turks that they need be very "nice" to the Americans as the United States will have much to say in the peace negotiations and are very powerful. As I am told that the Germans have largely instigated the Turks in their past conduct, this is, to say the least, interesting. As yet, as I have not been received by the Sultan, but will be on October 2, I have not seen any of the official Germans or official Turks except one or two.

I also learned, from two different sources, that there is much ill-feeling against the Germans and those who are in accord with them here, that this feeling is particularly strong in the army among both officers and men, and is shared by the people themselves to some extent.

It was openly rumored a few days ago that the Turkish army at Sivas, fighting the Russians, threatened to revolt, unless a separate peace was at once negotiated by Turkey. A large number of troops, I am told, have deserted. It is also stated that Talaat or Enver or both may be assassinated any day, as soon, in fact, as the committee of Union and Progress considers their usefulness at an end, or should decide that it was time to make a separate peace. But there has been talk about this for more than a year. The story of the differences between Enver and Talaat still grows. Enver wishes to sacrifice everything to the army. He is urging, according to latest reports, the abrogation of all exemptions from military service, despite the fact that such exemptions have been purchased at the rate of $300 a piece. Talaat, it is claimed, believes this policy dishonest, and, in addition, argues that the small number of exempted men are necessary, in any case, to carry on the commerce and industries of the country. It is not here, like in Germany and France, where women can take the place of men. The women of Turkey would not be permitted by custom, and are not fitted by training, to take over the work of men. There is great bitterness in Constantinople over Enver's threat to call the exempted men.

Closely allied with this subject, is the question of the scarcity of agricultural labor, of men and beasts on the farms. The government has given great publicity to a law passed to conscript agricultural labor and put it under military régime. Also a great deal has been said about the possibility of making machinery take the place of men and draft animals. All this, however, is very much up in the air, and it is doubtful whether anything can be done of consequence in this direction before the war's end to alleviate the food situation.

Very sincerely yours,

ABRAM I. ELKUS

867.00/802½

The Ambassador in Turkey (Elkus) to the Secretary of State

CONSTANTINOPLE, *November 17, 1916.*
[Received December 26.]

DEAR MR. SECRETARY: I have been acting as Ambassador since October 2, although I have been here since September 11, and have begun to have a fair insight into the workings of the Turkish Government.

The entire administration of affairs is in the hands of three men, Enver, Minister of War and Commander of the Army, Talaat, Minister of Interior, and Djémal, nominally Minister of Marine, but actually Commander-in-Chief of Syria and Asia Minor.

Enver has full charge of the war in Europe.

Talaat has full charge of all internal affairs, the finances, et cetera.

Djémal is absolute dictator of all affairs in Asia Minor.

Each resents the slightest interference by any of the others with his privileges and powers.

There are the usual other Ministers, Foreign Affairs, a Grand Vezier (Prime Minister), a Parliament consisting of Senators and Deputies, but they are all practically figureheads and forms. The will of these three men dominates everything.

All representatives of foreign powers are now requested to deal only with the Minister of Foreign Affairs. He really acts as a "buffer" for the three in control. He frankly says, when a request, or matter is brought to him, that it must be submitted to one or the other Department.

There is little, if any, system in administration and great delay about everything. To get a positive answer quickly to anything is an impossibility and almost so after weeks of negotiation. Delay . . . is the order as to everything. All the foreign powers find this true, and among the greatest complainants are the German and Austrian Ambassadors, who experience the same difficulties as the representatives of neutral powers.

As to military matters, it is stated that the Germans have a written agreement with the Turks, providing for the control by the German officers attached to the Turkish Army and that is the only instrument compelling obedience to German authority, although that is often thwarted.

The change recently made in the German Embassy, here, is due to the fact that the former Ambassador stated he could do nothing with the Turks . . .

To illustrate as to how matters are attended to here: Before I took charge, the Department requested the Embassy to obtain permission for American citizens, or the wives and children of such, living in Palestine, to leave Turkey on the *Des Moines*. The Chargé replied that no one had been allowed to leave Turkey, since the war began, except through Constantinople, and that it was not probable that the rule would be broken.

The Department urged this matter upon me personally and I took it up with the Grand Vezier, who was then acting as Minister of Foreign Affairs, in the absence of that Minister in Berlin, (where he remained two months endeavoring to conclude a new Treaty with Germany). After considerable urging and discussion, the Grand Vezier agreed to allow all American citizens to leave on the *Des Moines* from either Jaffa or another port to be designated by the War Department, which, he said, would be done in a few days.

. . . I wrote him a note the same day confirming the conversation and setting forth his promise fully and carefully. Then came the usual delay. "Military reasons required a few days delay". Then Halil, the Minister, returned and the matter must be taken up with him. He knew nothing about it. No records appear to have been kept and he would have to inquire. At last, after the sending of several notes, making several visits, an answer was received that the supplies on the *Des Moines* may be landed at Jaffa, but no one may leave on the *Des Moines*. When attention is called, and very emphatically, to the agreement of the Grand Vezier, the answer is blithely given, if he did say so, he had no authority. Of course, it was pointed out, that I could not go behind the authority of a Minister, that it was not in my province to go to the Minister of War, to find out if the Secretary of War or anybody else had agreed to this, et cetera. It took a great deal of argument and time to obtain an agreement to this simple proposition, and then there must be a consultation with the Grand Vezier to see if he did make the promise. Of course, I pointed out that the letter had not been denied and that it was clear and explicit.

Then again, we have to meet with the most childish constructions placed upon happenings in the United States and newspaper accounts there of happenings here, and interviews and speeches. For instance, I am told that the real trouble about the *Des Moines* is an alleged statement made by my predecessor, when he returned to the United States, that the Turkish officials were willing to sell Palestine or that he could buy it. This statement was widely circulated here and the Turks now believe that the United States has designs upon their territory. They cannot believe our aims are largely humanitarian and the protection of American interests here. In some way they have come to believe that an American cruiser coming to Jaffa and taking Americans away, must be connected with the plan to buy Palestine. Every little remark about Turkey, appearing in our press, eventually comes back here, enlarged, exaggerated and misconstrued.

The Turkish officials (now and especially since the election) express a desire to be very friendly with this Embassy and they showed that to some extent, in promising to exempt our Turkish employees from the military law just now enacted—but after considerable urging.

. . . .

For many years the Turks played off one foreign power against another. Usually the English against the French. Now there are indications of playing off the United States against Germany. The Germans know this and have suggested unofficially to me that we act in concert in such matters as we can agree upon. I have said, of course, submit what you wish to me and I will consult my government.

The financial situation here is bad and becoming acute.

A gold Turkish pound is worth $4.40 and it now sells for $7.20 in paper money in Constantinople. In the interior of Asia Minor it sells for $8.80 and even as high as $10.00 in paper. All gold has practically disappeared, and is hidden by those who have it. The gold in circulation was before the war about 53 million pounds, but now practically none is to be had.

We sell drafts on the United States at the rate of $3.75 to $4.10 for a Turkish pound paper, but as you will see this is at a great loss and therefore I have cabled urging that gold be sent here, if possible.

The interest on Turkey's national debt is now 25 million pounds annually. The annual revenues just before the war were 23 millions. The expenditures are now 30 millions. So you can see what is likely to happen. Besides, it is estimated 3 millions annually in taxes have been lost, because of the Armenian massacres.

The party in power, therefore, sees its only hope in continuing the war. That makes things appear safe for the present, as Germany must make new loans to keep Turkey as an ally.

The Germans, Austrians and Turks were greatly interested in the result of the election. Until Friday, November 10; it was reported that Hughes was elected and there was great rejoicing by the Germans particularly about this. The Turkish newspapers contained leading articles stating that Hughes might be "truly neutral", which they explained to be, prohibit sales of ammunition to England and permit Germany's submarine warfare, to break England's unlawful blockade. Then on Friday came the news that the election was in doubt, with chances in favor of the President. On Sunday, November 12, your telegram came informing us definitely of the result.

Enver, at present, is the most powerful of the ruling triumvirate. He is the Germanophil member, with German military backing, and the ever present argument of military necessity to enforce such measures, ruinous in the opinion of many, to the country's policy, as the general calling out of all the men up to the age of forty five.

But as a matter of fact, the Turks and Germans are not very good friends. . . . The Turks are already planning how they may best get rid of German supervision as soon as the war is over. But the likelihood is the Germans, if permitted by the Entente, will retain their control even after the war.

A movement against the Greeks of the Asia Minor littoral, similar to that against the Armenians, and a renewal of Armenian deportations is said to have begun with deportations into the interior. At Smyrna, the first deportation has been started, because of a revolutionary plot said to have been discovered by the Government. Three hundred Armenian families are reported as having been sent into the interior.

The food situation has grown worse. The price of bread has been raised again. All other food prices are being increased in proportion. Well-to-do people can still buy everything they need. But there is a distinct visible augmentation of misery among the poor.

The Jews, for the present, seem to be let alone. In Asiatic Turkey, Djémal is strongly opposed to the Zionists, as he believes they are a political party, and has sent two of their leaders from Palestine to Turkey. The talk about purchasing Palestine has helped to create this feeling and also unwise talk by Zionists in the United States.

I hope that these letters may be of some interest, but it is difficult, so far away, to know exactly what to write about.

Yours sincerely,

ABRAM I. ELKUS

867.00/804½

The Ambassador in Turkey (Elkus) to the Secretary of State

CONSTANTINOPLE, *March 2, 1917.*
[Received April 7.]

DEAR MR. SECRETARY:

. . . .

Notwithstanding the rupture with Germany, our relations with the Turkish Ministers independent of the business of the Embassy at the Sublime Porte, more especially that dealing with belligerent interests, continue to be cordial. It is reported to me from all sides that the Turks will not break off relations with the United States even if there should be war between Germany and America. As I have already telegraphed the Department, Talaat Pasha stated to me that he saw no reason why the friendly relations between Turkey and America should not continue, even if there was a rupture between America and Germany. Some days after that he told me that he had reported our conversation to the Sultan, and that His Imperial Majesty had thoroughly approved Talaat Pasha's statements and said he deeply desired the continuation of the friendly relations between the two countries. But Djavid Bey, the new Minister of Finance, was much more outspoken than the Grand Vizier. In the course of a quiet after-dinner confidential conversation at the Embassy, he told me the other day that even if there was a war between Germany and America, Turkey would not break off relations with America. Djavid said that it was only after the war had ceased that people would realize what a calamity it had been. This country would be short of men, would be under the burden of a tremendous debt, the revenues decreased and would have to look outside of Turkey for financial assistance in order to begin the work of construction. "Turkey's only hope is in the United States. The European countries will be unable or unwilling to help us financially." "On the other hand," he continued, "what can we expect to gain if we take part in a war against the United States? Absolutely nothing! I therefore guarantee 90% that if there is war between Germany and the United States, Turkey will stay out of it. At least that is our feeling and our intention to-day." And he looks upon the above reasons put forward by him as logical and convincing. I asked him what the Turks would do in case the Germans insisted on Turkey performing her duty as an ally to declare war against America. He said Turkey would simply refuse and if Germany still insisted Turkey would ask her to send her 3 to 400,000 troops to do the fighting, as otherwise the Turks would be unable to fight alone. The cordiality now demonstrated by the Ministers may be genuine and sincere, or may be only assumed and serving for some ulterior purpose. . . . Future developments will show whether this demonstration is sincere or not. If not sincere it may serve one of the following two purposes: it may be intended to mislead us, and for the purpose of having America help Turkey now or hereafter,—a repetition under another form of the assurances given to the British Ambassador in 1914 that Turkey would remain neutral—or it may be intended for the edification of Germany, a kind of a warning, if not a threat, to the overbearing ally that she is not the only great power and that if she is not more considerate towards the weaker ally, the latter can find—had found—other friends! Some Turks, however, not friendly towards the Union and Progress Committee have quite a different interpretation for these demonstrations of cordiality. According to what they say the Union and Progress leaders are aware that they will be held responsible for dragging Turkey into this war, which has proved to be disastrous for the Empire; that they will also be held responsible for the Armenian massacres, the persecution of the other non-Turkish races and for endless other misdeeds. Therefore seeing the approach of the day of reckoning and having no confidence in the ability or the willingness of their German ally to help them in the hour of need, they desire to make friends with America now, in order to protect themselves or at least have a friend when that day of reckoning comes.

But it is curious to hear that some German officers here have stated that even if war should occur between America and Germany, Turkey should continue her diplomatic relations with America. These officers are further stated to have said it is not desirable to have a war between Germany and the United States.

It is rumored that both in Turkish and German military circles here there is an apprehension that should war ever be declared between the United States and Turkey, the former can at once send troops and ammunition from the Philippines to the Persian Gulf and thus help the British in Mesopotamia or Palestine.

It may interest the Department to know some facts demonstrative of cordiality on the part of the Ottoman Ministers and other dignitaries. First of all, in the two private audiences which I have had with the Sultan, His Majesty has put aside all formalism and court etiquette and shown a kindly, friendly attitude towards me and towards those who accompanied me. All the Court officials, Chamberlains, Secretaries, Masters of Ceremony, Aides-de-Camp, have been friendly to me and to my family, most attentive in details and tried their best to make our stay in Constantinople pleasant. They have often called at the Embassy on the days when Mrs. Elkus is at home. The same is true of the officials of the Sublime Porte in their personal relations with us. All the principal ministers—except Chukri Bey, Minister of Public Instruction, who is chiefly responsible for the sinister policy of the Turkish Government in the so-called seizure of the French, British, et cetera, institutions, have been constant callers at the Embassy, both before and after the rupture with Germany. I can state that Talaat Pasha has shown more friendship and intimacy since that rupture. Both at dinners, lunches and ordinary at home days these Ministers, Senators and other dignitaries have thoroughly enjoyed themselves. I hear that a short time ago, since the rupture with Germany, Talaat Pasha gave instructions to the Press Bureau not to allow the publication of articles hostile to America; and if articles not exactly friendly have appeared we can be almost certain that they were in papers subsidized by certain foreigners.

A few weeks ago it was suggested with very complimentary remarks to confer an Ottoman order on Mr. Schmavonian, who, it was said had often avoided misunderstandings between the Embassy and the Sublime Porte. At Mr. Schmavonian's request I did not submit this matter to the Department, as he with very becoming modesty, said he did not think he ought to receive a decoration at a time when no other member of the Embassy staff would be authorized to receive one. It came to me as a surprise that the Grand Cordon (first class) of the Chéfékat order has just been bestowed on Mrs. Elkus. The Imperial Iradé was issued yesterday. As the law does not prevent her from accepting the order and as the wives of all my predecessors have received the same, I assume there can be no objection to her accepting this sign of courtesy and friendship on the part of His Majesty and of his Government. I could enumerate many other facts and instances showing indications on the part of the Ottoman Government of friendly and cordial conduct towards the Embassy.

Of course these things do not pass unnoticed and are variably commented upon in foreign diplomatic and Turkish circles.

I do not believe that these demonstrations of cordiality are seen with approving eyes either in Germany or in England. As much as I can judge from the Entente and German press, I think that these countries would prefer to see an enmity if not an actual break off between Turkey and the United States. Otherwise how could we interpret such unfounded statements as the following in the foreign press: that the American missionaries have been interned in Turkey, that the *Scorpion* has been sunk or seized, that the Department has had no news from the Embassy; or that I invited a number of diplomats to dinner to discuss political situation and all declined, et cetera? I can not say that the Germans here, more especially the military, have all been cordial to this Embassy. According to statements from Turkish sources, I am led to believe that at times they have sought to bring about friction and misunderstanding between us and the Turkish authorities.

I mentioned above the statements of Talaat Pasha concerning the continuation of friendly relations and approval of the same by His Majesty. I was told the other day by a neutral envoy here that the German admiral Souchon, who bombarded Odessa and thus brought about the war between Turkey and the Entente, stated to this diplomat that Talaat Pasha had told me in connection with the question of an eventual rupture of relations between Turkey and the United States, that Turkey would do exactly what Germany dictated. (This is at variance with what Talaat really said.)

Turks state to me that Germany does not wish to see here an Ambassador of a great power like the United States, who is too friendly with the Turks, because they wish to impress on the Turks that they are the only power that can protect Turkey, and the only friend Turkey has. I am told on the other hand that the Turks wish to emancipate themselves from this German guardianship.

The feeling in the civilian Turkish circles is far from being friendly to the Germans. In a conversation with a Turkish Minister, the latter said,

"really speaking the Germans had no friends, their manner is such that they can have no friends, that they have a wonderful military organization, of which they are proud, and through their organization they have a strong discipline in their own country holding the people under a permanent guardianship and obedience, and they imagine that they have the same power over all the world. In diplomacy they are poor and what success they have had has been through threat. They think of nothing but themselves and their own interest. They never take into consideration the feelings and interests of others. We are their allies. In this war we have rendered them signal services, and have acted towards them as gentlemen. What have we seen? What are they doing for us. Nothing. In all our dealings with them they raise difficulties. If we have negotiations concerning a loan or anything else, there is not a small point that can be raised in their favor which they would fail to raise. We went into the war without thinking of loans, expenses or other details. Had we asked the Germans at that time to take upon themselves all our war expenses, Germany would have agreed to do so, but as we did not raise that question, to-day we are borrowing money from the Germans and we are indebted to them to the amount of 100,000,000 pounds sterling just for the war expenses. As allies of the Germans, of course, we desire to see Germany win in this war, but do not want to see Germany have such a victory as to become the dictator of the whole world. That would be a misfortune for all."

I spoke to him about the food question in Germany, and whether the scarcity was such as to force the Germans to put down their arms. The Minister stated that according to his information the German Army was well fed; as to the civilian population, he believed, that through the wonderful organization which they have in Germany, it would be possible to feed them until the new crops. But in his opinion there was another question which was more serious for the Germans than that of the food supply. How long will the material for the manufacture of ammunition last? There is scarcity of coal and scarcity of copper.

These statements did not prevent him from saying that the way the Entente Powers had published their terms of peace was a most stupid piece of business. There were thousands of people in this country, who were against the war and longed for peace, and yet the Entente Governments say that they want to give Constantinople to Russia. All these people now want the continuation of the war.

He knew that there were no diplomats in Germany, that it was only through force that the Germans wanted to deal with every nation, but he had believed that in England and in France there were good diplomats. The way the latter acted in this matter showed him that there is a penury of statesmanship even in those countries.

While speaking of the friendly relations between Turkey and America, I told him that Turkey had many friends in America, but I added in order that these friends might in some way be able to be of any service to this country, there should be put an end to all Armenian massacres as well as Arab or Syrian or other persecutions. He at once stated that he agreed with me entirely. "These things should not have happened." He said he hoped that very soon we would see an amelioration in the condition of the Armenians, who would be allowed to travel and do business within certain zones. What happened was a most deplorable thing and he said you can be sure that it will not be repeated.

In conclusion I desire to inform you that when we first heard of Germany's last decision in regard to submarine warfare, the German Ambassador here told me that Germany was committing a serious mistake. He is since reported to have said that this warfare has proved ineffective.

It is difficult to know how much truth there is in these different and sometimes contradictory rumors. But I thought you would be interested to hear them. . . .

With kindest regards [etc.]   ABRAM I. ELKUS

INDEX

INDEX

VOLUME II IS INDEXED SEPARATELY

VOLUME II IS INDEXED SEPARATELY